THE MOSCOW STATE YIDDISH THEATER

Jewish Literature and Culture
Series Editor, Alvin H. Rosenfeld

Indiana-Michigan Series in Russian and East European Studies
Alexander Rabinowitch and
William G. Rosenberg, general editors

THE MOSCOW
JEWISH CULTURE
STATE YIDDISH
ON THE
THEATER
SOVIET STAGE

INDIANA UNIVERSITY PRESS
BLOOMINGTON & INDIANAPOLIS

Jeffrey Veidlinger

The author and the publisher with to acknowledge the generous support of
the Lucius N. Littauer Foundation.

This book is a publication of

Indiana University Press
601 North Morton Street
Bloomington, IN 47404-3797 USA

http://www.indiana.edu/~iupress

Telephone orders   800-842-6796
Fax orders   812-855-7931
Orders by e-mail   iuporder@indiana.edu

Library of Congress Cataloging-in-Publication Data

Veidlinger, Jeffrey, date
The Moscow State Yiddish Theater : Jewish culture on the Soviet stage /
Jeffrey Veidlinger.
    p.   cm. — (Jewish literature and culture) (Indiana-Michigan series in
Russian and East European studies)
Includes bibliographical references and index.
ISBN 0-253-33784-4 (cl : alk. paper)
1. Moskovskiĭ gosudarstvennyĭ evreĭskiĭ teatr—History. 2. Theater,
Yiddish—Russia (Federation)—Moscow—History—20th century.   I.
Title.   II. Series.   III. Series: Indiana-Michigan series in Russian and East
European studies

PN3035 .V45 2000
792'0947'31—dc21
00-035004
1 2 3 4 5   05 04 03 02 01 00

CONTENTS

Acknowledgments

I am most grateful to all my colleagues, friends, and family who have taken the time to support my work. First and foremost, I would like to thank Richard Stites, who inspired me to look at culture from a new perspective, and who saw this project through from its initial stage as a first-year graduate seminar paper to a dissertation and beyond. His enviable ability to edit the minutia of grammar while simultaneously envisioning and expanding the Big Picture has helped make me a better writer. I thank David Goldfrank, Catherine Evtuhov, Aviel Roshwald, and Andrzej Kaminski for being invaluable teachers and advisers at Georgetown; Abraham Ascher, Robert Weinberg, Regine Robin, and Steven Usitalo for their careful reading and critique of the entire manuscript; Ala Perelman-Zuskin and Nina and Natalia Vovsi-Mikhoels for their comments, for their assistance, and for generously providing many of the photographs included in this book; and Janet Rabinowitch and everybody at Indiana University Press for facilitating its publication. I also thank all those who have provided advice in numerous forms along the way: Lynn Mally, Zvi Gitelman, Karen Petrone, Vassili Schedrin, Joshua Rubenstein, Esther Markish, Louis Greenspan, Randy Law, Karl Qualls, Katya Nizharadze, Larry Fields, Alvin Rosenfeld, and John Efron. I am grateful to Georgetown University, the Social Sciences and Humanities Research Council of Canada, and the Lucius N. Littauer Foundation for providing generous financial support for this project.

I am also indebted to those abroad who have helped me uncover the documents that inform this work. In Moscow, I thank the staffs of the Russian State Archive of Art and Literature, the State Archive of the Russian Federation, the Russian Center for the Preservation and Study of Modern History, and the Bakhrushin State Theater Archive and Museum. In Jerusalem, I thank the staffs of the Israel Goor Theater Archives and Museum, the National Sound Archives, the Central Archives for the History of the Jewish People, and the Center for Research and Documentation of East European Jewry. I am also indebted to everyone at Merkaz Ha-Magshimim for cheap housing and great company. In Tel Aviv, I thank the staff of the Diaspora Research Institute. Back in the United States, the librarians of the Library of Congress, and particularly the Hebraic and Near Eastern Reading Room, merit special mention.

Segments of Chapters 1 and 2 were previously published as "Let's Perform a

Miracle: The Soviet Yiddish State Theater in the 1920s" in *Slavic Review* 57, no. 2 (Summer 1998). I am grateful to the journal for permission to reprint these segments.

Finally, I would like to thank my wife, Rebecca; my parents, Otto and Marilyn; my siblings, Daniel and Shira; and my uncles, aunts, and cousins for their unwavering support. I hope, as well, that my grandparents, Rabbi Abraham and Sophie Greenspan, Andrew Veidlinger, and Mary Vernon, all of whom grew up in Eastern Europe during the age of the Yiddish theater, would be proud. Their values, erudition, and love of Jewish culture profoundly influence this work. It is to their memory that this book is dedicated.

A Note on Transliteration and Translation

For Russian, I have used the Library of Congress system of transliteration without diacritical marks. For common personal names in the text, I have used spellings more familiar to American readers (Trotsky rather than Trotskii, for instance). In the notes and bibliography, however, I have adhered to the Library of Congress system.

For Yiddish words, I have used the YIVO system of transliteration throughout the text, except for names familiar to English speakers in a different form. Since the spelling of Yiddish was not standardized, some words were spelled differently on different occasions and in different places. For consistency, I have standardized the spelling of commonly used Yiddish words in the text. In the notes and bibliography, however, I have transliterated Yiddish words exactly as the authors wrote them.

Many of the people mentioned in this book used different names in different languages (Abram in Russian, Avrom in Yiddish, and even Abraham in English). For consistency, I have used the name by which I believe they are most widely known.

Unless otherwise indicated, all translations are my own.

THE MOSCOW STATE YIDDISH THEATER

Introduction: Soviet Jewish Culture or
Soviet Culture in Yiddish?

ELIEZER: I have traveled the entire land
   From border to border.
   I have also been in foreign lands where Jews live—
   There all is over:
   Many who never even dreamt of war,
   Are now ready to take up swords.[1]

※

BAR KOKHBA: The time has come. Enough talk!
   Because if not today,
   Who knows if tomorrow will already be too late?
   The battle cry: the time has come
   To free ourselves from the Roman yoke.[2]

※

(A struggle. Bar Kokhba arrives armed and throws himself directly into the melee. . . . From all sides armed Jews enter)

BAR KOKHBA: My brothers! I look at you
   Perhaps in numbers we are few
   Less men than the enemy, fewer arms we bear,
   Only with my head and right hand I swear
   And let us all in a single voice vow:
   With our arms, we will defeat him now.[3]

These words, written by the Soviet Yiddish playwright Shmuel Halkin and performed on the stage of the Soviet State Yiddish Theater of Moscow in 1938, were attributed to Bar Kokhba, the leader of a Jewish rebellion against Roman rule over Jerusalem in 132–135 C.E. When it was performed in Moscow with the support of the Soviet government, the Yiddish operatic play *Bar Kokhba* was already well known among Yiddish theatrical audiences. A previous version, performed by Abraham Goldfadn's troupe in 1882, had allegedly provoked Tsar Alexander III to ban all Yiddish theater in the Russian Empire the following year. The tsar's Ministry of Internal Affairs regarded the play as a subversive call for resistance to contemporary authorities and as an endorsement for the nationalist principle that the Jewish nation can only be free in an armed state of its own. Yet in 1938, at the height of Stalin's Great Terror, as Bolshevik zealots crusaded across the Soviet Union to root out imaginary vestiges of oppositional movements and autonomous institutions, official Communist newspapers praised the play as an affirmation of Soviet power and championed the Jewish rebel hero as a Bolshevik prototype. No one, not even the notoriously intolerant Soviet censors, left any written record expressing doubts that Bar Kokhba was anything but an exemplary defender of the international working class. The present-day historian must ask how Bar Kokhba was transformed from a Jewish nationalist into a Bolshevik prototype, and how complete that metamorphosis really was.

The juxtaposition of national motifs and Bolshevik themes was integrally related to Soviet nationality policies. Prior to the Revolution, Vladimir Lenin and Josef Stalin had fought against the Austrian Marxist and Jewish Bundist policy of granting minority nations broad cultural autonomy on the grounds that such "cultural-national autonomy . . . contradicts the internationalism of the proletariat and is in accordance only with the ideals of the nationalist petty-bourgeois."[4] Lenin believed that once the minority nations were freed from colonial oppression, their proletariat would assimilate with the proletariat of the dominant nation. Lenin did reserve for the minority nations the "right of self-determination," which he narrowly defined as the right to secede. Upon seizing power, however, the Bolsheviks were forced to reconsider their earlier platforms. On one hand, the right to secede from the union threatened to further dismember the empire they were inheriting, and on the other hand, their opposition to cultural autonomy threatened to alienate the minority nations on whose support the Revolution depended. Thus, while maintaining their earlier platforms in theory, the Bolsheviks began to reverse themselves in practice.

In order to spread its message and create a base of support among the non-Russian national minorities, the Party encouraged the communication of Communist ideals in local languages and discourses in a policy that became known as *korenizatsiia* (nativization). The origins of *korenizatsiia* began in November 1918 with the creation of the Commissariat of Nationality Affairs (Narkomnats), headed by Stalin, which was in charge of implementing Soviet policies toward the minority nations. By April 1918 Stalin had already reversed his previous opposition to "cultural-national autonomy" by advocating cultural autonomy in the fields of education, the courts, and administration in Central Asia and the Caucasus as a means of raising the cultural level of the native inhabitants. These policies continued over the next several years and were finally enshrined by a resolution of the Tenth Party Congress in 1921. There, the Party promised to help the minority nations "develop and strengthen their own Soviet statehood in a form corresponding to the national conditions of the people" and to "develop press, schools, theaters, clubs and general cultural-educational institutions in native languages."[5] In the 1930s, this objective was formulized with the slogan "national in form, socialist in content." Bolshevik thinkers hoped that with proper education, national awareness would soon be replaced with class consciousness. Minority languages and national forms were expected to become thin veils, subtly concealing the prototypical New Soviet Man who would educate the masses from behind a visage familiar to his audience.

The recent breakup of the Soviet Union into its national components has shown that these hopes ultimately remained unfulfilled. Instead, artists took advantage of the opportunity to utilize their national myths and languages to re-enact ancient battles for national independence, to revive long-forgotten heroes, and to recreate the halcyon days of the people's glory in order to ignite their audience's nationalist yearnings. Thus official nationality policies aimed at national integration inadvertently stimulated national distinctions and fostered the development of some minority nations.[6] Stalin and the Bolshevik leadership realized this danger themselves at an early stage in the Revolution, prompting Stalin to temporarily reject the slogan "national self-determination" in favor of the more limited slogan "the right of nations to secede." Even so, by the Tenth Party Congress Stalin was already fending off criticisms that the Party had artificially cultivated the emergence of national awareness in Belorussia and Ukraine.[7]

Bolshevik propagandists failed to realize that national forms—languages, myths, archetypes, and symbols—were semiotic systems that aroused pre-existing emotions and expectations among audiences familiar with the codes. Despite all attempts to divorce the signifier from the signified—to assign contemporary meanings to ancient myths—residues of the original sign remained intact within the understandings of the interpreters. National forms are not translucent veils behind which any character can hide; they are more like the masks of the commedia dell'arte, with recognized personalities that evoke common expectations among the audience, irrespective of the function they are purported to perform. Whether the mask is Harlequin, Charlie Chaplin's Little Tramp, St. Patrick, or Bar Kokhba, audiences expect certain behavioral patterns from recognized heroes and interpret their actions within this light. Chaplin's difficulty in adapting to the sound film, for instance, is symptomatic of this phenomenon—many audiences could not help but picture the Little Tramp tripping over his shoelaces during Chaplin's impassioned plea for peace at the end of *The Great Dictator*. Similarly, whether mouthing Marxist political platitudes or imparting consciousness to a proletarian uprising, Bar Kokhba retains certain preconceived character traits in any interpreter's understanding. To some audiences he eternally remains a reckless adventurer who brought disaster upon his people, whereas others see him as a national hero who proved that his people cannot be vanquished without a fight. National discourses can not be made incidental to the nation from which they emerged.

This book uses the example of the Soviet State Yiddish Theater of Moscow (hereafter Moscow State Yiddish Theater) to demonstrate how Jewish writers and artists were able to promote their own national culture within the confines of Soviet nationality policies during the period 1919 to 1949. I argue that while sharing many aspects of the state's educational ideals and class-based worldview, the Yiddish theater successfully resisted all attempts to turn its stage into just another platform of Soviet propaganda. Soviet politics on the Yiddish stage retained a distinctly Jewish orientation not merely by dint of being performed in what is almost exclusively a Jewish language, but also by virtue of overt and covert cultural contexts and signifiers. The theatrical personnel interpreted their assignments through their own national perspectives and conveyed meaning to their Jewish audiences by referring to shared cultural assumptions. Under the guise of conventional socialist realism, the Yiddish theater brought to life shtetl fables, biblical heroes, Israelite lore, exilic laments, and contemporary conundrums. I argue that whether depicting proletarian workers in the Soviet state or Jewish rebels in ancient Judaea, the Yiddish theater balanced its Communist aspirations with a distinct Jewish identity to varying degrees throughout its existence.

The means by which this "Jewishness" was manifested, however, varied throughout the theater's life. Chapter 1, which deals with the early history of the theater, demonstrates that the theater initially greeted the Bolshevik Revolution with enthusiasm and confidence. Its plays during the first half of the 1920s extracted and radicalized the existing social satire of pre-revolutionary Yiddish writers, such as Sholem Aleichem, Abraham Goldfadn, and Sholem Asch, fusing the Yiddish culture of the shtetl with a modernist framework. The second chapter argues that beginning in 1924, the theater's director, Aleksandr Granovsky, gradually became disenchanted with the progress of the Revolution as bureaucratic and political hurdles impeded his artistic creativity. In 1927 Granovsky started expressing his frustrations on stage by surreptitiously inserting hidden protests into the theater's productions in the form of Jewish symbols. Granovsky's frustrations came to the fore during the theater's 1928 European tour, as Chapter 3 shows, prompting the director to defect to Germany. Chapter 4 deals with Solomon Mikhoels's first years as the theater's director, during which time the corresponding objectives of the state and the theater, both of which sought to foster a new Soviet Jewish culture, allowed for the promotion of Yiddish writers such as David Bergelson and Peretz Markish, who situated socialist story lines within Jewish contexts. The leftist leanings of these writers and the prevalence of socialist themes in their works made them ideal candidates for the Soviet Yiddish canon. In several cases, Mikhoels also expanded upon Granovsky's technique of symbolically alluding to Jewish national themes within otherwise orthodox socialist realist productions. Chapter 5 shows that after a brief flirtation with translations of European classics in 1934–1935, the theater began to produce plays with more blatant national agendas in 1936. This new official tolerance toward expressions of national identity came on the heels of the 1934 Congress of Soviet Writers, which unleashed a celebration of ethnic diversity within the Soviet Union. The theater, however, was hardly free from molestation, as Chapter 6 shows. The Great Terror of 1937–1939 threatened the theater and consumed several peripheral figures, but remarkably failed to engulf the theater as a whole. Chapter 7 follows Mikhoels's activities as chair of the Jewish Anti-Fascist Committee during World War II, showing how the Nazi threat ignited the national sentiments of many Soviet Jews, including Mikhoels himself. By the end of the war, as Chapter 8 shows, Mikhoels had allowed his Jewish loyalties to emerge from behind his stage mask and manifest themselves in the public sphere. This provided Stalin with the occasion to build upon the wartime resurgence of Russian national chauvinism and channel those sentiments against the Jews, leading to the theater's ultimate destruction and the emergence of state-directed anti-Semitism, as discussed in Chapter 9.

Soviet Anti-Semitism

Thanks to the untiring efforts of interested foreign scholars who over the course of four decades have compiled testimonies and statistics on Soviet persecution of Jews, Western observers during the Cold War have been alert to the deplorable fate of post–World War II Soviet Jewry.[8] Activists in America, Europe, and Israel encouraged massive letter-writing campaigns to Leonid Brezhnev imploring him to free Natan Sharansky and other prominent Jewish *refusniks*, think tanks were dedicated to the dissemination of aid to Soviet Jewry, and Jewish schoolchildren around the world were encouraged to express solidarity with their persecuted co-religionists by wearing "Soviet Jewelry" (bracelets engraved with the names of Soviet *refusniks*). The pressure these groups exerted on the American administration probably contributed to the insistence of Ronald Reagan at his 1986 Reykjavik Summit with Mikhail Gorbachev that arms control be linked to human rights and to the subsequent release of Sharansky and other *refusniks*.

In their efforts to raise public awareness of the post-war Soviet regime's persecution of Jews, however, many of these scholars have overemphasized Jewish victimhood under the pre-war Bolsheviks. Jews certainly suffered during this period, but they did so as a result of residual popular anti-Semitism and Soviet persecution of religious institutions and alternative centers of power in general rather than as a result of any preconceived plan by the authorities to target Jews in particular. Synagogues were forcibly closed along with mosques, churches, and Buddhist *datsans;* former members of the Jewish socialist party, the Bund, were arrested along with former Mensheviks, Socialist Revolutionaries, and members of the Polish Socialist Party; rabbis were humiliated along with priests, imams, and village elders; the Yiddish language was purged of "Hebraisms" just as Uzbek and Tatar were purged of "Arabisms and Farsisms"; and "suspect" Jewish writers were silenced along with their Armenian, Russian, and Ukrainian colleagues. To be sure, many non-Jews blamed their woes on the "Jewish problem" and treated their Jewish neighbors accordingly. But on the whole, there is little evidence to suggest that prior to World War II the regime singled out Jews for punishment merely for being Jews.

In tandem with these anti-religious and anti-nationalist campaigns, a flourishing of secular Jewish cultural life emerged in the Soviet Union that has largely been ignored by foreign observers. Although official Soviet nationality policy initially denied the Jews national status on the grounds that they lacked a territorial homeland, the Jews were accorded many of the same rights as the official minority nations, including the right to use one of their own languages—Yiddish. As a result, during this period Jewish writers and poets composed epic works that were published by one of the world's largest Yiddish-language printing presses;[9] Yiddish folk singers and klezmer bands toured the country and released phonographic recordings;[10] ethnomusicologists recorded, arranged, and published the tunes of the Jewish shtetls;[11] Jewish research institutions, libraries, and museums were established in Kiev, Minsk, Odessa, Leningrad, Moscow, Georgia, Birobidzhan and Samarkand;[12] hundreds of thousands of Jewish students attended Yiddish-language schools[13]; and seven State Yiddish Theaters entertained audiences nightly. In an effort to solve the Jews' longing for a territorial homeland and to secure for the Jews the territorial underpinnings of nationhood, the Soviet Union even established a Jewish Autonomous Region in Birobidzhan in 1934, where Yiddish was promoted as an official language.[14]

All this changed drastically in the early morning of January 13, 1948, when Solomon Mikhoels, the director of the Moscow State Yiddish Theater and chairman of the Jewish Anti-Fascist Committee, was killed in a truck accident near Minsk. Few suspected that the accident had been orchestrated by the Secret Police and that Mikhoels was the first victim of what was to become Stalin's final purge —this time directed against the Jewish cultural community. With the murder of Mikhoels, the Soviet state adopted an official policy of anti-Semitism. Within the next two years, a group of prominent Yiddish writers and other public figures were arrested, Yiddish papers ceased publication, and the Yiddish printing press and all the Yiddish theaters were closed. This was followed by the 1952 execution of thirteen prominent Jewish activists, including several who had been involved with the Yiddish theater, and by the infamous Doctor's Plot the following year, in which a group of predominantly Jewish doctors were accused of attempting to poison leading Kremlin officials.

"I would have liked the Moscow State Yiddish Theater and its actors to be remembered not only in light of the tragic events which beset them, but principally for their artistic work," wrote Ala Perelman-Zuskin, the daughter of the actor Benjamin Zuskin.[15] Unfortunately, the tragic deaths of Mikhoels, Zuskin, and other members of the theater have overshadowed their life achievements. Mikhoels has come to be associated almost exclusively with the beginning of Stalin's purge of Jewish cultural figures and the onset of official anti-Semitism rather than with the theater to which he dedicated most of his life.[16] Aside from representing the beginning of a new era of oppression, however, Mikhoels's murder also represents the finale of an era of achievement and creative experimentation. During the thirty-year existence of the Moscow State Yiddish Theater, Mikhoels and the theater helped transform the Soviet capital into one of the most productive centers of Yiddish culture in the world.

Yet it has been maintained that throughout its existence the Soviet state— often personified in the figures of Stalin and Lenin or viewed as an outgrowth of Marxist ideologies—aspired to destroy Jewish culture. Many scholars have adopted an intentionalist argument, reasoning that from its inception the Bolshevik Party considered the liquidation of Jewish culture to be a theoretical and strategic imperative.[17] Chone Shmeruk, for instance, declared to the World Jewish Congress in 1973 that

> the political and ideological doctrine of the Bolsheviks did not recognize the existence of the Jewish people as self-evident and cast doubt on the existence of a specific Jewish culture. . . . Stage by stage, it reduced the various spheres of Jewish culture inherited from the pre-revolutionary period, denying the very

awareness of its existence at times both in theory and practice, at other times in practice only.[18]

Lenin's theoretical writings, especially his 1903 polemic against the Bund, have often lent credence to the intentionalist argument. The Bolshevik founder's off-hand remarks in favor of the total assimilation of the Jews have helped scholars trace a direct line from the formation of the Bolshevik Party as an alternative to the "Jewish Mensheviks" and the Bund to the pinnacle of Soviet anti-Semitism in the 1970s.[19]

Others maintain that "Lenin was an implacable foe of anti-Semitism throughout his political career."[20] The roots of anti-Semitism, they argue, must be found in the policies of Lenin's successor. Indeed, Stalin's famous definition of a nation as a "historically constituted, stable community of people, formed on the basis of a common language, territory, economic life and psychological make-up manifested in a common culture"[21] clearly excluded the Jews, who, until the 1934 foundation of Birobidzhan, lacked a territorial unit of their own. Many scholars have seen in Stalin's definition a theoretical pretext for his campaign against "root-less cosmopolitans" that would decapitate Soviet Jewry forty years later.[22] Others have subscribed to a "great man" theory of history by arguing that the roots of official anti-Semitism can be found in Stalin's psychological profile, that anti-Semitism was an integral component of Stalin's weltanschauung. These studies point to Stalin's seminary education, his limited contact with Jews during his childhood, his feelings of inadequacy when confronted with a group of Jewish revolutionary intellectuals during his youth, and his alleged paranoia as the factors that fostered the dictator's anti-Semitic tendencies.[23] The spread of Soviet anti-Semitism is thus seen as an intentional process surreptitiously planned by Stalin and gradually implemented according to some type of preconceived blueprint.

Although the view that Stalin was deliberately anti-Semitic has permeated much Soviet Jewish history, more general histories of Stalin's Russia as a whole have de-emphasized this aspect of his character. Robert Conquest, for instance, who could hardly be called an apologist, notes that Stalin's "view of humanity was cynical, and if he too turned to anti-Semitism it was as a matter of policy rather than dogma. . . . The 'anti-Semitism,' thus disguised, was in accord with Stalin's general exploitation of prejudices, and of the gullibility and pliability of men in general."[24]

Totalitarian Culture

In the years after World War II, the Soviet state began to deliberately discriminate against its Jewish population and to single out Jews and Jewish institutions for persecution. Although many Yiddish schools, courts, newspapers, and other institutions had been closed during the late 1930s as part of a general discrimination against all national minorities and religions, after World War II discrimination against Jews took on more specifically anti-Semitic dimensions. Soviet anti-Zionist propaganda was framed within an anti-Semitic discourse, quotas were placed on Jewish enrollment in institutions of higher learning, and thousands of Jews were persecuted as *refusniks* for requesting permission to emigrate. United in opposition to contemporary Soviet policies toward its Jews, Jewish intellectuals around the world began painting a picture of a totalitarian state founded on the principles of anti-Semitism. The totalitarian paradigm is by no means unique to scholars of Jewish history; some historians and political scientists, often influenced by Cold War hostility, have maintained to varying degrees that the Soviet polity was a nearly static entity controlled by a tight-knit Party dominated by a relatively uncontested ruler who sought to impose his own will upon the populace.[25] Others have shown that the Party itself was plagued by internal dissent (at least throughout its first decade in power) and was forced to compete with a plurality of voices from the populace as a whole.[26]

Most of the discussion has centered on the interplay between politics and ideology. However, the Bolshevik Party from its earliest days was equally concerned with the cultural front. Even Leon Trotsky, the commander of the Red Army, found time during the Civil War to write articles instructing the New Soviet Man on proper etiquette. Clearly Bolshevik leaders were concerned with creating a truly new and revolutionary social and cultural discourse. Despite a plethora of opinions, Soviet ideologists agreed on the fundamental premise that culture must serve a social function, but few agreed on the means of reconciling education with entertainment and channeling artistic creativity into social utility.[27] According to some advocates of the totalitarian schema, the reigning Party should have had little difficulty reforming the social habits of its subjects. Yet Peter Kenez has shown that despite their attempts to impose a new social discourse on the population, the Bolsheviks were plagued by financial limitations and a dearth of resources that often rendered their extensive network of propaganda largely ineffective.[28] The Party was ultimately unable to mold the masses at will. Yet by the early 1920s the cultural sphere truly had been revolutionized as the people attempted to perform and realize their own "revolutionary dreams." Artists, scientists, workers, peasants, professionals, women, Jews, and other ordinary citizens all expressed their enthusiasm and uncertainties about their future in their own way.[29] Despite Lenin's apprehensions, experiments in futurism, constructivism, suprematism, acmeism, Taylorism, and formalism proliferated in this explosion of the avant-garde.

One of the major sites of conflict was the theatrical stage, where a myriad of voices competed to design the ultimate proletarian set.[30] Some drama theorists, under the influence of Richard Wagner and Friedrich Nietzsche, sought a return to the mass spectacles of the Hellenic age by infusing religious content into theater. Others directed their attention toward the proletariat by constructing scenes derived from the factory floor—the milieu of urban workers—or they encouraged factory workers to form amateur theaters, thereby advocating a culture in which the people would be performers as well as spectators. Commissar of Enlightenment Anatolii Lunacharskii declared in 1925 a "return to [Aleksandr] Ostrovskii," indicating a preference for the realism of the nineteenth century. Others believed, simply, that ticket prices should be reduced to make theater affordable to the lower classes. In short, voices in the cultural sphere were no less fragmented than the voices in the political sphere.

The Jewish Avant-Garde

Recently some scholars have begun to look at the Jewish cultural front as well. In his influential work on the Jewish Section of the Communist Party in the 1920s, Zvi Gitelman noted that the iconoclasm of the "revolution on the Jewish street" was coupled with a constructive force, in which the Jewish Section attempted to modernize the shtetl through Yiddish courts, Party cells, and trade unions.[31] Others have shown that much of the creative experimentation that characterized Russian culture in general during the revolutionary era resonated within both Hebrew and Yiddish theater, film, art, and literature.[32] The Hebrew theater Habima produced one of the most memorable theatrical productions of the decade with its rendition of Solomon Ansky's *Dybbuk* in 1922, Marc Chagall fused avant-garde aesthetics with the Jewish heritage on canvas until his departure from the Soviet Union in 1922, and the writers of the Kultur-Lige brought Yiddish poetry in a modernist framework to the Jews of the former Pale of Settlement. The vibrant Jewish culture depicted in these works calls for a re-evaluation of the state's relation to Jewish artists and entertainers during the 1920s. Even Shmeruk noted that "we can see the period from the 1920s until 1941, the year of the German invasion of Soviet Russia, as the period when Soviet Yiddish literature flourished."[33]

Perhaps, therefore, the obliteration of Jewish culture should be pushed back at least to coincide with Stalin's Cultural Revolution or, to use his own term, "Great Break" of 1928–1931.[34] Indeed, it has long been contended among left-leaning circles that Soviet aspirations toward total power began only with Stalin's "betrayal of the Revolution," or "great retreat."[35] Subsequent explorations by Sheila Fitzpatrick and others into social life after the Cultural Revolution have revealed a less static and homogenized portrait of the Soviet 1930s. Revisionist historians have convincingly demonstrated that a deep chasm emerged between the state's ambitions toward totality and the implementation of its policies.[36]

The study of Soviet cultural life in the 1930s, and particularly of the state-mandated style of socialist realism, has also challenged totalitarian paradigms. Whereas most Western observers once regarded socialist realist art as a perversion of realism devoid of aesthetic merit, the methodologies of post-structuralist criticism, with their appreciation of popular culture and audience tastes, have encouraged critics to search for popular and familiar themes in socialist realist culture. This methodology helped scholars construct a narratology of socialist realist fiction that revealed polyphonic voices within the aesthetic, political infighting among its trustees and continuities between the avant-garde experiments of the 1920s and the artistic products of the 1930s.[37] Others have observed in the culture of the 1930s a diverse subculture, or popular culture, which entertained the people in their daily lives.[38] With few exceptions, these approaches have yet to be applied to

Jewish culture of the period after the New Economic Policy (NEP), or to the culture of the other minority nations.[39] Régine Robin, who has done work on both Russian and Yiddish socialist realism, is one of the few scholars who has appreciated the "richness of Jewish civil society in the Yiddish language until late in the 1930s."[40] Even among Yiddish specialists, the myth that socialist realist doctrines obliterated Judaic motifs from Yiddish culture has remained relatively unchallenged.

Thus many scholars continue to equate the rise of socialist realism and its correlative slogan, "national in form, socialist in content," with the decline of Jewish cultural expression. Michael Stanislawski, for example, argues in a colorful essay that "beginning in 1930 and 1931, all attempts at creating a Soviet Jewish culture were all but smothered in the general obliteration of artistic and cultural creativity throughout the Soviet Union."[41] Similarly, in his decoding of Der Nister's 1929 "Under a Fence: A Revue," David Roskies writes that the story "marked the end of Jewish fantasy, and for all intents and purposes Jewish messianic dreams, in the vast Soviet empire."[42] Lester Samuel Eckman anachronistically argues that during the late 1930s, "the petty trader, the speculator, the *luftmentsh,* became a common stereotype of the Jews, at the same time that Jewish professors, doctors, teachers and others were contributing much to the development and modernization of Russia."[43] Yet it was precisely during the 1930s that the characters of the petty trader, speculator, and *luftmentsh* were abolished from Soviet Yiddish literature to be replaced with workers, collective farmers, and Red Army soldiers. And the *luftmentsh* was not an invention of Soviet propagandists—rather he was a stock character of pre-revolutionary Yiddish literature, folk tales, and songs.

Other historians have chosen 1937 as the turning point, interpreting the Great Terror as either a patently anti-Semitic act or, at the very least, one that emphasized Jewish victimhood. "During the Great Terror," writes Louis Rapoport, "Stalinist agitators had stirred up anti-Semitic prejudice and brought it to a climax."[44] Similarly, Eckman writes: "At first, by dark hints and allusions, Stalin's agents stirred up anti-Semitic prejudice and brought it nearer the surface until it reached its climax during the period of the great purges in 1937–1939."[45] Others have seen a complete annihilation of Jewish culture during the purges: "It may be said without exaggeration that after the purge of the thirties not a single person with any authority whatsoever was left at liberty in Soviet Jewish journalism, culture, or even science."[46] It has been contended that Jewish culture was gradually curtailed until "toward the end of the 30s nothing was left of it,"[47] allowing Stalin to revel in the "total suppression of Jewish cultural life" as "fear and terror filled the hearts of every Jew in Russia, from the humblest citizen to the ranking Communist Party leader."[48]

The notion that Stalin and his agents deliberately provoked anti-Semitic discrimination as part of the Terror is not shared by most specialists on the purges. Indeed, despite acrimonious contentions over the periodization, motivations, processes, and scale of the purges, none of the specialists on the period argue that the Terror was specifically anti-Semitic in nature—that it singled out Jews for being Jews.[49] If Jews suffered disproportionately during the purges of the 1930s, it can be attributed largely to their heavy representation among the groups that were hardest hit—intellectuals and Party members. That is not to say that anti-Semitism was absent during this period. In fact, as Robert C. Tucker notes, hostility toward Jews became increasingly noticeable during the Great Terror.[50] Social hostility, however, should not be equated with the type of genocide imagined by Eckman and others. Students of the Soviet Union's other national minorities have held that ethnic persecution was a pervasive aspect of Soviet policies toward non-Russians in general. Only recently have specialists on the Jewish minority, such as Igor Krupnik, come to realize that "Jewish policy was a fairly integrated component of Soviet nationalities policy. Several other peoples were purged and promoted in roughly the same way, while a few had a far more tragic record of persecution by the communist state."[51]

Although the Cultural Revolution, the advent of socialist realism, and, later, the purges of the 1930s certainly curtailed the breadth of Jewish cultural expression, it must not be forgotten that some of the greatest achievements of Jewish culture in the Soviet Union were produced during this time, such as Der Nister's epic novel *Family Mashber* (1939) and the folk music collections of Moshe Beregovskii, Moshe Khashchevatskii, and Yekhezkel Dobrushin.[52]

The Denationalization of Jewish Culture

The paradox that Yiddish culture flourished in a state that allegedly sought to eradicate Jewish nationhood has often been reconciled by denying that these works can be considered "Jewish." It has been contended that under the dictates of socialist realism, Jewish artists rejected their Jewish heritage by "de-nationalizing" their art and purging it of Jewish motifs, making "Yiddish literature for the most part national only in its language medium."[53] Historian Benjamin Pinkus, for instance, writes of the 1920s that "the Soviet government planned to cut the Jews off from their past in order to de-nationalize them completely, and the means of doing this was to be a process of stifling Jewish culture."[54] The notion that Jewish national expression in the Soviet Union was curtailed, or even liquidated, beginning in the 1920s has been widely repeated. We are told that Jewish writers, artists, performers, and musicians were confronted with "the choice between rejecting the Jewish idiom or sinking into oblivion."[55] Although one could certainly write of "Jews in Soviet Culture," "Jews in Soviet Music," or "Jews in Russian literature," the notion of Jews in Jewish culture was rejected.[56]

Within this paradigm, Jews who achieved success in the Soviet Union were often dismissed as defectors from the national cause. The most intense criticism, ironically, fell on those who wrote in Yiddish rather than Russian. They were regarded as the fifth column, betraying the "Jewish cause" from within. While historians, literary critics, and others have searched for Jewish motifs and influences in the works of the Jewish writers Ilya Ehrenburg and Isaac Babel or the Jewish mass song composers Isaac Dunaevskii, Matvei Blanter, and Dmitrii Pokrass, all of whom achieved their fame within the Russian linguistic milieu, Yiddish writers, composers, and actors were dismissed for neglecting Judaic values and forsaking their heritage.[57] Thus Gregor Aronson could refer to Mikhoels as "a man who had never taken part in Jewish civic affairs," despite the fact that Mikhoels had led the Yiddish theater for two decades and the Jewish Anti-Fascist Committee for five years before being murdered for his Jewish activities.[58]

Although most scholars have placed the blame for this "de-nationalization" of Soviet Jewish culture firmly in Stalin's hands, some, like Ruth Wisse, have presented a more nuanced approach to the problem. She prefers to emphasize the role that Jews themselves played in attacking Judaism—what she calls "the voluntary anti-Jewishness of Jewish artists and Jewish commissars."[59] "Owing to its theoretical internationalism," she continues, "Communism offered modern Jews the unique opportunity of renouncing Judaism not through defection (conversion to another religion) or through assimilation (conversion to another nationality), but through gradual national self-transcendence."[60] By linking the decline of Jewish culture in the Soviet Union to the universal phenomenon of the "self-hating Jew," Wisse succeeds in refining the conundrum. Indeed, one need only think of Benny Goodman, Irving Berlin, and Louis B. Mayer to remember that Soviet Jews were not alone in trying their luck in a non-Jewish milieu. Wisse, however, retains the charge that "the harsh reality of totalitarianism notwithstanding, the Jewish writers and artists of Russia were freely exercising their own will in their adaptation to Communism and in their abandonment of their own civilization."[61] Although Wisse correctly highlights the voluntary nature of Soviet Jewish adaptations, she presents it as a stark choice between Communism and Jewish civilization, leaving no room for compromise or subtle shading.

The argument that Soviet Yiddish writers had rejected their Jewish heritage achieved predominance during the 1960s and 1970s. But it was first put forward in the 1930s by a group of Russian Jewish émigrés based in New York, who attempted to reconcile the existence of a Jewish cultural life in the Soviet Union with what they perceived as an official denial of Jewish national distinctness. Yiddish literary critic Shmuel Niger (1883–1955), for instance, maintained that the Soviet state stifled the development of a Jewish national culture by prohibiting Yiddish writers from expressing themselves as Jews.[62] He blamed socialist zealots (as well as Zionist activists) for rejecting a millennia-old tradition of Jewish bilingualism by promoting the exclusive use of one language. The essence of Jewish self-expression, he believed, rested in the ability to traverse between two linguistic cultures—Aramaic and Hebrew, Arabic and Hebrew, or Yiddish and Hebrew (not to mention Ladino, Spanish, and other linguistic cultures to which the Jews have belonged). While other peoples certainly possessed both a lingua franca and a vernacular, only among the Jews, he maintained, did the two linguistic cultures coexist in an equilibrium. He believed that Soviet Yiddish culture, with its complete rejection of the Hebraic tradition, was simply a crude translation of Soviet culture into the Yiddish language—there was no Soviet Jewish culture, only Soviet Yiddish culture. Only during World War II, when the same writers whom Niger had earlier criticized for forsaking their heritage began to openly express themselves as Jews did Niger reverse himself and come to see the Soviet Yiddish writers as modern "Marranos" (Jews forcibly converted to Christianity during the Spanish Inquisition, but who remained Jews in secret).

On the other hand, essayist Nakhman Mayzel (1887–1966) argued that a literary analysis of the works of many Soviet Yiddish writers reveals strong nationalist motifs and evokes nationalist sentiments.[63] Indeed, Mayzel, who emigrated to the United States after participating in numerous Yiddish cultural organizations in Kiev during the 1910s and editing the Yiddish literary journal *Literarishe bleter* (Literary Pages) in Warsaw in the 1920s, played a seminal role in popularizing the works of Soviet Yiddish writers in the West. Later Irving Howe was to continue Mayzel's mission by reintroducing Soviet Yiddish writers to a new generation of the American public. Howe, however, confined himself to the early works of these writers, noting that "it has seemed pointless to waste space by printing what Yiddish writers had to compose during the worst years of the Stalinist period—these should be familiar enough to anyone who has read equivalents in other languages. And there are some things it is better to leave in the past."[64] A similar policy was followed by Golda Werman, who has recently presented English speakers with a welcome translation of David Bergelson's early writings. Yet, following Howe, she too dismisses Bergelson's later works, which were written in a period when, she writes, "anything that touched on Jewish culture and the Jewish past was considered separatist and nationalistic."[65] Although Howe and Werman were pioneering in their identification of Judaic motifs in early Soviet Yiddish writing, they missed the opportunity to extend their observations into the 1930s and 1940s.

Secular Jewish Culture

The near-total eradication of public Judaic religious worship in the Soviet Union has contributed to the general impression that Jewish cultural life as a whole was wiped out. Because they equated the Judaic religious faith with the Jewish nation, many scholars believed that the obliteration of the latter necessarily followed from the deterioration of the former. The position that Jewish culture cannot exist in a secular framework—now largely rejected by all but the most Orthodox religious circles—was a fairly widespread belief in the early years of this century; it was shared by both the Orthodox, who believed that all Jewish life lay within Scripture, and by the assimilationists, who believed that the only obstacle to becoming true Germans or Americans was the synagogue. Abraham Idelsohn, for instance, one of the foremost scholars of Jewish ethnomusicology, had written of Jewish folk music that "if, by folk-song, we understand words and tunes of war and drink, of carnality and frivolity, then the Jews have no folk-songs. Jewish folk-song, like Jewish life in the last two thousand years, nestles in the shadow of religion and ethics."[66] There were others, of course, who chose to expand their definition of Jewish culture beyond the synagogue and into the marketplace. Ethnomusicologist Lazar Saminsky, for instance, argued that the folk musicians of the shtetl can be considered "Jewish" despite their secular orientation: "They were brought up on [Jewish] beliefs and customs, on [Jewish] tunes and melodic gusto.

. . . Their exploration and endeavors created a genuine foundation of Jewish musical culture."[67] Although religious symbols continued to play an important role in secular culture, they were often desanctified and reinterpreted as cultural rather than religious motifs.

The thesis that Judaic religious practice defines Jewish culture was violently thrown into question during World War II, not only as a result of Hitler's insistence that a people be defined by race rather than by cultural affiliation but, more important, by the nationalist sentiments that the Holocaust aroused in even the most fervent Jewish assimilationists. The subsequent founding, predominantly by secular labor Zionists, of the State of Israel and the flourishing of secular cultural life in the new state convinced the majority that Jewish culture need not be tied to religious faith.

There were some who replaced religion with language as the decisive factor. This view took a concrete form at the Czernowitz Conference of 1908, at which a group of European Jewish intellectuals determined Yiddish to be "a Jewish national language," and at the Tenth Zionist Congress of 1911, the first to be held primarily in Hebrew. Influenced by Herderian notions of collective culture, the participants of both conferences believed that a Jewish *Geist* could only emerge in a Jewish language. Both groups were united in their opposition to the German Jewish *maskilim* (enlighteners) who followed Leopold Zunz in asserting that any work produced by a Jewish author could be considered part of Jewish culture.[68] Others, like the literary critic Baal-Makhshoves (Isador Eliashev, 1873–1924), sought a middle way: "And what, in a nutshell, is the point?" he wrote in 1918. "It is that we have two languages and a dozen echoes from other foreign languages, but that we have only one literature."[69] Indeed, Baal-Makhshoves was one of the first critics to call for a more complex assessment of "Jewishness" in literature. It could hardly be forgotten, he wrote, that some of the greatest works of Jewish literature, such as Moses Maimonides' *Guide to the Perplexed*, written in Arabic, were not written in a "Jewish language." Instead Baal-Makhshoves defined a work's "Jewishness" by its content.

The presumption that there are identifiably Jewish literary themes and that one can express oneself as a Jew within a secular context and even in a gentile language has today become nearly universally accepted. Few would deny the influence of Judaism in the secular writings of Franz Kafka, Sigmund Freud, or Philip Roth, let alone the Yiddish writer Sholem Aleichem or the Israeli winner of the Nobel Prize for literature, Shmuel Yosef Agnon. The same can be said for the films of Woody Allen or the art of Marc Chagall, to name but a few examples. In fact, it has been contended that Judaic motifs can even be found in the mathematical reasoning of Albert Einstein and the rational musical system of Arnold Schoenberg.[70] Even though they were no longer writing religious commentary or divine praises, all the aforementioned figures share a talmudic obsession with interpretation and an insistence that everything has meaning. All are, in some form or other, mimetic of rabbinical writing. From a thematic perspective, identifiably Jewish values can be found in the works of all of these creators. Literary critics have presented varied views of Jewish literary motifs; some have identified an adherence to the code of *mentshlekhkayt*—a faith in the innate goodness of humanity and in its ability to actively bring about positive change.[71] Others have seen a profound appreciation for the contemporary significance of history or the notion of "tradition as continuity."[72] Others have searched for the intersection of oral storytelling and the written word;[73] while still others have emphasized generational conflicts and alienation.[74] Freud's Oedipus complex, Kafka's revolt against his "bourgeois father," Portnoy's carnal rebellion against his mother in Roth's *Portnoy's Complaint,* and Tevye's daughters' abandonment of their father's tradition in Sholem Aleichem's *Tevye the Dairyman* all emphasize familial relations and the tensions between parents and children as an essential component of self-definition. All also share a preoccupation with the individual's alienation from society and the defining of personal identity. Kafka's Joseph K., Roth's Nathan Zuckerman, Sholem Aleichem's Menakhem Mendl, and Agnon's lone writer in the Land of Israel all search in vain to find a place for themselves in an alienating society. Similarly, in their own ways, Einstein, Freud, and Karl Marx each sought order and meaning in an often hostile world.

Recently several literary critics have come to reject this thematic approach on the grounds that such themes should not be claimed as the exclusive property of the Jews—indeed, one need not look beyond Russia's own writers Fedor Dostoevsky and Ivan Turgenev for examples of the generational conflict in non-Jewish literature. Instead, they have sought to define a "semiotics of Yiddish communication," or have searched for Jewish archetypes in modern literature.[75] Although they are not the exclusive property of the Jews, the ubiquity of themes in Jewish writing such as uprootedness, alienation, generational conflicts, and historical memory should not be overlooked. These themes can be considered Jewish not only because of their common usage among Jewish writers, but also because of their biblical roots, ranging from Job's compulsion to find meaning in suffering to the familial conflicts between Joseph and his brothers to the pretext "because I am the Lord your God who brought you out of Egypt," which justifies modern obligations by referring to historical moments. Clearly there is no litmus test that verifiably identifies Jewish content. That being said, few would disagree that a group of Jews that performs Yiddish plays situated within a Jewish milieu, refers to Jewish themes and Jewish history, and whose audience is largely Jewish could be considered "Jewish." This was the case of the Moscow State Yiddish Theater.

Soviet Jewish Theater

As has been the case with much Soviet Yiddish culture, the history of the Moscow State Yiddish Theater has been largely unexamined. Art and theater historians have evaluated the theater's aesthetic approach to selected productions,[76] and anecdotal glimpses into Mikhoels's life can be gleaned from several biographies that his contemporaries have written of him.[77] There has not yet been an attempt, however, to assess the theater's relationship with the state during its heyday, to place the theater within the context of Soviet culture, or to examine the theater as a window into Soviet Jewish life.

One of the primary impediments to such a project has been a lack of sources. Soon after Mikhoels's death, his papers were seized from his office by the Secret Police and transferred to the Bakhrushin Theater Museum and Archive. In order to eradicate his legacy the Ministry of State Security ordered the theater's archives destroyed in 1953: a massive bonfire was lit that consumed large segments of the Yiddish theater's records. Satisfied that the deed had been carried out, the inspector departed before the blaze subsided. The fire was quickly extinguished and all archival remnants were collected and hidden. Only since Gorbachev unleashed his program of *glasnost* have these salvaged documents emerged from their hiding place and become available to researchers. These documents, which constitute the largest segment of the Moscow State Yiddish Theater collection at the Russian State Archive of Literature and Art in Moscow, are analyzed for the first time in this book.

The most important segment of the collection consists of the texts and synopses of most of the plays performed at the Yiddish theater. Although some texts did not survive the fire and others are missing segments or are partially burned around the edges, these documents allow for the first reconstruction of the theater's content. Indeed, most of the plays performed at the Yiddish theater were never published; it was impossible before the opening of this archive to make any judgment about their content. In addition to the scripts themselves, the artistic segment of the archive contains selected directorial notes, visual material, and musical compositions, allowing the modern researcher to reconstruct performances. The administrative segment of the collection, containing the theater's correspondence with the Union of Artists and the Commissariat of Enlightenment, reveals altercations between the theater and its overseers and attests to the director's early resistance to state interference. The protocols of the Yiddish Theatrical Society, also part of the administrative segment, establish the theater's pre-history as an autonomous association. Press releases, posters, programs, and financial reports have provided clues into how the public received their productions; and biographical information and salary lists have allowed the researcher to unmask the theater's participants. Finally, the collection contains the Committee of Artistic Affairs' archive on the Yiddish theater, including its correspondence, financial records, and the archives of the theater's liquidation committee.

In addition to the holdings of the Russian State Archive of Literature and Art, this book examines the correspondence between the theater and the Communist Party, housed at the Russian Center for the Preservation and Study of Modern History, and the Commissariat of Enlightenment's notes on the theater, housed at the State Archives of the Russian Federation. Both of these collections reveal the methods by which the state and the Party attempted to assert control over the theater and the means by which the theater resisted. Finally, material on the early history of the Moscow State Yiddish Theater can be found in the manuscript divisions of the Bakhrushin Archive in Moscow and the Public Library in St. Petersburg.

Other valuable sources have been brought to Israel by Russian immigrants. Among these sources are the immigrants themselves, who brought with them their own recollections. This study has benefited extensively from both formal interviews with participants in the theater and less formal talks with casual observers. When Mikhoels's daughters immigrated in 1972, they brought with them segments from their father's personal archives, which they had taken possession of before the documents were transferred to the Bakhrushin Archive. These have since been deposited in the Central Archives for the History of the Jewish People in Jerusalem. The personal archives of various writers and actors, including additional scripts, have also been deposited in Tel Aviv's Diaspora Research Institute by their families. Finally, the Israel Goor Theater Archive and Museum in Jerusalem has recently collected press reports on the theater and has obtained more segments of Mikhoels's personal archives, including stenographic reports of his most important speeches and his notes on staging. Thus for the first time, the texts of the Yiddish theater's plays and the theater's correspondences with state and Party organizations have become available for examination.

The new sources examined in this book demonstrate that the Moscow State Yiddish Theater expressed itself to varying degrees as a "Jewish" theater throughout its history. It was "Jewish" not only in the narrow sense that with few exceptions, its actors, designers, musicians, playwrights, administrative directors, and most of its audience were Jewish; but in the broader sense that it addressed distinctly Jewish concerns from a distinctly Jewish perspective. On its stage could be found folk legends of the East European Jewish masses, august defenders of ancient Judaea, talmudic parables of rabbinical wisdom, lyrical anecdotes of Zionist dreams, sacred prayers for divine intervention, and modern conundrums of the Jewish condition. The people who made the theater saw it as part of a cultural and historical continuum of Jewish culture, beginning with Abraham's covenant with God. The Moscow State Yiddish Theater interpreted its surroundings in light of Jewish memory and as exegesis of Hebraic texts—in the words of Yosef Hayim Yerushalmi, writing of medieval Jewish texts, they tended "to assimilate events to old and established conceptual frameworks . . . to subsume even major new events to familiar archetypes."[78]

The aesthetic, ideological, administrative, and political history of the Moscow State Yiddish Theater challenges the presumption that Soviet Yiddish culture only existed within an elusive and even deviant "denationalized" void. On the contrary, the theater proudly asserted and celebrated Jewish identity—sometimes with the overt blessing of the regime and at other times as a surreptitious challenge to authority. Through the use of allegorical language and symbolic allusions, the theater was able to project illicit messages past the censors, who often spoke no Yiddish and were unfamiliar with Judaic lore. Only those segments of the audience who were steeped within the Judaic tradition were capable of deciphering the theater's codes.

At the same time, the theater adhered to the principles of socialist realism and the goals of Soviet socialism. Its participants sought to create a renaissance of Jewish culture in cooperation with the "first socialist state" and in harmony with the ideals of the Revolution. Its performances genuinely scorned the aristocracy and bourgeoisie, lamented the fate of the downtrodden masses, celebrated the progress of socialist construction in the Soviet Union, and spoke to the broad masses, drawing upon their traditions and hopes. In short, the theater exhibited the three elements of socialist realism identified by C. Vaughan James in his study of the doctrine—*narodnost* (popular spirit), *partiinost* (social function in conjunction with the Communist Party), and *klassovost* (a class-based worldview).[79] These ideals, however, were not perceived to be incompatible with expressions of Jewish identity. Despite a theoretical denial of Jewish nationhood, in practice the Soviet state accepted the existence of a Jewish nation, for better or for worse. Stalin and the Bolshevik Party recognized Yiddish as the national language of the Jews and hence permitted and funded Yiddish Party cells, a Yiddish writer's union, Yiddish printing presses, Yiddish journals, and Yiddish theaters until after World War II. Similarly, the term "Jew" was enforced as a national designation to be stamped on passports, and a Jewish Autonomous Region was established in southeastern Siberia. When the slogan "national in form, socialist in content" was implemented, the Jews, like all other nationalities, were expected to communicate socialist ideologies to their audiences through national discourses. The Moscow State Yiddish Theater willingly complied. Although there were times throughout the period that either side of the equation predominated, in general the theater found a balance between its Judaic heritage and socialist yearnings. Only when the zealous guardians of proletarian art within the Communist Party placed *partiinost* above all else did some of the theater's participants realize that the model of Communism being implemented in the Soviet Union was far from a panacea and begin to search for alternative cures. These acts of resistance contributed, after World War II, to the ultimate destruction of the Yiddish theater.[80]

"Let's Perform a Miracle": The Creation of the Moscow State Yiddish Theater

1

In February 1917 the streets of Petrograd erupted in revolution. As Nicholas II, the last tsar of Russia, abdicated the throne held by his family for 300 years, a Provisional Government was set up to run the country until elections could be held for Russia's first democratically elected constituent assembly. Among the many who rejoiced at the collapse of the autocracy was a large segment of the Jewish population. Liberal democratic politicians governing for the first time over the world's largest concentration of Jews promised an end to their political, social, and cultural discriminations. Eight months later, the Provisional Government was overthrown by a small group of individuals belonging to a radical Marxist-inspired party calling themselves Bolsheviks. At the head of this "revolution" were two men: Vladimir Lenin, the founder of the Bolsheviks, and Leon Trotsky, the Jewish long-time radical activist and recent convert to Bolshevism. As of August 1917, five other members of the Party's twenty-one member Central Committee were of Jewish origin (Grigorii Zinoviev, Lev Kamenev, Iakov Sverdlov, Moisei Uritskii, and Grigorii Sokolnikov). Despite the Jewish Bolsheviks' total rejection of their Judaic heritage and identity, Jews and non-Jews alike quickly noticed the dispro-portionate number of Jews who constituted the upper echelons of the new Soviet government.

In spite of the new predominance of a select group of their co-religionists, most of the Jewish population was cautious in lending its support to the new Bolshevik regime. Even the majority of Jewish socialists were more likely to have supported either the Menshevik faction of the Social Democrats or the Bund, the Jewish socialist party. Many liberal Jews feared that the Bolsheviks would reverse the gains Jews had made under the Provisional Government, while Jewish mer-chants were wary of the Bolshevik promise to nationalize trade. The Zionists, for their part, protested Soviet nationality policy for failing to grant official recogni-tion to the Jews as a nation. The Jewish Orthodox and Hasidic populations, which constituted the vast majority of the Jewish population in the region, were the most distrustful; many had seen promising young rabbinical students abandon their religious studies, families, and traditions, enticed by the socialists' promises of a just society. On the other hand, the Bolsheviks were less offensive than the anti-Semitic and right-wing political parties that continued to threaten the shtetl.

In late 1917, for the first time, Lenin admitted the great significance of Jewish participation in the Revolution and formed the Commissariat of Jewish Affairs (Evkom), a division of the Commissariat of Nationality Affairs. The Commis-sariat of Jewish Affairs, along with parallel organizations for the Muslim, Polish, Latvian, Armenian, and Belorussian nations, was created with the goal of imple-menting Bolshevik policies and conducting propaganda among its national constituents. Soon after the establishment of the Jewish Commissariat, a Jewish Section (Evsektsiia), was formed within the Communist Party. Originally, the two organizations were expected to operate separately; the Commissariat of Jewish Affairs was to deal with affairs of the state and the Jewish Section with Party affairs. However, the fact that they shared a common director in the person of former rabbi Semen Dimanshtayn did little to help delineate their responsibilities. Within the next two years the Commissariat of Jewish Affairs declined in importance as most of its functions were taken over by the Jewish Section. By 1920 the Commissariat of Jewish Affairs was downgraded to a department; it was dissolved four years later along with the entire Commissariat of Nationality Affairs.[1]

Both the Jewish Section and the Commissariat of Jewish Affairs hoped to instill Bolshevik values, centered on communism and secularism, among the Jewish masses. In accordance with Lenin's nationality policy, the Jewish organs spread Bolshevik propaganda in the language of their constituencies—Yiddish. It was hoped that Yiddish propaganda would help persuade the masses of traditional Jews in the provinces to abandon their religious beliefs and embrace the new socialist dogmas. Given a 70.4 percent Jewish literacy rate according to the census of 1920—more than double the average for the Soviet population in general—Dimanshtayn believed that the Jews could be easily reached through the written media.[2] However, he failed to realize that they were also more likely to question written material that contradicted their own corpus of traditional works. The failure of the first Soviet Yiddish-language newspaper, *Di varhayt* (The Truth, January 1918–August 1918), proved to some that the creation of a new age required a new mode of discourse with no strong roots in the past.

Some believed that the Jewish discourse could be purified with a linguistic reform similar to the reforms of other Soviet languages. Such a reform was carried out in 1919–1920 by the Yiddish linguists Ilya Falkovitsh (1898–1979), Ayzik Zaretskii (1892–1956), and Nakhum Shtif (1879–1933). The overarching goal of the linguistic reform was to purify the Yiddish language through de-Hebraicization, just as the Central Asian languages had been purged of Arabisms and Farsisms, and through a reform of spelling, in which the consonantal endings were removed, a more phonetic spelling was adopted, the silent aleph was removed from the middle of words, and the gender of several words was changed.[3] The reform served as a literal break from both pre-revolutionary Yiddish and the Yiddish used in the capitalist world.

Those more committed to revolutionary iconoclasm saw linguistic reform as counterproductive. The reformers, they believed, were, to paraphrase Lenin, "revolutionaries in word and reformists in deed." The complete overhaul of tradition, the revolutionary iconoclasts maintained, required not only the expression of new ideas, but also a novel way of expressing those ideas; in short, the creation of a new mode of discourse. Russian poets, such as Andrei Bely and Aleksandr Blok, who united around the journal *Apollon*, followed the German modernists and French symbolists in believing that language was not a neutral force but rather that it imparted its own dated values onto society. They believed that in order to bring about societal change language must not only be reformed, but in some cases, abolished altogether in favor of nonverbal forms of communication, often epitomized by theater.[4]

Drawing from the example of the French Revolution, many Bolshevik and pre-revolutionary aesthetic philosophers associated theater with revolution: the events of 1789 had created a public for the bourgeois theater of Schiller and his notions of culture and morality; the 1848 Springtime of Nations was epitomized by Wagner's romantic extravaganzas and, later, Wedekind's erotic Christianity; and the final workers' revolution would, in turn, be remembered by its proletarian futurist theater. Theater was seen by these thinkers not only as a practical instrument of propaganda but also as a sacred festival. As early as 1904, the philosopher Viacheslav Ivanov, who after the Revolution would join the Theatrical Department of the Commissariat of Enlightenment, revived the myth of the theater as a temple in which rituals derived from Dionysian cults could unite Christ and man. This veneration of the "New Dionysus" was drawn from Wagner and Nietzsche, both of whom sought a return to the passion of the Hellenic mind.[5] Commissar of Enlightenment Anatolii Lunacharskii rejected many of Ivanov's cultic fantasies but still believed in 1920 that "there is no doubt that each epoch must have its own theater, and our great revolutionary epoch, approaching socialism, cannot but create its own theater, reflecting its passions, intentions, hopes, mishaps and victories."[6]

The chief proponent of this position within the Jewish community was Moshe Litvakov (1880–1939). In his youth, Litvakov had seemed an unlikely candidate for Bolshevik zealotry: he had received a traditional Jewish elementary education before studying in a yeshiva and joining the Poalei Tsion party, a labor Zionist movement advocating the establishment of a Jewish state in Palestine on socialist principles. In 1902 he moved to Paris, where he studied philosophy at the Sorbonne. Three years later he returned to Russia and quickly became involved in Jewish revolutionary circles. After the Revolution he became the head of the Jewish Writer's Section, a member of the Jewish Section, and a staff member of *Di varhayt*'s successor, *Der emes* (The Truth), assuming the task of editor in chief in 1924. In a radical shift from his earlier Zionist affiliations, Litvakov became a stalwart opponent of Zionism and the Hebrew language; he vehemently persecuted those who continued to champion either. His precise and methodological skill at literary criticism combined with his revolutionary zeal made him a valuable asset for the Jewish Section and helped gain him a great deal of influence on Jewish cultural life. As a member of the Moscow State Yiddish Theater's governing board, he was also able to influence the organization directly. His unrelenting politicizing would eventually earn him the hatred of all those who found themselves to be the targets of his criticism.

Litvakov's promotion of Yiddish theatrical arts was a paramount factor in the formative period of the Yiddish theater. Referring to the importance that rabbinical circles placed on written texts, he claimed that Hebrew literature could not be an art for the working people because it had been contaminated by the spirit of pre-emancipated Jewry.[7] The only medium appropriate for the expression of revolutionary ideas, he continued, was the theater. In reference to the Russian language theater, Lunacharskii had argued that theater first had to be purged of the bourgeois connotations it had acquired in its nineteenth-century heyday.[8] Indeed, Trotsky also wrote that theater "is perhaps the most conservative form of art."[9] But Litvakov and his supporters maintained that Yiddish theater was exonerated from this responsibility because it was a new art form emerging from a blank slate. Litvakov claimed that Jewish theater had no past and thus carried no traditional undertones—it was truly the forum of the Jewish future.

The myth that the Jewish theater was creating form out of void permeated the thought of many Jewish theater activists. Many even spoke of Soviet Yiddish theater in messianic terms. The founding of a Yiddish theater represented to them the birth of a new era and the emancipation of Judaism from centuries of oppression. The theme of cultural regeneration recurs throughout the speeches of those involved with the opening of the theater. Abram Efros wrote: "[The Yiddish theater is] a theater that is its own grandfather, father, and son. A theater that has not yet any past, present, or future and that must create for itself a past, present and future."[10] Solomon Mikhoels echoed him: "First and foremost, it must be understood that [the State Yiddish theater] was built up from a blank slate. . . . It cried out to live together with all the power of the Russian Revolution."[11]

While it is true that Yiddish theater had few bourgeois precedents to destroy, it did have a heritage in popular street theater and melodrama. Thus, some activists preferred to interpret the creation of the Moscow State Yiddish Theater in apocalyptic terms—it was not creating form out of void; it was a destructive force, destroying in order to create anew. It was in reference to this melodrama that Marc Chagall wrote: "Let us join forces and get rid of this rubbish. Let's perform a miracle."[12] This type of iconoclastic rhetoric was a common attribute of revolutionary discourse, expressed not only in the manifestos of the futurists but also in popular rituals and hooliganism.[13] Chagall was not the only member of the troupe to use religious imagery in his portrayal of the theater. Aleksandr Granovsky wrote: "What kind of theater will you be? What gods will you seek? We don't know our gods—we seek them. Perhaps we will make gods for ourselves."[14] Influenced by Ivanov and the playwright and drama theorist Nikolai Evreinov, Granovsky the theater director equated himself with a miracle worker capable of transforming the theater into a temple. The reference to god-building was an echo of pre-revolutionary rhetoric, propagated by such influential figures as Maksim Gorky and Lunacharskii, which linked religious millenarianism to socialist utopianism. Lenin's speeches on utopian dreams, the poetry and art of the futurists, the aesthetic philosophy of Ivanov, and the newest trends in Soviet theater all proclaimed the dawn of a "new world" and the need to "remake everything."[15]

Prologue

However, the claims of the progenitors of Soviet Yiddish theater that they were creating form out of void and initiating an apocalyptic rebirth were exaggerated. Jewish theater had long been prohibited by rabbinical authorities because of its common association with pagan ritual—a prohibition shared by pre-Renaissance Christian authorities. Jewish theater was further discouraged by *halakhic* (Judaic law) prohibitions on women singing and dancing in front of men and on men dressing as women. Thus, for many centuries, Jewish theater was restricted to the *purimspiel,* performed on the festival of Purim. This festival commemorates the victory of Esther and her cousin Mordechai over Haman, the royal adviser of Persia who had been designing a genocide of the Jewish people. During Purim, Jews are told to remember the banquet held by the Persian king Ahasverous by "drinking until they cannot tell the difference between Haman and Mordechai." It became traditional to masquerade as characters from the story, and it even became acceptable in more radical circles for men to dress as women.

During the Middle Ages, largely through the influence of Christian mystery plays, German *Fastnachtspielers,* English harlequins, and other folk carnivals, the Purim celebrations became more formalized as the festival turned into a Jewish mardi gras during which street parades would usher in the *purimspielers,* who would visit aristocratic neighborhoods demanding to put on living-room exhibitions. In addition to the traditional Esther story (which incidentally, also formed the basis of much non-Jewish theater, including the first recorded play in Muscovite history performed at the court of the seventeenth-century tsar, Alexis Mikhailovich) other legends, such as the story of Joseph, were gradually incorporated into the repertoire of the *purimspielers.* Many of the professional Jewish actors of the twentieth century, including Mikhoels, fondly recalled these *purimspielers* as an early influence.

Another important source of early Jewish theater was the wedding. The *badkhen,* the jester who played the role of master of ceremonies at Jewish weddings, would entertain the guests with witty jokes and sermons. The post-wedding party itself was also a free-for-all theatrical experience as fiddlers played lively klezmer music while men and women danced in separate quarters, impressing their peers through acrobatics and circus feats. This spontaneous conversion of the solemn religious ceremony into a festive event also served as an important basis for subsequent theater. The wedding scene would become an integral ingredient of virtually every Yiddish play; the audience would be disappointed if they left without one.

A final theatrical influence in the Ashkenazic Jewish tradition were the so-called Broder singers, itinerant bards who traveled through Eastern Europe performing pranks and short skits in marketplaces. The name derives from the Polish town of Brody, which hosted a thriving Jewish community immersed in enlightened thought. The first such entertainers emerged in the 1860s. Their shtiks appealed primarily to the lower-class *maskilim* because they satirized the Jewish upper classes and the pious Hasidic rebbes.

Not surprisingly, the first genuine Yiddish theatrical troupes emerged in Russia and Eastern Europe where the vast majority of world Jewry resided. While Yiddish had become the most commonly spoken language among Ashkenazic Jews since the fourteenth century, its use was mostly restricted to oral discourse; the sacred Hebrew language was reserved for scholarship and dignified writing. However, beginning in the 1860s several *maskilim,* influenced by the emergence of national vernaculars throughout the Russian, Hapsburg, and Ottoman Empires, sought to turn their own vernacular into a literary language. This movement was spearheaded by the novelist S. Y. Abramovitsh (1835–1917), known by his pseudonym Mendele Mokher Sforim (Mendele the Book Peddler). Mendele's poignant portraits of Jewish life in the shtetls of Eastern Europe not only immortalized his own name but also influenced the next generation of Yiddish writers who would revolutionize the Yiddish language and Jewish identity along the way. Among this group were the writers Sholem Aleichem (1859–1916), Sholem Asch (1880–1957), Isaac Leyb Peretz (1852–1915), Solomon Ansky (1863–1920), and the playwright Abraham Goldfadn (1840–1908).

Goldfadn, a free-thinking former ladies' hat salesman, is credited with having founded the first Yiddish language theater in Iasi, Rumania, in 1876. Whether or not Goldfadn's troupe was actually the first Yiddish theater has never fully been established. During the 1920s and into the 1930s many actors refuted Goldfadn's claim. For instance, Abraham Fishzon claimed to have been a member of a troupe in Berdichev in 1875, while others claimed to have been in Yiddish theaters in Warsaw and even Constantinople in 1870 and 1875, respectively.[16] There is little evidence to substantiate any of the stories—many troupes were camouflaged as German theaters, making it difficult to differentiate them from genuine Yiddish theaters, and opinions seem to have been formed more out of civic patriotism than historical research.

During the Balkan wars of 1875–1878, Goldfadn's troupe found its way into Odessa, where the large Jewish population greeted it with tremendous enthusiasm. Its presence stimulated the development of several other Yiddish theaters, all of which presented so-called *shund* (trash) entertainment, performing melodramatic comedies and operettas replete with couplets, vulgar witticisms, double entendres, crass jokes, bawdiness, and suggestive movements. Various attempts by journalists such as Osip Lerner (1847–1907), who became director of the Odessa Marinskii Theater in 1880, to aristocratize the theater by presenting high-brow art were merely mocked by Goldfadn's more popular troupe.

After the 1881 assassination of Tsar Alexander II, the situation of Jews in Russia worsened drastically. Anti-Jewish pogroms swept through the Pale of Settlement (the western provinces to which Jewish residence was restricted) and the reactionary Tsar Alexander III promulgated the May Laws restricting Jewish freedoms. In 1883, after a performance of Goldfadn's *Bar Kokhba* about the second-century Jewish rebellion in Palestine, the Ministry of Internal Affairs issued a ban on all Yiddish theater. The thriving theatrical community that had been forming around Goldfadn disintegrated as the actors returned to their former jobs or emigrated.

Indeed, many of the most prominent actors on New York's celebrated Second Avenue stages arrived in America during this period, along with 1.3 million other Jewish immigrants who flooded the Lower East Side. Among the émigrés were Goldfadn himself and several members of his troupe, including Jacob Adler, Sigmund Mogulesko, and David Kessler—all of whom would become leading stars of the Yiddish theater in America. It was not until the next wave of immigrants in the 1890s, which included Jacob Gordin and other former assimilationists, that New

York Yiddish theater would progress into a "dignified" art form that emulated the bourgeois stages of St. Petersburg and Berlin.

Meanwhile, back in Russia, several small traveling troupes continued to function despite the ban, often deceiving the authorities by advertising themselves as "German" troupes and simply fleeing from town to town whenever the authorities caught on. While most of these troupes were of an inferior quality, often merely recreating Goldfadn's plays from memory, one troupe stood out—that of Abraham Fishzon, which was active in the 1890s. One of the reasons for his success was his troupe's material basis. Unlike the majority of traveling troupes, Fishzon had the money to support his actors, allowing them to develop their skills and become true professionals. Fishzon's permanence also allowed him to develop a following, an achievement made difficult due to the impossibility of advertising.[17]

By the turn of the century a debate about the merits of Yiddish theater was brewing in the Russian press, particularly in the Jewish Russian-language journals *Voskhod* [Dawn] and *Budushchnost* [The Future].[18] The debate was sparked by a series of letters to the editor of *Voskhod* which told of several groups of Jewish youth banding together to perform plays in southern Ukraine. Most of these letters noted the predominance of the plays of Goldfadn due both to a lack of repertoire and the people's passion for historical plays. For instance, the author of one letter wrote that "among the local Jewish youth, small curious circles are emerging with the goal of putting on performances. . . . The Jewish public, for the most part, demonstrates an interest in plays of Jewish life in general, and of Jewish history, especially its heroic epochs."[19] Other letters noted that "curiously, the performances even interest the Russian population, but the Jewish intelligentsia still feels uncomfortable in their presence."[20] The same themes were echoed in a letter to the editor of *Budushchnost:* "[A group of] Jewish youth gave their first performance under the leadership of the artist Ariana-Mikhailova. The evening attracted a large public, Christians and Jews, who were quite satisfied with the young amateurs."[21]

However, many of the more conservative segments of the Jewish population, *maskilim* and religious Jews alike, still looked upon the theater with suspicion. The Orthodox opposed its flagrant violation of the legal and rabbinical bans, while many *maskilim* still regarded Yiddish theater as a fad popular only among the youth—true art, they maintained, must be expressed in the elevated languages of Goethe and Shakespeare, not the crass jargon of milkmen and housewives. The self-conscious aristocratic Jews of St. Petersburg were particularly adamant in their insistence on this rule; if it was not done in the celebrated salons of Berlin and Paris, they would not allow it to be done in Petersburg. Champions of Yiddish theater realized that the most effective means of convincing their opponents was to provide evidence of a European precedent. For instance, after witnessing a performance of an "eastern operetta" entitled *Daughter of Jerusalem* which was performed in Berlin, ethnomusicologist Iulii Engel wrote in *Voskhod* that this theater was in fact a Jewish theater: it was patronized by Jews, performed in Yiddish, dealt with Jewish themes, and used Jewish music and dance. The existence of such a theater, he argued, proved that fine art could be expressed in Yiddish.[22] Two years later, the discovery of another Yiddish theater in Austrian Lemberg, this time openly calling itself Jewish, buttressed Engel's argument: "I am convinced that a jargon theater can be established," the discoverer of the theater wrote, and "that sensible plays can be produced there, that these artists are tremendously talented and embody the living, genuine spirit of contemporary Jewry, and that there is no theater public more receptive and responsive than the Jewish theater public."[23]

Since the open publication of the existence of Yiddish troupes on Russian soil did not provoke a new police crackdown, many of these troupes became more self-confident, settling in the large Jewish population centers of Odessa, Vilna, Warsaw, Lodz, or Kiev. However, with the economic downslide of 1903, which was accompanied by a revival of anti-Jewish pogroms, many troupes either disbanded or fled to America. One exception, again, was Fishzon's troupe, which enabled Odessa to have a steady Jewish theater between the years of 1900 and 1904. As the existence of a permanent Yiddish theater in Odessa gradually became known, the Odessa liberal press occasionally even took to reviewing Yiddish plays.

After the 1905 Revolution, general theatrical journals joined the Jewish press in its call for the legalization of Yiddish theater.[24] However, a repertory problem remained: with no Yiddish dramatists, the troupes were consistently forced to perform revised versions of the old Goldfadn melodramas. In an effort to develop a Yiddish theatrical repertoire, the popular Yiddish writer Sholem Aleichem, who was residing in Warsaw, resolved to write a series of Yiddish plays and to solicit plays from other writers. "The day is near," he promised, "when one will no longer hear 'German' in the Jewish theater anymore. . . . The Jewish language, the true language of the people, Jargon [Yiddish], will take its place."[25] Simultaneously, in Warsaw, the Yiddish modernist Isaac Leyb Peretz began reviewing Yiddish plays in the press; his constructive criticisms and support helped guide young playwrights in the art of drama. However, Peretz's calls for the "democratization" of theater to make it more accessible to the masses were met with criticism from Sholem Asch, who preferred high art that catered toward the bourgeoisie.[26]

The same year, the director Spivakovskii, who had been collaborating with Sholem Aleichem, made a daring trip to St. Petersburg with his troupe, flaunting his rejection of the ban right in the tsar's capital, where he played Goldfadn's *Shulamis* and *Two Kuni-Lemls*. Most important, the tour gave the illusion that Yiddish theater was now permitted again. However, there was a constant awareness that the Yiddish theater was not experiencing a healthy growth due to a very limited repertoire and perpetual fear of a renewal of tsarist oppression, not to mention resistance from within the Jewish community.

In 1907 the crackdown finally occurred as the Ministry of Internal Affairs reaffirmed the ban and Yiddish theater was once again forced to go underground. By the time the ban was relaxed again two years later, a group of wealthy Jewish activists, who had profited from the economic opportunities offered by Russia's industrialization, could be found who were willing to patronize the theater. Furthermore, the efforts of Sholem Aleichem, Peretz, and others to promote the Yiddish language as a dignified vehicle of literary expression had been astonishingly successful. The most concrete expression of this achievement was the 1908

Czernowitz Conference in Hapsburg Bukovina, at which a prominent group of Jewish writers declared Yiddish their preferred language of expression.

In this atmosphere, a Yiddish Theatrical Society was formed in Warsaw by Peretz and the Bundist poet, pamphleteer, and playwright, A. Vayter (Isaac Meir Devenishskii, 1878 or 1879–1919). The society encouraged a young playwright named Peretz Hirschbein (1881–1948) to switch from Hebrew to Yiddish writing. In 1908 he moved to Odessa, where he founded the first professional Yiddish art theater, modeled on Constantine Stanislavsky's renowned Moscow Art Theater. While the troupe only lasted two years before Hirschbein emigrated, it had proven that a Yiddish art theater was viable and had produced at least one exceptional actor—Jacob Ben-Ami. After the dispersion of the Hirschbein troupe, Ben-Ami moved to Vilna, where he helped form the Organization of Yiddish Artists, which, in 1916, became the acclaimed Vilna Troupe. Even before its 1920 adaptation of Solomon Ansky's *Dybbuk,* the theater had achieved fame throughout Poland; eventually it became known throughout Europe. It 1924 it emigrated to America.

By 1912 there were sixteen Yiddish theatrical troupes in Russia; according to one estimate, by World War I there were a total of 600 Jewish actors and chorus members, 90 percent of whom lived in poverty. After the 1917 Revolution, the number of troupes greatly increased throughout Ukraine and Belorussia. Quite different in style and content from these amateur theaters was the Hebrew-language Habima theater, whose influences included the Vilna Troupe. The Habima troupe was formed in Bialystok in the years before the Revolution by the former Hebrew teacher Nakhum Tsemakh (1887–1939); it became a professional theater in 1918 after its move to Moscow and subsequent incorporation into Stanislavsky's art theater system. Over the next decade, the theater achieved world fame by producing Hebrew versions of Jewish mystical and folkloric plays, including Solomon Ansky's *Dybbuk,* about a ghost that haunts a yeshiva; David Pinski's *The Eternal Jew,* a messianic legend set after the destruction of the Jewish temple; Halpern Leyvick's *The Golem,* about a sixteenth-century rabbi who uses mystical powers to create and give life to an artificial man; and Richard Beer Hoffman's biblical drama *Jacob's Dream.* The theater aroused the ire of the Jewish Section through its use of the Hebrew language and insistence on mystical themes. Its continued existence, though, was ensured by the support it received from Lunacharskii and other high-ranking officials. In 1926 the troupe, while on a European tour, defected and eventually settled in Palestine.[27] Habima, though, was just one of many experiments in Jewish theatrical life that accompanied the Revolution. Raikin Ben-Ari, a member of Habima, recalls that "in the first period of the Revolution . . . an enormous reservoir of latent energy was uncovered: clubs, associations, reading circles, and dramatic groups sprang up by the minute."[28]

The Jewish Theatrical Society

The most significant of these associations was the Jewish Theatrical Society of Petrograd. The society actually crystallized in the months prior to the Revolution, when a group of activists associated with the Jewish Folk Music Society decided to form a society with the goal of "assisting in all manners the development of Jewish theatrical affairs" through legal means.[29] Motivated by the theory of "organic work," the society was one of many amateur societies founded by liberal Jewish philanthropists who hoped to construct a national socioeconomic and cultural infrastructure while remaining under Russian political rule.[30]

The Society's first meeting, held on December 1, 1916, was attended by a group of eighteen individuals, including writers Mark Rivesman and Lev Levidov and literary critic Shmuel Niger. The primary accomplishment of the meeting was the approval of a constitution outlining the society's objectives:

> 1) To coordinate the needs of Jewish theatrical affairs and of interested Jewish theatrical and stage workers
>
> 2) To bring public institutions and individuals concerned with the question of Jewish theatrical affairs together with the state
>
> 3) To establish theaters and theatrical ventures and to assist in the foundation of private theatrical enterprises
>
> 4) To promote, with the proper authorization, theatrical spectacles and concerts, and to organize tours in accordance with this goal.[31]

The committee also sought to organize lectures, conferences, and courses on Jewish theater; to establish museums, libraries, and exhibitions; to publish newspapers and books; to sponsor competitions; and to engage generally in the promotion of Jewish theatrical arts. Additionally, committees were formed to prepare a report on a Jewish theatrical repertoire and to investigate the logistics involved in establishing a theater school.[32]

The following week twenty-seven individuals met to discuss repertory questions in greater detail. Among those playwrights mentioned most often were Goldfadn, Asch, and Peretz.[33] On December 30, the group met again with some new members, including Solomon Ansky. At this meeting it was decided to form a library based on the donation of a private collection of Jewish plays and to begin the practical matter of creating a Jewish theater school. Due to the lack of capable Jewish directors, a motion to search for a prominent non-Jew to head the school was approved.[34] At a subsequent meeting several weeks later, some members began expressing their frustration, complaining that while the society had two million rubles at its disposal it had still not achieved any practical results; its plans were too ambitious. Rather than continue long-term plans for the foundation of a theater school, this group proposed a public reading of one of Ansky's plays.[35] The society decided to allocate funds toward short-term performances while continuing its search for a director.

When the society next met, on February 5, 1917, a resolution proposed that a Russian director be nominated as head of the theater school. In the meantime, the society would concentrate on the short-term goal of presenting public readings of Yiddish plays. The motion was greeted with almost unanimous enthusiasm. But as the debate on the motion concluded and the members prepared for the formal vote, an unknown newcomer to the society who was attending his first meeting stood up and dramatically objected. According to the stenographic report of the meeting, the orator declared:

> We . . . must have new people who will dedicate themselves fully to the new theater, for professionals will destroy it. . . . It is first necessary to open a theater school. Jewish theater has to be created from the beginning; it has nothing—we possess neither a voice nor a body. Having set about work, we absolutely must refuse creative pursuits. In the meantime academic work is needed, and actors, who are at least literate in respect to the stage are needed.[36]

Following a prolonged exchange of opinions, the Theatrical Society voted in favor of the proposed studio-school. After formally introducing himself as Aleksandr Granovsky, the future director of the Moscow State Yiddish Theater was put in charge of preparing a report on his proposed school.

Granovsky, however, had had little previous exposure to Yiddish culture and did not even speak the language—his German would suffice until he could pick up enough Yiddish with the help of his troupe. His background lay in the European modernist schools. He was, in the words of Mikhoels's daughter, "an esthete of European culture and reactions."[37] Avraham Azarkh, Granovsky's given name, was the son of Moshe Azarkh, one of the wealthiest Jews in Russia and one of a select few to whom the tsar had given the privilege of residing in Moscow. When Granovsky was an infant the family moved to Riga, where they assimilated into the dominant German population. Disappointing his father's professional aspirations for the youth, Granovsky moved to St. Petersburg in 1910 to study theater, where he was influenced by Vsevolod Meyerhold's experimental studio. In 1913 he moved to Germany and studied under Max Reinhardt, the founder of the Schall und Rauch cabaret and director of the Deutsches Theater who was known for his treatment of theater as spectacle and for his emphasis on pantomime, music, dance, and acrobatics. Upon his return to St. Petersburg, Granovsky co-directed Reinhardt's *Oedipus* and Shakespeare's *Macbeth* with Iury Iurev of the Aleksandrinskii Theater at the Cinizelli Circus. He and Iurev then collaborated with Gorky and the renowned opera singer Fedor Chaliapin to found a theater of tragedy. Although the plan never materialized, Granovsky's association with Chaliapin helped him direct *Faust* and *Sadko* at the Bolshoi Theater.[38]

Granovsky was uniquely qualified and willing to lead the Jewish Theatrical Society. The report he diligently prepared for the Society's next meeting envisioned the creation of a theatrical school modeled on Reinhardt's acclaimed studio. His recommendations were remarkably thorough. The first semester of the program would include lessons in voice, speech, rhythm, and gymnastics; the second semester would add theater history and Jewish history to the program. He recommended two hundred and fifty days of classes a year with three two-hour classes a day, and he planned for between twenty and forty students. His one condition was that no professional theater workers should be accepted into the school.[39] Tremendously impressed with the newcomer's progress, the Theatrical Society appointed Granovsky its director in March 1918.[40] With the recent arrival to Petrograd of the reputed theater activists A. Vayter and Mendel Elkin (1873–1962), the project got under way.

Soon after, the Commissariat of Jewish Affairs, in conjunction with the Theatrical Department of the Commissariat of Nationality Affairs, began work on founding a Yiddish-language theater in Moscow. They wrote to the Theatrical Department of the Commissariat of Enlightenment in October 1918:

> In the matter of building a new theater for the Jewish proletariat we are entering a new beginning. Jewish theater is simply *balagan* in which the primary place is occupied by operettas, melodrama, and feeble boulevard shows (fairground booth entertainment) with national-chauvinist content. . . . In all cities in which there are Jewish workers, social democrats are erecting dramatic circles in which there could be good strong dramatic work.[41]

In order to turn these circles into useful instruments of propaganda, the Commissariat of Jewish Affairs decided to establish a central theater-studio in Moscow to coordinate Yiddish theatrical activities throughout the country and to devise a repertoire of revolutionary Yiddish plays. A list of acceptable pre-revolutionary plays was compiled, consisting, once again, primarily of the works of Sholem Aleichem and Sholem Asch.[42] A subsequent report recommended the establishment of a theater school capable of teaching general knowledge as well as theatrical skills. Recommendations also included the publication of Yiddish plays and a monthly journal on Yiddish theater and the creation of a library of Jewish theater.[43]

While the Commissariat of Jewish Affairs had similar goals to those of the Jewish Theatrical Society, the disbanding of the Commissariat and the merger of the Theatrical Department with that of the Commissariat of Enlightenment in January 1919 forced the cancellation of the project. Instead, the Theatrical Department of the Commissariat of Enlightenment began working on a broad program to establish theaters among all national minorities. The Yiddish theater project was subjoined to an overly ambitious scheme envisioning national theaters for the Chuvash, Kyrghiz, Kazakhs, South Slavs, Czecho-Slovaks, Armenians, Kalmyks, Ukrainians, and Belorussians.[44] The project was never realized. Instead, once the Jewish Theatrical Society finally succeeded in forming a studio under the leadership of Granovsky, the Commissariat of Enlightenment simply nationalized it—along with all other independent theaters—under the auspices of its Theatrical Department.[45]

※

The role of the Jewish Theatrical Society in the establishment of the Moscow State Yiddish Theater has been much misunderstood. The notion that the Moscow State Yiddish Theater was unilaterally created by the Commissariat of Nationality Affairs owes its derivation to Soviet historians who were anxious to create a myth of the state as an omnipotent creator benevolently bestowing culture upon its progeny. Due to the suppression of any documents challenging this fiction, it has been repeated by even the most learned Western scholars. For instance, Beatrice Picon-Vallin wrote that "the Jewish Theatrical Society of Petersburg showed itself to be incapable of founding the new Jewish theater. It was the revolution which gave life to this project: the Commissariat of Jewish Affairs of Petrograd . . . [which] obtained the consent of Aleksandr Granovsky."[46] Another version has it that "in 1919, the Yiddish Section (Yevsektsia) [sic] of the Commissariat for Jewish Affairs[47] . . . planned a studio to train actors for a new Soviet Jewish theater of high quality."[48] Another version, spread primarily by Granovsky himself, maintains that he created the theater single-handedly. While this fiction was broadcast throughout Europe during the theater's 1928 tour, discerning critics were disinclined to believe it. Few, however, have followed the literary critic Nakhman Mayzel, who claims to have been present at a meeting of the Jewish Theatrical Society in the late summer of 1917 and who tells that the theater "was founded in the years 1917–1918 in Petrograd by a group of Yiddish theater activists and theater lovers."[49]

As the newly available transcripts from the Jewish Theatrical Society's first meetings reveal, the theater arose neither from the state's *diktat* nor from one man's whim; it developed through the combined efforts of a broad group of liberal Jewish intellectuals and philanthropists. Furthermore, contrary to the messianic cries of its founders, it did not suddenly spring out of a vacuum; it had evolved over the course of forty years, during which a large group of Jewish playwrights and actors sprawling over two continents gradually transformed a vernacular dialect into a literary language and inspired a theater-going public in the process.

The Yiddish Chamber Theater

On November 29, 1918, the journal *Zhizn iskusstvo* announced that a Jewish workers' chamber theater, headed by Aleksandr Granovsky, had been founded in Petrograd. Granovsky was one of many Soviet modernist artists who defined their system as a rejection of the values and aesthetics of previous epochs. Together with the supporters of Proletkult (Proletarian Culture Movement) and TRAM (Theater of Working-Class Youth), Granovsky was anticipating a redefinition of theatrical space that he believed would evolve as the proletariat usurped the stage from the bourgeoisie.[50] Rather than recruit participants through local theatrical societies, Granovsky advertised for actors by posting bills throughout the streets of Petrograd in the hopes of attracting the Jewish proletariat.[51] Because "the entire personnel of our theater came to us as raw material," Granovsky wrote, they were able to "abandon themselves to the joy of creation." He wanted to divest his theater of any remnants of the hated old world by assembling a troupe with no roots in the past. Indeed, many of the approximately thirty actors who came to the theater were amateurs, but few were of working-class backgrounds or had ever seen the inside of a factory. This parallels Lynn Mally's observations that the Leningrad TRAM "included people with less than pure factory credentials."[52] The majority were young men and women in their early twenties hailing from urban lower-middle-class families of the western borderlands. Typical of this breed were three star actresses who remained with the theater until its closing: Esther Karchmer, a recent gymnasium graduate who had been born in Vilna in 1899; Iustina Minkova, a former milliner born in Warsaw in 1897; and Leah Rom, the theater's star dancer, born in a small shtetl in 1894. The theater critic Osip Liubomirskii writes of the initial troupe: "The majority were people of the free professions. Prior to enrolling in the studio many of them had pretty honest jobs and decent lifestyles."[53]

Solomon Mikhoels [Solomon (Shloymo) Mikhailovich Vovsi], born in Dvinsk in 1890, was the oldest actor admitted into the studio. The large Vovsi family— Mikhoels was one of nine children (including a twin brother)—was exemplary of Eastern European Orthodox Jewry. He described his father as a "typical Jewish patriarch saturated with a deep fanaticism." His mother, in contrast, was an avid reader of secular Russian and Yiddish fiction.[54] Like many of the other male actors, at the age of four, Mikhoels was sent to *kheder* (Jewish religious primary school) where he studied the Bible, Hebrew, the Talmud, and the Mishnah. At the age of fifteen, after his family moved to Riga, Mikhoels enrolled in middle school, where he was to remain until 1908. In 1911, he enrolled in the Kiev Commerce Institute and upon graduating transferred to the faculty of jurisprudence at St. Petersburg University. After his graduation he was offered a job teaching mathematics at a Proletkult school. This career path was cut short, however, when in 1919 he heard about Granovsky's theater. The idea of becoming an actor was not new to Mik- hoels; he claimed to have been interested in theater from an early age. As a child he and his brothers attended the Dvinsk theater's Russian translation of *Hamlet*, and Mikhoels became further inspired after seeing a Yiddish troupe on tour. In imitation of their new heroes the young Vovsi brothers performed *purimspiels* for the family, and Mikhoels wrote a short play, *The Sins of Youth*, about a child who does not want to study, which he performed for the neighborhood children.[55] Later he informally studied Russian diction for fourteen years in the hope, he claimed, of eventually becoming an actor.[56] No doubt he reasoned the skills would also be of use as a legal orator. According to Mikhoels's brother, they also grew up in a musical family—their father was musically gifted and a great fan of cantorial music.[57] Mikhoels's bulging eyes and protruding forehead contributed to his ex- pressive face which, combined with his large gesticulating hands, constituted an ideal stage actor's physique.

Granovsky was prepared to run a tight ship. Unlike the transient Yiddish troupes who picked up extras at inns en route only to drop them off again at the next stop, Granovsky demanded commitment. In January 1919 he presented his employees with a one-year contract obligating them to attend all rehearsals. An additional clause required them to arrive at the theater five minutes before each rehearsal and forty-five minutes before each performance. Prospective employees also agreed to accept all roles assigned to them; Granovsky would tolerate no grumbling over bit parts. The Commissariat of Nationalities, in conjunction with the Theatrical Department of the Commissariat of Enlightenment, under whose auspices all state and private theaters were in the process of being nationalized, would pay each member 900 rubles per month—a nearly worthless sum given the

Bolsheviks' liberal use of the currency printing press.[58] In order to allow the group to supplement this "income" with a day job, rehearsals were scheduled only for evenings and Sunday afternoons.[59]

The ambitious director decided that his theater's initial repertoire would include seven different plays to be performed in three separate programs. Granovsky selected a challenging repertoire to show off his troupe's command of both European symbolist and *Haskalic* (Jewish Enlightenment) plays. He quickly proved himself to be a perfectionist; just days before the scheduled premiere, after the streets of Petrograd had been plastered with posters announcing the event, Granovsky decided he was not satisfied and delayed the performance for a week, forcing the reprinting of posters in the midst of a major paper shortage.[60] Finally, on July 3, 1919, the troupe put on its first performance, consisting of three plays: A. Magid's Yiddish translation of *The Blind* by the Belgian symbolist Maurice Maeterlinck (1862–1949)—a play Granovsky believed would prove that fine art can be expressed in the Yiddish language; and two plays by the Yiddish playwright Sholem Asch—*Sin* and *Prologue*.[61] The next night they performed *In Winter* and *Amnon and Tamar* by Asch and a symbolist short play written by Mikhoels entitled *The Builders*, which was about the Tower of Babel.[62] The final program consisted of just one play, a Yiddish translation of Karl Gutzkow's (1811–1878) *Uriel Acosta*. The play was staged by R. Ungern, a non-Jewish former director at the Theater of Artistic Drama and member of the World of Art school.

Uriel Acosta was the most noteworthy production of this first period. Written in 1846 by a member of the Young Germany school, the play is based on the true story of Uriel d'Acosta, a seventeenth-century *converso* (a Jew forcibly converted to Catholicism) who fled Portugal to Amsterdam, where he was able to practice Judaism openly. However, frustrated by the necessity of conforming to Judaism's strict rituals, he committed suicide. The play's criticism of the superstitious rituals which were perceived to accompany religion appealed to Soviet ideals. The play had long been the epitome of dignified drama in the Jewish repertoire and a popular choice for non-Jewish theaters as well. In 1881 alone three versions of the play were being performed within the Russian Empire, including a Yiddish translation by Osip Lerner. A Hebrew version was even performed at the eleventh World Zionist Congress in 1913. It is hardly surprising that Granovsky sought to prove himself with this classic of the European stage. In the words of Lulla Adler Rosenfeld, Jacob Adler's granddaughter, "Uriel Acosta from the actors' viewpoint may be called its Hamlet. No dramatic actor could reckon himself of the first rank until he had shown what he could do with Acosta, the great Rationalist, the martyr who faced excommunication to bring light to his people."[63]

Unfortunately, these early productions were largely unsuccessful. One anonymous critic who wrote an unpublished hagiographical portrait of Mikhoels was forced to admit: "This time, Mikhoels was not successful at portraying Uriel. The theater went along the path of aesthetics, the director wanted the stage to be a beautiful sculpture—'living pictures,' but not living people; he wanted an unhappy Uriel, and not a hero who is victorious over his thoughts."[64]

The only saving grace of the performances was their exceptional music. Influenced by Reinhardt's emphasis on harmony, Granovsky sacrificed his principles to hire professional musicians. Aleksandr Krein (1883–1951), who composed for *In Winter,* was born in Nizhnii Novgorod, to a family of professional musicians. His rich ornamentation of oriental motifs, which became apparent in his earliest compositions, attracted the attention of both the Jewish Folk Music Society and Russian musical critics. After working with the Yiddish theater for the next two decades, Krein turned to ballet; his *Laurencia* was performed by both the Kirov and Bolshoi Theaters in the 1940s. Joseph Akhron (1886–1943), who added a score to *The Blind,* was a graduate of the St. Petersburg Conservatory and a former member of the Jewish Folk Music Society. He continued to work for Yiddish theater before emigrating to California in the early 1920s. Driven by its musical success, the troupe supplemented its dramas with informal evenings of music that featured eclectic programs of revolutionary songs, klezmer dances, and Chopin marches.[65]

Having had little popular success, the troupe concluded by the end of the month that the assimilated Jews of Petrograd had little interest in Yiddish theater. It accepted an invitation from the Bund chapter in Vitebsk to move to the more Jewish town for the summer, where it met wider, but still limited, success.[66]

Two years had passed since the "Great October Socialist Revolution," and Petrograd was in shambles; hunger and fear enveloped the city for the second summer in a row. The government had fled the city of the Revolution to Moscow's Kremlin, the medieval tsarist fortress. Returning from a tumultuous countryside in the fall of 1919, Granovsky and his troupe discovered that the Jews of Petrograd had not increased their interest in Yiddish theater; nobody was willing even to provide them with an auditorium or rehearsal hall. Not to be deterred by such technicalities, Granovsky almost farcically insisted that his employees adhere to their contractual obligations and maintain the rigorous rehearsal schedule. Much of the troupe lacked their director's enthusiasm and optimism. Around half of them abandoned their leader and returned to the workforce. Indeed, the theater's opportunities in Petrograd were spent.

Scene Change: Moscow

"Passionate, frenzied, turbulent Moscow, the headquarters of the revolutionary country, the potential capital of the world . . . marching along the streets the chimera of dozens of directors, hundreds of artists, thousands of actors, barefoot dancers, circuses, dilettantes and adventurists metamorphose into reality."[67] Thus wrote Abram Efros (1898–1954), a Moscow theater and art critic who believed in the messianic mission of Yiddish theater to bring revolutionary ideals to the Jewish public. He was an ardent leftist who wrote of pre-revolutionary bourgeois art forms with utter disdain. Like Ivanov, Evreinov, and others, Efros praised theater for its Dionysian potential. He hoped to create a new stage capable of breaking down not only aesthetic traditions, but social barriers as well:

> The new type of production required a new scenic atmosphere. It was incumbent
> to change the traditional box . . . The question was one of conquering the air, of

vestiges of capitalist society, either through an inability or an unwillingness to adapt to the new world, many audience members looked upon the comical and quaint *luftmentsh* with compassion and empathy.

The small auditorium on Stankevich Street where the theater was housed is described by Zagorskii as a place that "produced the atmosphere of a chamber, a studio, or a laboratory. The feeling of intimacy and closeness between the theater and its audience for that first performance resembled the First Studio of the Moscow Art Theater."[87] In his sets Marc Chagall sought to emphasize this intimacy: he abolished the separation between performers and audience in a tribute to "collective action" by decorating the entire theater with oil paintings and ridding the stage of a front curtain. The open stage was an innovation of Meyerhold's, designed to emulate the street theater which he admired as a spontaneous expression of the people's celebratory mood.[88] It also paralleled similar developments in painting, such as the works of the artist Pavel Kuznetsov (1878–1968), who rejected frames for his paintings in the belief that art should not be separated from the everyday. Chagall's back mural depicted disjointed groups of figures moving away from the theater's entrance in a portrayal of forward motion—the expected course of the Revolution.

Chagall incorporated Jewish folk motifs into his art in an effort to veil revolutionary ideals in symbols familiar to his audience and to desanctify religious images. For instance, an acrobat wearing phylacteries standing on his head symbolizes the theater's goal of turning religion upside down and converting "unproductive" religious Jews into entertainers. A worker about to applaud represents the anticipated proletarian response and the conversion of Jews into workers. A ram's horn, a messianic symbol blown on Rosh Hashanah to welcome the new year, depicts the welcoming of the new age and equates messianic expectation with revolutionary utopianism.[89]

Each skit was staged with the high level of precision that was soon to become characteristic of Granovsky's system. The actors gestured in exaggerated movements, bending and flexing their bodies to the limits of human elasticity or rigidifying themselves like metal. Indications of personal feelings were concealed behind painted expressions. Overall they gave the impression of pantomime or marionettes controlled by an offstage puppeteer. Despite the similarities in their approaches to theater, Chagall and Granovsky proved to be personally incompatible and Chagall soon departed. Although Chagall only worked with the theater for this first production, his contribution to its aesthetic approach was seminal. The troupe learned from him the means by which syncopation can be transposed from music into three-dimensional art—a technique which was epitomized by Granovsky's biomechanics—and he introduced them to the fusion of folk art and modernism.

Much of the Soviet press criticized the performance for being too manufactured, thereby destroying the spontaneity and genuineness of Sholem Aleichem. One reviewer wrote, "Adonai, Adonai! What have they done with the good nature and gentleness of Sholem Aleichem?"[90] Hoping to enjoy the type of sentimental

Top: Marc Chagall, "Introduction to the Jewish Theater." © 2000 Artists Rights Society (ARS), New York/ ADAGP, Paris.

Opposite page: Marc Chagall's sets for *Mazel Tov,* 1921. Photo from O. Liubomirskii, *Mikhoels* (Moscow, 1938).

Left: Solomon Mikhoels as Reb Alter in *Mazel Tov,* 1921. Photo courtesy of Natalia Vovsi-Mikhoels.

and nostalgic portraits which had brought Sholem Aleichem international fame, much of the Jewish audience was also shocked and disturbed by Granovsky's savage mockery of their way of life. Some even accused the theater of anti-Semitism —a charge initially shared even by some members of the troupe itself.[91] However, the show was a popular success; it was performed over 300 times and *Mazel Tov* remained in the theater's repertoire for over a decade. In September 1921 *The Spoiled Celebration* was replaced with *It's a Lie* (written in 1906), about the vicious rumors of a rich and famous rabbi's personal affairs. Like its predecessor, the play mocked false piety.

On February 13, 1921, the theater premiered *Before Sunrise* by A. Vayter, the Yiddish theater activist who was murdered in a pogrom by Polish troops occupying Vilna during the Civil War. Eager to depict the popular Bundist as a revolutionary fighter, the Bolsheviks portrayed his death as an act of martyrdom. Set during the Revolution of 1905, the play was one of the first in the Yiddish language to put revolution on stage. As crowds amass on the streets in the early hours of a frigid night, Vayter takes us into the drawing room of one Jewish intellectual family as they contemplate the choices before them: while the younger generation is torn between the futures promised by the Zionists and Communists, their elders try to persuade them to return to their religious tradition. Granovsky worked closely with the Soviet Jewish writer Yekhezkel Dobrushin (1883–1952) in a rearrangement of the text to create a memorial for those, like their friend Vayter, whom they believed had been martyred for the revolutionary cause.

Dobrushin, the son of a lumber merchant from Chernigov, would become a regular collaborator with the Yiddish theater. He had first been introduced to socialist circles in the early 1900s when he was studying at the Sorbonne. In 1909 he returned to Russia and began writing Yiddish poetry and short stories. In 1920 Dobrushin moved to Moscow, where he became secretary of the Yiddish Writer's Union and a noted literary critic and playwright in his own right. During World War II, he worked with the Jewish Anti-Fascist Committee before being arrested in 1948. He died in prison, presumably in 1953.

The second production of the season was Sholem Asch's *God of Vengeance*, about a Jewish brothel owner who tries in vain to shield his daughter from his business. First performed by Max Reinhardt in 1907, the play's licentious content and sacrilegious undertones thrust it into the heart of a public controversy, earning it notoriety. Soon after, its performance by Rudolph Schildkraut (father of Joseph Schildkraut, the famous American stage and screen actor) on Broadway led to Schildkraut's arrest and helped bring about a congressional investigation into salaciousness in the theater.[92] In the 1940s Asch forbade its production. While Granovsky's decision to perform it was surely influenced by Reinhardt's production, the play's notoriety had reached Russia long before. A Russian-language version had even been performed in 1907 in St. Petersburg.[93] Granovsky sought to replace the play's salaciousness with pedagogy by using it to argue the intrinsic connection between sin and capitalism.

Finding a replacement for Chagall proved difficult for the theater. Granovsky and Efros finally agreed on a young unknown artist who had recently arrived in

Moscow from the south—Isaak Rabinovich (1894–1961). As Efros explained, he was desirable for four reasons: he was young, he came from a Jewish milieu, he appreciated the differences between theater art and canvas, and he was a revolutionary.[94] Despite its popular success, the troupe as a whole was receiving lukewarm reviews at best. Most critics, however, did recognize the exceptional ability of the theater's musicians, artists, and director. Granovsky was even invited to direct a German translation of Mayakovsky's *Mystery Bouffe,* a parody of the story of Noah's ark, at the Moscow Circus for the delegates to the Third Comintern Congress in June 1921.

The First Reviews

Due to its popular success, the Moscow State Yiddish Theater was quickly outgrowing its intimate theater hall. Within months of the theater's initial move to Moscow, Lunacharskii had taken it upon himself to help the theater find a larger auditorium. In March 1920, he had convinced the photo-cinema department of his commissariat to give Granovsky a building on the Arbat in exchange for a new building in Chistye Prudy. However, Granovsky refused the offer, insisting on the Sohn Theater in the Triumphal Garden.[95] While negotiations continued, Khaim Krashinskii proposed that they take the Romanov military club—a former noble palace on Malaia Bronnaia which had been confiscated during the Revolution and turned into a military club.[96] Krashinskii's proposal was accepted, and on September 15, 1920, the palace was put at the disposal of the Moscow State Yiddish Theater by the Presidium of Workers, Red Army, and Peasant Deputies of Moscow.[97] After over a year of renovations, the palace was converted into a 500-seat concert hall. The theater would remain there until its 1949 closing.

The renovations required a great deal of work and money, amounting to 25 million rubles.[98] As a result of these expenditures, the theater quickly encountered financial difficulties, forcing it to seek a grant of 3.5 million rubles in order to remain open. The request was given tentative approval by the Commissariat of Enlightenment,[99] but when Lunacharskii brought the issue before the Council of People's Commissars (Sovnarkom) in June 1922 it was rejected "on account of political considerations."[100] At this moment, the theater faced the very real possibility of imminent collapse. It was only saved thanks to the intervention of the Jewish Section, which was motivated by the theater's propaganda potential.[101] Moishe Rafes, a former Bundist who had become active in the Jewish Section, penned an appeal to the commissar of nationality affairs, Joseph Stalin:

> From considerations of a political character, I believe it necessary to ask you somehow or other to reconsider the decision of the Minor Council of People's Commissars (MSNK) which deprived the Moscow Jewish Chamber Theater of a subsidy.
>
> Having spent the past year in Warsaw and having had the opportunity to observe how the Jewish bourgeoisie and especially the conciliatory press use every triviality to systematically poison the Soviet Government, I can categorically confirm that the decision of the MSNK will be liberally manipulated by them. And the decision, really, will be little understood. . . .

We, at this time, are expending a great deal of energy and means to dissemi-
nate correct information abroad about the politics of the Soviet state. Three and
a half million rubles is not a large sum. Disregarding all reasoning of a cultural
and artistic character, I propose that out of considerations of a general political
character it is necessary to re-establish immediately the subsidy of three and a
half million to the Jewish chamber theater before news of this reaches America.[102]

Convinced of the need to maintain at least a facade of tolerance toward the
Soviet Union's national minorities before the American and Polish press, Stalin
acquiesced and granted the theater its required subsidy. The urgency with which
the letter concludes—"before news of this reaches America"—reveals the audience
to whom the state believed the theater was performing, regardless of who sat in the
concert hall. Fear of the effects of economic boycott, only partially alleviated by the
still-recent Treaty of Rapallo with Germany, kept the fledgling state on its best
behavior before the foreign press, forcing it to take great pains to hide its crimes.
Polish public opinion was also paramount in warding off a potential Polish attack
to retake the Soviet Union's new acquisitions on its western frontier, and it was
hoped that the large Polish Jewish population would look upon the Soviet state as
its protector. While no record of Stalin's response is available, the grant was given
to the theater that year. The issue was probably decided in July when the Council
affirmed the decision to include the Yiddish theater in the list of state academic
theaters.[103]

The first production at the new Malaia Bronnaia Theater was Moshe Litva-
kov's new translation of Gutzkow's *Uriel Acosta*, which premiered on April 9, 1922.
Granovsky's version differed immensely from the Petersburg production, which
Ungern had directed. The new adaptation was prepared by Moshe Litvakov and
Mark Rivesman, the literary director of the theater, based on a 1919 Yiddish
translation Abraham Muravskii had prepared for the Vilna Troupe and an 1880
Russian translation by Petr Veinberg. In the words of Zagorskii,

> In Petersburg . . . the central role was played by the actor, still only beginning to
> learn the actor's trade. In Moscow, A. Granovsky introduced into the production
> a Jewish player who had already acquired, while in the Chernyshevskii [formerly
> Stankevich] Hall, a fully mastered voice, movements and gestures. . . . In the
> Moscow version of *Acosta*, he introduced an ideological significance, a tragedy of
> mentality and not merely of emotion.[104]

The sets were designed by Natan Altman (1889–1970), an artist who came to
the Yiddish theater from Habima. While Altman's mother tongue was Yiddish,
his prominence rested on his involvement with non-Jewish Soviet culture. Born in
the town of Vinnitsa in Ukraine in 1889, Altman moved to Odessa in 1901, where
he enrolled in the Odessa Art School. Dissatisfied with the realist approach which
monopolized the school, in 1907 he returned to his native Vinnitsa, where the
contrasting shadows and lights of the town's narrow alleyways influenced his fas-
cination with the effects of light and atmosphere. It was here too that he began to
explore Jewish folk art, painting his "Old Jew" and "Young Jew." In 1911 Altman
traveled to Paris, where he familiarized himself with French impressionism and

was introduced to cubism. When he returned to St. Petersburg in 1913, Altman became one of Russia's first cubist artists and, after the Revolution, embraced futurism. He was commissioned to design the first Soviet postal stamp and designed the Uritskii Square (Palace Square) carnival celebrating the first anniversary of the Bolshevik Revolution.[105] In 1921 he moved to Moscow and became involved with theater, working with Meyerhold on Mayakovsky's *Mystery Bouffe*, and with Habima on *Dybbuk* before coming to Granovsky's theater.[106] Art critic Daniel Reznik wrote of Altman that he had an "organic ear for our revolutionary epoch. Altman is entirely in the present, he is through and through contemporary. He is the propagandist of the new aesthetic, the aesthetic of masterly skill, conscious of understanding and affection."[107] Abram Efros was the first art critic to recognize Altman with his 1922 work *A Portrait of Natan Altman,* the first book written about the artist. Efros praised Altman for his refusal to succumb to the World of Art style and for his rejection of the aristocratic art forms of Paris.[108] Throughout his work with the Yiddish theater, Efros maintained that Altman's art was the perfect complement to Granovsky's goals and ideals.[109]

For *Uriel Acosta,* Altman painted the walls of the theater black and left the stage empty except for several geometric volumes suggesting furniture. Abstract montages of geometric shapes and color represented the urbanized and industrialized future foreseen for the Soviet state. Influenced by Malevich's suprematism, Altman rejected realistic art, which he believed strove to imitate a dead past; he particularly rejected portrayals of concrete objects as representative of private property. According to Efros, the cubist set resembled Alexandra Exter's work for Tairov's theater, a worthy archetype.[110] It was in emulation of Tairov and Exter that Efros sought artists who could metamorphose themselves into "artists of the theater, a distinctive species, an organic composition of the production—a painter, sculptor, an architect capable of seeing and thinking in terms of scenic extension and dimensions."[111] Altman's abstract sets provided a provocative contrast with Granovsky's realistic staging and psychological probing.

Despite moderate success, the play was quickly overshadowed by the theater's other two new performances of the season: Goldfadn's *The Sorceress* and Sholem Aleichem's *Two Hundred Thousand.* Both of the new productions attacked capitalism, private property, and money, portraying the evil and misery that accompany them and the psychological price of acquiring unearned money. In addition, by combining modern biomechanical dance with traditional Jewish folk music, the theater once again sought to present familiar symbols in new contexts through a merger of modernism and folk arts.

The Sorceress premiered on December 2, 1922. The play opens at a birthday celebration for Mirele, the daughter of Reb Avremtse, a wealthy Jew. The party is ruined as a tsarist officer enters and arrests Avremtse, leaving Mirele in the care of her wicked aunt, Vasia. In collusion with a sorceress, Vasia kidnaps the child and takes her to Istanbul—allowing the troupe to display some exotic and exciting Turkish dance and music—and sells her into slavery. The play ends with a joyous reunion as Avremtse is released and Mirele's beloved succeeds in rescuing her.[112] The play, with its harrowing adventures, disastrous mishaps, narrow escapes, and intervention by characters possessing magical powers, was typical of the melo-drama of nineteenth-century Yiddish theater, ironically the epitome of the *shund* entertainment the Moscow State Yiddish Theater had been formed to combat. Similar productions, such as Mikhail Glinka's *Ruslan and Lyudmila,* were also still prominent on the Russian stage.

The text of Goldfadn's play was rearranged by Dobrushin and Litvakov. It was hoped that the revised script would help quell criticism from leftist circles attack-ing the theater's decision to produce a play written by the archetype of the old melodramatic Yiddish theatrical style.[113] Mikhoels argued that Goldfadn was a folk artist who wrote plays portraying genuine shtetl life, which, when combined with the newest stage styles, produced true revolutionary theater.[114] The staging, with laughter at inappropriate times and bombastic music during love scenes, also aimed to mock the melodrama of the original script. Litvakov, acting hypocriti-cally in light of his role in the arrangement, was not convinced. He complained that a theater which claimed to abhor and despise literariness should not have been performing a classic of old Yiddish melodrama. The public debate illustrates that the Party's control over the theater's repertoire was not yet complete. While still adhering to the Party's program in spirit, Granovsky was unwilling to allow Lit-vakov to dictate the means by which his ideology was expressed. Despite the negative press—or, more likely, because of it—the play was immensely popular and remained in the theater's repertoire until 1934. It was later revived in a new adaptation after World War II.

Over the next few years, as a Party line on Goldfadn became formulated, Litvakov's outright rejection would lose out to Mikhoels's conditional praise. Like the Moscow State Yiddish Theater, Goldfadn would be seen as a revolutionary who fought against the insipid rabbinicism of his era in an effort to promote sec-ular enlightened culture among the Jewish masses. However, the sentimentality and melodrama of his plays, which were geared toward bourgeois audiences, would remain a contentious subject.[115] Ironically, when *The Sorceress* premiered in New York in 1882 with Boris Thomashefsky's troupe, it also aroused a controversy, this time from the Hebrew Immigration Aid Committee, who feared that the por-trayal of the Jewish peddler as a swindler and thief would contribute to anti-Semitic feelings among non-Jewish New Yorkers.[116]

Once again, the highlights of Granovsky's production were the art and mu-sic—this time thanks to the efforts of Rabinovich and Akhron. Zuskin's starring role, as well, helped propel him into the limelight, ensuring him a position as Mikhoels's sidekick for years to come. Rabinovich assembled a constructivist set of scaffolding, ladders, and platforms protruding at various levels, making the stage resemble a construction site—a symbol of progress, and a setting familiar to a proletarian audience. Akhron arranged Goldfadn's songs and wrote an additional twenty new songs which he based on his own ethnographic studies in the former Pale of Settlement. Akhron's songs utilized the traditionally Jewish Dorian mode with an augmented fourth—the same scale made famous by Tevye's leitmotif in *Fiddler on the Roof.* "The Meeting of Mirele and the Sorceress," with its eerie introduction and oriental motifs bolstering Mikhoels wailing voice, was even released on phonograph. The juxtaposition of Akhron's folkish melodies and Rabin-ovich's futuristic sets emphasized the distinctions between old and new.

Granovsky's strict discipline and training produced remarkable results. The actors danced, climbed, crawled, jumped, flipped, and somersaulted over, under, and around the sets and each other. Choreographed like clockwork, the actors moved like cogs in a machine, sporadically bursting out of their syncopated robotic mime into wild and frenzied dance. They littered the stage, filling all its open space and crevices as they crawled along the scaffolding like nimble cats or pounced out of concealed pits like leopards on the attack. Hidden behind grotesque makeup, each individual ego was but a symbol for the social class it represented.

Granovsky's carnivalesque sacrilege manifested itself in his equation of the sorceress's spell with the Kol Nidre prayer sung on the eve of the Day of Atone-ment and in a mourning ceremony that is held for an earlock. Zuskin, in the role of Baba Iakhna, was dressed as a woman but wore arm phylacteries (the ritual dress prescribed for men) around his legs. While this female role was traditionally played by a man, a custom followed in New York as well as in Moscow, the wear-ing of phylacteries amounted to sacrilege. It could also be interpreted as a protest against the treatment of women in traditional Judaism by mocking the segment of the morning prayer declared by Jewish men while wearing phylacteries: "Blessed art thou, Lord our God, King of the universe, who hast not made me a woman." Further, by having both women singing and dancing on stage and a man dressed as a woman, the theater flaunted its defiance of Judaic law while simultaneously emphasizing its victory over the ancient repression of theater. The iconoclastic

The Sorceress, 1922. Sets by Isaak Rabinovich. Photo from *Das Moskauer Jüdische Akademische Theater* (Berlin, 1928).

mission was further represented by a funeral procession for the "Old Theater Habima" which passes through the town square.

Unfortunately, many Soviet reviewers were disappointed and could not refrain from comparing the theater unfavorably with Habima, whose production of Solomon Ansky's *Dybbuk* was rapidly achieving worldwide fame. One reviewer complained that Granovsky's excessive biomechanics distracted the audience from the play, making the performance appear to be more of a festival than an art theater.[117] Others complained that Granovsky's mechanized adaptation had destroyed the spirit and spontaneity of Jewish folk theater. [118] The British director Basil Dean, who saw the play on a trip to Russia, disagreed: "I believe that this production is one of the best examples of Russian theater," he wrote.[119]

In light of the negative response from the Yiddish press and the Jewish Section, the theater next returned to a less controversial author—Sholem Aleichem. In January 1923, when work began on *The Big Win* (which was written in 1915 and later renamed *Two Hundred Thousand*), the repertory decision was praised by both Dobrushin and Litvakov in *Der emes.*[120] Excitement was further generated through a gala four-year jubilee celebration in January, during which the theater presented the 150th performance of *An Evening of Sholem Aleichem.* The addresses given at the gala by Litvakov and Granovsky showed that this time the two were in total agreement. *Der emes* reported that the auditorium was filled with workers, students, literary figures, and artists.[121] The new production premiered on June 28, 1923.

Two Hundred Thousand begins at the house of the poor tailor Shimele Soroker, where his assistants Motl and Kopl continuously interrupt each other as they try to formulate new ways of expressing their shared love for Shimele's daughter Beylke. Meanwhile, Shimele is groveling to his landlord and his wife is staving off sundry lenders. The next evening, after winning 200,000 rubles in a lottery that day, Shimele, now insisting on being called by the more formal appellation Simeon Makarovich Soroker, throws a flamboyant ball to which he invites all the luminaries of the town. Making the rounds as the host of the evening, Shimele arranges a match between his daughter and the son of his wealthy landlord and invests in a nascent movie studio. Much to his chagrin, the next morning the illiterate former tailor discovers that he put one too many zeros on his check toward the founding of the studio, leaving him destitute once again with only memories of his night as one of the elite. The play ends happily as the landlord to whom Shimele promised his daughter reneges on the agreement, allowing her to marry her true beloved, Shimele's poor assistant.[122]

In contrast to the original Shimele, who gives much of his fortune to charity, Granovsky's protagonist lunges full force into the immoral and decadent lifestyle of the nouveau riche. Shimele was intended to arouse the disdain of the audience. Indeed, like Bolshevik agitators, Granovsky shunned any psychological complexities, preferring to portray characters as social types. The sharp contrast between the reformed Shimele and his working-class background was emphasized by a split stage which placed workers on ladders effortlessly floating above the bourgeoisie, whose obesity made them ever aware of the pull of gravity. A matchmaker parachuted onto the stage, alluding to a literal interpretation of the ubiquitous *luftmentshen*. In another scene, the obese swindler stood atop a table as the crowds swooned around him in reverence and musicians serenaded from the scaffolding above. A contorted menorah floated above center stage, mocking the false piety of the bourgeois clique.

As had now become common for the theater, prominent professional artists and musicians were recruited. Isaak Rabichev (1896–1957) designed the sets for *Two Hundred Thousand*. Rabichev was born in 1896 in Kiev and had studied at the Brodsky Art School until 1917, when he continued his art studies in Moscow. He had worked as a graphic artist for *Pravda* and had achieved fame designing agitational posters, the most famous of which were his "Proletarians of All Countries Unite" and "The Enemy Will Find No Place to Hide From the People."[123] But the most significant new recruit was Lev Pulver (1883–1970), whose musical compositions became the hallmark of the theater for the duration of its existence; they were even featured at the 1939 New York World's Fair. Pulver was born in 1883 in a shtetl on Russia's western frontier into a family of musicians. He graduated from the St. Petersburg Conservatory in 1908 before joining the Bolshoi Theater orchestra, where he served as violin soloist for fourteen years.[124] Songs like "Not Shimele! It's Semen Makarovich," with its Hasidic-style chant, and the lively wedding dance "Sher," with its syncopated rhythm, became staples of the theater.[125]

With its newfound niche among Moscow's major theaters and new home on the Malaia Bronnaia, the theater's trade union also decided, on September 15, 1924, to delete the word "Chamber" from its name, changing it to the State Yiddish Theater, also known by its Russian acronym, Goset.[126] The growth of the theater, combined with its new responsibilities, led to financial problems which left the troupe unpaid for extended periods of time. This was caused in large part by the exponential growth of the theater's staff; it doubled in just eighteen months and continued to increase. In March 1922, the theater's staff numbered only forty-eight people, including twenty-five actors and actresses. That number had increased to seventy-four in June of the same year and to eighty-seven by September 1923. The staff continued to grow, reaching a peak of one hundred and fifteen by 1924, including four department heads, forty-four artistic personnel, twenty-three orchestra members, eighteen administration personnel, fifteen technicians, five costume makers, three decorators, and two medical advisers.[127] Many of the new actors, such as David Chechik (b. 1893), were former members of the Kiev Kultur-Lige dramatic circle who relocated to Moscow with the organization's 1924 dissolution. Others, like Moshe Goldblatt (b. 1896), were graduates of the Yiddish theater studio. Salaries also increased, particularly those of the orchestra members and department heads. In 1924, twelve members of the organization had salaries of over 100 rubles a month: Granovsky at 360, Pulver at 287, Mikhoels at 230, and Zuskin at 115.50. Several members of the orchestra and management divisions, the lighting technician (Aron Namiot), and the chief makeup artist (Tubakov)

200,000, 1923. Sets by Isaac Rabichev. Photo from *Das Moskauer Jüdische Akademische Theater* (Berlin, 1928).

200,000, 1923. *Front, from left to right*: Eva Itskhoki, Evgeniia Epstein, Rakhl Imenitova, Esther Karchmer. *Back:* Benjamin Zuskin. Photo courtesy of Ala Perelman-Zuksin.

round out the list of top salaried members.[128] Wages for the rest of the staff were scaled in thirteen divisions. This situation did little to placate the grumbling bit actors, who were already complaining that they were experiencing worse hunger than they had during the Civil War.[129]

These financial and administrative difficulties impeded the theater's artistic work. Unable to put together a full-length play, the troupe resorted to performing a series of sketches: *Three Jewish Raisins,* written by Dobrushin and Nakhum Oyslender (1893–1962), premiered in March 1924. Oyslender was born in 1893 in Kiev and, like Dobrushin, was the son of a lumber merchant. After studying medicine in Berlin, he was mobilized into the Red Army as a military doctor. After the Civil War, Oyslender started writing symbolic Yiddish poetry. However, he would find his niche not as a creative writer, but as a literary critic and translator; *Three Jewish Raisins* was his first venture into dramaturgy. The reference to raisins was both a tribute to Goldfadn's famous song "Raisins and Almonds" and a synecdoche of wine—a symbol of merriment and life.

Each sketch mocked one of the major genres of Jewish theaters: *Prince von Fliasko Drigo,* about a love affair between a Chinese emperor and a poor Jewish woman from Odessa, poked fun at the melodramas popular among wandering Jewish troupes. In the spirit of Goldfadn, the play is an adventure-packed fantasy in which the two lovers narrowly escape certain death through a series of mishaps and encounters with bandits and pirates, only to be reunited in the finale. The second sketch, *Sarra Wants a Negro,* satirizing the American motto that "everything is possible in America," mocked the New York Yiddish theaters; and *A Night at a Hasidic Rebbe's,* the most successful of the three, parodied the mystical piety of Moscow's own Habima. This last sketch concludes after a wealthy rebbe explains to his eager neophytes how he has accumulated his wealth, and one student exclaims, "My God, how many poor people are needed so that one rich man can live the good life in this world!"[130] Once again Granovsky's staging emphasized the carnivalesque, mixing the sacred with the profane. By turning the ecstatic dance and singing of the Hasidim into theatrical gestures devoid of ulterior meaning, the movements were deprived of their spiritual significance. Such spiritual dance was also a large part of Habima's choreography, epitomized by plays such as *The Eternal Jew.* The popularity of the play was enhanced by Pulver's parody of Hasidic songs, using authentic melodies such as "When the Rebbe drinks, his students follow" which mocked the conformity of the sect. The first two sketches were later dropped from the repertoire, and the title *Three Jewish Raisins* was used to refer to a program consisting of Sholem Aleichem's *The Divorce Paper* (written in 1887), *Mazel Tov,* and *A Night at a Hasidic Rebbe's. The Divorce Paper,* Sholem Aleichem's first play, presents a conversation between two poor failures who conclude that "Life goes nowhere—feh!"

One critic praised *A Night at a Hasidic Rebbe's* for its intricate artistic content as well as its propagandist anti-religious message but was less impressed with the other "raisins": "Here they only dance and sing."[131] *Izvestiia,* in contrast, was full of praise: "One can say that it is the most joyous production of the season."[132] *Pravda* echoed this sentiment: "One can confidently say that of all the parody spectacles of the ongoing season this is the most successful, most joyous and wittiest."[133]

While the Soviet press praised the productions of these years for their strong social messages, some critics were dubious about the theater's potential to persuade Jews of the merits of communism. One reviewer wrote: "I suppose that to the Jewish theater all this is new and unusual and would be irreplaceable for the broad Jewish working masses in the provinces, but here in Moscow, alas, it is idle beauty."[134] Indeed, evidence suggests that the theater was not reaching its intended audience—the Yiddish-speaking religious Jews. In the words of Nahma Sandrow, "Laughter came in two waves: first from those who understood the jokes, and then from those to whom they had to be explained."[135] Russian-language synopses were sold to 60 to 80 percent of the audience each night,[136] brief summaries of all productions appeared in the major theatrical journals along with the cast lists, and the performances were so dominated by song, dance and decorations that they could be appreciated even without any understanding of the dialogue.[137] Furthermore, while the Jewish population of Moscow was rapidly increasing, it still only constituted 5.8 percent of the total Jewish population of the Soviet Union, and it was one of the most assimilated segments of that population.[138] The frequency of articles on the theater in the Russian press confirms that it was not exclusively of interest to Jews. The new theater building on Malaia Bronnaia was a stark contrast from

A Night at a Hasidic Rebbe's, from *Three Jewish Raisins,* 1924.
Photo courtesy of Ala Perelman-Zuskin.

the Bund hall where they played in Vitebsk for the summer; the Moscow State Yiddish Theater was placed in the heart of the downtown theater district—less than a kilometer from the famous Stanislavsky, Meyerhold, and Tairov theaters. In short, the theater was clearly addressing itself to a non-Yiddish-speaking audience. For central state organizations such as the Commissariats of Enlightenment and Nationalities, both of whom sought to use the theater as a showpiece to demonstrate for foreigners the thriving culture of Soviet national minorities, the ethnic composition of the in-house audience made little difference. However, for the Jewish Section, which hoped the theater would inspire traditional Jews to revolutionize their values and adopt new behavioral patterns, the lack of interest among the targeted audience was a significant problem to be rectified in the future.

Revolutionary Theater

Bolshevik thinkers of the 1920s believed that with appropriate content the theater could become an ideal medium for a revolutionary culture. It alone could present utopian visions in concrete forms: revolutionary heroes, right-wing foes, popular festivals, religious rituals, modern industry, and capitalist speculation could all be appropriately exalted or denigrated in a setting comprehensible to even illiterate masses. This sentiment was shared by the community of artists involved in the Soviet Jewish theaters of the 1920s. They were united by a common belief that the theater was the medium most suited to freeing Jewish society of what they saw as its insipid, rabbinical scholasticism and bourgeois philistinism.

The initial successes of the Bolsheviks in establishing control over the turbulent, war-torn country caught many of the self-appointed guardians of proletarian cultural purity off guard. Lacking the resources to create a network of Soviet, state-controlled cultural institutions, the Bolsheviks were willing, for the time being, to welcome those that emerged independently. Unsure how best to create and enforce a purely working-class culture, these enthusiasts were willing to tolerate a motley mix of interpretations. Typical of this ambiguity was the state's simultaneous funding of both the Hebrew-language theater, Habima, and the Moscow State Yiddish Theater. In such an open environment, the Yiddish Theater's symbolist staging, constructivist sets, folkish melodies, and popular texts were permitted to prosper relatively free of state interference.

The Moscow State Yiddish Theater's support for Communist ideals and compliance with Bolshevik nationality policies of the era, as well as its use of the language championed as the vernacular of working-class Jews, helped gain it an unprecedented degree of state patronage. However, while the theater was formed with the support of the state, the initiative came from Jewish artists whose own ideals corresponded roughly to those of the Soviet government.

As a result of its official sanction, the theater became a haven for artists working in all media. Those unsure of how to express their revolutionary ardor appropriately could be comforted that the theater provided a suitable forum. Those fearful of arousing suspicion of their apprehensions toward the new order could camouflage themselves among the theater's zealots. And those simply unable to make a living otherwise could join the state-funded theater. Once they became co-opted into the system, many members of the troupe adopted its ideology, confirming one scholar's conclusions about the Soviet propaganda system that "Soviet propaganda may not have convinced the masses but it succeeded in reinforcing the commitment of the propagandists."[139]

While the theater and its ideology attracted many artists to its stage, its effectiveness must also be assessed on the basis of its audience. As we have seen, the theater was preaching to the converted, or at least to the oversaturated—its message was hardly new to the intelligentsia and social luminaries who filled the Malaia Bronnaia Hall one night and migrated to the nearby Meyerhold or Tairov theater the next. Its large non-Jewish audience was probably captivated by the theater's exoticism, viewing its Jewish content no differently than they would the Gypsy entertainers who performed at expensive après theater restaurants. On the other hand, word of Granovsky's accomplishment was gradually reaching the influential Jewish communities of Warsaw, Berlin, London, and New York. Although many greeted the news of a Jewish cultural renaissance in Soviet Russia with skepticism, others were less cynical. After the expansion of the theater in the second half of the decade, the British journal *Theatre Arts Monthly*, for instance, would write that:

> Soviet Russia, alone among nations, claims three state-endowed Jewish theatres. Nor is the reason hard to find, for it stems from the Soviet policy of National Cultural Autonomy. According to this doctrine every nationality represented in Russia not only has the right to use its own language and develop its own culture but can also count on the State for active support in the exercise of this right.[140]

Comrades from the Center: State, Party, and Stage

2

As the actors of the Moscow State Yiddish Theater attained the status of stardom, they began to act accordingly; their youthful dreams of "performing miracles" were replaced with more adult concerns about personal finances and prestige. Their deference toward the unquestioned authority of Aleksandr Granovsky was replaced with a more weathered skepticism, encouraged by their union leaders. And the intimate friendships which fueled the collective in its early days were replaced with jealous tempers. To use Hannah Arendt's term, the troupe became atomized, but not as a result of the crushing momentum of a totalitarian movement. Rather, it was simply a prosaic clash of egos as some actors elevated their personal interests above those of the collective. This environment not only impeded the artistic development of the theater but also allowed the state to manipulate the internal discord and penetrate the theater's curtain, introducing its own characters both onstage and backstage in an effort to assert its agenda.

After its victory in the Civil War, the strengthened Soviet state was no longer satisfied with the often passive role it had played previously; as of 1924 it was prepared to reallocate its resources toward cultural enlightenment and propaganda. This was heralded by the November 1923 creation of the Central Repertory Committee (Glavrepertkom), the committee of censorship, as a division of the Commissariat of Enlightenment. Certainly Bolsheviks from Lunacharskii to Trotsky had realized the important propagandistic value of culture in general and theater in particular, but economic difficulties and concerns with more pressing problems hindered any concerted action on the cultural front during the Civil War. The Bolsheviks had no choice but to allow a wide array of cultural discourses to compete as the true expression of proletarian culture.[1] It was not until the New Economic Policy (NEP) provided the Party with sufficient breathing space that it could finally work toward the disposal of those whom Trotsky dubbed in his 1924 work *Literature and Revolution* the "fellow travelers of the revolution."[2]

But there was no general agreement regarding a definition of proletarian culture, even within the upper echelons of the Party; the well-known conflict between Aleksandr Bogdanov and Lenin was only the tip of the iceberg. As Trotsky put it: "The question is . . . in which case and between what should the Party choose. And this question is not at all as simple as the theorists of the 'Lef' [Left Front], the heralds of proletarian literature and the critics are pleased to think."[3] Indeed, while all Communist thinkers agreed with Lenin's oft-cited remark that culture must serve the Party's interests, none agreed on how to reconcile education with entertainment or how to channel artistic creativity into social utility. In their efforts to abolish the realism of the old, many artists created abstractions incomprehensible to the masses. While there was no definitive and consensual ideological answer (despite Trotsky's polemics) there was a political solution—to obtain Party control for the moment and defer repertory and stylistic decisions for later. In other words, to invert Marx's sociology by making political control the "base" rather than the "superstructure," from which cultural enlightenment would derive only secondarily. This is, in many ways, a paraphrase of the revised totalitarian argument regarding the supremacy of the regime's political power over socioeconomic factors, which claims that by 1932 each "sensitive field" of culture "was annexed by the regime and directly subordinated to its immediate political purposes. And in each case Stalin personally initiated the change."[4] But how was this achievement actually accomplished, and was Stalin truly the prime mover?

While the state's cultural organs wrangled over the terms by which proletarian culture would be defined, the Jewish Section of the Party was constructing its own project that was equally, if not more, pertinent to the Moscow State Yiddish Theater's future. The ultimate goal of the non-Jewish state organs with regard to the Yiddish theater was, as we have seen, to use the theater as a showpiece for the West, as a testimony to the state's tolerance and support of its national minorities. The goal of the Jewish Section, which was less concerned with foreign audiences, was to "educate" the Jewish masses of the former Pale of Settlement in order to wrench them away from their traditional religious lives in the shtetl and to integrate them into the expanding proletariat or convert them into collective farmers. As the foremost scholar of the Jewish Section writes, "By 1925–26 it was the Jewish Section which defined the scope and intensity of the revolutionary struggle for the modernization of Soviet Jewry and, in many cases, instigated and led it. . . . In effect, it was assigned a major role in determining the future of Soviet Jewry."[5] Consequently, its own division between the assimilationists, who anticipated the "withering away" of national peculiarities, and the nationalists, like Moshe Litvakov, who pursued a distinctly Jewish proletarian culture, was reflected in the Yiddish theater's development. Furthermore, the Thirteenth Party Congress in May 1924, which called for an increase in Party work among national minorities in their native languages, also provided the Jewish Section with the authorization it needed to expand its base, especially into the Ukrainian and Belorussian shtetls.[6] The Jewish Section's Yiddishization campaign, which had been harassing the Hebrew-language Habima theater from as early as 1920 (despite Lunacharskii's objections), ensured that Yiddish, rather than Hebrew, would be designated as the Jewish national tongue. This led to the final denouement of Habima—a process that was hastened by the death of its most prestigious director, Evgenii Vakhtangov (1883–1922) and by the recent successes at the Moscow State Yiddish Theater.

In the summer of 1924, confronted with the task of integrating the shtetl Jews into Soviet society, the Jewish Section founded the Committee for the Settlement of Jewish Toilers on the Land (KOMZET) and its non-Party corollary, the Society for the Settlement of Jewish Toilers on the Land (OZET, GEZERD), with the ultimate goal of enticing Jewish petty traders and unemployed workers to abandon the shtetls in favor of agricultural colonization on collective farms. Because the vast majority of Jews in the former Pale still held strong ties to rabbinical Judaism, Hasidism, or Zionism, the movement was accompanied by anti-religious and anti-Zionist campaigns. Within the next year, the Jewish Section mounted over 120 anti-religious campaigns, closed over 1,000 *kheders,* and arrested countless Zionist leaders. This "Face-to-the-Shtetl" movement provided a new impetus and direction for Soviet Jewish culture that resonated deeply within the Moscow State Yiddish Theater.

Face to the Shtetl

With the return to a partial market economy during the New Economic Policy (NEP), the theater quickly realized the benefits of pleasing those who held the purse strings. However, it was faced with an insurmountable quandary shared by any product geared toward a working-class constituency—the audience, by definition, lacks the funds necessary to serve as patrons. In the context of 1920s Russia, this meant catering to either Moscow's "Nepmen"—those entrepreneurs profiting from the restoration of private business—or to the state, which retained control of the economy's "commanding heights," including the credit industry, which was centralized under the state bank in 1918. Since the regime, which claimed to represent the proletariat, apportioned its funds according to political expediency, the theater was forced to choose between profit and politics: it could fill its coffers by charging the Nepmen in Moscow, or it could achieve its political goals by touring the poverty-stricken provinces, where the majority of unassimilated Jews resided, and offering discounted tickets to workers, thereby garnering state patronage. For the Moscow State Yiddish Theater the choice was obvious: as a revolutionary theater geared toward the working masses, it could hardly defile itself by coddling the Nepmen.

Following the line advanced by the Jewish Section's "Face-to-the-Shtetl" movement, the Moscow State Yiddish Theater took several steps to extend its reach into the former Pale: first, Litvakov helped found a Society for Friends of the State Yiddish Theater to organize a campaign to the shtetls. Its first meeting, on September 22, 1926, formulated the goals of the society—to publish a journal on the activities of the theater, to discuss general questions of Jewish culture, and to gather members and supporters for the theater. Between March and May 1927, the membership of the organization increased from 545 to 890 members, the largest contingent of whom were dependent wage earners (66 percent), followed by factory workers (16 percent). Students, artisans, and housewives rounded out the rest.[7] To supplement these activities a newsletter for the theater was established for distribution throughout the country.[8]

Second, the theater was reorganized as the nucleus of a network of Jewish theatrical institutions under the auspices of the Theatrical Department of the Commissariat of Enlightenment. The network corresponded to Granovsky's earlier vision, in which his Moscow studio was to serve as a training ground and model theater for other Yiddish theaters scattered strategically throughout the Soviet realm. To facilitate this project, the Moscow division was allocated three build-ings: the theater on Malaia Bronnaia, an artists' residence at the old theater on 12 Chernyshevskii (formerly Stankevich), and a school-studio on 6 Kuznetskii Most. Finally, in 1925, Ukrainian and Belorussian divisions of the State Yiddish Thea-ter were created in Moscow and later relocated to Minsk, the capital of the Belo-russian Soviet Socialist Republic, and Kharkov, the industrial capital of Ukraine. The Ukrainian division was directed by Efraim Loiter, the former director of the Kultur-Lige's theater section, while the Belorussian division was entrusted to Moshe Rafalskii, former director of the Unzer Vinkl theater.[9] Lacking Granov-sky's ties to high-level Party figures like Lunacharskii (whose cultural tastes were relatively conservative and who looked upon the new avant-garde proletarian cul-ture with a certain skepticism), the provincial theaters were more susceptible to the influence of the extreme left Proletkultists and the Jewish Section, both of which promoted a total break with pre-revolutionary culture and a singular emphasis on the most radical definition of proletarian culture. Thus, the repertoires of these theaters came to consist primarily of political works by contemporary Soviet Jew-ish writers that glorified the Soviet regime.

The radical politicization of the provincial theaters and their overwhelming dependence on orders from Moscow were deterrents to genuine experimentation and innovation. Financial difficulties and resistance from actors who were to be transferred to the provinces further hindered the development of these theaters. Indeed, rather than have talented Moscow-based actors transferred to the prov-inces, as Granovsky envisioned, more often than not movement was in the reverse direction as provincial hopefuls were called to the big city. Many participants in these theaters later went on to work for more central and prominent theaters, not the least of which was the Moscow State Yiddish Theater. This trend supports the hypothesis that those institutions, led by the Commissariat of Enlightenment, which preferred to use the theater as a showpiece for visiting foreigners were win-ning out over the more populist Jewish Section, which sought to direct its propa-ganda toward a domestic audience.

Lacking the charismatic stars who contributed to the popularity of their Mos-cow counterparts, these provincial theaters were destined to remain, for the time being at least, provincial in the full sense of the word. Shtetl audiences preferred to wait for the chance to see Mikhoels and Zuskin when they went on tour than satisfy their desire for entertainment with the lesser theaters. The wait usually proved worthwhile, as Granovsky's troupe began to spend its summers touring the former Pale. Over the summers of 1922 and 1923, with the aid of the Com-missariat of Enlightenment, it brought its message to Minsk, Vitebsk, Gomel, Kharkov, and Kiev. The following summer, the troupe was popular enough to be expressly invited by the community. The director of the Gomel State Theater in-vited Granovsky's troupe to visit, offering to pay 12,000 rubles and accommoda-tions for twenty shows,[10] while Minsk offered 15,000 rubles.[11] Hoping to capital-ize on his provincial popularity, Granovsky, in a letter to Litvakov, requested 5,000 rubles from the Jewish Section to help subsidize a tour of Ukraine, where his troupe's anonymity could not attract the capital investment the Belorussians were willing to risk.[12] Even Odessa, having heard of the theater through word of mouth alone, offered to pay 2,000 rubles a night and to house the theater in hotels rather than dormitories—a rare treat for the wandering stars.[13] In preparation for the theater's arrival, placards in Yiddish—a strong indication of the expected audience—were posted throughout the streets.[14]

The program for the 1924 tour included *Two Hundred Thousand, The Sorceress, Three Jewish Raisins, God of Vengeance,* and *An Evening of Sholem Aleichem* (*Agents, Mazel Tov,* and *The Divorce Paper*). Additionally, the theater added to its repertoire an evening of entertainment entitled *A Carnival of Jewish Comedy.* The program typically consisted of a variety of short sketches supplemented with musical performances. For instance, one program included a medley of Hasidic, Latin American, and African American music and dance; a sampling of folk songs from Vilna sung by the actress Leah Rom; a Jewish dance performed by Mariia Askinazi; a Hasidic musical ensemble; some klezmer music; and a short sketch.

During the 1924 tour—the one for which we have the best records—the theater played in Kiev, Gomel, Odessa, and Kharkov before returning to Moscow in September.[15] To accommodate large audiences, the theater sometimes played outdoors or on factory floors. Since tickets were sold at reduced rates for workers, students, soldiers, and members of Party organizations and special closed performances were given to union members, we can compile a fairly accurate assessment of the theater's success in attracting members of these targeted groups. But the figures are probably bloated because the report was prepared for the Jewish Section by the governing board of the theater, which had a vested interest in proving to its primary benefactor that it was reaching its intended audience. Furthermore, ticket purchasers could have exaggerated their worker background in order to receive the discounted tickets. Nevertheless, the statistics confirm a reasonable hypothesis—that in regions with high concentrations of Yiddish-speaking Jewish workers, the audience was comprised of Yiddish-speaking Jewish workers. Of seventy-three performances to over 91,000 people, between 65 and 80 percent of the audience were Jewish, and between half and two-thirds of all spectators received discounted tickets as either union members, workers, Party members, or Red Army soldiers.[16] Clearly the theater was reaching its targeted audience of Jewish workers in the provinces. Furthermore, each show was viewed by an average of 1,250 people, compared with under 300 a night in Moscow.

The Penniless Box Office

While the provincial tours, where the theater met its intended audience, were certainly effective propaganda, they were inevitably financial failures. The dream of using proceeds from the Moscow season to finance the politically expedient tours proved to be unrealistic; even in Moscow the theater could barely escape without a loss, let alone cover the costs of transportation and housing for the large troupe, now numbering 115.[17] In this light, it should come as little surprise that the

1924 tour concluded with a deficit of between 6,000 and 8,000 rubles, at a time when the theater was already almost 40,000 rubles in debt.[18]

Thus, in the fall of 1924, after the troupe's extended summer tour, Granovsky returned to Moscow as a supplicant: "We are the only theater in the USSR which accomplishes such significant political work while remaining artistically avant-garde. What theater can produce this kind of press? What theater can demonstrate such closeness to the Party?"[19] he demanded in an appeal to the Jewish Section for funds. In October the Council of People's Commissars approved, on the Commissariat of Enlightenment's recommendation, a grant of 50,000 rubles—40,000 to cover the theater's debt, and an additional 10,000 bonus for its "revolutionary portrayal of the Jewish bourgeois shtetl-dwellers, and its decisive war against clericalism and national chauvinism."[20]

Despite this assistance, financial difficulties were exacerbated by administrative and personal conflicts within the troupe. The grueling tour schedule began to have a negative effect on the actors, and the theater's trade union voiced its grievances against the director. In 1924 the kindling ignited into a huge flare-up between Khaim Krashinskii and Granovsky. Krashinskii was a minor member of the troupe's acting personnel, but he was the only member of the Communist Party in the troupe and the secretary of the theater's local union branch. He had come to the theater from the Commissariat of Nationality Affairs, where he had been secretary of the Jewish Department and had led the campaign against Habima in 1920–1921, accusing the Hebrew theater of being counter-revolutionary and Zionist.[21] His position against Habima had brought him into direct confrontation with Lunacharskii, who at the time continued to support the Hebrew theater for its artistic merits.[22]

After a minor argument, Krashinskii denounced Granovsky to the Jewish Section, complaining that the troupe's director had been tampering with the theater's accounts, that he did not allow the members of the troupe to develop artistically, and, most serious, that "the absence of a Party controller has resulted in an ideological bias in the past repertoire toward accommodating the theater to the side of the NEP public." He recommended that a working board be established over the theater, that Granovsky be dismissed from his role as financial director so that "the financial-administrative section can be put in the hands of a Party member," and that "a purge of actors in the collective be carried out, freeing the theater of bourgeois elements and replacing them with proletarian Communists."[23] Krashinskii became further infuriated when a commission appointed by the Jewish Section to investigate the charges absolved Granovsky but stated that "Kr[ashinskii] was not able properly to use his position as the sole Communist in the theater to resolve the crisis that arose in the theater. . . . In order to get his way, he took it upon himself to aggravate relations with the directorate."[24]

Dissatisfied with the resolutions of the committee, Krashinskii turned to the Moscow Union of Artists, an organization dominated by plebeian artistic workers notoriously hostile to the prestigious state theaters.[25] The union responded with its own investigation.[26] This time the commission upheld Krashinskii's position and recommended that Granovsky be relieved of his financial and administrative duties and be replaced with a Party member.[27] The Jewish division of the Commissariat of Enlightenment agreed with Krashinskii[28] but was countered by Comrade Palatnik, a member of the theater's governing board and a representative of the Jewish division of the Soviet of National Minorities, who sent a secret letter to the Jewish Section accusing Krashinskii of intentional troublemaking and of falsely denouncing Granovsky to the secret police.[29] Thus, a conflict which started as a clash of personalities was broadened to include virtually the entire Jewish state apparatus. This incident began a trend by which the disgruntled members of the theater would appeal to higher authorities in their squabbles with Granovsky, thereby legitimizing state and Party interference in the internal affairs of the theater. Each organ responded by appointing a commission to investigate and mediate; once invited in, these commissions were reluctant to withdraw. The Jewish theater was not alone in its struggle for administrative autonomy during this period. As Lunacharskii's influence declined, Party and union officials were successful in having their own candidates appointed to important posts throughout the Moscow theatrical establishment. According to Richard Thorpe, Party membership became one of the most important criteria in the appointment of many theater directors in 1924–1925, surpassing even artistic experience.[30]

Jewish Luck

By February 1925, the theater was finally ready to present its next full-length production—Granovsky's adaptation of Isaac Leyb Peretz's mystical play about the dawn of modernity, *Night in the Old Market,* which he turned into a tragedy about a wedding of the dead in a graveyard.[31] Preparations for the production lasted over a year due to a combination of the problems plaguing the theater's administration and Granovsky's insistence that the premiere be delayed until he was completely satisfied with the production—a process that involved over 250 rehearsals. When news was released that the theater was working on a play by Peretz, *Der emes* lamented the theater's decision to perform material from the pre-revolutionary past rather than utilize the works of the new generation of contemporary Soviet artists, such as Ber Orshansky (1884–1945), Aharon Kushnirov (1890–1949), and Ezra Finenberg (1899–1946), all of whose works were under preparation for performance at the Ukrainian State Yiddish Theater.[32]

Despite this public criticism, Litvakov and the Jewish Section continued to defend Granovsky before the trade union and continued their fund-raising for the theater. Granovsky's adaptation of Peretz's classic left little of the original author's intent; the play was reinterpreted to conform to the Jewish Section's new agenda. Heartened by its experience in the provinces and encouraged by the Jewish Section's "Face-to-the-Shtetl" campaign, the theater chose to use the play as an attack on the shtetl, which was symbolized by a cemetery. The juxtaposition of a wedding and a cemetery represented the belief that a new beginning cannot occur in a dead world. Starring Mikhoels and Zuskin, the play consisted of a plotless montage of eerie, disconnected images. As night falls in the cemetery, the dead rise from their graves to the sounds of the Kaddish, the Jewish prayer for the dead, mixed with the requiem mass. As the dead rise, they shout allusions to traditional Judaism: "The Kohanim [priestly clan] gather," "The horn of the Messiah," "The synagogue is taken over by the dead!" "Dead Ones with Torah bells!" "With Sukkos [huts built during the Festival of Tabernacles] pegs!" "With phylactery bags!" After the wedding, as dawn approaches, the wedding entertainer calls "Remain above the earth! Don't return to the graves!"—an appeal to abandon the metaphorical shtetls. However, fearing the rising sun and the new day, the dead return to their graves.

The attack on the shtetl was accompanied by an attack on religion. As the play ends a voice is heard from beneath the stage, shouting "God!" to which the wedding entertainer replies "Dead, your God. . . . He is Bankrupt!"[33] This line, which appeared only in Peretz's 1909 text, recurred twice in Granovsky's adaptation and was developed into a major theme. Once again, Granovsky alluded to the carnivalesque by transposing the sacred and profane through the *badkhens*. His *badkhens* were actually closer to the *payats*, another type of Jewish clown often portrayed in the *purimspiels*, who were known for inserting profanities into prayer.

The musical accompaniment, composed by Aleksandr Krein, consisted of dissonant perversions of traditional klezmer music sporadically interrupted by fragments of dialogue. His score comprised five major elements: 1) impressionist genre themes depicting the everyday life of the shtetl; 2) tunes drawn from the repertoire of the klezmers 3) modern motifs characterizing the growth of the Jews from the "old ghettos"; 4) religious elements drawn from Jewish liturgical melodies; and 5) dissonant themes depicting the triumph of the new world. The predominance of music in the production taught Mikhoels a lesson on the significance of restraining speech: "I act more remarkably when I am silent than when I am talking," he later remarked.[34]

Robert Falk designed a series of grotesque costumes that portrayed the undead zombies with dripping flesh. Falk (1886–1958), the son of a prosperous Moscow lawyer, began his career in the Moscow School of Painting, Sculpture, and Architecture in 1905. After traveling to Italy in 1910 he returned to Moscow, where he affiliated himself with the Jack of Diamonds group, where he met Chagall and Altman. Primarily a landscape painter, Falk found the transformation to theater difficult, but he adapted well and went on to work for Habima and the Belorussian State Yiddish Theater. Great care was taken in the construction of the costumes and sets, and Falk accompanied them with a large oil painting. A flurry of macabre colors graced the stage, which was set in the shadow of a huge wrinkled *hamsah* (Kabbalistic sign in the shape of a hand) that came down from the center of the stage, displaying Peretz's Hebrew initials. The costumes also emphasized the mechanical movements of the actors. While Falk's designs were among the most memorable in the theater's history, Efros was less than enthusiastic, disappointed by the artist's use of space. Several years later he wrote, "Falk and theater —two incompatible things."[35]

Solomon Mikhoels in *Night in the Old Market*. From Liubomirskii, *Mikhoels*.

Solomon Mikhoels and Benjamin Zuskin as badkhens in *Night in the Old Market*, 1925. Photo courtesy of Ala Perelman-Zuskin.

Robert Falk's sets for *Night in the Old Market,* 1925. From *Das Moskauer Jüdische Akademische Theater* (Berlin, 1928).

Night in the Old Market was one of the Moscow State Yiddish Theater's most popular productions, but it received ambivalent reviews from *Pravda,* which criticized it for merely stating the obvious and offering no solutions.[36] *Izvestiia* was also somewhat critical, worried that the theater was romanticizing the shtetl,[37] while another reviewer was concerned about the mystical-religious content of the play, which he felt the theater was unable to overcome completely.[38] However, most critics saw it as a successful continuation of the cycle of anti-religious, anti-shtetl productions, couched in the stylized and grotesque forms that had become the theater's hallmark.[39] Several reviewers reminded their readers that the reactions of Moscow and Leningrad audiences were of little significance, because the vast majority of Jews, for whom this production would have been most valuable, lived in the provincial shtetls.[40] Granovsky and his troupe continued to find favor in the eyes of the Commissariat of Enlightenment; in February of that year, Lunacharskii awarded Granovsky the honorary title of State Academic Theater Artist.[41]

The following summer the troupe once again toured the provinces. This time it supplemented its stage offerings with a motion picture directed to shtetl audiences. *Jewish Luck,* the theater's first venture into the new medium, was filmed on location during the summer of 1925. While Lenin regarded cinema as one of the most important art forms, in 1925 only ninety motion pictures were made in the

Soviet Union.[42] Thus, the Moscow State Yiddish Theater's invitation was a rare privilege shared by relatively few of the many ambitious artists who hoped to immortalize themselves on film.[43]

Granovsky first wrote of a desire to make a film in September 1924, beginning negotiations with Sovkino, the state film enterprise, soon after. The final deal was favorable to the theater: Sovkino agreed to provide transportation, costumes, 17,000 meters of Kodak film, and forty days in the Goskino factory for cutting and editing.[44] Granovsky and Grigorii Gricher-Cherikover (1893–1945) directed it, Natan Altman designed the sets, and Lev Pulver composed and conducted music for the premiere. The prominent Soviet writer Isaac Babel (1894–1940) was recruited to write titles. The film again starred Mikhoels and Zuskin.

The film follows Sholem Aleichem's hapless insurance salesman Menakhem Mendl as he experiments in matchmaking, only to inadvertently arrange a marriage between two women. The wedding, a traditional Jewish symbol of life and renewal, turns into a disaster, once again symbolizing the belief that a new beginning could not take place within the shtetl. The new medium allowed for a more forceful attack on shtetl life. Renouncing the carnivalesque and acrobatic features which had become the hallmark of his theater, Granovsky chose instead to present a "realistic" portrait of pre-revolutionary shtetl life in all its stagnancy. By claiming to present a candid, almost documentary, portrayal of the shtetl, Granovsky spurned anticipated attacks of exaggeration, especially from an American audience without firsthand knowledge of life in the former Pale. The sheer starkness of the dirty town of Berdichev as depicted on the crude grainy film was sufficiently unappetizing, especially when contrasted with the modern, revolutionary city of Odessa. Lest the audience miss the message of his straightforward narrative, Granovsky used cinematic tricks to highlight it; one scene shows a cemetery which fades out as the streets of Berdichev fade in, merging with the gravestones to equate the shtetl with a cemetery.

The film also attacked the treatment of women by traditional Jewish ritual, mocking the trade of women among matchmakers. During a dream sequence, Menakhem Mendl, imagining that he has become the greatest matchmaker in the world, is approached by the German Jewish financier and philanthropist Baron Maurice de Hirsch at an exclusive seaside Odessa café. The world-famous philanthropist humbly explains to the great matchmaker, "American bridegrooms are climbing the walls, there aren't enough brides to go around. Save America, Menakhem Mendl." After arrangements are made, a boxcar train full of women in wedding dresses, classified according to their physical characteristics—one car reads "fat"—arrives in Odessa. After the women are carried off the train and inspected, they are loaded—by crane—onto a ship bound for America.

Finally, the film sought to show the oppression of the poor by the rich in the traditional Jewish settlements. "Oy, it's tough for a poor Jew to get anything out of a rich man," and "You can't do anything without money," laments Menakhem. Other scenes mocked the social segregation of the rich and the poor and the economic stresses of marriage. While one woman complains, "My father wants me

The brides meet in *Jewish Luck,* 1925. Photo courtesy of
Natalia Vovsi-Mikhoels.

to marry a rich man," another written request for a match reads, "O.K. if the groom
is not yet a doctor."

Produced by the All-Ukrainian Photo-Cinema Administration and sponsored by the Society for the Settlement of Jewish Toilers on the Land, the primary
target audience was the shtetl Jews of Ukraine. However, an American audience
was also targeted. A version with English-language titles was prepared and the
film was made available for export, although it did not reach America until 1935,
when Worldkino released a dubbed version entitled *Menakhem Mendl* in Yiddish,
or *The Matchmaker* in English.[45]

One reviewer used the opportunity to discuss the potential the Revolution
had created for Jews. The satire of Sholem Aleichem, he explained, emerged out
of the difficulty of pre-revolutionary Jewish life. However, the Revolution gave
Jews all the institutions necessary for a new life:

> For us now, *Jewish Luck* has practically become a historical film. . . . Now in
> Belorussia . . . grand work is going on regarding the allotment of land to Jews.
> Collective farms are springing up, they are irrigating the land. . . . One need not
> feel sorry for the image of Menakhem Mendl's umbrella, one need not find
> romance in the past . . . but one must know of the old life.[46]

Backstage Backstabbing

Although the movie project was a massive undertaking for the troupe, only a
select few of its members were involved in the film. Those deprived of a chance at

eternal stardom on the silver screen became bitter. The problem was compounded by Mikhoels's refusal to join the local union on the grounds that he considered it to be merely a platform for petty political squabbles. Without the mediation of the theater's biggest star and a firm voice of authority, the union was left to indulge in its own jealous grievances. In one instance, the union called upon all members of the troupe involved with the movie to share their new income with the rest of the troupe—a move obviously opposed by those who were putting in the extra time and effort to conform to the rigorous schedule demanded by the filming. Furthermore, the irregular filming schedule, complicated by the need to work within Sovkino's calendar, threw off the normal rehearsal program, infuriating those who were forced to conform. Granovsky, in turn, criticized the troupe for failing to recognize the importance of the movie, the potential success of which could provide a firm financial basis for the theater in the future, thereby benefiting the entire troupe. At a subsequent meeting between the directorate and the union, the directorate reprimanded the union for abusing its power and called upon a commission to investigate its behavior. Thus, the union became embroiled against not only Granovsky, but against the entire directorate, leading to a sharp division between the local union, which was backed by the Moscow Union of Workers, on one side, and the theater's directorate, its governing body, the Jewish Section, and Granovsky on the other.[47]

A new flare-up took place when the trade union met to discuss problems affecting the directorate without Granovsky's presence. When Granovsky complained, one member of the troupe contemptuously replied: "We are not obliged to think about when Granovsky is busy with the movie."[48] Once again, the workers of the theater appealed to higher sources, writing a letter to the Jewish Section arguing that as a result of the movie, the repertoire for the coming season was being neglected.[49] The Jewish Section sent Moshe Litvakov to investigate the problem. The tension was in no way eased when Litvakov, addressing a general assembly of the theater's local union, reduced all of the collective's problems to Party matters which he claimed were not comprehensible to the masses, who were not members of the Party.[50] Members of the theater's union then insulted Litvakov in the presence of the Central Committee of the Jewish Section, leading to a further deterioration of relations.

The problem only worsened in September 1925, when in accordance with the state policy of *khozrazchet,* or self-finance, the theater was deprived of its extensive funding and ordered to fend for itself. On December 1, 1925 the Commissariat of Enlightenment and the Management of State Academic Theaters issued a joint declaration confirming the transfer of the Moscow State Yiddish Theater to self-finance and placing it under the supervision of the Management of State Academic Theaters, a division of the Commissariat of Enlightenment. While Granovsky was permitted to remain as director, he was henceforth obligated to remain within the limits set by estimates and plans and was required to receive special permission from the management for any activity deviating from the plan.[51] According to Granovsky, the theater's union used the resulting economic hardships to pursue a deliberate policy of discrediting the directorate before the Union of

Artists rather than helping to placate the troupe, which he believed was their role.[52]

Responding to complaints from the local union that Granovsky was failing to consider a repertoire for the coming season, the Management of State Academic Theaters appointed B. S. Shteiger to investigate. Shteiger, the prototype for Mikhail Bulgakov's distasteful informer Baron Maigel, was the special agent responsible for reporting on the actions of visiting entertainers. His report on the Yiddish theater concluded that its problems were common to all theaters and therefore did not warrant further action. However, he did use the opportunity to suggest material for a new repertoire, proffering plays by Isaac Babel, Yekhezkel Dobrushin, Abraham Veviurka, and the American playwright Halpern Leyvick. He also endorsed Granovsky's proposed repertoire, which included Babel's *Benye Krik*, Sholem Aleichem's *Doctor* (written in 1887), and Dobrushin's adaptation of Goldfadn's *The Tenth Commandment* (written in 1887).[53]

The theater also found itself harassed by the state for the first time when the city of Moscow ordered the conversion of Chagall Hall (the old theater on Stankevich) into a residence, prompting appeals from Granovsky and the Jewish Section to Lunacharskii.[54] The matter was brought up at the highest levels to the Council of People's Commissars.[55] Despite these protests, the Chagall murals, which had continued to decorate the hall, were moved to the storage room beneath the stage of the Malai Bronnaia Theater, thereby ending their public exhibition, and the historic Stankevich studio was converted into a residence for the troupe.

Financial problems also continued into the 1924–1925 season, during which the theater's debts rose to over 90,000 rubles, according to one estimate, the largest portions of which were salary expenses and tour deficits.[56] As a result of the long summer tour, the theater had played only seventy shows in Moscow over the regular season—not nearly enough to bring in the revenue necessary to cover the tour's losses. Indeed, the regular season brought in less than 60,000 rubles, a large drop compared to the nearly 140,000 rubles in profits the previous year.[57] However, recognizing the political expediency of the tours, the Management of State Academic Theaters, the Commissariat of Enlightenment, the Commissariat of Finance, and the Council of People's Commissars all approved a 30,000-ruble grant to help the theater eliminate its debts.[58]

The situation was worsened by the new frugality of the Council of People's Commissars with regard to the funding of state theaters. In late 1921, Lenin started to pressure Lunacharskii to reduce the expenses of the state theaters, even suggesting closure of the Bolshoi and Marinskii theaters.[59] The Yiddish theater was not immune to these cutbacks. Under the guise of a solution to the theater's poor financial standing, the Council of People's Commissars proposed removing the theater from the list of State Academic Theaters and moving it from its Moscow location to Belorussia, where they believed the larger Jewish community would be capable of supporting it. Realizing that the provincial Jewish communities were too poor to support the theater, Granovsky staunchly opposed the decision on the grounds that "a transfer is the same as killing it."[60] No doubt he was also concerned that if separated from the cultural center of Moscow, the theater would be doomed to parochialism. The Jewish Section agreed with Granovsky, prompting a letter from Sh. Palatnik to the Commissariat of Enlightenment, whose director sat on the Council of People's Commissars: "The liquidation of the Moscow State Yiddish Theater would be a great blow to all our Soviet cultural work among the Jewish masses," he wrote, emphasizing the theater's political importance.[61] The commissariat agreed and sent its own note to the council stating that it "cannot agree with this decree, on the grounds that moving the Moscow State Yiddish Theater from Moscow would effectively signify its liquidation."[62]

The theater also objected to the proposal to remove it from the list of State Academic Theaters and the protection to which this entitled it. In a letter to the Commissariat of Enlightenment, the theater's union for the first time suggested that the theater was being discriminated against on the basis of anti-Semitism: "The theater does not want to think it is an outcast only because it is a Jewish theater, but it thinks the exhaustive demands on it reveal such signs."[63] Similar accusations of anti-Semitism would be directed toward the Academic Theater organization throughout the decade. The charge was not launched lightly; the Management of State Academic Theaters was the only organization to be so accused by the Yiddish theater. For instance, in 1928, when one of the most famous actresses in the Maly Theater died (Mariia Nikolaevna Ermolova, b. 1853), all members of Moscow's theatrical society were invited to the funeral except for the members of the Jewish theater. The incident sparked a series of letters from Granovsky to the board of the Maly Theater, *Der emes,* and the Commissariat of Enlightenment. "Surely, in 1928, the word 'Jewish' is not still odious for the Maly Theater, or does the Maly Theater think that the death of Mariia Nikolaevna does not concern the 'non Russian' artists of Moscow?" he demanded.[64] Although there is no evidence that the state itself discriminated against the theater on the basis of anti-Semitism, it was inevitable that the theater would encounter anti-Semitic individuals, such as Shteiger, who sought to use their power to ostracize the Jewish theater.

In 1925 there clearly was ongoing tension between the Management of State Academic Theaters and the Yiddish theater; according to Granovsky, the management was withholding promised funds and violating orders to release the theater from its debts. Granovsky further charged that neither the manager nor his deputy had ever visited the Malaia Bronnaia Hall.[65] Shteiger shot back with the accusation that the Yiddish theater was operating at an overwhelming deficit largely because Granovsky was overpaying himself and misappropriating funds from the film by separating the film's account from that of the theater.[66] Granovsky correctly retorted that the film was being conducted under the auspices of Sovkino, not the Management of State Academic Theaters; therefore it was essential that the accounts be separate. Furthermore, the decision to separate the accounts had previously been approved by Shteiger himself.[67] The baseless accusation was probably a manifestation of Shteiger's anti-Semitism. Once again, the Jewish Section came to Granovsky's defense by sending a secret communiqué to the Commissariat of

Enlightenment warning that the Management of State Academic Theaters was manipulating figures to give the false impression that the theater was in dire financial straits and deliberately misrepresenting the matter of the film's income "to give the impression that Granovsky is a blackmailer."[68] Palatnik, however, added to the communiqué the recommendation that a Party member replace Granovsky as administrative-financial director of the theater.

Finding itself defeated in the first round, the management changed tactics by arguing that Granovsky's theater was a political rather than an artistic organization and therefore did not fall under its auspices. This line of reasoning, which discredited Granovsky as an artist, infuriated the director, who responded by tendering his resignation.[69] However, at the same time, he wrote to those institutions he believed were sympathetic toward him, the Jewish Section and the Commissariat of Enlightenment, hinting that he could be persuaded to retract his resignation if a commission were to investigate the Management of State Academic Theaters.[70] The Jewish Section quickly seized the opportunity to firmly establish its own control over the theater. While it sought to keep Granovsky as artistic director, it recognized an ideal opportunity to appoint one of its own to the theater's board of governors. "Granovsky must always feel the strong hand of the Communists near him," stated one internal Jewish Section memo.[71]

On March 13, 1926, Litvakov, Palatnik, and Granovsky decided to encourage the Commissariat of Enlightenment to set up a commission to investigate the internal problems of the theater.[72] When Litvakov wrote to the Commissariat of Enlightenment less than two weeks later asking to testify at the hearings, he was informed that the investigation had already been concluded.[73] The commission's findings were discussed at a meeting of the presidium of the Commissariat of Enlightenment on April 6th, when it was resolved that the Yiddish theater would remain in Moscow on the list of State Academic Theaters and that measures would be taken to relieve it of its debts. Specifically, it was decided to ask the Council of People's Commissars to ensure the theater's continued financial stability by providing a grant to pay off the theater's debts and an additional loan of 20,000 rubles. In return, the commissariat would force Granovsky to accept two assistant directors, who were to be appointed by the Jewish Section.[74]

This victory, however, proved to be short-lived. On May 28th the Council of People's Commissars rejected the proposal, providing only verbal encouragement that "measures of an internal organizational character be taken to lighten the theater's current financial position and secure its continued existence in Moscow."[75] As an afterthought, it also expanded the theater's credit with the State Bank. Nevertheless, the possibility of moving the theater to either Ukraine or Belorussia continued to be investigated.[76]

The question was finally brought to the highest level when the Jewish Section sent a report to the Politburo asking for its intervention:

> We believe it is our Party obligation to inform the Politburo that in the near future, the only national theater in the USSR—the State Yiddish [Theater]—will be closed. The closure can only be stopped with immediate help. This situ-

ation is a result of the political relationship of the Management of State Academic Theaters with the theater. . . . The Moscow State Yiddish Theater is not just a theater, but also is related to the working masses, the Party, trade unions, and Komsomol organizations. In the course of three years it has toured Russia, Ukraine and Belorussia on the invitation of local Party committees, executive committees and trade unions . . .

Regardless of all this, the theater has almost always in its existence been under the threat of closure. Even in 1922 the question of its removal was raised. . . . It was averted only through the interference of Comrade Stalin.

The letter went on to imply that the Management of State Academic Theaters, motivated by anti-Semitism, was sabotaging the theater by deliberately depriving it of the rewards lavished upon its competitors.[77]

The Politburo responded with a noncommittal letter, expressing sympathy with the theater. It praised the theater for being "deeply revolutionary, thoroughly Soviet and, at the same time, high art"; for capturing "the love of the Jewish working masses of Russia, Ukraine and Belorussia"; and for attaining "great fame . . . in America, Poland and Lithuania, clarifying the high standing of the culture of national minorities in general and of Jews in particular in the Soviet state." The loss of the Yiddish theater, it concluded:

could, in our opinion, prove to be very significant. It would provide sensational material for agitation by the yellow press against Soviet power on the basis of the "Jewish Question"; it would provide "evidence" that those culture-building measures taken by the Soviet state among Jews were temporary and ephemeral. It would especially undermine the campaign abroad to bring Jewish land workers to the USSR.[78]

Yet the Politburo declined to take specific measures to ensure the theater's survival.

The Jewish Section responded to the Politburo's report with a reiteration of its position—that taking the Yiddish theater off the list of state theaters and taking away its subsidy would be the equivalent of closing it.[79] Assessing the favorable situation in the Politburo, the Commissariat of Enlightenment once again wrote to the Council of People's Commissars to recommend that the theater remain in Moscow on the list of state theaters: "Leaving Moscow would not be favorable for its development because it would be doomed to work in isolation from the broad working masses of the Jewish people and because it has too much of an established audience here."[80] Of course, the Jewish working masses were, in fact, concentrated in Belorussia and Ukraine: according to the 1926 census 69.3 percent of the Soviet Jewish population lived in Ukraine, of whom 15.2 percent were classified as workers; while only 5.8 percent of the Jewish population lived in Moscow, of whom only 8.3 percent were workers.[81] A more credible motivation for keeping the theater in Moscow, the unrivaled center of Soviet cultural life, was expressed by the newly formed Society for Friends of the State Yiddish Theater. On December 16th, 1926, an appeal from the society appeared in *Der emes*:

It is no coincidence that in Moscow—in the center of our great union . . . in the new laboratory of the great revolution—also resides the laboratory of revolutionary art, thought, and feelings. One is connected to the other. . . . All those who love the State Yiddish Theater . . . should join the society and do all that they can to help and work for *our* theater.[82]

Whatever his personal motivation, Lunacharskii insisted that the theater must remain in Moscow and recommended a 50,000-ruble loan to wipe out its debts—especially those owed to the workers—and enable a new production to be mounted: he was convinced that, given the advance necessary for a new production, the theater would net a profit the coming season. The need for a new production was echoed by the theater's union,[83] which also insisted that the workers be paid all back wages first.[84]

Indeed, underlying the imminent collapse were real financial problems. Before the summer tour began, the workers had not been paid. They continued to demand equal payment, a system the directorate categorically refused to enforce. On June 25th, the union demanded that all back wages be paid prior to the commencement of the tour.[85] Despite attempts to quickly raise the necessary funds, it simply could not be done. Finally, an agreement reached on July 30th called for the union to distribute 14,500 rubles by the middle of August to help alleviate back wages.[86] When the directorate failed to come up with the funds, the theater workers refused to go to Minsk as scheduled.

The trade union then presented its grievances to the Moscow Union of Artists, now adding the complaint that the troupe had not been given its allotted two-week vacation. The vacation incident was sparked when actress Rakhel Imenitova left for the Crimea without permission from the directorate, prompting the theater's governing board to sanction her. The local union adopted the position that Imenitova had gone on sick leave, not vacation, but added that vacations were long overdue.[87] The directorate responded by arguing that a tour of Leningrad was necessary to raise the money required to pay the troupe: if a vacation were to force the cancellation of the Leningrad stint, they could not be paid. Imenitova then took the matter to the courts, which ruled in her favor and ordered the directorate to give the troupe a two-week vacation and pay its obligations immediately after their tour of Leningrad.[88] The theater's local union responded with a declaration stating: "The general gathering of workers of the Moscow State Yiddish Theater categorically protests against the methods of the directorate which systematically breaches all agreements concluded with the union on its obligations to the workers."[89] The Union of Artists backed it up by ordering the workers to be paid by October 15th and by unilaterally replacing Granovsky as administrative-financial director of the theater with one of their own people, Comrade Plomper. Regarding the vacation problem, the Union of Artists ordered the workers to be given vacations on a rotating basis until the start of the new season on January 1st.[90]

Granovsky, who had become visibly exhausted and had succumbed to the idea of an assistant director in August, still resented the union's move, arguing that he wanted only an assistant, not a replacement, and that the union did not have the authority to intervene.[91] He preferred that the Commissariat of Enlightenment or the Jewish Section, both of which he knew to be sympathetic toward him, appoint him an assistant.[92] The Management of State Academic Theaters, for its part, continued to hope that one of the new personnel would eventually become director.[93] But Granovsky insisted that the Union of Artists did not have the authority to replace him and that the financial and artistic apparatuses of the theater were indivisible and must remain so. Thus, Plomper's status as administrative-financial director was recognized only by the union. The solution proved to be short-lived; by January the union had turned against Plomper, ordering him to pay the workers' wages and provide them with regular vacations.[94]

The entire conflict was essentially about the theater's autonomy with respect to Party organizations. Although Shteiger's attack on the theater may have been motivated by anti-Semitism, the general trend toward curbing institutional autonomy reflected the climate within the Soviet cultural realm. Michael David-Fox has shown that by the mid-1920s, the Party had made significant headway in consolidating its control over formerly autonomous institutions of higher learning, while Lynn Mally has shown that through the introduction of trade union control in 1925, the Proletkult also lost the remaining vestiges of its autonomy.[95] Although the Party and its organs were divided among themselves with regard to their attitudes toward the Yiddish theater, all agreed that it required greater Party supervision. Each organ was willing to manipulate any internal dissension within the theater to promote its own agenda. Granovsky, for his part, viewed all such moves as an intolerable obstruction of his creative independence. Granovsky's ordeal forced him to re-evaluate his faith in the promise of Soviet art.

The New Repertoire

On the positive side, the truce allowed for the preparation of two new productions in 1926: Goldfadn's *The Tenth Commandment* and a play by the contemporary Soviet writer Abraham Veviurka (1887–1935) entitled *137 Children's Homes*. The *Tenth Commandment* was a modern adaptation of Goldfadn's play, reoriented toward the ideological needs of the Soviet state. The story tells of two angels, one Evil and one Good, who place a wager on the expediency of the Tenth Commandment: "Thou shalt not covet thy neighbor's wife." The Evil Angel, arguing that the commandment is no longer applicable, wagers that he can find a righteous person who breaks the commandment. When he shows how the German bourgeoisie exchange wives for sport, the Good Angel quits in despair. Mikhoels, as the Evil Angel, was entrusted with a carnivalesque role that mocked the traditional Jewish distinctions between good and evil.

Settings ranging from heaven to modern Palestine and Germany also allowed Granovsky to insert contemporary political commentary into the text. The play was highly symbolic in its satirical criticism of Zionism, religion, the bourgeoisie of Europe, and especially the Second International (1889–1914). One scene shows the Orthodox Jews praying for the health of the Second International:

> God save the Second International
> Shelter and Secure it

From Moscow Tsars
From Red Stars
From Comintern
From Profintern
From whatever the Communists want to become.[96]

The play also pokes fun at capitalism in the West with songs like "Berlin, Berlin":

In Berlin, Berlin, Berlin
Is a crisis of a sort
One spreads money all over
As it bursts bank after bank
While people are sick and suffer . . .
Capital must be preserved
While six million do not eat.[97]

The chilling reference to the number six million becomes eerily prophetic when taken in conjunction with a following verse:

In Berlin, Berlin, Berlin
Is the power of a sort
Which is called Sturm und Drang
And they do all that Hitler wants.[98]

While the play was overtly propagandist, it was full of the song, dance, and humor of Goldfadn's original. It was a popular production, taking in an average of 786 rubles per show over the course of the year,[99] and it received favorable reviews. "*The Tenth Commandment,*" wrote an *Izvestiia* critic, "is the first Jewish revolutionary operetta."[100] *Trud* saw it as a criticism of the false piety of modern Europe with an element of hope that would precede the expected world revolution. "It is done by the brilliant director Granovsky with great taste and rhythm and excellent staging and flow. . . and all this goes on with spirit, joy, and much activity."[101] All reviews complimented Rabinovich, Pulver, and the choreographers for their contributions to the production.[102] "The theater is standing on the correct path and with every production is gaining still more sympathy for the new Jewish society," wrote *Pravda.*[103] One critic praised it for being comprehensible to a broad audience.[104] However, some, like Litvakov, voiced criticisms of the play, attacking Granovsky for his penchant toward musical comedies. He wrote that Granovsky "uses music to evade the concrete word."[105] He also noted that the operetta style of the production "is the true quintessence of bourgeois artistic culture. New methods and means must be found for operetta art and Granovsky in *Though Shalt Not Covet* has not found them."[106]

In the fall of 1926, the theater began to lean toward more proletarian-oriented productions. Veviurka's *137 Children's Homes,* based on his short story, which appeared in the Yiddish journal *Oktober* (October) under the title *Comrade Shindel,* told of a young woman from a shtetl who falls in love with Comrade Shindel, played by Mikhoels, a smuggler impersonating a local Party boss who claims to be collecting money for the establishment of orphanages but in fact is trafficking contraband hidden in phylacteries. When Shindel's assistant loses the phylacteries in which the contraband is hidden, Shindel is forced to buy up all the phylacteries in the town, in the hope that someone has come across his. The Jews all willingly trade in their phylacteries and even offer to sell their guest all other types of religious paraphernalia. Mocking the value placed upon phylacteries as family heirlooms and the sacredness of the leather straps, one seller parts with his with the words:

> And now I give you the holy tefillin (phylacteries) of my holy zayde (grandfather). I received them from my zayde. My zayde received them from his zayde and his zayde got them from his great zayde and his great zayde got them from his great great zayde and so on higher, higher, and still higher—a huge chain of zaydes all the way back to Ezrah the Scribe.[107]

137 Children's Homes was intended to raise awareness of the ongoing attempts of counter-revolutionaries to undermine the new regime through illegal activity. The use of religious artifacts for speculation was intended to equate religion with capitalism. It was also intended to urge Jews to reject their so-called "old rags" (prayer shawls) and "bourgeois psychology" and instead reorient their resources toward political and community goals, such as the establishment of orphanages. Once again Altman painted sets, while Aleksandr Krein wrote the music.

The show was the theater's biggest failure, both critically and financially.[108] It was performed only fifteen times during the season, taking in a petty average of 311 rubles per performance, well below the theater's 700-ruble average.[109] The play lacked song and dance and did not flow as previous plays had. Judging by the extensive doodles on Mikhoels's personal copy of the script, even the star had trouble staying alert during rehearsals. The response of the Soviet press was also critical, reflecting the increased earnestness about the portrayal of political themes in art. Reviewers, such as Mikhail Zagorskii, no longer felt that shtetl life should be portrayed at all, even for educational purposes—it was simply too horrible for a comedy.[110] *Pravda* wrote, "The absence of a large theme in the production and the unsuccessful dramatic choice does not move the theater forward and does not make the 'modern' play an event in the life of the Moscow State Yiddish Theater."[111] *Izvestiia* simply called it an "unsuccessful play."[112] Critics complained that it was obvious from the very beginning that the comrade was a fake. Even Altman's art was criticized as being poor realism; it was too minimalist, consisting simply of a few chairs and tables scattered around the stage.[113] In a more probing review, Litvakov attributed the play's failure to an unsuccessful text. While he believed that the original short story was an interesting anecdote, "from an anecdote does not come a plot. . . . There is no development, no dynamic—Shindel comes in and wanders around; Jews come in and wander around. . . . The dialogue is shallow and banal." He complained that Shindel was portrayed as having "absolutely no revolutionary intent. He is a character full of old Jewish associations." He remarked that there were too few examples of the new Soviet man in the play, and those that existed were "chiefly clay golems." Indeed the entire play, he wrote, "is not revolutionary and owes nothing to the revolution. . . . One can transfer the same story to any place."[114] Perhaps, though, Litvakov's objections stemmed from ulterior motives.

There is an alternative interpretation of the play which radically changes the message. The final draft of the script approved by the requisite censors was entitled *200 Children's Homes;* the version of the script used by the actors contains handwritten corrections replacing every reference to 200 with 137. Indeed, the play underwent several title changes, from *Comrade from the Center* to *200 Children's Homes* to its final *137 Children's Homes.* The last-minute change was probably deemed to be merely an insignificant adjustment of the facade. Yet Granovsky prided himself on being a symbolist and often claimed that every word and gesture on his stage was full of significance. He would hardly have picked a random number. Perhaps, then, the number was a cryptic reference to Psalm 137—one of the best-known of all Biblical passages:

> By the rivers of Babylon, there we sat down, yea we wept, when we remembered Zion. We hung our lyres upon the willows in its midst. For there they who carried us away captive asked us for a song: and they who spoiled us asked us for mirth, saying, Sing us one of the songs of Zion. How shall we sing the Lord's song in a foreign land? If I forget thee O Jerusalem, let my right hand forget her cunning. If I do not remember thee, let my tongue cleave to the roof of my mouth; if I do not set Jerusalem above my highest joy.

The psalm, which contains the most stirring Zionist oath as well as one of the most impassioned exilic laments, also bemoans the inability of the exiles to perform music in a foreign land. This is noteworthy because the play was performed immediately after a campaign against Yiddish dramatists who adhered to the style of musical comedy. This type of harassment ultimately led the director to reject his earlier belief that the Soviet Revolution was the harbinger of a Jewish cultural renaissance. While Granovsky never expressed any sympathy with Zionism, even after his defection two years later, the allusion to this psalm is likely a surreptitious expression of his distaste toward the limitations being put on Jewish creativity in the Soviet state.

The Jewish Don Quixote

As the popularity of the Yiddish theater expanded beyond the Jewish community, it steered its thematic goals accordingly, prodded by its detractors' allegations of "nationalism" and "bourgeois sympathies." In November 1926, Granovsky announced the debut of his new program embracing the best works of the Revolution—regardless of their Jewish content[115]—interspersed with some universal dramatic classics.[116] Granovsky, who since the theater's debut of Maeterlink's *The Blind* in 1919 had adamantly insisted on joining the ranks of world art through the performance of universal classics, welcomed the opportunity to prove his versatility. His adaptation of *Trouhadec,* by the French playwright Jules Romains (1885–1972), which premiered in January 1927, proved that a complete break with Jewish culture—both in terms of content and provenance—could still produce fine

Trouhadec, 1926. Photo from *Das Moskauer Jüdische Akademische Theater* (Berlin, 1928).

art. Romains, most famous for his *Dr Knock,* written in 1925, was the founder of Unanimism, a movement which sought to promote the ideals of universal brotherhood and group consciousness by viewing the world in terms of groups rather than individuals. Granovsky's production was the first time that the work of Jules Romains was performed on stage. The play begins on a Monte Carlo terrace where Yves le Trouhadec, a French professor, joins a group of academicians, to whom he professes his love for the Parisian actress Mlle. Rolande. When the extravagant and lavish Mlle. Rolande arrives, Trouhadec realizes that in order to court her successfully he will need to raise his income bracket. Thankfully, the casino is a short walk away. Winning big in the casino and entranced by the many beautiful women, Trouhadec forgets Rolande until she reappears on the scene, now jealous of her paramour's successes. Realizing his beloved is now within his reach, Trouhadec organizes a banquet for her. However, while preparations are under way, his gambling luck runs out, leading him to bankruptcy; he is saved from suicide only by the prospect of ruining an expensive banquet. Trouhadec decides that he will dedicate his life to writing a book—*Roulette: The Only Useful Profession,* when one of the barons he had befriended offers him a job as police commissioner of Monaco Principality. Having moved up the social ladder, Trouhadec renounces his private life and forms a Party of Gentlemen of which he names himself president. As a leader of aristocratic society, he decides he must marry a baroness. However, his plans are foiled when a pregnant Rolande appears, demanding that Trouhadec take on his paternal responsibility.[117]

Natan Altman depicted the flamboyant costumes of the European urban upper class as he had seen them in his travels—through the eyes of a destitute Soviet

Jew whose own tattered clothing was but a mockery of fashion. Lev Pulver, for the first time, incorporated episodic music as well as songs drawn from modern European music. However, the play was made by Mikhoels, whose poignant reading of the contradictions of Trouhadec's personality added a new dimension to the play: on one hand the protagonist is a serious professor and would-be academician, while on the other he is a vain adventurist caught up in the irrationality of the roulette wheel. This hint of psychological complexity, which Granovsky's previous stylized system had avoided, proved to be a success.

The press praised the production for its portrayal of bourgeois life in contemporary Europe.[118] *Pravda* wrote, "The basis of the growing success of this production can be found in its inclusion of high skill."[119] Zagorskii called it a "splendid success."[120] However, the production caused consternation and a split within the Society for Friends of the State Yiddish Theater, some of whom believed that non-Jewish themes would help make the theater world-class, while others feared the loss of its national essence.[121] This ambivalence was epitomized by Moshe Litvakov. On one hand he celebrated the production as a step toward solving the theater's repertoire problems, seeing the play as a "poignant satire against contemporary bourgeois society"; on the other hand he berated the absence of any workers on the stage. "The conclusion," he wrote, "is that on the whole *Trouhadec* is, so to speak, a permissible production in the Moscow State Yiddish Theater, a production with great worth, especially for the inner professional training of the troupe. But . . . the theater must finally begin to present productions with concrete revolutionary content."[122]

Yet for its next production the pendulum swung in the opposite direction; the theater returned to Jewish themes, creative experimentation, and a renowned Yiddish writer—Mendele Mokher Sforim, the "grandfather of Yiddish literature." Dobrushin converted Mendele's unfinished short story *The Travels of Benjamin III* into a play and added an ending. The play, which premiered on April 20, 1927, starred Mikhoels as Benjamin, a naive simpleton from the shtetl of Tuneiadovka (Droneville), who, like Cervantes' Don Quixote, resolves to set out in search of the faraway places cited in popular literary tales. In this case, it is the "Black Jews" (one of the lost tribes of Israel) in the Land of Israel that captures the young hero's attention. After enticing his friend Senderl, a meek househusband in perpetual fear of his wife, with a promise that when Benjamin becomes king he will make Senderl viceroy, the two secretly steal away in the middle of the night to begin what they believe will be a heroic and historic adventure. After what seems to them like an eternity of harsh travel, they spot a town ahead, which Senderl presumes must be Istanbul. Realizing how far they must be from home and how close to the Land of Israel, Benjamin dreams about how posterity will compare him to the other great adventurers such as Alexander of Macedon. The dream sequence, designed by Robert Falk, depicts the Promised Land as a fantastical fairy land inhabited by creatures who are half men, half beast.[123] Upon entering "Istanbul," they meet a neighbor from Tuneiadovka who casually informs the two journeyers that their wives are looking for them and inquires what business brought them to Glupskie (Dimwit-town), a village in the region of Tuneiadovka. The excursion finally reaches its conclusion when the two approach a familiar site. "How did we get back to Tuneiadovka?" asks Senderl, to which Benjamin wisely replies, "The earth is round."[124] The two adventurers find that their real homeland is in Russia.

The play sought to convince Jews to abandon the shtetls and begin productive lives and to discredit the increasingly popular option of emigration to Palestine. Mocking the Zionist claim that Palestine is more of a homeland than Ukraine, Pulver incorporated the Zionist anthem and future national anthem of Israel, Hatikva (The Hope), into a traditional Ukrainian melodic motif. Mikhoels' portrayal of the "Jewish Don Quixote" represented an important change in direction for the theater toward the type of constructivist realism being made popular by Tairov.[125] Building upon the approach he set as Trouhadec, Mikhoels attempted to delve into the psychology of his character, seeing him as a complex individual— an ambitious youth "with his wings clipped,"[126] rather than as a social type. It was the first performance in which Mikhoels's sympathetic portrayal of the character, combined with Pulver's authentic shtetl tunes, transcended Granovsky's symbolism. The adaptation of realism was received positively by most critics. One wrote, "It is a joyous show. . . . It can agitate, be comprehended by, and captivate the audience. . . . It is, for this theater, a viable beginning."[127]

Despite the play's overtly anti-Zionist intent, many audience members were probably inspired by Benjamin's heartwarming search for a better life in Zion. The fantastical land portrayed in Benjamin's dream could also be interpreted as a tribute to the biblical land of miracles. Indeed, during the theater's European tour, at least one reviewer was touched by what he saw as the Zionist inspiration behind *The Travels of Benjamin III*. A. S. Lirik, writing for the Yiddish paper *Haynt* (Today), rejected any satirical interpretation of the play and saw it simply as a genuine homage to the Zionist dream:

> Is this the same regisseur who showed us *Two Hundred Thousand* and *The Sorceress*? There there was satire and ridicule, here there is pure childish humor; there they were comedians and joyous acrobats, here they are children, grown children, clever children, but with the purity of the genuine folk. . . . Here the Yiddish actors do not look like marionettes, but like people. . . . A good angel also prompted Granovsky to present *Benjamin III* not in the style of satire, only in the spirit of his popularity. What can be more popular than the dreams of generations, and which dream is stronger among Jews than the dream of the Land of Israel?[128]

The success of the 1926–1927 season dispelled any rumors of collapse and put a temporary end to financial difficulties. The debt was also reduced by a long season, lasting 239 days, in which the theater gave 192 performances (not including the summer tour). Four new productions (*Trouhadec, The Tenth Commandment, 137 Children's Homes,* and *The Travels of Benjamin III*) also helped draw audiences. In total over 47,000 spectators attended the theater, averaging 244 a night. Notably, the theater was still only filling half its seats—its financial success was more attributable to the sheer number of performances than to its nightly attendance. With over 600 hours spent in nearly 100 rehearsals, the troupe earned this success

The Travels of Benjamin III,
1927. The letters on the
curtain spell Mendele in
Yiddish. Photo courtesy of
Ala Perelman-Zuskin.

Left to right: Benjamin
Zuskin as Senderl, Solomon
Mikhoels as Benjamin, in The
Travels of Benjamin III.
Photo courtesy of Ala
Perelman-Zuskin.

The Dream Sequence from *The Travels of Benjamin III.*
Photo from Solomon Mikhoels, *Stati, besedi, rechi.*

through hard work.[129] The season ended with another successful tour, during which the theater played to an estimated 71,000 spectators.[130] Once again, the tour proved that there was more interest in Yiddish theater in the provinces than in Moscow.

Revolution on Stage

With the approach of the tenth anniversary of Bolshevik power, the theater was obligated to celebrate the occasion by "putting the Revolution on stage." Granovsky chose to sidestep the sensitive issues surrounding the portrayal of the Bolshevik Revolution by turning to more remote political upheavals. For despite the flurry of festivals which celebrated its victory, the narrative of the "Great Socialist October Revolution" was only now being canonized in art with Sergei Eisenstein's film *October.* Many knew that the chronology of events as they occurred the night of October 25, 1917 was simply too mundane to form the creation myth of the utopian state. The action was not the stuff of dreams or drama: there were no mass demonstrations, no street fights, no barricades, and no live cannons fired from offshore ships. Granovsky was by no means the first to be confronted with this enigma, nor was he the first to opt to ignore it. Sergei Tretiakov's *Roar China!,* for instance, which was among the first productions to show a revolution on the stage, shunned the story of the Bolshevik seizure of power in favor of depicting a remote Chinese rebellion against Western imperialism.

Following this model, Granovsky chose to produce Lipe Reznik's *Uprising,*

81

which premiered November 7, 1927. Reznik's original text was a symbolist drama set in an unnamed valley town where a mystical "general-engineer" defends his revolution against a counter-revolutionary center. Granovsky placed the play in a concrete setting, turning it into a historical representation of the Dutch colonization of Java and an uprising against the British overlords. It was a bland depiction of the clash of cultures and class struggle which accompany imperialism. According to Moshe Goldblatt, Mikhoels, realizing the script's shortcomings, deliberately sabotaged his chance of being assigned the lead role by giving a pitiful performance at the script's preliminary reading in the presence of the author. As a result, the lead was given instead to Goldblatt, who, in light of Granovsky's strict discipline, could not refuse.[131]

The play surpassed even *137 Children's Homes* as a popular and critical failure. The performance compared unfavorably with similar productions running simultaneously in Moscow (*Dzhuma Mashid*, about colonialism in India, at the Korsh Theater and *Kauchuk*, about colonialism in South America, at the Proletkult theater), and the absence of Mikhoels from a lead role contributed to the Yiddish theater's dwindling audience.[132] Litvakov complained that Granovsky's adaptation turned the play into a completely different piece of work: "In *Uprising* the theater handled all the ideology correctly, it did everything to give the play and the performance an appropriate ideological direction. But it could do nothing, because the entire structure and content of the play conflicts with the regisseur's intentions."[133] Others simply felt the play was boring or unsuccessful, often noting its excessive melodrama and affectations and weak character development.[134] The turn away from specifically Jewish-oriented productions to general Soviet themes also detracted from the theater's uniqueness, a point not lost on some reviewers, one of whom cautioned that "the theater must remain a Jewish theater . . . and not just a theater in the Yiddish language."[135]

The new year could hardly have started worse for Granovsky. On January 2nd, the commission which had been invited to investigate the continuing battle between the directorate and the theater's union issued its conclusions. The commission found that the theater still had a total debt of nearly 200,000 rubles, despite having received almost 50,000 rubles in subsidies. The primary cause of the debt, it continued, was poor management on the part of Granovsky, who had allowed his staff to balloon to ninety people. Specifically, it found that 50 percent of the budget allocated for salaries went to a fourteen-member administrative section and that the eighteen-member orchestra was disproportionate for the size of the theater—another attack on Granovsky's emphasis on music. Most important, it found that the "non-Party-member director, Granovsky" had led the theater into conflict with its trade union by systematically violating his agreements. Thus, the commission recommended that, pending the approval of the Moscow Union of Artists, Granovsky be formally replaced with Comrade Plomper as administrative-financial director.[136]

An infuriated and frustrated Granovsky responded the same day with a defiant letter. He refused to recognize the authority of the union and said that the theater had no need of a Party director since there were already two Party members on the theater's board of governors (Litvakov and Palatnik). He then disputed each point of the commission's report, noting, for instance, that there were only ten members of the administrative department of the theater and that they did not consume nearly 50 percent of the budget; that the total deficit of the theater was under 150,000 rubles; and that the money spent on the music section, which had only fifteen orchestra members, was absolutely essential.[137] According to the theater's accounts, Granovsky's version was closer to the truth. There were eleven administrators who consumed under 20 percent of the total budget, while the fifty-seven-member artistic division (including all actors) received nearly 70 percent of all wages. Indeed, Mikhoels, whose salary now came to 400 rubles a month, had over-taken Granovsky, whose salary lingered at 360, as the highest-paid member of the staff. Ten other actors received salaries of over 100 rubles a month.[138] In this light, Granovsky criticized the integrity of the commission, pointing out that it had made its decision based on only one twenty-minute conversation with the theater's director. Finally, he objected to being referred to as "the non-Party-member Granovsky."[139]

Several days later, Granovsky received another order, this time from the Commissariat of Enlightenment, demanding that he reduce his staff.[140] While the staff of the theater had fallen from its high of 115 in 1924, it remained relatively over-staffed.[141] Thus, on January 11th, an ad hoc commission to reduce the staff of the Moscow State Yiddish Theater was gathered together under the auspices of the Management of State Academic Theaters. It was decided to release three members of the administrative section, one member of the technical department, and three members of the artistic division.[142] Regarding the last category, it was easily decided to release the choreographer and one actress who was away on a vacation for which she had not received permission. However, the third choice posed a problem, because both Rakhel Imenitova and E. Z. Vayner had only been in four of the last seven productions. Eventually, Granovsky's argument that Vayner should be retained because she had been in the theater since its founding was accepted and Imenitova was laid off. The official decision, which was issued in the name of the Management of State Academic Theaters, was then sent to the Commissariat of Enlightenment and the Union of Artists for approval, which they gave.[143]

Imenitova, for her part, felt that the decision to fire her was based on a personal vendetta of Granovsky's, who still held a grudge against her for the vacation incident several years earlier. Thus, on February 15th, two days after she was officially released, Imenitova filed suit in the People's Court against the directorate of the theater.[144] The legal suit quickly divided the theater once again, reviving the old divisions between the directorate and the troupe.[145] The March 26th decision of the People's Court found that the defendant had been unduly fired and called for her reinstatement as well as for reimbursement of her lost salary and legal fees, despite the fact that the decision had been approved by all the requisite supervisory organizations.[146]

Bogged down by ongoing administrative, financial, and legal difficulties, and with extensive planning for his upcoming European tour, Granovsky had little time in early 1928 for artistic concerns. These distractions contributed to what Goldblatt called a severe lack of discipline during the preparations for the next production.[147] Despite these difficulties, Dobrushin and Oyslender's adaptation of Sholem Aleichem's story "It Doesn't Work," premiered in March 1928 under the title *Luftmentshen.* The play represented Mikhoels's third attempt at portraying Menakhem Mendl. This time, the hapless *luftmentsh* travels the world in a fruitless effort to eke out a living. In Odessa he speculates among the Jewish poor, in Kiev he speculates among the rich Jewish capitalists, and in America he discovers that the "Land of Opportunity" is a myth. When our hero, now in the role of a diplomat, gains an audience with the Turkish sultan—an allusion to those political Zionists who believed that a Jewish homeland could be established in Palestine with the permission of the sultanate—the audience could only laugh at the absurdity of the situation. Stylistically, the theater sought to remind the audience that they were watching a spectacle. For instance, characters in different villages used the same telegraph machine to dispatch messages to each other, and characters wrote letters without a pencil. However, many of the workers in the audience failed to understand the meaning of such subtleties, relegating them to carelessness or prop shortages.[148]

In Marxist Jewish literary criticism, Menakhem Mendl had come to symbolize the archetype of the *luftmentsh.* He was, as Sholem Aleichem himself wrote, proof that "everything built in air and wind must eventually come crashing down."[149] However, the political situation had made the public less tolerant of subtle innuendoes; political leaders preferred broad attacks. Mikhoels was only able to justify his decision to interpret Menakhem Mendl as a comic figure, rather than as a tragic and vicious capitalist, on the grounds that parasites like Mendl were a dying type and no longer required the reticence of earlier times.[150] Nevertheless, by returning to the Jewish shtetl past, the theater was falling behind the political demands of the day. "[The Moscow State Yiddish Theater] cannot continue returning to the theme of the Jewish past," wrote one critic. "The circle is closed. The bankruptcy of the old Jewish shtetl world has been unmasked for ever. If still after *The Travels of Benjamin* the Moscow State Yiddish Theater succeeds in lyrically creating the dying-out days of old, then it is only the last echo, the dying echo of a requiem of the past."[151] *Pravda* was equally critical of the production's theme:

> The Moscow State Yiddish Theater has not emerged out of the Pale of Settlement, the lyrical humor of life in the Jewish towns. . . . In short, [*Luftmentshen*] is not a failure, but it is not an achievement—it is treading in place. Maybe, and even probably, *Luftmentshen* will find its public. But it is nonetheless necessary for the theater to reconsider continuing along this path.[152]

Despite their harsh criticism, reviewers were unable to concede that the show was a popular failure. For instance, *Izvestiia* wrote: "It cannot be said that the material for this production is bad. The literary reworking of the text by Dobrushin was done with great thoroughness. . . . Mikhoels plays his role wonderfully. . . . The music of Pulver enlivens the spectacle and is the most effective part of the play."[153]

One reviewer, who saw the play in Odessa and wrote for *Der emes* had, perhaps, not yet been briefed on the Party line. He could hardly contain his enthusiasm:

> Mikhoels plays Menakhem Mendel. This is not an uneventful play from the other world. . . . This is savage satirical humor, a sharp protest, a verbal exclamation against any economically inept epoch, in which a thousand Menakhem Mendels choke themselves and march on without any ground under their feet. . . . Mikhoels does not play Menakhem Mendel; rather he lives together with him, he aches together with him, he rages together with him.[154]

While haughty critics in Moscow could freely celebrate the Revolution's role in wiping out the vestiges of the *luftmentshen,* provincial Jews needed only to look at themselves to appreciate the play's poignant candor.

The question of whether the Soviet state played a preventive or prescriptive role in the culture of the New Economic Policy era continues to be debated among

historians. Since E. H. Carr's monumental history of the Bolshevik Revolution,[155] the era of the NEP has generally been seen as a period of transition during which the state retreated from its aspirations of total control of culture.[156] However, a few scholars have argued that it was during the period of the NEP that the Party began the Cultural Revolution that would bring culture under the state's firm control. Michael Fox, for instance, argues that:

> an entire system of ad hoc commissions was developed to report to the Politburo or Central Committee on issues of special importance. . . . The result was that artistic and scholarly groups were closely monitored, and altercations negotiated. . . . The high Party leadership, therefore, did not merely set major policies, but was deeply involved in the picayune of cultural affairs. . . . The important thing about such seemingly insignificant squabbles was that they were inevitably tied to the institutional turf battles surrounding censorship. Just as Party leaders could become involved in such disputes, so could Party and state institutions.[157]

Fox's observations are apropos in many ways. However, Fox assumes a commonality of purpose among these ad hoc commissions. This was rarely the case. The turf wars waged among the Commissariat of Enlightenment, the People's Court, the unions, and the Jewish Section enhanced the theater's autonomy while limiting each individual institution's say. Like a manipulative child who turns to Mom when Dad says no, the troupe could shop around for the permission it required. Nevertheless, each organ's persistent need to display its own power and the resulting constant reversals of policy led to an atmosphere of incessant harassment, impeding Granovsky's autonomy. While Granovsky could, perhaps, have reached an arrangement of mutual interest with a single organization—as he achieved with Litvakov and the Jewish Section—the varying objectives and universal aspirations toward hegemony of each organ placed them in opposition to one another, making a compromise with one anathema to the other. The ironic consequence was that the confusion regarding delineation of duties led to an indefatigable, yet ultimately ineffective, discipline.

This process began in 1924–1925 as Granovsky started to lose control over the day-to-day activities of his troupe. While various organs of the state, such as the Management of State Academic Theaters, the Commissariat of Enlightenment, and the Union of Artists, issued declarations transferring aspects of the theater's operations to their control, they did not interfere in the everyday functioning of the theater unless invited to do so by members of the troupe. As the theater staff took advantage of the many bureaucratic checks on its director by appealing to higher authorities, the organs of the state were given the opportunity to intervene by invitation, thereby increasing their legitimacy as a superior authority. While the process began with Krashinskii's appeal to the Moscow Union of Artists, Granovsky himself finally succumbed to such tactics. His final act of desperation—his appeal to the Central Union of Artists—gave the union the legitimacy to issue its declaration relieving him of his post as head of the administrative-financial division. That is not to say that the decision was not politically motivated.

By literally asking for its intervention, Granovsky forfeited his final say. However, as we shall see in the next chapter, Granovsky's capitulation was not complete; he was merely biding his time, waiting for the opportunity to reassert his authority.

We must note that at this stage no restrictions were placed on the theater's repertoire or stylistic approaches. Indeed, a list of permissible productions circulated in 1928 included virtually the entire corpus of Yiddish theater—over 100 different playwrights were represented.[158] However, this leniency hardly stemmed from any democratic notions of artistic freedom; it was simply an unavoidable consequence of the Party's own confused understanding of the nature of proletarian culture, since an orthodox cultural discourse had yet to be formulated. In the interim, the Party had to be content with limiting the administrative autonomy of the theater, thereby placing the regime's political control above and beyond the enforcement of any cultural ideology. The suppression of the Moscow State Yiddish Theater's administrative autonomy coincided with similar measures taken against all independent institutions, regardless of their political or ideological affiliations. It was a fate shared not only with such prestigious institutions as the Proletkult, but also with a wide range of informal voluntary organizations ranging from local literary circles to sports clubs.

In the case of the Moscow State Yiddish Theater, neither the state nor the Party unilaterally imposed itself upon a helpless organization. On the contrary, the initiative to curb the theater's autonomy was taken by low-level workers seeking self-promotion by discrediting their superiors, thereby entering into a dialogue with the state to the mutual advantage of the workers and the state. In this instance, however, it must be remembered that the initiative was spearheaded by Khaim Krashinskii, the troupe's only Party member. As such, his actions can be interpreted as those of either a low-level worker in the troupe—one of the common people—or as a functionary of the ruling Party. Furthermore, while his actions were supported by the theater's trade union and therefore could be seen as the collective expression of the entire troupe, one must not forget that the union—of which he was secretary—often used coercive methods to maintain its membership. Thus, the initiative to curb the theater's autonomy was taken by a single low-level worker who acted as a member of the Communist Party to seek promotion either within the Party or the theater by discrediting his superiors and enforcing his own opinions on the collective through his control of the union. The state and Party were able to keep their hands clean by allowing one of their minions to do their dirty work.

In the larger arena of cultural outreach, the theater expanded its influence during the latter half of the 1920s into the working-class populations of the provincial shtetls. Nevertheless, it failed to become a genuine workers' theater on a par with its allegedly "bourgeois" competitors in New York. The Yiddish theaters of America catered to the very same lowbrow habits that Granovsky sought to reform. Whether they were coming from the sweatshops of the Lower East Side or the factories of Moscow, weary laborers preferred the "beerhall" theaters of Second Avenue, where they were encouraged to heckle and swoon over their beloved stars for the sheer sake of entertainment, over the Malaia Bronnaia "Temple" where they were instructed to remain silent and absorb the pedagogical lessons of the anonymous actors and agitators.

The Moscow State Yiddish Theater was a small but integral part of the vast program of propaganda upon which the Soviet state and the Jewish Section relied to entice the shtetl Jews. It functioned in conjunction with more conventional forms of persuasion, such as Yiddish Party cells, trade unions, courts, books, pamphlets, periodicals, schools, and violent coercion. While the problems associated with many of these methods have been amply documented, Jewish Party membership did increase dramatically throughout the 1920s, and Jewish agricultural settlements flourished briefly in the latter part of the decade.[159] Perhaps the theater was able to motivate the populace where traditional forms of agitation failed.

Wandering Stars: Tour and Reconstruction

3

In April 1928, the Moscow State Yiddish Theater embarked on a nine-month tour of Europe. During its absence, Stalin began the implementation of his "Second Revolution," or "Cultural Revolution," during which he attempted to transform every aspect of Soviet society, from the production of pig iron to the repertoire and aesthetic techniques of the Yiddish theater. The First Five-Year Plan, implemented in 1929, aimed to centralize all decision making in the hands of an elite few. The first step in this process was the removal of local specialists, those enterprising and creative individuals who operated the factories, supervised the workshops, financed the business firms, and directed the theaters. All remaining vestiges of autonomy held by cultural and political institutions were to be eradicated as the state asserted its control. In May and June 1928, during the theater's absence, the Shakhty trial, at which a group of mining specialists was accused of sabotage, preceded a turn against the alleged Europeanized intelligentsia and their claims of cultural superiority. The icons of the Revolution—its generators, celebrators, propagators, and supporters, from Leon Trotsky to Maksim Gorky—were rejected by zealous workers and Party activists as deviationists—whether from the right or the left was irrelevant. Factory workers joined in the chorus, along with the Communist press and the associations of proletarian musicians and writers, in jeering Prokofiev, Meyerhold, Eisenstein, and Granovsky as relics of an age gone by with nothing left to contribute to the new Revolution—which this time was to be carried out by the workers alone.

The Soviet theater and its personnel did not escape the stringent demands placed on society. In August 1928, Mikhail Chekhov, the pre-eminent Russian actor and playwright, defected, while Meyerhold, in Europe over the summer, was persuaded to return to Moscow and attempt to revive his ailing theater only through the direct intervention of Lunacharskii. Mayakovsky's *Bedbug*, which premiered at the Meyerhold Theater in early 1929, was quickly met with harsh criticism from the Union of Proletarian Writers. However, the great director's calamitous fate was delayed, thanks to the tremendous popular success of his new production. A young Dmitry Shostakovich, who was working with Meyerhold on the production, also became the subject of intense slander. Even the hallowed halls of the Bolshoi were not immune to the whirlwind of change. The Yiddish theater, too, was to undergo its most striking transformation during this turbulent period. In the words of prominent theater critic Pavel Markov, "The slogan of Cultural Revolution is being enthusiastically and triumphantly carried into execution."[1]

The Best-Laid Plans

The notion of a European tour was appealing to both Granovsky and the Party, albeit for very different reasons. Granovsky, craving recognition from his alma mater, had begun plans as early as 1923 to tour Germany.[2] The director was always more at home in the cosmopolitan capitals of Europe than in the poverty-stricken shtetls of the former Pale or the ostracized capital of Revolutionary Russia. Natalia Vovsi-Mikhoels wrote of Granovsky that "life in the Jewish shtetls, on which practically the entire repertoire of the Jewish theater was founded, was totally strange and incomprehensible to him."[3] He disdained Russia for what he saw as its parochialism, debilitating bureaucracy, and marginality.[4] His correspondence provides evidence that he yearned for the fraternity of the European salons he had abandoned. He composed lengthy intimate personal letters to German friends and continued to network extensively with German colleagues. In short, Granovsky was more interested in showing European society how he could make Jews dance than in showing the Jewish masses how to become productive factory workers in service of the Soviet state.

Throughout the 1920s, Granovsky concentrated on enhancing his prestige abroad: he sent costumes and photos for inclusion in an exhibition in Vienna;[5] he planned an exhibition of his theater in America;[6] and he repeatedly sent press releases and photos to European newspapers. He even kept German-language letterhead on hand. Much to his chagrin, many of his plans met with frustration. For instance, while Granovsky was able to elicit articles about his theater in several Yiddish- and Russian-language Berlin newspapers, such as *Eko* (Echo) and *Nash mir* (Our World), the German-language papers from which he most sought recognition politely replied that the Yiddish theater would not be of interest to their readership.[7] Furthermore, the pictures that were published in *Nash mir* were accompanied with the mistaken caption, "The Jewish chamber theater, Habima," confusing Granovsky's troupe with his rival, the Hebrew-language theater.[8] A British paper even failed to identify the theater whose photos it featured.[9] It became increasingly clear to Granovsky that in order to get the international recognition he craved he needed to take his troupe on the road.

The state, as well, had strong reasons for wanting a tour. In the late 1920s, with the likelihood of world revolution fading, the diplomatically isolated Soviet Union became desperate for allies. With increasing anti-Semitic incidents spreading through Europe, it was hoped that the Jews of the world, particularly the influential Polish Bund and New York Worker's Circle socialist movements, could be persuaded to lend their support to the Soviet Union.

In early 1924 Granovsky began negotiations with Harry Winitsky of the New York socialist Yiddish paper *Frayhayt* for a tour of America, which he hoped could follow a tour of Germany.[10] The paper was already intensely involved with Yiddish theater; it had sponsored the New York communist Yiddish troupe which was to become the Artef (Workers' Theater Society) Theater directed by Benno Schneider—ironically, a former member of Moscow's Habima. On the paper's recommendation, Granovsky turned to the theater activist Mendel Elkin, an expatriot Belorussian Jew living in New York.[11] Since 1907, Elkin had been involved with a group of Yiddish theater activists in Minsk that had included A. Vayter, Ari Ben-Ami of the Hirschbein theater, and Peretz Hirschbein himself. He was later associated with the founding of the Jewish Theatrical Society of Warsaw, together with Vayter, Isaac Leyb Peretz, and Scholem Asch. In 1923, Elkin moved to New York, where he helped found the Yiddish Theater Society and the Unzer Teater troupe of the Bronx, whose short-lived existence ended in 1926 with bankruptcy.[12]

Elkin's arrangement with Granovsky involved an exchange in which the Soviet troupe would come to North America over the summer and fall of 1924, where they would play in New York, Chicago, Boston, Philadelphia, St. Louis, Toronto, Montreal, and Winnipeg, while a New York troupe would tour the Soviet Union.[13] Originally Elkin hoped to send the renowned actor Maurice Schwartz and his Yiddish Art Theater, but eventually decided to allow Edwin Relkin (1880–1952), the leading Jewish theater agent famous for making the Café Royale in the Lower East Side his office, to decide the matter.[14] While the Jewish Section approved of the tour in principle,[15] the ten months it took the Jewish Section to debate the matter left Granovsky's American and German partners frustrated, leading to a break in relations.[16] Any attempts to re-establish relations were thwarted when the Soviet Central Committee of the Union of Artists forbade the American troupe to tour without prior approval of its repertoire.[17] The American union was equally inflexible, first by refusing to give permission for Relkin to tour communist Russia[18] and then by refusing to allow Granovsky's troupe to visit New York during the theatrical season for fear of the competition it posed to local troupes.[19] The problem was resolved only after Elkin convinced the American union that Granovsky's troupe was geared toward a specific audience and would not pose any competition.

Negotiations once again hit a snag over financial differences. Granovsky initially demanded $25,000,[20] but eventually lowered his costs to $16,000.[21] The price still proved to be too high for Elkin.[22] Granovsky, not realizing the high price of advertising in the United States, demanded a publicity campaign beyond Elkin's means. He required well-published books in Yiddish and English, bilingual glossy programs and librettos with photos, and extensive advertisements in the Russian, Yiddish, and English press: "We are not intended only for the attention of the Jewish public. Our forms and principles are undoubtedly new also for the English theater," he wrote.[23] When Elkin indicated he was approaching bankruptcy, Granovsky appealed to his acquaintance Leon Talmy (Layzer Talmovitsky, 1893–1952) for help.[24] Talmy was a one-time Territorialist (supporter of Jewish autonomy within the Diaspora) from Russia who was active in the American Communist Party during his residence in the United States in 1912–1917 and 1920–1932.

Talmy's response was not encouraging:

> Relkin terminates the agreement on the grounds that it is too great a risk. . . . All other Broadway managers have said that they think it is too great a risk. They point out that it would require a very broad advertising campaign to generate interest. In general, the condition of Broadway is now extremely unfavorable toward foreign theaters, especially Jewish ones. The other possibility is to try to interest private individuals who are able to partially finance you. Personally, I am skeptical of these.[25]

Talmy went on to advise Granovsky to focus on the Jewish theaters of Second Avenue. But without Broadway, Granovsky was not interested. Attempts by Dobrushin to reopen negotiations with different contacts, notably with the Yiddish dramatist Halpern Leyvick, met similar fates.

Just over a year later, Granovsky renewed contacts after setting a new date for his world tour. Negotiations began in September 1926 when Palatnik, as a member of the theater's governing board, wrote to the Jewish Section asking the Party's opinion on the possibility of a European and American tour to take place the following summer and fall.[26] Over the next few months, Granovsky wrote some twenty letters to Berlin, Prague, New York, Buenos Aires, Vienna, London, Warsaw, and Amsterdam searching for sponsors.[27] Plans to tour Britain fell apart after the British government refused to grant visas to the troupe on the grounds that they would provide competition for the local theaters. Huntley Carter, the renowned theater critic and Granovsky's British sponsor, suggested that the real motive lay in a fear of Communist propaganda.[28] After receiving favorable responses from two Berlin firms, Granovsky wrote to the Jewish Section, which had not yet replied to Palatnik's request. He stressed that many other Soviet theaters had recently received permission to travel abroad, hinting that a denial of his request would be construed as anti-Semitic.[29] The Jewish Section turned the matter over to the Commissariat of Enlightenment, which waited a year before approving the tour in early 1928 with three conditions: that a fixed time period be confirmed, that the troupe "attach to the tour a character which reflects favorably on Soviet art abroad," and that Granovsky actively work to enhance the foreign reputation of the Soviet Society for the Settlement of Jewish Toilers on the Land.[30] While waiting for a response from the Commissariat of Enlightenment, Granovsky had also continued secret negotiations with several American firms[31] before deciding to return to Mendel Elkin, giving him power of attorney in the spring of 1927.[32] On January 28, 1928, the theater finally received official permission from the Commissariat of Enlightenment to go abroad.[33]

On March 12, 1928, the governing board of the theater, now consisting of Granovsky, Palatnik, Litvakov, and Lazar Vayn, met for the last time before the tour to discuss seemingly mundane matters. Regarding the repertoire for the coming season, it was decided that Granovsky would continue to rehearse Sholem Aleichem's *Luftmentshen* during the tour and that a new play by a Soviet author would be added later. Granovsky then insisted that Vayn be dispatched to Europe at a later date to allow the director to take a vacation while abroad. Finally, it was decreed that Mikhoels be given a vacation due to illness and that an understudy be trained for Mikhoels should his illness continue.[34]

The protocols from this meeting, particularly Granovsky's concern with finding replacements for himself and Mikhoels, indicate that he might have been planning to defect well in advance and that he may have even planned to take Mikhoels with him. The harassment the director had experienced over the previous two years, culminating with the reference to him as "the non-Party director" and his forced dismissal from the post of financial-administrative director foreboded a bleak future. His antagonistic response to the commission's report had

done little to bring him back into favor. This hypothesis also explains his obsession with securing permission for the tour; it was his only opportunity to carry out
such a plan.

Indeed, the suspicious character of Mikhoels's sudden illness was not lost
on the Central Committee of the Communist Party. In early March, the Central
Committee abruptly denied passports for the troupe, citing rumors of defection.
The problem was resolved only through the joint intervention of a number of Jews
prominent in the Communist Party, including Semen Dimanshtayn, former head
of the Commissariat of Jewish Affairs; Aleksandr Chemeriskii, secretary of the
Jewish Section; Palatnik; and Litvakov. In a letter to the Central Committee of the
Party, they vowed to "fully vouch for the conduct of the theater abroad" and suggested that Vayn be dispatched to monitor the troupe—ironically the very same
suggestion that had gotten Granovsky in trouble in the first place.[35] Granovsky left
Moscow on March 21st without delay, to be followed by the rest of the troupe two
weeks later. Since the European segment of the tour was to be preceded by a tour
of the Soviet Union's western provinces, Vayn stayed behind to oversee repairs of
the theater hall and to finish some accounting business; he had plans to join the
theater in Berlin in October.

Meanwhile, on April 4th, Comrade Waldman, a member of the Union of
Artists stationed in Berlin with the Soviet diplomatic corps, discovered that the
German firm with which Granovsky had contracted was not solvent. His suspicions grew when he discovered that the 10,000-Mark advance stipulated in the
contract had never arrived. On further investigation he found that Granovsky had
requested that the money be placed into a German account rather than be sent to
Russia. Upon interrogation, Granovsky insisted that the money was needed in
Germany to purchase supplies abroad. However, all foreseeable supplies had been
brought from Russia—at great expense; the 10,000 Marks seemed to be just the
right amount of money one would need to start a new life in Germany. But for the
time being, the Party, worried that any moves to cancel the tour at this point would
be construed as anti-Semitic by the foreign press, accepted Granovsky's explanation and the tour continued.[36]

Europe

From the first instant the troupe set foot on non-Soviet soil, its conduct was
provocative. Huge crowds met the performers at the Warsaw train station, fueling
the egos they had acquired as theater stars. Many of the actors were also met by old
friends and family dressed in traditional religious garb. At least one actor reported
feeling self-conscious and ashamed in front of his Orthodox brethren; whereas in
the Soviet Union modern dress was regarded as a sign of enlightenment, among
many Polish Jewish circles it was still seen as indecent. The actors' piety was further stirred by the timing of their arrival, which coincided with the first night of
Passover. Several actors accepted invitations to attend a seder that night, the feast
commemorating the Exodus from Egypt. The actor Moshe Goldblatt recalled the
effect the seder had on him: "The seder night! A world of nourishment and mem-

ories from childhood years." Conveniently forgetting his own role in promoting Communist propaganda, Goldblatt continued: "For ten years in Soviet Russia they inundated us day in and day out with anti-religious propaganda and inculcated our consciousness with negative and even abhorrent attitudes toward the Jewish tradition, rites, holidays and way of life. We had even begun to believe in this."[37]

While no performances were scheduled for Poland—the troupe hoped to perform there on their return trip—Granovsky, Zuskin, and Mikhoels accepted interviews with the Yiddish literary magazine *Literarishe bleter*. In their first open interviews with the foreign press, the performers belittled the state's role in the development of the theater. In an issue dedicated entirely to the Moscow State Yiddish Theater, Granovsky provided the lead article, "Our Theater," in which he portrayed the theater as his own independent creation; other articles repeatedly referred to "The Granovsky Theater." Zuskin was quoted as saying, "The theater came to life around the person of A. Granovsky." Throughout the journal, the theater's adaptations of Sholem Aleichem, Peretz, Goldfadn, and Mendele were celebrated, while no reference was made to the contemporary Soviet plays. Further, the journal published an article on the theater by David Bergelson, a Soviet Yiddish writer who defected to Berlin in 1921. Although Bergelson would be valued as a pro-Soviet writer upon his return to the Soviet Union in 1934, he was out of favor with the Kremlin in 1928, and his association with the troupe was not viewed favorably in Moscow.[38]

The troupe's behavior in Berlin, where it would spend the next six weeks giving its first European performances, was no different. The actors, accustomed to dormitories and cafeterias, were overwhelmed at their Berlin accommodations and amazed at the extravagance of European life. Goldblatt recalls the first night in Berlin when several actors were invited to dinner at the residence of a friend of Granovsky. It was Goldblatt's first live encounter with the European bourgeoisie, whose decadence and iniquities he had mocked on stage for the last ten years: "At a colossal table, around which could sit no less than a dozen people . . . a huge number of different foods, baked goods, fruits and drinks were laid out on the table. The lavish cut glass and porcelain dishes in which all the delicacies were placed was enrapturing."[39] Initially, the young actors were astonished by the ease with which "Herr Professor Granovsky" fit into this alien environment. But during an evening of stimulating conversation, the director revealed his family secret to the actors—that he was a "class enemy," having been born into one of the wealthiest bourgeois Jewish families in the Russian Empire. Henceforth, those present that evening would see their mentor in a different light.

The troupe's Berlin premiere of *Two Hundred Thousand*, which was attended by a large segment of the German cultural intelligentsia, particularly those of Jewish extraction, was an instantaneous popular success. Goldblatt recalls that

> when we thought that the stormy ovation and the cries of "Bravo" and "Granovsky" would never end, people immediately set out to find the person being honored and almost forcefully shoved him onto the stage where he remained standing bewildered with a pale jelled face until his wife yelled to him with a

hoarse voice from behind the curtains: "Aleksei, give another bow. Why are you just standing there like a groom under the *chuppah*?"[40]

"The greatest triumph which the theater found in Berlin with its first performance," Goldblatt later wrote,

> was the stir within the Jewish population of Berlin. . . . How the German Jews, who with great contempt and scorn looked upon the *Ostjuden* [Eastern Jews], suddenly, to their great surprise, [found out that] an inferior backward caste can have a cultural institution that stands no lower, and is possibly even higher than, a lot of institutions in Western Europe.[41]

The troupe anxiously awaited the first reviews. Goldblatt, the actor to whom Granovsky entrusted the critical task of perusing three editions of each of Berlin's fourteen daily newspapers for reviews, described the director's state of mind at the time:

> Knowing Granovsky's erratic nervousness that he had nightly exhibited, I was completely surprised by the soberness and almost indifference with which he read about yesterday's premiere and about his great success with the audience. . . . I could not understand how a director could nonchalantly read through a review of his production. . . . But, subsequently it turned out that Granovsky's callousness was artificial and external. When we saw him later he had lost sleep for a considerable time and had stayed awake the entire night smoking countless cigarettes. So much so that in the morning a thick cloud of tobacco hung over his room.[42]

The initial reaction of the press was rewarding. Alfred Kerr, an assimilated Jew who was Germany's leading theater critic, exclaimed, "This is great art. Great art. . . . Not a dead point the whole evening. . . . Amazing."[43] The Yiddish press, while appreciating the high caliber of art, was skeptical about the troupe's politics. For instance, Herman Swet wrote in *Der moment*: "All of Germany is praising the theater to the skies!" He credited Granovsky with retaining artistic integrity and forgoing "propositions from the Soviet propaganda machine."[44] While intended as a compliment, such statements inflamed Moscow. A. S. Lirik felt similarly:

> Who believed that Sholem Aleichem's hero Shimele Soroker, the simple folkish man, who wins the big win and later loses it, that he, the poor tailor of the shtetl, would be transformed into a symbol of the revolution against the old world? . . . [The actors] climb and crawl on the stage like nimble cats. They dance and move like the best acrobats. . . . One must have respect for the high technical culture in their play. . . . but their one-sidedness is their curse. Only in revolutionary Russia, where man is dead and only the masses, the collective, live; only there where mechanisms and machines are a cult to which man bows down, only there could they rise and develop as a theater. . . . There is no joy; only exaggeration and satire.[45]

One critic who saw the show later in Frankfurt was turned off by the troupe's lighthearted approach to deep philosophical problems, insinuating that it would be more appropriate for a cabaret than a theater. "One cannot compare these acrobats with Habima," he wrote. "Their approach to art is very lighthearted while Habima is deep. . . . [The Moscow State Yiddish Theater] is entertaining, but one must not extract theoretical obligations from them. . . . It is a joyful fair. One should be permitted to smoke and drink beer [here]."[46]

The premieres of *The Sorceress* and *The Travels of Benjamin III* also received rave reviews, but the critics continued to fault the troupe for its agitational propaganda. A group of actors within the troupe suggested that the theater forego its planned performance of *Trouhadec,* the most pedagogical of its productions, in favor of a repeat performance of one of the lighter plays. However, the suggestion was withdrawn when the troupe was visited by a Soviet "diplomat," who disciplined the actors for their resistance to the planned performance.[47] As expected, the new premiere of *Trouhadec* received negative reviews from critics, who chastised Granovsky for deviating from the Jewish classics.

The financial and popular success of the tour was immediately apparent back home, prompting an optimistic Council of People's Commissars to wipe out the theater's debts to all state organizations with the hope that the tour would make up for all lost funds.[48] Yet Moscow was not pleased with the political and agitational success of the tour. Soon after Granovsky's arrival in Berlin, word reached Moscow that he was attempting to renegotiate contracts with the tour's sponsors. Suspicious of the director's motives, Palatnik and Litvakov, on behalf of the Jewish Section, sent a telegram to Granovsky in which they reiterated that "A trip to America is categorically forbidden."[49] Additionally, the Jewish Section and the Commissariat of Enlightenment decided to dispatch Vayn immediately to Berlin. On May 25th, Vayn sent a telegram to Granovsky asking the director to obtain a French visa for him and to have it sent to Berlin.

Vayn arrived in Berlin on June 5th, not realizing that the theater had just departed for Paris.[50] After explaining to the French embassy that he was with the Yiddish theater, he was assured that in that case he must already be in Paris where the theater was currently performing. Aggravated, Vayn had no choice but to monitor Granovsky's activity on the basis of irregular reports from Granovsky himself until he could obtain a French visa. Occasionally, however, rumors reached Vayn through other channels. For instance, he heard from a member of the diplomatic corps of the Union of Artists, who had just returned to Berlin from Paris, that Granovsky was "sick six days a week and healthy one day." Yet rumors were spreading that Granovsky was working on a film. Vayn recommended to Litvakov that Granovsky take a vacation. But he realized that his recommendation unfortunately could not be fulfilled because he, Granovsky's assistant director, was detained in Berlin.[51]

In the meantime, Vayn snooped around the German capital, where he discovered that Granovsky had failed to report one-tenth of his revenue from the Berlin shows.[52] Granovsky was up to even more unorthodox financial dealings in Paris: on June 5th he negotiated an agreement that included a trip to America, by which his sponsor would pay debts and expenses of the European segment of the tour in return for a percentage of the profits from the American leg of the tour.[53]

On June 14th, Vayn was still waiting for his visa in Berlin. In a letter to Litvakov he accused Granovsky of sabotaging his visa application:

> Today is the eighth day that I have been sitting in Berlin and I still have no visa.
> . . . I have sent two telegrams to Aleksei Mikhailovich [Granovsky]. In answer, on
> Monday (June 2) I received a telegram from Aleksei Mikhailovich in which he
> wrote "regarding the visa, you should receive an answer today." Today is Thursday and still no visa. I cannot judge what type of measures Aleksei Mikhailovich
> has taken toward dispatching a visa to me. . . . Does Aleksei Mikhailovich want
> me to come? Of course not. I explained the situation to the representative of [the
> diplomatic corps of the Union of Artists] in Berlin, Comrade Simok. In answer
> to Simok's suggestion that I come there, Granovsky answered, "Why does he
> need to?"[54]

When Vayn sent a threatening telegram to Granovsky, the director replied from his Parisian haven, "I am not used to receiving letters written in that tone and if you repeat it again, I will throw your unread letter into the wastebasket."[55] Indeed, Granovsky surely knew Vayn's motives and was in no hurry to facilitate them. He must have relished the idea that the man entrusted with the task of reporting his every move to the Communist Party was 500 miles away, entirely reliant on his own efforts to bring them together. Further, Granovsky had proven that he had the means of obtaining visas; during this same period he obtained a visa for Robert Falk, who had remained in Berlin after the rest of the troupe's departure for personal reasons.[56] Granovsky later admitted that when the French Embassy asked him for a guarantee that Vayn was not a member of the Communist Party, he had refused to give it.[57]

At the end of June the theater was still receiving positive reviews from the press. *Pravda* even reprinted excerpts from European reviews, particularly those which emphasized the Party line that such art could only develop with extensive state funding and support.[58] However, such articles were the exception. The majority of the foreign press, while praising the theater's artistic merits, denied that it represented a flowering of autonomous Jewish culture in the Soviet Union. For instance, Nakhman Mayzel, the influential theater and literary critic, did not believe that the theater was showing its true face to Europe. Writing in the Warsaw Yiddish paper *Haynt*, he argued:

> They bring the quintessence of Jewish identity from Moscow. The theater is
> under the direct influence of the Jewish Section which in theory wants to annihilate all that is Yiddish . . . but Granovsky understands that the old Mendele,
> Sholem Aleichem, Peretz, and Goldfadn are safe and more interesting that the
> young Veviurka and Reznik. . . . The Moscow Yiddish Theater is going around
> the world clothed with such old classics instead of showing the new revolutionary Moscow.[59]

Zionists, Rabbis, and Nationalists

During the course of the summer of 1928 several scandals rocked the troupe, leading to demands from Moscow that the theater return. The scandals involved three incidents in particular during which members of the troupe violated their instructions to avoid circulating among "anti-Soviet elements." The first was the troupe's attendance at a Shavuot (Feast of Tabernacles) banquet in Mannheim given by an unnamed Jewish organization sympathetic to rabbinicalism. This was followed by a meeting of Zuskin and Mikhoels with Sholem Asch. Finally, Zuskin, Mikhoels, and Goldblatt met with Chaim Weizmann, the president of the World Zionist Organization and future president of Israel. Understandably, Litvakov was infuriated—his trusted anti-Zionist, anti-rabbinical, anti-nationalist troupe had been holding meetings with the world's leading Zionists, rabbis, and nationalists. He was particularly disturbed by the meeting with Weizmann. He was undoubtedly familiar with the Zionist's attitude toward the Soviet Union. Weizmann had recently written in reference to the Birobidzhan project: "The whole fantastic project of setting up a Jewish Republic in Russia is a second matter which attempts to pervert humanitarian efforts of American Jews into a political action serving Soviet purposes."[60] Further, Litvakov likely knew that Weizmann was in the process of bringing Habima, currently stationed in New York, to Palestine to serve as the Palestinian national Hebrew theater.[61] Despite Weizmann's preference for Hebrew, it is possible that he had similar plans for the Yiddish theater.

In order to put pressure on the theater, the Soviet government released information to the local and foreign press that the theater's tour had accumulated a debt of 45,000 rubles—a figure Granovsky categorically denied.[62] In September rumors that the troupe would soon be recalled to Moscow reached Europe. The rumors prompted a letter from the theater's local union to the theater's governing board (Palatnik and Litvakov), with copies sent to the Union of Artists, in which the local union denied any involvement in Granovsky's alleged schemes and plans to defect: "The Moscow State Yiddish Theater collective has acted with the highest political and professional discipline throughout the entire tour. We, the local trade union, are sure that there is not one worker in the theater who does not wish to return with the theater to Russia."[63] Benjamin Zuskin also sent his own letter to Litvakov justifying the illicit meetings:

> I have reason to believe that you believed me and still believe now, so believe me that I am writing you the truth about the tour. Believe me, Moisei Ilyich, that all the information which you have on the movements of our actors in Europe has not a single basis [in fact]. . . . Every one of us remembers and knows that he is a Soviet citizen.

The Mannheim Shavuot banquet, he explained, occurred after the troupe had been stuck in Frankfurt for four days unable to perform due to a lack of ticket sales during the Jewish holy days. After a week with no income, the troupe was literally starving and thus could hardly turn down the invitation to a banquet. The "tea with Asch" incident, he continued, was a chance encounter; Mikhoels and Zuskin were invited to David Bergelson's Berlin apartment, not realizing that Scholem Asch would be there. Explaining the Weizmann incident, Zuskin wrote that one night after a show,

Weizmann came behind the curtains to thank us and express his delight. He saw and spoke to Mikhoels, me, and, I believe, Goldblatt, since we three stayed behind on stage. The others were already removing their makeup. What, in your opinion, should we have done? Turned our back to him and left?[64]

If Weizmann offered the troupe a haven in Palestine, his offer was rejected.

Negative reports of the theater's conduct, however, continued to flood the office of the Jewish Section. Continuing his investigation into Granovsky's behavior, Vayn discovered that immediately after arriving in Berlin, the director had contacted a number of Soviet émigrés, including Vassilii Kandinsky, and had largely ignored the collective, preferring to circulate in bourgeois German and Russian émigré circles. This conduct is confirmed by Goldblatt's memoirs. Forced to rely on hearsay and press reports, Vayn wrote:

> In all his speeches and interviews, Granovsky did not once mention that the theater was formed thanks to the union and strength of the Soviet state and workers, emphasizing always that the theater is his doing—if it were not for him there would be no theater. The press always calls it "Granovsky's theater." Furthermore, when asked what he thought of the USSR, Granovsky replied, "I do not interfere with politics. I am an artist. To me it is all the same who is in power."[65]

As we have seen, the accusations were largely true. However, even Vayn could not deny that the tour had been an immensely popular success.

America or Moscow?

The tide began to turn in more than one way in Vienna. The theater's stint in the city was generally ignored by the German press, while the response from the largely assimilated Jewish quarter was "cold and indifferent."[66] To make matters worse for Granovsky, on September 10th—after five months of waiting in vain for a visa—Vayn finally caught up with the troupe. Also, after a month of futile attempts to get information from Granovsky, Palatnik was dispatched to Berlin to investigate further. The meeting between Vayn, Granovsky, and Palatnik took place on October 11th. Palatnik wanted to know if Granovsky planned to continue the tour to America, where the missing money from the Berlin tour was, and how the theater had managed to accumulate a deficit when it had a guarantee from its German sponsors. Granovsky denied that there was any guarantee, arguing that the Commissariat of Enlightenment's information was incorrect. He further insisted that all subsequent arrangements had also been approved by Waldman of the diplomatic corps of the Union of Artists. Regarding the question of America, Granovsky admitted he had made a lucrative agreement with a French firm, insisting "I did not know that Moscow was against an American tour." Furthermore, he pointed out that the contract had been signed while he was still in Moscow. Indeed, Granovsky had signed a contract with the French firm in Moscow, but without consulting the Commissariat of Enlightenment and without including an American tour. After further interrogation, Granovsky admitted he knew the American tour was prohibited:

We had begun to play in Belgium and Holland and on the fifth or sixth day in Antwerp a telegram arrived from Comrade [Aleksei] Sviderskii [saying] that the American tour is prohibited as is the rest of the European tour. I wrote Sviderskii a letter stating that first of all I completely do not understand why he does not approve the maximum favorable agreement. Secondly, I do not understand why currently three directors of academic theaters sit abroad and conclude agreements on tours to America—yet for the Moscow State Yiddish Theater this is forbidden. Thirdly, what kind of principles could interfere with a trip to America and to New York, where there are so many Jews? Why is the agreement that I first succeeded in concluding so advantageously to us not being approved? In conclusion, I asked him to release me from the theater.[67]

He went on to relate that when he told the French firm that Moscow was forcing the cancellation of the contract, it threatened to take the theater to court. Granovsky reiterated that the deficit problem would be solved with a trip to New York. The panel was not fazed by the prospect of a lawsuit. Vayn and Palatnik agreed to place all responsibility for forfeiting the contract on Granovsky, while the government would deny any involvement.

The next day Palatnik sent a report to Litvakov along with a stenographic record of the meeting with Granovsky. His advice was to take every measure possible to return the troupe to Moscow immediately before the situation got further out of hand. Describing the director's mood, Palatnik wrote that Granovsky was convinced there was a mole close to the theater, that he felt the Soviet press was slandering him, and that he believed he could not return to the Soviet Union with impunity.[68] Palatnik advised Litvakov to "write something kind," to Granovsky which would open the path for a discussion of his return. Regarding the rest of the troupe, he wrote:

The artists, for the most part, have been unfaithful abroad. The success, improving their material position, has largely regenerated them so that they are not averse to touring endlessly. . . . For the present there are still corners of the earth with Jews where they can play. Zuskin is included in this group of artists. The other group wants to return to Moscow, as long as it can be guaranteed they will not go hungry. Regarding Mikhoels, they say he will return to Moscow.[69]

The solution, he believed, was to begin a slanderous campaign in the press, which would scare the troupe into behaving for the sake of their families in Moscow:

What do we need now? In no circumstances should we hush up the state of unrest in the Moscow State Yiddish Theater's tour. It must be published in *Der emes* (and not only in *Der emes*, if possible) but also in all provincial papers, through letters from comrades and articles. If possible this question must be considered in meetings, carried out in resolutions, etc. In a word, conduct a campaign along the lines of that carried out against Meyerhold. But it must always be remembered that such a campaign must not cut off the path to a return of Granovsky and the theater. At the same time, bear in mind arrangements should Granovsky not return to the Soviet Union. . . . I am also writing to the Friends of the State Yiddish Theater to publish an open letter to Granovsky, which will be composed by us.[70]

Two versions of the fraudulent letter, in Russian and Yiddish, were preserved. The letter states:

> The theater has had enormous success abroad and nobody has any doubt that the objective accomplishments were successful—Soviet [*sic*]. For it is clear even to our enemies that only under the regime of proletarian dictatorship, only under the national politics of Soviet power, could it be possible that a state over the period of several years would spend around a million rubles so that a Jewish theater can form and develop into a first class theatrical collective, beginning with its art director and ending with the last extra. But . . . the political character of the theater is currently being distorted.

> The artistic stagnation and ideological conservatism that the theater has found abroad conflicts with the goal the theater expressed in its farewell evening in Moscow—that the bourgeoisie will admire the theater's art and feel their class hatred. On the contrary, the theater has become the love of the Jewish bourgeoisie abroad.[71]

Articles criticizing the theater's conduct on its foreign tour were also appearing in a wide variety of newspapers and theatrical journals. For instance, Lunacharskii wrote an article in *Vecherniaia Moskva* (Evening Moscow), in which he acknowledged the troupe's popular success but criticized Granovsky for not adhering to proper ideology in his contact with the press. Leaving open a channel, he hinted that if their behavior improved, a tour to America would be possible.[72] The article was widely reprinted, appearing in *Der emes* and *Literarishe bleter*.[73] It soon became apparent, however, that the campaign against the theater was becoming counterproductive. Palatnik's next report to Litvakov stated that the troupe was becoming less willing to return to Moscow. "The artists," he wrote, "do not want to return to Moscow soon because they are afraid of the mood in Moscow. . . . The theater will be humiliated, said Mikhoels." The artists, he continued, were virtually certain that Granovsky would not return with them and feared for their future without him. Practical concerns also figured into the equation: the theater had no new productions prepared and the Malaia Bronnaia Hall was still under renovation.[74]

The Jewish Section was alarmed by this newest report: a mass defection would do irreparable damage to the Soviet Union's reputation in the foreign press. After the recent defection of the Habima troupe while on tour, the Moscow State Yiddish Theater remained the Communists' most valuable show piece with which they could prove to the world that the Soviet Union was free of chauvinism toward any group. They had spent countless resources touting the theater as simultaneously anti-rabbinical, anti-Zionist, anti-nationalist, and pro-Soviet, all as a spontaneous expression of the actors' beliefs and ideals. A mass defection would have proven the opposite to the Western press. The Party was determined to take all measures necessary to ensure the return of the troupe, preferably with Granovsky, but without him if necessary.

Palatnik formulated a two-step scheme: first, in order to turn the troupe against Granovsky, he personally awarded the artists all outstanding wages, hinting that Granovsky was responsible for the delay.[75] He then gave Granovsky an off-the-record commitment to an American tour, provided the troupe first return to Moscow: "I strictly took the position that the theater should return to Moscow and only from there go on to America. I suggested that Granovsky together with Mikhoels come to Moscow, and *once there I will not agree to a trip to America* [Palatnik's italics]."[76] Regarding Mikhoels, Palatnik explained, "I took a candid tone with Mikhoels—yes or no? Return now or not? This candid presentation of the question instilled hostility in Mikhoels toward me, but on the other hand he announced that he will return to the USSR."[77]

By October 27, 1928, a week later, Palatnik was optimistic. Granovsky had promised to return and to "write a letter to the papers" denouncing his past activity.[78] Palatnik believed it was genuine; Granovsky had consistently denied rumors in the German and Russian press that he, Mikhoels, and Zuskin were defecting.[79] Yet the German press continued to report that the three were planning to extend their stay in Germany to make a film adaptation of *Benjamin* entitled *The Modern Quixote*, despite the Jewish Section's opposition.[80]

Thus, in early November the troupe's mood was positive: the theater was playing in Berlin to consistently full houses, and Broadway was looking closer.[81] After investigating the contract with the French firm, Palatnik concluded that Granovsky was right—a tour to America would be a gold mine. The catch was that Granovsky was the gold; without him the theater was an empty shaft. Palatnik noted that Granovsky's dismissal from the post of director "even if he remains head of art . . . would lead to the possibility of a political scandal and the disintegration of the theater. I therefore decide that in my opinion we should negate the question of an American tour."[82] Once again, the Commissariat of Enlightenment forfeited financial success for political utility. They could no longer allow Granovsky to retain his position.

On November 24th, in all likelihood having made his decision to defect, Granovsky signed off all administrative and financial control of the theater to Palatnik in an agreement that stated:

> 1) As of November 24, all financial matters and judicial rights of the director of the theater are handed over to the managing representative of [the Commissariat of Enlightenment], Comrade Palatnik, until a director is appointed from Moscow.

> 2) Aleksandr Mikhailovich Granovsky will be the artistic director of the theater until the end of the tour abroad and all rights relating to the internal artistic life of the theater will remain under the management of Granovsky.

> 3) Questions of internal administrative orders (hiring and firing artists, questions of salaries, etc.) will be decided jointly by the managing director and the artistic director.

> 4) Questions relating to political appearances (speeches) of the theater (participating in various banquets and speeches in the name of the theater) are decided by the directing manager and the artistic director.[83]

Throughout December, the Jewish Section continued its attempts to bring the theater home, while slowly accepting that it was likely to lose Granovsky. It began to concentrate its efforts on securing the return of the rest of the troupe, Mikhoels and Zuskin in particular. On January 1, 1929, Vayn wrote to the Jewish Section:

> Why does Granovsky insist on an American tour? Granovsky does not want to return to the USSR now: he is afraid of responsibility for his fiscal problems and politics, etc. Apart from that he now does not intend to put forward a new repertoire, etc. The arrival of Granovsky in the USSR would be a failure in his theatrical career. . . .
>
> Keeping in mind all the above indicators, *it is not possible to allow a tour.* In the theater a schism may occur, like that which happened with Habima. . . . Thus, it is essential to *immediately send a telegram to the plenipotentiary, about taking measures to return the theater to Moscow.* [Vayn's italics][84]

The Jews of New York would continue to wait in vain for the troupe's appearance.[85]

Finally, in the middle of January, the troupe—without Granovsky—returned to a frigid Moscow. Granovsky remained in Germany, where he worked in the film industry, remaining ever close to controversy. One of his films, *The Sorrow of Life* (1931), about a woman who experiences severe complications during childbirth and is forced to undergo an emergency operation, was banned in Germany for fear it would discourage women from having children. Throughout the decade, Granovsky also worked with the Deutsches Theater in Berlin, directing, among others, Molière's *Le Bourgeois Gentilhomme.*[86] Both Natan Altman and Robert Falk, who had accompanied the theater on its tour, remained in Europe with Granovsky. Falk worked on the film *Taras Bulba* (1930) with Granovsky and lived in Paris for ten years before returning to the Soviet Union in 1937. Altman stayed only three years, returning to his homeland in 1931. Granovsky's wife, Aleksandra Azarkh, returned to Moscow, where she joined the staff of the Yiddish theater school. In March 1937, Granovsky died at the age of forty-seven in Paris. No obituary appeared in the Soviet press, but Nakhman Mayzel wrote in *Haynt:* "He was an interesting and very complicated man. He possessed a restless spirit—he had in him a bit of an adventurer. At the same time he was as naive as a child."[87] While his name was soon forgotten by the Soviet press—at first spoken of only with derision and, later, not spoken of at all—he was fondly remembered by his students. Joseph Schein, a former student of the Yiddish studio recalls:

> In the family of Yiddish actors, Granovsky was remembered silently with love and appreciation. He put his life into his performances, and into the acting of his students, who remembered how Sasha (Aleksandr) would capture a scene in a production and how he would interpret a character. His heritage brought us pride for many years.[88]

From the perspective of the Party, the tour was largely a failure, and the troupe would never again be permitted to leave the Soviet Union. The foreign press, by and large, treated the actors as talented individuals who were able to develop artistically in spite of their citizenship rather than as a result of it. Jewish papers, in particular, rejoiced at the performances but were wary of confusing fantasy with reality. They were alert to the fact that the theater was presenting only the best face to the Western world and was hardly representative of the state of Jewish society in the Soviet Union as a whole. While they were impressed with the theater, they refused to view it as a microcosm of Soviet society or even of the Jewish Section. European Socialists continued to view the Jewish Section as a cartel of traitorous Bundists, Zionists were unwilling to forgive its repression of the Hebrew language, and religious Jews around the world continued to despise its anti-religious campaigns. Upon its return to Moscow, the troupe was presented with both more unified cultural policies and a state that was more willing to carry them out.

The Jewish Section (soon to become a victim of the Cultural Revolution itself with its 1930 dissolution) and the Commissariat of Enlightenment treated the troupe with an unprecedented degree of condescension, manipulation, and authoritarianism. With nobody around to listen, these organs could assert themselves without fear of being challenged. While the troupe could mock this bellicosity with flagrant disobedience abroad, upon its return it was confronted with a fait accompli: the Party had used the troupe's absence to unilaterally restructure the theater in accordance with Stalin's "Cultural Revolution." In their attempts to persuade the troupe to return to Moscow, Palatnik and Litvakov used a combination of the carrot and the stick. They manipulated the publicity-craving actors by threatening negative press campaigns while simultaneously promising a sham trip to the coveted American shores as a reward for proper behavior. Although the younger actors succumbed to the tricks, the more experienced and skeptical director did not. The chasm between Granovsky and the Party, which had first cracked open with Granovsky's adaptation of *137 Children's Homes,* proved to be irreparable.

The Cultural Revolution

Having finished its European tour and subsequent expedition to the Jewish heartland, the Moscow State Yiddish Theater returned to an altogether different Moscow. The theater's absence coincided with the climax of a major social and political turning point in the history of the Soviet Union, generally known as the Cultural Revolution. The primary impetus toward the Cultural Revolution of 1928–1929 was the emergence of a new class of upwardly mobile individuals from predominantly working-class or peasant backgrounds who felt that the Revolution was fought for their benefit but was instead being led by bourgeois intellectuals with their own agendas. The Shakhty trial engrossed the country and signaled the start of a new campaign against "bourgeois specialists" and intellectuals and the "rightist deviationists" within the Party who tolerated them. Over the course of the year, the "soft line on culture" that the Party had pursued during the NEP years hardened into a militant repression of all non-Party and non-proletarian elements within the cultural sphere. The ensuing class war and social purging of intellectuals expedited the promotion of the upwardly mobile proletariat.[89]

Because the Moscow State Yiddish Theater was abroad on tour at the start of the Cultural Revolution, its day of reckoning was delayed until its return and, after that, until the termination of its annual summer tour of the provinces. However, when it returned to Moscow in the fall of 1929 the theater was hit with a vengeance. Not only was it subject to the usual harsh requirements being forced upon every Soviet institution from factory to cinema, but with the departure of Granovsky as artistic director the theater also faced the unavoidable task of its own internal reconstruction.

The most pressing demands made upon the theater were with regard to its administration. As was the case throughout the state, non-Party specialists, and particularly intellectuals, were purged from positions of power and replaced with Party members who were usually younger and had fewer European contacts and who had lived their formative years under Soviet power. In the case of the Yiddish theater, purging the top administrative personnel was unnecessary because Granovsky, who had concentrated all administrative and financial responsibilities in his own hands, had already defected. The state easily appointed a loyal bureaucrat, S. S. Somov, to take on the role of administrative director. While Somov proved to be popular with the troupe, which complimented him for making everyone feel like "old comrades," his tenure lasted less than a year.[90]

Next, the theater was placed firmly within the framework of the newly revamped "proletarian state." The first step taken in this direction was the order that the department of art and literature, having reorganized itself administratively, should see that the theater begin to work on fulfilling orders from the organs of the Party, the soviets, and the professional unions. The theater was urged to strengthen its relations with worker organizations and told to strive to ensure that 85 percent of its audience be members of Party and union organizations and that 32 percent of the audience be factory workers.[91] In order to achieve this goal, the Society for Friends of the State Yiddish Theater was revived as a liaison between the theater and the workers. Concrete measures were also taken to introduce workers to the theater: ticket prices were reduced by 10 percent, special coupon booklets were distributed to workers providing a 50 percent discount on tickets,[92] and special performances were given in factories throughout the country. Additionally, workers were given the opportunity to meet with and exchange ideas with the actors through informal meetings and lectures. One writer explained the purpose of these meetings:

> Workers are not just interested in questions of artistic method and the path of the theater, but also in how actors live. When [the worker] learns how much our comrades work and how they study, when we explain to him that from early morning [the actors attend] theater circles on Marxism and art and Leninism; that the group studies plays, fencing, dance and movement, after which rehearsals go for between two and three and a half hours, then there is a break, lunch, and

in the evening a performance—the workers understand how complicated and stressful the working days of the actors are.[93]

Workers were also invited to join the repertory committee and to attend rehearsals so that they could express their opinions prior to production. One such worker expressed his opinion in a factory journal:

> Earlier, during tsarism, we Jews had no rights and were an oppressed nation. We had no possibility for our development. We could not have useful occupations. . . . Only the October Revolution removed our chains; it allowed us to breathe freedom, and created for the Jews and all oppressed nations the conditions for a happy working life. . . . We would like to see on the stage of the Jewish theater the real life of the new man and not the man of air. We would like to see Jewish shock workers, Jewish Communists, Jewish collective farmers, the culture of Jewish engineers, students, and musicians. We would like to see a person with the new socialist understanding.[94]

Additionally, the theater building was turned into a de facto Jewish cultural center; it presented special commemorative evenings of interest to Jews, hosted meetings, and entertained Moscow with other Jewish theatrical and musical troupes during summer tours.

Next, measures were taken to increase working-class representation among the theater's staff. To make way for the new cadres, the theater was ordered to lay off fourteen members of its staff, reducing the total number to seventy-five for the 1928–1929 season. Half of those released were members of the artistic division, while only three members of the bloated administrative division were laid off.[95] On August 1, 1929, the theater, along with all other state theaters, was given specific instructions from the Commissariat of Finance on the means of calculating payments for workers.[96] In the Yiddish theater, the order meant a reduction of total salaries by nearly 10 percent. The upper echelons were hit hardest; the director's salary dropped from 360 rubles to 225 rubles per month.[97]

In keeping with the principle of creating a new cadre of theater workers, the Soviet State Yiddish Theater School was completely revamped and turned into a certified four-year technicum, bringing it in line with similar technicums at Moscow's other major theaters. During the First Five-Year Plan, the Commissariat of Enlightenment began to issue universal standards for Soviet theatrical schools, requiring each to teach general subjects, such as history, politics, economy, art, and Marxism-Leninism, in addition to their specialized programs. Thus, students devoted a great deal of attention to studies unrelated to the theater. The curriculum, however, retained all the basics of a theatrical education—diction, staging, dance, rhythm, stage movement, music, Yiddish, acting, Yiddish theater history, European theater history, and makeup.[98] "It is not possible today to be a good actor without having a fixed baggage of culture and knowledge," Mikhoels once explained.

> The audience looks through the actor as does an X-ray machine. The actor, on the stage, reveals himself, before all else, as a man, entirely naked. His body

Left to right: Solomon Mikhoels, Benjamin Zuskin, Yekhezkel Dobrushin, 1930.
Photo courtesy of Ala Perelman-Zuskin.

cannot compensate for any part he plays. One will immediately realize the important thing: if he is a man of culture or a crass youth.[99]

The technicum became an integral part of the theater; it was also the largest Yiddish theater school in the world. In its first year as an accredited institution, the school received fifty applicants for the fall session.[100] Mikhoels himself devoted a large portion of his time to cultivating his love of Jewish theater among the students. Many students fondly recalled the director's lively talks on diverse subjects. The other teachers included many of the older actors in the troupe as well as representatives of Moscow's literary and artistic Jewish elite, such as the playwright Yekhezkel Dobrushin, the writer Moshe Broderzon, and the director Efraim Loiter. The leader of the practical acting department was Aleksandra Azarkh, Granovsky's estranged wife. Benjamin Zuskin also played a leading role, tutoring his students on the practical elements he derived from his academic work on Yiddish literature. Perhaps the most difficult role fell upon Sara Rotbaum, who taught a master class on phonetics and diction. Because students came from all corners of the Soviet Union, Romania, and Lithuania—and even several from as far away as Canada and Uruguay—their Yiddish dialects and accents varied immensely. It was her task to standardize their accents and present a uniform language to the theater's audiences.

Mikhoels the Director

The next major step in the theater's reconstruction was the appointment of a new artistic director to replace Granovsky. The obvious choice was Solomon Mikhoels. Not only was he the most talented, competent, and popular member of the troupe, but the Commissariat of Enlightenment also regarded him as an ideal candidate to help carry out its reconstruction. Although Mikhoels retained a preference for the Yiddish classics, he was willing to use the stage to promote the work of his colleagues, enhance the prestige of the cultural community to which he proudly belonged, and nurture the development of Soviet Jewish culture. Peretz Markish, an author who would become a regular contributor to the repertoire of the theater, praised Mikhoels for having the courage and vision to introduce audiences to young and unproven writers.[101] By giving such writers a large and already acclaimed forum to present their newest works, the theater's contribution to the maintenance of Yiddish literature throughout the 1930s and beyond cannot be overstated. The Soviet authorities, for their part, demanded repertoires from contemporary Communist playwrights reflecting the "great achievements" of the Bolshevik Revolution.

From a political perspective, Mikhoels was an odd choice. His credentials as a Communist were severely lacking. He was not a member of the Communist Party and never would become one. In contrast to the majority of Soviet Jewish cultural figures—David Bergelson, Peretz Markish, Moshe Litvakov, Natan Altman, and others—Mikhoels was never a radical ideologue of any kind. He joined the theater out of a love of theater and Jewish culture, not out of identification with the proletarian bases of Granovsky's vision. Even within the theater, Mikhoels shunned political activity of any kind—he ardently refused to join even the theater's own trade union. He never expressed any grandiose vision of the theater as a temple for the new proletariat as Granovsky had. He simply sought to entertain.

Mikhoels's roots lay in traditional Jewish life. As a youth, he showed no interest in the socialist and populist circles that had enticed so many Jewish intellectuals; he spent his time studying with Hebrew grammarian Rabbi Isaiah Hertz Gordon and writing his own Hebrew poetry. In one messianic poem he wrote with his brother, Mikhoels even envisioned a Jewish redemption in Jerusalem. His first attempt at acting, at the age of twelve, was in a play called *The Hasmoneans* that a youth group in Dvinsk presented for Hanukkah.[102] While he drifted away from the Hasidic lifestyle in which he was reared, he never rejected Judaism outright. He retained much of his early religious education and never tired of peppering his lectures with rabbinical adages or retelling Jewish folktales to anyone who would listen. Even when presenting formal addresses to Party organs in an official capacity, Mikhoels could rarely resist entertaining his audience with a diversion into Jewish folklore or elucidating a point with biblical and talmudic references. During World War II, Mikhoels even took to carrying a Bible with him. Like millions of Jews around the world, Mikhoels had eschewed his religious practice but continued to embrace the ethical principles of Judaism and to celebrate *Yiddishkayt* and the Jewish cultural heritage. He identified himself as Jew above all else and circulated primarily within a Jewish milieu.

The only hurdle the state needed to overcome was a renewed danger of defection on the part of Mikhoels. In June 1929 Mikhoels received an invitation to Berlin from the German Communist director Erwin Piscator. Piscator, an admirer of the Proletkult movement, had often written of the need to revive Yiddish leftist theater in Germany in emulation of his Moscow counterparts.[103] Together with the Modernist architect Walter Gropius, he was seeking collaborators for his Total Theater project when the Moscow State Yiddish Theater arrived in Berlin. Piscator was planning to stage Walter Mehring's *The Merchant of Berlin* (about a poor Jew who exploits the inflationary crisis of 1923 for personal gain) and sought to cast a native Yiddish speaker as the play's protagonist. Mikhoels had greatly impressed Piscator and likely would have made an ideal candidate. The role remained unfulfilled in the summer of 1929, when Piscator traveled to Moscow for the foundation of the International Association of Workers' Theaters. According to Piscator's biographer, the director sought Mikhoels's collaboration on the project.[104] When he could not bring Mikhoels to Berlin, Piscator instead hired New York Yiddish actor Paul Baratoff, who came to Berlin specifically to star in Piscator's play. Piscator would continue to seek Mikhoels's collaboration throughout the 1930s, most notably for his 1936 plan to found a German-language theater in the Soviet German Volga Republic.

Mikhoels, for his part, likely felt betrayed by Litvakov's subterfuge in inducing the return of the troupe with sham promises of a trip to America. Further, the drastic changes and new climate which had emerged throughout the country during the theater's brief absence unnerved even the most loyal Bolsheviks. The immediate motivation for Mikhoels's frustrations, however, was a meeting of the theater collective, held in May 1929, during which the future of the theater was debated. A report of the meeting published in *Der emes* indicates that the troupe was alert to the dangers it faced. Oyslender, for instance, called for leniency from the leftists, warning that the old repertoire should not be discarded too hastily. Two other members of the troupe demanded artistic autonomy: "It is our theater, it has been ours and it will remain ours . . . The collective must stand on its own healthy feet."[105] Although Sviderskii, the head of the Central Arts Administration, gave Mikhoels the requisite permission to travel to Berlin for four months, the permission was retracted because of Somov's objections.[106]

Mikhoels continued to resist following the Party line, as reflected in his response to the Party's efforts to rewrite the theater's history in accordance with the values of the Cultural Revolution. Trade union journals such as *Vecherniaia Moskva* and *Rabochii i iskusstvo* (The Worker and Art) took the lead in this project. They chastised the theater for its behavior under the "rightist" and "bourgeois" director, Granovsky, and reproached him for his defection. However, as Mikhoels often reminded the public, Granovsky had not officially defected; he continued to insist that he would return after completion of the movie.[107] The critical retrospectives in the press of Granovsky's tenure made it clear he was no longer welcome—no doubt playing a role in confirming his decision not to return. Mikhoels, however, did not want the theater's past to be denigrated. He argued that the theater did not need to be "saved from Granovsky"; it had always reflected the revolutionary mood of the times, as evidenced by *Trouhadec, The Travels of Benjamin III, The Tenth Commandment,* and *Luftmentshen.* The editors of the trade union journals were not convinced: "The skill and indisputable service of Granovsky does not in any sense excuse him from his responsibility for the delayed turn of the theater toward the [mood of] current days."[108]

The campaign against the theater's past spilled out of the press and into other public forums as well. One of the most critical organizations was the Union of Artists. In 1929, the Presidium of the Moscow regional Union of Artists met to discuss the Moscow State Yiddish Theater. One press report summarized the meeting:

> The Presidium verified that the Moscow State Yiddish Theater does not reflect the life and work of the Jewish working masses in the post-revolutionary era, except for some attempts (*137 Children's Homes* and *Uprising*); and that although the Moscow State Yiddish Theater has a revolutionary significance in the combat against old lifestyles, it does not, in this measure, satisfy the needs of the Jewish working masses.[109]

Further, in a dispute held at the theatrical workers' club in January 1931, Litvakov charged the theater with failing to move beyond the days of the NEP and compromise with bourgeois art forms. The classics, on which the theater had so heavily relied, he continued, no longer had meaning in today's world. Mikhoels once again countered by reminding the audience that under Granovsky the theater had always sought to portray social characteristics while inventing new revolutionary aesthetic forms. He further emphasized that while he now sought to present new plays by contemporary writers, this was not to be done at the expense of dismissing elements of traditional Jewish national theater and musical motifs.[110] Eventually, Mikhoels would give up his ardent public defense of Granovsky, preferring to simply rewrite the history of the theater without his mentor.[111]

In his statements behind closed doors, however, Mikhoels remained loyal to his former teacher and director. For instance, in one speech to the Committee of Artistic Affairs in the mid-1930s, Mikhoels openly contradicted the director Sergei Radlov, who accused the theater of formalism:

> Sergei Ernestovich [Radlov], speaking of our theater, argued that he finds clear examples of formalistic expressions in the acting of a number of Granovsky's productions. I must put forward a contrary point. Granovsky, who staged a number of our productions, today has become a person who is subject to categorical condemnations and not only in view of what he did in theater. In the first place, and above all else, he is subject to condemnation because he betrayed the trust of the Party and the government and betrayed his own collective. I am compelled to say about this that in my opinion, in spite of everything, Granovsky possessed a high level of mastery and to take this away from him would be absurd.[112]

While Mikhoels then went on to criticize elements of Granovsky's formalism, his ardent defense of his teacher's talent and his recognition that Granovsky was being denounced out of political rather than artistic motivations is notable.

As he watched the campaigns progress against his avant-garde colleagues —Meyerhold, Granovsky, Shostakovich, and others—Mikhoels quickly learned that in order to revive the Yiddish theater, he had best follow the state's criteria. Mikhoels, however, should not be seen as merely a handmaiden of the state; all the official requirements were consistent with his own goal of cultivating a Soviet Jewish cultural renaissance. There was nothing inherently repugnant—either morally or aesthetically—about showcasing the works of contemporary writers. Indeed, it is a commendable objective shared by the finest theaters throughout the world. The same can be said of cultivating relations with the working class and offering opportunities for the lower classes to explore the theater. Similarly, Mikhoels's rejection of his predecessor's artistic methods allowed the new director to develop his own distinct system. Throughout Europe and North America stylized class-based character traits were gradually being replaced with profound psychological inquiry as the "world-historical role" of Marx gave way to Freud. It was this correlation between official requirements and Mikhoels's own dreams that would make him an exemplary director who was valued by his superiors and loved by his people.

The Court Is in Session: Judgment Postponed

4

As part of the Cultural Revolution and the general overhaul of Soviet society that accompanied the beginning of the First Five-Year Plan in 1929, the Moscow State Yiddish Theater was subjected to an increased level of aesthetic censorship and Party control. The theater responded by hiding Jewish themes beneath the surface of its plays. It presented a series of socialist-realist productions with cryptic Jewish subtexts, attained through the use of Jewish archetypes, symbols, and allegory.

During the period of the NEP, the Party adopted a "soft line on culture," a relatively passive system of censorship geared primarily toward preventing "harmful" material from being disseminated. Indeed, throughout the 1920s, the Commissariat of Enlightenment did not possess any centralized arts administrative organ. The Central Management of Literary and Publication Affairs (Glavlit), founded in 1922, was initially the state's only organ of censorship. In an effort to protect the integrity of theater from zealous officials, Lunacharskii had resisted the centralization of theater administration. Thus, the Management of State Academic Theaters, directly supervised by the commissar, was responsible for the administration of all state theaters, while most other theaters were subordinated to the Central Repertory Committee. The theaters of the extreme left (TRAM, Proletkult, and the Theater of Revolution), on the other hand, were placed under the supervision of the city soviet. Thus, the pre-revolutionary state theaters and the Moscow State Yiddish Theater were technically given favorable status, angering the leftist advocates of proletarian culture.

The Cultural Revolution of 1928–1929 led to the ascendance of more militant and repressive cultural policies. Since 1926, voices from within the Communist Party had been urging the Party to take an active role in directing literary and artistic affairs. In 1927, Platon Kerzhentsev, an old Bolshevik formerly active in Proletkult and later appointed to the central committee of Agitprop, recommended that the Commissariat of Enlightenment set up a central arts administration. The suggestion was received favorably and in April 1928 the Central Arts Administration (Glaviskusstvo), headed by Aleksei Sviderskii, was founded by order of the Council of People's Commissars as a supervisory organ over all artistic institutions in the country. Several months later, the Management of State Academic Theaters, under whose auspices the Moscow State Yiddish Theater had functioned, was abolished and replaced with a Department of Literature, Art, and Theater, headed by P. I. Novitskii, former head of the art section of the Central Sciences Administration (Glavnauka). With the departure of Lunacharskii from the Commissariat of Enlightenment in 1929, the left wing of the Party was given free reign over cultural affairs, during which time it firmly strengthened Party censorship.[1]

Henceforth all repertory decisions were taken out of the hands of the board of governors and the artistic director of an individual theater and were instead to be decided by the Commissariat of Enlightenment's Central Repertory Committee and the Central Arts Administration. Not only did the Repertory Committee play an important part in the selection of repertoires but it was also a ubiquitous presence during the rehearsal stage, ensuring that a proper interpretation of each play was adopted. Representatives from the Repertory Committee would attend dress rehearsals, sitting obtrusively at a long green felt table set halfway back in the house, accompanied by the director and his assistants.[2]

With the institutional framework of censorship in place, the state sought to compel theaters to abide by the rules of an aesthetic style, known as socialist realism, whose formulation was only in its burgeoning phase. The resolution "On the Reconstruction of Literary and Artistic Organizations" issued on April 23, 1932, represents the culmination of the Cultural Revolution in the aesthetic sphere. This was followed by the 1933 publication of Gorky's *On Socialist Realism* and the First Writers' Congress the following year, at which socialist realism, a term that had slowly been entering Soviet parlance since the 1920s, was declared the sole acceptable form of art in the Soviet Union. Any objective meaning of socialist realism was, in the early 1930s at least, marred by a cacophony of voices, each defining the new aesthete according to its own vision. Writers seeking to interpret the slogan drew from a variety of sources, including the fiction of Emile Zola, Fedor Dostoevsky, and Honoré de Balzac; the drama of Aleksandr Ostrovskii and William Shakespeare; the epic sagas of Scandinavia; the folklore of the Russian village; the heroism of Hellenic mythology; and, of course, the novels of Maksim Gorky and Fedor Gladkov. The only consensus was that artistic products should appeal to the masses.[3]

The Yiddish theater, when told to appeal to the people, was forced to consider to which people it should appeal. Was it to gear itself toward the minority of Jews who were working in the factories? To the even smaller minority who had joined collective farms? To the proletariat as a whole—Jewish and non-Jewish alike? Or to the vast majority of Jews who had not yet joined the ranks of the rural or urban proletariat? Further, how was it to appeal to the people? Was it sufficient to address them in Yiddish—the mother language of the older generation, but a language rapidly decreasing in use among the youth? Or was the theater required to address problems specific to Jews? Was it permissible to draw upon the national myths of the Jewish people? In short, what role was the national specificity of the theater to play in its productions? These dilemmas were shared by all cultural institutions in the state, particularly those of the minority nations, each of which tried to deal with the new demands in its own way. The slogan "national in form, socialist in content," was eventually adopted as a guideline. Once again, though, the slogan's conciseness left little room for elaboration.

Describing the effects of the new style on theater, American theater critic Norris Houghton wrote:

> The nature of the theater underwent a change during this period: it ceased to be agitational and turned propagandist. It paid less attention to satirizing and condemning the old and more to depicting the new. . . . A certain amount of guidance seemed necessary. For the accomplishment of this two-fold program, therefore, the government, through the agency of its Commissariat of Education, tightened its authority over the theater.[4]

While the Yiddish theater had already anticipated the turn toward realism in its production of *The Travels of Benjamin III*, it was a far cry from the type of socialist realism required by the state—for *Benjamin* was still a classic tale of the shtetl written by a pre-revolutionary writer. Socialist realism demanded that the theater orient itself toward contemporary themes that reflected the strength and growth of socialism in the Soviet Union. This foreboded a difficult adjustment for the Moscow State Yiddish Theater: its two previous plays on modern themes, Reznik's *Uprising* and Veviurka's *137 Children's Homes*, had been particularly weak artistic productions and had brought the theater its two greatest failures. Its return to the classics of Yiddish literature, such as *The Travels of Benjamin III* and *Luftmentshen*, was a response to this failure.

The problem with the new repertory demands, which was immediately recognized by all critics, was that the type of revolutionary plays demanded by the state had not yet been written. In an influential article published in the Yiddish journal *Prolit*, Osip Liubomirskii urged, "Our art in general and the theater in particular must become infected with the same enthusiasm that propels contemporary times from factory to factory, from plant to plant, from collective farm to state farm." There were virtually no plays, Liubomirskii continued, that reflected the actual problems of the day as they related to the complex social processes that had emerged from the ideological and psychological class struggle. The reason for this absence, he argued, was that virtually all Jewish writers in the Soviet Union were of petit bourgeois origins and were unable to break with this past. No modern Soviet dramaturgist or writer was able accurately to portray the modern class struggle from the vantage point of the factory worker. For instance, in an effort to write a proletarian play, Kushnirov turned to the historical past in *Hirsh Lekert,* while others, such as Lipe Reznik in his *Uprising,* depicted revolutionary eras in other countries. The solution Liubomirskii proposed was to facilitate the growth of worker clubs and amateur dramatic circles from which new proletarian writers could be recruited. Further, he argued, a concerted effort was needed to work out a Jewish national form consistent with socialist content.[5] Much of the theater's subsequent history was guided by this effort.

The new state guidelines led to a renewed debate among writers and artists regarding the role that Jewish national form should play in art. Censorship of Jewish themes in Russian-language literature made it clear that topics such as popular anti-Semitism, Zionism, and Jewish religious life were taboo, while any literature in the Hebrew language was now firmly banned.[6] The role of Jewish themes in

Yiddish literature was less clear. Opinions ranged from those who believed that "national" only referred to language—Gorky's *Mother* performed in Yiddish, for instance, would satisfy the criteria—to those who anticipated a more substantial tribute to national myths, history, and ideology.[7] All shared the conviction, though, that pre-revolutionary material, such as the plays of Sholem Aleichem, Goldfadn, and Peretz, would no longer suffice, even if performed in the revised and modernist forms Granovsky had favored. It was clear that understanding these Jewish stories with socialist intentions was no longer enough; the theater would now have to try to give Jewish meaning to what were primarily socialist stories.

The Moscow State Yiddish Theater experimented with several different ways to incorporate the new values. Between 1929 and 1935 the theater oscillated between three broad approaches to socialist realism. The first was "national" in the narrowest sense—plays in the Yiddish language telling of socialist construction. Jews numbered among the characters, sometimes even playing a dominant role, but the themes were universally "Soviet." It was the basest type of national culture, what the Georgian writer Nikolo Mitsishvili called "pale copies of Russian literature, and as restrained in the choice of new subjects as in the search for national forms."[8] These plays exemplified what can be called "Soviet culture in the Yiddish language." The second type of play was outwardly similar to the first, but was marked by its identifiably Jewish subtext. The Yiddish theater, which had flirted with allegorical allusions to Jewish lore under Granovsky, responded to increased censorship by hiding its Jewish associations between the lines of the text. Typically, the narratives of these plays paralleled great moments in Jewish history or contained symbolic references to Judaic concepts. The third type of production—of which there are but two examples in this period—were translations of European drama. Although these plays were generally considered politically sterile, I will argue that in at least one case—Shakespeare's *King Lear*—the theater continued to use allusion in an effort to criticize the power that was trying to convert the Jewish theater into a theater of translation.

Workers on Stage

The theater's new aesthetic style under Mikhoels's directorship was immediately apparent:

> On the Jewish stage, they acquired their own reflection of revolutionary romanticism, the heroic battles of the Civil War, industrial and collective farm development, the theme of Soviet patriotism. They found a place for the new heroes of our day—revolutionaries, workers, collective farmers, Soviet intelligentsia, fighters and commanders of the Red Army. They began to sound the ideas of international worker solidarity and the brotherhood of nations.[9]

When the now largely working-class audience entered the theater hall on October 11, 1929, for the premier of Yekhezkel Dobrushin's *The Court Is in Session,* they were immediately confronted with a new Yiddish theater. They no longer saw grotesque figures veiled behind cosmetic masks. Gone too were the bizarre metal ladders and platforms leading nowhere. This time they saw silhouettes of themselves in their workplace. Rabinovich, who returned as designer, flooded the stage with blue-collar workers—robust men in grimy caps and gray cloth vests interacting among wooden sets depicting a bustling workroom. They could also recognize the music as their own. Gone was the traditional Jewish music based on the folkloric and klezmer motifs that their parents had sung in the shtetl. For the first time, Lev Pulver drew his inspiration from the melodies of the new audience—worker tunes and army songs that gave the music a simpler, but harsher, feel.[10] Refrains such as:

> Red Army soldiers, hey, red brothers,
> Let us sing, hey, red songs.
> In the army we learn and we get ready
> To spread among the people throughout the land.[11]

and

> Work is meaningful, work is meaningful!
> When the plane planes and the knife cuts,
> Ay, ay, ay, work is better
> When the plane planes with a sharp knife[12]

were a far cry from the theater's earlier folk songs, although by no means without precedent in traditional Yiddish tunes—artisanal songs of labor can be found among the earliest collections of Yiddish folksongs.[13] Even the light dialogue and simple language were more in tune with the discourse of the working class. In concert with the movement toward the "normalization of language," Dobrushin sought to draw his vocabulary from the idioms of the people rather than the argot of the intelligentsia.[14] Only the staging by Fedor Kaverin (1897–1957), who had previously worked with the Maly Theater, still retained the accentuated, almost biomechanical style of acting complete with exaggerated movements, although in a far more subdued form.

Benjamin Zuskin, as Niome Burman the joiner, brought a new character type into the repertoire of the theater—the hard-working blue-collar laborer. The plot of *The Court Is in Session* revolves around Niome, the shtetl-born son of a Jewish déclassé merchant, who leaves the old life to join the Red Army. After being released from the army, Niome is convinced that he can do more to help build communism. With the public good in mind, he gathers a group of young labor enthusiasts together to form a collective artel and rebuild a local mill. "Will the mill be ours?" asks one lad. "Ours" replies Niome's companion, Sonia. The conflict of the play emerges when Niome falls in love with a non-Jewish woman, Anastasia, knowing that his parents will not approve. When Anastasia asks her beloved why he has not written about her to his parents, the young man replies that his parents are religious Jews, and therefore he cannot speak of love with them. "Why? Religious Jews don't love?" asks the young gentile woman. "They love, only they conceal it," replies Niome, to which Anastasia marvels at these "strange people," but continues to insist on being allowed to meet them. Niome is finally forced to tell her the truth: "They hate Russians." Again Anastasia is dumbfounded, musing,

"They love you and you love me and they hate me? Strange people!" Sure enough, upon hearing of their son's new beloved, the young hero's parents disown him. However, he easily finds a new family among his worker comrades. The play takes place in a flashback, as the young couple tell their story to a court in the hopes of suing Niome's parents for child support for their newborn son.[15]

From the moment the play was announced, the Soviet press in general, and the workers' press in particular, was unanimous in its praise for the new direction upon which the theater was finally embarking. *Rabochii i iskusstvo* wrote that "The play *The Court Is in Session* is an important, leading example of the turning point in the work of the Moscow State Yiddish Theater."[16] Others were more specific: "The old man Burman and the speculator Droibkin . . . are not new [characters] for the Moscow State Yiddish Theater; we have met them in earlier performances . . . But Burman's son Niome (who is demobilized from the Red Army) and Anastasia (his Komsomolka wife) are figures we are seeing for the first time."[17] Similarly, Isaac Nusinov argued that despite several weak characters, in its portrayal of the New Soviet Man the play represented a great step forward for the theater and for Soviet Jewish art in general.[18] While they could hardly restrain their praise for the political importance of the new production, many critics did not even bother to mention the aesthetic quality of the play—it was of little relevance. The theater's Yiddish-speaking supporters, on the other hand, were more interested in such "trivialities." Zagorskii and Liubomirskii, both of whom had written books on the Yiddish theater, praised Kaverin for "partially retaining the style of the Moscow State Yiddish Theater. He only changes the distribution of color and light and even sometimes suppresses the eccentric style of the text. And this is correct."[19]

The most important criticism of the play was with regard to the theater's characterizations of the New Soviet Man. Niome is intended as a "positive hero" to replace the perennial *luftmentsh* of the former era. He is designed as a didactic model to be contrasted with his parents, who represent the obsolete generation. However, Niome is a mere silhouette when compared to the psychological depth of the older generation. This weakness can, at least partially, be attributed to the writers' and actors' own personal experiences. As George Lukács noted in his critique of socialist realism, "It is evident that writers will tend to present an inside picture of the class on which their own experience of society is based. All other social classes will tend to be seen from the outside."[20] Indeed, it is a truism that writers write best about their own experiences. This posed a problem for Soviet Jewish writers and actors, virtually all of whom were of petit bourgeois heritage and had little experience in the factories, the Red Army, or on collective farms.[21] In addition to their own personal experiences, the troupe had spent a decade perfecting the portrayal of the shtetl Jew, a character whose contradictory and sympathetic characteristics had already been formulated so well by Sholem Aleichem and Mendele Mokher Sforim.

The new generation lacked the dimensions of their elders. For instance, Liubomirskii wrote that "the weakness of the play is that Dobrushin, like the majority of our Soviet dramaturgists, knows and can show the old life and the old types, but he still cannot manage to embrace the growth of the new, of our youth, with convincing artistic forms."[22] Workers who wrote about their reactions to the play in the proletarian press were similarly unconvinced, complaining that they could not understand the motives that would impel a child born of déclassé merchant parents to abandon everything and join the Red Army.[23] The audience could also empathize with old Burman, a poor Jewish merchant struggling against the drastic changes occurring around him to maintain his culture and to instill the morals of his own upbringing in his offspring, because he was a character close to their real lives. Niome, in contrast, was a chimera. Although there certainly was a new generation that rejected its parents' erudition in favor of assimilation, its transformation was never as complete as that portrayed in the play. Jews participated actively in the industrial drive of the First Five-Year Plan by flocking en masse to factories, but the type of assimilation portrayed by Dobrushin in *The Court Is in Session* was typically hindered by anti-Semitic resentment.[24] Niome was too detached from his people; too unaffected by his parents' pleas and sufferings. He showed no remorse or hesitation. The enthusiasm and ease with which he disowned his parents and blended into the Soviet working-class gentile world, where he was welcomed with open arms and joyous song, was simply unconvincing. He was a difficult character to portray because he did not exist. Indeed, Western socialists commonly criticized Soviet socialist realism for portraying what "ought to be" rather than "what is." The genre encouraged writers to portray the exceptional as typical, in anticipation of future realities.[25]

Conflict between generations was a useful theme for the theater because it allowed the portrayal of the beloved older generation alongside the less believable new generation. It is, of course, a timeless literary theme, but it was particularly poignant during the volatile period of the Revolution and Civil War as children rejected the political and moral values of their parents. Thus, it found its way into countless contemporary Russian plays as well, notably Boris Lavrenev's *Breakup* and Konstantin Trenev's *Liubov Yarovaia* (in which a Bolshevik woman reveals the identity of her husband, a White officer, to her superiors, which leads to his arrest.) It was at this time that the first generation to have been born in the Soviet Union was coming of age and beginning to marry and start families of their own. Those who had been educated in the new ideology of the Soviet state were being encouraged to revolt against any vestiges of pre-revolutionary values that remained within the family.

For the Jewish playwrights of the early 1930s, the theme was particularly appealing. By ostensibly using the older generation as negative heroes and foils to the youth, the theater was able to continue depicting the idealized stereotype of the shtetl Jew which was so popular among its audience. The *luftmentsh* could no longer be the hero of the play, but he could at least continue to entertain the audience as a negative foil.

The placement of proletarian characters on stage was coupled with renewed efforts to put workers in the audience and to solicit material from proletarian writers. The theater initially concentrated its efforts on attracting workers during its summer tours. Over the summer of 1930 it toured Berdichev, Kiev, Odessa, and Kharkov, where it played extensively in factories for proletarian audiences.[26] In their absence, Moscow was treated to a tour of the Belorussian State Yiddish Theater; they played a total of thirty-five shows to 15,000 spectators.[27] Further, the summer tours acquired greater prestige by featuring premieres. In Odessa, for instance, the theater premiered *The Dams*, staged by Kaverin and written by former Red Army soldier and factory worker Hershl Orliand (1896–1946). The theater had high expectations for the play; Orliand was the only Soviet Yiddish writer with genuine proletarian credentials.

The story "The Dams" first appeared serially in *Di royte velt* (The Red World) in late 1927 and early 1928. The play is a bland socialist realist production about a heterogeneous group of Jews, non-Jews, workers, and peasants who overcome all their differences and the harsh conditions of the time to build a dam in a malaria-infested locale.[28] The play exalted the participation of formerly poor shtetl dwellers in the process of socialist construction. At the same time it was saturated with overtones of social conflict between old, worn-out intellectuals and enthusiastic youth; Jews and Ukrainians; men and women; and foremen and workers. Personal conflicts and love triangles added further confusion to the already entangled plot.

Der emes wrote of the play that "one can say that *The Dams* is for the theater a historical performance; with it the theater has finally established itself with two feet firmly and securely on a new revolutionary-proletarian ground."[29] However, the Russian-language press disagreed, noting that in its adjustment to revolutionary themes the theater was losing its Jewishness, which was its raison d'être: "The State Yiddish Theater is without doubt currently going through an artistic crisis. The production *The Dams* provides patently obvious evidence of this. . . . There is nothing here either genuinely proletarian or genuinely Jewish," wrote one critic, calling Orliand's text "a weak play" and Kaverin's staging "unsuccessful and chaotic."[30] Despite the confounding plot, however, audiences were able to enjoy the many mass scenes at the construction site, as well as Pulver's music with its Polish motifs.

The weak play was symptomatic of a continual repertory crisis within Yiddish theater, a crisis shared by many Russian-language theaters as well. Put simply, playwrights could not produce new plays as quickly as the Commissariat of Enlightenment could issue new directives. While the theater had two new plays scheduled for the 1931 season—Peretz Markish's *Do Not Grieve!* and M. Daniel's (Daniel Meyerovich, 1900–1941) *Four Days*—it was clear to all involved that these two plays were among the only remaining works with both artistic merit and appropriate themes. Given that there were only a limited number of Soviet Yiddish authors, only one of whom was a professional dramaturgist (Dobrushin), the implementation of the new repertoire was sure to be difficult.

The following year, 1931, the theater performed *Do Not Grieve!* by Peretz Markish. Markish was born into a poor family in the town of Polonne in Volhynia in 1895. He received a typical Jewish education, studying in *kheder* and working as a choirboy in a synagogue before moving to Odessa and later to Kiev. At the age of fifteen, Markish had already begun writing poetry in Russian. In 1916, he was drafted into the tsarist army, and spent time fighting at the front. In his youth in Kiev, Markish had been involved with the Yiddish socialist artistic groups Kultur-

Benjamin Zuskin in *Do Not Grieve!*, 1931.
Photo courtesy of Ala Perelman-Zuskin.

Lige and Our Own. In 1921 he moved to Warsaw, where he became an editor and frequent contributor to the leftist expressionist magazine *Khaliaster* and was one of the founding members of the Yiddish literary journal *Literarishe bleter*. During the 1920s he spent time in Paris, London, Berlin, and Palestine, where he refined his artistic style; he returned to the Soviet Union in 1926. As one of the most prolific Soviet Yiddish writers he was often called upon to write for the theater, always working in close cooperation—which often turned into bitter, but friendly, disagreement—with Mikhoels on the staging of his plays. A tremendously charismatic figure, Markish was often called upon to be a spokesman for a variety of organizations.[31]

Do Not Grieve! had first been performed in Russian at the former Korsh Theater under the title *Land*. The play was about a struggle among the déclassé population of a Jewish shtetl between those who embrace the Revolution by joining the toiling masses at a Jewish collective farm and those who still cling to the life of the former *luftmentshen*. The young collective farmers embrace communism by joining the Komsomol (Communist Youth League) and go on to play a meaningful role in the fight against kulaks, while the *luftmentshen* linger in their squalor.

Do Not Grieve!, co-directed by Sergei Radlov (1898–1964) and Mikhoels, was again criticized for displaying richly developed older characters but relatively hollow youth. While praising Markish, many critics warned of the biblical motifs which occasionally appeared in his works. Many also felt that the play's theme was a little behind the times: "*Do Not Grieve!* sketches only the first steps of the Jewish workers on the land and of course does not reflect the current situation of the Jewish village and its fight for collectivization,"[32] wrote one critic. In general, the Yiddish production was compared unfavorably with that at the Korsh Theater.[33] Once again, the positive heroes were not real. The enthusiastic Jewish collective farmers could only be chimeras; only about 5,000 Jews joined collective farms during the great drive to collectivize during the summer of 1929.[34] While the numbers increased over the next few years, the statistics indicate that few were able to adjust to agrarian life—the percentage of gainfully employed Jews on collective farms declined from 10 percent in 1930 to 6.7 percent in 1935.[35]

National Archetypes

In 1930 the theater turned to the already renowned Yiddish writer David Bergelson. Bergelson (1884–1952) was born into a Hasidic family in the town of Okhrimovo, near Uman, Ukraine, in 1884. During his youth, he received a strictly Jewish education, studying the Talmud, the Bible, and Hebrew in a local *kheder*. Although he began writing in Hebrew and Russian, he achieved great popularity with his first Yiddish novel, *At the Depot* (1908). After embracing socialist ideals, in his *When All Is Said and Done* (1913) and *Departing* (1920) Bergelson turned toward works that sensitively portrayed the poverty and hopelessness of the old Jewish life. As one of the leaders of the Kiev Kultur-Lige, Bergelson also edited the two-volume poetry anthology *Our Own* (1918–1920). In 1921 he emigrated to Berlin to escape the horrors of the Civil War. Throughout the 1920s, Bergelson was an active Communist in Germany, working for the Communist Yiddish paper *Frayhayt* (Freedom) and publishing novels in support of the Soviet Union. *The Deaf*, his first major dramatic work, was loosely based on a short story he had written in 1907. The dramatic version was first performed in Gomel in 1929; it was later performed in 1930 in Vilna under the title *The Flour Mill*. It was the production of the play at the Moscow State Yiddish Theater, which premiered in January 1930, however, that would be most remembered. Mikhoels starred as the Deaf.

The Deaf was one of many Soviet plays which sought, in the words of Konstantin Rudnitsky, "to show ordinary, average people who were not heroes, who did not speak or behave heroically, but who were nevertheless capable of rising to the heights of heroic action."[36] Like much contemporary literature, it showed that "little heroes" were capable of "big deeds."[37] The play was exemplary of the spontaneous revolutionary enthusiasm that was still being tolerated in 1930. The deaf protagonist of Bergelson's play, who is never given a formal name, is a simple inarticulate mill worker who lost his hearing in an accident at the mill due to the negligence of the mill owner, Shimon Bika. He lives alone in his silent world with few concerns about the outside world beyond the welfare of his only daughter, Esther, whose mother was worked to death at the mill. Plagued by emotional and physical pain, the Deaf silently accepts his lot. The play begins as the Deaf discovers that Esther, who is employed as a servant in Bika's house, is pregnant by Bika's son, Mendel, who has seduced her.

Grieving, the Deaf remains silent until he hears of a plan to bring in new machinery and lay off half the workers. No longer able to control himself, the Deaf reaches his limit. "Bika is my enemy," he stutters in a rambling soliloquy which serves as his meek epiphany, "I am perpetually envious of him. He is my enemy. Come here, come here. If Bika is killed, I will be happy. Yes, yes, I will be happy. Nu, and when I . . . when I alone . . ." He stops in mid-sentence before continuing "The blood goes to my head. I do not sleep at night, I do not sleep."[38]

In the next scene, he is thrust into the forefront of a futile rebellion in which he radicalizes the working masses and calls for a violent attack on Bika. However, when the Deaf breaks into the mill owner's home with an axe, he is easily apprehended and arrested, leaving the workers to continue their futile strike. Seemingly fated to linger in obscurity as just one of the injured working masses, the Deaf's pent-up anger, frustration, and desperation suddenly explode, thrusting him into the forefront of a revolution and turning him into a working-class hero.

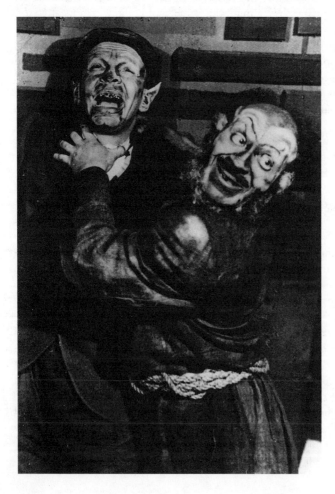

Benjamin Zuskin and Solomon Mikhoels in *The Deaf,* 1930. Photo courtesy of Ala Perelman-Zuskin.

The play, staged by Sergei Radlov, was the first representation of Yiddish realism in Soviet theater. The much-suffering Deaf is a tragic figure whose life has been devastated by the evil forces of capitalism as represented by the ruthless, yet religiously pious, mill owner. His only joy in life is his daughter, Esther, by whom he measures any semblance of hope he encounters in his pitiful life. "Nu, already twenty-three years I have worked for him," he ponders in a reflective moment. "I became deaf by him. I hear nothing. But sometimes when she, Esther, speaks to me I hear. She Esther. Esther." In the words of Liubomirskii: "He perceives in a vague manner, but he does not understand. It is the tragedy of a single individual."[39] Some critics, failing to recognize the poignancy of the plot, felt that the theme of a poor maiden falling in love with a rich capitalist reeked of melodrama.[40] Most critics, however, recognized the revolutionary significance of the production. One wrote that the play "decisively exposes the Jewish bourgeois nationalists, who contend that amidst the united Jewry there were never class antagonisms."[41] While biomechanics was no longer an acceptable aesthetic means of expressing the new realism, rhythm remained an integral part of the theater's training. "The only language of the actor," Mikhoels once said, "is rhythm."[42] Pulver's music strove to help the actors attain perfect rhythm and to capture the difficulty with which the protagonist communicates.

Aside from its overt revolutionary significance, the play retained a strong Jewish subtext by paralleling in many ways the biblical Book of Esther, another tale of a young woman and her guardian's love. Like the biblical Esther, Bergelson's Esther is a poor person whose only source of love is her male guardian. As a result of her extraordinary beauty her fortune changes when she is brought into the camp of the overlord—the Persian king in the Bible, the mill owner in the play. In both versions, her guardian is left on the other side of the real or metaphorical palace wall, where he discovers a plot within the palace to destroy his people, either through death (the Bible) or the loss of livelihood (the play). Together the two Esthers and their two guardians attempt to foil the plan. Both stories focus on a banquet: it provides the setting for the entry scene for the biblical Esther and the place where the Deaf prepares to attack the mill owner. At this point, however, the two stories diverge. While the Book of Esther is one of the most optimistic books of the Bible because the evil plan is foiled and its culprit is hanged, Bergelson's play ends in tragedy. The biblical story emphasizes the pride and dignity of Esther and her uncle: it is the uncle's stubborn refusal to bow down to the minister that precipitates his plan for genocide and it is Esther's continued identification with the Jewish people that prompts her to halt the genocide. The Deaf, in contrast, has adopted a subservient and fatalistic attitude toward his oppressor, making his final vanquishment an inevitable product of his lifelong capitulation. By neglecting both God and his people, the Deaf pre-ordains his own failure. By paralleling the Book of Esther, Bergelson's lyrical play nevertheless hinted at the optimistic history of the Jewish people and their ability to survive.

The 1930 production of the play at the Moscow State Yiddish Theater added a new symbolic reference to nationalist themes. Mikhoels, as the Deaf, developed what he called a gesture leitmotif in which he would begin to raise his hands to the stars, but on the way his right hand would get distracted and wipe the sweat off his brow. After a moment, he would become lost in thought as his right hand lingered in a clenched fist resting limply over his head, where it would remain for extended periods of time. Mikhoels repeatedly emphasized the importance of this one gesture in his discussions of the play.[43] He argued that this gesture symbolized his character's high aspirations that were unable to reach fruition because of his preoccupation with his labor, leaving him perpetually frustrated, seemingly fated to a life of inaction. However, this gesture, combined with the stuttering voice Mikhoels used to speak the meager few words his character utters during the course of the play, can be seen as a symbolic reference to Psalm 137 and one of the Zionist movement's themes: "If I forget thee, O Jerusalem, let my right hand lose its cunning, If I do not remember thee, let my tongue cleave to the roof of my mouth."

Solomon Mikhoels as *The Deaf,* 1930. Photo from O. Liubomirskii, *Mikhoels.*

The fate of the Deaf parallels that of Soviet Yiddish literature in general. His true feelings, which he is unable to express overtly, are forced deep within his inner self, only to reveal themselves periodically through symbolic expressions. While the image of the tongue-tied Deaf with his right arm resting limply above his head was a mundane pose to the vast majority of the secular and non-Jewish audience, who saw it merely as indicative of a "tortured soul," it can also be seen as a value-laden symbol, evoking the longing of the Jews for an end to their Diaspora existence.

Over the summer of 1931, the troupe toured the Jewish heartland again, concentrating on strengthening its relations with worker organizations by performing at factories, collective farms, and military camps, where they gave a total of 143 performances,[44] to an audience of which it was estimated that 80 percent were workers.[45] These tours were becoming more educational: members of the troupe often delivered special lectures on Jewish literature and theater. Troupe members also attended similar lectures provided for them by representatives of non-Jewish local theaters and worker organizations.

Upon their return to Moscow, the Jewish worker's club Kommunist announced that it would sponsor the November premiere of *Four Days*, for which tickets would be distributed only at factories to ensure that workers were given the first opportunity to see the new show. Preparations had begun during the summer tour. *Four Days* was written by M. Daniel and was based on his novella *Iulis*, a Civil War story situated in 1919 Vilna during the German occupation. The play was written in honor of Iulis Shimeliovich (1890–1919), a former Bundist who had become an active member of the Commissariat of Jewish Affairs and editor of the journal *Kommunist* after the Revolution. In 1919 Shimeliovich and eight other Bolshevik activists committed suicide in Vilna.[46] The play draws its name from the four days the Bolshevik partisans within the city were forced to wait before the expected arrival of the Red Army. Outwardly the play sought to exalt the role of the Bolsheviks in defending the Revolution against the perceived treachery of the Bund and the Polish Socialist Party. The play begins with subtle foreshadowing when, amid the cries of starving children, one little boy says "I heard from an adult that soon the soviet will build a revolution in the city, kick out the German occupiers, and then everyone will eat meat for lunch." Meanwhile, Bundists and members of the Polish Socialist Party take up arms and put up placards calling for workers to help build the Revolution. The children watch the opposition parties, but the scene ends with a child dreaming of one day becoming a Bolshevik.

Most of the play's action takes place within the Vilna soviet as the Bundists and Polish Socialists split from the Bolsheviks, led by Iulis, over the issue of whether the soviet should remain only the organ of the working class or expand itself, as the Bolsheviks desire, to be an organ of government as well. The excitement peaks as one nationalist asks, "To whom does Vilna belong? To Warsaw or Moscow?" to which one Bolshevik hero responds, "To the working class of Vilna!" Unconvinced, the Polish Socialist Party and the Bund split from the Bolsheviks and stave off the Red Army, allowing the Whites to take control of the city. During the final exciting battle scene, the Bolshevik partisans, who begin their rebellion from within the city, wait in vain for the Red Army to back them up. Realizing they have been betrayed by the opposition parties, they commit suicide before the counter-revolutionary forces are able to capture them.[47]

In the playbill, Mikhoels took the rare step of including a foreword, in which he explained that the theater was attempting to go in a new direction in accordance with the new demands of the working class to portray the first few days of the Revolution, to present heroes appropriate to the new times, and to elaborate on the differences between the various socialist parties. Daniel also wrote a foreword in which he explained the earnestness of the topic, dedicated the play to the martyred Bolshevik heroes, and explained that the play was meant to represent the real life of everyday Jews during the Civil War period. The earnestness of the topic was further demonstrated by the length of the playbill, which consisted of a whopping seventeen pages of pedantic commentary.[48]

The play was in many ways a risky production—it was one of the first plays mounted by the theater by an unproven Soviet Jewish writer. For these reasons, some, like Peretz Markish, who owed much of his world fame to Mikhoels's willingness to experiment with unproven artists, would look back on *Four Days* as one of the theater's most significant productions. It was the first play, he argued, that allowed for the combination of the new Soviet socialist art and the developing Yiddish theater. It represented the development of a new form in the Moscow State Yiddish Theater, he continued—psychological realism.[49] In significant ways the risk paid off. The ideological and political content of Daniel's play was universally praised by critics as the archetype of Yiddish revolutionary plays, while the character of Iulis was cited as a "wonderful example of a Bolshevik."[50] *Der emes* wrote of the play:

> Iulis is the Moscow State Yiddish Theater's first success on their path to overcoming the crisis that has overcast it for so long, and that has surrounded all the major moments of its theatrical life—repertory, directorial and internal collective work.... For the first time on the stage of the Moscow State Yiddish Theater there is a play about class struggle, about the important question of the proletarian revolution, about the actions of the working class, about proletarian dictatorship.[51]

Iakov Grinvald echoed this sentiment: "The new production is a meaningful attempt in the theater's life and provides evidence of the genuine attempts to include new themes, which continue along the lines of *Do Not Grieve!*"[52]

However, the onstage production of *Four Days* was far less successful than hoped. *Literaturnaia gazeta* wrote:

> The production has a profound international significance.... It is a victory for the theater. But this victory is still unfulfilled, still indecisive.... In this production there is still a strong contradiction between the essence and the expression of the idea.[53]

Indeed, Mikhoels's portrayal of Iulis was one of his weakest performances. In contrast to his more convincing characters, like Menakhem Mendel, Benjamin, and the Deaf, Iulis is not a product of the simple Jewish folk, brought up on Talmudic erudition and shtetl yarns. On the contrary, he is a sophisticated Marxist who em-

Four Days, 1931. *Left to right:* Daniil Finkelkraut, Benjamin Zuskin, Solomon Mikhoels, Eva Itskokhi. Photo courtesy of Ala Perelman-Zuskin.

braces the Revolution not out of frustration, innocent hope, or genuine sympathy, but out of an academic conviction based on the laws of dialectical materialism. He was the first professional Bolshevik to find his way onto the Jewish stage; yet it was this very professionalism and commitment to the cause which made the character unbelievable. Iulis, like Niome Burman, was a flawless prototype for the New Soviet Man, but he was not real. His ardent and unwavering principles did not allow for the kinds of tragic indecision and psychological contradictions Mikhoels had portrayed so well in *The Deaf*. This flaw was particularly acute during the final suicide scene. "The basis of the play's weakness," wrote one critic,

> is its central point—the death of Iulis and his comrades. The death does not seem entirely justified. Its inevitability is not motivated fully and from all sides, and the audience does not accept the tragedy of the situation with the necessary poignancy.[54]

Der emes agreed, noting that the suicide was an "ideological error," and that "Iulis is a proletarian revolutionary who is capable of the greatest sacrifice, but who does not completely possess the necessary Bolshevik duty to fight."[55] Indeed, the confidence with which he takes his life seemed remote to an audience which had witnessed some years before the paralyzing vexations and doubt that Uriel Acosta had undergone when confronted with a similar decision.

Surely the author knew that mass suicide under siege was hardly the type of heroism required of committed Bolsheviks (although suicide and sacrifice were later incorporated into Bolshevik heroism). One must ask, then, why this tragic ending was included. The answer may lie within a symbolic interpretation of the text, which alludes to an altogether different moral ideology. *Kiddush ha-shem* (sanctification of God's name, or martyrdom) is a well-recognized motif in Jewish literature and history. In this case, a play about a group of ideologues who wait under siege for the enemy to approach, deciding at the last minute to take their own lives rather than be captured, particularly evokes the story of Masada as told by Josephus Flavius, the historian and commander of the Jewish army in Galilee. The fortress of Masada, which fell in 73 C.E., was the last holdout of the Jewish rebellion against Roman rule in Palestine. After the failure of the rebellion in Jerusalem, a group of Zealots led by Eliezer ben Yair fled to the fortress of Masada, where they were able to resist Roman encroachments. However, with time on their side, the Roman legions were easily able to surround the fortress, put it under siege, and slowly vanquish it. When the end was imminent, the 960 Zealots decided to take their own lives rather than become slaves of the Romans. Seen within this light, the narrative takes on a nationalist significance, linking the Bolshevik protagonists who outwardly reject the nationalism of the Bundists and Polish Socialists to the greatest Jewish nationalists—the rebel Zealots. Once again, a play mounted by the theater evoked one of the proudest moments in Jewish national history.

The reference to Masada is particularly timely because the story had only recently begun to re-emerge in the Jewish collective memory after centuries of neglect. The narrative of Josephus had largely been forgotten by Jewish historians, although it continued to be published in numerous translations throughout the centuries. Another chronicle of the rebellion, *The Book of Jospian*, had preserved the narrative in a modified form—Jospian reports that the Jewish rebels fought to the death. However, after the first Hebrew translation of Josephus in 1862, the myth of Masada as an example of mass suicide under siege was revived. Beginning with the 1923 publication of a new Hebrew translation of his war chronicles,[56] Masada became an integral Zionist symbol. The popularity of Josephus's version among the Jewish populace was further enhanced by Selig Kalmanowitsch's first Yiddish translation[57] and, most important, by the 1927 publication of Yitzhak Lamdan's epic poem *Masada*. The poem, which uses Masada as a metaphor for Zion, tells of a Jew who flees oppression in Russia to rebuild the Land of Israel. Its popularity rapidly spread throughout Europe. By the late 1920s a Zionist journal entitled *Masada* had emerged in Europe and the mountain itself became a popular pilgrimage site for Zionist youth. Given the contemporary popularity of Masada as a Zionist symbol, the Yiddish theater's cryptic reference was easily accessible—although by no means obvious—to an audience literate in Jewish mythology.[58]

In both *The Deaf* and *Four Days*, the Moscow State Yiddish Theater's "Jewishness" was forced beneath the surface. The depiction of the revolutionary struggle of the proletariat and their vanguard against the evil forces of capitalism in the two plays was balanced with Jewish archetypes and structures underlying the manifest text. To the casual observer, these plays displayed no elements of Jewish form other than language; it mattered little whether or not Iulis and the Deaf were even Jewish. They fit the model plot of contemporary socialist realism and contained no overt taboos. But beyond the text lurked powerful images of Jewish nationhood.

The Costs of Reconstruction

Repertory difficulties and difficulties embracing the new style continued to plague the theater. It had not produced one resounding success since its European tour, and the two plays that were moderately well-received—*The Deaf* and *Four Days*—were really short stories rather than dramatic scripts. As a result of these difficulties, a political-cultural committee similar to those already in place at other theaters was established to help the troupe recognize appropriate material. The committee determined and implemented all artistic decisions, thereby reducing the authority of the theater's individual artistic director and dispersing that authority among the various outside organizations that had a vested interest in the theater.

On February 19, 1932, the Yiddish theater's political-cultural committee met for the first time. Boris Volin, a representative from the Commissariat of Enlightenment, chaired the conference, and Zuskin served as secretary.[59] The committee was composed of representatives from the Soviet of Nationalities, the Commissariat of Enlightenment, *Der emes*, the Union of Proletarian Writers, selected trade unions, and selected factories. Representing the Moscow State Yiddish Theater itself were Pulver, Mikhoels, Zuskin, and the actors Abraham Baslavskii, Rakhel Imenitova, and Yosef Shidlo. This intensified censorship of the theater would, for the time being, restrict its ability to refer to Jewish themes.

Among those represented on the political-cultural committee were many writers with the Jewish background required to decipher the theater's covert code, particularly Moshe Litvakov and Isaac Nusinov. Nusinov (1889–1950) was a former Bundist who, like many of his fellow revolutionaries, had fled to central Europe before the war to escape tsarist persecution. After the Bolshevik Revolution, Nusinov returned to Russia and joined the Communist Party in 1919. He was active in the Kiev Kultur-Lige before moving to Moscow in 1922, where he made his mark as a Yiddish literary critic. Litvakov, like Nusinov, was an experienced literary critic who would likely have recognized the Judaic motifs in the troupe's productions. But to point them out publicly after the fact would have been counterproductive. Litvakov had been a vocal supporter of the theater from its inception and had vouched for the troupe's political orientation before his superiors in the Party. He was also an old acquaintance of Mikhoels.

While both Nusinov and Litvakov had prior connections with the theater, neither had had the power to decisively influence productions. In 1932 political criticism had not yet become a death sentence, but it would likely have had adverse effects on the state's support for the theater. Litvakov did not want to force the closure of the theater he had done so much to promote, he merely wanted to reform it in accordance with the ideology of the Party. He probably still believed that the best means of convincing the troupe to discard its nationalist orientations lay in private persuasion rather than public humiliation. The political-cultural committee gave him this opportunity.

At its first meeting, the committee debated the suitability of mounting Dobrushin and Nusinov's *The Specialist*, even though rehearsals had virtually finished and the premiere was slated for a mere ten days later.[60] By threatening to cancel a production on such short notice, the committee immediately established its power. It was decided that the theater should perform one act the following day at a factory and allow the workers to express their opinions, which would leave the theater with a "full week" to make any changes. Dropped for production for the 1932 season were Peretz Markish's *The Fifth Horizon*,[61] Ernst Toller's (1893– 1939) *Flame from the Boiler* (which was to have been guest-directed by Piscator),[62] and two plays on the theme of industrialization by Markish and Orland. The committee then approved a motion to undertake much-needed renovations at the theater hall. It was also decided to arrange a meeting with a committee of Yiddish writers (Litvakov, Mikhoels, Markish, Nusinov, Dobrushin, and others) who had been appointed the previous month to prepare for the celebration of the fifteenth anniversary of the October Revolution, for which a "significant sum" had already been set aside.[63] Finally, two subcommittees were arranged: one for public relations and one to make repertory decisions. Members of the troupe were notably absent from the repertory commission.[64]

On March 12, 1932, the theater premiered *The Specialist*. It was another weak play, with an oversimplified plot about anti-Soviet sabotage. Mikhoels starred as Berg, an engineer who feels that the Soviet state is failing to give him the respect he deserves. As a bourgeois specialist, Berg scorns the notion of sacrificing his own exaltation for the betterment of the community. This attitude quickly leads him into an anti-Soviet group of saboteurs who believe they can neutralize the Soviet state through vandalism.

One reviewer wrote that the play demonstrates "the costs of reconstruction. The blame for this goes, in the first place, to a production built upon literary material of a low quality."[65] The problem with the play, as many critics and workers pointed out, was that the authors failed to provide a convincing motive for the sabotage. No doubt many of the thousands of innocent workers falsely arrested for sabotage during the 1930s could have made the same point. Even the educational value of the play, some critics complained, was outdated—the theme of bourgeois specialists, they argued, had reached its apogee several years earlier, despite the fact that non-Party specialists continued to be arrested and harassed throughout the decade. Other critics felt that the problem with the work went beyond the poor script. Iakov Grinvald, for instance, argued that in addition to using a second-rate text, the theater was not making enough of an effort to reconstruct its artistic methods and was still adhering to elements of the grotesque.[66] Indeed, even Markish was unable to restrain himself from criticizing the acting, noting that Mikhoels "rambled."[67]

As it returned to Moscow from its first summer tour in Baku and the Donbass region, the theater faced a future full of doubt. While the theater had three approved plays scheduled for the new season: *Who Is Against Whom?* by Markish; a play in progress by Daniel about the German revolutionary movement; and a play by Ber Orshanskii on the theme of the Civil War,[68] the season was delayed due to the sudden approval by the Moscow soviet for renovations at the Malaia Bronnaia Hall. The renovations, which the troupe had hoped would be done while it was absent during its summer tour, began only upon the troupe's fall return. The the-

Benjamin Zuskin and Esther Karchmer in *The Specialist.* Photo courtesy of Ala Perelman-Zuskin.

ater remained closed until the following April, forcing the cancellation of the entire season. The process of renovating a theater in the Soviet Union often outlasted the life of a troupe. For instance, Meyerhold, who moved out of the Sohn Theater in 1931, fell victim to Stalin's purges in 1938 before his new theater was completed. The renovations of the Yiddish theater allowed the state to bide its time while it decided on the future of the theater. In the end the renovations were a tremendous improvement to the theater. The entire hall was mechanized and electrified, the stage was enlarged, and a rehearsal hall, dressing rooms, set workshop, and permanent curtains were added.[69]

While the theater was closed, the center of Jewish Moscow's cultural life moved to the Jewish worker's club, Kommunist, where workers were "entertained" with oral readings of Marxist newspapers and occasionally treated to guest appearances by members of the State Yiddish Theater, who would perform scenes from recent and classic productions.[70] Instead of the theater, Soviet Jewish cultural patrons could also entertain themselves with Mikhoels's second major motion picture production—*The Return of Nathan Becker*, which was released in 1932. Two years later a Russian version of the talkie was released. The film, although not affiliated with the Yiddish theater, was written by Peretz Markish. It told of a Russian emigre living in America who returns to his homeland along with an African American friend, played by Kador Ben-Salin, to help build socialism in Magnitogorsk. The first scene shows a ship leaving from New York against a backdrop of montages of Manhattan decadence that included advertisements for cosmetics and billboards showing scantily clad women. The contrast with the shtetl where they arrive is immediately apparent. The shtetl is a decrepit ghost town in which a lone violinist plays a lethargic tune as panhandlers and peddlers loiter aimlessly. Mikhoels, playing Nathan's father, decides to join the two men in the construction business. Once in Magnitogorsk, Nathan is shocked to see workers studying theater and relaxing. After they explain that cultural enlightenment is a vital aspect of work, a skeptical Nathan, brought up on the American ideal of relentless work devoid of recreation, challenges some Soviet workers to a "shock worker" contest to see who can produce the most in the least amount of time. The contest is framed in a celebratory atmosphere, with montages of typical circus scenes, showing that work is an amusement in Magnitogorsk. When, predictably, the American loses to his more skilled and energetic Soviet counterpart, Becker is mortified and tells his wife, who had resisted the move from the beginning, that they are returning to America. His wife, however, has since fallen in love with Magnitogorsk. She struggles to determine how much time she has left to enjoy the "Magnetic Mountain," but is confused by the four-day work week and the absence of a religious Sabbath. In the end, Becker decides to stay, realizing that he can work and learn to improve himself—"Father, you know," he reflects, "here they work not only with their heads, but also . . . " and he motions to his heart. The final scene shows Mikhoels, the old Jew, sitting atop a construction site with his new African American friend, teaching him how to *nign* (hum Ashkenazic melodies) with elaborate hand gestures.[71]

One purpose of the film was to convince Jews to leave the shtetls and join industrial production. Its makers also hoped to encourage emigration from a depressed America to a prospering Russia by painting a rosy picture of race relations in the Soviet Union, contrasting it with both the failure of Jewish assimilation and the ubiquitous race riots of America. Although the U.S. Department of State was concerned about the propagandist value of the film,[72] it was eventually brought to America and opened in New York in April 1933. *Der emes* called the film "a pitiful failure," arguing that the dialogue was corny and labored and that the complex prose of the language was incomprehensible to workers. Furthermore, it argued that the contrast between the shtetl and Magnitogorsk, which forms the basis of the movie's social message, was anachronistic; by the time Magnitogorsk was founded, the argument continued, the old shtetl life had been entirely eliminated —a point Mikhoels, who spent every summer touring through these "non-existent" shtetls, could well have protested.[73]

There is little doubt that the Moscow soviet's decision to undertake renovations on the theater during the season was also motivated by political concerns. As we have seen, despite its efforts, the theater was not adapting satisfactorily to the new repertory requirements. Closing the theater for several months might give it an opportunity to begin anew on a repertoire specially selected by the political-cultural committee. Because there was no available repertoire, writers had to be commissioned for specific jobs—a very time-consuming project. Thus, while in January 1933 the theater announced that its next new production would be David Bergelson's *Midat ha-din* (A Measure of Strictness),[74] the premiere of the play did not take place until October 3rd—over a year after the theater's closure.

The play tells the story of Fillipov, an overworked Bolshevik leader deployed at the Polish border who succeeds in suppressing the counter-revolutionary activities of socialist revolutionaries, bandits, and smugglers through the implementation of strict discipline. The central conflict revolves around Fillipov's battle with Lemberg, a particularly ruthless speculator. The play ends when Fillipov's murder at the hands of counter-revolutionaries is avenged by a mob of angry workers. Bergelson originally wrote the story as a novel while living in Berlin in 1924–1925. The novel was then serialized in the Soviet Yiddish literary journal *Di royte velt* in 1928. As Bergelson explained, there were fundamental differences between the morals and ideologies of the novel and the play, largely as a result of the changes which took place in the construction of socialism in the Soviet Union between 1928 and 1932. He noted that while in 1928 there was a need to dwell on the old life (represented by the clericalism of Lemberg), in 1932 the old had been completely destroyed, and therefore the play was more concerned with glorifying the new (represented by Fillipov). The vilification of Lemberg was more complete in the play, which left no room for the audience to sympathize with the character's reluctance to part with the old life. "In the book," wrote Bergelson, "Lemberg is not entirely unmasked. Under his piety, the disgusting speculator still remains unexposed. But in the play all his masks are removed."[75] The play, he argued, was intended not only as a historical justification for Civil War violence, but also as a warning to those who believed that the war had been won and that the Revolution could let down its guard.

The artistic presentation of the play saw Mikhoels's first use of the split stage. A similar device had been used by Meyerhold in the 1926 production of *Roar China!,* but Meyerhold's split stage was used primarily to display the antagonisms between the British and Chinese. Mikhoels, on the other hand, sought to emulate Eisenstein's film montages through the depiction of two or more parallel events suggesting cognitive or emotional associations to the audience. For instance, when Fillipov catches Lemberg red-handed smuggling leather across the border, the audience simultaneously sees a Red Army division marching barefoot in the background, reminding them that Lemberg's crime is not victimless; he is stealing from the brave soldiers defending the people.[76] Another divided scene showed a battle between Reds and Whites on stage right, while to their left two contrabandists calmly played chess; each move of a figure on the board corresponded to a genuine battle and loss of life to the players' immediate right. While the counter-revolutionaries lounged around at home, the heroic Red Army soldiers fought for their own lives and the liberty of all Soviet citizens. The split stage was also used to enhance the subjectivity of the performance. For instance, in one scene, Mikhoels divided the stage into parts, one of which was set at a border patrol station and the other in a shtetl, and allowed characters from the two sets to converse with each other through space and time. The play was full of mass scenes, calling for 45 roles.

One critic wrote of the premiere, "It has been such a long time since such a dignified, celebratory mood prevailed in the Moscow State Yiddish Theater."[77] In Litvakov's review for *Der emes,* he praised Bergelson's play for being truly revolutionary and uniting the writer's creativity with an appropriate class-centered worldview. Litvakov saw Fillipov as a Christ-like figure seeking an apocalyptic destruction of the old world in order to usher in the new messianic era through his own martyrdom.[78]

Once again, though, the play had an ambiguous subtext that alluded to a different interpretation. The title of the play, *Midat ha-din,* was accurately translated into Russian as *Mera strogosti,* which can be translated into English as *A Measure of Strictness* or *Stern Judgment.* These translations, however, fail to reflect the nuanced meaning of the Hebrew term *midat ha-din.* In the Kabbalah (mystical Judaism), the term is used to refer to those attributes of God that demonstrate his vengeance in opposition to his mercy. In effect, the term is often equated with Satan—it is the source of all evil in the world. Certain Hasidic sects that were dominant in the Ukrainian regions in which Bergelson was reared raised the notion of *midat ha-din* to include the concept of redemption. According to this doctrine there are two states of Jewish existence: that dominated by *midat ha-din* and that dominated by *midat ha-hesed* (a measure of benevolence, or divine grace). According to historian Raphael Mahler:

> The basic idea in all Hasidic doctrine of this period in Galicia is the primacy of
> the kabbalistic notion of *midat ha-hesed* (divine grace). . . . All the calamities of
> the *galut klali* (the exile of the Jewish people) as well as of the *galut prati* (the exile

of the individual Jew), derive from the dominance of *midat ha-din* (stern judgment) over *midat ha-hesed.* . . . If, according to the Hasidic teachings, all the woes of the Jewish people and of each individual Jew are caused by the domination of the power of *midat ha-din,* this domination reveals itself first of all in the oppression of the Jews by the gentile nations.[79]

Thus, by use of the term, Bergelson equates Soviet power with the evil of *midat ha-din,* or exilic oppression. Bergelson's support for the Bolshevik system of justice as expressed in the text of his novel is mitigated by this symbolic interpretation. Although this should not be regarded as deliberately subversive (Bergelson wrote the novel in Berlin where he was free from censorship), it does suggest that Bergelson's support may have been more equivocal than a straightforward reading of his novel suggests.

Despite the relative success of Bergelson's second play, the fact remained that an acceptable Yiddish theatrical repertoire was not emerging. Even the successes did not reflect well on Yiddish dramaturgy per se—both Bergelson plays were adaptations of earlier novels, as was Daniel's *Four Days.* While Yiddish plays were being written by Soviet writers, each had its own ideological offense. New plays by Dobrushin and Veviurka, for instance, were dismissed for being overly mystical and messianic, while even some revolutionary plays about the Civil War and socialist construction, such as Ezra Fininberg's *Youth* and Veviurka's *Naftali Botvin,* were dismissed for ideological errors. Other plays that sought to follow the same formula as Markish's *Do Not Grieve!,* such as Veviurka's *The Steppe Is Burning* or Dobrushin's *On the Sixty-Second,* were less successful as artistic products.[80] Even Mikhoels was becoming frustrated by the low artistic quality of the new plays. According to Isaac Babel, "[Mikhoels] was extremely disapproving of the plays of Soviet dramatists, which he contrasted with the repertoire of old and classic plays."[81]

After almost two years of its existence, the political-cultural committee proved to be largely ineffective and was, predictably, paralyzed by its own internal turf wars. Furthermore, more Yiddish state theaters had arisen throughout the country. It was becoming clear that a central organization was needed to coordinate the activities of the various Yiddish theaters. Ia. O. Boiarskii, the head of the Union of Artists, recognized this opportunity by calling a general meeting with the directors of all the Yiddish state theaters in December 1933. He began the session by explaining that

> as a result of the territorial dispersion of the Jewish theater audiences in various national republics, the Central Committee of RABIS (The Union of Artists) is the only all-union organization, working in the sphere of culture, which can and must organize this historical first meeting of workers in Jewish theater.[82]

In other words, since the theaters were not solving their own problems, the Union of Artists would take it into its own hands to dictate solutions. The potential Jewish audience, Boiarskii theorized, was undergoing a process of denationalization, in which they were assimilating with general Soviet society and were no longer interested in parochial theater. Mikhoels was the first to challenge this assumption, recognizing that it was a dangerous contention coming from outside sources. Further, the repertory problem was not reflected in any loss of audience, Mikhoels argued, despite figures from the Central Theater Ticket Office to the contrary. Hinting that the state ticket office was deliberately sabotaging the Yiddish theater, Mikhoels cited one example in which prior to a performance the cashier had reported that only four seats had been sold, yet when the curtain opened the house was full. This sentiment was echoed by the directors of the Kiev and Birobidzhan Yiddish theaters, who reported that most of their shows regularly sold out. Furthermore, in the Jewish Autonomous Region of Birobidzhan, continued its director, assimilation was simply not an issue.[83]

Despite these objections, Boiarskii passed a resolution stating that henceforth all additions to the ongoing repertoire should be restricted to translations of accepted European and Russian classics, at least until an appropriate Jewish repertoire was created. New productions of the Moscow theater would consist only of two plays: Shakespeare's *King Lear* and a work by the French playwright Eugene Labiche (1815–1888). The theaters were permitted, however, to continue performing Jewish plays already in the repertoire. Before the meeting closed, Mikhoels warned that "if we turn ourselves into a theater of translation, then to us, as a Jewish theater, there is nothing more to be done. Our path is unique—it is only compatible with the creative growth of Jewish theater and Jewish drama."[84]

The Classless Society

By the time the First All-Union Congress of Yiddish Theaters convened in late 1934, there were eight Yiddish theaters scattered throughout the Soviet Union, many of which were staffed by graduates of the Moscow Yiddish Theater technicum. In addition to the older theaters of Moscow, Minsk, and Kiev (which had been transferred from Kharkov in 1931), new troupes had emerged in Odessa, Birobidzhan, Tashkent, Stalindorf (in the Volga German Republic), and Simferopol (in the Crimea). The latter two were the newest additions, both of which had been founded with the support of the Society for the Settlement of Jewish Toilers on the Land to serve as collective farm theaters.[85] Mikhoels, chairing the congress, followed the Party line against his prior objections and called upon his colleagues to turn away from the Yiddish classical repertoire and begin presenting strictly contemporary Soviet plays. Once again he refrained from denouncing the theater's earlier period, noting that the era of experimentation had "found a new aesthetic, new method, new rhythm, and new stage language."[86] His about-face, though, suggests that Mikhoels was becoming wary of his future.

Mikhoels was conspicuously absent from the directorate of the theater's newest production, turning the job over to French director Leon Mussinak and to Aleksandra Azarkh. *The Millionaire, the Dentist, and the Pauper* (formerly entitled *The Thirty Million of Mister Gladiator*), a lighthearted vaudeville by Labiche that poked fun at the decadence of Western European high society, premiered in November 1934. When the American millionaire Yucatan leaves his wife behind and arrives in Paris with his secretary and his son, there is no end to the hilarious and

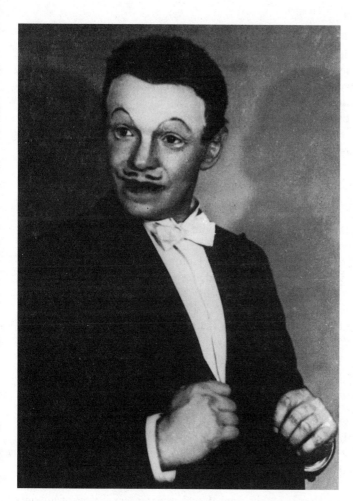

Benjamin Zuskin
as Anatol in *The
Millionaire, the
Dentist, and the
Pauper,* 1934.
Photo courtesy
of Ala Perelman-
Zuskin.

outrageous adventures they encounter. The audience is told: "Once the Spanish discovered America, and now the Americans, with their dollars, will discover Europe." The plot of the play revolves around the seductress Suzanna's attempt to marry Anatol, Yucatan's son, in order to get his money—a scene dominated by Dobrushin's song "Less Love, More Money." However, Yucatan himself has already set his eyes on the seductress. At a gala ball, receiving news of his wife's death, Yucatan rejoices because he is now free to pursue his new prize, and steels himself for the task of removing his son and rival. However, the plan fails and Yucatan is left alone.

Writing in *Izvestiia,* Mussinak described the play as a modernized reinterpretation of the vaudeville, which not only revealed the comedic irony of Labiche, but also underlined the bitter irony of his play, turning it into a tragicomedy.[87] While some critics agreed with the director's assessment,[88] the majority was less enthusiastic. Grinvald, for instance, wrote that it had neither political nor social value, but was, nevertheless, a pleasant performance.[89]

Like Meyerhold's production the same year of *The Lady of the Camellias* by another French writer, Alexandre Dumas, *The Millionaire* sought to present an artistic portrayal of the slavery of women under capitalism. Incidentally, another translation from the French, this time of Balzac's *A Bachelor's Establishment,* was playing simultaneously at the Vakhtangov Theater. The Yiddish theater was not alone in its confusion regarding appropriate Soviet repertoire. Lacking a model of the type of integrative propaganda demanded by socialist realism, theaters throughout Moscow preferred to delay the adoption of the program for as long as possible by staging French vaudevilles.

Always anxious to help those in the arts overcome difficult times and find appropriate repertoires, the state once again intervened by establishing yet another committee to assert its authority over the arts—the Committee of Artistic Affairs, attached directly to the Council of People's Commissars. The political-cultural committees for individual theaters which had previously decided collectively on all artistic questions were relegated to a formality; all genuine considerations of an artistic character were henceforth to be decided by the new Committee of Artistic Affairs. The organization was headed by Platon Kerzhentsev, the leftist former Proletkult activist and deputy head of Agitprop, who was assisted by Boiarskii. With supervisory powers over all elements of art in the country, the committee did not restrict itself to repertory matters. Henceforth each theater would have to submit requests for approval of every move: hiring a new stage manager, giving a vacation or sick leave to a staff member, presenting a new production, raising a salary, disciplining a member of the group for lateness, and giving a bonus, to name but a few of the thousands of requests which flooded the committee. Each dress rehearsal would be attended by a member of the committee, and representatives from the Department of Propaganda, the Central Committee of the Party, and the Repertory Committee who would discuss the play and "recommend" any changes.

In addition, the Party organization of each theater, consisting of all staff members who were members of the Communist Party, was given increasing authority, regardless of the ranks of the Party members within the troupe. Thus, for instance, Juri Jelagin, a former member of the Vakhtangov Theater orchestra, explained that the most powerful personages in his theater became the barber, a couple of stagehands, the manager of the dining room, the editor of the theater's newsletter, the manager of the laundry room, and one of the bass tuba players.[90] The Moscow State Yiddish Theater was in a similar state. Of its members, only seven were Party members, none of whom were actors, directors, or musicians.[91]

Although the troupe began to lose even more control over its destiny, it was placated by the type of state privileges that characterized the "classless society" of the 1930s. Living the high life, the former students, workers, and struggling artists who became the Moscow State Yiddish Theater had little desire to risk trading in their privileged life for possible Siberian exile. The life of the privileged artists is colorfully described by Jelagin:

Thousands of innocent people were placed under arrest, the prisons were crowded, in the villages peasant uprisings and desperate attempts to resist hated collectivization were suppressed with incredible cruelty. Denunciations, lies and fear were all around, and the immense country was in the grip of famine. Yet, backstage in the Second Art Theater, life was dominated by noble, warm friendliness, by a total absence of jealousy and intrigue, by unselfish service to art and by faithful devotion to the theater and its ideals.[92]

Norris Houghton echoes him: "If it can be said that an aristocracy exists in the classless society of the Soviet Union, then the artists of the theater are a part of it."[93]

The Moscow State Yiddish Theater was no exception to this rule. As with Shimele, the poor tailor who changes his name to Semon Makarovich Soroker after winning the lottery, the actors in the Yiddish theater troupe adopted more formal appellations. The program for *King Lear* listed the actors' names with first initials for the first time (patronymics would later be added), accompanied by state-awarded titles. By 1935 Mikhoels had been made a People's Artist of the Russian Republic, while Goldblatt, Shidlo, Shteiman, Rotbaum, Minkova, Zuskin, Pulver, and Radlov were all Honored Artists of the Republic. In the mid-1930s there were approximately 500 Honored Artists, a title endowed upon the fortunate by the Council of Peoples' Commissars upon recommendations from the Commissariat of Enlightenment. In the words of Norris Houghton:

> These honors are not empty ones. They bring with them certain privileges. . . . The right to have one's own apartment is granted to honored artists[,] some of whom occupy alone or with their families apartments of four or five rooms. A few of the great People's Artists have an entire house. They all may have one or two servants.[94]

Indeed, many of the more senior members of the Yiddish theater had moved out of the Stankevich residence into luxury apartments on Moscow's prestigious Gorky (Tverskaia) Street or Arbat Street. The honor additionally relieved the recipient of a great deal of work. For instance, while the average member of the Yiddish theater attended anywhere from 100 to 140 rehearsals during the 1936 season, Honored Artist Iu. Ia. Minkova attended only fourteen, while Honored Artist S. D. Rotbaum was only present for thirty-three.[95]

Mikhoels, especially, had achieved "star status." Polish Yiddish actress Ida Kaminska, who never forgave Mikhoels for his unwillingness to help her find a job during World War II, recalled her first impression of the actor during this period:

> Mikhoels sat in his dressing room like an emperor, surrounded by young actresses. One of them fanned him, another served him coffee, a third asked him what he wanted. Everyone fawned over him. I don't recall anyone dancing around a prima donna the way they crowded around Mikhoels.[96]

The King and the Fool

The 1935 production of *King Lear* was perhaps the theater's most famous performance in its history. Preparations for the production began in March 1934,

Solomon Mikhoels
as King Lear.
Photo courtesy
of Ala Perelman-
Zuskin.

when Shmuel Halkin (1897–1960), a Soviet poet known for his historical subjects, was commissioned to provide a Yiddish translation.[97] Les Kurbas, the Ukrainian director and former student of Max Reinhardt, was originally slated to stage the production. His arrest, however, delayed the scheduled fall 1934 premiere and forced the theater to search for a new director. The play finally premiered under the directorship of Sergei Radlov on February 5, 1935.

Sets were designed by Aleksandr Tyshler. Tyshler (1898–1964) was born to an atheist family of Jewish background in the town of Melitpol. After moving to Kiev, he enrolled in the Kiev Art School in 1912, and upon finishing became involved with the art studio of Alexandra Exter. After joining the Red Army to fight in the Civil War, Tyshler moved to Moscow, where his dynamic series of paintings on Civil War and fantasy themes caught the attention of M. Rafalskii, director of the Belorussian State Yiddish Theater, who invited Tyshler to join his theater as designer. After working with Rafalskii on the theater's production of Veviurka's *Naftali Botvin* and Bergelson's *The Deaf,* Tyshler began to supplement his work on the Belorussian State Yiddish Theater with the Red Army Theater, the Kharkov State Yiddish Theater, and others. In 1933, Tyshler accepted Mikhoels's invitation to design sets for *King Lear* while simultaneously working on *Richard III* for the Bolshoi Theater and the *Death of Tarelkin* for the Maly Theater. For *Lear,* Tyshler constructed a two-story stage, depicting a medieval village with a castle and sculpted figures.

Although hardly new to the Russian theater, Shakespeare was seeing a revival in the 1930s. The Vakhtangov Theater had presented its severely criticized production of *Hamlet,* with music by Shostakovich, in the early years of the decade and in 1936 had premiered *Much Ado About Nothing.* By the late 1930s, *Othello* had been performed in Kirghizia, Georgia, Buriat-Mongolia, Tadzhikistan, Armenia, and Moscow. In 1934, *Twelfth Night* was being performed at the Second Moscow Art Theater and *Romeo and Juliet* at the Theater of Revolution. Other productions of *Romeo and Juliet* could be seen in Yaroslav and Magnitogorsk. An Uzbek translation of *Hamlet* premiered in 1938 and the play was also performed in Kursk, Stalingrad and Tbilisi.[98] However, the idea of Mikhoels playing Lear was met with skepticism from most tragic actors of the period.[99] One director, perhaps skeptical of Mikhoels's ability to portray a British king, suggested that he relocate the narrative to Palestine—a notion categorically rejected by the actor.[100]

One of the reasons for Shakespeare's renewed popularity in the 1930s was that such tried and true plays, so familiar to any theatergoing public, seemed to the authorities to be politically safe. A 1929 list of acceptable dramatic productions released by the Central Repertory Committee gave *King Lear,* along with fourteen other Shakespearean plays, a rare "A" rating, indicating that it was "most acceptable."[101] Directors were able to take advantage of this lax attitude toward Shakespearean productions to manipulate his plays subtly into political protests. Because of their remote historical content, Shakespeare's historical tragedies were particularly suited for allegorical intent. Boris Pasternak's translation of *Hamlet* is probably the most well-known attempt by a Soviet writer to use Shakespeare as "a lyrical confession camouflaged as translation," in the words of Vladimir Markov. Pasternak's translations, Markov continues, were "not only alien to the atmosphere of socialist realism, but some lines sound outright defiant."[102] Despite the Marxist doctrine of linear history, the early Bolsheviks were wary of history repeating itself: it is well known that Lenin, for instance, studied the Paris Commune carefully for fear of repeating its mistakes and often used Napoleon Bonaparte as a symbol of military dictatorship, even coining the term "Bonapartism," later used by Trotsky as an attack on Stalin's Russia. Bolshevik propagandists themselves often used historical episodes as allegories for contemporary threats and victories: Sergei Eisenstein's *Alexander Nevsky* (1938), which painted a horrifying picture of barbarian Teutons as German fascism threatened Europe, is perhaps the most recognized example of this type of art. Even earlier theatrical productions, such as Tretiakov's *Roar China!* and the Yiddish theater's own *Uprising,* had depicted the revolutionary struggle in other regions as a metaphor for Russia's own Revolution. Thus, official Soviet discourse had already created a precedent whereby historical events could be understood as representing contemporary issues. With the intensification of Soviet censorship, historical commentary became a convenient means of critiquing the modern regime as well. As A. Belinkov wrote in his Aesopian text *Iurii Tynianov:* "At the end of the twenties a certain segment of the Russian intelligentsia began to see analogies between the modern age and revolutionary eras of the past."[103] Belinkov wrote these lines in a text which, itself, has been interpreted as an allegorical "essay on the nature of despotic and totalitarian power."[104]

Benjamin Zuskin as the Fool. Photo courtesy of Ala Perelman-Zuskin.

Thus, it is not in the least far-fetched to interpret *King Lear* as an allegorical critique of Stalin's tyranny. This interpretation is given further credence by the onstage production of the play at the Moscow State Yiddish Theater. The show trial which opens the play as the self-centered and autocratic yet insecure king demands verbal adulation was reminiscent of Stalin's growing cult of personality and the earlier Soviet show trials of Socialist Revolutionaries, Mensheviks, and bourgeois specialists. Lear's misdirected expulsion of the only daughter who truly loves him and his misguided trust in those who seek to betray him leads to his own tragic downfall. Was Mikhoels warning Stalin that his own campaign against the Old Bolsheviks and alliances with the new guard would only lead to doom? Was Mikhoels also making a reference to the strife in Stalin's family which led to the death of his wife in 1932? Mikhoels's own commentary on the play helps to underscore this interpretation:

> The tragedy for me does not begin with the expulsion of Goneril, but rather in the expulsion of Cordelia, that is, in the first act. . . . The tragedy of Lear is the bankruptcy of his former false and stagnant feudal ideals; and in the agonizing advent of the new, more progressive and truthful ideology.[105]

By transposing the tragedy from Goneril and Regan's rejection of Lear to Lear's rejection of Cordelia, Mikhoels blames Lear rather than his daughters for the outcome. The tragedy, Mikhoels insists, is a direct consequence of the king's impotence and the bankruptcy of his ideals; it cannot be blamed on his subjects' acts of sabotage. If we replace Lear with Stalin and feudal with Communist, Mikhoels's comments can be read as a scathing critique of Stalin's Russia. By emphasizing that the central point of the play is not the betrayal by Lear's daughters, but rather Lear's betrayal of the one daughter who is faithful to him, Mikhoels emphasizes the allegorical element—the true "enemy of the people" is the king who exiles his faithful servants, as Stalin was doing to the intellectuals who helped build the Revolution. Although the process of extracting ideological premises from all art was a mandatory game in 1930s Russia, the explicit message of Mikhoels's analysis is contradicted by an allegorical reading which sees Lear as Stalin and the bankrupt political system he adheres to as Bolshevism.

This interpretation is buttressed by later Soviet analyses of the play. Grigori Kozintsev's 1965 essay on *King Lear*, based on a 1941 essay published in *Teatr*, argues that the theme of one tyrant replacing another is a timeless theme, equally applicable to Shakespeare's era as it is to Lear's. By suggesting that Shakespeare chose a historical ruler as a metaphor for the reigning monarch (Elizabeth I), Kozintsev seems to be covertly inviting his readers to do the same, implying that Lear can be a commentary on Stalin's Russia:

> The events of the tragedy should be perceived as taking place in a real world of tyranny, rather than in the vacuum of fabular convention. . . . By blending periods and locales, he [Shakespeare] was able to compare, emphasize, and generalize. . . . In order to bring contemporary processes into full relief, the shadow of another epoch was cast on the principals and on the course of events. The story of the old hero was repeated in a new time and with a totally different quality.[106]

143

Kozintsev continued:

> One form of oppression succeeded another. . . . New rulers cut down medieval
> detention stocks in the name of the free development of new forms of production
> and the free (though already unlimited) oppression of man by man. . . . Hordes
> of vagabonds, terrible caravans of human grief, roamed the country. They were
> ragged, exhausted from hunger, and vainly sought work. They dragged them-
> selves along the roads, leaving by its edge the corpses of those who did not have
> the strength to go farther. So went the future army of hired labor. It had already
> begun to be disciplined to the new order.[107]

The allegorical elements were also emphasized in the performance. Liubomirskii describes Mikhoels's entrance as Lear:

> If not for the crown, it would be difficult to believe that he is a king: a modest,
> flabby, solemn old man, who comes down, stooping, and quietly approaches the
> throne. He stands by the throne as if he wants to recollect something. Having
> seen the jester on the throne, he glances perplexedly, grasps the jester by the ear
> and calmly lifts him slightly above the throne. He begins to laugh with a sarcas-
> tic, weak giggle, and sits on the throne.[108]

This triumphant first scene was a subtle tribute to the carnivalesque. Additionally, it can be seen as an allegory of 1930s Russia. While the Fool sits triumphantly on the throne, the wise play the role of comedians on a stage. The line
"Thou wouldst make a good fool"[109] uttered by the Fool to Lear, becomes a dominant theme. The interplay between Zuskin as the Fool and Mikhoels as Lear was
one of the most celebrated elements of Radlov's production. In the words of Mikhoels, "We do not play two roles, we play together a single role, only two sides of
it."[110] On a simplistic level, the blurring between Lear and Fool can be seen as an
attempt to equate Stalin with a fool. On a more profound level it can be seen a
challenge to Stalin's tidy division of the world between Good and Bad, We and
They, Red and White. The theater had been developing this type of Janus-faced
character since it introduced the character of Benjamin, who can be seen as half
Don Quixote and half Little Tramp. The notion of ego and alter-ego, which was
repeated throughout the theater's plays beginning with the tragicomedy of *Night
in the Old Market,* presented contradictions that challenged the tidy divisions of
Stalin's world. "There is one remarkable trait in Shakespeare's heroes," Mikhoels
wrote. "This is the internal dialect of their manners. Shakespeare did not simp-
lify character types, rather, he complicated them. He always brought contradictions into their mindset, contradictions which he wanted to prove [were recon-
cilable]."[111] Indeed, the theater's emphasis on the psychological contradictions of
individuals could not have been more removed from the stylized social types
Granovsky had earlier sought to extract from Sholem Aleichem and Goldfadn.
Mikhoels described the psychological contradictions of Lear through a musical
analogy: "[Shakespeare's art] is never a monody, and it is the actor's task to hear the
separate notes making the character. . . . They may be separated by quite an in-
terval; on the other hand, contrasting and diametrically opposed notes may coin-

Solomon Mikhoels
and Benjamin
Zuskin as Lear
and Fool. Photo
from Solomon
Mikhoels, *Stati,
besedi, rechi.*

cide in time."[112] The internal contradictions within the character were further underlined on stage. In the words of Grinvald:

[The] greatness [of Mikhoels's Lear] was not external but internal. Mikhoels's Lear was carried away by the beauty of his soul, purified by the torments of suffering, and enlightened by the rays of the new truth. . . . Lear appeared to Mikhoels as an example, thought up by Shakespeare, of the embodiment of a meaningful and deep philosophical idea. The artist saw this idea as a conflict between the human ego, imagining itself as omnipotent and invincible, and the reality of the objective world, before which the individual's arrogant ego is pitiful and weak.[113]

Mikhoels also developed the leitmotif of a gesture in *King Lear,* a technique first used in *The Deaf,* in which he would repeat a particular gesture which summa-

145

rizes the character's innermost thoughts. Lear would giggle, evoking his reaction at first seeing Cordelia; feel for tears on others' faces, foreshadowing the tears on Cordelia's cheeks; and put his hand over his head, as though searching for the crown which he no longer possesses. This gesture perhaps best conveys the pathos of Act 1, Scene 4, when Lear curses Goneril as he slaps himself on the belly "so the house resounded with those slaps."[114] After uttering this famed curse, Mikhoels once again reaches for his discarded crown before breaking down into tears. He has realized that without the crown he is nothing.

Mikhoels's Lear loves to sing, which allowed Pulver to utilize sixteenth-century Renaissance English music. In particular, he has a favorite hunting song. The metaphor of hunting is deprived of its regal and grandiose associations, becoming instead a simple song enjoyed by an old man. The song takes on greater significance later in the play. Finding himself in captivity with Cordelia, Lear finds intense joy simply by looking into his daughter's eyes and holding her hands. After the death of Cordelia, Mikhoels's Lear is unable to giggle; instead he quietly hums the hunting song to himself. Liubomirskii notes that Mikhoels's Lear is happier in prison with Cordelia than he had ever been before; he finally outgrows his habit of reaching for his crown. Furthermore, Lear refuses to isolate himself, at least intellectually, from the realistic problems confronting those who do not share his position in life: poverty, hunger, and cold; Mikhoels underscores his sympathy for the "poor wretches" of Act III, Scene 4.

Mikhoels's performance firmly placed him among the ranks of Russia's greatest artists—a fact immediately recognized by all critics. "Before you unfolds the play of an artist," wrote *Leningradskaia pravda*, "an artist of world standard, whose name you must place among the ranks of the great names of the artistic stage— from Mochalov to Ermolova, together with Rossi and Salvini."[115] "*King Lear* in the Moscow State Yiddish Theater's presentation is one of the best Shakespearean productions in the Soviet theater," wrote *Pravda*.[116] "Mikhoels has entered the ranks of the greatest actors of the world" echoed Karl Radek, writing in *Izvestiia:*

> This presentation, in the first place, is a great cultural victory for the Jewish population of the USSR. *King Lear* at the Moscow Jewish Theater enters the highroad of great culture and great art, just as the Jewish poor, who are participating in the industrialization and collectivization of our country, have entered the great path of socialist construction.[117]

Other critics seem to have appreciated the symbolic elements. For instance, Grinvald praised Mikhoels for drawing "a clear picture of the death, of the failure, of the feudal world."[118] Rozentsveig echoed him: "Shakespeare saw the death of the feudal princedoms, he saw the failure of the system."[119] Radek, though, asked "What is it? A personal human tragedy or a symbol of the social crisis at the end of the sixteenth century?"[120] The play was so successful that less than four years later, in December 1938, the theater celebrated its 200th performance of *King Lear*.[121] After this production, Litvakov could write that the Moscow State Yiddish Theater was "one of the greatest theaters in the world."[122]

Audiences and Censors

The theater struggled during the early 1930s to define and interpret the slogan "national in form, socialist in content" in a manner advantageous to itself and acceptable to the increasingly influential censors. Initially Mikhoels mimicked the style of productions being performed at Russian theaters and concentrated on the officially condoned theme of socialist construction in the Soviet Union. These productions, however, failed to attract large audiences. Whereas during the NEP the theater's Semitic exoticism and modernist experimentation had attracted many non-Jews, in the early 1930s the Yiddish theater was rapidly transforming itself into a clone of Moscow's other theaters, differentiated only by its language. Those who did not speak Yiddish were no longer rewarded with exotic treats for sitting through an incomprehensible production. Jews also became less interested in the theater because it ceased to reflect the peculiarities of their own existence. While the Jewish audience could identify with the negative hero, the *luftmentsh* or the parent whose children were rejecting tradition, the positive hero—the New Soviet Man—was still a chimera. This uneasiness was a factor of what Régine Robin calls the "impossibility" of the socialist realist aesthetic. "The positive hero," she writes, "can only be a horizon, a limit to be reached in indeterminacy, a goal."[123] The socialist realist discourse urged the portrayal of "what ought to be" rather than "what is," thereby eliminating the possibility of drawing examples from the real world. Socialist realism did not require the actor and dramatist to replicate life, as its name implies, but rather to construct an idealized vision of the future as determined by ideological and political propaganda that was not even of their own making. Further, the realist designation abhorred the stylized masks of agitprop behind which actors in the 1920s had hidden, thereby excusing themselves from probing the psychology of their characters.

In response to these problems, the theater began to perform productions with which their Jewish audience could better identify. First, the theater turned toward better-known authors, such as David Bergelson and Peretz Markish. Second, it adopted the generational conflict as its pet theme, allowing the continued portrayal of the familiar Jew who loved learning and tradition. Finally, the theater began to present productions that mirrored recognizable Jewish stories and legends and that contained Jewish subtexts and archetypes. Although the text of these plays continued to refer to socialist realist themes, the subtext alluded to stories more enthralling than the construction of dams.

It is difficult to determine what portion of the audience, if any, was able to recognize these connections and read the theater's subtext. Certainly large portions of the theater's audience, particularly those who saw the theater during its provincial tours, had received traditional Jewish educations prior to the Revolution and therefore possessed the necessary cultural and linguistic tools required to decode the plays. Up until 1917, virtually every Jewish boy attended a *kheder* or Talmud Torah where, in the words of Zvi Gitelman, they "mastered impressive amounts of traditional lore and developed outstanding powers of reasoning as well as a lifelong commitment to the study of the Torah."[124] Young women, as well, had received religious instruction through Yiddish storybooks and religious texts prior to the Revolution. Those who received their education after 1917 had less formal exposure to traditional Judaism, but many of those living in Ukraine and Belorussia had still been reared in religious homes and functioned in a predominantly Jewish milieu. Many Jewish children continued to receive their primary education in Yiddish at the new secular schools, and a few had probably attended some of the clandestine religious schools that continued to exist into the late 1920s.[125] Because of the informal networks by which Jewish tradition was transmitted after the Revolution, it is difficult to determine with any precision what percentage of the population possessed the tools necessary to appreciate the theater's subtext. Even if it is assumed that a large segment of the theater's audience had extensive Jewish backgrounds—an assumption that holds more for the theater's provincial audiences than for those in Moscow—this alone by no means indicates that they understood the productions in allegorical terms. It is worth remembering, however, that in an environment of strict censorship audiences are more responsive to hidden codes and contexts, because they recognize that certain ideas cannot be conveyed overtly.

The censors, on the other hand, seem to have lacked even the most basic skills required to carry out their work effectively. With the 1930 dissolution of the Jewish Section, the Party lost its chief conduit to the Jewish community. Henceforth the theater was supervised by the Central Repertory Committee, whose officials lacked the Jewish Section's familiarity with Jewish life. In fact, the theater itself was forced to hire translators to translate each play into Russian for approval by the censors, suggesting that the censors did not even read Yiddish. While there is no evidence that the translators deliberately doctored their translations, the meaning of certain terms, such as *midat ha-din*, were simply lost in translation. The fact that the censors needed translations also suggests that they were unfamiliar with other aspects of Jewish culture to which the theater's plays referred. Despite their strong presence, the censors seem to have rarely interfered with the theater directly. Although they played an active role in suppressing Hebrew literature and Jewish topics in Russian literature, the censors were less conspicuous in the realm of Yiddish. This can be attributed both to a lack of staff with the necessary linguistic skills as well as to the Party's own ambiguous policies with regard to Jewish themes in Yiddish literature. Having deprived itself of the Jewish Section's guidance in formulating policies about Yiddish literature and culture, the Party seems to have been just as confused about the slogan "national in form, socialist in content" as was the theater.

The ubiquitous presence of censorship itself, even if it did not directly touch their work, was sufficient to keep Yiddish writers on their toes. The theater's relationship with its censors can be gleaned from an anecdote told by Yiddish poet Abraham Sutzkever, who fled Vilna to Moscow in 1944 and was asked by Mikhoels to write a play for the theater. Sutzkever recalls that he told Mikhoels he was concerned about the censors: "At these words of mine Mikhoels laughed, not only with his face, but with his entire body. . . . 'You are mistaken, Abraham, the censor has nothing to do with us, because in every writer's head sits his own censor.'"[126] In other words, as long as they were not antagonized, the censors left the theater alone. As Peretz Markish wrote:

> [Mikhoels's] elaborate creation process allows him to attain the highest grade of artistic independence and freedom and gives him the possibility of manifesting his own artistic individuality and the social philosophy of the time and society in which he lives.[127]

Mikhoels understood that his theater's raison d'être was its "Jewishness." He had clearly seen, since the 1927 production of *Uprising*, that without Jewish content the theater would fail, both financially and ideologically. His motives, however, cannot be reduced to pure opportunism. Jewish culture remained close to Mikhoels's heart; throughout his tenure as director of the theater, the promotion of Jewish culture in the Soviet Union increasingly became his pet cause. Mikhoels was able to turn his theater into a Jewish cultural center where the greatest Soviet Jewish artists, directors, actors, musicians, and writers could all find a faithful audience.

Where Are the Maccabees? The Heroic Past

5

One of the problems discussed at the First Writers' Congress of 1934 was the application of socialist realism to non-Russian culture. Ethnic writers were warned against producing mere facsimiles of Russian culture, on the one hand, and becoming self-contained, on the other. A synthesis of the two extremes was found in Gorky's call for a return to folklore. Artists and writers were urged to draw from the cultural traditions with which their people identified, to express themselves with *narodnost,* a popular spirit.[1] Russian novelists revived the themes of peasant *lubok* literature, balalaikas became the musical instrument of choice, Ukrainian dance troupes performed in colorful peasant dress, and olympiads and *dekada*s showcasing the folk cultures of different nationalities proliferated. The proponents of folklorism sought to construct a new supernational culture that would encompass the universal myths of all people of all time. It was this struggle to create a universal Zeitgeist devoid of all indeterminacies that has prompted Régine Robin to call socialist realism "an impossible aesthetic."[2] A further impossibility inherent in the aesthetic was the notion of *narodnaia kultura,* a term which can be translated as "people's culture," "folk culture," "national culture," or even "mass culture." The urge to appeal to the *narod* was by no means new to Russian aesthetic ideology. It can be traced back to the 1874 "Going-to-the-People" movement, during which thousands of Russian students flocked to the countryside alternatively to learn from or to teach the people. This dichotomy between the *narod* as teacher and *narod* as student persisted well into the 1930s. During the 1920s, theater activists such as Meyerhold and Granovsky drew from the fairground, the carnival, and popular theatrical traditions (such as the *purimspiel*) in an effort to incorporate the spontaneity of the "common folk" into their art, while others delivered Bolshevik literature into rural reading rooms.

Yet despite its celebration of cultural diversity and exoticism, the regime sought to divorce cultural production from the ideology behind it; culture was permitted to be national, but not nationalist. In other words, Soviet folklorist culture was expected to present "kitsch nationalism," a superficial recognition of a nation's cultural idiosyncrasies that was devoid of political or religious implications.[3] Official recognition of a nation's unique cultural traditions was not expected to validate that nation's claim to distinctness, and certainly not to sovereignty. This phenomenon of divorcing cultural production from broader sociological issues was hardly restricted to the Soviet Union. In fact, postcolonial literary criticism contends that Western attitudes toward the "Orient" reek of similar condescension.[4] Thus, official Soviet nationalities policy continued to deny the existence of a Jewish nation in theory, while simultaneously promoting a diluted Jewish national culture.[5]

National motifs were to be used solely as a medium through which socialist themes could be communicated. Regardless of the language and dress of the protagonists, the structure of all socialist realist novels remained the same. On Moscow's stages and in the pages of Soviet novels, young men and women became "questing hero[es] in search of consciousness."[6] They learned to be "conscious" workers by enlisting in the Red Army to defend "the Great October Revolution," by wresting produce from a hostile nature with the help of their trusty tractors, and by mining coal to fuel their motherland's ever-expanding industrial production. These "boy meets tractor" novels, however, were largely absent from the Yiddish stage. Certainly audiences saw young Jewish workers leading their parents to a state of "revolutionary consciousness," but the action was more likely to take place in the home, that sanctuary of Jewish life, than in the factory or the field. Socialist realism in the Yiddish theater was geared toward the peculiarities of Jewish life.

The plays presented at the Moscow State Yiddish Theater in the latter half of the 1930s can be characterized first and foremost by their definite "Jewishness." After divorcing itself from Jewish content with its 1935 production of *King Lear,* the Yiddish theater returned to its roots with a vengeance in the latter half of the decade. This period saw not only a return to the pre-revolutionary Jewish playwrights that had dominated the stage in the 1920s—Sholem Aleichem and Abraham Goldfadn—but also a renewed attempt to have contemporary Jewish playwrights deal with specifically Jewish themes. No longer were Jewish motifs to be clandestinely hidden beneath socialist story lines—they were now openly proclaimed and celebrated on stage as an expression of folklorism and popular spirit, provided that they adhered to certain rules. The first such works appropriated the folklore and popular heroes of the nineteenth-century shtetl and transformed them into didactic illustrations of the merits of communism and Soviet policies.

As the decade progressed, the theater became more willing to cross the line from national content into nationalist content. It began to move away from quaint socialist fables drawn from shtetl life to politically charged legends of ancient Judaea. The integration of national form into Jewish art posed a unique problem in that much of what could be called Jewish form was based on either religion or the Jewish longing for Zion, both of which were strictly taboo topics. "I do not understand why a Georgian or an Uzbek theater may present a national epic, but we may not," Mikhoels protested.[7] The answer was obvious and Mikhoels doubtless knew it. There was nothing unpatriotic or anti-Soviet about Georgian poets dreaming of their ancient capital Mtskheta or about Uzbek bards singing of the Shir Dar Madrasa of Samarkand—both were integral features of the Soviet Union of which all its citizens could be proud. But a Jew longing for Jerusalem was an altogether different matter—not because he was a Jew, but because he looked beyond the Soviet realm for inspiration. All Soviet citizens were invited to share in the glory of the halcyon days of Mtskheta and Samarkand, but the lore of Judaea and Samaria was the exclusive property of the Jews. Plays depicting the halcyon days of Jewish civilization in ancient Israel implicitly glorified the golden era of Jewish statehood and implied a degeneration of society since the beginning of exilic existence. The theater's spokespeople officially presented these plays as socialist realist examples of the class struggle within the Jewish community, although the texts themselves were rife with subtexts and coded symbols asserting genuine national pride.

Other plays were situated in Russia and resuscitated the shtetl Jew, a character, whether adored or despised, who had remained close to the hearts of Jews and non-Jews alike. While the characters were portrayed first and foremost as Soviet citizens or subjects of the tsar, to many audiences it likely made little difference whether their heroes were of proletarian or aristocratic stock—the important fact was that they were Jews. While the nationalist structure of these plays was less explicit, they were in many ways a greater challenge to the mythology of Jewish assimilation and integration. For in contrast to the historical plays that validated Jewish nationhood by harking back to ancient Judaea, these plays acknowledged the unique predicament and distinctness of the contemporary Jewish population of the Soviet Union.

Fifteenth Jubilee

In March 1935, the Moscow State Yiddish Theater celebrated its fifteenth jubilee with a momentous gala. A jubilee committee was established, headed by such luminaries as the new Commissar of Enlightenment Andrei Bubnov (who replaced Lunacharskii in 1929) and Ia. O. Boiarskii. Representatives from the Jewish cultural community included David Bergelson, Itzik Fefer, Peretz Markish, and Moshe Litvakov.[8] The gala event was typical of contemporary Soviet commemorative events: a series of bland policy speeches "entertained" the invited guests, and for the finale the Moscow State Yiddish Theater performed a scene from *Two Hundred Thousand,* into which greetings to the theater were inserted from major factories and collective farms.[9] In honor of the jubilee, the first acts of *Two Hundred Thousand* and *The Divorce Paper* were broadcast on the radio.[10] Additionally, the theater and its administrative director, Ida Lashevich, were honored by the Commissariat of Enlightenment. The Soviet Telegraph Agency (TASS) credited the theater with being "one of the best theaters in the world."[11]

Der emes celebrated the jubilee by inviting factories and collective farms throughout the Soviet Union to send their greetings to Mikhoels and his troupe. The workers of Kalinindorf District, for instance, saluted the theater with hails of "Long live the nationality policies of Lenin-Stalin! Long live socialist culture! Long live the State Yiddish Theater and its talented collective! Long live our greatly beloved Stalin!" The festive mood of the paper, however, was tempered by a short article—doubtless included as an ominous warning—which reported on a plenum held by the Union of Soviet Writers in which Yiddish dramaturgy was criticized for failing to portray the New Soviet Man.[12]

The festivities surrounding the theater's anniversary provided an ideal opportunity to formulate an official interpretation of the theater's history. According to this schema, first formulated by Mikhoels at the All-Union Assembly of Jewish Theaters, the recent translations of Shakespeare and Labiche were hailed as the enlightened culmination of a three-part history of the theater. During the first period, 1920–1929, the theater performed avant-gardist versions of Yiddish literary classics. The second stage, 1929–1934, saw a turn toward Soviet Jewish writers who portrayed the Civil War and the Revolution, while for the third and final stage, the theater raised itself to the exalted level of performing standard classics of non-Jewish theater. This standardized interpretation of the theater's history became the sole acceptable means of discussing the topic. It was repeated in virtually every speech and article written by Mikhoels over the course of the year, it appeared in reviews and articles on the theater in the press, and it appeared on the cover of librettos from the period.[13] For instance, Intourist's libretto of *King Lear* contained the unintentionally ironic statement that "the theatre could not content itself . . . with themes drawn from the past, even though treated from a revolutionary standpoint. . . . The theatre has been searching for new Soviet themes and consequently for new artistic methods."[14] How exactly Shakespeare, a sixteenth-century British playwright, could write plays on "Soviet themes" was unclear.

Yet there are many indications that some people, including Mikhoels, were not satisfied with this paradigm. Indeed, despite the resounding success of *King Lear,* it was difficult for those who hoped for a flowering of Yiddish culture to accept that the highest level of this renaissance would be characterized by translations of European classics. One need only recall Mikhoels's warning that "if we turn ourselves into a theater of translation, then to us, as a Jewish theater, there is nothing more to be done" as evidence that he would not be satisfied with only translations.[15] It seemed like more of a retreat than a leap forward. Mikhoels often reminded his audience of the theater's attempts in 1926–1927 to produce contemporary Soviet plays on revolutionary themes.[16] This deviation from the theater's path of development did not fit into the ascribed dialectical periodization. Further, it contradicted the estimation of Granovsky as an ardent counter-revolutionary. Behind closed doors, Mikhoels's defense of Granovsky was unwavering. Referring to the requirement of denouncing past excesses, he allegedly once remarked to Liubomirskii that "to dictate to the theater to deny its history is the same as dictating it to deny itself."[17]

Some outspoken critics shared Mikhoels's concern. For instance, Zvi Friedland had the audacity to deny that socialist principles could be extracted legitimately from Shakespeare. In *Literaturnaia gazeta,* he argued that the theater should return to Jewish tragicomedies:

> The combination of tragedy and comedy in the productions of the Jewish Chamber Theater played a great educational role for its audiences. It helped them purify their internal world from the remnants of capitalism. The role of the Jewish Chamber Theater has still not been adequately evaluated. This theater is a significant factor in the international education of the working masses.

Friedland continued that with *King Lear,* however, "the theater, it seems, has entered into a denial of itself."[18] He then singled out *Night in the Old Market* as one of the theater's finer productions, praising it for convincing the audience of the tragedy of the old Jewish life through an enjoyable performance. This was a stark contrast to the politically correct interpretation of the play, which regarded it as a text adulterated with mystical and religious dogma. Not surprisingly, Friedland's article provoked a repudiation in *Sovetskoe iskusstvo*.[19]

After the jubilee the theater completed its plan for the year 1935, which included a summer tour in which the theater played forty-two shows in Leningrad to a total of 70,000 spectators and performed nearly sixty shows in Ukraine.[20]

The Wailing Wall

The theater's repertory decisions over the following year reveal a great deal of uncertainty about its future. Between May 1935 and February 1936, no fewer than twelve different plays were announced in the press, including new ones by Kushnirov, Daniel, Bergelson, and Reznik; an adaptation of Babel's *Sunset;* and translations of Pushkin.[21] The theater's first play after the jubilee reflects much of this uncertainty. The new production, which premiered in November, was Shmuel Halkin's Yiddish translation of Lev Mizandrontsev's *Wailing Wall*, staged by Vasily Fedorov. Mikhoels was conspicuously absent from the production. The performance was entirely devoid of the type of symbolism and avant-garde theatrics that had characterized earlier productions. Even the music, composed by Moshe Milner, the musical director of the Kharkov State Yiddish Theater, sought to authentically recreate Middle Eastern melodies, while A. M. Gusiatinskii's realist art left little room for the audience's imagination.

The play's message was clear and straightforward. It was the theater's first specifically anti-Zionist production since *Benjamin*. However, this time rather than poke fun at the fantastical dreams of Zion, the play offered a more sober pedantic criticism of the perceived political implications of Zionism, representing an early manifestation of the motifs that characterized Soviet anti-Zionist propaganda after the creation of the State of Israel.[22] In particular, the play overemphasizes the role of Jewish capital in financing Jewish colonization of Palestine and equates the Arab population with the downtrodden proletariat, while the *khalutzim* (Jewish pioneers) are portrayed as capitalist imperialists. This was a stark contrast with the theater's earlier depictions of Jews. For fifteen years, the Yiddish theater had been stereotyping Jews as pitiable paupers and *luftmentshen*. Suddenly the very same Jews were transformed into the epitome of Western financiers, who, having already pillaged the wealth of the European proletariat, were beginning to look elsewhere for regions to exploit.

The play begins in the port of Jaffa as a group of Jewish colonizers from Germany disembark from their ship exuberantly singing Zionist songs. One such *oleh* (immigrant to Israel) is Leo Berns, a fictional German Jewish poet, who decides to settle in the colony Derekh Tikvah (The Road of Hope), where his brother resides. When he arrives he learns that his brother has been killed during an attempted expropriation of Arab land. Berns learns of the frequent Arab raids on the colony and is surprised at the extent of Arab-Jewish hostilities. At a meeting of the colony, he learns of the Jewish policy of appropriating Arab land with the ultimate goal of capturing the Wailing Wall (the last remaining wall of the second Jewish Temple) by annexing Jerusalem to a Zionist state. Only one member of the colony objects to the planned expropriation, for which he is summarily banished from the colony. The next act takes the audience to a neighboring Arab settlement, where the villagers realize they must defend their land with violence. The Jews take the initiative, however, with a pre-emptive strike against their Arab neighbors. In the final scene a lone Jew and Arab befriend each other and come to understand that they are not enemies. The only enemy is the Wailing Wall.[23]

Pravda, accentuating the struggle between the poor working Arabs and the rich bourgeois Jews, complimented Fedorov for not being distracted by the "Eastern exoticism" of Arab life and for adhering to "social truths," but criticized the play for weakly portraying the class differences among the Jewish immigrants.[24] This sentiment was shared by most critics, many of whom used the opportunity to lambaste the "bourgeois movement of Zionism" for its oppression of the "Arab proletariat."[25] One critic noted that "the audience knows from the papers that rich Jews are striving to buy up Arab land for the needs of colonists and that this has only led to a new explosion of national strife. All this is true. All this happened in actuality, but in the past authors have not properly provided all the details of contemporary life in Palestine."[26] Indeed, it was not easy to portray the struggle for Palestine—a land in which every stone is sacred for having been walked upon by prophets and a land whose own history provides the source of national awareness for countless peoples—as a class struggle in which national and religious connotations were only secondary.

Jewish Robin Hoods

Over the next two years, the theater presented two plays that drew from the folk tradition of social banditry. Eric Hobsbawm has defined "social bandits" as "peasant outlaws whom the lord and state regard as criminals, but who remain within peasant society and are considered by their people to be heroes, champions, avengers, fighters for justice."[27] Common figures in most cultures, bandits were ubiquitous in pre-revolutionary Russian popular culture; they symbolized the freedom of the individual over the strictures of society and the arbitrariness of tsarist law. The Russian folk heroes Stenka Razin and Emelian Pugachev both symbolize this spirit of revolt. However, as Jeffrey Brooks notes, social bandits were rare in Russian fiction.[28] Russian fictional bandits certainly challenged authority, but they did so out of gluttony rather than for the good of society. Social bandits were more common in Jewish folk traditions, where they realized the spontaneous rebellion of the poor against their oppressors.[29] They appeared in early *purimspiels,* in Sholem Asch's *Motke the Thief,* in Joseph Opatashu's *Romance of a Horse Thief,* and especially in Isaac Babel's *Benya Krik.* These stories told of "noble robbers" who fought to "right societal wrongs."[30] They exalted the egalitarianism of folk justice and heroized those who sought to mete it out.

Moshe Kulbak's (1896–1940) *Boytre the Bandit* was first performed in 1936 during the Yiddish theater's summer tour of Smolensk, Leningrad, Odessa, and the Donbass region; it premiered in Moscow in October. The play was based on Schiller's *Robbers,* in which the noble robber Karl Moor sacrifices his own life to save a poor man. The play was Mikhoels's first attempt to deal with pre-revolutionary Russian Jewish life since he became the theater's director. In his biography of Mikhoels, Matvei Geizer describes how the play was added to the repertoire:

> Once, in January 1936, while returning home after a performance, Mikhoels noticed a stalker. Some "strange character" followed him through the public garden of Tverskaia Street. Now when Mikhoels approached the door of his entrance, the "strange character" silently called to him: thin, dark eyes, very sweet and shy, he took a portfolio out of his briefcase and said: "I ask of you, read it. Just read. I don't dream of greatness and I don't expect anything." The stranger revealed himself to Mikhoels as somebody very familiar. It was the renowned Jewish poet, Moshe Kulbak, and in the portfolio was his play *Boytre the Bandit*.[31]

Born on a farming community near Vilna, Kulbak was one of the few Jewish intellectuals with practical agricultural experience. His poetry celebrated the return of Jews to the soil and promoted agricultural pursuits. Kulbak received a typical Jewish education, studying in *kheder* and then yeshiva. In 1919 he moved to the city of Vilna, and then Berlin. Although he was only in his early twenties, Kulbak's expressionist poetry was already being read throughout the Yiddish-speaking world by the time he returned to Vilna in 1923. Kulbak immigrated to Soviet Minsk in 1928, hoping to take advantage of what he thought were liberal cultural and political conditions in the Soviet state. During the 1930s, Kulbak turned to socialist realism and sought a more gentle humor in emulation of Sholem Aleichem. *Boytre*, written in 1933 and published two years later in the literary journal *Shtern*, was one of only two dramatic works written by the prolific writer. In addition to being performed at the Moscow State Yiddish Theater, the play was performed in 1937 at the Artef Theater in New York.

The play is set in the year 1829 during the reign of Tsar Nicholas I, a period remembered bitterly by Jewish victims of tsarist oppression. The plot centers around the conflict between the hero, Khaim Boytre, a Robin Hood–type folk thief, and Aron Wolf, the head of the *kahal* (Jewish communal government). Boytre's rebellion against the rabbinical kahalic authority begins when Wolf rejects Boytre's suggestion that the community raise money to help the poor and provide medication for the sick. Wolf insists that the *kahal* should respect the tsar's directives and concern itself solely with spiritual matters: "Jews are responsible at present only for peace within their home," he explains. "The king has insisted on this."[32] To spite the elder's intransigence, Boytre woos Wolf's daughter, winning her over by his courage in challenging the dominant authority. The poor and downtrodden celebrate their victory. The play ends, however, as Wolf summons mercenaries to attack Boytre, who is killed in the ensuing battle.[33]

Kulbak portrayed Jewish history in early nineteenth-century Russia as a "prison of nations." His Marxist interpretation of history was most evident in the illumination of class conflict within the Jewish community. The play scoffed at the vision of the *kahal* as a unified organization, highlighting instead the very real social conflicts permeating the institution.[34] It also addressed the inadequacies of national autonomy by showing how the nominally autonomous *kahal* was unable and unwilling to resist the evils of the tsarist regime. Kulbak suggested that protection from despotism cannot be found in national self-government, but rather must be sought in the international class consciousness suggested by Boytre's joint Cossak-Jewish partisan army. As Mikhoels explained, "In counterbalance to several of our old works that idealized the past and sketched it in mild lyrical tones, in this production the theater strives to show the accumulation of rage and the hate felt toward the oppressors."[35] The oppressors in this case were the rabbinical authorities who controlled the *kahal* and allegedly used their dominance over the organization to perpetuate the economic status quo. The *kahal* is portrayed as an institution whose very purpose is the maintenance of power for the privileged. Boytre's request that it use its influence to redistribute resources on an egalitarian basis threatens the very foundations of the institution and its power structure. Boytre's insistence that one's first loyalty must be to the community and not the family also conformed with contemporary Soviet demands that led young children to denounce their parents to the secret police.

On a less structuralist level, the play represents a continuation of the theater's more traditional themes—the ability of romantic love to overcome all obstacles and the conflict of generations. The play was not merely a front for a social ideological lesson, but was also an episode from real life. Thus, most observers classified the play as a romantic rather than a historical drama. For instance, Iakov Grinvald wrote that while it is set in a historical time frame, it is not a historical play: "It is a poetic play on a historical theme, in which we are given living historical sketches . . . a romantic drama."[36]

Stylistically, the play was the closest to Granovsky's method that the theater ever produced under Mikhoels's directorship. Mikhoels sought to recreate a *purimspiel* atmosphere. The play was full of exciting crowd and festive wedding scenes. Zuskin, as Boytre, played his first real non-comedic role and succeeded, according to all accounts. Mikhoels and Tyshler devised a mise-en-scène depicting the poverty and hopelessness of life in the Pale; somber colors in the backdrop contributed to the gloom of the setting. Tyshler was praised for finally abandoning any semblance of stylism and truly embracing realism.[37] Pulver also spiced his Jewish folk songs with more experimental, almost atonal, strains, producing an eerie feel devoid of the gaiety of traditional klezmer music.

The reaction of the press was tremendously positive. "In Kulbaks's play," raved one critic,

> the theater gave a genuine reproduction of Jewish life in the "prison of nations"—tsarist Russia. There we see the great social conflict between the Jewish rich and the Jewish poor. . . . The author has built a play on Jewish legends and has liberally used the rich folklore of the Jews. It has made the play accessible and comprehensible to a mass audience.[38]

Grinvald echoed him: "The Moscow State Yiddish Theater has given us a superb production. We highly recommend that not only Jews see it, but all of Moscow."[39] Critics also appreciated the revamped portrayal of shtetl Jewry, as the *luftmentsh* gave way to the bandit-hero. "*Boytre the Bandit* firmly rejects any of the idealization of the old life that can be found in the theater's prior works,"[40] wrote one critic. "There has not yet been on the Jewish stage a production on par with *Boytre the Bandit* in terms of the strength of its heroic inspiration," agreed *Izvestiia*.[41] Some, however, criticized the theater for returning to the old Jewish shtetl after having found moderate success in the portrayal of contemporary revolutionary movements with *Four Days* and *The Deaf*.[42]

M. Gershenzon's vaudeville *Hershele Ostropoler*, performed in 1937, again drew from the folk tradition of the noble robber and exalted the leveling of popular justice. In contrast to the violence of Boytre and typical folk bandits, Hershele Ostropoler was a cunning fool who helped the downtrodden and outsmarted the elites through his wits and chutzpah. The legends of Hershele were widespread throughout the Pale of Settlement; they were favorite stories of children and parents alike. Even Isaac Babel had featured Hershele in his short story *Shabos-nakhamu*.[43] Through his cunning, humor, and folkish charisma, Hershele could always be counted on to outmaneuver the rich in favor of the poor. In Gershenzon's adaptation, Hershele defeats the miserly moneylender Kalman. Berl, a young would-be groom who has starved himself for weeks to save enough money for a wedding ring, comes to Kalman, who is holding Berl's grandmother's ring as a pledge. Kalman insists on charging an exorbitant price for its redemption and is unwilling to compromise. Hershele then makes his appearance, promising to obtain the ring for the couple. He steals a golden cup, an umbrella, and a sack from Kalman. When Kalman brings a policeman to arrest Hershele for stealing the cup, Hershele replies that the moneylender is out of his mind; the cup does not belong to him. To prove his point, Hershele explains to the policeman that Kalman thinks everything is stolen from him, at which point, on cue, Berl enters holding Kalman's umbrella and Bunem, the bride-to-be, enters with Kalman's sack, sending Kalman into a frenzy and convincing the policeman that the moneylender is out of his wits. Berl receives his ring back and the wedding takes place with all the traditional merriment.

The play, which was Zuskin's first attempt at directing, received generally positive reviews. Grinvald appreciated the play as a simple, festive, life-affirming satire of the old shtetl life.[44] A. Khasin, reviewing the play for *Der emes*, wrote: "Here the gifted dramatist has the opportunity to create a character like the old Charlie Chaplin. For instance, here it was necessary to express artistically the entire range of folk buffoonery . . . and to combine the socialist character with the nationalist form of Jewish folk traditions." He praised Gershenzon for raising the folk text to a new dramatic level by adding realistic dialogue, pathos, and new comedic situations. However, Khasin felt that overall the production was a bit careless. This may have been due to Zuskin's inexperience or to the short period of rehearsals. But Khasin noted that the play demonstrated two very important points —first, that "Zuskin can and must work as a director," and second, that "actors like [Ilya] Rogaler and [Isaak] Lure who have until now only played episodic roles can play, and play well, lead roles."[45]

Jewish bandits and their ethos of folk justice, centered on a Robin Hood–like concern for the social welfare of the underprivileged, recreated the pastoral shtetl.

By drawing from epic themes, the plays of Gershenzon and Kulbak, like Babel's cycles, transformed the resigned and meek shtetl Jews into robust heroes. The bandits boldly challenge their oppressors and through sheer nerve bring justice to the people. However, popular justice and spontaneous leveling reeked of anarchism. It was not the means by which those who claimed to represent the conscious vanguard of the proletariat would reconstruct society. The Bolshevik version of history rejected the spontaneous redistribution of wealth, the "Black Repartition" that Russian peasants and populists had imagined would level society. The collectivization drive of the late 1920s and early 1930s had forcefully and violently demonstrated that individual paupers were not to appropriate the property of their former landowners. The means of production were not to be seized by the needy; rather, they were to be nationalized by the state according to a central plan. Further, the romanticization of folk violence implicit in Boytre's struggle for justice was intolerable to a regime which vehemently needed to preserve its own monopoly on violence. Thus, the notion of folk justice was rejected by the reigning power in favor of its own laws. This official rejection of the tendency to heroize and romanticize social bandits would eventually silence both those like Babel, who made a career of tales of violence, and those like Kulbak, who merely dabbled in the genre.

The Weasel and the Well

One night sometime in 1937, Stalin's right-hand man Lazar Kaganovich (1893–1991) attended a performance of *Boytre the Bandit*. After serving as a Party functionary in Turkestan, Kaganovich had risen quickly within the Party leadership under the personal patronage of Stalin himself. As head of the Ukrainian Communist Party from 1925–1928 and head of the agricultural section of the Party thereafter, Kaganovich was largely responsible for implementing collectivization. When he returned to Moscow in 1928, he was appointed to the Secretariat of the Central Committee, and in 1930 he became First Secretary of the Moscow Party Committee. During both collectivization and the Party purges, Kaganovich had proven his ability to effectively carry out Stalin's most ruthless orders, which earned him Stalin's unrivaled trust. It was not Kaganovich's sheer power, however, which most disturbed the Yiddish theater troupe. Unlike most official Party representatives who occasionally observed the theater, Kaganovich was Jewish and spoke Yiddish fluently. He had received a typical Jewish education in his native Ukrainian town of Kabana. His father was a tailor; his paternal grandfather a cantor. He was able to understand and appreciate every linguistic and cultural nuance. Further, despite his background, Kaganovich was not known to be a friend of the Jews.[46] One negative word from this illustrious guest, and the entire theater could be closed down and its participants arrested. Joseph Schein reports that during the curtain calls, Kaganovich was absent from his box—an ominous sign. After a private conversation with Mikhoels, he appeared backstage to chastise the theater:

> It is a shame to me, a shame.... Look at me, at what I am.... I am a Jew, my father was also one: exalted, bright, healthy. Why do you drag down such Jews on your stage? Deformed, lame, crippled?! . . . Such Jews summon sensations among the

audience. I want you to summon sensations of pride in today and yesterday with your plays. Where are the Maccabees [the leaders of the Jewish revolt in 160 B.C.E. who rededicated the Temple]? where is Bar Kokhba [the leader of the Judaic revolt against Roman rule in 132 C.E.]? . . . Where are the Birobidzhan Jews who are building themselves a new life?[47]

Schein described the reaction among those backstage:

Some of the younger members were hearing these names for the first time and did not understand what kind of Jewish revolutionaries he was talking about and demanding from the theater. For the elders it sounded like a provocation. Only an hour ago, nobody would dare even think about them for fear of being accused of nationalism or counter-revolutionary activity.[48]

It was one o'clock in the morning by the time Kaganovich left the theater. Despite the late hour, Mikhoels immediately contacted Halkin—the one writer whom he could rely upon to bring to life the heroic age of Jewish history on such short notice. Within months, Moshe Kulbak was arrested and his play was removed from the repertoire of the Yiddish theater. The author perished three years later in a Siberian labor camp.[49]

Kaganovich, indubitably acting with Stalin's support, had strong reasons for encouraging heroism. The glorification of the past was a theme whose growing prevalence was noticeable not only in Yiddish culture but also in Russian culture as a whole. With the rise of fascism in Germany, the dream of a worldwide social-ist revolution was firmly put to rest. The Soviet Union could no longer be pro-moted as a harbinger of world communism. On the other hand, by the late 1930s the political system in place was no longer threatened by internal enemies—Sta-lin's grip on power was virtually untouchable. Thus, Soviet propaganda largely abandoned the image of the Soviet Union as a bastion of communism keeping capitalist forces at bay. The new threat had little to do with economic forces and everything to do with German and Japanese military might. The upcoming battle was perceived as a war to preserve the Russian motherland from foreign enemies. Russian patriotism was promoted in conjunction with Russian chauvinism. For instance, on March 13, 1938 the Council of People's Commissars and the Central Committee approved a resolution authorizing the compulsory teaching of the Russian language in all schools.[50] In an effort to rouse the people's patriotism, the Soviet state saturated its propaganda with the historical heroism of the nation's defenders. Films such as Eisenstein's *Alexander Nevsky* drew from the distant past to resuscitate historical figures as models of patriotism. Personal valor and mili-tary might were the character traits most valued for the coming confrontation, and it was the goal of Russian and Yiddish culture to provide heroic examples of this type.

It did not take long for Mikhoels to construct his own rhetoric that glorified the Jewish past along the lines of Kaganovich's model:

The main question which is now brought to the attention of the Moscow State Yiddish Theater is the question of the [Jewish] people. The people are not like they have been portrayed in the past. The Jewish people are a powerful and healthy people, a people who have undergone thousands of years and have lived to be free, thanks to the great October Socialist Revolution, thanks to the nationality politics of Lenin and Stalin. . . . Heroism—this word represents for us the fundamental task.[51]

Kaganovich's chastisement came as a relief to Mikhoels, who had always expressed a great deal of pride in the Jewish past. Whereas previous references to the glory days of Masada and the Jewish revolts could only be surreptitiously inserted into his plays, Mikhoels was now being given license to openly proclaim his pride in Jewish heroism. Certainly the comic character of the *luftmentsh* had always appealed to Jewish sentiments, but few proud Jews could forget the halcyon days of the Maccabean revolt. Further, the authorization to explore historical themes freed the theater from the narrow confines of its previous repertory requirements. Since Mikhoels had become director of the theater, his repertoire had largely been confined to plays situated within a period of roughly thirty years, from the 1905 Revolution to the present. The cycle of productions portraying socialist construction and revolutionary enthusiasm, which never reached the aesthetic quality of the theater's earlier productions, was becoming even more stale. Kaganovich's proclamation thus unleashed in Mikhoels a barrage of emotions that materialized on the stage of the Yiddish theater. Grinvald recounts the ease with which this new vision was incorporated into the theater's repertoire:

> The Jewish theater, which is guided by Mikhoels, is beginning to see in its people not only poor, downtrodden, oppressed people, but also proud heroes, brave and selfless fighters for national independence, for freedom. Returning to the past, the theater finds in the history of the Jewish people the greatest military leaders, masculine, freedom-loving fighters with weapons in their hands, raised against the oppressors and enslavers. Moving toward the present with their new repertoire, which incorporates better productions of Soviet Jewish writers, the theater sees and shows its audience the current happiness of the Jewish people, clear examples of socialist construction, defenders of the Soviet homeland, and healthy, strong, new people full of optimism.[52]

Masculinity became a major theme in the Yiddish theater for the first time. The meek househusbands in perpetual fear of their overpowering dominant wives who had whimpered on the Yiddish stage for decades were replaced with robust, virile, gallant youth. This reworking of the male prototype is a familiar component of nationalist movements. Just as Soviet and German youth joined gymnastic societies under the belief that physical exercise was an integral component of *Bildung* or *kulturnost,* Jewish nationalists around the world sought to expand Jewish education beyond the *kheder* and into the gymnasium.[53] Zionist sports and gymnastics clubs in particular sought to produce, in Max Nordau's words, *Muskeljudentum* (muscular Jewry), physically capable of farming and defending the future Land of Israel.[54] In this sense, the Moscow State Yiddish Theater shared with Zionist culture a desire to remake the Jewish male. Both cultures looked toward the same historical episodes for inspiration: the Maccabean revolt, the Bar Kokhba revolt, and the pre-exilic Jewish state in Palestine.

Over the next two years, the troupe would present two plays situated in the halcyon days of pre-exilic Judaea in which the national content was foregrounded in both the text and the performance. The productions, *Shulamis* and *Bar Kokhba*, were both written by Shmuel Halkin and were based on plays by Goldfadn. No Yiddish author was better suited for the task of reviving Jewish national history than Halkin. Halkin has long been recognized as one of the most nationalist of Soviet Yiddish writers: "Among the Soviet Yiddish writers," wrote American Yiddish literary critic Nakhman Mayzel in 1958, "Shmuel Halkin has remained the most complex and sophisticated, the most profound and the most Jewish."[55] Noted Soviet Yiddish literary critic Aron Gurshteyn (1895–1941) agreed, noting that Halkin's poems "strove toward the threads of old Jewish culture, toward the metaphorical imagery of ancient Jewish literature, among which the Bible is given the first place."[56]

Halkin was born in the Belorussian town of Rogachev in 1897. His father, a lumber inspector, taught him a love of nature and philosophical appreciation for physical labor that would permeate much of his early writing. As a youth, Halkin began writing Hebrew poetry on the theme of nature. Fleeing the wartime devastation of Rogachev, Halkin moved to Kiev, where he met David Hofshteyn and Peretz Markish. It was there that he began to write in Yiddish, publishing his first poems in the Minsk literary journal *Shtern* in 1921. He moved to Moscow the following year. Between 1922 and 1935, Halkin published four original poetry collections. In contrast to the majority of Soviet Yiddish writers, Halkin rejected shtetl life as his primary subject matter, preferring instead biblical and historical themes. For this reason, he was criticized in 1929 by a group of proletarian literary critics led by M. Altshuler. Although Litvakov initially defended Halkin, when charges of nationalism resurfaced two years later Litvakov joined the critics and helped convince Halkin to recant his earlier work.[57] The author, however, found that his creative impulse was integrally linked to a national stimulus. Deprived of Hebraic motifs, Halkin found that he had difficulty writing. Although he continued to sporadically publish poetry in various anthologies and journals after 1935, he began in the mid-1930s to turn his attention to translations of European classics, most notably his translation of *King Lear*, and to adaptations of canonical works such as Goldfadn's plays.

Shulamis, perhaps Goldfadn's most famous play, was based on the legend "The Weasel and the Well." The legend, often cited as "one of the most popular and important stories in Jewish culture,"[58] traces its origins to Talmudic times.[59] The fable tells of a young woman who falls into a well while wandering in the desert. Her screams are heard by a young warrior who rescues her, falls in love, and vows to marry her after completing his campaign. In need of the two witnesses required by Jewish law to confirm an oath, the lovers decide to use the well and a nearby weasel. The warrior then breaks his vow and marries another woman, who bears him two children—the first of whom is killed by a weasel and the second of whom dies after falling down a well. Realizing that he is cursed, the warrior returns to and marries his betrothed, who has remained faithful, discouraging suitors by feigning insanity. The fable was eternalized by a Talmudic reference in which Rabbi Hanina uses it as an example to illustrate the importance of abiding by God's covenant. If a vow to a weasel and a well must be taken so seriously, he writes, imagine how earnestly one must adhere to a vow before God.[60]

The fable was first adapted into a play, *The Lovers of Zion,* in the early 1880s by Joseph Lateiner, a rival of Goldfadn's. Not to be outdone, Goldfadn quickly responded by writing his own play, under the title *Shulamis*—a reference to the heroine of the Biblical Song of Songs, usually interpreted by rabbinical commentators as a symbol for Zion or the Jewish people. First performed in the southern Ukrainian town of Nikolaev, Goldfadn's play was so popular it has since been performed in Yiddish, Russian, Ukrainian, Polish, Hungarian, and German. "Raisins and Almonds," a lullaby from the play, has become one of the most beloved of Yiddish songs. The original text was written during Goldfadn's so-called nationalist period, the point at which the playwright rejected Haskalah in favor of a more romantic nationalism. By setting the story in Biblical Judaea, Goldfadn was making a political statement in favor of the nationalist Zionist camp. The play is set against the backdrop of a war of national liberation as the Hebrews defend the Land of Israel from foreign invaders. While the Moscow State Yiddish Theater had previously performed plays by Goldfadn, it had never before attempted one from his nationalist years.

Before production on Halkin's adaptation even began, Litvakov waged a campaign against the play within the theater collective, eventually bringing several actors to his side. He berated Mikhoels for neglecting contemporary themes and for clinging to historical myths. He was likely also wary of Halkin's interpretation and eager to prove to the leftists who had attacked him in 1929 that he no longer supported Halkin's nationalism. Mikhoels ardently defended the production against his critics throughout the week-long assembly which met to evaluate the play. He argued that the play was chosen in response to Gorky's call at the 1934 Writers' Congress for literature that drew upon the folk traditions of the people. *Shulamis,* he maintained, was simply a historical work that depicted the efforts of two lovers to overcome the class antagonisms permeating the Jewish community. Mikhoels's efforts to premiere the production on time were relentless; he spent his days before the assembly listening to reproaches and his nights with the troupe in rehearsals that sometimes lasted until three in the morning.

When the play finally premiered—on schedule—Mikhoels and Halkin exceeded Litvakov's worst fears. Like Goldfadn's play, Halkin's version is set in Biblical Judaea. *Shulamis* thereby became the first play performed on the Yiddish stage, and the first major work by a Soviet writer, to be set in Biblical Judaea. Not only did Halkin revive the Jewish homeland for Soviet audiences, but he also reinvented the Jewish people. There are no *luftmentshen* in Halkin's world. On the contrary, the Jewish people are armed shepherds with the will and the strength to defend their land from powerful invaders. The play opens as a group of shepherds take up arms to defend Judaea against a fearsome invading enemy. They are inspired by the patriotic song of the folksinger:

> Bows and arrows—taught in the hand,
> Freedom must remain for our land.
> For our land and for our right,
> Judaea will not lack might.[61]

Halkin establishes in the very first scene the position that the Jewish state must protect itself from enemies by force of arms—a powerful and provocative assertion in the Soviet context of the late 1930s.

Like Goldfadn's text, Halkin introduces the shepherdess Shulamis, who follows her father Monoyekh on his way to war. Upon reaching the desert, Monoyekh instructs his daughter to return home. But first, he and the folksinger warn her to beware of the "well of the beloved two"—an innovation of Halkin's. According to the folksinger, a childless Canaanite man rich in sheep and cattle had come across a well in the desert while traveling with his veiled wife. When the two approached the well, his wife removed her veil to take a drink. As she was drinking, the shepherd caught a glimpse of his wife's unveiled face in the water's reflection and was so overcome by her beauty that he fell into the well.[62] This folktale, which does not significantly contribute to the plot of the play, was probably inserted as an allusion to the biblical Abraham. Not only is Abraham recognizable as the childless shepherd from ancient Canaan, but the tale itself is borrowed from a popular fable that tells of Abraham's journey from Canaan to Egypt. According to fable, Abraham was so pious that he never looked at his wife's face, until one day he caught a glimpse of her face reflected in a stream and was overcome by her beauty.[63] Halkin thereby surreptitiously brings Abraham into his play to prepare us for his next major innovation.

Predictably, after departing from her father, Shulamis, dizzy with thirst, falls into a well. She is saved by the great hero himself, Avessalom, who is on his way to Jerusalem to fight the enemy. Upon gazing at the face of Shulamis, the warrior immediately falls in love and pledges to return to marry her after his campaign. At this point, Halkin makes a drastic departure from both the Talmudic parable and Goldfadn's play. Rather than make their oath before the weasel and the well, in Halkin's version the two swear before the "heavens and the earth."[64] Thus, the entire ironic structure of the narrative is removed. In Halkin's play Avessalom will not have two children who are killed by a weasel and a well—it would be meaningless. This conspicuous alteration can be seen as an ellipsis, a marker indicating to those who are familiar with the parable that something is awry. Instead of the expected oath, the audience is confronted with a far more serious oath; in fact it is the very oath about which Rabbi Hanina warned in his commentary on the parable —a vow before God.

The oath before the heavens made in the Canaanite desert also alludes to the Biblical covenant between God and Abraham—the defining moment in Jewish history in which God is said to have granted the Jewish people the land of Israel in return for their eternal allegiance. Indeed, the Covenant has often been compared to a betrothal between Israel and God. In this case, God is represented by the heavenly witness to the oath and Shulamis, like her Biblical namesake, is a symbol

Shulamis, 1937. *Left to right:* S. Fabrikant as Tsingtang, Eda
Berkovskaia as Avigail, Mark Shekhter as Avessalom.
Photo courtesy of Ala Perelman-Zuskin.

for the people of Israel. The reference is strengthened by the folksinger's earlier
allusion to Abraham. The oath to the heavens and earth is also reminiscent of
Moses's song, "Ha'azinu," which begins the penultimate weekly portion of the
Torah with the phrase, "Give ear, O heavens, let me speak; Let the earth hear the
words I utter." The song, allegedly composed by Moses at the border of the Promised Land, celebrates the return of the Jewish people to Zion and the fulfillment
of God's promise to Abraham. By simultaneously alluding to both God's initial
covenant with Abraham and his ultimate fulfillment of the vow many generations
later, Halkin establishes a nationalist and religious subtext in his work. Seen in this
light, Halkin's play is transformed into a warning to those who believe that the
Covenant in the Canaanite desert can be broken without consequence.

Further, in Halkin's version Avessalom does not intentionally betray Shulamis by marrying another, but is forced into an arranged marriage with Avigail, a
Jerusalemite maiden, against his will. While this addition can be seen as an added
attack on the strictures of religious tradition, it can also be seen as a symbol for the
Jewish condition. Shulamis, as the betrothed, becomes a symbol for Zion—often
portrayed as a bride—while Avigail represents any substitute for the Promised
Land. Like Avessalom, the interpretation continues, the Jewish people were forcefully taken away from their beloved Zion and made to pledge allegiance to another.

Just as Avessalom can never be content with his new bride, so the Jewish people can never be content with the Diaspora or with a substitute for Zion—a possible reference to the Jewish Autonomous Region in Birobidzhan.

To underline this interpretation further, two characters were added to the text for its onstage performance—a talking dog and a talking cat—both of whom served as a chorus, accentuating the action taking place on the stage. Neither character is represented in Halkin's published text; both appear only in an unpublished addendum to the script. The two were largely extraneous, adding little to the plot development. Their addition was severely criticized by countless critics. Their presence in a production which was touted as a "historical" play—an already absurd classification given that the play does not represent a genuine historical episode and does not even take place in any clearly defined historical era—seemed to be nothing more than a rejection of the "historical" classification and an insinuation that the play had allegorical connotations. The only major function of the two animals in the plot was to remind Avessalom of his oath and help convince him to return to Shulamis. When the two animals hear of his marriage to Avigail in Jerusalem, the dog urges "We must remind Avessalom of the promise he gave to Shulamis. I am heading to Jerusalem. . . . I don't believe, I don't believe that in his heart the warrior can live as a traitor. I am going to Jerusalem to Avessalom. I suggest you follow me." The dog then proceeds to bark the musical "oath theme," linking Jerusalem (Zion) to the oath. This scene, which ends the second act, facilitates the reunion of the two lovers that forms the basis of the third and final act.[65] Thus, the just conclusion of the story is made functionally contingent on the journey to Jerusalem. Further, the simple utterance of the phrase "I am going to Jerusalem. I suggest you follow me," can be seen as a subtle hint, directed not only toward the dog's feline companion, but toward the entire audience. Indeed, it was common practice in Soviet Aesopian writing to express taboos by attributing them to another through quotation. In this case, the phrase is further distanced from the author by being attributed to a dog.

Shulamis exalted the freedom, romance, and heroism of pre-exilic Judaic life. Yet the majority of critics, failing to recognize the play's significance, praised the theater for abandoning the national limitations of the productions that had filled the stage during Granovsky's tenure. One critic wrote that "*Shulamis* has a profound significance for the theater's creative history. *Shulamis* signifies a novel improvement in the Moscow State Yiddish Theater's ideological and artistic growth. It is a new step on the path of reconsidering and surmounting its conception, which it inherited from its former director, Granovsky."[66] *Izvestiia* echoed this sentiment: "This performance will no doubt take its place in the history of Jewish theater as a step on the path of overcoming the traditions of national limitations, characterized by the list of its old plays."[67] This dichotomy can be attributed to the theater's publicists, who chose to deny the nationalist aspects of the play and touted it instead as a historical representation of the class struggle. Because the vast majority of theater critics and censors lacked the linguistic and cultural tools required to understand the complete text, they were forced to rely on the synopses provided by the theater, Mikhoels' public statements, and the Russian translations of each play that the theater submitted to its censors.

The only prominent critic with the linguistic and cultural tools necessary to appreciate the play's varied meanings was Litvakov, who published the first segment of his two-part review of the play over a month after its premiere—a suspiciously long delay. Hinting at the play's dichotomous meaning, he wrote:

> Why not set down to produce a new play, and a new production on a Soviet theme, or on a theme of the Revolution, of socialist construction, of the participation of Jews in the greater revolution? . . . *Shulamis* is the first alarm for the Moscow State Yiddish Theater. It is noted that the theater and, above all, Comrade Mikhoels must pay heed to the alarm and draw from it the necessary conclusions.[68]

Arguing that the "historical play" could just as easily be set in the days of King David or in post-biblical Israel, Litvakov was the only critic to question the historicity of the play. His review is punctuated with hints that he found the play inappropriate and even subversive. It was probably his uncertainty which led to the delayed review; Litvakov perhaps debated the merits of publicizing his conclusions. Alternatively, he could have been advised against such a course of action by his superiors. Nevertheless, Litvakov was satisfied with the stylistic elements of the production. He praised Mikhoels for discarding Granovsky's "stereotypical positions, gestures and mimics" and authoritarian methods, noting particularly the new director's willingness to allow the actors greater freedom in their interpretations. "In a word," he declared, "Mikhoels's system of expression is entirely different from that of Granovsky." He also praised Mikhoels for preventing the music from dominating the production: "The Moscow State Yiddish Theater is becoming a dramatic theater rather than an opera theater; it is a spoken theater, not a singing theater."[69]

Indeed, stylistically the production was fresh and gratifying. On a simple level the play represented a return to a typical theme of Jewish literature: a betrothed couple becomes separated as a result of an engagement made without their consent and are then reunited. Many actors were given their first leading roles, giving the troupe a new look, and Mikhoels's willingness to allow the actors to develop individually was producing concrete results. One critic ascribed the superior acting to the training the troupe had received in performing Shakespeare.[70] Many reviewers enjoyed the music and dance of the play.[71] Generally, the production was praised for being a refreshing return to the spontaneity of Goldfadn, rehabilitating the playwright from the reputation he had earned through Granovsky's stylized interpretation of *The Sorceress*.[72]

The new style was enhanced by the fact that the theater welcomed a new designer for the production. While Mikhoels had wanted Tyshler to continue as designer, the Committee of Artistic Affairs had vetoed his decision, appointing instead Vadim Ryndin, an artist famous for his design of Vsevolod Vishnevskii's *An Optimistic Tragedy* at the Kamerny theater in 1932. While Ryndin's colorful architectural sets were a worthy feat, they were inappropriate for a production in which the action unfolds in a desert and at a well. Some, however, failed to appreciate the irony. One critic wrote that Ryndin "was very successful in his laconic brevity and in painting the severe colors of the legendary biblical desert landscape and the graphic stylization of the ornaments in the foreground of the curtain." Others were less enthusiastic. One critic wrote that Ryndin did not understand the legend of Shulamis: "Everything [all the art] was done painstakingly but coldly; with talent but without emotion."[73] Despite these criticisms, the play had a long and successful run. Having pulled off its first nationalist production, the theater became even more daring for its next performance.

Bar Kokhba

In March 1938 the theater presented another production from Goldfadn's "nationalist" phase: Halkin's adaptation of *Bar Kokhba*. The choice was ironic in and of itself. It was Goldfadn's 1882 performance of this play which had purportedly led Alexander III to ban Yiddish theater. The fact that the play had been recognized, even by Alexander III, as a dangerously nationalist production immediately made it a controversial production for the Moscow State Yiddish Theater. For centuries, the rabbinic tradition had marginalized Bar Kokhba, emphasizing the failure of his call to arms while highlighting the teachings of his supporter, Rabbi Akiba. The emergence of a Bar Kokhba hagiography was precipitated by the Zionists' search for new national heroes. As one scholar has written:

> The transformation of Bar Kokhba from a dubious leader of a failed revolt to a prominent heroic figure from Antiquity is an important feature of the Zionist reshaping of the past. . . . While the rabbinical tradition tends to project a negative image of the leader of the failed revolt and to highlight his controversial character, the new Hebrew tradition portrays a heroic image of a courageous and resourceful man who succeeded in rallying the nation behind him in order to liberate it from oppressive Roman rule.[74]

The heroism of Bar Kokhba was revived by the Zionist movement and invoked repeatedly by prominent Zionists, from the Hebrew poet Chaim Nachman Bialik to the first prime minister of Israel, David Ben-Gurion. The Revisionist Zionist youth movement even appropriated the name of the site of Bar Kokhba's last stand—Betar. The Zionist projection of the hero was maintained not only by Kaganovich, who included Bar Kokhba in his call for new Jewish heroes, but also by Halkin and Mikhoels. In order to emphasize the break with traditional interpretations of the failed rebellion, a conversation about Josephus Flavius was inserted into the first scene of the text. Senator Lucius, an emissary from Rome, asks Bar Kokhba if he is familiar with Josephus's negative interpretation of Simeon Bar Giora, a controversial Jewish rebel who in 67 C.E. declared the freedom of all Jewish slaves, to which Bar Kokhba replies: "[Josephus] spread lies about us throughout Rome. He wrote his book in Rome and for Rome. For us he is a Roman and for Rome he remains a Jew. If you ask a child in the street he will know the name of Bar Giora."[75] Perhaps Halkin meant to imply that just as Josephus corrupted the heroic image of Bar Giora, so early rabbinical commentators had corrupted the image of Bar Kokhba. In his public statements, Halkin claimed that his interpretation of the uprising debunked the "myth" that it was a national movement and showed instead that it was a class rebellion. He claimed that his text emphasized that the rebels were comprised of lower-class artisans. Halkin claimed that rather than a Jewish uprising against the destroyers of the Temple, the uprising was fought on behalf of all the downtrodden who were enslaved by the imperialist Romans. Halkin also claimed to emphasize the internal conflicts within the Jewish community, particularly the struggle of the young fighters against the elders, who opposed the uprising for fear of surrendering their wealth and religious traditions.[76] "Bar Kokhba," wrote M. Shekhter, who played the lead role, "is the spirit of the people, reflecting their hopes and struggles for freedom. He is close to the people, always with the people. . . . His personal life, the personal happiness of Bar Kokhba, is dependent on the fate of the people and subordinated to the happiness of the people."[77]

These themes were reiterated by many critics who wrote about the production in Soviet papers. "The heroic poem of S. Halkin is one of the best dramatic works of Soviet Jewish literature and its high quality guarantees a successful production," wrote one.[78] Commentators believed that the play was particularly successful in its reinterpretation of the Bar Kokhba myth. "He [Halkin] strove not only to write a colorful episode of remote history," wrote another critic, "but also to present it to Soviet viewers through the prism of a Marxist historical understanding . . . to free Bar Kokhba from the captivity of lies put out by clerics and assimilationists."[79] Similarly, another warned that "the Zionists want to appropriate the glory of Bar Kokhba for themselves," but that thanks to Halkin the hero had been reinstated to his proper place in the Marxist canon.[80] *Pravda* saw the play as an affirmation that "the theme of the battle for freedom and independence is international."[81]

The play begins in a city square as Bar Kokhba and Hillel drill themselves in preparation for battle. Pnina, the daughter of Eliezer, an elderly rabbinical scholar whose submission to the Roman overlords is mocked by the younger generation, watches in admiration. Eliezer and the Roman overlord Lucius then arrive. As he approaches Bar Kokhba, Eliezer states, "Your power, Bar Kokhba, would be fitting for the study of Torah."[82] Lucius then questions Bar Kokhba, asking if it is true that he can catch stones, to which the warrior replies: "I don't only catch the stones, I throw back those stone that are aimed at me. You can be sure of that!" A worried Lucius waits until he is alone with Eliezer before assessing the situation: "He speaks against Rome and will not be satisfied with talk. He is leading the entire youth down that road; also many elders are among them." When Lucius asks Eliezer whether he, too, would fight with Bar Kokhba, the old rabbi replies: "My good, sir, such accusations are groundless."[83]

The first scene sets the tone for the rest of the play: Bar Kokhba is portrayed from the start as a clever, well-educated warrior—self-assured and confident, yet still intent on training himself and others through vigorous physical exercise. In contrast, Eliezer indicates from his first words that he opposes the rebellion. However, the people side with Bar Kokhba. As one enthusiast explains to Eliezer: "Be-

169

tween you, Rabbi, and the people a wall has arisen."[84] Repeated references to both
Eliezer's age and Bar Kokhba's youth firmly establish a generational conflict. Anti-
religious themes also permeate the play. Eliezer, the rabbi, is portrayed as a traitorous villain who prefers to retain his position under Roman sovereignty rather than
risk his livelihood for his people's freedom. Bar Kokhba, on the other hand, gives
no thought to God. When the rabbi blesses his troops, Bar Kokhba snaps: "God!
Only do not help our enemies. For us, we can do without your help."[85]

With the next scene, set in a blacksmith shop, Halkin establishes the working-class origins of the rebellion. The audience is also introduced to a token non-
Jew who supports the rebellion. But the theme of internationalism is never fully
developed, despite the theater's claim that it was radically reinterpreting the story
as an ecumenical rebellion. Non-Jews play no significant role in the revolt. This
does not stop Bar Kokhba from defending the rights of the non-Jews within his
kingdom, but they become beneficiaries of the rebellion only through Bar Kokhba's
justice and impartiality. The victorious Jewish leader grants equality to his non-
Jewish subjects as a privilege; they do not earn it as a right. This becomes evident
after Bar Kokhba's initial victory, when one of his assistants issues a decree ordering the expulsion of the Syrians from the land. Bar Kokhba chastises him: "Where
do you get the right to give this order? . . . Not only Jews are fighting with us, but
also Greeks, Syrians, all those who are not content with Rome fight together with
us. . . . The Syrians and the Parthians and the Greeks, they want to be free from
Rome just like we do."[86]

Although Halkin makes it clear that non-Jews will benefit from the rebellion,
the crucial decision to take up arms is made solely by Jews for the benefit of Jews.
Eliezer's assessment of the situation is based on his impressions of Jewish suffering rather than class oppression. As he states in the second act, during which the
decision to go to war is made:

> I have traveled the entire land
> From border to border.
> I have also been in foreign lands where Jews live—
> There all is over:
> Many who never even dreamt of war,
> Are now ready to take up swords.[87]

Bar Kokhba replies with the language of war:

> The time has come. Enough talk!
> Because if not today,
> Who knows if tomorrow will already be too late?
> The battle cry: the time has come
> To free ourselves from the Roman yoke.[88]

This call to arms is soon followed by a stage direction indicating the exclusive
participation of Jews: "A struggle. Bar Kokhba arrives armed and throws himself
directly into the melee. . . . From all sides armed Jews enter." Bar Kokhba then
addresses the assembled Jews:

My brothers! I look at you
Perhaps in numbers we are few
Less men than the enemy, fewer arms we bear,
Only with my head and right hand I swear
And let us all in a single voice vow:
With our arms, we will defeat him now.[89]

As the assembled Jewish fighters prepare to depart, Rabbi Akiba lays his hands upon Bar Kokhba and blesses him, to which Bar Kokhba responds:

I swear by your name, Simeon Bar Giora,
I swear by all the holy beloved names,
For you, for us—for all, we will take revenge![90]

By alluding to Bar Giora and the other "holy beloved names," Halkin places the Bar Kokhba rebellion within the context and tradition of Jewish revolts against Roman oppression.

The musical score, choreography, and art of this scene emphasized that only Jews undertook the rebellion. Tyshler, who returned to the theater after Ryndin's brief tenure as designer, was condemned for constructing a simple set of palm trees and ancient ruins, alluding to the destruction of the Jewish Temple, the stimulus that provoked the Jewish revolts.[91] Pulver drew all his musical themes from Eastern European Jewish folk music rather than attempt to reproduce music from the era of the play's narrative, as he had done in several previous productions. "Pulver's music," wrote Potapov, "was, as always, melodious, but the composer did not find his niche in this performance. It is difficult to blame him for relying on folklore, for hardly any musical documentation is preserved from the period, but the music should be closer to the theme of the production."[92] Zhivov suggested that the play would have been more successful without music and dance altogether.[93] Aron Gurshteyn wrote that despite the success of Halkin's text, the aesthetic presentation of the play was somewhat "distasteful." "Why do Jews suddenly break into a dance when they are called upon to revolt?" he asked. "The people call to rebellion, they prepare themselves for a battle, and suddenly a dance—this suggests that these are a strange people."[94] This comment seems somewhat inappropriate for a musical based on song and dance. Perhaps Gurshteyn, a specialist on Goldfadn who would have noticed the inconsistencies in Halkin's "reinterpretation" of the play, was using this general critique of the musical genre to hint at a more substantial criticism of the production.

Other diatribes against the anachronism of using folk material in a historical production support the hypothesis that the song and dance were intentional non sequiturs with allegorical implications. The anachronistic song and dance could have served as a marker for the audience, indicating an ulterior message. While Bar Kokhba calls upon all oppressed peoples to join in his rebellion, the distinctly Eastern European Jewish dance that signifies inclusion in the group essentially excludes the participation of non-Jews, marginalizing their role in the rebellion. The idea of ancient Parthians joining in on the Hasidic-style dance would have appeared absurd to any audience. Through this technique, the theater may have

Aleksandr Tyshler's sets for *Bar Kokhba*, 1938.

sought to emphasize the Jewishness of the uprising while maintaining publicly that the uprising was ecumenical.

The final scene, which depicts the melee between the rebels and the Romans, also emphasizes the national element of the uprising. The battle is fought between the Jews and the Romans (there are no non-Jewish rebels present), while rich and poor Jews alike die for the cause. Bar Kokhba's last words, also the final words of the play, pay tribute to his people, his folk: "He who dies for freedom for his people is destined to remain alive forever. In battle, in battle! The battle is not yet over." As the curtains close, a fellow rebel kisses the hero, alluding to the Biblical parable that recounts how God recalled Moses to heaven with a kiss.[95] Bar Kokhba thereby is equated with Moses, the most important Jewish prophet, who led his people from slavery in Egypt to freedom in the Land of Israel. Once again, Mikhoels succeeded in using "national form" to promote nationalist content.

The Conscious Family

In addition to patriotism, Soviet culture of the mid-1930s sought to instill optimism and a sense of stability in the population. The kinetic energy of the revolutionary years, epitomized by the utopian projects of the futurists and other avant-garde artists, was repudiated, as were the individuals who supported it. Stability replaced dynamism as the overarching value of the regime. The June 1936 prohibition on abortion, for instance, represented a return to conservative family values that emphasized familial responsiblity.[96] Following Stalin's famed statement that "life is getting better, life is getting happier," the betterment of life became a dominant theme in Soviet culture. Artists painted cornucopian images of pastoral life, rife with mirthful peasants, while daring aviators conquered the sky on the silver screen. Citizens were encouraged to interpret their surroundings in light of the radiant images projected in novels and on stages while ignoring the view outside their own windows. Socialism, Stalin declared, had been achieved and won. In this mythical best of all possible worlds, there were no longer innately evil provocateurs and saboteurs. All individuals were capable of goodness under socialism. Those who sinned did so simply because they had fallen under negative influences, often portrayed as the work of foreign agents. Everybody could be reformed—could reach a state of revolutionary consciousness—with proper breeding. Rapid pardons came to those who recanted their past transgressions—at least on the stage and screen.

The Moscow State Yiddish Theater's productions of Peretz Markish's *Family Ovadis* and Sholem Aleichem's *Tevye the Dairyman* both highlighted the optimism of the Jewish people, but from a particularly Judaic philosophical and sociological perspective. From a structuralist perspective, these plays resemble contemporary socialist realism. Their plots parallel those of *Chapaev* and *Mother,* as described by Katerina Clark: "the tale of how an ignorant, superstitious peasant progresses in 'consciousness' and knowledge under the tutelage of a formed and 'conscious' mentor."[97] Both plays, however, deal with human suffering from what is essentially a Jobian perspective, a philosophical quandary that has permeated

Jewish thought for centuries. Like the biblical Job, the lead characters accept their suffering and question its causes while retaining an essential faith in the goodness of their world.

Like *Shulamis* and *Bar Kokhba,* these productions exalted Jewish life; but they differed from Halkin's plays in that they drew from themes popular in pre-revolutionary Yiddish secular writing rather than ancient Hebraic lore. They centered on the conflict of generations within the family rather than national uprisings and wars of independence. On one hand, this shift can be seen as a weakening of national significance because the plays move away from the halcyon days of Jewish national existence. But on the other hand, it can also be interpreted as an even greater exclamation of national endurance in its affirmation of the continued distinctness of the Jewish community in modern times. It was one thing to portray a united Jewish nation in antiquity but quite another to imply that the Jews remained a distinct society in the contemporary Soviet Union.

The protagonists of both plays were characters reared in the shtetl whose children choose instead to embrace the newer radical ideology of socialism. The older generation is confronted with the choice of either rejecting their children or accepting the deterioration of their time-honored traditions. Both plays emphasize the perseverance of the traditional Jewish family. The emphasis on family life in general and marriage in particular was representative of Jewish traditional values. Since the beginnings of Yiddish literature, the family had been the center of nearly all narratives, while every great Yiddish story ended with a wedding. As David Bergelson wrote in 1945, "Among Jews, a nation that has long been unable to enclose itself with territorial frontiers, the next value—that is the family—has been strengthened even more. Hence the particular significance of family life among Jews; hence the particular affectation with which they marry off their children."[98]

Peretz Markish's *Family Ovadis* premiered on November 7, 1937, the twentieth anniversary of the Revolution. In 1936 Markish had been urged by the Committee of Artistic Affairs to write a play on the topic of Birobidzhan.[99] The project of establishing a Jewish Autonomous Region in Birobidzhan, a region in the southeastern extreme of Siberia, was initiated in 1928 by Mikhail Kalinin, the president of the USSR. The goal of using the region as a solution to the 2,000-year-old Jewish exile was supported by Dimanshtayn and the Jewish Section; it even got backing from some American Jewish organizations. Others, however, saw the project as a transparent attempt to exile the Jewish population to the margins of civilization and as competition for the Zionist project. Between 1928 and 1933 nearly 20,000 Jews migrated to the region, 60 percent of whom quickly returned to western Russia. In 1934 the region was officially designated a Jewish Autonomous Region and attempts to encourage migration increased. But the Jewish population never exceeded 20,000 and Jews remained a minority in the region.[100] Although Markish's play glorifies the region in accordance with contemporary propaganda, there are indications that the author's own sentiments were quite different. In 1934 Markish visited the region but was unimpressed with what he saw:

"What type of stupid Jew would move to Birobidzhan from Moscow?" he asked during his 1952 interrogation. "I did not believe that any intelligent Jew would go to live in Birobidzhan when they have everything here."[101] Perhaps it was for this reason that Markish set his original text in an unnamed borderland. For its performance at the Moscow State Yiddish Theater, though, the action was moved to Birobidzhan. Once given the order to publicize Birobidzhan, Soviet Jewish luminaries were unanimous in their public support.[102]

The play revolves around Zayvl Ovadis, played by Mikhoels, and his five sons: Motka, a Party worker; Shleymka, a border guard; Borukh, a factory worker; Kalman, a lumberman who works with Zayvl; and his eldest son, who has emigrated to Palestine. The play begins as the family prepares for Kalman's wedding. As they anxiously await news from Shleymka, they receive instead a letter from Zayvl's eldest son, who wishes to return to his Soviet homeland. The letter sparks a debate within the family as Avram, Zayvl's father, laments the hard life of Jews in the Soviet Union, pointing to the fact that their town does not even have a train station. Motka reminds Avram of the situation of Jews in the rest of the world: "Do you really think the Germans or Poles or Romanians are patting the Jews on the back? And in Palestine they don't slaughter Jews?"[103] On the wedding day, the family finally receives the long-awaited news of Shleymka. But the news is tragic—he has been killed in a border dispute while fighting for the Red Army. The wedding seems to be ruined and the newlyweds cursed until Motka justifies his brother's martyrdom: "Shleymka did not die, father. . . . Shleymka gave his life for himself and for all of us because twenty years ago others gave their lives for him. He is not dead. . . . He will forever live in the hearts of all."[104] Motka is right, the family realizes, and the death turns into a blessing for the newlywed couple as they decide to enlist in the Red Army to begin a new and better life. In the final dramatic scene—which takes place in the newly built local train station—the commander of the Red Army hands Kalman his dead brother's rifle with the words, "By command of our people's committee, the rifle of the fallen hero of the frontier guards, Ovadis, is given to his brother Kalman Ovadis to defend the border of our socialist fatherland. . . . So, Kalman Ovadis joins in today's patrol for Stalin."[105] The play ends with Zayvl coming to terms with the new socialist "truth."

The story exhibited many traits common to socialist realist fiction. Most important, it is ritualized to conform to the master plot identified by Katerina Clark. It is the tale of how a naive simpleton gradually emerges into a state of revolutionary consciousness with the guidance of a mentor. Zayvl's skepticism toward the changes occurring around him is assuaged as he comes to realize, with the help of his sons, that he can be truly free only under socialism. Further, the heroic ending of the play was a common structure of socialist realist fiction of the 1930s. As construction on the long-awaited train station is completed, a ceremony is performed in which the torch carried by the martyred Shleymka is transferred to his brother Kalman, who in a graveside oath promises to continue his brother's quest.[106] Markish's play also adheres to the Party line on Birobidzhan, despite the myth's gross inaccuracy. The actual arduous conditions and barren surroundings of the region are invoked only in the bitter ramblings of the grandfather. Instead, the district, which over half of all Jewish colonizers had abandoned by the play's premiere, is depicted in purely fantastical terms.

While deriving key elements from official paradigms, however, the play forms its own independent master plot, derived primarily from a Jewish context. Ubiquitous themes in Russian literature of the period—epic quests, "tractor romances," and conflicts with nature—are notably absent from the play. Most socialist realist literature was structured around occupational units—the factory, the collective farm, or the military unit. Most Jewish contributions, on the other hand, followed the model of family sagas, in which the family unit becomes a microcosm for society. The character of Zayvl was a complex psychological portrait. Brought up in

Solomon Mikhoels as Zayvl Ovadis in *Family Ovadis,* 1937. Photo from Solomon Mikhoels, *Stati, besedi, rechi.*

the former Pale of Settlement, Zayvl lacks the means to comprehend the changes occurring around him. Although he cannot blame his eldest son for being lured by Zionist promises, he sympathizes more with his younger sons, who seek a niche for themselves in their homeland. "For forty years I have been walking on a path, on a foreign path . . . and the foreign path has become my own, and my children have become foreign," he laments.[107] Zayvl's lament is clearly a reference to the forty years that the ancient Israelites spent in the desert before reaching the Promised Land. Like the Jews of Exodus, Zayvl realizes that his life is a life of wandering. His generation will not live to see the Promised Land—that privilege must await the next generation. Birobidzhan will never be Zayvl's Promised Land; it will always remain a "foreign path." Thus, the central theme, from a structuralist perspective, can once again be reduced to the conflict of generations. The Birobidzhan setting is merely a skeleton in which the universal theme of alienation of parents from their children is inserted. Seen from this perspective, the play's structure resembles that of *King Lear* more than that of *Chapaev*. Markish himself emphasized this point: "In a certain way he [Mikhoels] changed the idea of the dramatic material, stripping it down to the most base conception of the production. Thus, the grandfather becomes the [head of the] entitled nest, from where the son and grandchildren are separated. He established the conflict of generations."[108]

Once again, the theater succeeded in preserving its favorite character type—the old shtetl Jew—while ostensibly embracing the revolutionary youth. As had been the case countless times before, the theater was faulted for its overly sympathetic portrayal of the dying generation. One reviewer wrote that "the basic deficiency in *The Family Ovadis* is that the younger generation is reduced to a type, the young hero of the play lacks individuality."[109] Clearly Mikhoels's poignant and lyrical portraits of the old Jewish life were not easily transferable to the new revolutionary youth. Even those who appreciated the play emphasized the pathos Markish evoked for the Jewish past: "Peretz Markish is one of the most talented contemporary Jewish poets. . . . He knows the Jewish people very well, their past and present . . . and because Markish feels and understands the past of his people, he can sketch their future. . . . *The Family Ovadis* is one of the best performances of the Moscow State Yiddish Theater's entire history, one of the most meaningful productions by Soviet dramaturgists."[110] "Without doubt," wrote another critic, "the honor goes to Peretz Markish. On the stage of the Jewish theater he brought forth living people."[111]

This pattern was repeated the following year with the theater's production of Sholem Aleichem's *Tevye the Dairyman*, performed in honor of the eightieth anniversary of the writer's birth. The epic-length play—it lasted nearly five hours—was to become one of the theater's most memorable performances in its history. After a ten-year hiatus, the theater returned to Sholem Aleichem and his poignant picture of the Jewish shtetl. The rehabilitation of Sholem Aleichem can be attributed primarily to the newly raised status of the Yiddish humorist's supporter, Maksim Gorky, who once wrote of Sholem Aleichem that he is "an exceptionally talented satirist and humorist."[112] Armed with Gorky's quotations, Soviet literary critics reassessed their attitudes toward the writer who was once criticized for romanticizing pre-revolutionary Jewish life. Commentators apologized for erroneously labeling Sholem Aleichem a naive humorist, for only seeing the dreams of his shtetl heroes but none of their sufferings, and for missing the author's satirical side, in which he embedded socialist messages into his work. One critic wondered how the writer now recognized as a revolutionary prophet could have been interpreted merely as "a good-natured humorist who stands on the sidelines of the battle."[113] Now they saw in Sholem Aleichem's characters heroic models for the New Soviet Man. "Tevye," Mikhoels explained, "is a profound example of the people. . . . In our theater we searched for and found a healthy animated life, which we brought to this great folk presentation."[114] The new approach to Sholem Aleichem was reflected not only in the plays of the Yiddish theater, but also in the festivities and observances that surrounded the celebration of what would have been Sholem Aleichem's eightieth birthday in 1939.[115]

Tevye, one of Sholem Aleichem's most famous plays, was popularized contemporaneously in the United States through Maurice Schwartz's motion picture of the same name. The play achieved world fame in 1964 when a musical version by Sheldon Harnick and Jerry Bock opened on Broadway under the title *Fiddler On the Roof*. The well-known story line involves a poor dairyman, Tevye, living in a late nineteenth century Russian shtetl, whose daughters each choose to reject his traditional Jewish lifestyle by marrying for love outside the community. In the version performed at the Moscow State Yiddish Theater, Hodl marries Perchik, a revolutionary whom she follows to Siberia; Khava marries a Ukrainian peasant; and Beylka marries a wealthy miser. The play ends with the eviction of the Jewish community from the shtetl by tsarist police.

The opening mise-en-scène, devised by Isaak Rabinovich, depicted a poverty-stricken peasant hut surrounded by a breathtaking pastoral setting. Tevye exits the hut through its splintery wooden door, stares at the clear blue sky longingly and exclaims "Oh Lord!" before slowly mounting his gaunt horse to begin his daily deliveries. This scene became a recurring theme of the play. The door of the hut is repeatedly opened and closed as people come and go throughout the play; each of Tevye's beloved daughters will leave through that door. The door represents both a real and a metaphorical division between the poverty of traditional Jewish life, represented by Tevye's decrepit home, and the prosperity of the socialist future, represented by the pastoral scene outside. Tevye's constant appeals to God simultaneously reflect his own doubts and hopes. While he knows he will never get a reply, he persists in this futile exclamation. Tevye is not a dreamer; he expects nothing more from the world than his lot. He is not a *luftmentsh* like his cousin, Menakhem Mendl. He is a family man burdened with a real job. In the words of one critic: "Menakhem Mendl wanted to become like [Israel] Brodsky [1823–1888, a rich Jewish industrialist], but Tevye did not dream of this. He knew that Brodsky is Brodsky and Tevye is Tevye."[116]

But Tevye and his simple faith did not make the transition to socialist realism unscathed. Rather than using Sholem Aleichem's original text—he had turned the popular story into a play in 1915—Mikhoels used an adaptation of the text

Solomon Mikhoels as Tevye in *Tevye the Dairyman,* 1938.
Sets by Isaak Rabinovich. Photo from Solomon Mikhoels,
Stati, besedi, rechi.

composed by Oyslender and Dobrushin. M. Zhivov once asked why the theater
used an adaptation rather than the original text.[117] The answer was clear: Sholem
Aleichem's story of Tevye was a humorous portrait of shtetl life, not a model of
socialist realist art. It took Dobrushin and Oyslender's adaptation to turn it into
one. As Jacob Weitzner recently noted, "Tevye's amused and skeptical attitude
toward the 'whole they called revolution, the good of the collective, the triumph of
the working class' disappeared."[118] In Sholem Aleichem's version, Tevye's love for
his daughters and concern for their happiness obliges him to accept their decisions,
helping him overcome the traditions he values most in life. In Dobrushin and
Oyslender's version, however, Tevye does not come to this decision through his
own reflection. He is not motivated by a love and respect for his daughters' judgment; rather Perchik—the trained revolutionary and the vanguard of the proletariat—convinces him of the merits of dialectical materialism. This new device
firmly places Sholem Aleichem's story within the canon of socialist realist fiction
as the protagonist achieves socialist consciousness with the guidance of a mentor.

Tevye also exemplified socialist realism in its staunch optimism. Faced with
numerous obstacles, both prosaic and dramatic, the socialist realist positive hero

Solomon Mikhoels and Leah Rom in *Tevye the Dairyman,* 1938.
Photo from Solomon Mikhoels, *Stati, besedi, rechi.*

retains his confidence in the progress of socialist construction. Tevye's faith in humanity is equally steadfast. Comparing Tevye to the biblical Job, who refuses to abandon his faith in God despite a series of tragedies that befall him, the critic S. Nels wrote that he was inspired by "the inexhaustible folk optimism of Mikhoels's heroes who have sustained the deepest tragedies."[119] "Of course this optimism," explained Mikhoels, "is not accidental. In this optimism is enormous strength, the strength of the people."[120] Sholem Aleichem aided the artist in his ultimate goal: "to infect [the workers] with a flame of passionate hope."[121]

The new version also treated relations between Jews and gentiles from a more Soviet perspective, emphasizing the "friendship of nations." Much of the prejudice in Tevye's attitude toward the conversion of Khava was removed from the play. For instance, as Weitzner observes, "Sentences that expressed the comical tension between Tevye's traditional Jewish outlook and the Gentile world were cut."[122] Similarly, a new segment was added in which, after being evicted by the tsarist police, Tevye forms a friendship with his Ukrainian neighbors, and together they realize that the source of their difficulties is the tsarist regime. Pulver's music, which combined authentic Ukrainian motifs with traditional Jewish tunes, also helped to emphasize the unity between the oppressed Ukrainian and Jewish populations of the Pale. In his composition, Pulver built upon the Jewish ethnomusicological work of Moshe Beregovskii, who had written several articles on the affinities between Ukrainian and Jewish folk music.[123] By incorporating Beregovskii's work into the play, Pulver emphasized the fraternity between the Jewish and Ukrainian peoples. This type of synchretic structuralism that searched across ethnic boundaries for cultural and linguistic similarities was a common attribute of contemporary Soviet academia, epitomized by the Japhetic theory of the linguist Nikolai Marr (1864–1934).[124] It was also a path often chosen by Soviet Jewish artists who attempted to balance themselves between the crime of "national nihilism," a denial of one's national history, and "bourgeois nationalism," undue emphasis on one's national history.[125]

From its first performance, the response to the play was radically different than responses to the theater's plays of the previous five years.[126] Kh. Tokar wrote in *Sovetskaia ukraina:*

> This production does not resemble at all the old plays of Sholem Aleichem or of the Moscow State Yiddish Theater. In the previous productions there were only attacks, even malice, insults to the old shtetl way of life. In reading anew Sholem Aleichem, the theater spotted and picked out a close-up of Tevye. . . . This production, apart from the directorial success of Mikhoels, brought creative satisfaction to the entire collective. They are not the masks of the Moscow State Yiddish Theater on the stage; they are living, lush, realistic types. People speak simply, honestly, warmly, and sincerely.[127]

Moshe Khashchevatskii called it "the Moscow State Yiddish Theater's best work in years, one of the best efforts of all Soviet theatrical art."[128] Eidelman echoed: "This production deeply touched the literary and theatrical society of Moscow and met with the warmest reception among the mass audience. . . . *Tevye the Dairyman* is not only one of the greatest successes of the Moscow State Yiddish Theater, but of all Soviet theatrical art."[129] Markish wrote that with Tevye, Mikhoels "finally crowned the entire path of his actorial and directorial art."[130] Itzik Fefer, writing in *Der emes,* praised Dobrushin and Oyslender for purging the play of its old interpretation while retaining "the purity of Sholem Aleichem's humor" and "the profound lyricism of the work."[131] The play was so popular that special performances were regularly given, including a radio montage[132] and a special showing at the Palace of Culture in Moscow.[133]

Both *Tevye the Dairyman* and *The Family Ovadis* resemble the prototypical socialist realist novel of the late 1930s. From a narratological perspective, they follow many of the structural elements typical of the socialist realist novel. Most important, the plays follow the development of their protagonist from naivete into a state of revolutionary consciousness, as he gradually comes to understand and accept the new "truths." Both plays also instill in the audience a profound optimism both in humanity's potential to reform and in the "victory of socialism." Tevye manages to retain his faith in humanity, and particularly in Jewish humanity, despite the series of crises that mar his path. He is indeed comparable to the biblical Job, only his faith lies in the spirit of the people rather than in God; the Jobian theme is transposed to a Soviet context. Both plays also underscore official

Solomon Mikhoels as Tevye. Photo courtesy of Ala Perelman-Zuskin.

interpretations of the events they characterize. Just as *Family Ovadis* echoed newspaper accounts of Birobidzhan, *Tevye the Dairyman* portrayed shtetl life as morally bankrupt and poverty-stricken. The Jews are given no respite from the afflictions of tsarist Russia; their pathetic existence is made bearable only by the people's optimism.

Like *Family Ovadis*, though, *Tevye* firmly retains its "Jewishness." Again the play was framed around the traditionally Jewish family unit. The theme of both plays, the conflict of generations, allowed the theater to portray the otherwise taboo subject of pre-revolutionary Jewish life. The traditional Jew was portrayed with a pathos absent in the portrayal of the younger generation. Both plays evoked sympathy for the elder generation and their traditional Jewish lifestyle while portraying the youth as stick figures devoid of psychological depth. The poignant portraits of Tevye and Zayvl, which were particularly acute in the sections of the plays before they accepted the values of the new world, were uncharacteristic of the pre-conscious hero. While the two eventually come to terms with the new way of life, their characters remain firmly within the old lifestyle. Other motifs common to Jewish secular literature permeate both plays. For instance, a wedding, a ubiquitous motif in Yiddish literature, serves as the setting for the climax of both plays: in *Tevye,* his daughter's marriage to Perchik introduces the hero to the mentor, while Shleymka's death before the wedding in *Family Ovadis* helps Zayvl realize the importance of the cause for which his son was martyred.

A Nation among Nations

The Moscow State Yiddish Theater embraced Gorky's call for folklorism. This license gave the theater the opportunity to move away from both stale depictions of socialist construction and Civil War in the Soviet Union and from translations of European classics. After a brief period of readjustment, the theater began celebrating pre-revolutionary Jewish folk heroes and exalting the popular justice of social bandits and pranksters. These plays, however, were merely kitsch —they divorced the folk motifs from the nationalist ideology behind them; they appropriated national signifiers, but left behind the signified. Ironically, it was one of these productions—Moshe Kulbak's *Boytre the Bandit*—that impelled Lazar Kaganovich to chastise the theater. Kulbak's subsequent arrest, along with many other members of the Minsk group with which he was associated, forced the theater to remove the play from its repertoire and redirect itself. Kaganovich's warning to the theater, however, may have been motivated by politics as well as by aesthetics. Perhaps Stalin's closest associate had foreknowledge of the arrest of Kulbak and sought to warn Mikhoels to avoid any association with the doomed writer. In order to prevent the purge of Kulbak and the Minsk group from spreading to the Moscow State Yiddish Theater, Kaganovich had to put an immediate end to the production of *Boytre the Bandit.* In the process, he heralded the theater's new approach to Jewish national themes.

In 1936, Bolshevik artists and writers began probing pre-revolutionary epic myths and tales for national heroes to be recast as Soviet prototypes. The Moscow State Yiddish Theater, for its part, was encouraged to introduce its audience to Jewish national heroes who could serve as historical models to be emulated and admired—provided that their struggle for freedom was expanded to include all oppressed people. The Judaean desert, however, could not appear on the stage without evoking the most profound national sentiments of the Jewish people. The 2,000-year-old Judaean state had too many national associations to become merely another arena for the class struggle. Although structurally the plays can certainly be linked to the narratology of socialist realism, their meaning lies elsewhere. Audiences entrenched in Judaic lore could easily look past the theater's platitudes that extolled the ecumenicism of ancient rebellions and see instead the greatest moments in the Jewish struggle for a national home unfold on the stage. Shmuel Halkin, who had already proven his nationalist sympathies, did his part to underline the national significance of the historical episodes he recreated through the use of metonymy and irony.

The theater did not limit its defense of Jewish national distinctness to antiquity; plays like *The Family Ovadis* and *Tevye the Dairyman,* in which contemporary Jewish concerns were central to the narrative, tell a similar story. By addressing specifically Jewish concerns—migration to Birobidzhan and the conflict between socialism and rabbinicism—the theater was acknowledging the distinctness of Jewish life. On the Yiddish stage, Jewish heroes no longer lived in the same context as their non-Jewish neighbors—they no longer rebelled against despotic mill owners, overcame arduous conditions to construct dams or flocked to collective farms with the general Soviet population. They were no longer simply Yiddish-speaking Soviet citizens. They now shared their own national history distinct from that of the general population, and they confronted social conundrums of their own. In short, they became a distinct nation.

One Generation Passes Away: The Great Terror

6

At the twentieth jubilee celebration of the Moscow State Yiddish Theater in March 1939, Jewish and non-Jewish luminaries celebrated what they claimed was a renaissance of Soviet Jewish life—a victory made possible, they declared in platitudes, by the triumph of Stalin's nationality policies and the realization of socialism. "Our people," declared Peretz Markish,

> to whom the Great October [Revolution] gave a homeland, the right to life and a human existence, began constructing a new socialist culture. . . . On the fields of Birobidzhan, the Crimea, Kherson, and the Caucasus, our Jewish collective farmers are living a cultured and prosperous life. Alongside others, the sons of our people are leading an unyielding and joyous struggle for a new life in the factories, the plants, and the mines; in the unbounded space of the great socialist homeland.[1]

Fefer echoed him: "You remember how they [the heroes of Sholem Aleichem and Mendele Mokher Sforim] used to ask: Where is the road to the Land of Israel? . . . I am fortunate that I can say to our grandparents and great-grandparents: There is a road! The road has been found! It is the road to our socialist homeland, the homeland of Lenin and Stalin."[2] Even local Stakhanovites were invited to submit their own feelings on the theater's victory to local papers and trade journals. One, mimicking contemporary propaganda, wrote: "This event is only possible in our country, the country of Stalin's constitution, where all nationalities have equal rights, where all people live happily in a civilized manner, where the people's talent flourishes. I am of the Jewish nationality and cannot but voice my emotional happiness on this occasion."[3] Yet some, like Moshe Kulbak and Moshe Litvakov, could not address the assembled crowd: they had been killed, along with millions of other victims, in what came to be known as the Great Terror.

On January 20, 1936, an article entitled "Muddle Instead of Music" appeared in *Pravda* that condemned Dmitry Shostakovich's opera *Lady Macbeth of Mtsensk District*. Over the next two months a series of articles in *Pravda* made it clear that the state's interest in the political content of art would henceforth extend to artistic form and style.[4] Within a year the Second Moscow Art Theater and the Simonov Theater had been closed, while other theaters were "merged," a euphemism for firing half the employees of both theaters. With the approach of the twentieth anniversary of the October Revolution, all Soviet theaters were instructed to perform a production in celebration of the event. Meyerhold's pick for his theater, *One Life*, based on Nikolai Ostrovskii's *How the Steel Was Tempered*—an archetypical socialist realist novel—was rejected by Platon Kerzhentsev, the director of the Committee of Artistic Affairs. On December 17, 1937, *Pravda* published an ar-

Left to right: Solomon Mikhoels, Evgeniia Epstein, and
Eda Berkovskaia at the twentieth jubilee celebration, 1939.
Photo courtesy of Ala Perlman-Zuskin.

ticle entitled "A Foreign Theater," denouncing Meyerhold for "formalism," a term
that originally denoted an emphasis on aesthetic form over political content but
that had since expanded to include any artistic work deemed offensive by socialist realist zealots. In early 1938, the Meyerhold Theater was closed. Meyerhold
was arrested in June 1939 and was executed the following year. Zinaida Raikh,
Meyerhold's star actress and wife, was brutally murdered in the couple's apartment
soon after her husband's arrest. Kerzhentsev himself was purged in 1938. The
Great Terror had invaded the theatrical space.

Meyerhold's fate was shared by countless others who perished in the Soviet
prison system in 1937–1939. Because of their disproportionate representation
among the intellectual community and the Party elite, the Jews bore a special fate.
Many of the most prominent Jewish members of the Party were the first to be
accused of "anti-Soviet sabotage"—including Trotsky, Kamenev, Zinoviev, and
Radek. The latter three were executed after dramatic show trials, in which the
tortured prisoners were forced to confess to outrageous crimes against the state
they had helped found. Within the next two years the purges spread through the
lower ranks of the Party, wiping out nearly 60 percent of the representatives to the
Seventeenth Party Congress of 1937 and nearly 80 percent of the Party's Central
Committee. Any Party organization with a semblance of autonomy was viewed
with suspicion, particularly those representing the national minorities. For instance, of the eighty-six members of the Ukrainian Central Committee in 1937,

only three survived the purges. The former members of the Jewish Section were no exception. In 1937 Moshe Litvakov was arrested as a Gestapo agent. He died in prison several weeks later. Within a year, the entire Jewish Party apparatus had been liquidated and its members arrested: Moshe Rafes, Mikhail Levitan, Semen Dimanshtayn, Aron Vaynshtayn, and Aleksandr Chemeriskii, along with many others, all shared Litvakov's fate. At the same time, those Jewish institutions attached to the Party and its organs were shut down, including the Yiddish Communist paper *Der emes*, the Society for the Settlement of Jews on the Land, the Committee for the Settlement of Jews on the Land, the Communist children's paper *Yunge gvardia*, and others.

Although Party functionaries were targeted over cultural figures, the latter were not immune to the purges. As accusations of foreign espionage engulfed the cultural intelligentsia, the Jews, with their well-known international contacts, became an easy target. Over the summer of 1937 Soviet prosecutors fabricated a center of Jewish terrorism in Minsk, purportedly aimed at the revitalization of the Bund with the support of foreign powers. Among the first victims of this purge were Yiddish literary critics Yashe Bronshtein (1906–1937) and Max Erik (1898–1937). Soon after, Izi Kharik (1898–1937), a prominent poet and editor of the Yiddish literary periodical *Shtern*, was arrested.

These developments have led many scholars to identify a "policy of state anti-Semitism pursued over the years by Stalin's totalitarian regime."[5] Jewish Party activists, however, were arrested en masse alongside their non-Jewish colleagues, and the purge of Jewish cultural figures was largely restricted to the Minsk group. Despite the calamitous effect the purges had on Jewish culture and society, Soviet Jewish culture was no more destroyed by the purges than was Russian culture. Indeed, the primary targets of the purges were not ethnic minorities; rather they were Party functionaries, military officers, technical specialists, factory and collective farm managers, and the intelligentsia. Because of both the disproportionate percentage of Jews in the latter category and the international prominence of the intelligentsia, the impression that Jews were specifically targeted during the purges has become commonplace. In fact, if the purges did discriminate against the national minorities, then it was the peoples connected to neighboring states who were singled out. As Terry Martin has recently noted, "The terror did not target those stateless diasporas, whose coethnics did not live in concentrated communities adjacent to the Soviet Union, such as Jews, Assyrians, and Gypsies."[6]

Although the late 1930s saw the decline of many aspects of Jewish life, particularly in the realms of education and religious life, secular aspects of Yiddish culture continued to flourish through the State Yiddish theaters, Der Emes Yiddish printing press, and the remaining Yiddish literary journals. The most important of these was probably the Moscow State Yiddish Theater, around which Jewish artists, writers, actors, directors, musicians, and dancers from all over the country united. Mikhoels's role in fostering this miraculous development by balancing official demands with Jewish national expression cannot be overstated. Beginning in 1937, Mikhoels became the indisputable leader of the Soviet Jewish cultural community. As Bergelson aptly noted during his 1952 trial: "There was not a single evening of Yiddish literature [at the Jewish Writer's Union] at which Mikhoels did not make a speech. . . . After [the death of] Litvakov, Mikhoels took all the reigns of power in his hands."[7] Although Bergelson made this statement as part of a forced confession, the statement nevertheless accurately reflects Mikhoels's prominence within the Jewish community. Not only did the staff of the theater emerge from the purges relatively unscathed, but so also did many other figures associated with the theater: writers Peretz Markish, Shmuel Halkin, and David Bergelson; composers Lev Pulver, Moshe Milner, and Aleksandr Krein; and artists Aleksandr Tyshler, Isaak Rabinovich, and Robert Falk were all saved, although Falk, who had spent ten years in Paris before returning to the Soviet Union in 1937, was ostracized by the Union of Artists. In fact, most of Moscow's Yiddish cultural community was left untouched. The same writers, such as David Hofshteyn, Der Nister, Lev Kvitko, and Itzik Fefer, who dominated the Yiddish literary scene prior to the purges continued to do so after. The Moscow Jewish cultural community in general and its State Yiddish Theater in particular miraculously weathered the massive havoc that resulted in the murder of countless public figures and ordinary citizens during the Great Terror.

The theater's survival was a product of both external and internal circumstances. Recent scholarship has shown that once Stalin awakened dormant social pressures with his initial show trials, the purges ballooned out of control. Turf wars, political infighting, center-periphery competition, urban-rural friction, personal feuds, and even class antagonisms were all "settled" with grassroots denunciations—each of which unmasked a whole new set of "criminals." While Stalin tacitly condoned the process and fueled it with spy mania and paranoia, he was aided by spontaneous terrorism from below. As the numbers of victims mounted into the millions, the purges lost any deliberate direction. The line between life and death was often drawn by chance alone.[8]

On several occasions, the storm approached the Yiddish theater, only to die out before engulfing it. With no guiding force, the tempest was unable to stay on course. Mikhoels's own actions also contributed to his security. By declining to participate in the rituals of denunciation and political flattery, Mikhoels remained largely alee from the tempest of the purges. When necessary he condemned ideas and systems, but he refrained from implicating individuals. Regarding his theater's conduct, Mikhoels did what he could to avoid antagonizing the censors, while at the same time making no radical departures from his theater's past that could indicate a need to hide previous indiscretions. He was indubitably aided by the murder of Litvakov and other Yiddish scholars loyal to the Party, which left nobody among the political censors capable of deciphering the theater's nationalist codes.

Face the Music

The continued existence of the Yiddish theater throughout the purges was by no means pre-ordained. Like virtually every other organization that existed in the

Soviet Union, it too came under attack for ideological deviations during the late 1930s. The attack against it, however, was half-hearted at best and never reached a critical momentum. Rather than begin with a direct attack on Mikhoels's theater itself—the most prominent bastion of Jewish identity in the Soviet Union—the brewing campaign against Jewish culture began from the sidelines; it gradually encircled the theater but never engulfed it. The same technique had been used on several other prominent institutions. *Pravda*'s attacks on Soviet theater, for instance, had been preceded by a campaign against music. Thus, when the Committee of Artistic Affairs began to construct an assault on Jewish music, there was reason for concern among all Jewish artists.

The early 1930s had seen a flowering of Jewish music, epitomized by the ethnomusicological work of Moshe Beregovskii, the new a capella group Iudvocans (Jewish Vocal Ensemble), the proliferation of Jewish motifs in Russian popular music, and, of course, the Moscow State Yiddish Theater's own music, which was achieving mass popularity through phonograph recordings. With the advent of socialist realism, however, Jewish composers began to be criticized for neglecting what David Bergelson called "the folk songs of the new Soviet man." The debate on Jewish music came to the fore with Iudvocans's February 1936 tour of Moscow. Iudvocans had emerged in Kiev as a small a capella group with no Party ties. Its growing popularity and tour of Moscow brought the troupe's autonomy to the attention of the Committee of Artistic Affairs. Mikhoels and other Jewish cultural activists were invited to attend a discussion on Jewish music, during which Bergelson, Litvakov, and the composer Aleksandr Veprik each criticized the choral group for clinging to the music of the shtetl over newer Soviet themes. Mikhoels was the solitary defender of the troupe: "Artistic individuality is not doomed in the a capella. This is its specialty and in this rests its greatness," he declared.[9] Mikhoels likely understood that any criticisms leveled against the music of Iudvokans would soon be used against his theater as well.

Despite Mikhoels's objections, the discussion concluded with the declaration that Soviet musicians must work toward strengthening Soviet Jewish music by establishing state patronage and by promoting dialogue between composers and lyricists. In other words, the state would work toward curbing the autonomy of Jewish musicians. The point was re-emphasized the following year when another major conference on Jewish music was held. This time, discussion centered around the music of the Moscow State Yiddish Theater, which was criticized for relying too much on Pulver, thereby ignoring other talented musicians. In more general terms, the Committee of Artistic Affairs announced that Jewish music was not evolving satisfactorily as a result of poor organizational work: "There is very good vocal and musical craft, but it is all unorganized and has a scattered character. It is not regulated, not controlled, and not supported by the Committee of Artistic Affairs," noted the Committee's music inspector.[10] Several months later, a special inspector was appointed to oversee the development of the music of national minorities; he was given specific instructions to pay particularly close attention to Jewish music.[11]

189

The Return of the Past

The attack on music was soon followed by an attack on the theater's art; it was criticized for displaying elements of formalism. While Granovsky's work had long been regarded as formalist, in 1936 the first attacks on a performance produced under Mikhoels's directorship began to appear. The theater was criticized for allowing elements of formalism to appear in the art for *Midat ha-din*.[12] Once again, Mikhoels defended the production before the Committee of Artistic Affairs, arguing that its popular failure was not due to formalism: "I also believe that this production was conventional, although it was unsuccessful. . . . It was not understood. But the popularity of a production still does not make it formalistic." However, Mikhoels's argument was not well received. A committee representative responded with the curt statement: "It is formalistic and symbolistic."[13]

Having warmed up with attacks on the music and art of the theater, the Committee of Artistic Affairs next turned its attention toward the nucleus of Jewish culture—the Moscow State Yiddish Theater. In 1936 the Committee of Artistic Affairs began evaluating the theater's history and concluded that it had been tainted with formalism under Granovsky's tenure. Over the next three years, as the campaign against formalism in art intensified, the committee sporadically turned its attention to the theater's past transgressions. Mikhoels himself was not directly charged with any iniquities. In fact, he was praised for having repudiated Granovsky's heritage. Nevertheless, he repeatedly defended his theater's conduct, standing alone against both his accusers and those from within the theater who chose to recant. The recurring charges, leveled at times directly by Kerzhentsev, indicate that the committee was preparing the ground for a campaign against the Moscow State Yiddish Theater. However, Mikhoels's refusal to provide the firsthand evidence necessary to publicly disgrace the theater impeded the committee's progress. In many cases, Soviet prosecutors were greatly aided by confessions and recantations uttered by the victims in vain hopes of amnesty. Without such cooperation, the task was made more difficult—although it was by no means impossible.

On October 17, 1936, a discussion was held between the troupe and Boiarskii to discuss the future path of the theater. The meeting, described by *Sovetskoe iskusstvo* as "friendly and candid," lasted longer than five hours. Boiarskii explained that the need for cultural construction was shared by all national theaters, including the Jewish theater, and that "the Moscow State Yiddish Theater must seriously contemplate its repertoire and the principles of its creative work." He outlined three themes that he believed were appropriate subject matter for the theater: 1) the portrayal of historical Jewish folk heroes, particularly between 1905 and 1917; 2) Jewish folklore—"but they must be genuine folk plays and genuine folk music"; and 3) didactic themes about the current state of Soviet Jewry, as expressed in Peretz Markish's works on Birobidzhan. He also stressed that the theater was founded on the principles of formalism under Granovsky and that more of an effort must be made to repudiate this past. In the discussion that followed, Goldblatt and Dobrushin both defended the theater's past, arguing that the theater had moved beyond the legacy of Chagall and Granovsky long ago. However, the message that the theater was still riding on the formalist reputation of Granovsky was prevalent—and Boiarskii sought to make that clear.[14]

Even after receiving this admonition, Mikhoels remained an apologist for Granovsky. Formalism, he contended, is defined as a "departure from reality . . . as Plekhanov said, 'art for art's sake.'"[15] Granovsky's plays, he continued, did not fit this definition.

> [Granovsky's plays] infect the theater hall with optimistic happiness. . . . Many call *The Sorceress* a formalist production. I disagree with this. . . . We have no productions full of formalism, with the possible exception of *Night in the Old Market*. We have productions with elements of formalism. . . . What saved these productions from being engulfed by elements of formalism, regardless of the fact that there are even individual elements removed from reality? They were saved by the great intimacy of the actors. I would say these productions were saved by their relation to the theater hall, they were saved by the popular spirit of the productions, their connection to the people's songs, to the people's character.[16]

Allegations of formalism continued to plague Mikhoels over the next two years. The theater's twentieth jubilee, for instance, provided an opportunity for a reassessment of its role in Soviet society; in various retrospectives and speeches delivered on the occasion its past was officially deemed to have been formalist. This interpretation was formulated by Khrapchenko, the new head of the Committee of Artistic Affairs, who was the keynote speaker at the theater's twentieth jubilee gala. He fêted the theater as "one of the most outstanding and most interesting theaters in our country" and praised it for being "one of the clearest affirmations of the creativity of the national politics of Lenin and Stalin." But at the same time, Khrapchenko inserted an ominous phrase, noting that the theater "went through a complicated and difficult road, not avoiding formalist influences and errors."[17] The official interpretation of the theater's history was repeated in countless retrospectives. Halkin, for instance, wrote that "Granovsky was a formalist director, a despotic director, freely and unceremoniously repressing every actor's attempt to gain creative independence." Halkin, however, was careful to ensure that Mikhoels was spared any association with his former mentor: "Mikhoels and the other better actors of the Moscow State Yiddish Theater were already then striving toward realistic art in spite of the influence and demands of the theater's director." The entire Granovsky era, Halkin explained, could be interpreted as a "battle between the realist actors and the formalist director."[18] Nusinov echoed him: "The war for realism and popular spirit in the Moscow State Yiddish Theater ended with victory when Mikhoels, who from the theater's origins had placed this principle in his creative art, became the theater's director."[19]

Mikhoels defended his mentor once again, both in his written commentaries and his speeches. In one retrospective, he emphasized that the theater was founded on popular principles: "From its first steps the theater began to collect, cultivate, and popularize all types of folk creativity. The music, dance, and ethos of the theater were drawn from the rich source of Jewish folklore."[20] In his speech at the gala he conspicuously ignored the accusations of formalism: "Twenty years of the Moscow State Yiddish Theater! If in 1916 someone were to suggest such a name for a theater, with such a collection of adjectives—"Moscow," "state," "Yiddish" —this would surely not be believed."[21] Mikhoels deliberately cited the theater's most realist production under Granovsky to de-emphasize its formalism: "After only five months the students presented the production *Uriel Acosta*. The spirit struggled with the mind for the liberation of the mind, for the creative mind."[22] Mikhoels ended his speech by connecting the theater's prosperity to the national policies of Stalin—a mandatory conclusion. His address was enthusiastically received by the audience of Jewish luminaries and other invited guests: "It is difficult to broadcast what took place in the theater when S. Mikhoels spoke inspiringly about the human genius—Stalin. A sheep's squall roared in the hall," recalled one observer.[23]

Despite the obvious temptation to portray himself as a hero who liberated the theater from Granovsky's formalism, Mikhoels continued to downplay any negative tendencies the troupe may have exhibited during its first decade. His ardent defense of his mentor's talent and his recognition that Granovsky was being denounced out of political rather than artistic motivations are notable. Mikhoels was probably motivated by a combination of genuine moral concerns and the understanding that once a climate of denunciation permeates an organization, it quickly becomes contagious. He likely believed, perhaps naively, that so long as he denied that Granovsky was a criminal, he could not be prosecuted for his associations with his mentor. Further, the Soviet secret police were not known for their willingness to forgive past transgressions. It was essential that Mikhoels avoid any admission of prior guilt.

The campaign against formalism in theater intensified at the First All-Soviet Conference of Theater Directors, which was convened under the auspices of the Committee of Artistic Affairs in June 1939. "The Soviet people," declared Mikhail Khrapchenko in his opening address,

> are waiting for theatrical productions that reflect the great deeds of the heroic people of our country. We need new dramatic material that will show the wealth of the Soviet man's internal world, the wealth and beauty of the Soviet people's life. We need art of a great idea, of great feeling, bright and diverse art.[24]

In fact, the conference was convened primarily to rout formalism out of the theatrical space. Yet not everyone followed the Party line. Mikhoels, for instance, gave one of the most memorable speeches at the conference, criticizing the very foundations of socialist realism.[25] In the words of British theater director and author Joseph Macleod, the conference "was notable for the stand taken by the veteran Jewish actor Mikhoels. He thought too much emphasis was being laid on the rational, and not enough play being given to the imagination."[26] Meyerhold, who spoke on the second day of the conference, took a more bellicose and ultimately foolish position against the anti-formalist crusade. He was arrested days later.

The official order for the liquidation of the Meyerhold theater, published in *Teatr* to serve as a warning for all, accused it of adopting "a position alien to Soviet art" and of being "bourgeois and formalistic through and through."[27]

Once the campaign against formalism in theater was officially sanctioned, it unleashed a slew of accusations from below: petty bureaucrats and provincial know-it-alls scrambled to prove their vigilance by being the first to find fault in art. For the Moscow State Yiddish Theater, renewed allegations came from the unlikely site of Dnepropetrovsk in the Donbas region of southeastern Ukraine, where the theater had toured in the summer of 1939. An article in the local press criticized the theater for "national distinctness," for playing only to Jewish audiences, and for being incomprehensible to non-Jews.[28] In the relatively provincial town of Dnepropetrovsk, the local press did not shy away from anti-Semitic innuendoes. The theater's administrative director at the time, Abraham Baslavskii, responded to the attack with self-criticism by apologizing for the theater's past transgressions and anti-Soviet behavior:

> Several years ago in the Moscow State Yiddish Theater there was a single Communist. . . . In addition, the direction of the theater was for a long time in the hands of an enemy who tried to use the theater for the falsification of Jewish history. As a result, plays such as *Boytre the Bandit,* which presents the rich revolutionary Jewish people in an ugly light, appeared in its repertoire.[29]

Mikhoels, on the other hand, recognized that attacks on the theater's cliquishness were merely veiled attacks on its Jewishness. He used his own pen to defend his theater, arguing that his audience was not limited to Jews but included all Soviet citizens:

> No, our audiences reason differently. They say: No matter what language these actors use, if it is a stage language, a Soviet language, we will understand them, just as in Moscow they are understood by Kyrghiz, Uzbeks and Kazakhs. . . . Our audience is immediately pleased that the hearts of the Moscow State Yiddish Theater's actors beat with the same rhythm of their own hearts, that their breath is the same as ours. With this rhythm and breath they feel a great love toward the motherland and toward Soviet art.[30]

In essence, Mikhoels was right; in one week in neighboring Voroshilovgrad the theater played to an estimated 7,000 spectators—hardly the size of a parochial audience. Clearly, the Yiddish theater was still attracting both Jews and non-Jews, as it had always done. Yiddish, he insisted, is a Soviet language and like all Soviet languages is capable of cutting across ethnic barriers. This rhetoric was derived in part from Marr's theory of linguistic internationalism, which argued for a typology of language based on class rather than ethnicity.[31] Baslavskii's statement indicates that Mikhoels's vigilance was well merited. Whereas previous allegations had concentrated on Granovsky's tenure, Baslavskii included *Boytre the Bandit*—one of Mikhoels's productions. It was indeed a small step from recognizing that Granovsky had committed errors to asserting that Mikhoels was guilty as well.

Arrests

In her biography of her father, Natalia Vovsi-Mikhoels recalls the fear that permeated the family during the year 1937: "The animated conversations of our nocturnal gatherings were beginning to know tense silences. We listened to every unexpected noise in the staircase. . . . That year, we hardly slept. . . . Every day, we learned of a new arrest of our friends or acquaintances."[32] The purges began to encircle the theater with the 1937 arrests of Litvakov and Ida Lashevich, the theater's administrative director. Both were loyal members of the Communist Party. Vovsi-Mikhoels remembers that "that night, after the arrest of Ida Lashevich, Papa did not close his eyes."[33] The purges were also rapidly enveloping the Yiddish theater school. At least four students were arrested, while others were constantly harassed and questioned about their comrades. One of its students, Joseph Schein, describes his experience at the school during this difficult time:

> Today is Monday, the theater's day off, so Mikhoels is with us. Seven in the evening, everyone sits in their place in a semi-circle. We look around and wait with impatience for his arrival. Suddenly we hear his patterned step. He arrives, bringing with him a celebration. Deliberately, he lays out the box of Kazbek [cigarettes], smokes a cigarette and considers, through the smoke, his surroundings. Suddenly his eyes cloud and harden on one place. We know what he is thinking: one of us is absent again, having missed several days—an enemy of the people—the third in the last few months. His short finger raps on his box, he goes to the window, opens it wide and stands a minute in thought. We are all silent with him. Now, we are united in the same thought.[34]

Mikhoels, Zuskin, and probably many other members of the troupe feared for their lives during this period, as was only natural, given the fate of their close associates. Both Mikhoels and Zuskin suffered from severe insomnia, living in perpetual fear of the dreaded midnight knock on the door that signaled the arrival of the secret police. Hints abound that the two were under suspicion—and that they knew it. For instance, Isai Belikov, a theater critic and close friend of Mikhoels, was in Birobidzhan in June 1939 when Polina Zhemchuzhina (the Jewish wife of the Soviet Union's foreign minister, Viacheslav Molotov, and a leading Party official in her own right, as well as an acquaintance of Mikhoels and Zuskin) visited the region. In a letter to Mikhoels's second wife, Anastasiia Potoskaia, he wrote: "Zhemchuzhina spent a day here on her way from Vladivostok to Moscow and I was with her for several hours. She asked about the health of [Mikhoels] and of Zuskin who, it turns out, visited her two days before her departure to the Far East, [and] complained of insomnia, etc. I assured her that the insomnia had ended. I don't know whether V. L. [Zuskin] will thank me for that."[35] Only Zhemchuzhina could have helped him with the type of insomnia he and Mikhoels were suffering. Mikhoels and Zuskin had good reason to lie awake at night in 1939. Evidence recently released from the archives of the KGB has confirmed that Commissar of Internal Affairs Lavrentii Beria was concocting a plot to connect Mikhoels with Isaac Babel, who had been arrested in May for conspiring with foreign agents against the Soviet Union. After his arrest Babel was forced to sign a confession implicating both Mikhoels and Sergei Eisenstein.[36] By spring 1939, however, the momentum of the purges was slowing as the threat of foreign enemies superceded the threat of the enemy from within. As the Soviet state began to prepare for the possibility of war, the purges fizzled out, giving those, like Mikhoels, who were lucky enough to have survived thus far some breathing space. Three months later, with the signing of the Soviet-German non-aggression pact, the Soviet leadership convinced itself that the danger of war had been averted. The mass arrests and executions that had characterized the late 1930s did not begin again until after World War II. Notably, after the 1948 death of Mikhoels, Zhemchuzhina may have been one of the first to inform the remaining members of the theater that Mikhoels's death had not been an accident. Perhaps she was passing on inside information to the two theater activists even in 1939.

Benjamin Zuskin and Eda Berkovskaia (his wife), 1930s. Photo courtesy of Ala Perelman-Zuskin.

Motivated by fear of repression, the theater was willing in 1938 to make the concessions necessary to ensure the survival of its members. This included succumbing to the morally humiliating task of denouncing one's colleagues. In March the collective issued its only statement of denunciation to the press, condemning those who had been "unmasked" as "enemies of the people."[37] In private, however, Mikhoels discouraged such behavior. When his daughter tore up her Komsomol application after being told that she would need to renounce many of her friends whose parents had been arrested, Mikhoels applauded her.[38] In public Mikhoels would not take such reckless risks. In October 1938, for instance, he delivered a radio address entitled "The Lie of Religion" in which he applauded "the people of Russia—all nations in the country" for having "shown the world their superiority over the Bible and God."[39] Nevertheless, the director continued to use biblical imagery in his speeches and continued to entertain his friends and acquaintances with biblical stories and Judaic parables. He even kept a copy of the Bible in his desk, which he carried in his pocket during his 1943 trip to America.[40] Even at the All-Soviet Conference of Theater Directors, Mikhoels drew from a wide range of Hebraic sources, including the Bible, the Talmud, and philosophy of the Haskalah. In addition to couching his arguments in Judaic parables, he had the audacity to present the Bible as a forerunner of Soviet values. "I believe that there is no greater passion of humans than the passion for understanding," he declared. "There is no greater joy than the joy of comprehension. One old book very correctly speaks of

Benjamin Zuskin, 1939. Photo courtesy of Ala Perelman-Zuskin.

this. That book is the Bible. It speaks about understanding, about joy, and about intervention in the world."[41] This Janus-faced attitude toward the Bible—rejecting it as a "lie," while endorsing its values and wisdom—was typical of Mikhoels's ambiguous position regarding the role of religion, a dichotomy shared by many other Soviet Jewish activists. When called upon to do so, he could prate anti-religious platitudes, but his subsequent words and deeds betrayed him.

Along with the intrusion of politics into the theater's backstage, a new militancy and strictness appropriate to the era began to permeate the theater's rehearsals, stifling the previously creative environment. The troupe's schedule came to resemble that of the early Granovsky era, when the workers had complained to the Union of Artists that their director was overly authoritarian. But this time the schedule was set by the very same organizations that had lent a sympathetic ear a decade before. The informal atmosphere that had previously characterized many of the rehearsals under Mikhoels was abandoned in favor of strict regimentation. One worker, for instance, was put under scrutiny for coming four minutes late to a rehearsal, while another was docked nine days' pay for coming thirty-five minutes late.[42] Each of these infractions was duly reported to the Committee of Artistic Affairs by the theater's administrative director, which in turn approved all discipline and kept close records of all offenses. Thus, the theater came to resemble, both onstage and offstage, a formal Party gathering rather than a creative environment.

Restless Old Age

The political climate in late 1938 required caution and compromise from those who were still left among the living. The arrest of Litvakov and the liquidation of the Minsk center foreboded a difficult time for Yiddish culture. Mikhoels made his biggest artistic concession by performing the theater's first contemporary play with no connection to Jewry whatsoever—L. Rakhmanov's *Restless Old Age*, translated from Russian into Yiddish by Halkin. The play was prepared hastily upon the order of the Committee of Artistic Affairs, which had vetoed the theater's planned repertoire—Der Nister's translation of Gogol's *Wedding* and a new play by Markish on the Civil War.[43] Instead, the theater was given a month to prepare *Restless Old Age*, a play which had already been performed in numerous Russian theaters and had even been made into a motion picture entitled *Baltic Deputy*. The production was a pre-ordained failure: there was little that the Yiddish theater could add to the mediocre script that had not already been done in other interpretations of the play, and Moscow audiences were already tiring of the drama. The decision to perform the play was supported only by the Party and Komsomol organizations of the theater, indicating the ascendancy of the theater's Party organization.[44] The repertory decision was justified by Baslavskii: "This, the theater's first presentation of a translation of a Russian play, opens new creative possibilities for the theater. . . . [The play] touches upon one of the current problems regarding the participation of the intelligentsia in the Revolution."[45] *Sovetskoe iskusstvo* rationalized the decision in more jaded terms: "The theater need not lock itself into the narrow circle of national themes. It must produce plays from the life of different nationalities in our country. . . . It is necessary to put on the stage of the Moscow State Yiddish Theater plays about Lenin and Stalin."[46] This was the most concrete denial of the theater's national peculiarity to date. The Yiddish theater, which for twenty years had entertained and educated Jews and non-Jews alike with plays drawn from national themes, was being forced to deny its heritage. Thankfully, the production of Rakhmanov's play turned out to be only a short hiatus.

Restless Old Age begins in Petrograd in 1916 at the house of the great botanist Dmitrii Polezhaev, who is working on a method of combating crop failure. As Polezhaev returns from an academic conference, his star student, Misha Bocharov, is arrested by the tsarist police, thereby threatening the completion of Polezhaev's manuscript. The following year, Polezhaev receives a new assistant whose weak scientific work is coupled with a foolish distrust of the new Bolshevik government. Polezhaev's project is finally saved from the new assistant's incompetence when in February 1918, Bocharov, who has since become an esteemed Bolshevik Commissar, returns to Polezhaev and helps him complete and publish his work. However, the star student informs the professor that he has returned only temporarily; he must return to the front to fight for Bolshevik power. Before departing, though, he sends the first copy of the book to come off the press to Lenin as a gift. As the curtains close, the phone rings. It is Lenin himself, calling to personally congratulate the author of the marvelous book he had just finished reading.[47]

The play, with only five major parts, was performed without the participation of either Mikhoels or Zuskin: it was staged by Isaak Kroll and starred Daniil Finkelkraut and Iustina Minkova, two longtime members of the troupe. It is possible that Mikhoels's absence from this new production was a deliberate decision on his part. He had shown during the theater's 1927 performance of *Uprising* that he would not take part in any production he believed was pure propaganda devoid of artistic merit. The absence of the theater's traditional stars, however, gave some of the troupe's less visible members an opportunity to prove themselves. For instance, Finkelkraut, who had been a member of the troupe since 1922, had never before been given such an important role. He was received warmly by the press: "The artist Finkelkraut can be congratulated on his triumph. He entirely succeeded in the role of Professor Polezhaev," wrote *Pravda*.[48]

After the All-Soviet Conference of Theater Directors, a campaign was begun to increase Party membership among the troupe. Prior to the campaign, only seven members of the Communist Party were on the payroll of the Yiddish theater, none of whom were members of the artistic personnel. However, within four months, four of the troupe's leading actors joined with great fanfare.[49] Over the next few years, the theater and its school would recruit primarily among Party members, and non-Party members admitted into the school would be encouraged to join before graduation.[50] Notably, neither Zuskin nor Mikhoels were among the new recruits. Both continued to resist membership in the Party, as they had done since the theater's inception, despite all apparent benefits of membership. Another means of encouraging greater Party influence on the theater was the recruitment of new cadres to the theater through the Yiddish theater school, which graduated a record eighty actors and five directors during 1938.[51] The push to join the Party in the Moscow State Yiddish Theater followed a similar effort in the Yiddish Writer's Union, during which Peretz Markish had joined as well.

The Banquet

Soon after the *Restless Old Age* fiasco, the Moscow State Yiddish Theater once again found common ground with the Communist Party and the Soviet state in their mutual hostility toward fascism. Hitler's Reich inadvertently provided the Yiddish theater with a concrete mission, capable of revitalizing and exciting both the Jewish masses and the troupe itself. Speaking at the theater's jubilee celebration, Zuskin anticipated the theater's intended thematic direction for the coming season. He contrasted the victory of socialism in the Soviet Union with the rise of fascism in the West: "During these days, when in the fascist countries Jews are being subjected to barbarian, brutal persecution, the jubilee of the Jewish theater in the country of socialism is an especially joyous event, a celebration of great political significance."[52] As Europe prepared for the prospect of a major confrontation with Hitler's Reich, Soviet propaganda in general, and Jewish propaganda in particular, took on a conspicuously anti-fascist tone. From the start, Mikhoels was an active participant in anti-fascist propaganda. Although the theater had made passing mention of the rise of fascism in Weimar Germany as early as 1926 with *The Tenth Commandment*, Mikhoels's first significant anti-fascist role was in Grigori Roshal's (1899–1983) 1938 film *The Family Oppenheim*. Based on Lion Feuchtwänger's 1933 novel *The Oppermans*, the film follows a prominent German Jewish family as they are asphyxiated gradually by the anti-Semitic climate of their homeland.

In a similar vein, the theater began preparations for an anti-fascist and anti-Zionist play by Markish, *The Oath*, about a Jewish family that flees persecution in Germany, hoping to find a safe haven in Palestine. Soon after their arrival in the Promised Land, they realize that they have no future there either. Disappointed with the promise of Zion, they flee to Spain to help fight in the Civil War. The title of the play referred to the oath taken by Jews fleeing the Spanish Inquisition never to return to Spain.[53] The play, however, was never finished. In the summer of 1939, anti-fascism became a taboo subject in the Soviet Union.

Spring 1939 began with a purge of Jewish diplomats. On May 3rd, Maksim Litvinov, the Jewish architect of the "collective security" alliance with Western Europe against Germany, was dismissed as the Soviet Commissar of Foreign Affairs. Within a month, his successor, Viacheslav Molotov, began making positive overtures to Berlin. Negotiations continued throughout the summer. On August 23, 1939, German Foreign Minister Joachim von Ribbentrop arrived at the Kremlin to sign a non-aggression pact with the Soviet Union. In the pact's secret protocol, Stalin and Hitler agreed to rearrange the map of Eastern Europe between themselves. Stalin firmly believed that by sheltering Russia beneath Hitler's wings, he had guaranteed his people peace and security. Immediately after the conclusion of the pact, all anti-fascist activity in the Soviet Union was banned. *The Family*

Oppenheim was removed from theaters, *The Oath* was canceled, and the Moscow State Yiddish Theater was left without a repertoire and without a direction. The pact was a tremendous blow to the Yiddish theater, both for genuine ideological reasons and for having destroyed its repertoire overnight. As a result, the theater spent the next two years struggling for direction, unable to develop any specific themes. Mikhoels had been taught that the times were too tumultuous to settle into any single ideology.

The theater's most ambitious production in the immediate pre-war period was *The Banquet*, based on a segment from Markish's 1929 novel *One Generation Passes Away, Another Generation Comes*. The title of the novel was drawn from the opening lines of the biblical book of Ecclesiastes:

> One generation passes away, another generation comes: but the earth abides forever. The sun also rises, and the sun goes down, and hastens to its place where it rises again. . . . That which has been is that which shall be; and that which has been done is that which shall be done: and there is nothing new under the sun. . . . There is no remembrance of things past, nor will there be any remembrance of things that are to come among those who shall come after.

The reference to Ecclesiastes helps frame the novel within the theme of continuity and tradition in spite of external change. This was a powerful theme in the context of revolutionary Russia, a state which claimed to be the first to break with all traditions and continuities. Markish's reference to the cyclical nature of time reveals a covert or even subconscious skepticism regarding the Revolution's potential to construct a new world. Perhaps it was for this reason that the reference to Ecclesiastes was abandoned for the production of the play. Without this allusion, the pessimistic intonation of the play is removed.

Markish's original novel told of the continuity of generations, as the elder generation of the shtetl, represented by the character of Mendel, passes its traditions and heritage to the new generation, represented by Mendel's son Ezra. The original novel was filled with biblical references and allusions, prompting American critic Nakhman Mayzel to write of it: "The entire idea, the tendency of the novel is thoroughly Jewish, nationally Jewish."[54]

The novel is set in a Ukrainian shtetl in 1919, where the population is being terrorized by Whites and Ukrainian bandits. Red partisans, Jews, Ukrainians, and Russians alike flee into the forest for shelter. The villagers must fend for themselves against the White bandits while they await aid from the Red Army, which is approaching the village. In order to gain time while awaiting rescue from the Red Army, the old man Mendel invites the bandits to a banquet, hoping to keep them occupied until the rescuers arrive. The banquet is ruined, however, as the bandits terrorize the women of the village. As Mendel comes to the defense of one woman, he is captured by the bandits. He is bound by his hands and feet ("just as Abraham bound Isaac at the Akedah," as Markish wrote in his original text, referring to Abraham's willingness to sacrifice his only son to prove his faith) and killed.[55] However, by detaining the bandits until the arrival of the Red Army, Mendel's deed saves the village.

Mendel's death represents the culmination of the novel's theme. The elder generation passes on and is martyred by the grace of God for the sake of the future of the new generation. It is a structure that has permeated Jewish history for centuries, connecting Mendel to Abraham, Bar Kokhba, the Maccabees, and all other Jewish heroes who gave their lives for the preservation of the faith and its people. Markish repeatedly invokes this chain of continuity throughout the novel. Yet, as the reference to Ecclesiastes implies, each sacrifice only begins another cycle. Ezra's generation, the reader surmises, will once again be forced to sacrifice itself for its children. This prophecy is proven true with the death of Ezra at the end of the novel—a segment absent from the stage production.

The stage version completely abrogates the nationalist and religious implications of Mendel's martyrdom. Even Mendel's dying words were rewritten to give the play an optimistic and internationalist tone. In the novel, Mendel leaves a testament for his son that reads in part, "there is no greater glory than to die for one's people"—a strong statement of national pride.[56] In the stage version, however, Mendel addresses the Cossack ataman, his murderer, with the words:

> My people have gone through centuries—they carry suffering on their path to a new bright life—they suffer, but humanity does not abandon them. You may think, Ataman, that it is terrible for me to die at the hands of a bandit. Who are you? You are hardly the son of your people. Your people are great and glorious and became parents to our children, became parents to my Ezra—my people will live.[57]

Thus, in the words of one critic, Mendel fights for "genuine internationalism, organic harmony with the consciousness of his national virtues, fearlessness, wise optimism, and a belief in a better future, in the happiness of all working people."[58] With the removal of the reference to Ecclesiastes and the cyclical nature of time, the audience is permitted to believe that a better future is truly dawning. Only those familiar with Markish's original Yiddish novel—which was a best-seller in its time and was even reprinted in Moscow in 1938—could truly appreciate the skepticism implied in the original title. Thus, the nationalist implications of the sacrifice are not only removed, they are replaced with an internationalist theme—the brotherhood between Jews and Ukrainians. The hostility between the Ukrainian bandit and the Jewish villager is portrayed as an isolated incident with no historical precedent.

Yet despite these revisions, the play retained much of Markish's original biblical and historical motifs. As Iogann Altman noted in *Izvestiia*, "Peretz Markish, though in a barely perceptible way, took old heroic motifs: the stoicism of Job; ... the bravery of Bar-Kokhba, who rose up against the Romans; the great teachings of Maimonides, who enlightened the people." Comparing Mendel to the Conversos who died for their religious ideals in sixteenth-century Portugal, Altman continued, "Mendel dies like they [the Conversos] died earlier in Portugal. But he had found a new idea—internationalism."[59] The plot was also reminiscent of a Hasidic legend told about the Gerer Rebbe, who allegedly invited Russian troops stationed in his town to a banquet in order to denounce two anti-Semitic

Polish military engineers.[60] Indeed, the structure of inviting one's enemies to a banquet in order to dupe them is a recurring theme in biblical literature, appearing in both the Book of Esther and the apocryphal Book of Judith. Further, the play represented a return to the time-honored theme of the conflict of generations, the conflicting ideals of fathers and sons.

The play was a critical success. *Izvestiia* praised the theater for rewriting the story of the Jewish shtetl by replacing the *luftmentsh* with heroic individuals.[61] *Pravda* wrote that "Markish's play *The Banquet* is a passionate tale of manhood and international brotherhood. And the Moscow State Yiddish Theater is successful in creating a passionate, exciting production."[62]

For its next production, the theater returned to the theme of Jewish participation in the collective farm movement. While hardly a novel subject—collective farm romances had saturated Russian stages for over a decade—it promised little chance of official objections on ideological grounds. Two plays were considered: Dobrushin's *Elka Rudner* (about the founding of a joint Jewish–non-Jewish collective farm) and Halkin's *Hero* (about Jewish migration to collective farms).[63] The troupe eventually settled on Halkin's *Hero,* the title of which was changed to *Arn Fridman.* The plot revolves around three related conflicts. The first is between Arn Fridman, a former teacher, and his son Lev, both of whom have abandoned the shtetl to become collective farmers. While Arn hopes to rebuild Jewish life on the basis of socialist activity and toil on the land, Lev initially resents being torn away from the shtetl. The second conflict is between Lev and his beloved Golde, who is turned off by Lev's disdain for the collective farm and is enchanted instead with the young poet and combine operator, Zeml, whose name is a play on the Russian word for land. The third conflict is between Arn and Sender, Golde's father and a former shopkeeper, who is causing trouble on the collective farm by insisting that he live only for himself. Essentially, all the conflicts are based on the fundamental disagreement of whether Jewish collective farming can provide a solution to the dilemmas of Jewish existence.

In one representative exchange between Arn and Sender, Sender posits that "a collective farm is new work, it is not a new life." Arn counters him by explaining, "No, a collective farm is not just new work, but also a new life, a new page in history." Arn's defense of the collective farm as a "new life" becomes a recurring theme throughout the play, restated in virtually every scene. The conflict between the two models culminates when Sender threatens to abandon the collective farm. Arn confronts him:

> Sender does not understand that yesterday, today, and tomorrow our people have only one goal in life and this goal must not be forsaken—freedom. This is what our people have sought for a thousand years. Our people have found themselves on the land, taken a new life away from slavery and the difficult life of oppression and exploitation. The strength of our people must raise us to a new socialist reality. We must do it for our children, for otherwise what will become of them? ... Sender works well, but his work is not for the service of the people, he thinks only of himself.

Benjamin Zuskin
and Shapiro in *Arn
Fridman.*
Photo courtesy of
Ala Perelman-
Zuskin.

The play climaxes when a fire occurs in the wheatfield. While Arn heroically ex-
tinguishes the fire, Sender sits in the corner of the field embracing a sheaf of grain.
In the denouement, Lev joins the Red Army as Arn provides him with some parting words: "Be healthy, my son. Serve your motherland faithfully and don't forget
that far away, far away in the Crimea, Jews live on your land, and among them,
close to you, is Arn Fridman."[64]

The play is based on a typical socialist realist structure and draws its form from
classical epic drama. Once again, a naive simpleton (Lev) is convinced by a mentor
(Arn Fridman) to embrace the Revolution and join in its defense. The play presents the most stylized heroes and villains to appear on the Yiddish stage. Arn's
commitment to the socialist cause is unwavering, while Sender's utter selfishness

provides an ideal obstacle to Lev's enlightenment. The final scene in which the newly anointed hero leaves his family behind to start a new life in the Red Army is the Soviet equivalent of the Hollywood cliché of walking into the sunset.

The text was Halkin's weakest play to date, likely a function both of the rapidity with which the script was written and the mundane theme about which the play was commissioned. Halkin had already proven that his dramatic strength lay in reinterpreting classics, and his poetic strength lay in his subtle ability to conjure images of the Jewish past. In *Arn Fridman*, Halkin could not apply either of these skills. Having just witnessed the height of the Great Purges and the death of many of his close associates, Halkin probably presumed that this was not the time to test the censor's limits. The poet likely composed this play to prove his loyalty to the Soviet state; it certainly could not have been to impress his audience with a creative triumph. Critics aptly complained that Halkin merely marked time in the crescendo leading up to the fire[65] and that the play was bereft of any detail or dramatic characterization.[66] The production's only merits were the superb acting of Zuskin and Finkelkraut and the return of Natan Altman as artist. His backdrop was a scenic painting of rows of telephone lines that stretched past great mountains and a golden sun into the blue Crimean horizon. The juxtaposition of electrification and nature reinforced the Promethean ideal of conquering nature while retaining a pastoral landscape, and alluded to Lenin's dictum that communism equals Soviet power plus electrification of the countryside. Heaps of bread and stockpiles of machinery littering the stage also presented an idealized picture of a countryside that was in reality perpetually on the verge of starvation.

Despite two weak new productions from the 1939–1940 season, the theater continued during its 1940 summer tour to attract large audiences. In Leningrad, for instance, it played to over 50,000 people between May 10th and June 5th.[67] When it returned to Moscow that fall, the theater had made little progress in its search for a means of overcoming political difficulties.

Solomon Maimon, the theater's second production of one of M. Daniel's plays, premiered in 1940. It told of the eighteenth-century Jewish philosopher of the Haskalah who fought against rabbinicism in favor of secular knowledge and scientific rationalism. Solomon Maimon (1754–1800) was recognized as a brilliant scholar from his early childhood in Lithuania, where the local rabbinical authorities offered to ordain him as a rabbi at the exceptional age of eleven. Maimon refused the honor, instead marrying the daughter of a wealthy Jew at the age of fourteen. In search of an alternative to rabbinical Judaism, Maimon turned toward the study of the esoteric Kabbalah, and later briefly joined a Hasidic sect. However, he found both paths ultimately unsatisfying. At the age of twenty-five, Maimon abandoned his family and left for Königsberg, where he hoped to study medicine. His heretical criticisms of rabbinical Judaism, however, alienated him from the community, forcing him to flee to Berlin, where he was treated with equal disdain. After flirting with apostasy, Maimon began writing philosophical treatises, in which he championed the rationalism of the Enlightenment over what he saw as the pedanticism of Talmudic scholasticism. After several years of wandering,

Benjamin Zuskin as Solomon Maimon, Iustina Minkova as his wife,
and Etta Kovenskaia as their daughter in *Solomon Maimon.*
Photo courtesy of Ala Perelman-Zuskin.

Maimon eventually settled in Berlin, where he joined the circle of Moses Mendelssohn, the most prominent figure of the Haskalah.[68]

Daniel's play focuses on the disputes between Maimon, played by Zuskin, and the Jewish community, both in its rabbinical and enlightened manifestations. The central conflict focuses on the altercation between Maimon and his erstwhile mentor Moses Mendelssohn. Maimon is disappointed with Mendelssohn's continued defense of Orthodox Judaism as "revealed legislation." In contrast to Mendelssohn, whose objective was the dissemination of Hebraic knowledge to the German public, Maimon hoped the intellectual current would flow in the opposite direction. While the historical Maimon sought a fusion between the rational elements of Judaism and the philosophies of the German Aufklärung, Daniel's Maimon seeks a more complete rejection of Judaism. In Daniel's text, Maimon receives his guidance not from the great philosopher of Berlin but rather from a simple pauper in a hotel, who convinces him that man is his own master and the measure of all else in the universe. The episode was based on a true story in which Maimon, after being banished from Berlin the first time, befriended a local beggar with whom he studied the art of panhandling for six months. Maimon's epiphany, imparted by the pauper, was Daniel's own invention, probably inserted to portray

Maimon's enlightenment as a product of working-class mentality. The play portrays Maimon as a nascent revolutionary who struggles against the dominant authorities that seek to keep the Jews in the dark age. He confronts and discredits the rabbis, the *kahal,* the *szlachta* (Polish nobility), the Kabbalists, the Hasidim, and the philosophers of the Berlin salons and their aristocratic patrons, only finding solace in near-total assimilation.[69]

Mikhoels linked the play to the rationalism of the French Revolution and Jewish emancipation. He emphasized the theme of "human understanding and the formation of world views based on the true comprehension of reality."[70] It was the theater's first attempt since *Uriel Acosta* in 1922 to animate the philosophical premises of Jewish rationalism and the complexities of apostasy. However, when compared to *Acosta,* the play fell short. "Daniel failed to find pathos in the battle between the hero's spirit and mortal body," wrote one reviewer.[71] Both *Pravda* and *Izvestiia* complained that Maimon's obsession with complex philosophical questions obscured his personal psychological struggles and, more important, his material struggle against the bourgeois oppressors and rabbinical authorities.[72] Another reviewer wrote: "The historical hero is not believable. . . . The art is not convincing. Before us, in essence, we find abstract truths. It is difficult to discern who Maimon fights against and for what."[73] Maimon's cause, however, was clear—he fought in the name of Jewish rationalism. A more forthright objection might have been that Daniel's Maimon does not frame his battle in terms of the class struggle. The poverty-stricken hero attacks his bourgeois and aristocratic enemies on the level of abstract philosophy rather than social justice. In other words, one could say that the play was decidedly un-Marxist. Daniel ignored a perfectly suitable opportunity to depict the materialist bases of the class struggle in historical perspective and chose instead to emphasize the primacy of ideology.

The play was also a popular disappointment. Philosophical debates in Berlin salons simply did not make for captivating entertainment. Pulver's lyrical music, Robert Falk's mass scenes, and superb acting by the troupe (including some new cadres who appeared in lead roles) did little to help the fundamentally weak theatrical experience. Yet, in a way, Maimon exhibits many of the same traits as the theater's previous protagonists. He exemplifies the same stubborn optimism and faith in humanity as Tevye and Zayvl Ovadis. As one reviewer noted, Maimon exhibits an "independent search for truth, bravery and human rights . . . the fearlessness and humanity of man, unbending in the battle to unravel the secrets of the universe."[74]

Goldfadn and Sholem Aleichem

The theater's relatively shoddy productions of the previous two seasons were beginning to have adverse effects on its popularity. As a result, the theater chose to return to the classics of nineteenth-century Yiddish literature, to Goldfadn and to Sholem Aleichem. Both had retained their charm through the years. The theater had, of course, built its reputation on these writers, and Mikhoels's portrayal of Sholem Aleichem's Tevye only a few years earlier had been the theater's greatest achievement since *King Lear.* Although neither author possessed the impeccable revolutionary credentials required of most authors under socialist realism, they were at least "men of the people" and instilled "the optimism of the people" in all their work. Both also addressed themes that corresponded to Soviet mores—a social concern for the downtrodden masses and a sensitive disdain for the aristocratic and rabbinic upper classes. They were regarded in Jewish circles with the same esteem as pre-revolutionary Russian masters such as Nikolai Gogol and Aleksandr Ostrovskii, both of whose plays also saw revivals in 1939.

The one hundredth anniversary of Goldfadn's birth gave the theater an ideal opportunity to return once again to one of its favorite playwrights. This time, the theater performed a vaudeville based on Goldfadn's *Two Kuni-Lemls.* The play was revised for production at the Yiddish theater by Zalman Shneer-Okun, a well-known collector of Jewish folk songs. According to Jewish theater legend, when a rival of Goldfadn's in Romania wrote a play entitled *Two Schmil Schmelkes* based on the German play *Nathan Schleimiehl* for performance by his own troupe, Goldfadn hired the novice playwright, put him on salary, discarded his play, and wrote a new adaptation.[75] The play was a simple tale about a young woman whose parents betroth her to a bumbling Hasid against her will. The woman, instead, falls in love with an uneducated commoner. The two lovers are able to overcome all the obstacles put in their way. The play ends happily as the commoner appears at the wedding ceremony disguised as the groom, and convinces everybody—including the real groom!—that he is the bride's intended.[76] The play satirized the fanaticism of the Hasidim and mocked the sway of tradition, a point appreciated by several critics.[77] However, despite some popular success, it was a critical failure. Aron Gurshteyn, for instance, wrote that "In the new Goldfadn production, the Moscow State Yiddish Theater unfortunately does not display the independence and originality that characterized its earlier performances. . . . We repeat again, we do not demand 'philosophy' from such plays, but we do legitimately demand taste, culture, and some type of united point of view. . . . We also legitimately demand that the production reflect our times."[78] The film director Grigori Roshal lamented that "in this play there is nothing new and nothing deep."[79] Others did note that "this vaudeville, of course, is a light, colorful, happy production and is received well by the audience."[80] The play was a distraction, light entertainment. Unfortunately, the play failed to elicit the desired public response.

The theater's return to Sholem Aleichem with his *Wandering Stars* promised to remedy the situation. Dobrushin's adaptation of Sholem Aleichem's play premiered in June 1941. It told the story of the development of Yiddish theater from its origins in late nineteenth-century traveling troupes. The play follows a troupe of eight actors who struggle to overcome the tradition of melodrama, the so-called *shund* (trash) theater. They seek to raise the theater to a new level of artistic merit worthy of "Shakespeare and his successor Goldfadn." Implicit in the battle against *shund* was the struggle against the entire lifestyle of the shtetl. Seeking to establish themselves as respectable "cultural tsars," "pedagogues," "philosophes," and "philologues," the enthusiastic artists emigrate from tsarist Russia to London and then to America. They are disappointed to find that the conditions for the development of a new art style are even worse in America than in Russia; the "Land of Opportunity" is rife with speculators, commercialism, and greedy corporations.[81]

Tyshler's art reflected the squalor of the poor actor's lifestyle. The actors performed on a stage of mud and lived in wretched hotels. In imitation of the ad hoc curtains used by the wandering theaters, he constructed a curtain sewn from old bedding. This lifestyle contrasted sharply with the scenes of New York, for which Tyshler painted a backdrop of skyscrapers. I. Bachelis called Tyshler's art "the best he has done for the theater."[82] Pulver once again returned to a symbolist interpretation of old Jewish melodies and utilized leitmotifs, such as his "Come, come to me," which opened the production. The play starred Zuskin and introduced Etel Kovenskaia, who at the age of fifteen performed in her first major role as Reysl. The press greeted the return to Sholem Aleichem enthusiastically. "The

Benjamin Zuskin and Sonia Binnik in *Wandering Stars.* Photo courtesy of Ala Perelman-Zuskin.

director, S. M. Mikhoels, fully reflecting all the social depths and satirical point-edness of Sholem Aleichem's production, produced a colorful, dynamic production."[83] The presence of several younger actors in lead roles was also a much-appreciated addition to the theater.[84] By 1947 *Wandering Stars* had been performed over 200 times.[85]

The Winter of Discontent

Mikhoels's plans for the coming season, most of which were not to reach fruition due to the Nazi invasion of 1941, indicate both an attempt to recreate an international success on a par with *King Lear* and a turn away from specifically Jewish topics. As he had done several times before when confronted with a serious repertory crisis, Mikhoels considered adapting world classics to the Yiddish stage; plays by Gogol, Gorky, and Molière were considered. Additionally, Daniel was commissioned to write a play about Karl Marx.[86]

Eventually the theater settled on Kushnirov's Yiddish translation of *The Span-iards* by the Russian romantic writer Mikhail Lermontov (1814–1841). The play, a tragedy set during the Spanish Inquisition, tells of the humanist freethinker Fernando, and his love for Emilio, the daughter of the noble Don Alvarets. When Don Alvarets refuses to allow his daughter to marry Fernando, Fernando is forced by an Italian Jesuit in the service of the Inquisition to kill his beloved. Fernando later meets his own end at the hands of the Inquisition authorities. The play's climax occurs when the suspicions of Don Alvarets are borne out, and we discover that Fernando is himself a Jew.

Although the play was not drawn from a Jewish repertoire, Lermontov's play displayed many of the Yiddish theater's favorite themes: there is a generational conflict between the class-conscious and xenophobic parents and the innocent, lovesick youth; a young couple's love is hindered by the forces of tradition; and, finally, the truth of international brotherhood is revealed as ethnic and religious barriers are overcome. The play was also full of contemporary relevance. As Mikhoels explained, the social and national differences between Fernando and Emilio continue "even in our day, when in the capitalist world a biological chasm exists between people [of different nationalities], a chasm that can separate loving individuals."[87] Mikhoels was indubitably referring to the plight of Jews under Nazi rule. Indeed, the entire play can be seen as a reflection of Jewish life under the Nazis, in which the Third Reich became a modern-day inquisition. At a time when anti-fascist productions were taboo and the Soviet Union was allied in a non-aggression pact with Germany, though, such an interpretation was dangerously provocative. In addition, one need not look too far to see the similarities between the momentum of the Inquisition and the momentum of the Bolshevik Revolution, both of which inspired overzealous supporters to unleash their fury on the innocent.

The play was greeted enthusiastically by the critics, many of whom praised Robert and Valery Falk for their sets and the return of Aleksandr Krein as composer. Krein's recreation of Spanish Renaissance motifs combined with vocals drawn from Jewish folk music was particularly appreciated.[88] Yet despite these positive reviews, the play failed to bring the theater the success it desperately needed. While on tour in Leningrad in May 1941, Mikhoels wrote to his wife complaining, "Here in the meantime things are joyless. At *Tevye* on the opening day of the tour the hall was only fifty percent filled. At *Maimon, The Spaniards,* and *Kuni-Lemls* there were even fewer."[89]

Mikhoels firmly believed that his next project would finally bring the theater the attention he was craving. Drawing upon the success of *King Lear,* he began another attempt at Shakespeare. Although he had often dreamed of playing Hamlet, by the late 1930s he began to realize he was too old for the part.[90] Instead, he once again chose a historical tragedy with uncanny contemporary relevance— *Richard III.* In June 1940, he reassembled the same team that had produced *King Lear:* Halkin for the Yiddish translation[91] and Radlov for the staging.[92] Mikhoels himself decided to star as Richard—his first new role since Tevye in 1938. As early as April 1939, Mikhoels wrote in *Literaturnaia gazeta* of his desire to tackle the problem of evil epitomized by Richard III: "I would like to try my luck at the psychological dilemma of nature, at a character that is the spiritual example of the enemy, of the enemy of all humanity, of the enemy of beauty, of the enemy of moral strength and stability, of our current enemy."[93]

The term "current enemy"—probably a reference to Hitler—was equally applicable to Stalin. The evil Richard, duke of Gloucester, who craves violence and viciously destroys enemies and friends alike in his megalomaniacal quest for power eerily resembled the Soviet dictator. The play begins as Richard plots to usurp the crown from his brother, King Edward IV, who lies ill. Richard succeeds in turning all other contenders for the crown against each other. The evil duke connives to have his other brother, the duke of Clarence, imprisoned and murdered, while blaming the incident on internal enemies and saboteurs—the queen's kin. Having established a new threat, Richard succeeds in having the queen's family imprisoned and murdered. Banishment to the Tower of London becomes a metaphor for execution. Shakespeare informs us through dramatic irony that none will survive their sentence. Throughout his terror, Richard maintains an aura of piety, expressing surprise and outrage at the extent of the growing bloodbath. Through such deception and intrigue, he is able to solicit the support of the people of London, who prevail upon him to accept his leadership of the realm. Despite this genuine popular support, Richard's coronation only leads to an intensification of the terror. Under the guise of defending the realm against further killings, Richard hires Tyrrel, perhaps Shakespeare's most evil creation, to complete his terrorizing purges by murdering his closest kin—his nephews and wife. As an army led by Henry of Tudor amasses to crush the new king and his reign of terror, Richard responds by intensifying the massacre.

After the de-Stalinization of the late 1950s and early 1960s, Eastern European intellectuals began subtly to compare Richard III with Stalin. Khrushchev's 1956 Secret Speech on the excesses of Stalinism made the publication of these interpretations possible, but such interpretations may have informed earlier readings of the tragedy as well. Jan Kott, a Polish professor of drama and one of the leaders of the Polish anti-Stalinist movement of the 1950s, wrote in 1964 that "a reader or spectator in the mid-twentieth century interprets *Richard III* through his own experience. He cannot do otherwise."[94] Shakespeare's "grand mechanism," Kott continued, in which the same tragedy is repeated in each historical play, is "the image of history itself."[95] It is, he asserted, "the world we live in."[96] Commenting on the scene in which a messenger who appears at his door in the middle of the night urges Hastings to support Richard's bid for the crown, Kott hints at a comparison with the secret police, notorious for their midnight arrests: "Shakespeare's genius shows itself also in the way he depicts the events occurring at four A.M. Who has not been awakened in this way at four A.M. at least once in his life?"[97] He continued to detail the show trial of Hastings, who, professing his love of the king and faith in royal justice, is nevertheless left alone with his executioners to meet his fate. More recently, Richard III has been interpreted onstage as an allegory for twentieth-century dictatorship, most notably in the Royal National Theatre's 1990 production.[98] Given the play's self-evident similarities to Stalin's reign of terror, it is remarkable that the Yiddish theater's preparations were permitted to continue so long. Ultimately, the play was never performed. It was stricken from the repertoire in 1942.

Theater of Survival

The late 1930s were ambivalent years for Mikhoels and the theater. On one hand, it was during this period that the purges approached the Yiddish theater, causing Mikhoels and Zuskin numerous sleepless nights. On the other hand, though, it was during this period that Mikhoels truly emerged as one of the greatest representatives of Soviet art and was showered with praise by the state. At the theater's twentieth jubilee, Mikhoels was honored with the Order of Lenin, the highest prize awarded to Soviet citizens. The Order of the Red Banner was given to Zuskin and Pulver, and additional awards were distributed to other prominent members of the troupe. Additionally, Mikhoels was named a People's Artist of the Soviet Union, Zuskin and Pulver became People's Artists of the Russian Republic, and five other members of the troupe were named honorary artists of the Russian Republic.[99] The awards were coupled with monetary bonuses: 85,000 rubles were allocated for distribution to the troupe, of which Mikhoels received 10,000. An additional 15,000 rubles was set aside for the convocation of a gala celebratory ceremony.[100] In 1940, Mikhoels's fiftieth birthday was celebrated with all the pomp due a first-class celebrity. The theater school was attracting an unprecedented number of students. In the words of the school's director, "even parents enroll their children in theater school [to become an actor]. It is no longer just a rebellious act."[101]

These honors, however, were accompanied by debilitating official responsibilities. Mikhoels's time was increasingly divided between his theater and his official assignments, forcing him to leave much of the day-to-day affairs of the theater in the hands of others and to absent himself from the stage. While retaining artistic control of the theater, Mikhoels did not appear on stage in any new play after

Tevye in 1938. Furthermore, Mikhoels's personal life sustained several major set-backs. Waking up to find that one of his close associates had been arrested was becoming increasingly routine, forcing him perpetually to be on guard for his own safety. As if this was not enough, his first wife's sister and surrogate mother to his children, Elsa Kantor, passed away in 1940, leaving him alone to take care of his young children. His only solace, as he confessed to Sergei Prokofiev, was in his work.[102] It is no surprise that in this atmosphere the artistic creativity of the theater suffered.

Mikhoels's remarkable ability to retain official favor throughout the purges and the seemingly asylum-like stature of his theater led to trumped-up rumors that he had a preferential relationship with Stalin. His friends and acquaintances were constantly seeking his protection, a favor Mikhoels was simply unable to provide. While he tried to extend his theater's shelter to as many different writers, musicians, and artists as possible, he knew that he could not save everybody. "Sometimes it seems to me that I alone am responsible for my whole people," he once remarked to his wife.[103] Mikhoels, however, had no preferential relationship with Stalin. This realization has prompted several scholars to attempt to account for Mikhoels's survival and the perseverance of his theater by arguing that the theater was saved due to its importance as an instrument of propaganda.[104] It is alleged that Stalin propped up the theater as a "showpiece" to dispel criticism that the Soviet state was anti-Semitic; Soviet propagandists could boldly point to Mikhoels's visibility as evidence of the prosperous state of Jewish national culture under Soviet rule. Although there is certainly evidence to suggest that Stalin considered the effect the Yiddish theater was having on the public opinion of world Jewry in the early 1920s, there is little to suggest that this incentive continued into the 1930s. After the establishment of the Jewish Autonomous Region, Birobidzhan seems to have largely usurped this role.

In fact, after the theater's 1928 European tour there were few attempts to promote the theater abroad. It was forbidden to continue its tour to America, where a Soviet Yiddish theater of its caliber would have greatly impressed anti-Soviet Jewish circles, both socialist and otherwise. Further, Granovsky's custom of dispatching press releases to European and American theatrical journals was abruptly discontinued under Mikhoels's tenure. Indeed, the theater's only production widely publicized abroad was *King Lear*. The Elizabethan classic, however, could have done little to convince foreigners that Jewish culture was flourishing under Soviet rule.

A variant of the "showpiece" theory contends that prominent Jewish figures were kept alive to elicit Western support in the event of a war with Germany. This theory, however, implies that during the Great Purges Stalin was planning strategically for the eventuality of a war with Hitler. But historians have shown that the Nazi invasion of the Soviet Union caught Stalin unprepared in spite of the many warning signals he received.[105] His lack of strategic planning is evidenced most obviously by the purges of the Red Army military command that decapitated its control center. Indeed, after the Molotov-Ribbentrop non-aggression pact, Stalin had little reason to believe that war was imminent. In the pre-war period, it would have been far more logical for Stalin to have targeted Jews to please his new ally. Hitler, no doubt, would have been most pleased to hear of the liquidation of the Moscow State Yiddish Theater. If the Soviet dictator had been motivated by anti-Semitism, this would have provided an ideal time for the liquidation of the Yiddish theater and its participants.

Ultimately, any logical resolution to the paradox of why the theater survived during the Great Purges implies that its survival can be explained through rational reasoning, and consequently that those who did not survive were murdered for strategic purposes. Recent scholarship, however, has argued convincingly that the purges were directed less by an intentional policy and more by the chaos of socio-political forces.[106] Once begun, the terror took on a momentum of its own, engulfing all those who crossed its path, while leaving many who stood in the eye of the storm alive. The upper echelons of the Party, it has been contended, unleashed pent-up anger and frustration among lower ranks both inside and outside the Party, which led to a climate of denunciation and self-criticism to which the secret police responded. It was this bottom-up momentum that facilitated the extent of the Great Purges.

Neither Stalin nor any of his associates ever designed a blueprint that indicated precisely who would be targeted and who would be saved. Stalin seems to have been no more concerned with the existence of the Moscow State Yiddish Theater than he was with the millions of petty bureaucrats, collective farm chairmen, factory foremen, and other ordinary citizens who were victimized. The evidence presented here that several campaigns against the theater were unleashed but ultimately failed indicate that its survival was not part of a grand design but was rather simply a product of the chaotic nature of the purges. After 1936 the theater was a subject of official criticism because of its history of alleged formalism. Such criticisms were usually forebodings of the imminent doom of an institution. In subsequent years the state cracked down on other Jewish cultural products, particularly music and art, but never completely annihilated them. Simultaneously, Mikhoels was implicated in the Babel affair and rightly believed himself to be in imminent danger. Yet, in all cases, the process was never completed. Armed with a combination of skill and luck, the theater managed repeatedly to deflect all attempts to liquidate it until its temporary survival was ensured by the Nazi invasion.

Despite their lack of concern for legal processes, Soviet prosecutors were notoriously dogmatic in soliciting denunciations and self-criticisms of their victims. Mikhoels ardently refused to participate in this type of ritual. On numerous occasions in which he was expected to play his part by denouncing Granovsky and recanting previous "errors," the director steadfastly refused. Somehow he understood that once he became a participant in the ritual, he would not be able to excuse himself from subsequent performances. He minimally played the part required of him by denouncing formalism in his speeches, but he refused to provide examples and never singled out particular individuals. He also prudently avoided the other extreme, resisting opportunities to make grandiose speeches defending himself and others. On the other hand, those who condemned him for deviations, such as Litvakov and Kerzhentsev, became victims themselves. Mikhoels took a great gamble by opting out of the ritual.

The director also possessed a remarkable ability to remain aloof from politics. Mikhoels repeatedly resisted political activity throughout his career, beginning with his refusal to join the theater's trade union in the early 1920s. Mikhoels had never been a member of any organization with an explicit political program. He was more of a mediator than an ideologue. By all accounts, this skill helped him gain the admiration and cooperation of his subordinates. The incessant squabbling that had permeated the troupe during Granovsky's tenure disappeared under Mikhoels. In contrast to his erstwhile mentor, Mikhoels actively sought to put less-experienced members of the troupe in lead roles and to use the works of a wide variety of Yiddish writers. His subordinates had little reason to resent him.

Mikhoels was not alone in this refusal to participate. Others, such as Isaac Babel, followed a similar policy. In contrast to Babel, however, Mikhoels continued working as usual. He neither participated nor remained suspiciously silent; he continued to work as though oblivious to the world around him. Although Mikhoels's refusal to participate in the ritual of the purges may have helped buy the theater time, ultimately the theater was saved only because the momentum of the terror was curtailed by the invasion of Hitler's Wehrmacht.

Brother Jews: Mikhoels and the Jewish Anti-Fascist Committee

7

On the morning of June 22, 1941, the Moscow State Yiddish Theater was performing a matinee of *Shulamis* at the Kharkov Red Army House while on tour. During the intermission, a messenger arrived to announce that the Soviet Union had been invaded by Hitler's Wehrmacht. Operation Barbarossa, as the onslaught was called, signaled the start of nearly four years of the most destructive war ever to be fought on Russian soil. Within the next two years, the vast majority of the audience, which was mostly composed of soldiers and officers, would be killed, along with an estimated 27 million Soviet citizens. The agitated actors were ordered to finish the show before boarding a train to Moscow. Not far from Kharkov, the train was bombarded by enemy fire but managed to continue into the capital.[1] The theater remained in Moscow, where it entertained a public deceived into believing that victory was at hand with revivals of its most popular productions. In the immediate aftermath of the war's outbreak, political expediency was replaced by the need to keep the population calm and entertained.

Since committing to a policy of non-aggression with Germany, the Soviet Union had accrued substantial territorial gains: the secret protocols of the Molotov-Ribbentrop treaty had allotted eastern Poland, Bessarabia (Moldova), Estonia, Latvia, and Finland to the Soviet sphere of influence (later Lithuania was added). By June 1940, as France fell in the West, the Baltic republics, Bessarabia, and eastern Poland had been annexed to the USSR, while Finland had been forced to concede territory around Leningrad after a costly winter war. Along with territorial enlargement came a population increase of approximately 17 million people. The 1.4 to 1.5 million Jews inhabiting the newly occupied territories, including approximately 250,000–350,000 refugees from western Poland, constituted a significant minority in the region.[2] The new citizens increased the number of Jews in the Soviet Union by over 30 percent. Although many residents of the occupied territories, particularly ethnic Poles, looked upon the Red Army as a hostile invading force, many ethnic minorities, including many Jews, initially hoped that Soviet sovereignty would put an end to ethnically based discrimination and halt further German advances into the regions of Eastern Europe densely populated with Jews.

Meanwhile, in August 1940, Hitler turned his attention to an aerial bombardment of Britain, hoping for the quick collapse of British defenses. By December, however, he realized that Britain would not fall as long as Soviet forces remained poised to the rear. Thus, the following spring he turned, once again, to the East. A lightening attack on the Soviet Union, he believed, would force Churchill to sue for peace. Despite repeated warnings of an imminent German invasion from the British and American governments, German deserters, and even Soviet military intelligence, Operation Barbarossa caught Stalin by surprise. Stalin chose to ignore all warnings, preferring to rely upon the pact he had made with Hitler in 1939. Although the Five-Year Plans of the 1930s had re-armed the Soviet Union and increased industrial and military production at great financial and human costs, the Red Army, the Russian people, and the Soviet economy were ill-prepared to defend their land against Nazi invaders. Stalin had always expected war to break out some time in the future, perhaps with Japan, but had not anticipated a surprise invasion from the West.

The invading Wehrmacht established air supremacy in hours, swept rapidly through the Baltic republics, and entered Belorussia and Ukraine within weeks. After disappearing from public view for almost two weeks following the invasion, Stalin reappeared to deliver a radio address on July 3rd in which he called upon the Red Army, the Navy, and all Soviet citizens to defend every inch of the Soviet land and to leave the invading army with only a "scorched earth." "All the strength of the people must be used to smash the enemy. Onward to victory!" he promised.[3] Within three and a half months, however, the Wehrmacht's three-pronged attack against Moscow, Leningrad, and Ukraine had largely destroyed the Soviet airforce, demolished thousands of tanks, taken prisoner or killed hundreds of thousands of soldiers, and caused unprecedented civilian casualties. The Wehrmacht had penetrated central Russia, pulverized Soviet border defenses, swept through Ukrainian villages, captured the ancient capital of Kiev, and laid siege to Leningrad in a blockade that would last nearly 900 days. In late September, the German Third Panzer Group was brought down from Army Group North and moved toward Moscow together with the Fourth Panzer Group from Army Group Center. During the second and third weeks of October the Soviet forces defending Vyazma and Bryansk had been destroyed, and the Kremlin was almost within sight of the Nazi field commanders.

While the Yiddish theater continued to function in theory during this period, the situation was chaotic. Sporadic air raids interrupted performances as the citizens of Moscow took refuge beneath the city in the newly constructed Moscow subway. By October 15, the Wehrmacht was less than seventy-five miles away from Moscow, forcing the evacuation of many Moscow institutions. The Moscow State Yiddish Theater, together with a number of other Jewish organizations, including other Yiddish theaters and the Jewish Writer's Union, were evacuated to the Uzbek capital of Tashkent, where it would remain until October 3, 1943.[4] In Tashkent, the Jewish actors became an integral part of the Uzbek cultural community, and Mikhoels guest-directed the Uzbek national theater in one of its most successful seasons. Mikhoels's most important contribution to the war effort, however, was his role in unifying Soviet Jewry as head of the newly formed Soviet Jewish Anti-Fascist Committee (JAFC).

The "national awakening" of Soviet Jews under the guidance of the Jewish Anti-Fascist Committee during the war has been well documented; but it has usually been seen as a complete reversal of previous trends rather than as part of an ongoing cultural development that had been brewing on the Yiddish stage for over a decade.[5] When examined in isolation, the committee appears as "the sole Jewish organization in the country ... which succeeded in uniting, for the first time in the history of the Soviet Union, the best writers, artists and researchers involved in Yiddish culture."[6] Shimon Redlich, for instance, the foremost scholar of the Anti-Fascist Committee, notes that because "the JAFC was the only central Jewish structure in Soviet Russia, it was inexorably connected to the fate of Soviet Jewry."[7] Certainly the Anti-Fascist Committee emerged during the war as the most important Jewish structure in Soviet Russia; however, it shared a stage with several other central Jewish structures, including the Yiddish Writer's Union and the State Yiddish Theater, the latter of which had united the best Yiddish writers and artists long before Mikhoels turned his attention to the Jewish Anti-Fascist Committee. The committee did not instigate an about-face in the political beliefs of its activists, but it did license Jewish writers, artists, and actors to proclaim national solidarity in a public and international forum for the first time in over a decade.

Brother Jews

Soon after the Nazi invasion, it became evident to those at the apex of power that the Soviet Union desperately needed international aid. Britain, however, was too busy fending off a Nazi attack of its own to render sufficient assistance, while Roosevelt remained suspicious of Stalin's motives and wary of his proven aggression and violation of human rights. But several Jewish organizations, such as the World Jewish Congress and the Jewish Agency for Palestine, were willing to engage any resource available, including alliance with the Soviet Union, "to assure the survival and to foster the unity of the Jewish people."[8] Stalin hoped that by advertising the achievements of Soviet Jewry to the world he would be able to attract contributions from world Jewry in general and the World Jewish Congress in particular. Solomon Mikhoels played a fundamental role in this mission, not only as director of the Moscow State Yiddish Theater, but also as chair of the Jewish Anti-Fascist Committee. During and after the war, Mikhoels's activities as a public figure became increasingly intertwined with his theatrical endeavors. His activities both within the Soviet Union and abroad on behalf of the Anti-Fascist Committee were integral to the future of the Yiddish theater.

Two months after the German invasion, Mikhoels took the lead in organizing a Jewish resistance movement within the Soviet Union. His first action was to organize a mass Jewish rally in Moscow. In a letter to Solomon Lozovskii, deputy chief of the Soviet Information Bureau, a department set up at the beginning of the war to oversee all war-related propaganda, he wrote:

> We, members of the Jewish intelligentsia, consider it appropriate to organize a Jewish rally aimed at the Jews of the USA and Great Britain, and also at Jews in other countries. The purpose of this rally would be to mobilize world Jewish public opinion in the struggle against fascism and for its active support of the Soviet Union in its Great Patriotic War of liberation.[9]

The letter was co-signed by several other prominent members of the Jewish intelligentsia, many of whom, like David Bergelson, Peretz Markish, Benjamin Zuskin, and Shmuel Halkin, had previously been associated with the Moscow State Yid-

A group of actors in the radio studio. *Sitting, from left to right:*
Solomon Mikhoels, Sara Rotbaum, unidentified radio announcer,
unidentified radio announcer, Liia Rozina, Lev Pulver.
Standing, from left to right: unidentified radio announcer, David
Chechik, unidentified radio announcer, Iosif Shidlo, Daniil
Finkelkraut, Iakov Kukles, unidentified radio announcer.
Photo courtesy of Ala Perelman-Zuskin.

dish Theater. Drawing from lessons he had learned as early as 1923, when the
Jewish Section of the Communist Party petitioned Stalin to subsidize the theater
"before news of this reaches America," Mikhoels formulated his request in terms
of its effect on American audiences. The strategy worked. On August 24, 1941, the
radio rally was broadcast. The speakers included the most prominent Jews in the
Soviet Union: Mikhoels, Markish, Bergelson, Nusinov, Rabinovich, Tyshler, Halkin, Zuskin, Ilya Ehrenburg, Sergei Eisenstein, and others. In their remarks, the
orators, headed by Mikhoels, appealed to the unity of world Jewry to continue
the fight against fascism. The speakers displayed a remarkable understanding of
Nazi atrocities against the Jews in the German-occupied territories.[10] "Mountains
of murdered corpses and ashes remain of every shtetl where Jews nested for nearly
a thousand years," declared Markish, "Everywhere [the Nazis] bring death and
destruction. Everywhere they carry despair and tears. Children and women and
the elderly they cut like grass and rape and trample under foot."[11]

As the prophesies predicted in the early plays of the theater, which equated
the shtetls of the former Pale of Settlement with cemeteries, began to be realized

in the here and now, Mikhoels's rhetoric suddenly transformed those same shtetls into bastions of genuine Jewish culture. Bergelson even heroized an elder of Lodz —the very same type of religious authority figure whom the theater had spent two decades denigrating and mocking. In stark contrast to the typical Soviet speech, Mikhoels made no reference to the unity of the working class of the world. Appealing to the bourgeois Jews of America and England he warned: "Jews, my brothers, remember that here in our battlefields, your fate as well as the fate of your countries is being decided."[12] The next day *Pravda* devoted a full-page spread to the meeting, with a banner headline that read: "Brother Jews of the Entire World."[13]

For the first time since the Revolution, Soviet Jewish activists openly hailed the existence of a united Jewish nation whose people were scattered throughout the world. The brothers of Soviet Jews were no longer Ukrainian peasants and Russian factory workers, but British and American Jewish philanthropists. Although the unique status of Jews within the Soviet Union had been officially recognized since the mid-1930s with the establishment of the Jewish Autonomous Region and the toleration of literature and theater dealing with national themes and Jewish distinctness, never before had Soviet Jews been permitted to openly assert their solidarity with Jews beyond the borders of the USSR.

On the surface the appeal to the Jews of the entire world appears no different than similar declarations made to the "youth of the entire world" and "scholars of the entire world." But neither world youth nor world scholars shared the same sense of community and solidarity as the Jews. Aside from sharing aspects of a common culture, language, and religion, many Jews in North America were Russian émigrés themselves and still had relatives and friends in the Soviet Union. Additionally, neither youth nor scholars were threatened by Nazism to the same extent as the Jews. The external threat was a strong unifying factor among Soviet Jewry. For decades they had been kept isolated from their co-religionists around the world, forced to withstand any threat to their nationhood without the support of their kin. After the German invasion of Poland, however, many Polish Jews fled across the river Bug into Soviet territory, reintroducing themselves to their Soviet "brethren." This first contact with their co-religionists beyond the Soviet pale in a quarter-century helped revive the national awareness of Soviet Jews.

After the August rally, Mikhoels was recognized within the Soviet Union as the de facto leader of the Soviet Jewish community, a position he used to foster a sense of solidarity among Soviet Jews and to persuade the Soviet Information Bureau to indulge him. Mikhoels's status as a public figure was institutionalized when he was appointed chair of the newly formed Jewish Anti-Fascist Committee. Mikhoels would use this position to act as a liaison between the Soviet state and Jews both within and beyond the Soviet Union. World Jewry, including the Soviet Jews, were thereby recognized as a distinct political interest group that merited its own semi-autonomous institution that could provide them with political representation.

The idea of setting up such a committee, on the model of Aleksei Tolstoy's All-Slav Anti-Fascist Committee, was initiated by Henryk Erlich and Victor

Alter. Both were former leaders of the Polish Bund who had fled their native Poland before the German invasion, only to be arrested and sentenced to death in the Soviet Union. After spending two years in prison, however, they were unexpectedly released in September 1941. Both were internationally renowned figures, respected by supporters and opponents alike, and the darlings of the American Jewish labor unions. Upon their release they began negotiating with Lavrentii Beria and Stalin regarding the possibility of establishing a Jewish anti-fascist committee.[14] They suggested that Erlich serve as chair, Mikhoels as vice-chair, and Alter as secretary. While he approved in principle of the proposed organization, Stalin did not trust the two former Bundists. On December 4th, Erlich and Alter were arrested again and taken to Kuibyshev prison. Eleven days later, on December 15th, Lozovskii appointed Mikhoels as chair of the Jewish Anti-Fascist Committee and literary critic Shakhno Epshteyn (1883–1945) as secretary.[15]

The prime objective of the Jewish Anti-Fascist Committee was to garner the support of American and British Jewry for the Soviet war effort. This was accomplished through numerous appeals to the unity of world Jewry—even the committee's newspaper was entitled *Eynikayt* (Unity). As Mikhoels said at the second radio rally: "Fellow Jews of the entire world! Even though we are separated by the Atlantic and Pacific Oceans, the oceans of blood for which the Nazis are responsible—the blood of our mothers and children, of our brothers and sisters—these oceans of innocent blood have confirmed the blood ties between us."[16] Within weeks of the August rally, it became apparent that the appeals were having the desired effect on foreign Jewish organizations. Even the U.S. Department of State interpreted the establishment of the committee as "a rapprochement between Soviet Russia and Zionist groups."[17] These sentiments were given further credence when the first secretary of the Soviet Embassy in Ankara visited Palestine with his press attaché, which represented the first official contact between the Yishuv (Jewish settlement in Palestine) and the Soviet Union. The visitors were welcomed with a ceremony at which both the Internationale and Hatikvah were sung together for the first time at an official Soviet reception. One banner draping the stage read, "The Land of Israel is the citadel of the national social renaissance of the Jewish people"—a mighty challenge to the historical attitude of the Soviet Union toward Palestine. While no representatives from the Jewish Anti-Fascist Committee were permitted to attend the ceremony, a message from the committee was read to the assembled guests.[18] The rally also provoked a response from Chaim Weizmann, chair of the World Zionist Organization. In a letter to the Jewish Anti-Fascist Committee dated September 8, 1941, Weizmann wrote, "We send our fraternal greetings. You may assure all your fellow citizens that the Jews of the world will not fail the common cause."[19] Similarly, throughout America, Jews responded to what many saw as an end to Soviet anti-Zionism and anti-religious policies. The Russian War Relief, headed by Edward Carter, and the National Council of American Soviet Friendship, liberal organizations sympathetic to Soviet causes, utilized the atmosphere created by the Moscow August radio call to rally Jewish support for their cause of soliciting military and medical supplies for the Soviet army. The plan to send to Russia planes and tanks named after historical

Jewish heroes, such as Bar Kokhba, elicited a particularly strong response, even though such transactions were already covered by the American Lend-Lease treaty that had been extended to the USSR in September 1941—although without the heroic names. As the *Chicago Jewish Chronicle* noted, "Every Tom, Dick and Harry, it seems, is now busily engaged in raising money for Russian war relief without authorization and without sanction."[20]

Other American Jewish circles, particularly Orthodox, Revisionist Zionist, and labor organizations, however, were more skeptical of the Russian government's desire to maintain amicable relations. For instance, the New Zionist Organization of America, noting the large number of Zionists imprisoned in Russia for their political beliefs, cautioned that "Russian diplomats expressed their sympathy for the sufferings of the Jewish people, but beyond that, nothing was forthcoming from the Russian government."[21] Similarly, the American labor movement refused to forgive the arrest of Erlich and Alter. The American Federation of Labor, along with the *Jewish Daily Forward* and the Workmen's Circle, petitioned American Assistant Secretary of State Breckenridge Long to intercede on behalf of Erlich and Alter.[22] While Long took the matter seriously, the Soviet embassy refused to discuss the matter with him, arguing that since Erlich and Alter were Polish citizens, the United States had no jurisdiction over them.[23]

On February 23, 1943, Maksim Litvinov, now the Soviet ambassador to the United States, wrote to William Green of the American Federation of Labor informing him that "for active subversive work against the Soviet Union and assistance to Polish intelligence organs in armed activities, Ehrlich [*sic*] and Alter were sentenced to capital punishment in August 1941," and that the sentence had been carried out.[24] In fact, Erlich had hanged himself in his cell several months earlier, while Alter had been executed on February 17th.[25] The execution shocked American Jewish labor activists and reinforced their suspicions of the Soviet Union. In response, the American Federation of Labor and the Congress of Industrial Organizations held a protest rally against the Soviet Union on March 30, 1943, in New York. The assembly, which was addressed by New York Mayor Fiorello La Guardia, among others, was attended by an estimated 2,500 people.[26] The Erlich-Alter affair seriously threatened to disturb any American Jewish rapprochement with the Soviet Union.

Furthermore, the appointment of Mikhoels as chair of the Anti-Fascist Committee was met with great skepticism on the part of British and American organizations. While Erlich and Alter were renowned political activists, trusted and admired around the world, Mikhoels's international fame was far more restricted. Few abroad knew him personally, and information regarding his theater was scant. For instance, the British Foreign Office was unable even to correctly identify Mikhoels's name, let alone his qualifications, and erroneously held him responsible for the arrest of Erlich and Alter: "It soon became obvious that the Soviet authorities meant to use the Jewish Anti-Fascist Committee as a tool for their propaganda" stated one British Foreign Office assessment. "The very same person who denounced V. Alter and H. Erlich to the Soviet authorities, a certain Hoels [*sic*], has been appointed Secretary General of the Jewish Anti-Fascist Committee."[27]

Not only was the representation of Mikhoels libelous, but the report also incorrectly stated that the Soviet government had set up an anti-fascist committee in Palestine. Soviet authorities quickly realized that if the Jewish Anti-Fascist Committee was to garner the trust of foreign Jewry, Mikhoels would need to be introduced to the world.

Menakhem Mendl Meets the Archbishop of Canterbury

In an effort to pressure the American government to open a second European front and increase the flow of military aid to the Soviet Union, the Soviet Information Bureau decided to send a delegation from the Jewish Anti-Fascist Committee to America and Britain. It was hoped that the delegates would be able to deflect attention away from the Erlich-Alter affair and convince Western Jewry that racial discrimination and anti-Semitism had been eradicated in the Soviet Union. The idea of sending a Jewish delegation abroad was discussed as early as August 1942, when Epshteyn suggested that a member of the Jewish Anti-Fascist Committee be sent to England and Palestine.[28] The proposal was rejected. Over the next year, however, as relations between Western Jewish organizations and the Soviet Union sharply deteriorated over the Erlich-Alter affair, the decision was re-evaluated. The ideal opportunity for such a visit came when the American Committee of Jewish Writers, Artists, and Scientists—headed by Albert Einstein and popular Yiddish columnist Ben Zion Goldberg (who was also the son-in-law of Sholem Aleichem)—together with the Jewish Council for Russian War Relief invited representatives from the Jewish Anti-Fascist Committee to the United States. This time the Soviet Information Bureau accepted the invitation. Soon after, Lozovskii and Deputy Commissar of Defense Aleksandr Shcherbakov met to decide on the delegation. Three names were initially discussed: Ehrenburg, who was regarded as too essential to be sent away; Markish, who was not believed to be trustworthy enough; and Epshteyn, whom Lozovskii believed was compromised in foreign eyes by his Party activities. Shcherbakov suggested dispatching Mikhoels on the grounds that he was an effective orator with an understanding of political language, and, most important, because he was not a member of the Communist Party and therefore would be regarded with minimal suspicion by his American hosts.[29] It was also decided to send the Yiddish poet, committed Communist, and future Secret Police informant Itzik Fefer (1900–1952), who could be trusted to keep an eye on Mikhoels's activities abroad. The United States quickly granted the two visas.

Mikhoels was immediately suspicious of his companion. Before departing, he wrote to his wife: "I will find myself practically alone . . . for the other colleague who is accompanying me can hardly be counted on for support and assistance. And the picture there is getting more complex every day."[30] Mikhoels's daughter has also testified that she recalls many allusive comments made by her father that indicate he knew of Fefer's mission.[31] According to historian Gennadi Kostyrchenko, however, it was not until 1944 that Fefer was recruited by the Ministry of State Security.[32] Regardless of whether or not he was officially employed by the ministry at the time of the American excursion, he could certainly have been counted on to provide information about Mikhoels's whereabouts.

Mikhoels was given little forewarning of the mission, probably to prevent him from making any subversive plans. As a result, the theater was left in disarray. Soon after his departure, the actor wrote to his wife:

> The way they uprooted me, and didn't give me a chance to get ready, is driving me crazy. I've left behind my infinitely precious and dearly beloved, my indispensable companion, and the children.... I've left the theater behind, with hardly any plans, without future prospects, without a leader.[33]

Before they were dispatched, Lozovskii spoke to the two delegates: "You are Soviet men first and foremost, and then Jews. When you arrive in America, you will be seen not only as Jews, but also as Soviet men. Not only the Jewish community and Jewish papers, but the entire American press will watch you because you will appear as Soviet men, regardless of your national membership."[34] The two were warned to keep in close contact with the Soviet consulate and not to hold any meetings without the permission of the consulate. According to Goldberg, the two were also instructed personally by Molotov, Stalin, and Kalinin.[35]

The journey to America in the midst of a world war was by no means a simple trip. Because of flight restrictions over European airspace, the trek took the pair through sixteen countries on five continents before returning to Russia in December 1943. The two departed by air from Moscow in May 1943 and traveled to Teheran, where they stayed for over two weeks.[36] It is possible that in Teheran Mikhoels came into contact for the first time with representatives from the Yishuv. Less than a week before Mikhoels's arrival in Teheran, a Jewish delegation from Palestine had presented the Red Army with military supplies at a ceremony in Teheran. Teheran remained a point of contact between the Yishuv and the Soviet Union throughout the war. It is unclear, though, whether the representatives of the Yishuv were still in Teheran at the time of Mikhoels's arrival.

Following their stay in Teheran and a brief stopover in Iraq, Mikhoels and Fefer unexpectedly were forced to land at Lydda Airport in Palestine.[37] Although the two were not permitted to leave the airplane as it sat on the runway, the brief visit seems to have been profoundly meaningful to Mikhoels. According to the testimony of his daughter, Mikhoels managed to smuggle out of the plane a brief note written in Hebrew to family friends who had settled on Kibbutz Afikim, in which he expressed his solidarity with the Zionists, writing, "I want to kiss the air and land of Israel."[38] Abraham Sutzkever also recalled Mikhoels telling him how he was touched by this trip, and how he "kissed the air" of Israel.[39]

From Palestine, Mikhoels and Fefer proceeded to Egypt, where they toured Cairo and the Giza pyramids. Departing Cairo, they followed the American military airways routes south through the Sudanese desert to Khartoum, across central Africa to British Nigeria and the Gold Coast, then flew across the Atlantic to Brazil. From Brazil they proceeded north to Puerto Rico and then to the Dominican Republic, where they stayed in Trujillo. The delegation finally arrived in Miami in June. Both travelers often spoke of the duration of the journey, which lasted exactly forty days, a number rich in Biblical imagery. As Fefer wrote in a letter to his family: "This number is mentioned more than once in Jewish history in the Bible. The Jews wandered in the desert for forty years after their difficult departure from Egypt on their way to the Promised Land; the Flood lasted forty days and forty nights."[40] Mikhoels, too, was fond of recalling the precise duration of the journey, as if to link his mission to the Egyptian Exodus, with himself playing the role of Moses. Both, he seemed to be saying, were historic journeys which would free the Jewish people from slavery and lead them to the Promised Land.

The delegation's first official stop was in Washington, where they attended a ceremony at the Soviet embassy. They then proceeded to New York, Philadelphia, Boston, Pittsburgh, Detroit, Chicago, Kansas City, San Francisco, and Hollywood. They also visited Mexico City and made several stops in Canada. Finally, on their way back home, the delegation spent several weeks in England. They returned to Moscow on December 10th.

The official segment of the delegation commenced in earnest when they arrived in New York. The two repeatedly issued addresses to American Jewry, appealing to their "brother Jews" for assistance in the Soviet war effort. Publicly, the delegates emphasized two themes: that racial prejudice and anti-Semitism had been eliminated in the USSR and that the Soviet army could defeat Hitlerism with the support of world Jewry. The most important event in their itinerary was a rally held at New York's Polo Grounds on July 8th. The *New York Times* estimated attendance at 47,000 people.[41] The event was most significant in that it was the first time Soviet Jews were permitted to present a united front with world Jewry in all its religious and Zionist manifestations. From the moment the ceremony began with singing of the Star Spangled Banner, Hatikvah, and the Internationale, the rally took on a blatantly nationalist tone. Besides Mikhoels and Fefer, other speakers included such prominent Jewish activists as writer Sholem Asch, Ben Zion Goldberg, Rabbi Stephen Wise, James Rosenberg (chairman of the Joint Distribution Committee), and Nahum Goldmann (director of the World Jewish Congress). Ecstatic greetings were also issued from the British Jewish Fund for Soviet Russia.[42]

Reports in *Pravda* emphasized that the "friendly pronouncements toward the Soviet Union and the Soviet government were met with resounding approval. References to the name of Comrade Stalin and the Soviet people as an example of a people united solidly around its leader evoked especially warm ovations."[43] This interpretation was echoed in a report to the U.S. Office of Strategic Services, which stated that "every mention of Russia, the Red Army, and Stalin was greeted with enthusiastic applause" and that "when the Soviet anthem was played, the majority of the audience sang the words."[44]

In addition to public appearances, Mikhoels held private audiences with a wide range of prominent Jewish and non-Jewish cultural figures. Few, if any, Soviet citizens had rubbed shoulders with such an illustrious community, representing such a wide array of ideologies. This would become a stigma that would haunt Mikhoels in the post-war era. By the end of his tour of America and Britain, Mikhoels had had substantial meetings with Sholem Asch, Marc Chagall, Charlie

Left to right: Itzik Fefer, Albert Einstein, Solomon Mikhoels, USA 1943. Photo courtesy of Natalia Vovsi-Mikhoels.

Chaplin, Theodore Dreiser, Albert Einstein, Lion Feuchtwanger, John Gielgud, Ben Zion Goldberg, Thomas Mann, Paul Muni, Max Reinhardt, Paul Robeson, and Upton Sinclair, to name but a few. Mikhoels also visited the grave of Sholem Aleichem, about which he wrote an article entitled "The Beloved Sholem Aleichem Spoke to Me."[45]

In addition, Mikhoels was given audiences with some of the most prominent political and religious figures of the time, including La Guardia and the Archbishop of Canterbury.[46] Official representatives of the American government, however, remained suspicious of the delegation. Although the reception committee had invited Franklin Delano Roosevelt to issue a statement, the president declined the offer.[47] The Roosevelt administration had remained aloof from the Russian war relief effort in general, on the grounds that the Lend-Lease treaty covered all necessary aid to Russia.[48] Furthermore, it was confused about the delegation's sponsorship. The administration received no official information from the Soviet embassy regarding the delegation prior to its arrival, and was therefore understandably confused when Mikhoels and Fefer suddenly arrived, claiming to be on an official mission from the USSR. The Foreign Nationalities Branch of the Office of Strategic Services reported on the delegation's sponsorship:

Statements published in the Yiddish and Anglo-Jewish press immediately after the arrival of the two visitors asserted that they had been sent by the Jewish Anti-Fascist Committee of Soviet Russia, a group of outstanding Jewish Communist leaders and writers of which Michoels [*sic*] is chairman. In daily press announcements and advertisements they are generally described simply as cultural ambassadors or artistic delegates. . . . Press announcements sent out by the Committee of Jewish Writers and Artists speak of Michoels and Feffer [*sic*] as an "official delegation from the USSR" and make no reference to the Jewish Anti-Fascist Committee. The *Information Bulletin* of the Soviet Embassy has made no mention of their presence in this country."[49]

Yet the report notes that "they have been received at the Soviet Embassy in Washington and at the Soviet Consulate in New York." In general, the report concluded that "the precise nature of their mission here has been left obscure."[50] The administration received little enlightenment from established Jewish organizations. One report, for instance, stated that since their sponsorship was unknown, "no organization with the prestige, standing, and tradition of the American Jewish Committee can give its official recognition to this delegation from the USSR."[51] The director of the Jewish Institute, which was associated with the American Jewish Congress, contended that "there is no doubt these two men are trying to do a good Soviet propaganda job by endeavoring to [c]reate the impression that Jewish life in Soviet Russia is a paradise."[52] Much of the administration's information about the delegation came from hostile sources. For instance, one report characterized the Committee of Jewish Writers and Artists as a "communist front organization."[53] The Office of Strategic Services also looked toward the *Jewish Daily Forward*, which wrote that Fefer was a "100% communist and has taught the Soviet Jews to hate the Jews of other countries."[54] Some Polish intellectuals, on the other hand, argued that "one of the objects of the above two delegates [Mikhoels and Fefer] was to spoil the good relations between Poles and Jews in this country."[55] Given so little official intelligence on the delegation, the administration had no choice but to ignore it.

The British Foreign Office was similarly skeptical. It also complained that British contributions to the war effort were being overlooked:

We seem to get small credit from them [Mikhoels and Fefer] for our own not inconsiderable share in the same enterprise, and as American Jewry is so pro-Zionist and the Soviet Government so firmly opposed to Zionism, this demonstration of devotion strikes me as unusual, even allowing for some artistic license in the Soviet reports. . . . If Jews in America think that anything they can do will cause the Soviet Government to deviate from its settled policy on as important a matter as the treatment of Jews here, they must rate their influence and powers of persuasion uncommonly high.[56]

"So, we meet again, Dr. Weizmann"

Despite being snubbed by the American Jewish Committee and most Jewish socialist organizations, Mikhoels and Fefer did manage to establish contact with a dizzying array of Jewish public figures and official representatives of the Jewish community.[57] Some of these meetings would later be used as evidence of Mikhoels's nationalist aspirations and the failure to report them would be used to condemn Zuskin to death, even though Zuskin may not have even been informed of the meetings.[58] The first such meeting was with James Rosenberg, the head of the American Jewish Joint Distribution Committee. Rosenberg, who in 1926 had visited several Jewish agricultural settlements in the Soviet Union, hoped to persuade the delegation to accept funds earmarked for distribution to Jewish settlements. He also suggested the creation of a Jewish autonomous region in the Crimea and donated 500,000 dollars to the Soviet Union Relief Fund for this purpose. When Mikhoels returned to the Soviet Union, he raised the idea with Lozovskii, who approved in principle. Discussions to that end reached very high levels before being thwarted.[59] The "Crimean Affair" was later used as evidence of the Jewish Anti-Fascist Committee's alleged anti-Soviet nationalist aspirations.

The most important meetings the two held, however, were with leaders of the Zionist movement. For instance, Chaim Weizmann, who spent much of the war in the United States, spoke at a welcoming reception in New York and remained in contact with the delegation until his departure for London in July 1943.[60] Meyer Weisgal, Weizmann's personal representative in the United States and director of the Jewish Agency for Palestine in New York, even managed to clandestinely arrange a private meeting with Mikhoels. After injuring himself at a rally, Mikhoels was taken to a hospital in New York. With Fefer attending official engagements, Mikhoels was left alone for the first time in his hospital bed. Weisgal took advantage of this opportunity to sneak Mikhoels out of the hospital for a full evening of candid conversation.

In his memoirs, Weisgal recalls that the meeting was arranged at the request of Max Reinhardt. He later told Natalia Vovsi-Mikhoels, however, that Weizmann was also present. The omission of this crucial fact in Weisgal's published work can be attributed to concern for the welfare of Mikhoels's daughters, who were still living in the Soviet Union at the time of publication. Weisgal's published recollection of the incident is also tainted with several other errors; most notably, he erroneously dates the encounter to 1942 and credits Reinhardt with having directed Mikhoels in *The Travels of Benjamin III.*

Weizmann, who had met Mikhoels during the theater's 1928 European tour, likely suspected that Fefer was acting as an impediment to Mikhoels's candor. His suspicions were proven correct. According to Weisgal, Mikhoels was initially very tense and fearful of being discovered, "but as the night wore on, and the alcohol produced its effect, he lost his way, began to weep, and to lament the lot of the Jews of Russia. . . . Later he confided to Joe [Brainin, a member of the American Committee of Jewish Artists, Writers, and Scientists] that he had only played the drunk, otherwise he could not have summoned up the courage to say what he did."[61] In what was probably the most frank conversation Mikhoels managed to have during the entire trip, he expressed a great deal of pessimism about the future of Soviet Jewry. "Jewish culture has no future in the Soviet Union," he declared. "At present it is difficult, but it will become worse." In addition, the group spoke

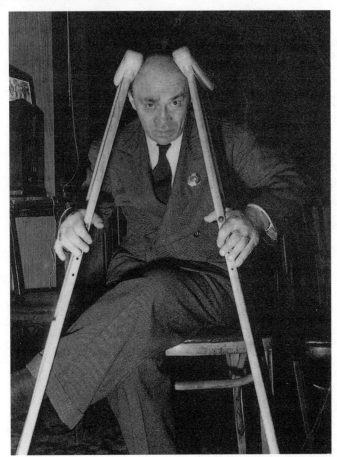

Solomon Mikhoels
with his broken
leg, USA 1943.
Photo courtesy
of Natalia Vovsi-
Mikhoels.

at great length about Palestine, and Mikhoels showed great interest and knowledge of the debates regarding the foundation of a Jewish state.[62] The Soviet secret
police later found out about this meeting and used it as evidence against Weizmann's sister, Maria, during its 1952 investigation of her.[63]

Nahum Goldmann, the director of the World Jewish Congress and an active
Zionist, also played an influential role in the delegates' trip by acting as a liaison
between the Anti-Fascist Committee and the U.S. State Department. He met
with the delegates on several occasions, during which he brought up a wide range
of topics that were well beyond the delegates' authority, including Jewish emigration from the USSR and Soviet treatment of Jewish POWs.[64] Goldmann openly
sought to use the visit as an opportunity to gain Soviet sympathy for the establishment of a Zionist state and publicly invited the two delegates to visit Palestine.
Both Weizmann and Israel Meriminsky, a representative of the Histadrut (Pales-

tinian labor union), later repeated the invitation. According to Shimon Redlich, who interviewed Meriminsky about his meeting with Mikhoels,

> Mikhoels was extremely moved by his direct encounter with a representative of the Yishuv. Mereminsky reported that, while Mikhoels clearly indicated his personal feelings in regard to Palestinian Jewry, he kept hinting that neither he nor his Committee made the important decisions. Mikhoels repeated several times in the course of the conversation that he was a "messenger only" and that the JAC was already "doing more than it could."[65]

Similar responses are recorded in reports to the Office of Strategic Services. For instance, one report states that "at a private and confidential meeting with some Jewish leaders, confronted with the question of the Soviet attitude towards Palestine, the two delegates in a rather pathetic way begged the Americans to 'leave them alone' and not cause them any trouble with questions [about topics] which was [*sic*] none of their business to discuss."[66]

Numerous reports state that Mikhoels became agitated when confronted with questions about Palestine, probably indicating his frustration at being unable to openly express his thoughts and feelings. Yet throughout the trip, Mikhoels gradually became more courageous in his responses. For instance, in Britain, when asked specifically about Soviet attitudes toward the possible establishment of a Jewish state in Palestine, Mikhoels was forthright. "I speak for myself," he replied, "I am not qualified to speak in the name of the USSR. It is certainly a matter of our common interest, of the interest of the Jewish masses, that the union between our lands remain as tight forever as it is today.... And I could add ... rest assured that if England decides to create a Jewish republic in the Land of Israel, without doubt there will be no obstacles on the Soviet side."[67] According to his daughter, the night before his return to the Soviet Union, Mikhoels also met with an in-law who discussed with him the possibility of settling in Palestine.[68]

There are several indications, ranging from the aesthetic content of the theater's productions to his actions at the Lydda Airport that Mikhoels harbored Zionist sympathies even prior to his arrival in America. His sudden outspokenness in England indicates that these sentiments were exacerbated by his experiences in America. In addition to receiving numerous entreaties from the world's leading Zionists during his tour, Mikhoels also made observations of his own which could have further convinced him that the only solution to the "Jewish question" lay in the foundation of a Jewish state. During the early twentieth century, four general ideologies were put forward as solutions to the "Jewish problem": religion, socialism, democratic capitalism, and Zionism. Mikhoels's rejection of religion from an early age was complete; he clearly did not believe that a retreat into religion and isolationism was a solution to the Jewish problem. As he lived through the Soviet purges, Mikhoels also became convinced that socialism as practiced in the Soviet Union would fail to provide a shelter for world Jewry. This left two options: democratic capitalism and Zionism. However, his firsthand glimpse into American life and his subsequent observations reveal a genuine distrust of the American model. His numerous official accounts of the visit provided him with an opportunity to vent what seem to be carefully formed criticisms of capitalist society. His use of concrete examples indicate a genuine disgust with what he saw as a racist society obsessed with the excesses of consumerism. He seems to have become convinced that democratic capitalism as practiced in America could not provide an attractive solution to the "Jewish question."

In numerous speeches, Mikhoels noted the effects of American racism and anti-Semitism. From the beginning, Mikhoels, who spoke no English, found that he was better able to relate to African Americans, who, he wrote, were more likely to be proficient in French. He was also attracted to African American culture, noting that his favorite play was *Porgy and Bess*—written by the Jewish composer George Gershwin, based on DuBose Heyward's novel.[69] Needless to say, he was disturbed by the living conditions and segregation of African Americans.[70] Conversations with Paul Robeson, the African American Shakespearean actor, convinced him that racism was deeply rooted in America. Similarly, despite the high visibility of Jews in American life, Mikhoels noticed a strong anti-Semitism lurking beneath the surface. He was particularly struck by the informal segregation of Jews, noting that there were even separate hotels and vacation spots for Jews. As O. Litovskii wrote, "His stories about the life of American Jews, although there was nothing unexpected for me, conveyed how harsh and bitter nationalism and anti-Semitism are."[71] Mikhoels was also disturbed by the excesses of capitalism. He commented that Americans treated their cars like gods and prayed in the language of dollars.[72] As a trained lawyer himself, Mikhoels also took an interest in the American legal profession: "A jurist is not someone who attempts to observe the law. On the contrary, he is someone who devotes his life to getting around the law," he quipped about American judicial proceedings.[73]

He was perhaps most disturbed, however, by what he saw as the pitiful stature of theater and art in the Western world. He was amazed that there was no theater of quality in either Miami or Washington. His only real exposure to American theater was in New York, where he was shocked that even Max Reinhardt, who had taken American citizenship in 1941 after fleeing from Germany, was unable to recreate his European successes. According to Mikhoels, Reinhardt was so disappointed with his American efforts that he discussed with Mikhoels the possibility of emigrating to the USSR.[74] Broadway, Mikhoels proclaimed, "is the street of sin."[75] He was particularly struck by the American interest in the private lives of its actors—"in what [they are] like as [people], in [their] experiences, in what [they smoke], in what type of linen [they wear], in what type of toothpaste and toothbrush [they use]."[76] He was further disturbed by the reluctance of American actors to take political stands: "The phrase: 'I am not concerned with politics' I heard from representatives of the American intelligentsia many times," he lamented.[77] Even Charlie Chaplin, whose political statements in the *Great Dictator* would lead to a congressional investigation against him, claimed to Mikhoels that he had no interest in politics.[78] Nevertheless, Mikhoels was fascinated by Chaplin and the two spent a full day together in Hollywood. Mikhoels was further disturbed by what he saw as a lack of Shakespearean productions in America; he was amazed when he visited the Folger Shakespeare Library in Washington to discover that he was only the second actor to visit the library.[79] Even in England, Mikhoels was amazed to discover that Shakespeare was no longer performed. When he met John Gielgud, the great actor complained to Mikhoels that the British no longer understood Shakespeare. The Archbishop of Canterbury repeated this comment when he met with Mikhoels: "Shakespeare can no longer be understood because the Bible has been forgotten. Without the Bible, Shakespeare cannot be understood." Mikhoels agreed, commenting on the influence of the Bible on his own portrayal of King Lear.[80] The cultural life of the Western world, Mikhoels firmly believed, was hopelessly decadent.

A Nationalist Nation

Mikhoels's agreement with the archbishop's estimation of the Bible reveals one of the unorthodoxies in the Soviet representative's thinking. During the war, Mikhoels became increasingly aware of the role that Jews and Judaism played in both world politics and his own life. As the chairman of the Jewish Anti-Fascist Committee, Mikhoels had unequaled access to information about the state of Jewry in Eastern Europe. Indeed, according to some sources, he was the first to make the claim that the Germans were manufacturing soap from the flesh of their Jewish victims, and he often displayed bars of soap allegedly made from human fat at mass rallies in America. He had unparalleled access to information being disseminated throughout the Soviet Union—through official and non-official channels—and to American and British intelligence as provided to him by his hosts. Letters from refugees constantly flooded the Jewish Anti-Fascist Committee headquarters, and Mikhoels met with numerous refugees who survived the journey to Moscow—sometimes through Mikhoels's personal intervention. Mikhoels was one of few Soviet citizens to have had an inkling of the extent of the Holocaust prior to the liberation of the concentration camps. Along with many others who were affected by the Jewish condition during World War II, Mikhoels seems to have come to believe that the Jewish people could only survive in a state of their own.

This sentiment, which is consistent with the nationalist pride Mikhoels had always demonstrated as director of the Yiddish theater, gradually and surreptitiously surfaced during his tour of America and Britain. The decadence and veiled racism that he perceived in America convinced him that the *goldene medine* (Golden State) would ultimately fail to protect the interests of European Jewry. Numerous conversations with the world's leading Zionists, including his old acquaintance Chaim Weizmann, further inspired him with Zionist convictions. Although Mikhoels was never able to assert Zionist ideologies openly, repeated references to his anxiety and uneasiness when the question of Palestine was broached indicate a sympathetic, or at least a complex, disposition. After his departure from Britain, Mikhoels gave his most tangible endorsement of the Zionist project by asserting that the Soviet Union would offer no resistance to the establishment of a Jewish state in Palestine.

Even without any substantial statement of Zionist sympathy, Mikhoels's activities abroad contrasted sharply with Soviet notions of nationality. Although on one hand Stalin unleashed a flurry of nationalist chauvinism, interpreting the war as a battle between Russians and Germans, on the other hand, internal Soviet propaganda endorsed the notion of a superethnic Soviet nation formed upon the principle of the "brotherhood of all Soviet peoples." Mikhoels's references to his "brother Jews" across the ocean, however, professed a solidarity with a people beyond the Pale, thereby breaching the Soviet national paradigm. The appeal to world Jewish unity implied that the Jews were exempt from the prototype of Soviet nationhood. The unity of the Jewish nation, he declared, cut across political and ideological borders—even the barrier between the Communist and capitalist worlds was penetrable.

The Soviet Information Bureau certainly encouraged Mikhoels and his associates to politicize and publicize their previously covert nationalism. Stalin's sudden need for Western support after the onslaught of Hitler's Wehrmacht persuaded him that his own Jews could be used as sirens, attracting ships of Jewish wealth and assistance to Communist shores. Mikhoels, therefore, was entrusted with the task of collecting information about Nazi atrocities against the Jews and was sent abroad to solicit support for the Soviet war effort. The knowledge and experiences he obtained through these missions bolstered Mikhoels's long-felt national awareness. The official sanction he received, however, did little to help him promote overt nationalism within his theater during the war.

Our People Live: The Yiddish Theater during World War II

8

In stark contrast to the information being disseminated abroad, internal Soviet propaganda sought to diminish both Jewish achievements and Jewish victimhood in the war. This phenomenon was intricately connected to a general revival of Russian national chauvinism and patriotism. On November 6, 1941, Stalin delivered his famous "Holy Russia" speech, in which the ethnically Georgian leader embraced the national heritage of "Mother Russia." He spoke of "the great Russian nation—the nation of Plekhanov and Lenin, of Belinsky and Chernyshevsky, of Pushkin and Tolstoy, or Gorky and Chekhov, of Glinka and Tchaikovsky, of Sechenov and Pavlov, of Suvorov and Kutuzov."[1] Increasingly, Stalin would speak of the Russian people as "the elder brother in the family of the equal Soviet peoples"[2] a slogan later parodied by George Orwell's farcical maxim, "all animals are equal, but some animals are more equal than others." Henceforth, official Soviet culture aspired to revive previously taboo nationalist sentiments among its population.[3] The unofficial order to invoke nationalism and patriotism was a logical and effective means of inspiring the population during the crisis of war. Love of one's country and fellow people, the desire to emulate historical heroes and to defeat age-old foes, devotion to religious symbols, and sentimental longings for serenity all encouraged civilians and soldiers alike to make great sacrifices for the common good of the nation.

Stalin's open declaration of Russian national chauvinism was echoed in the cultural sphere. Playwrights such as Vladimir Soloviev, Aleksandr Afinogenov, the Tur Brothers (Leonid Tubelskii and Pëtr Ryzhei), and Konstantin Simonov, to name but a few, sought to instill hope and patriotism in Russian citizens while emphasizing the excitement of war over the devastating havoc it brings. Plays, like Simonov's spy story *The Russian People*, embodied all the essential ingredients for a bombastic, patriotic, wartime drama: heroic Russians, romantic love, death-defying exploits, secret missions, and villainous traitors. Others, like Soloviev's *Field Marshall Kutuzov* inspired viewers with examples of historical military heroes who overcome the odds to lead the Russian people to victory.[4] Documentary newsreels, radio broadcasts, and newspaper reports all worked to ensure that, whether defending the frontier or minding the home front, modern Russians were portrayed as giants standing on the heads of giants.

It did not take long for anti-Semitic undertones to emerge from the national fervor. Rumors of Jewish intrigue and self-interest helped Soviet propaganda account for Stalin's dire misjudgment of August 1939. The Russian people needed to be convinced that Stalin had not erred but rather had been betrayed. Yet a betrayal by Hitler would have implied that Stalin's decision to trust the Führer had been erroneous in the first place. Thus, the Russian people were permitted to believe that they had been forced into the war by the one group with the most to gain from a second front against the Germans—the Jews. Unchecked rumors were permitted to spread that the Jews had somehow betrayed Stalin and forced Russia into the war for their own parochial interests. The same Jews, it was contended, then retreated into the Soviet interior, forcing Russian soldiers to fight their war. These reports were fueled by Nazi propaganda, broadcast throughout the occupied territories and spread into the heartland by hearsay. Soviet news bureaus did little to stifle the rumors and even sustained them by belittling Jewish involvement at the front. The notion that Jews were contributing little to the Soviet war effort was given some rationalization by the fact that several major Jewish organizations had been evacuated to the Soviet interior. It was of little consequence that countless non-Jewish governmental, administrative, industrial, and cultural organizations had also been evacuated.[5]

Prior to its evacuation, the Moscow State Yiddish Theater was reorganized, both artistically and administratively, to convert it into an instrument of Soviet wartime propaganda. In October 1941, the Committee of Artistic Affairs removed the theater's administrative director and his deputy. While both were Party loyalists, both had had previous connections to the theater before their appointments. Thus, the committee could have had suspicions that their loyalties were to the theater first and the committee second. They were replaced with G. B. Fishman and A. B. Vitis, who served as administrative director and deputy director, respectively.[6] Fishman was a long-time member of the Party and had served in the Odessa Committee of Artistic Affairs before taking on the directorship of the Yiddish theater. The two were to remain loyal overseers of the theater on behalf of the government and would fulfill their future role as directors of the Commission to Liquidate the State Yiddish Theater with equal zeal. Next, the theater was rewarded with financial compensation. While the State Bank had turned down a request for a loan on December 1, 1941, on the flimsy grounds that the loan application failed to follow the proper channels, the Committee of Artistic Affairs intervened on December 31st to ensure that the theater received its required stipend.[7]

Next, the theater's repertoire was modified to reflect contemporary concerns connected with the war. Productions that had been in the works for several years, such as Shakespeare's *Richard III*, Markish's *Kol Nidre*, and Halkin's *The Musician* (about a bright young musician who was murdered by monarchists), were deemed "out of date" and canceled on account of "the artistic demands of the war."[8] Additionally, the film *Prestige of an Empire*, based on the notorious anti-Semitic Beilis trial of 1913, was canceled by Agitprop in 1941. The film was written by Lev Sheinin, the famous detective novelist and chief of the Department of the Office of Investigation. It was to be directed by Eisenstein, and Zuskin was to play the role of Beilis. Eisenstein had even spent several months in 1940 working on the film.[9] Now that a new threat had emerged from the West, however, it was considered counterproductive to dwell on the threats of the tsarist past. The theater had also planned to perform a stage adaptation of Lion Feuchtwanger's *The Oppermans*.[10] Mikhoels had already played the role in Grigori Roshal's 1938 motion picture. As

Nazi crimes against the Jews intensified during the war, however, Feuchtwanger's 1933 portrait of the persecution of Berlin Jews seemed inappropriately tame. Even at his most pessimistic, the author was simply unable to imagine the extent of Nazi brutality. "Today," wrote Mikhoels in a letter to Feuchtwanger, "the heart demands still more. It demands still more fervor."[11] The play was more likely canceled because it drew attention to the distinct plight of Jews under Nazi rule—a major Soviet taboo during the war.

The theater's repertoire was instead forced to mirror Soviet interpretations of the war. The theater's portrayal of the war provides an early example of the official myths that would come to characterize Soviet interpretations of the Holocaust in the occupied territories. Based on a study of articles on the Holocaust from the Soviet Yiddish journal *Sovetish heymland,* which began to appear in 1961, Zvi Gitelman outlined four recurring themes: "(1) Gentiles frequently saved Jews in occupied territories; (2) the Jews who resisted did so for universal, not parochial, reasons; (3) there was much cooperation among all nationalities against the Nazis; (4) the only collaborators with the Nazis were fascists."[12] Additionally, the fact that the Nazis targeted Jews over all other nations was hidden from the Soviet people. Soviet propaganda showed, in Ilya Ehrenburg's words, "the solidarity of the Soviet population, the rescue of individual Jews by Russian, Belorussians, Ukrainian, and Poles. . . . Such stories help heal terrible wounds and raise the ideal of friendship among peoples even higher." At the same time, Ehrenburg continued, "It is essential to show that Jews died bravely, highlighting all the instances of active or passive resistance; the underground organizations of the ghetto; the escapes and uprisings; and the Jewish partisans, who, after escaping death, took vengeance on the murderers of their loved ones."[13] These motifs, which all serve to underline the theme of interethnic unity in the Soviet Union, can be found in most of the Yiddish theater's wartime productions. The theater idealized the fraternity of all nations in the Soviet Union. However, the flip side of Jewish-gentile unity was a diminution of Jewish-gentile distinctions. Soviet theater—in contrast to some Western-oriented Soviet propaganda—ignored the fact that the German fascists were motivated by anti-Semitism. The enemy, it was contended, made no distinction between Jews and non-Jews.

Tashkent

The relocation of the Jewish cultural institutions to Central Asia provided an ideal setting for the construction of a myth of national friendship between the Jewish and Central Asian peoples. In reality, the people of Tashkent were far from unanimous in welcoming the nearly 400 Jews associated with the Yiddish theater who converged on the city during the period of evacuation.[14] The arriving Jews were often greeted with anti-Semitic taunts and even occasional acts of violence.[15] Uzbeks were not alone in their animosity toward the Jewish evacuees. As the news spread that so many Jewish intellectuals were safe in Central Asia, other Soviet citizens came to resent the Jewish evacuees, characterizing them as "draft dodgers"—a term that was sometimes extended to include all Soviet Jews, despite the fact that Jews served in disproportionately high numbers in the Red Army.[16] However, the troupe contributed more than its fair share to the war effort. Many members of the Yiddish theater chose to abandon their Tashkent haven to volunteer for military service, while others volunteered to be dispatched to the front in brigades that entertained the troops.[17]

Those who remained in Tashkent did their best to contribute to the Uzbek community. For instance, Mikhoels delivered several lectures, served as a consultant for the Tashkent theater, and even guest-directed an Uzbek play written by Khamid Alimdzhan, one of the new Soviet Uzbek writers who emerged in the late 1920s.[18] In return, the Uzbek government lauded the theater: the Central Committee of the Communist Party of Uzbekistan and the Council of People's Ministers of Uzbekistan honored Mikhoels with the title People's Artist of Uzbekistan; Zuskin and Tyshler were made Honorary Artists of Uzbekistan; and several other artists were given distinctions.[19] In addition to introducing itself to Uzbek culture, the Yiddish theater introduced the Uzbeks to Jewish culture. In January 1942, the theater began regular performances in Tashkent, presenting selections from its past repertoire, including *Tevye the Dairyman, Shulamis, King Lear, Wandering Stars,* and *Two Kuni-Lemls.*[20] The Yiddish theater played an integral role in the wartime flowering of the cultural life of Tashkent. In the words of Aleksandr Deich, "Mikhoels, it can be said, was the chief of all Tashkent theaters."[21] This fact was even recognized by Alimdzhan himself. In his farewell article to the thousands of evacuees, he wrote in *Pravda vostoka:*

> The people will never forget the winter of 1941–1942 in Tashkent . . . [when] people of science, literature, and art lived and worked in Tashkent in an atmosphere of Stalinesque friendship of peoples. The Yiddish theater in Tashkent for the first time presented an Uzbek play . . . [and] Zuskin at the Yiddish theater enraptured audiences with the role of the Fool in Shakespeare's *King Lear.* The public was delighted by high examples of stage art.[22]

The theater also continued its own creative development in Tashkent. By its first spring in evacuation, it had already begun planning for new productions.[23] The plays that the theater premiered in Tashkent celebrated, in Mikhoels's words, the "new ideological patriots of our great country" and aimed to show how "the Stalinist epoch strengthened the creative spirit of [different] peoples."[24] Its first production, *Khamza,* demonstrated the myth of fraternal relations between Jews and Uzbeks. The play was written by Amin Umari and Kamil Iashen, who, after his first play, *Two Communists* (1928), was recognized as one of the foremost Uzbek playwrights. Khamza Khakimzade Niiazi (1889–1929), the play's hero, was a real-life Uzbek poet, playwright, and composer. Khamza was most famous, however, for founding the first serious Uzbek theater, which emerged out of an amateur troupe he assembled in 1915. Iashen's play concentrated on this aspect of Khamza's life. The flowering of Khamza's troupe and its subsequent emergence as a professional theater, the Muslim Youth Musical-Dramatic Troupe, was portrayed in much the same terms as the emergence of the Yiddish theater: as a consequence of the October Revolution and of Soviet support for the culture of its national minorities.[25] Like many of the seminal figures in Soviet Yiddish literature, Khamza received a typical religious education—in his case through the Muslim *madrasa* rather than the Jewish *kheder*. Like the Yiddish theater, Khamza's early productions drew from pre-revolutionary vernacular literature. Later, he helped create a Soviet Uzbek repertoire that extracted contemporary political significance from local folklore. His most important dramatic works included *Landowner and Farmhand* (1918) and *The Secrets of Yashmak* (1927), a defense of the Muslim women's liberation movement. After Khamza's death the Tashkent theater was named in his honor. In addition to being one of the founders of modern Uzbek culture, Khamza was also portrayed as a genuine revolutionary. Iashen's play follows the Uzbek hero as he builds canals, fights for international socialism and the full emancipation of women, and challenges religious fanaticism, bourgeois nationalism, and feudal-era laws and rituals. The final scene depicts Khamza's tragic death at the hands of a mob of religious fanatics. The play ends with the lines: "We will transform the arid earth into a blossoming orchard! Music! What more than music! . . . The songs of Khamza will forever live in the hearts of the people."[26] The production was received positively, and the Yiddish theater's hagiographical portrait of the Uzbek hero was held up as a shining example of the "people's strength."[27]

Structurally, the play repeated many of the themes the Yiddish theater had addressed over the preceding decades, merely substituting Muslim for Jewish tradition. For instance, Khamza advocated emancipation from the strictures of religious fanaticism just as Boytre, Maimon, and Arn Friedman had done in the Yiddish theater's earlier productions. Furthermore, Khamza's championship of secular culture and theater as a means of liberating the population from religious scholasticism paralleled the theme of *Wandering Stars* as well as the State Yiddish Theater's own history. Both served as examples of the flowering of national culture under the Soviet regime. Finally, both Khamza and Mikhoels used their public stature to promote broader social awareness among their people. While Khamza's epitaph could well serve for Mikhoels's own epitaph several years later, the means of their final defeat were entirely different.

The theater also adopted a syncretic approach to national cultures, consciously drawing parallels between modern Uzbek and Jewish history and demonstrating the kinship among all Soviet peoples. For instance, as Pulver had incorporated Ukrainian and Jewish musical motifs in *Tevye*, the musical score of *Khamza* found common themes in Uzbek and Jewish folk music. The incorporation of Uzbek cultural motifs demanded mutual cooperation between Uzbek and Jewish artists, whose ability to work harmoniously together was held up as an example to be emulated by all. For instance, the Yiddish poet and novelist Der Nister (Pinhas Kahanovitz, 1884–1950) worked closely with Iashen in his translation of the text; Sarra Ishanturaev, the star actress of the Khamza theater, and Mannon Uiger, the celebrated actor and co-founder of the Uzbek TRAM, assisted Efraim Loiter in the staging of the production;[28] and the Uzbek folk artist Mukkary Turgunbaeva worked with Iampolskii to put Uzbek dance to Jewish music.[29] Thus, offstage as well, the play exemplified Uzbek-Jewish unity, and by extension, the unity of all Soviet peoples benefiting from Stalin's nationality policies.

237

An Eye for An Eye, 1942.
Left to right: Iustina Minkova,
Benjamin Zuskin, Nina Sirotina.
Photo courtesy of Ala Perelman-Zuskin.

Eda Berkovskaia in *Khamza,* 1942.
Photo courtesy of Ala Perelman-Zuskin.

These themes continued into the theater's next production—Peretz Markish's *An Eye for an Eye,* which premiered in the fall of 1942. The play was a passionate attack on fascism, arguing that the Nazis can only be defeated by the solidarity of all oppressed peoples, backed by the strength of the Soviet army. The first scene opens as a Nazi soldier forcibly marches a group of Poles into the town square, yelling "Faster, swine!" "The order is fulfilled," he heartlessly announces to his superior. "They are all in the square. There is no resistance! It can begin!" The Nazi colonel then addresses the Poles: "Eight hundred years ago this town belonged to the German knights of the Teutonic order. After that the city was befouled by the black Slavs, who rose against the good will of the Northern German race."[30] As the gathered masses look on, the colonel removes a statue of Adam Mickiewicz, the greatest Romantic poet of Poland, from the town square, symbolizing the German destruction of Slavic culture.

In the next scene, the oppression of the Poles is juxtaposed with the oppression of their Jewish neighbors. Markish takes the audience into the Jewish ghetto, where a family huddles together in their living room. Tyshler's sets depicted rickety broken portraits in the family room, which represented the destruction of the family's heritage. The family watches as night falls on the street and a Jew is beaten by a Nazi soldier, who, watching the Jew fall to the ground in pain, yells, "Get up, vermin!"[31] The repulsive spectacle is interrupted as the Pole Stanislaw enters the house, explaining that he is working for the Polish underground against the fascists: "Not one Pole will die before biting through the throats of three fascists," he promises.[32] He has come to recruit partisan fighters, and convinces the Jewish children, Binyomin and his sister Vigda, to join them. "We no longer need the halo of the laws of Moses and Israel!" declares Binyomin,

> We need to tie our lives to the battle. . . . We must swear to ourselves not to die until we pay back our ruin, until we settle accounts for our pain and shame, until we die off from hanging, and are dangling in the windows, until our unburied corpses litter the street. For our dishonored sisters and destitute children. An eye for an eye!! This must be our vow![33]

On the surface, Binyomin's impassioned speech asserts the goals of the partisan movement as portrayed in Soviet lore. True to Soviet propaganda, he openly discards the "laws of Moses and Israel" and the traditions from which they emerge. Yet at the same time, his battle cry is drawn from the very same tradition he renounces—the biblical injunction of "an eye for an eye." This incongruity illustrates the torn identity of many Soviet Jews during the war. On one hand, they recognized the military benefits of Soviet power and felt a loyalty to the state they called home; but on the other hand, the shared experience of oppression under Nazi ideology united them with their co-religionists abroad, and the emergence of Russian nationalism excited their own national identity. Just as many Russians invoked the vicious laws of Ivan Grozny to nourish a sense of historical continuity and fuel modern bellicosity, many Jews turned to a reinterpretation of the laws of Leviticus to justify their own pugnacity.

The play provides a perfect illustration of the ways in which the propaganda themes identified by Gitelman were staged. First, the Jews resist the fascists for universal rather than parochial reasons—they do not fight for the survival of the Jewish people; but rather for the victory of the interethnic forces of communism over fascism. Second, for all their evil characteristics, the Nazis are ironically portrayed to be racially blind—they make little distinction between Jews and Poles. Their world is divided only between Communists and Fascists. The Jewish and Polish responses are similarly juxtaposed; they fight together for their common purpose. The partisan movement is portrayed as a glorious example of Jewish-Polish cooperation. Third, the Jews are saved only through the kindness of the gentiles, who graciously invite them into the partisan movement. Finally, the Soviet army is depicted in nearly messianic terms. It is a deus ex machina, in anticipation of which the mortals on stage await with an unwavering faith.

Although the play conceals any Polish-Jewish discord, the Jewish community itself is sharply divided along generational lines. The elder *maskilim* are convinced that the German rationalism of Kant and the Aufklärung will eventually triumph over the madness of the Third Reich, while the elder Orthodox Jews have faith that God will not allow them to suffer any longer. Only the youth are drawn to the partisans, convinced that their salvation lies in their own military might. This generational conflict tied Markish's newest play to the theater's favorite theme, one of the most durable subjects of Jewish literature. However, in contrast to Markish's earlier portraits of the old generation, this time the audience is given little reason to pity those who wait in vain for God's help while the youth risk their lives in battle.

Dobrushin's *Marvelous History* provides another example of Soviet wartime propaganda as reflected on the Yiddish stage. The play emerged from a commission Dobrushin received from the Yiddish theater in 1942 to write a play about the partisan war in Ukraine.[34] The text was approved by the Committee of Artistic Affairs in February 1944.[35] The play follows a Jewish family in Ukraine, the Grossmans, as their town is surrounded by Germans. While Esther Grossman and her son are captured by the enemy, her husband Shimon escapes. By accident, Shimon manages to cross enemy lines and stumbles into a Red Army camp, where he finds his daughter Leah and her fiancé, Lieutenant David Novak. After Shimon reveals how he managed to cross the front line, the Russian commander sends Leah into the German camp to steal the enemy's operational plan. Leah completes the mission successfully, stealing the relevant documents from the German commander's residence. On her way back to the camp, she is aided by a group of partisans, who shoot the German commander.[36]

The play reflects only a partial view of the reality of Nazi atrocities. The cooperation of Jews and gentiles in the face of their shared (and identical) experience of oppression was once again highlighted as the theme of the play. Jews and non-Jews are lumped together both as victims and as anti-fascist fighters. Certainly, this was one aspect of reality; but at the same time it conceals the greater part of the whole in which Jews were singled out for annihilation. With the exception of one episode, in which Shimon relates a story about the destruction of the Jewish Temple, implicitly comparing the event to the Nazi invasion, the play makes no reference to the singling out of Jews for special treatment by the enemy. Not only are Jews and non-Jews lumped together as victims, but no distinction is made between their responses; gentiles risk their lives to save their Jewish neighbors. The Grossmans, for instance, are saved by a broad coalition of nationalities, including the Russian commander of the Red Army and the Ukrainian partisans. On the other hand, not a single Ukrainian collaborates with the Fascists against the Jews. The falsehood of this paradigm was well documented by Mikhoels and the Jewish Anti-Fascist Committee at the time. The committee had been receiving numerous letters from the occupied territories in which the collaboration of "friendly" nations was described. For instance, one letter from a collective farm in the Stalindorf district stated "135 Jews were killed by the German fascists with the collaboration of local police and traitors from the local population. Their entire inventory and property was plundered by several 'kind' neighbors."[37] Rather than put such atrocities on stage, Mikhoels and the Yiddish theater instead celebrated the role that gentiles played in saving Jewish lives. Once again, the Nazis were portrayed as being blind to any racial or ethnic differences among people; their battle was ideological rather than racial in the play.

The Lighter Side of War

Theater audiences were also entertained with more light-hearted and sentimental plays drawn from the canon of pre-revolutionary Yiddish classics. In the words of Mikhoels, "From time to time the theater returns to the classical legacy of humanity and the classical legacy of our folk, falling back on them as living sources from which new strength, new understanding, new knowledge, and new skills are extracted."[38] Most important, however, these humorous productions provided a much-needed outlet for a war-weary audience.

One such production was Dobrushin's adaptation of Sholem Aleichem's "The Enchanted Tailor" (written in 1900). The play starred and was staged by Zuskin, who took over as artistic director when Mikhoels was preoccupied with the Jewish Anti-Fascist Committee.[39] The story was first introduced to Russian audiences in 1928 with the motion picture *Laughter through Tears*, directed by Grigori Gricher-Cherikover. It tells the story of a poor tailor, Shimen-Eli, whose penchant for misquoting Talmudic and biblical sayings and stern criticisms of the wealthy and respected members of the town earn him the derision of the community, including his wife. After she nags the tailor to buy a goat so that the children can have milk for supper, Shimen-Eli agrees, pointing out: "A wife has to be obeyed, you know. It says so in the Talmud in black and white," and he recites Aramaic-sounding gibberish in imitation of the language of the Talmud. On the way to the neighboring village where he is to buy the goat, he stays at an inn where the keeper is put off by his pretensions. On the return trip, having purchased a fine goat, the innkeeper decides to play a trick on the pseudo–talmudic scholar and replaces his she-goat with a male. Upon arriving home, his wife is furious to see that Shimen-Eli has allowed himself to be tricked. The poor tailor returns to the neighboring village; but on the way, the innkeeper switches the goats back, so that when Shimen-

Eli accuses the vendor of tricking him, he is instead accused of slander. Once again Shimen-Eli returns to his native village, and once again the innkeeper switches the goats. In the end, the two villages, each vouching for the honesty of their own, decide to take up arms against each other, and poor Shimen-Eli, convinced that he is cursed by a spirit, becomes mortally ill with insanity.[40]

The play's social message was more akin to the themes the theater had tried to impress upon its audience in the early 1920s than to socialist realist structures. Like *Two Hundred Thousand, The Sorceress,* and *An Evening of Sholem Aleichem,* the play was a simple light-hearted attack on the notorious *luftmentshen.* Once again, Zuskin aimed to portray the hopeless poverty-ridden shtetls of the former Pale. Shimen-Eli, unsatisfied with his simple pauper's lifestyle, allows himself to be persuaded to try to enlarge his small fortune by investing in a goat—a move that would greatly enhance his prestige. However, like many of Sholem Aleichem's

Benjamin Zuskin as Shimen-Eli in *The Enchanted Tailor,* 1944. Photo courtesy of Ala Perelman Zuskin.

other characters who try to get ahead in life, the poor tailor's attempts are doomed to failure. The subtle mockery of rabbinical learning, talmudic scholarship, and naive mysticism are also typical of Sholem Aleichem, and had been one of Granovsky's favorite themes. At the same time, the production allowed an orthodox Marxist interpretation: the goat can be seen as the means of production—Shimen-Eli's attempts to gain the means of production for himself are doomed to failure because the proletariat cannot gain access to the means of production without revolution. However, while Marxist notions certainly can be extracted from the plot, the play is far from the socialist realist productions of the 1930s, epitomized by *The Deaf, Midat ha-din,* and *Four Days.* Like *Tevye,* the production evokes pathos more than laughter. It was presented as a lyrical and realist tragedy rather than as a humorous anecdote.[41] Its performance is indicative of a relaxation of pedagogical requirements from the state and a newfound tolerance for sentimental tales from folk traditions. According to TASS, the performance was met with great success.[42]

When it returned to Moscow in fall 1943, the theater continued with its lighthearted programs, presenting Dobrushin's adaptation of Goldfadn's *Capricious Bride* (written in 1877) and a collection of short Isaac Leyb Peretz sketches, which was presented in conjunction with the Soviet State Yiddish Theater School. *Capricious Bride* told of a young woman whose ideals of romance give way to a deeper appreciation of love and companionship when she falls for an older man. The play was representative of the type of sentimental middle-class values that came to dominate much post-war Soviet culture as the regime satisfied the people's demands for relaxation, stability, and conservatism.[43]

Holy Alliances

As Mikhoels and the Anti-Fascist Committee strove to solicit international support for the Soviet war effort, the Yiddish theater sought to delve into the past for other instances of Jewish-Christian alliances. David Bergelson's *Prince Reuveni* was one such example. Mikhoels hoped to turn *Reuveni* into the theater's greatest triumph, surpassing even *King Lear.* "No mise en scène, with the exception of *Lear,* occupied my father for such a long time," wrote Mikhoels's daughter.[44] However, despite the theater's best efforts, it was never performed. Indeed, the last few years of Mikhoels's life were dedicated almost exclusively to the production of this ill-fated play. The Committee of Artistic Affairs gave permission for the theater to commission the play in February 1944,[45] and Bergelson was given the commission the following September.[46] Two months later the theater began rehearsals,[47] and in February 1945 the production was given an official go-ahead by Khrapchenko.[48] However, by December it had not yet premiered, and it was once again approved for the 1946 season.[49] The play continued to be included in the theater's plans for the remainder of its existence, and rehearsals were held just days before Mikhoels's death.

The play is about David Reuveni, a controversial sixteenth-century advocate of Jewish-Christian unity, regarded by many as an impostor. David Reuveni was a popular subject for Jewish writers, appearing in novels by Max Brod and Joseph

Opatashu and in a play by David Pinski. Reuveni belonged to a group of Kabbalists who were convinced that the messianic age had begun and the world was on the verge of redemption. Most of our sources on Reuveni come from his contemporary, Yosef Hakohen (1496–1578), who chronicled Reuveni's remarkable life, allegedly based on Reuveni's diary. According to his biographer, in 1524 Reuveni appeared in Europe, claiming to be a princely emissary from a Jewish state in Arabia. He appealed to Pope Clement VI and the Holy Roman Emperor Charles V to ally with the Jews for a war against the Turks with the goal of liberating Palestine from Muslim rule. While both rulers were suspicious of the self-styled prince and his purported kingdom, they greeted their guest with all the pomp worthy of a visiting head of state and entertained his proposal. In Portugal Reuveni also met with a Converso named Diego Pires, who was so enraptured with Reuveni's plan that he reconverted to Judaism and changed his name to Shlomo Mulkho (King Solomon). However, their plan to save European Jewry from the Inquisition and to liberate Palestine ultimately failed. Both were eventually arrested by Charles V; Mulkho was burned at the stake in 1532 and Reuveni died in a Spanish prison several years later.[50]

Bergelson's version makes no apology for its nationalist significance and repeatedly stresses the theme of Jewish perseverance in the face of potential disaster. It exhibits, in the words of Shmuel Rozshansky, "a stirring lyricism of a national vision."[51] The Jewish people, Bergelson's Reuveni contends, will survive only by taking up arms: "The people will continue to live! . . . You fight, my people, that means—you live, my people,"[52] commands Reuveni. On the surface, though, Bergelson's interpretation downgraded the religious and messianic significance of the Reuveni story. For instance, Reuveni scoffs at the rich Jewish merchants who seek martyrdom by the grace of God and who die with a prayer of God's Oneness on their lips. It is much more fruitful, he contends, to die with a sword in one's hand. "This is the war ideology of the Soviets," wrote one American critic. "This is also Reuveni's ideology."[53] The theme of Jews and non-Jews uniting against a common foe also conformed to what Gitelman identified as one of the recurring themes of Soviet interpretations of the Holocaust.

At times, however, the subtext of the play contradicts its overt anti-religious stance. The play's anti-religious significance, for instance, becomes ambiguous when Reuveni dies with the Hebrew words of a Yom Kippur prayer on his lips: "Who will live and who will die." Once again, the ambiguity of Soviet Jewish existence surfaces as the protagonist in his final breath symbolically returns to the faith he rejected in life.

The entire play can also be seen as a roman à clef in which Reuveni is an allegorical representation of Mikhoels, who had recently returned from his own quest for Christian support abroad. Like Reuveni, Mikhoels had suddenly appeared in the Western world as an emissary from a forgotten Jewish community in the East. Seeking Western support against a common enemy, both Mikhoels and Reuveni pledged that their own people would fight in unison with the West and promised an end to animosities and differences between their own kingdoms and

their potential allies. Only through Jewish unity and Jewish-Christian cooperation, they contended, could the evil foe threatening Europe be defeated. Indeed,
many of Reuveni's impassioned speeches closely resemble the appeals Mikhoels
made at the anti-fascist radio rallies. Both also railed against religious fanaticism
and passivity. Could, then, Reuveni's final monologue, with its prayer and implicit
return to the Jewish faith, have been a clandestine declaration of Mikhoels's epiphany? If so, it was a confession he would never be able to make. Despite his best
efforts, the play was never performed.

While such a messianic theme may have been acceptable during the war, once
the war was finished, blatant nationalism was no longer acceptable. By the time the
play was ready to be performed, in early 1945, the Soviet army was advancing well
into Europe toward the American forces. As the two armies prepared to meet, the
Soviet Union no longer sought cooperation with its erstwhile Western allies. The
world Jewish unity that the Soviet regime had sought to promote during the war
had lost its strategic imperative. Nevertheless, Mikhoels continued rehearsals and
repeatedly received official permission to keep the play in the theater's repertoire.
When Mikhoels departed Moscow for his ill-fated journey to Minsk, he left on
his desk the script of *Prince Reuveni* and Machiavelli's *The Prince*, which he was
reading for background on Renaissance Europe.[54] Mikhoels, the modern Reuveni,
was about to fall to the Machiavellian trap of the modern Prince Stalin.

War in the Post-war World

As the military war drew to a close, theater was catapulted into a new front:
"The war continues in the ideological front," stated Mikhoels.[55] In February 1944,
the Committee of Artistic Affairs met to approve the theater's future repertoire. It
was decided that the theater should henceforth deal with themes relating exclusively to "The Great Patriotic War."[56] The importance of wartime themes was
further enhanced several months later when in connection with the twenty-sev-
enth anniversary of the October Revolution, the Committee of Artistic Affairs
ordered all theaters to present for approval plays about "the historical victory of the
heroic Red Army over the fascist aggressors."[57]

In 1944 alone, the Moscow State Yiddish Theater commissioned Shmuel
Halkin, Aleksandr Borshchagovskii, Abraham Sutzkever, David Hofshteyn, and
David Bergelson to write plays glorifying the victory of heroic Jews who unite with
non-Jews to defeat the enemy.[58] In addition, over the next few years, the theater
would either commission or adapt plays on war themes by Peretz Markish, Moshe
Pinchevskii, Vasili Grossman, Moshe Broderzon, Itzik Fefer, Grigori Linkov, and
Isaak Hoberman.[59] Most of these plays were never performed, some for ideological reasons, some on account of poor aesthetic quality, and others simply because
the authors did not complete the text before the theater was destroyed.

The victorious campaigns of the Red Army during 1944 genuinely impressed
upon Soviet citizens a new hope. The unbounded enthusiasm that overtook Soviet Jewish culture as the Red Army marched toward Berlin was not merely man-

dated by the state, but in fact seems to have genuinely permeated the thinking and attitudes of many Soviet Jews after their country's victory over Nazi forces. Soviet Jewish writers and citizens celebrated the triumph of the Jewish people over Nazism and the perseverance of the Jewish nation. Since the mass graves, the crematories, and the annihilation of six million Jews was not yet common knowledge, the strength of life and dignity could still be celebrated.

Ben Zion Goldberg describes the mood of the theater at the time of his 1946 visit:

> The house was always sold out in advance. I had to reserve my seat a few days beforehand, and when I failed to do so, I had to be accommodated by an extra chair in the aisle. Backstage, the atmosphere was devotional as well as theatrical. The actors were votaries in a service. They spent six to ten months rehearsing and studying a new play. I was present at one such session; it might have been a graduate seminar in dramatic arts where professor and students analyzed the inner meaning of every line and movement.[60]

Mikhoels, too, could hardly contain his excitement. Yitzhak Rosenberg, a member of the Czechoslovakian government delegation to the World Jewish Congress, commented on his impressions of Mikhoels in November 1944: "He was a charming person, hospitable, generous with his time and a very good listener. . . . Mikhoels expressed an optimistic outlook on the future of the Jewish people, and this boundless optimism combined with his excellent personality left a marked influence on me."[61] The Moscow State Yiddish Theater appeared to be heading for another victorious post-war decade. New personnel were hired, the continuing staff were given pay raises,[62] and the theater school accepted sixty young hopefuls to help carry the troupe into a post-war world. The theater also began preparing new productions to entertain the next generation. In the two years after the conclusion of the war, the Moscow State Yiddish Theater commissioned nearly twenty different plays, enough to last at least ten years in the best of times.[63] The titles of some plays the troupe planned to present speak volumes for the optimistic mood of Yiddish playwrights: Pinchevskii's *I Live*, Bergelson's *I Will Live* (which was performed at the New Yiddish Folk Theater of New York in 1945), Fefer's *To Life*, Hoberman's *Life Is Worth Living*, Halkin's *For Life and Unto Death*, and others. This proliferation of life-affirming plays can be attributed to both official pressure and genuine enthusiasm on the part of the writers.

This euphoria was expressed in the theater's first post-war production—*Freylekhs* [Joy], an allegorical celebration of Jewish perseverance. The prize-winning production was commissioned to the Yiddish folklorist Zalman Shneer-Okun in January 1945.[64] The theater once again turned its attention to that time-honored symbol of life and renewal, the Jewish wedding. The production was a symbolist recreation of the traditional wedding ritual, virtually devoid of any narrative. The play can most appropriately be described as a succession of images. Its opening scene recalled the creation myth, particularly in its Kabbalistic interpretation, as seven dim lights—evoking the seven days of creation—emerge from

Benjamin Zuskin in *Freylekhs,* 1945. The Hebrew words, ôkol
khasan ve kol khalahö, are part of a traditional wedding song.
The photo was partially burnt during the fire set in the Yiddish
Theater archives by the Secret Police in 1950.
Photo courtesy of Ala Perelman-Zuskin.

the void. The lights then reveal human forms, just as the light of the Divine Presence created Adam Kadmon (Primal Man), and suddenly burst into a flurry of
color. Tyshler set the prologue in complete darkness. The audience gazes at the
void in expectation and contemplation, until "in the black square of the stage,
seven solitary lights burn."

Their dim light falls on faces and hands, holding these lights. The faces are
tense, their appearance is of concentration. Above shines a single star. Its bluish
shining twinkle fights with the quiet melancholy of the wandering lights. The
sound of a requiem fills the expanse. This *Yortsayt*—a ceremonial rite for the
remembrance of the dead—expresses sorrow and vows to be a grateful and eternal memorial. But suddenly a *badkhen* appears—the spirit of a wedding. His
ringing voice breaks the ceremonial melody—"extinguish the light, blow out the
melancholy."

The Requiem melody transforms itself. Joyful, ceremonial music is heard. A
bright light bursts into flame. It lights up the entire stage. A demand for light.
Faces are revealed with heads proudly raised. They wear bright clothing. This,
the voice of the folk jester, who moves, writhing like quicksilver, and who sees the
wisdom of the people's faces. With great agitation he speaks of the sorrow which

envelopes every blessed person with thoughts of the dead, who were torn from life in the war of liberation. Let us share in a pre-eminent memorial which will be the joy of life, an affirmation of victory, and a celebration of the new life, which was fought for by the victorious people, who are immortal.[65]

The stage then fills with jesters, dressed in costumes that are completely black on one side and a patchwork of colors on the other. "Our people live!! Let's celebrate a wedding!" declare the *badkhens,* as they usher in a carnival of song and dance. The wedding guests then begin to arrive: an officer returning from the front, a mother who has lost her only child, and an old soldier who had been recruited into the tsarist army.[66] A series of dances follow, beginning with the dance of the elders and ending with the dance of the future grandchildren, symbolizing the revitalization of the Jewish community through the next generation. Even the old soldier's beard was a symbol of rejuvenation. The long, scraggly beard he wears in the first scene gradually becomes shorter throughout the play, until at the end of the wedding he shaves, revealing a youthful visage. The play ends in a polar image of its beginning. Gradually a rainbow of colors merges, as in a prism, into a single shaft of white light.

Once again, the theater emphasized the new themes of universalism and world unity. Pulver's music incorporated a wide range of international rhythms— klezmer merged with flamenco, African American, and Arabic motifs—many of which Mikhoels had picked up on his American tour. This eclectic flavor was both an affirmation of the new expanded post-war world, and a lament for the destruction of the old world. Klezmer music and all that it symbolized was a phenomenon of the past. The Eastern European shtetl, which the theater had satirized and condemned for decades, was finally defunct. But contrary to early utopian visions, the shtetl Jews had not been converted into New Soviet Men in the factories of the future. Instead they were burned to ashes in the furnaces of Auschwitz. But Mikhoels sought to emphasize that Jewish life would renew itself as it had done so many times before. As new centers of Jewish life emerged in South America, North America, and even Palestine, the community, like its music, would adapt. Like Jewish life, the spirit of the music perpetually fluctuates between mourning and joy, between death and life, until at the wedding banquet life triumphs in a festival of song, dance, and laughter. The play was a celebration of life in the face of death; it was Mikhoels's affirmation of the strength of human dignity and freedom; it was a commemoration of the people's victory over Hitler, enlarged into a victory of humanity over inhumanity.

One reviewer wrote of the play that "in my opinion, the only production in which this [Jewish national] form can be sensed, seen, and felt is the Moscow State Yiddish Theater's most recent production."[67] Boris Shimelovich, a prominent doctor and member of the Jewish Anti-Fascist Committee, praised the production in a letter to Mikhoels, writing, "After the greatest tragedy in the history of the Jewish people, there is a theater in the USSR with a full house—with the call, 'Freylekhs.' You know, my friend, this is highly significant and very promising. This means that our people live, we are living, and we shall live—we, its sons and daughters."[68] The show was awarded the Stalin Prize, the country's most presti-gious theatrical award. By September 1948, it had been performed over 200 times and had been seen by an estimated 140,000 people.[69]

Moshe Broderzon's (1890–1956) *Holiday Eve,* presented at the Yiddish the-ater in 1947, once again celebrated the perseverance of the Jewish spirit in the aftermath of the world war. Broderzon had been commissioned in October 1946 to write a play about the Soviet people's victory over the Fascists.[70] The play had been approved by the Committee of Artistic Affairs in late January 1947 and pre-miered the following spring.[71] Broderzon was born in Moscow in 1890 to a wealthy religious family. At the age of nine he had moved to Lodz, where he attended *kheder* and became a bookseller while writing poetry with a group of young Yid-dish poets who called themselves, appropriately, "The Young Ones." Broderzon's political satire, written for Yiddish cabaret theaters, helped make him one of the leading Yiddish humorists in Poland. By the age of twenty-eight the "Prince of Young Yiddish" was known throughout Poland. Returning to Moscow before World War II, he sought membership in the Union of Soviet Writers, to which he was not admitted until 1945. This made it possible for his play *Holiday Eve* to finally be performed, under Zuskin's direction, at the Moscow State Yiddish Theater.[72]

Like *Marvelous Story,* the play tells of a Jewish woman, Nekhama, who is caught behind enemy lines and finds herself confined to a ghetto. Through the in-tervention of the Red Army, she is saved from being deported to a concentration camp, but the rest of her family does not share her fortune; they perish in the Holocaust. After the German retreat, Nekhama meets a fellow Jew who has also lost his family. While Nekhama has lost her faith in humanity and succumbs to a suicidal depression, her new companion is full of energy and a thirst for creative activity. Eventually, Nekhama learns that life must be permitted to emerge victo-rious. In the words of one critic, "Our Soviet accomplishments save this woman, and return her to the world of living people and living feelings."[73] Like *Freylekhs,* the play affirms life and sends the message that the people must rebuild and move beyond the atrocities of the war. This message was not only apt for the Jewish survivors of the Holocaust, but would also become a mantra of post-war Soviet objectives in general. Having lost an estimated 27 million citizens during the war, and witnessed the devastation of more than 70,000 villages and the destruction of the state's economic infrastructure, the need to rebuild was paramount in the post-war Soviet mentality.[74]

Itzik Fefer's *Sun Doesn't Set,* which premiered on February 15, 1947, again celebrates war heroism.[75] The play was about "the struggle of Soviet Jewish people in the difficult conditions of German occupation."[76] Fefer wrote of the play:

> Along with the spirit of suffering in the [Jewish] people lives a spirit of resis-tance, a spirit of struggle for life and freedom, a spirit of war for justice against their enemies. The spirit of struggle for life and freedom, which has lived in the people for a thousand years, was made especially clear during the days of the Great Patriotic War—and not only in the ranks of the heroic Red Army, but also

deep in the interior and in partisan forests. Even in the sheltered ghetto, sons and daughters of the Jewish people heroically struggled against the enemy. Here a Stalinist friendship of peoples played a decisive role, at the head of which stood the great Russian people. Here a great role was played by the Soviet Union, which stood as a new land for an ancient people.[77]

A short review in *Eynikayt* heralded the play's "great success," a bland phrase which came to be used increasingly to describe the theater's productions during the period of its deterioration.[78]

In June 1947 the theater presented Peretz Markish's new play, *Uprising in the Ghetto*, about the April 1943 Warsaw ghetto uprising. Soviet propagandists hoped to use the Nazi razing of the Warsaw ghetto, in which over 30,000 Jews were annihilated, as a means of diverting attention away from the newly discovered Katyn mass grave, containing the bodies of thousands of Polish officers murdered by the Soviets.[79] The heroism of the ghettos was a popular theme among Soviet Jewish writers: "The Ghetto of Vilnius" by Abraham Sutzkever and the poem "Shadows of the Warsaw Ghetto" by Fefer all glorified the uprisings. As early as July 1944, the Moscow State Yiddish Theater began work on a play about the Warsaw ghetto uprising. Initially Halkin was commissioned to write the play;[80] however, the theater chose instead a text written by Markish.

Markish's text once again followed many of the wartime propaganda themes as well as some more traditional themes of the Yiddish theater. First, the text emphasizes the cooperation among different nationalities in the fight against the German enemy, particularly the role of righteous gentiles in helping save Jews. The play focuses on one underground division led by two young Bolsheviks, one Jew and one non-Jew—Hirsh Glik and Andrei Semibrat. Second, the play argues that the Nazi war was motivated by fascist ideology rather than racism. Third, the play emphasizes the internal dissension within the Jewish community; the primary conflict of the play is not between the Jewish underground fighters and the Nazis, but rather between the fighters and the Judenrat, led by Hirsh's father, Wolf Glik, and a conglomeration of elder Jewish oligarchs. While the fighters seek confrontation with the enemy, the Judenrat pleads patience and accommodation with the German overlords of the ghetto. The tragic conclusion of the play depicts the liquidation of the ghetto. The play was intended as a reaction against the new Jewish literary tendency to portray the Jews under Hitler's domination as "a mass of people, weak and subdued, inclined toward their tragic fate." Markish sought to show that the Jews of the ghettos retained their strength and perseverance against a seemingly indestructible enemy. "This strength," stated one critic, "is the idea of communism, which inspires all peoples."[81]

Unbeknownst to the theater, on October 7, 1946—several months before the play's premiere—Aleksandr Shcherbakov, the head of the Soviet Information Bureau, wrote a secret report to Aleksandr Kuznetsov, secretary of the Central Committee, in which he criticized Markish's text for being too nationalistic and for implicitly arguing for the establishment of a Jewish state. According to the report,

In a play by the same author, *Uprising in the Ghetto,* sent for publication in the U.S.A. by the Jewish Anti-Fascist Committee, the girl Naomi declares: "Everything has been taken away, except our sight, so that we can see everywhere that we are different. . . . Every threshold burns you with inhospitality. . . . "

Naomi explains this "homelessness" of the Jews. "A piece of our own country," evidently national territory, would change the situation.[82]

The same letter noted the nationalist implications of *Prince Reuveni,* on which Mikhoels was still working: "The thought runs throughout the play that the salvation of the Jewish people lies in organized strength, supported by their own state."[83] The letter was subsequently sent to Secretary of Ideology Andrei Zhdanov, who could not have been pleased with the information it provided. Later, *Holiday Eve* would also be singled out for nationalist implications;[84] although not until after Broderzon had been arrested.[85] Indeed, as the warmth of Yalta chilled into the Cold War, "Brother Jews" became "Rootless Cosmopolitans," and those suspected of the crime of promoting international harmony during the war were promptly silenced.

During and after World War II, the Moscow State Yiddish Theater utilized all its resources to excite anti-German sentiments among its audience and to inspire the people with tales of heroism, escape, and triumph. Soviet audiences and foreign observers were assured that the Red Army would emerge victorious due to the feelings of brotherhood that Stalin had inspired among all Soviet peoples regardless of race or creed. It was this unity, the myth asserted, that motivated Poles, Ukrainians, and Russians to risk their lives to save Jews and that induced Uzbeks to welcome Jews and Russians into their haven away from Nazi aggression. Yet, in the real theater of war, Jews fell victim not only to Nazi genocide, but also to Polish collaborators, Cossack brutality, and Russian discrimination. Even Uzbek hospitality often gave way to taunts and assaults. Soviet citizens were taught that the invading Nazis would make no distinction between Russians, Uzbeks, or Jews in their murderous campaign. Yet in Wannsee and Berlin, the Nazis planned the total annihilation of the Jewish race, and in Birkenau and Maidanek their Final Solution was implemented. In the aftermath of the war, the Moscow State Yiddish Theater celebrated life, while the Allied armies liberating the camps somberly uncovered mounds of mass graves revealing the remains of millions of emaciated human beings.

This Is a Bad Omen:
The Last Act

9

The Great Patriotic War, as World War II was known in Soviet parlance, unleashed a flood of patriotism and national pride among Soviet citizens. National minorities in general and Jews in particular were initially led to believe that they could share in the post-war exultation, as they had shared in the burdens of the war. However, Secretary of Ideology Andrei Zhdanov and his cohorts cultivated their own version of racial intolerance, drawing upon the people's latent chauvinism, and eliminated the national minorities from the Soviet ideal of nationhood. Their task was facilitated by the resurgence of conventional patriotism toward "Mother Russia," which had supplanted Communist ideological convictions during the war as the defining factor of Soviet identity. Although the Moscow State Yiddish Theater sought to elevate the role of ideology in the war by drawing battle lines between fascism and communism and by showing Jews, Russians, Poles, Ukrainians, and Uzbeks fighting side by side, these images were effectively countered by Stalin's speeches, Soloviev's films, and especially Ehrenburg's articles, which painted a historic and bifurcated struggle between Germans and Russians. Despite the fact that the most efficient spokesman for this model was himself a Jew, Ehrenburg's readers often chose to exclude his co-religionists in their ideal of Russian identity. Thus, when the tank battles ended, the dust settled, and the ashen remains of human lives were buried, Stalin pledged a "Big Deal" with the middle class of Russian extraction: in return for their acquiescence to the ruling regime, they would be permitted to enjoy the fruits of their victory within their own value system.[1] By the time Mikhoels and his associates realized that they had been excluded from the deal, it was too late.

Russian national chauvinism, Nazi propaganda, and rumors of Jewish treachery during the war all helped unleash a latent anti-Semitism in the post-war Soviet Union. The first inkling of what was to come could already be seen in the months after the Nazi invasion, when on August 17, 1942, Georgii Aleksandrov, director of Agitprop, prepared a report entitled "The Selection and Promotion of Personnel in the Arts," in which he argued that many institutions of Russian art "turned out to be filled by non-Russian people (mainly Jews)."[2] In particular, the report cited the disproportionate number of Jews represented in the Bolshoi Theater, the Moscow and Leningrad State Conservatories, and the Moscow Philharmonic. Indeed, Jews were overrepresented in the arts.[3] As Juri Jelagin explains, the arts was "the only Russian profession which had not been subjected to the cruel class and social discrimination prevalent during the first two five-year plans of the Stalin era."[4] Many children of the déclassé and "class enemies," two other groups in which Jews were overrepresented, were able to find careers in the arts when other doors were closed. In response to Aleksandrov's report, the Committee of Artistic Affairs responded by "purifying" artistic institutions of Jews, beginning with the Moscow State Conservatory's director, Aleksandr Goldenweizer.[5] It did not take long for other national minorities to be affected by Stalin's new chauvinism. Over the summer of 1944, for instance, Tatar, Bashkir, and Kazakh historians were warned against expressing excessive nationalism.[6]

As the world war gave way to the Cold War, Russian national chauvinism emerged as a dominant legitimizing factor for the regime. Russians were taught to redirect their hatred of fascism toward a general hatred of the West and of all things foreign. In August 1946, Zhdanov began a campaign to rid Soviet culture of "foreign" (non-Russian) influences. Over the following winter, numerous measures were enacted to ensure that Soviet citizens relinquish their contacts with the West. Soviet prisoners of war, who were forcibly repatriated in accordance with agreements reached at Yalta, were summarily shot by NKVD troops or shipped to work camps in Siberia for the crime of having seen the West, ethnic minorities in the borderlands were systematically "resettled," and on February 15, 1947, marriage between Soviet citizens and foreigners was prohibited by law. As had been the case countless times before, attacks on foreign elements in music presaged a general attack on culture. Beginning in 1948, composers Dmitry Shostakovich, Sergei Prokofiev, and Aram Khachaturian were criticized for using non-Russian ethnic musical motifs. In its most absurd form, the purge of non-Russian national motifs even permeated the sciences. The Soviet Academy of Sciences decided that Russians were responsible for the invention of virtually every technological innovation from the radio to the airplane. By 1950, Trofim Lysenko's phony genetics had been endorsed by Stalin to the exclusion of all others, leading to the persecution of all those who continued to believe in the results of Western bourgeois "experimentation." Many of the persecuted scientists, like Lina Shtern, were Jewish. This fact was by no means accidental, as evidenced by the official criticism of their scientific methodology—that it was plagued by a "perfidious Zionist character."[7] In 1952 Shtern stood side by side with Zuskin, Bergelson, Markish, Fefer and others during their trial for anti-Soviet sabotage.

The Jewish Anti-Fascist Committee's Yiddish-language newspaper quickly jumped on the bandwagon, supporting what amounted to a denial of its own position. On September 24 an article in *Eynikayt* criticized several Jewish authors, including Halkin, for overt nationalism.[8] Mikhoels once again refused to mouth government platitudes; rather, he was a vocal opponent of Zhdanov's anti-cosmopolitan campaign. Inebriated with hubris, Mikhoels accused some of the most revered plays of the wartime period of exhibiting Russian chauvinism in a speech to the Committee of Artistic Affairs. He criticized *Russian People,* for instance, of speaking only of Russian patriotism rather than of Soviet patriotism which includes, he wrote, "Russians, Ukrainians, Georgians and Uzbeks," notably leaving out the Jews.[9] When criticized for having a lack of Soviet productions in his theater's repertoire, Mikhoels was unapologetic: "I ask, 'Haven't we presented our Soviet authors? Haven't we presented Soviet plays? We have. But we have not presented enough, and the most important defect is that the classic plays continue in the repertoire for ten to fifteen years, but the contemporary Soviet plays are quickly removed from the repertoire.'"[10] In other words, the theater could not be blamed if contemporary Soviet productions failed to attract audiences that were as large as the audiences for Yiddish classics. As he had done so many times before, Mikhoels responded to pressure defensively, refusing to act the part expected of him. Rather than demean himself with self-criticisms and apologies, Mikhoels refused to admit any wrongdoing. This time, however, his status had changed. He was no longer merely a Jewish actor; now he was the head of the Jewish Anti-Fascist Committee with extensive contacts around the world and an emerging political agenda of his own. It was for this crime that he was summoned to Minsk in January 1948.

The Jewish Anti-Fascist Committee in the Post-war World

After his return to the Soviet Union from his expedition to the West, Mikhoels continued to use the Anti-Fascist Committee to undertake a wide range of projects in support of his people. Essentially, he sought to turn the committee into a Jewish cultural-political center. One of the first projects in which he participated under the auspices of the committee was the compilation of a Black Book of Nazi atrocities against the Jews. The project, which anticipated the publication of the book in Yiddish, English, Spanish, French, German, and Russian, was undertaken with the assistance of several American, British and Palestinian Jewish activists, including Albert Einstein, Dr. Stephen Wise, Lion Feuchtwanger, Chief Rabbi of the British Empire Dr. Joseph Herman Hertz, and Sholem Asch. The Russian side included Halkin, Bergelson, Markish, Ehrenburg, Grossman, and Abram Efros, in addition to Mikhoels.[11] However, it soon became apparent that the Black Book Committee was unwilling to follow the conventional Soviet interpretation of World War II. Some of its members expressed a desire to break the taboo against emphasizing Jewish victimhood. For instance, in one meeting Efros declared: "The book must tell that there was a murder of an entire people. Germans killed a large number of other people too, but what we had here was total annihilation." Grossman's response was that "if the book as a whole is about Jews, then we should avoid the use of the word 'Jew.' . . . We can write 'they assembled people,' or 'people went to the square,' or 'five people fell,' without writing the word 'Jew.'"[12] But by the time the English version of the book was published (the only version to be released in Mikhoels's lifetime) Grossman had acquiesced. The second chapter of the book openly emphasized the distinct fate of Jews under Nazism: "The German fascists plotted the destruction of the Jews as an integral part of their program to enslave the world. From the very outset of their bloody adventure, the Nazis schemed to tear up the roots of German and world Jewry."[13] In contrast to the image projected in Mikhoels's theatrical productions, the Black Book emphasized the racial elements of the Holocaust. The battle was no longer between fascists and Communists as on the Yiddish theater's stage; it was now between Germans and Jews:

> All this the Germans—we must speak of Germans as a whole and not purely of the Nazis—did wantonly and deliberately. . . . The plan to exterminate a whole

people numbering millions, to do so not as an act of war, but as part of an effort wholly unconnected with war, to wipe out systematically a group of human beings with whom the murderers had been living in close association and from whose association they had derived substantial advantages—such a plan was unknown in history up to the attempted extermination of the Jews.[14]

Further, the book valorized the role of the Palestinian Yishuv in saving Jews. The chapter on resistance began by describing how the "shock troops from Tel-Aviv . . . quietly entered the continent and spread out through the occupied countries to organize Jewish resistance groups, to train them in sabotage, and to set up an underground railway to smuggle Jews to safety."[15] This was anathema to Soviet sensibilities, which preferred to assert the Soviet Union's unique status as the savior of the Jews.

In June 1947, just as the Der emes printing press was preparing 50,000 copies of the book for publication in Russia, the presses were stopped by order of the Central Management of Literary and Publication Affairs. Justifying the decision, Aleksandrov wrote:

Running through the whole book is the idea that the Germans plundered and murdered Jews only. The reader unwittingly gets the impression that the Germans fought against the USSR for the sole purpose of destroying the Jews. . . . The idea itself of some kind of non-existent order of priorities is incorrect. In documents of the Special State Commission for ascertaining and investigating the heinous crimes of the German fascist aggressors, it was convincingly shown that Hitler's ruthless slaughters were carried out equally against Russians, Jews, Belorussians, Ukrainians, Latvians, Lithuanians, and other peoples of the Soviet Union.[16]

Once again, Mikhoels played the foreign press card, appealing to Zhdanov to reverse the decision of the Department of Propaganda and to hasten the publication of the book on the grounds that "the reactionary press is attempting to remove responsibility from the German fascists for the annihilation of the Jewish population in the temporarily occupied territories, placing heavy blame for these crimes upon the local non-Jewish population."[17] But his appeal was rejected.

The second project with which Mikhoels involved himself was the distribution of foreign aid within Russia. Mikhoels had been receiving many appeals for help from Jewish communities and individuals throughout the country who felt they could not turn to any other organization.[18] Mikhoels chose to take their concerns to Molotov himself, writing: "The Jewish population, with rare exception, is being completely ignored by local authorities in the distribution of this kind of aid." As usual, Mikhoels did not appeal to Molotov's humanitarian instinct; rather he asked for assistance because "the Jewish pro-fascist *Forward* [Yiddish daily newspaper] in New York is calling on Jewish organizations to stop the campaign to send assistance to the Soviet Union."[19] As a solution to the distribution problem, Mikhoels suggested that the Jewish Anti-Fascist Committee supervise distribution. Although Molotov recommended that a committee be set up to investigate the irregularities, he was reluctant to augment the authority of the committee in domestic matters: "The JAFC was not created to handle such matters and the committee apparently does not have a completely accurate understanding of its functions."[20] Its function was to raise money, not to allocate it. Later requests by Mikhoels to allow American donations to be earmarked for certain destinations were categorically rejected, officially on the grounds that "singling out Jews from the general population of the Soviet Union for special treatment will create conditions for anti-semitism."[21]

Mikhoels also sought to use the Anti-Fascist Committee as a liaison between the Jewish population and the Soviet government. The most pressing problem was the resettlement of Jews who had fled the western provinces in advance of the Nazi invasion. Many seeking to return to their homes were met with hostility by the local inhabitants, who were fearful of retribution for their wartime conduct or who had profited from the Jewish absence by usurping abandoned Jewish property. Once again, Mikhoels was informed of the situation through numerous letters which poured into the offices of the Jewish Anti-Fascist Committee.[22] According to one report from a committee meeting, "Peretz Markish maliciously declared that 'the Jews are once again in a ghetto.' . . . Unfortunately, S. M. Mikhoels, who was chairing the session, never spoke out about it."[23]

Later, the 1920s proposal to resettle Jews in the Crimea was revived under Mikhoels's name, although Mikhoels's actual contribution to the project remains unclear. In February 1944, in the so-called Crimean Brief (actually two slightly different letters sent to Molotov and Stalin), Mikhoels, Epshteyn, and Fefer suggested "the creation of a Jewish Soviet Socialist Republic on the territory of the Crimea."[24] The appeal represented an about-face for Mikhoels, who had long voiced his objection to the establishment of a Jewish autonomous region in Birobidzhan. He justified the change in approach by calling attention to the "insufficient mobilization of [Birodidzhan's] full potential." He also pointed out that "for a great part of the Jewish population . . . their places of origin were turned by the fascists into cemeteries that can never be brought back to life, where their families and friends lie. . . . During the war certain capitalist vestiges became intensified in the psyche of certain strata of various nationalities, including their intelligentsia. One of the most striking expressions of these relics is new outbursts of anti-Semitism."[25]

Mikhoels also retained his foreign ties after the war and continued to represent himself as a Soviet delegate to world Jewry. Between 1944 and 1948 he requested permission to attend a meeting of the World Jewish Congress in New York (1944), a Jewish Conference in Helsinki (1946), a World Congress of Jewish Culture (1946), a conference on Jewish Culture in Poland (1946), an International Conference of Anti-Fascist Organizations in Paris (1947), and a meeting of the Jewish Democratic Committee of Romania (1947).[26] Lev Sheinin, who had served as an assistant to the Soviet prosecutor at the Nuremberg Trials, also requested that Mikhoels accompany him to Nuremberg. Each of these requests was rejected by Mikhail Suslov, the head of the Central Committee's Foreign Policy Department.

Mikhoels's public actions demonstrated a profound interest in the reconstruction of Jewish life in the Soviet Union after the war. His private statements, on the other hand, reflected both his growing pessimism in the fate of Soviet Jewry and his increasing Zionist sympathies. Abraham Sutzkever, for instance, recalls one evening in 1946 when he was a guest at Mikhoels's home. After the other guests retired for the night, Sutzkever and Mikhoels were left alone. Mikhoels filled two glasses with vodka, handed one to Sutzkever and gave a toast: "Lekhaim, Abraham, to the people of Israel." Sutzkever then took out a letter he had brought with him that was written by Isaac Leyb Peretz to the writer Yehoash (Solomon Bloomgarten), who had translated the Bible into Yiddish before his departure for Palestine. Sutzkever read the letter:

> We wish you wholeheartedly a fortunate trip and we wish you health. Take us with you in your heart and your thoughts. . . . And say our names to the hills of Judaea, the Cedars of Lebanon and all that remains—there is no land we would rather live in. Zion is our path. The world with Zion at its peak is our future.

After a pause, Sutzkever writes, Mikhoels repeated the words, "'there is no land we would rather live in' with a quivering lower lip, as though he were studying a role." After a moment in silence, Mikhoels continued, "You know, when I was flying to America in July 1943, flying over the land of Israel, I kissed the air." The conversation then turned to Mikhoels's trip to America. When Sutzkever asked Mikhoels what he had talked about with Einstein, Mikhoels replied that Einstein had asked if there was any anti-Semitism in Russia. "And what, Comrade Mikhoels, did you answer?" Sutzkever describes Mikhoels's response: "'I answered him'—and a bitter ironic smile filled his face—'that our constitution, as everyone knows, prohibits anti-Semitism.'" This exchange gives an idea of Mikhoels's ability to overtly state one thing while covertly communicating another—a skill he used adroitly both on and off the stage.[27]

American Spy and Zionist Agent

As the Soviet Union braced for the Cold War by demonizing the West and beginning its campaign against "rootless cosmopolitans" who "kowtow to the West," Mikhoels's travel requests were used as evidence of criminal activity. Like the millions of repatriated Soviet POWs sent to Siberian camps upon their return, Mikhoels was tainted by having seen the West. For this reason Viktor Abakumov, an agent of the Ministry of State Security, was put in charge of the Mikhoels case. Abakumov had made his reputation heading Smersh (Death to Spies), the department responsible for imprisoning those who had come in contact with the West during the war. He was a close confidant of Stalin and would soon be appointed Minister of State Security.

Before Stalin intervened and transferred the Mikhoels case to Abakumov, the Central Committee of the Communist Party debated the future of the Jewish Anti-Fascist Committee. Since as early as 1946, the Central Committee had been discussing the possibility of disbanding it on the grounds that it had overstepped its boundaries by continuing to promote the interests of Soviet Jews and by retaining extensive foreign contacts with Zionist and bourgeois Jewish organizations.[28] Further, the Central Committee began to receive reports alleging nationalist motifs in Soviet Yiddish literature, including Markish's *Uprising in the Ghetto* and Bergelson's *Prince Reuveni*.[29] Due in part to personal antagonisms and turf wars within the Central Committee, however, no direct action was taken against either the Jewish Anti-Fascist Committee or its chairman. It seems that Aleksandrov and Suslov wanted the committee disbanded, but were opposed by Molotov and Aleksandr Kuznetsov, the Central Committee's secretary. Zhdanov, for his part, sought to restructure the committee rather than completely destroy it.

As the Central Committee was debating the Anti-Fascist Committee's future, however, the Ministry of State Security under Abakumov's direction had already begun to act independently (although with Stalin's approval) against it. With the eventual liquidation of the Jewish Anti-Fascist Committee in mind, the Ministry planted Grigori Kheifetz in the organization as a spy. Together with Itzik Fefer, who was already reporting on the committee's activities to the Ministry of State Security, he helped the prosecutors formulate a case against Mikhoels and his associates. The Ministry of State Security was acting in total isolation from the Central Committee, as evidenced by one proposal that circulated within the Central Committee that recommended the removal of Fefer from the Jewish Anti-Fascist Committee on the grounds that he was a former Bundist. Had the Central Committee been aware that Fefer was a stooge of the Ministry of State Security, such a recommendation would not have been permitted.

Rather than dabble in Yiddish literary criticism, as the Central Committee was attempting to do, Abakumov preferred to fabricate a case against Mikhoels based on the actor's personal connections. Indeed, the Russian secret police had known for centuries that the simplest way to indict an individual was to establish associations between the accused and known criminals. This type of "evidence" had sent countless loyal Bolsheviks and ordinary citizens to their deaths during the 1930s and would soon be used against Moscow's leading Jewish intellectuals. The "criminal" with whom Abakumov decided to link Mikhoels was Evgeniia Allilueva, the ex–sister-in-law of Stalin's ex-wife Nadezhda. Abakumov charged that Allilueva had used Mikhoels and the Jewish Anti-Fascist Committee to submit incriminating information on Stalin's private life to U.S. intelligence officers. Stalin was able to connect Allilueva to Mikhoels through Isaak Goldshteyn, the nephew of I. L. Peretz and an acquaintance of Allilueva. Although Goldshteyn and Mikhoels had only met twice, once at the theater in 1945 and again in the autumn of 1946, Goldshteyn was a friend of Z. G. Grinberg, who in turn was a close associate of Mikhoels in the Anti-Fascist Committee. The connection was sufficient for Stalin's henchmen to construct a charge of conspiracy against the trio. On December 10, 1947, Allilueva was arrested and accused of spreading slander against Stalin. Five days later, Goldshteyn was also arrested. According to trial records and rehabilitation reports from the KGB archive, which were collected by Gennadi Kostyrchenko, throughout December Goldshteyn was continuously beaten and tortured until on January 9, 1948—less than a week before Mikhoels's murder—he signed a confession stating that he was acting as an agent of Mikhoels and was entrusted with collecting information on Stalin's private life from Allilueva and passing it on to Mikhoels, who in turn was passing it on to anti-Soviet American Jewish organizations.[30] It is worth noting that there was a far more direct connection between Allilueva and Mikhoels in the person of Polina Zhemchuzhina, Molotov's wife, who had been a close friend of Nadezhda Allilueva before the latter's death in 1932 and was an associate of Mikhoels. The new purge, however, had not yet reached the level of Molotov's wife. Her arrest did not occur until the following year.

The perseverance with which Abakumov fabricated a case against Mikhoels seems bizarre, given that the actor would be killed in secret. The intelligence-gathering operation would have been more in keeping with a show trial than a clandestine murder. This has led some observers to conclude that a show trial was being planned but was abandoned at the last minute.[31] Kostyrchenko counters this argument on the grounds that a show trial would have brought publicity to Stalin's personal life, complicated Soviet diplomacy, and turned Mikhoels into a martyr and could therefore not have been contemplated.[32] Stalin, however, had never before feared making martyrs of individuals. His murderous purges were never before softened by diplomatic concerns, and with ultimate control over the testimony of defendants, he had little to fear about what the discovery process would reveal of his private life. Kostyrchenko's explanation implies that the process was well thought out in advance. This, however, does not seem to be the case. According to the time schedule constructed by Arkady Vaksberg, the decision to kill Mikhoels was made after the arrest of Goldshteyn.[33] Thus, some event must have occurred that discouraged the prosecutors from continuing the investigation and hastened the need to murder Mikhoels.

This defining event was probably a speech Mikhoels made in which he gave voice to his long-held Zionist sympathies. On November 29, 1947, after Britain announced its intention to end its mandate in Palestine, the future of the region was put to a vote in the United Nations. The Soviet Union, represented by Andrei Gromyko, joined with thirty-two other nations to approve the establishment of a Jewish state in Palestine. In the ensuing euphoria, Mikhoels overcame his usual caution to openly celebrate the United Nations resolution. According to Mikhoels's daughter, in December 1947 during a jubilee ceremony for Mendele Mokher Sforim, Mikhoels and Zuskin performed a segment of their 1927 play *The Travels of Benjamin III*. Mikhoels spoke: "Benjamin departed in search of the Promised Land and asked a villager he met along the way how to get to Eretz [the Land of] Israel . . . and right here, not very long ago, since the debate of the United Nations, Comrade Gromyko has answered this question."[34] The tumultuous applause lasted a full ten minutes. According to Mikhoels's daughter, the next day they heard a recording of the ceremony on the radio, but Mikhoels's speech had been deleted. "This is a bad omen," Mikhoels remarked. Indeed, a newspaper advertisement confirms that on Saturday, December 27th, the Union of Soviet Writers sponsored an evening at the Politechnical Museum dedicated to Mendele Mokher Sforim on the occasion of the thirtieth anniversary of his death. Mikhoels, along with Bergelson and Dobrushin, were listed as the speakers.[35] According to the time line established by Vaksberg, the decision to send Mikhoels to Minsk was taken sometime between December 31st and January 2nd.[36] Vaksberg, however, is unable to find the precise stimulus that led Stalin to make the final decision.

Although it seems that Mikhoels's increasing outspokenness and the apparent encouragement he was receiving from the Jewish community as a whole had come to Stalin's attention earlier, the Mendele affair was probably the last straw. After such a provocative statement in favor of Jewish nationalism and Zionism, Stalin likely decided that the time had come to act.

The fact that the statement came from Mikhoels was particularly important because it lent credence to the assumption that Mikhoels harbored Zionist sympathies and gave new meaning to his contacts with Western Zionists. Further, by linking his endorsement to one of the theater's earliest productions, Mikhoels contradicted years of denying that the Moscow State Yiddish Theater's plays could be interpreted as nationalist. In a single statement, Mikhoels undermined years of public denials and confirmed that the plays of the Moscow State Yiddish Theater could be given nationalist interpretations sanctioned by Mikhoels himself.

More important, Mikhoels's statement of support for the partition plan was the first time that any Soviet Jew had publicly endorsed the establishment of a Jewish state in Palestine before a Soviet audience. It was a serious misjudgment. Soviet diplomatic support for the United Nations partition plan was by no means intended as an official endorsement of Zionism. The decision to support the partition plan was based solely on the diplomatic imperative of forcing the British out of the Near East. The Jewish state, Stalin and Gromyko believed, would act as a counterweight to the pro-British leanings of the region's Arab populations. Further, they hoped that the new Jewish state would look toward the Soviet Union for support and give the USSR a beachhead in the region. Soviet recognition of the State of Israel was no more intended as an endorsement of Zionism than Stalin's wartime alliance with Britain and America was intended as an endorsement of democratic capitalism. While Mikhoels was astute enough to refrain from celebrating the American Dream during the war, he failed to display the same common sense in 1947. The tumultuous applause that greeted Mikhoels's statement doubtless indicated to the Soviet authorities that Zionism was striking an emotional chord within the Jewish population. In order to prevent Zionist euphoria from getting out of hand, it was imperative that Mikhoels be silenced as soon as possible. Thus, the planned show trial on the charge of "American espionage" was abandoned in favor of a quick clandestine assassination.

Mikhoels, though, could not have been so naive as to have thought that such a statement was permissible. Perhaps, therefore, his statement was a deliberate provocation. Knowing that his days were numbered, Mikhoels could have decided to use what he believed would be his last public appearance to its utmost effect. Indeed, there is evidence to suggest that Mikhoels suspected he was under investigation prior to the Mendele evening. Lidiia Shatunovskaia, a theater historian and friend of the Alliluev family, for instance, recalls that on December 27th—the day of the Mendele celebration—she bumped into Mikhoels on Tverskaia Street, and he said to her: "This is the beginning of the end."[37] That night Shatunovskaia and her husband Leonid Tumerman were arrested. Shatunovskaia was later charged with passing sensitive information about the Alliluev family to Mikhoels, who in turn passed the information to "American-Zionist" intelligence.[38] It is difficult to determine whether Mikhoels somehow knew about Shatunovskaia's impending arrest, or if their brief encounter on the street was observed by secret agents and thereby provided a necessary link between Mikhoels and the Alliluev family. In other words, Mikhoels's remark to Shatunovskaia could have become a self-fulfilling prophecy. Indeed, Shatunovskaia and Mikhoels were not such close friends. It seems to be too much of a coincidence for the two to have accidentally met on the street hours before Shatunovskaia's arrest for conspiring with Mikhoels. It is far more likely that Mikhoels was being followed by agents searching for "evidence" to be used in a show trial against him. But after Mikhoels's reckless speech that night, the authorities must have realized that a show trial would be too risky.

Around January 2, 1948, Mikhoels was instructed to travel to Minsk as a member of the Stalin Prize Committee to review a play that was nominated for the Stalin Prize. The testimonies of several of Mikhoels's acquaintances indicate that Mikhoels suspected he would never return to Moscow. According to Zuskin's testimony at his trial, about two or three days before the trip to Minsk, Mikhoels made Zuskin sit at the director's desk and said, "Here, you will be sitting in this chair soon, very soon."[39] The academician Pëtr Kapitsa, an old acquaintance of Mikhoels with whom he had not spoken in several months, also recounts how he received a farewell call from Mikhoels the day before he left for Minsk.[40] Prior to his departure for Minsk, Mikhoels was informed that his companion would be Vladimir Golubov-Potapov, the executive secretary of the theater journal *Teatr* and a man with connections to the Soviet security apparatus. On January 7, 1948, the two boarded a train from Moscow's Belorussian Station.

On January 11, 1948, Mikhoels called his family in Moscow and informed them that he had seen Fefer in the Minsk hotel where he was staying, but that Fefer had mysteriously hidden to avoid being spotted. Fefer was supposed to be in Moscow continuing work at the Jewish Anti-Fascist Committee. His sudden appearance in Minsk was an ominous sign and provided early evidence of the poet's involvement in the sinister plot.

Most of our information regarding the events of the night of January 12th and 13th comes from testimonies by Abakumov and his deputy Sergei Ogoltsov, which were given to Lavrentii Beria during his 1953 investigation into the Mikhoels incident. Abakumov recalled:

> It was then well known that Mikhoels had arrived in Minsk together with a friend, whose name I can't remember. When this fact was reported to I. V. Stalin, he immediately gave the order to carry out the liquidation in Minsk itself under the guise of an accident, that is, that Mikhoels and his companion were to die in an automobile accident.

The story is continued by Ogoltsov:

> It was decided that agents would invite Mikhoels to visit an acquaintance at night, send a car to the hotel where he was staying, take him to the suburban

country house of L. F. Tsanava, liquidate him there, transport his body to a remote street in a thinly populated area of the city, lay it on the road leading to the hotel, and have it run over by a truck. . . . That's the way it was done.[41]

On January 27, 1948, Lavrentii Tsanava, a high-ranking member of the Belorussian NKVD, was awarded the Order of Lenin "for exemplary execution of a special assignment from the government."[42]

The Show Must Go On

The two bodies were found the next morning lying face down in the snow on a deserted Minsk road. The bodies were soon brought back to Moscow. Boris Zbarsky, the director of the Lenin Mausoleum laboratory and a professional embalmer, was entrusted with the task of preparing Mikhoels's body. Beginning on January 15th at four in the afternoon, the body lay in state at the auditorium on

The last photo of Solomon Mikhoels. 11 January 1943. Photo from Solomon Mikhoels, *Stati, besedi, rechi.*

Malaia Bronnaia Street. Visitors crowded into the theater until midnight to catch a last glimpse of Mikhoels, and the following morning the body was displayed again until the funeral began at noon. During those two days over 10,000 people came to pay their respects, and over 100 telegrams were sent to the theater from all over the world.[43]

The outpouring of emotion after Mikhoels's death was remarkable. *Eynikayt* dedicated two full issues to publishing the thoughts and reminiscences of Mikhoels's friends and admirers. Ilya Ehrenburg, for instance, wrote a tribute to "a great actor and a wonderful person" entitled "He Lived for his People." In a less genuine article, Fefer wrote: "Mikhoels came from the people, lived with the people, and wanted to stay with the people. Mikhoels was always connected to the people, and it is not by accident that he revealed himself to everybody on the theater's stage. He sought a tribune and he found one. . . . Mikhoels loved his people with an open and pure heart."[44] Other contributors included Yekhezkel Dobrushin, Alexander Fadeev, Nakhum Oyslender, Boris Zbarsky, Benjamin Zuskin, Peretz Markish, and Moshe Goldblatt, to name but a few.[45] The following week two memorials for Mikhoels were conducted at the theater. The director's brother spoke about their childhood together and about Mikhoels's early love of theater, Azarkh spoke about their early days in Petrograd and about her companionship with Mikhoels at the Petrograd School of Theater, and Dobrushin spoke about Mikhoels's first attempt at directing with *The Travels of Benjamin III.*[46] In May 1948, scholarships were established by the Committee of Artistic Affairs in honor of Mikhoels at the Soviet State Yiddish Theater School and the Lunacharskii Institute.[47] Allegedly to ensure that Mikhoels's death did not have a negative impact on the ongoing revival of Jewish culture, on February 17, 1948 the Committee of Artistic Affairs officially appointed Zuskin as director of the Moscow State Yiddish Theater.[48]

The official deification of Mikhoels after his death was a ploy designed to hide official complicity in the murder. Soviet prosecutors were relentless in their efforts to conceal the anti-Semitic nature of their campaign behind the myth that Stalin's nationality policy provided for the triumph of all national cultures. Yet this public adoration, in both official and unofficial quarters, was coupled with messages passed along behind closed doors as the Ministry of State Security began preparing for the total destruction of Jewish culture in the Soviet Union. The liquidation of the Moscow State Yiddish Theater, ostensibly for "financial reasons," was a carefully contrived procedure, designed to hide any anti-Semitic motivation. Two months after Mikhoels's murder, Abakumov prepared his final report on the Jewish Anti-Fascist Committee in which he wrote, "Mikhoels and his like-minded colleagues, as revealed by intelligence work and an investigation of Jewish nationalist matters, used the Jewish Anti-Fascist Committee as a cover for carrying out anti-Soviet activity." Mikhoels was accused of engaging in anti-Soviet activity after his return from America and of trying to establish a Jewish state in the Crimea.[49] With the intensification of the Zhdanovshchina (the campaign of Russian chauvinism named after Andrei Zhdanov) and the veiled anti-Semitic campaign against "rootless cosmopolitans," the Moscow State Yiddish Theater's fate was sealed. As the year progressed and the Zhdanovshchina intensified, many Jews "in the know" began to suspect that Mikhoels was actually murdered. Rumors to that effect began circulating among the theater staff just days after the murder, stimulated by an anonymous phone call to the theater and statements made by Zhemchuzhina at the funeral. However, the majority of Moscow's Jews continued to believe that Mikhoels's death was a tragic accident. The American Embassy in Moscow, on the other hand, doubted that the death was accidental. Noting the preponderance of clandestine Zionists in Belorussia, the embassy suggested in a dispatch to the Department of State that Mikhoels may have been murdered by Jewish Zionists who opposed his anti-Zionist stance.[50]

Although one would expect the sudden attention lavished upon the theater after Mikhoels's death to have stimulated an increase in the public's attendance at the Yiddish theater, the opposite was the case. The decline in the Yiddish theater's attendance, however, was not a product of popular lack of interest, but rather a product of the Committee of Artistic Affair's calculated decision to force the theater into bankruptcy. First, the committee revised the theater's repertoire for the coming year. Rather than perform a series of plays by some of the most noted contemporary Jewish writers, including Grossman and Fefer, as previously planned,[51] the committee ordered the theater instead to rework two of its former classic productions: *Hershele Ostropoler* and *The Sorceress*,[52] both of which were popular failures due to the fact that few potential audience members had missed previous versions during their long runs. Second, the committee ordered the theater to perform Yiddish translations of contemporary Russian plays, a policy that had actually begun in the months preceding the murder of Mikhoels. This indicates that the decision to force the closure of the Yiddish theater was actually taken in tandem with the stillborn decision to try Mikhoels for anti-Soviet sabotage.

The theater's final production before Mikhoels's murder was Aleksei Brat and Grigori Linkov's *Tumultuous Forest*, which premiered in November of 1947. The play was a revised version of Linkov's *War to the Home Front of the Enemy*, a Russian play about a Jewish partisan who dies in battle. The play drew its name from the "legendary valor" of the partisans who turned the forests into a staging ground for battle.[53] This weak production repeated many of the theater's wartime themes, particularly its emphasis on the unity of all Soviet peoples in the face of fascism. Similarly, the theater's first new production after Mikhoels's murder was a Yiddish translation of Vitenzon and Zinger's *Zoria Belinkovich*, again originally written in Russian. Structurally, the play was almost identical to *Tumultuous Forest*; it told of a Jew during World War II who is killed fighting fascism, only this time the hero was the commander of a submarine rather than a partisan. Both plays retained a semblance of Jewish content by featuring Jewish heroes, but they had little else "Jewish" about them. These two translations of Russian works were an ominous sign of the decline of Yiddish culture. At a time when Yiddish writers were at their most productive—the theater had just commissioned numerous prominent Yiddish writers to compose promising plays—the theater was forced to bypass its traditional sources and perform bland Russian plays by obscure writers instead.

Tumultuous Forest, 1947. *Left to right:* I . Gross, Benjamin
Zuskin, and Etta Kovenskaia.
Photo courtesy of Ala Perelman-Zuskin.

The only new play by a Yiddish playwright was Isaak Hoberman's *Life Is Worth Living,* a comedy about a man who talks incessantly, thereby revealing his stupidity. Little information is available on this production other than two reviews, one of which lamented an unfortunate choice of repertoire and a bland script.[54] *Eynikayt,* on the other hand, reported in an unusually short review that the production was met with "great success."[55]

The Committee of Artistic Affairs also took a number of administrative measures to ensure the theater's financial failure. In early 1948, in an effort to boost ticket sales, the theater had begun offering subscription tickets, entitling the subscriber to buy a set of ten tickets for reduced prices.[56] However, when rumors spread that the list of subscribers was being handed over to the Ministry of State Security, subscriptions dwindled. The project was finally canceled when ticket distribution for all theaters was centralized on November 20, 1948, leaving individual theaters with no discretion to conduct their own promotions.[57] The central ticket cashier subsequently was able to fabricate attendance: potential patrons could be told that the production was sold out when in fact no tickets had yet been sold or a full house could be reported as "empty." Unable to force the troupe into bankruptcy, Ministry of State Security officials finally resorted to hiring people to loiter conspicuously on the sidewalk of the Malaia Bronnaia to spread the rumor that audiences were being photographed for the State Security records. This was enough to empty the auditorium for good.[58]

The theater, however, proved to be more resilient than the Committee of Artistic Affairs and the Ministry of State Security expected. Although attendance fell significantly and the theater exceeded its allowed losses,[59] it managed to stay afloat by drastically reducing its staff and adding performances to its already grueling schedule.[60] But the committee was relentless in its efforts to force the theater into bankruptcy. In the summer of 1948 it ordered the theater to tour Leningrad and Odessa,[61] where it would perform thirty-four times during June and July.[62] The theater's regular summer tour was an integral component of its artistic and political mission but was inevitably a financial failure because of the costs associated with travel. The theater was customarily reimbursed for its losses by the state, which regarded these tours as essential propaganda. This time, however, the theater was given no financial relief.

Next Year in Jerusalem

In the fall of 1948, a series of events again connected with the establishment of Israel unleashed the final storm that would ultimately destroy the Moscow State Yiddish Theater, the Jewish Anti-Fascist Committee, and the last remnants of Jewish cultural life in the Soviet Union. By October 1948, it was obvious that Mikhoels was by no means the sole advocate of Zionism among Soviet Jews. The revival of Jewish cultural expression during the war had fostered a general sense of boldness among the Jewish masses. Many Jews remained oblivious to the growing Zhdanovshchina and the threat to Soviet Jews that the brewing campaign against "rootless cosmopolitans" signaled. Indeed, official attitudes toward Jewish culture were ambivalent during this period. On the surface, Jewish culture seemed to be supported by the state: public efforts had been made to sustain the Yiddish theater after Mikhoels's death, *Eynikayt* was still publishing on schedule, and, most important, the Soviet Union recognized the establishment of a Jewish state in Palestine. To most Moscow Jews, the state of Soviet Jewry had never been better.

This general euphoria became most evident after the establishment of the State of Israel on May 14, 1948. The first open declaration of solidarity with Israel appeared on May 20th, when *Eynikayt* published an open letter of congratulations to Chaim Weizmann, the new provisional president of Israel.[63] Soon after, the offices of the Jewish Anti-Fascist Committee were flooded with letters of support from ordinary Soviet Jewish citizens; some asked for help to emigrate to Israel, some offered financial assistance, some offered to enlist in the Israeli army, and others simply expressed support. Many letters suggested using the Jewish Anti-Fascist Committee as a central organ to coordinate emigration, financial aid, and arms shipments to Israel.[64] Kheifetz passed on the names of all signatories to the Central Committee of the Communist Party.[65] One report stated that "a series of letters clearly reflect nationalist sentiments. The authors of these letters do not distinguish between Jewish citizens of the USSR and Jews living in capitalist countries and, apparently, consider Israel to be their true homeland, tending to put it above the USSR."[66]

The situation spun out of control with the arrival in Moscow of Golda Meir (Meyersohn) and the first Israeli mission to the Soviet Union. They arrived on September 2nd, one month before the Jewish High Holidays. On Rosh Hashanah (October 2nd), Meir attended religious services at Moscow's Choral Synagogue. In her autobiography, Meir described the scene in front of the synagogue:

> It [the street] was filled with people, packed together like sardines, hundreds and hundreds of them, of all ages, including Red Army officers, soldiers, teenagers and babies carried in their parents' arms. Instead of the 2,000-odd Jews who usually came to synagogue on High Holidays, a crowd of close to 50,000 people was waiting for us. For a minute, I couldn't grasp what had happened—or even who they were. And then it dawned on me. They had come—those good, brave Jews—in order to be with us, to demonstrate their sense of kinship and to celebrate the establishment of the State of Israel.[67]

Because most of the crowd was unable to fit inside the synagogue, a spontaneous street celebration erupted, forcing the closure of much of downtown Moscow for the afternoon as jubilant Jews celebrated the first New Year of the Jewish State. Ten days later the scene was repeated for Yom Kippur services. As the services concluded with the traditional blowing of the shofar and the chant of "Next Year in Jerusalem," the crowd erupted into a frenzy: "A tremor went through the entire synagogue," recalled Meir.[68] On September 16th, Meir also attended the Moscow State Yiddish Theater, where an Israeli flag was being displayed. As a gesture of support, she bought several season tickets to distribute to those who could not afford them. Meir also brought out the most nationalist sentiments among those with whom she met. For instance, Polina Zhemchuzhina spoke with Meir in Yiddish—much to the chagrin of the State Security trying to report on her conversations—and expressed solidarity with the Israeli state. The exuberant reception of the Israeli mission was unprecedented in Stalin's Russia. Spontaneous assemblies were unacceptable in Stalin's ritualized society. The fact that this gathering was focused on both a foreign nation and a religious holiday only added to the anathema. The Jewish reaction to Meir's visit firmly convinced Stalin that the Jews were a fifth column who would betray the Soviet Motherland for the Zionist homeland.

The Liquidation of the Moscow State Yiddish Theater

On November 20, 1948, just over a month after Yom Kippur, the Central Committee of the Communist Party ordered the Ministry of State Security to disband the Jewish Anti-Fascist Committee. Within days, the committee's offices were closed down, *Eynikayt* ceased publication, the Der Emes Yiddish printing press was destroyed, and Yiddish radio broadcasts were discontinued. The Moscow State Yiddish Theater, for its part, was ordered by the Committee of Artistic Affairs to embark upon a return engagement to Leningrad for an unprecedented December tour—a move the committee expected would firmly bankrupt the theater.[69] A similar ploy was used to liquidate the Ukrainian State Yiddish Theater. After the war, the Ukrainian State Yiddish Theater was ordered not to return to Kiev but instead to relocate to Chernovtsy in former Rumanian territory. The move was expensive, requiring an entire restructuring and the purchase of a new auditorium. Just when the theater was getting settled in its new home, it was ordered to go on tour. After all tour expenses had been paid, bringing the theater into a debt which could only be recovered through a highly successful tour, the theater was ordered to cancel the tour and return to Chernovtsy. After three performances of, appropriately, Sholem Aleichem's *Wandering Stars*, the troupe was liquidated.[70]

Some probably recognized the Leningrad tour ploy for what it was. Zuskin, who had fallen ill at the height of the Great Purges, once again succumbed to illness. He was hospitalized on December 20th and never returned to his post at the theater.[71] On December 24, 1948, he was arrested in his hospital bed by the Ministry of State Security for attempting to promote "Jewish nationalism" and "anti-Soviet behavior." The evidence presented by the Ministry of State Security after a search of his apartment at 9 Tverskaia Street consisted of a French Jewish journal, several documents listed in the report simply as "documents," an "autobiography," notes on the staging of plays for the Yiddish theater, and a notebook in Yiddish. Apparently, the fact that the director of the Moscow State Yiddish Theater had notes on staging and a notebook in Yiddish was sufficient evidence for his arrest. On December 29, 1948, the Committee of Artistic Affairs officially released him from the staff of the theater retroactively as of December 24th.[72]

The same day, the committee issued a declaration to the theater ordering it to produce a repertoire that reflected "important real-life Party-oriented themes on current Soviet affairs, demonstrating aesthetically the basic character traits of Soviet people, the high moral and aesthetic principles of Soviet society . . . the great victory of the Soviet people and the Bolshevik Party in the Patriotic War . . . the heroism of post-war construction . . . the Soviet intelligentsia and their patriotism, and the struggle against the servility of bourgeois Western culture." The theater was given less than a month to turn over a new repertoire.[73] The order to prepare for the future was a charade. Behind the scenes, the Committee of Artistic Affairs was already preparing for the theater's ultimate destruction even as it approved new scripts for the theater.[74] Two days after issuing its repertory directives, the committee issued regulations for the "liquidation of the Moscow State Yiddish Theater," calling for the immediate convocation of a liquidation committee to be appointed by the Committee of Artistic Affairs in conjunction with the Ministry of Finance and the Union of Artists. The order was signed by F. V. Evseev, the deputy director of the Chief Management of Dramatic Theaters of the Committee of Artistic Affairs, and by N. Bespalov, assistant director of the Committee of Artistic Affairs.[75]

The Ministry of State Security simultaneously embarked upon its own mission to arrest the most prominent remaining representatives of Soviet Jewish culture. Fefer was arrested the same night as Zuskin, the night of December 23rd and

24th. The following month, between December 24th and January 28th, David Bergelson, Yekhezkel Dobrushin, Shmuel Halkin, Solomon Lozovskii, Peretz Markish, Der Nister, Isaac Nusinov, and other members of the Jewish Anti-Fascist Committee were arrested. Soon after, the Yiddish theater school was closed, and its director, Moshe Belenkii, arrested. In early 1949, the Jewish Writer's Union was closed, along with most remaining Yiddish publications. By the summer of 1949, the last remaining bastions of Jewish culture were the State Yiddish Theaters. However, one by one, they too were closed: the Belorussian State Yiddish Theater, the Birobidzhan State Yiddish Theater, and the Ukrainian State Yiddish Theater. The Moscow State Yiddish Theater was the last to be closed.

With its most prominent authors in prison, the theater was ordered by the Committee of Artistic Affairs to remove all works by the arrested authors from the repertoire and to refrain from using any material from their works for new productions or educational purposes.[76] On March 9, 1949, the theater was ordered to balance its books by cutting expenses[77] and further reducing its already emaciated staff.[78]

On February 23, 1949 the Committee of Artistic Affairs informed the Central Committee that "the Moscow State Yiddish Theater causes the state great losses and cannot work in the future in self-sufficient conditions"; it recommended that the theater be closed within the week.[79] The attached documents showed that attendance in 1948 was less than 50 percent of capacity and that in the first two months of 1949 it had dropped to less than a quarter of capacity. The stated reason was that "the children and youth, almost without exception, do not attend Yiddish plays."[80] In preparation for the liquidation of the theater, all members of the troupe were required to fill out forms listing their travels abroad and naming any relatives they had who lived abroad. This information was then passed on to the Ministry of State Security.[81] The Committee of Artistic Affairs also drew up negative reviews of several plays and passed the information on to Agitprop,[82] which in turn wrote a report for Stalin and Malenkov:

> Lately the theater has fallen into a complete ideological and artistic decay. The theater's repertoire is extremely unsatisfactory with regard to its ideological-artistic quality and is limited by the narrow frames of its national subjects. The theater has not staged the works of the classic Russian playwrights or the plays of modern Soviet authors. Its repertoire is littered with ideologically defective plays by nationalist playwrights. (The theater has produced plays by the repressed authors Fefer, Markish and Dobrushin.)
>
> . . . The theater personnel is littered with people who are not good artists and are not worthy of political confidence. After S. Mikhoels's death, V. Zuskin —now repressed—was appointed artistic director of the theater. Neither the producer nor the actors who are cast are great masters. Out of 55 artists there are only 4 Communists and 6 Komsomol members. Many artists are immigrants from abroad and through their relatives have connections abroad.
>
> . . . The Department of Propaganda and Agitation considers it expedient to accept the suggestion of the Committee of Artistic Affairs of the Council of Ministers of the USSR (Comrade Lebedev) regarding the liquidation of the

Moscow State Yiddish Theater. We ask that the Decree of the Central Committee of the Communist Party of the Soviet Union (Bolsheviks) on this question be approved.[83]

The Central Committee, however, declined to decide the matter at that time.

On June 30, 1949, the Committee of Artistic Affairs issued a report concluding that the theater had failed to complete the plan. The attached statistics, however, indicated that the theater was faring significantly better than implied in the committee's charges; it had exceeded its performance plan by 8 percent, performing 309 rather than the required 286 shows; and its revenue for the 1948 season was 2,080,000 rubles, significantly higher than the 1947 intake of 1,154,000 rubles. The report concluded that "as a result of not completing the plan, the theater shall withhold salaries."[84] Truly, the theater had not fulfilled the financial plan, which called for an absurdly high intake; but considering that over the course of the year it had lost its star and director and had been forced to undergo a complete restructuring, it is remarkable that it was still able to surpass its intakes from the previous year. However, even though the theater had lost its second director in two years, its chief writers were gone and their material no longer allowed to be performed, and a general atmosphere of fear and terror kept audience members away, during the first half of 1949 the theater lost only 446,000 rubles,[85] compared with a loss of 682,000 rubles the previous year[86]—this from a theater which even in its best days ended seasons with a deficit. On August 10, 1949, a new circular was released to all of Moscow's theaters stating that the management of the Yiddish theater had not followed its instructions to present an estimate for the coming year, and thus "for the manifested lack of discipline and breach of financial estimates, the assistant director of the theater, Comrade Vitis, A. B., will be placed under observation."[87] On September 12th, nevertheless, the committee permitted work to begin on a new production—A. Vitov's *Near Another's Estate*.[88]

But the effort was in vain. On November 14th the committee issued its final order to liquidate the theater as of December 1st on account of its unprofitability. By that date, the Committee of Artistic Affairs had apparently received approval from the Central Committee. The order stated:

Order no. 959
Committee of Artistic Affairs of the Council of People's Ministers of the USSR

November 14, 1949

The Moscow State Yiddish Theater finished the 1948 year with losses of 1,247 thousand rubles and for the ten months of 1949 has allowed losses of the sum of 815 thousand rubles.

Attendance at the theater, both in the years 1948 and 1949 has been at a completely unsatisfactory level, and is currently at 13.7 percent capacity. For many performances only thirty to forty spectators are at the theater. The opening of a new production did not raise the audience's interest. The allocation of subscription tickets for the theater's performances in the same period has brought a general debt in excess of one million rubles.

I order:

1) The liquidation of the Moscow Yiddish Theater as of December 1, 1949 on account of its unprofitability.

2) The formation of a liquidation committee, consisting of M. M. Zorin as chair, G. B. Fishman, F. B. Rainov, and A. B. Bekman, to implement the liquidation of the Moscow Yiddish Theater.

3) The liquidation commission to direct the liquidation of the theater as of 15 December of this year; to present a liquidation balance to the Head Management of Dramatic Theaters; to organize with the Moscow Yiddish Theater a systematic tour and farewell show; to secure the maintenance of the theater's building, administration and service personnel; and to pay its way in full without any subsidy.[89]

The following day, the Chief Management of Dramatic Theaters issued a declaration to the Moscow State Yiddish Theater ordering the cessation of all theatrical activity.[90] All workers in the theater were paid in full until December 28, 1949.[91] Alternative jobs were found for many of the theater's former actors, while others were refused jobs. Some directors, however, such as Yurii Zavadskii, the director of the Mossoviet Theater, defied government orders and accepted a few actors, such as Etel Kovenskaia, who had fallen into disgrace after the Yiddish theater's closure. Kovenskaia was later fortunate enough to be able to emigrate to Israel, where she performed on both the Hebrew and Yiddish stages. According to her friends, however, her heart always remained with the Moscow State Yiddish Theater.[92] All playwrights under commission who had not yet been arrested were partially paid for their work through the intervention of the Union of Soviet Writers. Special considerations were taken to help members of the orchestra find employment in other theaters.[93]

Throughout the next year, the liquidation committee sold the theater's assets to pay off its debts. The inventory of assets, encompassing 203 pages, ranged from a cupola valued at 25,000 rubles to fake moustaches valued at two and a half rubles each.[94] On January 21, 1950, the liquidation committee, which had been working out of the Malaia Bronnaia Theater, was ordered to vacate the premises within two days.[95] One of its last acts, on May 29, 1950, was to turn the buildings on 2 and 4 Malaia Bronnaia, which had housed the Moscow State Yiddish Theater and served as a Jewish community center for Moscow's Jews since 1923, over to the Theater of Satire.[96] The liquidation committee was itself liquidated by order of the Committee of Artistic Affairs on July 1, 1950.[97]

August 12, 1952

The former heroes of Jewish culture were received in prison with interrogation and torture before being left to languish in solitary confinement for three years. Some, like Der Nister and Isaac Nusinov, perished from the harsh conditions. As for the others, they were left alone until July 1951, when Abakumov was arrested and the investigation was turned over to Mikhail Riumin, the new Minister of State Security. Unbeknownst to the prisoners, Riumin approved a set of accusations in March 1952, which were formally approved by Stalin in April. Due to severe illness, Halkin was excused from trial and sentenced to ten years' imprisonment. He survived to be rehabilitated after Stalin's death. As for the other prisoners, on May 8th they were recalled from their cells and brought before a military collegium of the Soviet high court. After being convicted of having conspired with Mikhoels to engage in active anti-Soviet nationalist activity, all but one of the defendants were put to death. The verdict was pre-ordained by direct order of the Politburo. In 1955 the Soviet Supreme Court established that the charges were blatantly falsified,[98] and in 1988 direct responsibility for the fabrication was placed on Georgy Malenkov, chair of the People's Council of Ministers: "It has been established that direct responsibility for the illegal repressions of persons accused in connection with the 'Case of the Jewish Anti-Fascist Committee' lies with G. M. Malenkov, who was directly connected with the investigation and the court examination."[99]

On August 12, 1952 Benjamin Zuskin, Peretz Markish, David Bergelson, Itzik Fefer, and nine other prominent Jews were executed for engaging in "anti-Soviet nationalist activity." Dobrushin perished in prison the following year. All of Fefer's efforts to save himself by cooperating with the authorities and emphasizing his own credentials as an informant were in vain. The massacre was preceded by a six-week secret trial in which the defendants were forced to confess to the crime of "collaboration with the nationalist Mikhoels." Mikhoels, the prosecutor asserted, was "a nationalist who dragged theater and art down into the swamp of Zionism." "In 1937," the prosecutor continued, "the activity of the theater took on a nationalist character." "From this one can draw the conclusion that Mikhoels led the theater toward nationalism."[100] The transcript, however, contains no concrete evidence of a nationalist direction in the theater. Indeed, references to the Yiddish theater are few and far between. The trial was not about theater. In fact, Zuskin's futile defense rested primarily upon the proposition that he was an actor: "I am an actor, and my fault is that all my attention concentrated on this actorial work."[101] By the time Zuskin was interrogated, he had learned that his prosecutors had little interest in the aesthetics or ideology of the Yiddish theater. Even if they cared to investigate, they had little hope of discovering any evidence, having killed off the only loyal Communists with the linguistic and cultural tools necessary to interpret the Yiddish theater's plays. Thus, rather than deconstruct the theater's repertoire, the prosecutors preferred to take Mikhoels's guilt for granted and simply spend the six weeks of the trial establishing each defendant's relationship with Mikhoels or with other defendants. For instance, rather than delve into any detail regarding Markish's artistic output, they proved the playwright's guilt with the fact that Fefer, a self-confessed enemy of the state, had visited Markish's apartment.

The Moscow State Yiddish Theater and its writers had exhibited nationalist sentiments in their works since the late 1920s. Yet despite this "crime" they had managed to survive the Great Purges intact. As long as expressions of national identity remained on stage and in Yiddish they were rarely noticed and thus provoked little official opposition. Once these sentiments were taken off the stage

Solomon Mikhoels memorial plaque on the Malaia
Bronnaia Theater today. The plaque reads: "In this building,
from 1922 to 1948, People's Artist of the USSR Solomon
Mikhailovich Mikhoels worked as an actor and artistic
director of the State Yiddish Theater, Goset."
Photo by author.

and into the public sphere, however, they could no longer be ignored. The eventual downfall of Mikhoels and his theater can be attributed to both the ideological changes brought about by the war and the participants' own politicization of their nationalist feelings. Mikhoels and others flaunted their national convictions both within the Soviet Union and abroad, declared their solidarity with world Jewry, and established and maintained contacts with the world's leading rabbis and Zionists.

Jewish expressions of national pride were most publicly represented in the Jewish Anti-Fascist Committee. Thus, the committee served as the linchpin around which the trials of 1952 were conducted. It was alleged that the Jewish Anti-Fascist Committee "became the center of Jewish nationalist activity."[102] According to a statement Zuskin was said to have signed on March 4, 1952, the Jewish Anti-Fascist Committee "was converted into a nationalist espionage center, leading a struggle against the USSR."[103] It was based on connections to the JAFC that the list of defendants was officially drawn, although some, like Zuskin, had only marginal roles. Yet many of the theater's stars and writers played an integral role in wartime propaganda through the Jewish Anti-Fascist Committee. During the war and for several years afterward, the Yiddish theater became institutionally, personally, and ideologically associated with the JAFC. Indeed, it was this intrusion into politics which ultimately led to the theater's destruction.

Thus, Mikhoels and others involved with the Jewish Anti-Fascist Committee and the Yiddish theater genuinely overstepped their boundaries during and after World War II by openly asserting their Jewish identity and expressing approval for their state's recognition of a Jewish homeland in Palestine. Mikhoels had broken the unstated pact he had made with the Soviet regime by maintaining extensive contacts with the West, by insinuating an identification with Zionism, by acting as a liaison between the Jewish citizens of the Soviet Union and the state, by glorifying Jewish participation in World War II, and by asserting Jewish distinctness within the Soviet Union. While these expressions would not have been a crime under any just system of law—and would not have merited death under the post-Stalin Soviet regime—they were deemed the most heinous of crimes under Stalin's ruthless tyranny. Yet to those who knew Mikhoels, his loyalty to both his people and his state were not contradictory. "Yes, he was Jewish," wrote O. Litovskii of Mikhoels:

> He performed in the Jewish language, but he performed emotionally. He was comprehensible and accessible not only to the Jewish public, but also to the Russians and not only because he spoke the language of art, but also because this Jewish actor did not know any homeland other than Russia. . . . Mikhoels was a Russian Jew, and he belongs simultaneously to Jewish and to Russian theater. . . . There he sits before me, together with his wife and friend Anastasiia Pavlovna Pototskii, chuckling, criticizing the Committee of Artistic Affairs, and telling stories about some type of utterly unusual drink to which a Georgian treated him. This is how he remains in my memory. . . . Solomon Mikhailovich Mikhoels, a great figure in Jewish, Russian and world culture.[104]

Conclusion: The Moscow State Yiddish Theater

The Soviet State Yiddish Theater was characterized throughout its existence by an inherent tension between its socialist principles and its nationalist yearnings. The Jewish activists who established a Yiddish art theater in pre-revolutionary Russia hoped to "enlighten" the Jewish masses by imparting their own secular notions of *Bildung* and social justice through legal channels. Soon after the Bolshevik Revolution, these theater activists found a willing partner in the Communist Party and its Jewish Section. With official state patronage, Communist dogmas could be fused with national symbols and artistic talent to create a potent instrument of agitational propaganda and public awareness. The theater and its supporters hoped to transform traditional and provincial Jews into collective farmers, proletarians, and Soviet citizens.

The honeymoon was short-lived. The newly accessible archives of the theater reveal that after only a few years of partnership, discord emerged between the theater, its trade union, the state, and the Party. Already by 1925, Aleksandr Granovsky, the theater's director, found himself inundated with bureaucratic impediments and petty squabbles. Self-satisfied Party activists and cocky young stars showed themselves to be more interested in self-promotion than in "civilizing" the pious Jews of the provinces—a sentiment shared by the theater's director himself. As disagreements emerged over finances and administrative matters, disgruntled cliques sought Party mediation and intervention. Having established a measure of administrative leverage, the Party proceeded to extend its influence to the theater's thematic and aesthetic content by demanding realist plays that promoted socialist construction and revolutionary consciousness. The theater responded by presenting plays that on the surface conformed to the Party's demands, but which could also be interpreted as surreptitious tributes to Jewish nationalism and protests against what was becoming an oppressive regime. The theater's censors failed to detect any ulterior messages but continued to pressure the troupe into conformity. During the theater's 1928 European tour, Granovsky, frustrated that his artistic judgment was being overruled by Party bureaucrats, defected to Germany.

When the troupe returned to Moscow in late 1928, Solomon Mikhoels, its star actor, was named to succeed Granovsky as director. At the same time, the theater's administration was reorganized to enhance Party influence, making forthright disagreements with the state more difficult. Fresh interpretations of the theater's forgotten and suppressed plays, however, reveal that the tension between the theater's national heritage and socialist ideology was merely pushed beneath the surface. Hindered by a lack of appropriate dramatic material, Mikhoels and the theater's literary directors reworked pre-revolutionary plays into timely political satires and encouraged contemporary writers to produce suitable material. Within

Mikhoels's first four years as director, the theater acquainted Moscow audiences with the works of some of the finest contemporary Yiddish writers: David Bergelson, Peretz Markish, M. Daniel, Yekhezkel Dobrushin, and Hershl Orland. With a series of plays glorifying the Revolution, the Civil War, and socialist construction, the theater garnered significant Party patronage. Mikhoels, however, refused to turn the Yiddish theater into a clone of Moscow's other theaters. He insisted on interpreting contemporary events through the prism of Jewish history, assimilating Judaic lore into his productions and alluding to nationalist Jewish archetypes. All these symbols were hidden from the censors, who were unfamiliar with both the Yiddish language and the Judaic heritage.

In the mid-1930s, faced with criticism that the theater was failing to produce successful socialist productions, Mikhoels retreated to Yiddish translations of European classics. Although his rendition of Shakespeare's *King Lear* met with popular and critical acclaim, Mikhoels feared that the theater was forsaking its national orientation. With the proclamation of the slogan, "national in form, socialist in content," Mikhoels was given license to return to Jewish folk traditions. Notes from the director's personal archives, however, show that the Yiddish theater faced a unique quandary in applying the slogan. In contrast to the history of the USSR's other national minorities, the halcyon days of Judaic lore lay in the ancient state of Judaea, well beyond the Soviet realm. Alone among the Soviet national minorities, the Jews possessed a heritage that could not be shared with other Soviet citizens—their homeland lay beyond the Soviet border. Revivals of Jewish national lore, therefore, could be construed as assertions of lost Jewish sovereign rights in Palestine, especially with the rise of Zionism as a viable political movement. The theater initially restricted itself to the nineteenth-century folk traditions of the Eastern European Jewish masses living within the Russian Empire.

Only in 1937, as Kaganovich and others began calling for the resurrection of historical heroes, did the theater begin to celebrate the lore of Judaea on its stage. Suddenly Jewish revolts against foreign rule became appropriate material. Although the theater publicly proclaimed that these productions should be seen as examples of the class struggle in historical perspective, its audiences could be inspired by scenes of Jews taking up arms to defend their sovereignty from oppressive regimes. Whether or not these scenes pertained to the modern predicament of Soviet Jewry was left up to the interpretation of the audience.

The Yiddish theater's efforts to integrate national awareness into its art was not unique. Similar efforts were put forward by other Jewish figures unconnected with the theater, including the novelist Der Nister (in his epic work *The Family Mashber*) and the ethnomusicologist Moshe Beregovskii. A glance at the cultural output of some of the Soviet Union's other minority nations reveals similar ambitions. The Armenian theater's 1940 presentation of Deremik Demirchyan's play *Native Land* (about the tenth-century Armenian ruler Gagik's heroic defense of Catholic Armenia against Byzantine invaders) can be seen as a metaphor for modern Armenia's resistance to Russian hegemony—the characterization of Russia as the "Third Rome," the heir to Byzantium, was a commonplace in Russian historical thought.[1] Wartime products of local patriotism also abound. The 1942 Stalin Prize–winning Georgian film *Giorgi Saakadze* (about the seventeenth-century nationalist hero) was one such example. The patriotic pride that Russian historical art inculcated in its audience has been well documented,[2] but the notion that local heroes instilled similar sentiments among the minority nations has only begun to be explored. Indeed, as George Liber has shown in his intriguing study of the effects of *korenizatsiia* (indigenization) in the Ukraine, the policy of nurturing local cultures often led to the genesis of nationalist movements.[3] This phenomenon has even prompted at least one scholar to declare that "it was Stalin who became the true 'father of nations.'"[4]

During World War II, as Soviet patriotism gave way to Russian chauvinism, the theater's two roles as Soviet agitator and Jewish advocate collided. In the late 1930s, the theater's efforts to find a new raison d'être with its promotion of anti-fascism was thwarted by the Soviet-Nazi non-aggression pact of August 1939. The anti-fascist theme was revived again soon after the German invasion of the USSR in June 1941. While Mikhoels, as chairman of the Soviet Jewish Anti-Fascist Committee, promoted Jewish unity around the world and raised awareness of the European Jewish predicament, his theater downplayed Jewish victimhood and championed Soviet nationality policies on its stage. Initially, the two facets coalesced only in their mutual support of the Soviet war effort as the sole means of liberating world Jewry from fascist hands. However, recent testimonies indicate that during Mikhoels's 1943 tour of North America and Britain, he began to explore alternative solutions to the "Jewish problem," including the establishment of a Jewish state in Palestine.

After the Allied victory, Mikhoels and the theater firmly rooted themselves on the side of Jewish nationality issues. The archives of the Jewish Anti-Fascist Committee reveal that Mikhoels sought to use his newfound political influence to engage the Soviet government in Jewish national issues, such as the resettlement of Jewish war victims, distribution of American aid, and geopolitical support for the Zionist cause. Similarly, the theater celebrated peace with a production glorifying Jewish perseverance, survival, and unity. Soviet patriotism among the Russian majority, however, had degenerated during the war into a Russian chauvinism that firmly excluded the Jews. Soviet Jewish activists, recently liberated from the threat of Nazism, found themselves victims of discrimination and anti-Semitism on the part of a society trying to stabilize and redefine itself. Not realizing the extent to which the tide had changed, Mikhoels, the theater, and the Anti-Fascist Committee flaunted their national pride, striking emotional chords among the Jewish minority. A distinct society of Jews, however, proved to be incompatible with Soviet collective mores as they developed during the regime's final stab at totalitarianism and mass conformity. With their extensive international contacts and vested interest in Near Eastern geopolitical affairs, the Soviet Jewish leadership was one of several groups who straddled the new binary division of the world between East and West. When the final curtain was lowered on the Yiddish stage, it fell with the force of iron.

Notes

Abbreviations Used in Notes

CAHJP   Central Archives for the History of the Jewish People, Jerusalem, Israel

CRDEEJ   Center for Research and Documentation of East European Jewry, Jerusalem, Israel

DRI   Diaspora Research Institute, Tel-Aviv, Israel

GARF   Gosudarstvennyi arkhiv rossiskoi federatsii
State Archive of the Russian Federation, Moscow, Russia

GPB   Gosudarstvennaia publichnaia istoricheskaia biblioteka, rukopisnyi otdel
State Public Historical Library, Manuscript Division, St. Petersburg, Russia

GTsTM   Gosudarstvennyi teatralnyi muzei im. A. A. Bakhrushina, rukopisnyi otdel
Bakhrushin State Theater Museum, Manuscript Division, Moscow, Russia

IGTAM   Israel Goor Theater Archives and Museum, Jerusalem, Israel

NARA   National Archives and Records Administration, College Park, Maryland

NSA   National Sound Archives, Jerusalem, Israel

RGALI   Rossiiskii gosudarstvennyi arkhiv literatury i iskusstva
Russian State Archive of Literature and Art, Moscow, Russia

RTsKhIDNI   Rossiiskii tsentr khraneniia i izucheniia dokumentov noveisheiistorii
Russian Center for the Preservation and Study of Modern History, Moscow, Russia

TsGAOR Ukr   Tsentralnyi gosudarstvennyi arkhiv Oktiabrskoi revoliutsii, Ukraina
Central State Archive of the October Revolution, Kiev, Ukraine

Introduction

1. Shmuel Halkin, *Bar-Kokhba* (Moscow: Der Emes, 1939), 50.
2. Ibid., 52.
3. Ibid., 58.
4. V. I. Lenin, *Sochineniia*, 38 vols. (Moscow: Foreign Language Publishing House, 1953–1955), 19: 490.

5. *Kommunisticheskaia partiia sovetskogo soiuza v rezoliutsiiakh i resheniiakh sezdov, konferentsii i plenumov TsK* (Moscow: Izdatelstvo politicheskoi literatury, 1970), 2: 252.

6. For recent discussions of Soviet nationality policies and their role in nation building see Yuri Slezkine, "The USSR as a Communal Apartment, or How a Socialist State Promoted Ethnic Particularism," *Slavic Review* 53, no. 2 (Summer 1994): 414–52; Terry Martin, "The Origins of Soviet Ethnic Cleansing," *Journal of Modern History* 70 (December 1998): 813–61; and Francine Hirsch, "Toward an Empire of Nations: Border-Making and the Formation of Soviet National Identities," *Russian Review* 59, no. 2 (April 2000): 201–26.

7. J. V. Stalin, *Works*, 13 vols. (Moscow: Foreign Language Publishing House, 1953–1955), 5: 48–49.

8. For some of the better works of this type on Soviet Jewry see Benjamin Pinkus, *The Jews in the Soviet Union: The History of a National Minority* (Cambridge: Cambridge University Press, 1988); Solomon M. Schwarz, *The Jews in the Soviet Union* (Syracuse, N.Y.: Syracuse University Press, 1951); Salo Wittmayer Baron, *The Russian Jew under Tsars and Soviets* (New York: Macmillan, 1964); Jacob Frumkin, Gregor Aronson, Alexis Goldenweiser, and Joseph Lewitan, *Russian Jewry (1917–1967)* (New York: Thomas Yaseloff, 1969); Lionel Kochan, ed., *The Jews in Soviet Russia since 1917* (London: Oxford University Press, 1970); Yaacov Ro'i, *The Struggle for Soviet Jewish Emigration, 1948–1967* (Cambridge and New York: Cambridge University Press, 1991); Zvi Gitelman, *A Century of Ambivalence: The Jews of Russia and the Soviet Union, 1881 to the Present* (New York: YIVO Institute, 1988); and Nora Levin, *The Jews in the Soviet Union since 1917: Paradox of Survival*, 2 vols. (New York: I. B. Tauris, 1990).

9. An average of over 450 Yiddish-language books were published a year between 1928 and 1935 (the years for which statistics are available). Most were probably published by Der Emes printing press. See Schwarz, *The Jews in the Soviet Union*, 139. Some of the most widely known Yiddish writers working during this period include David Bergelson, Peretz Markish, Der Nister, Shmuel Halkin, Leyb Kvitko, David Hofshteyn, and Moshe Broderzon.

10. Some of the more prominent Yiddish singers included Zinovii Shulman, Marina Gordon, Sidi Tal, Clara Vaga, and the a capella group Iudvokans. Some of their recordings can be found at the National Sound Archives of Israel in Jerusalem.

11. For some of their published works see Moshe Beregovskii and Itzik Fefer, *Yidishe folks-lider* (Kiev: Melukha farlag far di natsionale minderhaytn in USSR, 1938); Yekhezkel Dobrushin and A. Yuditskii, *Yidishe folks-lider* (Moscow: Der Emes, 1940); Moisei Khashchevatskii and Der Nister, *Yidishe folkslider* (Odessa: Kinderfarlag, 1940).

12. The largest Jewish research institutes were the Institute of Jewish Culture in Kiev, which was active from 1929 to 1948, and the Jewish Section of the Belorussian Academy of Science, which functioned from 1924 to 1935.

13. According to statistics compiled by Benjamin Pinkus, there were 800 Yiddish-language schools in the Soviet Union in 1927 with 107,000 pupils. In 1939, there were 75,000 pupils in Yiddish schools. See Pinkus, *The Jews in the Soviet Union*, 109.

14. For more on Birobidzhan see Robert Weinberg, *Stalin's Forgotten Zion: Birobidzhan and the Making of a Soviet Jewish Homeland—An Illustrated History, 1928–1996* (Berkeley: University of California Press, 1998).

15. Ella Perlman, "Introduction" in Beth ha-tefutsot, *The Closed Curtain: The Moscow Yiddish State Theater*, catalogue from exhibit at Diaspora Museum, Tel Aviv.

16. For recent works dealing with the execution of Mikhoels and the post–World War II liquidation of Jewish cultural and social institutions see Arkady Vaksberg, *Stalin against*

the Jews, trans. Antonina W. Bouis (New York: Alfred A. Knopf, 1994); G. Kostyrchenko, *V plenu u krasnogo faraona* (Moscow: Mezhdunarodnye otnosheniia, 1994); Shimon Redlich, *War, Holocaust and Stalinism: A Documented Study of the Jewish Anti-Fascist Committee in the USSR* (Luxembourg: Harwood Academic Publishers, 1995); Mordechai Altshuler, "The Agony and Liquidation of the Jewish State Theater of Belorussia (1948–1949)," *Jews in Eastern Europe* 3, no. 25 (Winter 1994): 64–72; V. P. Naumov, *Nepravednyi sud. Poslednii stalinskii rasstrel* (Moscow: Nauk, 1994); Aleksandr Borshchagovskii, *Obviniaetsia krov* (Moscow: Kultura, 1994); and Fedor Liass, *Poslednii politicheskii protsess stalina ili nesostoiavshiisia genotsid* (Jerusalem: F. Liass, 1995).

17. The terms "intentionalist" and "functionalist," borrowed from the discourse of historians of Nazi Germany, are equally useful in describing two approaches to the development of Stalin's Great Terror. In German historiography intentionalists maintain that the Holocaust derived from a concrete plan devised by Hitler himself prior to World War II, whereas functionalists believe that the Holocaust gradually evolved as a consequence of Nazi-inspired anti-Semitism and Germany's changing fortunes during the war. In the Soviet context, intentionalists argue that the Great Terror was planned by Stalin in advance, whereas functionalists posit that the purges were impelled by the changing socioeconomic forces of the 1930s. For a functional approach to the Holocaust, see Martin Broszat, *The Hitler State: The Foundation and Development of the Internal Structure of the Third Reich* (London: Longman, 1981). For an intentionalist approach to the Holocaust see Eberhard Jäckel, *Hitler's Weltanschauung: A Blueprint for Power* (Middleton, Conn.: Wesleyan University Press, 1972).

18. Ch. Shmeruk "Jewish Culture in the Soviet Union in Historical Perspective," in *Jewish Culture in the Soviet Union: Proceedings of the Symposium Held by the Cultural Department of the World Jewish Congress* (Jerusalem: World Jewish Congress, 1973), 20.

19. Naomi Blank, "Redefining the Jewish Question from Lenin to Gorbachev: Terminology of Ideology?" in Yaacov Ro'i, ed., *Jews and Jewish Life in Russia and the Soviet Union* (Essex: Frank Cass & Co., 1995), 51–66; Thomas E. Sawyer, *The Jewish Minority in the Soviet Union* (Boulder, Colo.: Westview, 1979), 10–15.

20. Lester Samuel Eckman, *Soviet Policy towards Jews and Israel* (New York: Shengold Publishers, 1974), 29.

21. Joseph Stalin, *Marxism and the National and Colonial Question: A Collection of Articles and Speeches* (London: Lawrence and Wishart, 1936), 8.

22. Vaksberg, *Stalin against the Jews,* 3–14.

23. Pinkus, *The Jews in the Soviet Union,* 143–44; Louis Rapoport, *Stalin's War against the Jews* (New York: Free Press, 1990), 1–40; Vaksberg, *Stalin against the Jews,* 15–33.

24. Robert Conquest, *The Great Terror: Stalin's Purge of the Thirties* (London: Macmillan, 1968), 76–77. See also Isaac Deutscher, *Stalin: A Political Biography* (1949; 2nd ed., New York: Oxford University Press, 1966), 605–606.

25. Conquest, *The Great Terror;* Adam Ulam, *Stalin: The Man and His Era* (New York, 1973); Richard Pipes, *The Russian Revolution* (New York: Vintage, 1990); Robert Tucker, *Stalin in Power: The Revolution from Above* (New York: Norton, 1990); L. B. Schapiro, *The Communist Party of the Soviet Union* (1960; 2nd ed., New York: Vintage, 1971); Hannah Arendt, *The Origins of Totalitarianism* (1951; reprint, New York: Meridian Books, 1958); Zbigniew Brzezinski, *Ideology and Power in Soviet Politics* (New York: Praeger, 1962); John Armstrong, *The Politics of Totalitarianism: The Communist Party of the Soviet Union from 1934 to the Present* (New York: Random House, 1961).

26. Stephen F. Cohen, *Bukharin and the Bolshevik Revolution* (London: Wildwood House, 1974); Robert Vincent Daniels, *The Conscience of the Revolution: Communist Oppo-*

sition in Soviet Russia (1960; reprint, New York: Clarion Books, 1969); Sheila Fitzpatrick, Alexander Rabinowitch, and Richard Stites, eds., *Russia in the Era of NEP: Explorations in Soviet Society and Culture* (Bloomington: Indiana University Press, 1991); Diane P. Koenker, William G. Rosenberg, and Ronald Grigor Suny, eds., *Party, State, and Society in the Russian Civil War: Explorations in Social History* (Bloomington: Indiana University Press, 1989); Moshe Lewin, *Lenin's Last Struggle* (London: Faber & Faber, 1969).

27. William G. Rosenberg, *Bolshevik Visions: First Phase of the Cultural Revolution in Bolshevik Russia* (Ann Arbor: University of Michigan Press, 1984).

28. Peter Kenez, *The Birth of the Propaganda State: Soviet Methods of Mass Mobilization, 1917–1929* (Cambridge: Cambridge University Press, 1985).

29. Richard Stites, *Revolutionary Dreams: Utopian Vision and Experimental Life in the Russian Revolution* (New York: Oxford University Press, 1989); Lynn Mally, *Culture of the Future: The Proletkult Movement in Revolutionary Russia* (Berkeley: University of California Press, 1990); James von Geldern, *Bolshevik Festivals, 1917–1920* (Berkeley: University of California Press, 1993); Abbott Gleason, Peter Kenez, and Richard Stites, eds., *Bolshevik Culture: Experiment and Order in the Russian Revolution* (Bloomington: Indiana University Press, 1985); Katerina Clark, *Petersburg: Crucible of Cultural Revolution* (Cambridge, Mass.: Harvard University Press, 1995).

30. Konstantin Rudnitsky, *Russian and Soviet Theater 1905–1932* (New York: Thames and Hudson, 1988); A. Anastasev, *Istoriia sovetskogo dramaticheskogo teatra* (Moscow: Institut istorii iskusstv, 1966); J. Douglas Clayton, *Pierrot in Petrograd: The Commedia Dell'Arte/ Balagan in Twentieth-Century Russian Theatre and Drama* (Montreal and Kingston: McGill-Queen's University Press, 1993); Lynn Mally, "The Rise and Fall of the Soviet Youth Theater TRAM," *Slavic Review* 51, no. 3 (Fall 1990): 411–30; A. V. Lunacharskii, *O teatre i dramaturgii* (Moscow: Iskusstvo, 1958); Lars Kleberg, *Theatre as Action: Soviet Russian Avant-Garde Aesthetics*, trans. Charles Rougle (London: Macmillan, 1993).

31. Zvi Y. Gitelman, *Jewish Nationality and Soviet Politics: The Jewish Sections of the CPSU, 1917–1930* (Princeton: Princeton University Press, 1972), 321–71.

32. For a modern approach to the Hebrew-language Habima theater, see Vladislav Ivanov, "Poetika metamorfoz: Vakhtangov i Gabima," *Voprosy teatra* 13 (1993): 188–222; and Vladislav Ivanov, "Teatr Gabima v Moskve: na vesakh Iova," *Znamia* 12 (1995): 168–92. For Yiddish film see J. Hoberman, *Bridge of Light: Yiddish Film between Two Worlds* (New York: Museum of Modern Art, 1991), 87–102; and J. Hoberman, "The Crooked Road of Jewish Luck," *Artforum* 28 (September 1989): 122–25. For inquiries into Soviet Jewish art in the 1920s see Ruth Apter-Gabriel, ed., *Tradition and Revolution: The Jewish Renaissance in Russian Avant-Garde Art, 1912–1928* (Jerusalem: The Israel Museum, 1988); and Susan Tumarkin Goodman, ed., *Russian Jewish Artists in a Century of Change, 1890–1990* (Munich: Prestel, 1995). For surveys of the Soviet Yiddish theater see Béatrice Picon-Vallin, *Le théâtre juif Soviétique pendant les années vingt* (Lausanne: Editions la cité, 1973); Mordechai Altshuler, ed., *Ha-teatron ha-Yehudi bi-Verit ha-Moatsot* (Jerusalem: Hebrew University Press, 1996). For a post-structuralist analysis of Soviet Yiddish literature see Régine Robin, *L'amour du Yiddish: écriture juive et sentiment de la langue (1830–1930)* (Paris: Editions du Sorbier, 1984), 175–245.

33. Ch. Shmeruk, "Yiddish Literature in the U. S. S. R.," trans. Miriam and Alfred A. Greenbaum, in Kochan, *The Jews in Soviet Russia,* 244.

34. The term Cultural Revolution was first applied to the era of 1928–1931 in Sheila Fitzpatrick, *Cultural Revolution in Russia, 1928–1931* (Bloomington: Indiana University Press, 1978), and was expanded in her collection *The Cultural Front: Power and Culture in Revolutionary Russia* (Ithaca: Cornell University Press, 1992). Recently some scholars have

sought to expand the term to include the entire 1920s, arguing that the third front of culture was an integral aspect of Soviet educational policies after 1920. Stalin's Great Break is thus seen as the culmination of a decade-long process of education and upbringing. See, for instance Michael David-Fox, *Revolution of the Mind: Higher Learning among the Bolsheviks, 1918–1929* (Ithaca: Cornell University Press, 1997).

35. Leon Trotsky, *The Revolution Betrayed: What Is the Soviet Union and Where Is It Going?* trans. Max Eastman (New York: Harcourt & Brace, 1937); Isaac Deutscher, *The Prophet Outcast: Trotsky, 1929–1940* (Oxford: Oxford University Press, 1963); Deutscher, *Stalin;* Roy Medvedev, *Let History Judge: The Origins and Consequences of Stalinism,* ed. D. Joravsky and G. Haupt, trans. C. Taylor (New York: Alfred A. Knopf, 1971); Nikolai Timasheff, *The Great Retreat: The Growth and Decline of Communism in Russia* (New York: Dutton, 1946).

36. Sheila Fitzpatrick, *Stalin's Peasants: Resistance and Survival in the Russian Village after Collectivization* (New York: Oxford University Press, 1994); Moshe Lewin, *Russian Peasants and Soviet Power* (London: Allen & Unwin, 1968); William G. Rosenberg and Lewis H. Siegelbaum, eds., *Social Dimensions of Soviet Industrialization* (Bloomington: Indiana University Press, 1993); Stephen Kotkin, *Magnetic Mountain: Stalinism as a Civilization* (Berkeley: University of California Press, 1995); Lewis Siegelbaum and Ronald G. Suny, eds., *Making Workers Soviet* (Ithaca: Cornell University Press, 1994).

37. Régine Robin, *Socialist Realism: An Impossible Aesthetic,* trans. Catherine Porter (1986; reprint, Stanford: Stanford University Press, 1992); George Lukács, *The Meaning of Contemporary Realism,* trans. John and Necke Mander (1963; reprint, London: Merlin Press, 1979); Katerina Clark, *The Soviet Novel: History as Ritual* (Chicago: University of Chicago Press, 1981); Boris Groys, *The Total Art of Stalinism: Avant-Garde, Aesthetic Dictatorship, and Beyond,* trans. Charles Rougle (Princeton: Princeton University Press, 1992); Hans Günther, ed., *The Culture of the Stalin Period* (London: Macmillan, 1990); C. Vaughan James, *Soviet Socialist Realism: Origins and Theory* (New York: St. Martin's Press, 1973); and John E. Bowlt and Olga Matich, eds., *Laboratory of Dreams: The Russian Avant-Garde and Cultural Experiment* (Stanford: Stanford University Press, 1996).

38. Richard Stites, *Russian Popular Culture: Entertainment and Society since 1900* (Cambridge: Cambridge University Press, 1992), 64–97; James von Geldern and Richard Stites, eds., *Mass Culture in Soviet Russia: Tales, Poems, Songs, Movies, Plays and Folklore, 1917–1953* (Bloomington: Indiana University Press, 1995), 123–330.

39. The New Economic Policy (NEP), which lasted from 1921 to 1928, allowed for private enterprise in small industry while the state retained control of finance and large industry. It was accompanied by a relaxation of cultural policies.

40. Robin, *L'amour du Yiddish,* 191.

41. Michael Stanislawski, "The Jews and Russian Culture and Politics," in Goodman, *Russian Jewish Artists,* 23.

42. David G. Roskies, *A Bridge of Longing: The Lost Art of Yiddish Storytelling* (Cambridge, Mass.: Harvard University Press, 1995), 229.

43. Eckman, *Soviet Policy,* 38–39.

44. Rapoport, *Stalin's War,* 54.

45. Eckman, *Soviet Policy,* 38–39.

46. Levin, *The Jews in the Soviet Union,* 324; Frumkin, Aronson, Goldenweiser, and Lewitan, *Russian Jewry (1860–1917),* 181.

47. Smeruk "Jewish Culture in the Soviet Union," 20.

48. Eckman, *Soviet Policy,* 44.

49. J. Arch Getty and Roberta Manning, eds., *Stalinist Terror* (New York: Cambridge

University Press, 1993); J. Arch Getty, *Origins of the Great Purges: The Soviet Communist Party Reconsidered, 1933–1938* (Cambridge: Cambridge University Press, 1985); Conquest, *The Great Terror;* Gabor Tamas Rittersporn, *Stalinist Simplifications and Soviet Complications: Social Tension and Political Conflicts in the USSR, 1933–1953* (Chur, Switzerland: Harwood Academic Publishers, 1991); Martin, "The Origins of Soviet Ethnic Cleansing."

50. Tucker, *Stalin in Power,* 490–91.

51. Igor Krupnik, "Soviet Cultural and Ethnic Policies toward Jews: A Legacy Reassessed," in Ro'i, *Jews and Jewish Life,* 68–69. See also Martin, "The Origins of Soviet Ethnic Cleansing," 853.

52. Beregovskii and Fefer, *Yidishe folks-lider;* Dobrushin and Yuditsky, *Yidishe folks-lider;* Khashchevatskii and Der Nister, *Yidishe folkslider.*

53. Shmeruk, "Yiddish Literature," 256.

54. Pinkus, *The Jews in the Soviet Union,* 106. For similar interpretations, see Baron, *The Russian Jew under Tsars and Soviets;* Schwartz, *The Jews in the Soviet Union;* Levin, *The Jews in the Soviet Union;* Ro'i, *Jews and Jewish Life.*

55. Jack Miller, ed., *Jews in Soviet Culture* (New Brunswick, N.J.: Transaction Books, 1984), 73.

56. Miller, *Jews in Soviet Culture;* Joachim Braun, *Jews in Soviet Music* (Jerusalem: Hebrew University Press, 1977); Efraim Sicher, *Jews in Russian Literature after the October Revolution: Writers and Artists between Hope and Apostasy* (Cambridge: Cambridge University Press, 1995).

57. For some examples of Judaic motifs in the writings of Ehrenburg see Anatol Goldberg, "Ilya Ehrenburg" in Miller, *Jews in Soviet Culture,* 183–213; Joshua Rubenstein, *Tangled Loyalties: The Life and Times of Ilya Ehrenburg* (New York: Basic Books, 1996); William Korey, "Ehrenburg: His Inner Jewish Conflict," *Jewish Frontier* (March 1968): 25–31. For some examples on Babel see Efraim Sicher, "The Jewishness of Babel," in Miller, *Jews in Soviet Culture,* 167–82; Walenty Cukierman, "Isaak Babel's Jewish Heroes and their Yiddish Background," *Yiddish* 2, no. 4 (1977): 15–27; Alice Stone Nakhimovsky, *Russian-Jewish Literature and Identity; Jabotinsky, Babel, Frossman, Galich, Roziner, Markish* (Baltimore and London: Johns Hopkins University Press, 1992), 70–106. For the Jewish roots of the mass song see Joachim Braun, "Jews in Soviet Music," in Miller, *Jews in Soviet Culture,* 65–106: 78–81.

58. Gregor Aronson, "The Jewish Question during the Stalin Era," in Frumkin, Aronson, Goldenweiser, and Lewitan, *Russian Jewry,* 193.

59. Ruth R. Wisse, "By Their Own Hands," *New Republic,* February 3, 1997, 38.

60. Ibid., 35.

61. Ibid., 43.

62. Shmuel Niger, *Yidishe shrayber in sovet-rusland* (New York: S. Niger Book Committee, 1958); Shmuel Niger, *Di tsveyshprakhikayt fun undzer literatur* (Detroit: Louis La Med Foundation for the Advancement of Hebrew and Yiddish Literature, 1941).

63. Nakhman Mayzel, *Dos yiddishe shafn un der yidisher shrayber in sovetnfarband* (New York: Yidisher Kultur Farband, 1959).

64. Irving Howe, and Eliezer Greenberg, eds., *Ashes Out of Hope: Fiction by Soviet-Yiddish Writers* (New York: Schocken Books, 1977), 25.

65. David Bergelson, *The Stories of David Bergelson: Yiddish Short Fiction from Russia,* ed. and trans. Golda Werman, foreword by Aharon Appelfeld (Syracuse: Syracuse University Press, 1996), xxiii.

66. Abraham Zebi Idelsohn, *Jewish Music in Its Historical Development* (1929; reprint, New York: Tudor Publishing Company, 1944), 358.

67. Cited in Nakhman Mayzel, *Yidishe tematik un yidishe melodies bay bavuste muziker* (New York: Yidishe Kultur Farband, 1952), 13.

68. Michael Brenner, *The Renaissance of Jewish Culture in Weimar Germany* (New Haven: Yale University Press, 1996), 16–17.

69. Baal-Makhshoves, "One Literature in Two Languages," in Hana Wirth-Nesher, ed., *What Is Jewish Literature?* (Philadelphia: The Jewish Publication Society, 1994), 74.

70. Robert N. Goldman, *Einstein's God: Albert Einstein's Quest as a Scientist and as a Jew to Replace a Forsaken God* (Northvale, N. J.: Jason Aronson, 1997); Alexander L. Ringer, *Arnold Schoenberg: The Composer as Jew* (New York: Oxford University Press, 1990).

71. Josephine Zadovsky Knopp, *The Trial of Judaism in Contemporary Jewish Writing* (Urbana, Chicago, and London: University of Illinois Press, 1975), 6–29.

72. Yosef Hayim Yerushalmi, *Zakhor: Jewish History and Jewish Memory*, foreword by Harold Bloom (1982; reprint, Seattle and London: University of Washington Press, 1996); Robert Alter, *After the Tradition: Essays on Modern Jewish Writing* (New York: Dutton, 1969); Irving Howe, *World of Our Fathers* (New York: Harcourt, Brace, Jovanonich, 1976).

73. Roskies, *A Bridge of Longing.*

74. Irving Malin, and Irwin Stark, eds., *Breakthrough: A Treasury of Contemporary American Jewish Literature* (New York: McGraw Hill, 1964).

75. Wirth-Nesher, *What Is Jewish Literature?*

76. For reviews, background information, and exhibition catalogues of Marc Chagall's artistic work with the Moscow State Yiddish Theater see Jüdisches Museum der Stadt Wien, *Chagall: Bilder-Träume Theater 1908–1920* (Vienna: Brandstätter, 1994); *Marc Chagall and the Jewish Theater* (New York: Solomon R. Guggenheim Foundation, 1992); and Matthew Frost, "Marc Chagall and the Jewish State Chamber Theatre," *Russian History* 8, no. 1–2 (1981): 90–99. For analyses of other selected productions of the theater see Mel Gordon, "Granovsky's Tragic Comedy: *Night in the Old Market*," *Drama Review* 29 (Winter 1985): 91–122; Picon-Vallin, *Le théâtre juif;* and Altshuler, *Ha-teatron.*

77. Yekhezkel Dobrushin, *Mikhoels der akter* (Moscow: Der Emes, 1940); Aliah Folkovitsch, *Mikhoels, 1890–1948* (Moscow: Der Emes, 1948); Matvei Geizer, *Solomon Mikhoels* (Moscow: Prometer, 1990); Iakov Grinvald, *Mikhoels: kratkii kritiko-biograficheskii ocherk* (Moscow: Der Emes, 1948); Osip Liubomirskii, *Mikhoels* (Moscow: Iskusstvo, 1938); Peretz Markish, *Mikhoels* (Moscow: Der Emes, 1939); Natalia Vovsi-Mikhoels, *Mon père Salomon Mikhoels: souvenirs sur sa vie et sur sa mort*, trans. Erwin Spatz (Montricher, Switzerland: Les Editions Noir sur Blanc, 1990); M. Zagorskii, *Mikhoels* (Moscow: Kinopechat, 1927).

78. Yerushalmi, *Zakhor,* 36.

79. James, *Soviet Socialist Realism.*

80. For more on resistance see *Kritika: Explorations in Russian and Eurasian History,* New Series 1, no. 1 (Winter 2000).

1. "Let's Perform a Miracle"

1. For more on the history of the Jewish Sections see Zvi Y. Gitelman, *Jewish Nationality and Soviet Politics: The Jewish Sections of the CPSU, 1917–1930* (Princeton: Princeton University Press, 1972).

2. Nora Levin, *The Jews in the Soviet Union since 1917: Paradox of Survival* (New York: I. B. Taurus, 1990), 47.

3. For more on the reform of the Yiddish language see Gennady Estraikh, *Soviet Yiddish: Language Planning and Linguistic Development* (Oxford: Clarendon Press, 1999).

For a discussion of the rationale behind Soviet national linguistic reform in general see Yuri Slezkine, "The USSR as a Communal Apartment, or How a Socialist State Promoted Ethnic Particularism," *Slavic Review* 53, no. 2 (Summer 1994): 430–32.

4. For a discussion of German symbolism and theater see Peter Jelavich, *Munich and Theatrical Modernism: Politics, Playwriting and Performance, 1890–1914* (Cambridge, Mass.: Harvard University Press, 1985), 2–3.

5. Viacheslav Ivanov, *Rodnoe i vselenskoe* (Moscow: Respublika, 1994), 26–51.

6. A. V. Lunacharskii, *O teatre i dramaturgii* (Moscow: Iskusstvo, 1958), 129.

7. Moshe Litvakov, *Funf yor melukhisher yidisher kunst teater, 1921–1925* (Moscow: Shul un bukh, 1924), 21. See also his "Der tsushtand un di oyfgabz fun der sovetish yidisher literatur," *Literarishe bleter,* January 13, 1928, 37–39; and Moshe Katz, "Di vegn fun dem yidishn teater," *Baginen* (1919): 69.

8. Lunacharskii, *O teatre i dramaturgii,* 127–50.

9. Leon Trotsky, *Literature and Revolution* (Ann Arbor: University of Michigan Press, 1960), 237.

10. Abram Efros, "Evreiskii teatr," *Teatr i muzyka* 9 (November 28, 1922): 110–11.

11. Solomon Mikhoels, "Mikhoels-Vovsi vegn dem teatr," *Literarishe bleter* 17 (April 27, 1928): 318–20.

12. Marc Chagall, *My Life* (New York: Orion Press, 1960), 159.

13. See especially, D. Burliuk, Aleksandr Kruchenykh, Vladimir Mayakovsky, and Viktor Khlebnikov, "Poshchechina obshchestvennomu vkusu," in Vladimir Mayakovsky, *Polnoe sobranie sochinenii* (Moscow: Gosvdarstvennoe izdatelstvo khudozhestvennoi literatury, 1955), 244. The most comprehensive monograph on the Futurists is Vladimir Markov, *Russian Futurism: A History* (Berkeley: University of California Press, 1968). For a more specific analysis of Futurist eschatologies, see Michel Aucouturier, "Le Futurisme Russe ou l'art comme utopie," *Revue des études slaves* 56, no. 1 (1984): 51–60. For discussion of the various forms of iconoclasm in the Russian Revolution, see Richard Stites, "Iconoclastic Currents in the Russian Revolution: Destroying and Preserving the Past," in Abbott Gleason, Peter Kenez, and Richard Stites, eds., *Bolshevik Culture: Experiment and Order in the Russian Revolution* (Bloomington: Indiana University Press, 1985), 1–24. For a discussion of pre-revolutionary hooliganism as iconoclasm, see Joan Neuberger, *Hooliganism: Crime Culture and Power in St. Petersburg, 1900–1914* (Berkeley: University of California Press, 1983).

14. GTsTM, f. 584, d. 4 (goals of Jewish Theater Society).

15. For a general discussion of god-building, see Richard Stites, *Revolutionary Dreams: Utopian Vision and Experimental Life in the Russian Revolution* (New York: Oxford University Press, 1989), 37–46.

16. See Zylbercwaig, "Iz dos yidishe teater gegrindet in Berditshev, Iosi, gor in Konstantinopol?" *Literarishe bleter* 8 (February 24, 1928): 149–50; L. Dushman, "Iz dos yidishe teater gegrindet in Varshe?" *Literarishe bleter* 13 (March 30, 1928): 269.

17. For more on the early history of Yiddish theater see Nahma Sandrow, *Vagabond Stars: A World History of Yiddish Theater* (New York: Harper and Row, 1977), 1–131; Lulla Adler Rosenfeld, *The Yiddish Theatre and Jacob P. Adler* (1977; reprint, New York: Shapolsky Publishers, 1988); B. Goren, *Di geshikhte fun yidishn teater* (New York: Max N. Mayzel, 1923); and Hershel Zohn, *The Story of Yiddish Theater* (Las Cruces: Yucca Tree Press, 1979).

18. See for example *Voskhod* 20, nos. 17, 36, 61, 93 (1900); 22, nos. 45–48 (1902); and *Budushchnost* 12, no. 28 (1900); 13, no. 12 (1901); and 14, no. 32 (1902).

19. *Voskhod* 20, no. 93 (1900): 14.

20. *Voskhod* 20, no. 17 (1900): 18.

21. *Budushchnost* 13, no. 12 (1901).

22. Iulii Engel, "Evreiskaia truppa v Berline," *Voskhod* 20, no. 61 (1900): 30–32. See also R. Brainin, "Evreiskii teatr v Berline," *Budushchnost* 12, no. 28 (1900).

23. M. Sukennikov, "Lembergskaia dramaturgiia," *Voskhod* 22, no. 45 (1902): 36; See also *Voskhod* 22, nos.47-48 (1902).

24. *Teatr i iskusstvo* 1905 no. 1; *Teatralnaia Rossiia* 1905 no. 1.

25. Cited in Nakhum Oyslender, *Idishe teater, 1887–1917* (Moscow: Der Emes, 1940), 59.

26. Ibid., 58.

27. For some recent work on Habima in Russia see Vladislav Ivanov, "Poetika metamorfoz: Vakhtangov i Gabima," *Voprosy teatra* 13 (1993): 188–222; Vladislav Ivanov, "Teatr Gabima v Moskve: na vesakh Iova," *Znamia* 12 (1995): 168–92; and Zippora Shehori-Rubin, "Habimah in Russia: Theater with a National-Zionist Mission, 1918–1926," *Shvut: Studies in Russian and East European Jewish History and Culture* 6, no. 22 (1997): 79–103.

28. Raikin Ben-Ari, *Habima* (New York: Thomas Yoseloff, 1957), 15–16.

29. RGALI, f. 2307, op. 2, d. 530 (protocols of the dramatic section of the Jewish Theater Society, 1916–1918), l. 1.

30. For more on Jewish organic work in early twentieth-century Russia, see Christoph Gassenschmidt, *Jewish Liberal Politics in Tsarist Russia, 1900–1914: The Modernization of Russian Jewry* (New York: New York University Press, 1995).

31. RGALI, f. 2307, op. 2, d. 529 (founding principles of Jewish Theater Society, 1916), ll. 1–5.

32. RGALI, f. 2307, op. 2, d. 530, l. 1.

33. Ibid., ll. 17–21.

34. Ibid., l. 27.

35. Ibid., l. 46.

36. Ibid., l. 47.

37. Natalia Vovsi-Mikhoels, *Mon père Salomon Mikhoels: souvenirs sur sa vie et sur sa mort*, trans. Erwin Spatz (Montricher, Switzerland: Les Editions Noir sur Blanc, 1990), 39.

38. GTsTM, f. 584, d. 7 (list of Granovsky's work, 1920–1930).

39. RGALI, f. 2307, op. 2, d. 530, l. 48.

40. Ibid., l. 49.

41. GARF, f. 2306, op. 24, d. 510 (correspondence between Collegium of National Minorities and Theatrical Section of Commissariat of Enlightenment, October 1918–May 1919), ll. 3–4.

42. Ibid., ll. 5, 10.

43. Ibid., ll. 3–11.

44. Ibid., l. 35.

45. For an explanation of this process in general, see Sheila Fitzpatrick, *The Commissariat of Enlightenment* (Cambridge: Cambridge University Press, 1970), 139–61.

46. Béatrice Picon-Vallin, *Le théâtre juif soviétique pendant les années vingt* (Lausanne: Editions la cité, 1973), 53.

47. The Jewish Section was, in fact, directly subordinate to the Communist Party, not the Commissariat of Jewish Affairs. The Commissariat was an organ of the state while the Section was an organ of the party.

48. Sandrow, *Vagabond Stars*, 226.

49. Nakhman Mayzel, *Dos Yiddishe shafn un der yidisher shrayber in Sovetnfarband* (New York: Yidisher Kultur Farband, 1959), 38.

50. For Proletkult, see Lynn Mally, *Culture of the Future: The Proletkult Movement in Revolutionary Russia* (Berkeley: University of California Press, 1990). For TRAM, see Lynn Mally, "The Rise and Fall of the Soviet Youth Theater TRAM," *Slavic Review* 51, no. 3 (Fall 1992): 411–30.

51. Irina Avanesian, "Master," *Teatralnaia zhizn* 10 (May 1990): 17.

52. Mally, "The Soviet Youth Theater Tram," 415.

53. Osip Liubomirskii, *Mikhoels* (Moscow: Iskusstvo, 1938), 8.

54. Efim Mikhailovich Vovsi, "Vospominaniia," IGTAM, uncatalogued manuscript, 3.

55. Ibid., 19–20.

56. GTsTM, f. 584, d. 128 (autobiography of Solomon Mikhoels).

57. Efim Vovsi, 5.

58. GTsTM, f. 584, dd. 129–132 (contract of E. B. Abramovich).

59. GTsTM, f. 584, d. 129.

60. RGALI, f. 2307, op. 2, d. 436 (posters, 1919–1923).

61. Ibid.; Avanesian, "Master," 17.

62. GTsTM, f. 584, d. 51 (*Stroitel,* a play by Solomon Mikhoels).

63. Rosenfeld, *The Yiddish Theatre,* 101. See also, Dalia Kaufmann, "Uriel Acosta le-karl gutzkov al ha-bimah ha-yehudit (1881–1922)," in Mordechai Altshuler, ed., *Ha-teatron ha-Yehudi bi-Verit ha-Moatsot* (Jerusalem: Hebrew University Press, 1996), 205–24.

64. CAHJP, P166, t. 2 (unpublished anonymous review of Uriel Acosta).

65. GTsTM, f. 584, d. 77 (program for concert performance, Moscow 1920).

66. RGALI, f. 2307, op. 2, d. 11 (letter from Vitebsk Bund on visit of Jewish theater, August 26, 1919).

67. Abram Efros, "Khudozhniki teatra Granovskogo," in Felix Dektor and Roman Spektor, eds., *Kovcheg: almanakh evreiskoi kultury* (Moscow: Khudozhestvennaia literatura; Jerusalem: Tarbut, 1991), 226.

68. Abram Efros, *Kamernyi teatr i ego khudozhniki,1914–1934* (Moscow: Nauka, 1996), xvi.

69. GTsTM, f. 584, d. 1 (Granovsky's manuscripts).

70. Vovsi-Mikhoels, *Mon père Salomon Mikhoels,* 28.

71. GTsTM, f. 584, d. 1.

72. Ibid., l. 2.

73. RGALI, f. 2307, op. 2, d. 15 (correspondence between Granovsky and Narkompros, 1921–1928), ll. 114–15.

74. A later call for auditions outlining the requirements can be found in "Tsum oyfnom in melukhishin yidishn teater tekhnikum," *Der emes,* September 23, 1923.

75. GTsTM, f. 584, d. 127 (autobiography of Benjamin Zuskin).

76. Efros, "Khudozhniki," 223.

77. Cited in Ruth Apter-Gabriel, ed., *Tradition and Revolution: The Jewish Renaissance in Russian Avant-Garde Art, 1912–1928* (Jerusalem: The Israel Museum, 1988), 148.

78. Abram Efros, *Iskusstvo Marka Shagala* (Moscow: Gelikon, 1918).

79. J. Douglas Clayton, *Pierrot in Petrograd: The Commedia Dell'Arte/Balagan in Twentieth-Century Russian Theatre and Drama* (Montreal and Kingston: McGill-Queen's University Press, 1993), 235.

80. For an analysis of the role of carnival in the Moscow State Yiddish Theater see Picon-Vallin, *Le théâtre juif,* 126–37.

81. Solomon Mikhoels, *Stati, besedi, rechi* (Moscow: Iskusstvo, 1981), 152.

82. Maksim Gorkii, "M Gorkii—Sholom Aleikhemu," in U. A. Guralnik, ed., *Sholom Aleikhem. Pisatel i chelovek* (Moscow: Sovetskii pisatel, 1984), 8.

83. A. V. Lunacharskii, "Genii smekha i pevets bednoty," in ibid., 37.

84. For an English translation see *Marc Chagall and the Jewish Theater* (New York: Solomon R. Guggenheim Foundation, 1992), 164–71.

85. M. Zagorskii, *Mikhoels* (Moscow: Kinopechat, 1927), 14.

86. A. Colin Wright, "'Superfluous People' in the Soviet Drama of the 1920s," *Canadian Slavonic Papers* 30, no. 1 (March 1988): 2.

87. Zagorskii, *Mikhoels*, 11.

88. Rudnitsky, *Russian and Soviet Theater 1905–1932*, 44–45.

89. Jüdisches Museum der Stadt Wien, *Chagall: Bilder-Träume Theater 1908–1920: Jüdisches Museum der Stadt Wien* (Vienna: Brandstätter, 1994); *Marc Chagall and the Jewish Theater.*

90. See, for example, E. Iantarev, "Vecher Sholom Aleikhema," *Teatr i muzyka* 11 (December 12, 1922): 236.

91. Efros, "Khudozhniki," 227.

92. See David S. Lifson, *The Yiddish Theatre in America* (New York: Thomas Yoseloff, 1965), 92.

93. "Drama vertepa," *Svoboda i ravenstvo* 22 (April 12, 1907): 22–24.

94. Efros, "Khudozhniki," 232–33.

95. RTsKhIDNI, f. 445, op. 1, d. 52 (correspondence between Jewish Section and Narkompros regarding Habima, July 1920–March 1921), l. 15.

96. Ibid., l. 16.

97. RTsKhIDNI, f. 445, op. 1, d. 60 (correspondence between Jewish Section and Moscow State Yiddish Theater, September 1920–December 1925), l. 1.

98. Ibid., l. 8.

99. Ibid., l. 15.

100. Ibid., l. 19.

101. Ibid., l. 18.

102. Ibid., l. 17.

103. GARF, f. 2306, op. 1, d. 1232 (petition to Sovnarkom to include Jewish theater among state academic theaters), l. 1.

104. Zagorskii, *Mikhoels*, 21.

105. James von Geldern, *Bolshevik Festivals, 1917–1920* (Berkeley: University of California Press, 1993), 93–102.

106. Boris Ignatevich Arbatov, *Natan Altman* (Berlin: Petropolis, 1924).

107. Daniel Reznik, "Natan Altman," *Di royte velt* 15 (October 1925): 115–21.

108. Abram Efros, *Portret Natana Altmana* (Moscow: Shipovnik, 1922), 40.

109. Efros, "Khudozhniki," 240.

110. Efros, *Kamernyi teatr*, ix.

111. Ibid., xxviii.

112. RGALI, f. 2307, op. 2, d. 459 (librettos); RGALI, f. 2307, op. 2, dd. 299–300 (*The Sorceress*).

113. Yekhezkel Dobrushin, "Teater un kunst: Goldfadn in yidishn kamer teater," *Der emes*, December 2, 1922.

114. Solomon Mikhoels, "Goldfaden i evreiskii kamernyi teatr," *Zrelisha* (October 17, 1922).

115. Yekhezkel Dobrushin, "Dray datn," *Di royte velt* 4 (April 1926): 91–94.

116. Rosenfeld, *The Yiddish Theatre*, 217.

117. Mikaelo, "Evreiskii kamernyi teatr Koldunia" *Teatr i muzyka* 11 (December 12, 1922): 234–35.

118. A. Kushnirov, *Zrelishcha* 17 (1922); See also M. Bleiman, "Kolduniia," *Leningradskaia pravda* (August 22, 1926); Andrei Sobol, "Novyi den evreiskogo teatra," *Teatr i muzyka* 12 (December 19, 1922): 297–99.

119. "Di oyslandishe teater-kritik vegn dem melukhishn yidishn teater," *Der emes*, January 8, 1927.

120. Yekhezkel Dobrushin, "Teater un kunst," *Der emes*, January 21, 1923.

121. "Der 4-tn yortog fun melukhishn yidishn kamer teater," *Der emes*, January 24, 1923.

122. RGALI, f. 2307, op. 2, d. 439 (foreign-language librettos, 1922–1944); RGALI, f. 2307, op.2, dd. 302–303 (*Two Hundred Thousand*).

123. GTsTM, f. 580, d. 545 (biography of I. B. Rabichev).

124. RGALI, f. 2307, op. 1, d. 98, ll. 7–23 (biographical information on Lev Pulver).

125. NSA, uncatalogued recording.

126. RTsKhIDNI, f. 445, op. 1, d. 60, l. 40.

127. RGALI, f. 2307, op. 2, d. 12 (list of theater employees), l. 16.

128. RGALI, f. 2307, op. 2, d. 26 (material regarding conflict between trade union and Moscow State Yiddish Theater, 1926–1929), l. 16.

129. RTsKhIDNI, f. 445, op. 1, d. 60, l. 42.

130. RGALI, f. 2307, op. 2, d. 176 (*Three Raising*), ll. 24–28.

131. Em. Beskin, "Tri iziuminki," *Novyi zritel* 15 (1924); See also A. Gvozdev, "3 iziominki–10ia zapoved," *Krasnaia gazeta* 23 (August 1926).

132. R. D., "Tri iziuminki v evreiskom kamernom," *Izvestiia*, April 8, 1924.

133. I. T., "Evreiskii kamernyi teatr," *Pravda*, April 3, 1924.

134. "Brambilla na bronnoi," *Pravda*, February 14, 1923. See also "200,000," *Izvestiia*, October 8, 1923.

135. Sandrow, *Vagabond Stars*, 238.

136. Mel Gordon, "Granovsky's Tragic Comedy: *Night in the Old Market*," *Drama Review* 29 (Winter 1985): 92.

137. James de Coquet, "200,000, comédie musicale interpretée par le théâtre académique juif de Moscou," *Le figaro* [Paris], January 13, 1928.

138. Gitelman, *Jewish Nationality*, 382.

139. Peter Kenez, *The Birth of the Propaganda State: Soviet Methods of Mass Mobilization, 1917–1929* (Cambridge: Cambridge University Press, 1985), 254.

140. Louis Lozowick, "Russia's Jewish Theatres," *Theatre Arts Monthly* XI (June 1927): 419–22.

2. Comrades from the Center

1. Richard Stites, *Revolutionary Dreams: Utopian Vision and Experimental Life in the Russian Revolution* (New York: Oxford University Press, 1989); Lynne Mally, *Culture of the Future: The Proletkult Movement in Revolutionary Russia* (Berkeley: University of California Press, 1990); William G. Rosenberg, *Bolshevik Visions: First Phase of the Cultural Revolution in Bolshevik Russia* (Ann Arbor: University of Michigan Press, 1984); James von Geldern, *Bolshevik Festivals, 1917–1920* (Berkeley: University of California Press, 1993).

2. Leon Trotsky, *Literature and Revolution* (Ann Arbor: University of Michigan Press, 1960), 56–115.

3. Ibid., 221.

4. Martin Malia, *The Soviet Tragedy* (New York: Free Press, 1994), 233.

5. Zvi Gitelman, *Jewish Nationality and Soviet Politics* (Princeton: Princeton University Press, 1972), 324–25.

6. Ibid., 330.

7. GTsTM, f. 584, d. 142 (protocols of Society for Friends of the State Yiddish Theater, December 22, 1926).

8. *Teatr i muzyka* 35 (October 9, 1923): 1119.

9. *Teatr i muzyka* 8 (April 17, 1923): 721. For the most comprehensive study of these theaters see Mordechai Altshuler, ed., *Ha-teatron ha-Yehudi bi-Verit ha-Moatsot* (Jerusalem: Hebrew University Press, 1996).

10. RGALI, f. 2307, op. 2, d. 15 (correspondence between Narkompros and Granovsky, 1921–1928), ll. 16, 18.

11. Ibid., l. 25.

12. Ibid., l. 26.

13. Ibid., ll. 37–38.

14. RGALI, f. 2307, op. 2, d. 438 (posters from tours, 1921–1924).

15. Ibid.

16. RTsKhIDNI, f. 445, op. 1, d. 60 (correspondence between Jewish Section and Moscow State Yiddish Theater, September 1920–December 1925), ll. 24–25, 57–58, 82.

17. RGALI, f. 2307, op. 2, d. 12 (list of theater employees, 1920–1937), l. 15.

18. GARF, f. 406, op. 12, d. 1460 (financial plans for state theaters for 1925–1926 season), l. 37.

19. RTsKhIDNI, f. 445, op. 1, d. 60, l. 31–33.

20. GARF, f. 259, op. 8b, d. 12 (protocols of Sovnarkom RSFSR, September 19, 1924–October 7, 1924), ll. 1–3.

21. RTsKhIDNI, f. 445, op. 1, d. 52 (correspondence between Jewish Section and Narkompros regarding Habima, July 1920–March 1921), l. 9.

22. Ibid., l. 4.

23. RTsKhIDNI, f. 445, op. 1, d. 60, ll. 52–54.

24. Ibid., ll. 45–46.

25. The Union of Artists was composed primarily of non-artistic workers from the former municipal and private theaters. See Richard G. Thorpe, "The Academic Theater and the Fate of Soviet Artistic Pluralism, 1919–1928," *Slavic Review* 51, no. 3 (Fall 1992): 405–406.

26. RTsKhIDNI, f. 445, op. 1, d. 60, l. 160.

27. Ibid., l. 162.

28. RGALI, f. 2307, op. 2, d. 26 (material regarding conflict between trade union and Moscow State Yiddish Theater, 1926–1929), ll. 14–18.

29. RTsKhIDNI, f. 445, op. 1, d. 183 (correspondence from Jewish Section regarding Jewish theater, 1926–1927), l. 65.

30. Thorpe, "The Academic Theater," 398–99.

31. For recent evaluations of this play see Mel Gordon, "Granovsky's Tragic Comedy: *Night in the Old Market*," *Drama Review* 29 (Winter 1985): 91–122; and Khone Shmeruk, "Be-lailah ba-shuk ha-yashen me-at Y. L. Peretz be-teatron ha-yehudi be-Moskvah," in Altshuler, *Ha-teatron*, 239–53.

32. "In melukhishn yidishn kamer-teater," *Der emes*, December 18, 1923.

33. Gordon, "Granovsky's Tragic Comedy," *Drama Review* 29 (Winter 1985): 92–94.

34. Osip Liubomirskii, *Mikhoels* (Moscow: Iskusstvo, 1938), 101.

35. Abram Efros, "Khudozhniki teatra Granovskogo," in Felix Dektor and Roman Spektor, eds., *Kovcheg: Almanakh evreiskoi kultury* (Moscow: Khudozhstvennaia literatura; Jerusalem: Tarbut, 1991), 238.

36. P. A. Markov, "Noch na starom rynke v evreiskom teatre," *Pravda*, February 13 and 14, 1925).

37. Er., "Noch na starom rynke," *Izvestiia*, February 13, 1925.

38. V. B., "Noch na starom rynke," *Krasnaia gazeta* (Leningrad), September 11, 1925.

39. Simon Dreiden, "Noch na starom rynke," *Leningradskaia pravda*, December 12, 1926; "Noch na starom rynke," *Novyi zritel* 50 (1924); Em. Beskin, "Dosadnaia opechatka," *Vecherniaia Moskva*, Feburary 11, 1925.

40. Dreiden, "Noch na starom rynke."

41. RGALI, f. 2307, op. 2, d. 3 (Lunacharskii on awarding Granovsky honorary title, February 1926).

42. Denise J. Youngblood, *Soviet Cinema in the Silent Era, 1918–1935* (1980; reprint, Austin: University of Texas Press, 1991), 240–41.

43. J. Hoberman, *Bridge of Light: Yiddish Film between Two Worlds* (New York: Museum of Modern Art, 1991), 92. Incidentally, the honor was shared with Habima, which had been invited to appear in a film adaptation of Sholem Aleichem's *The Deluge*. However, facing more pressing problems, Habima declined the offer.

44. RGALI, f. 2307, op. 2, d. 15, l. 67.

45. Hoberman, *Bridge of Light*, 191.

46. Viktor Shklovskii, review of *Evreiskoe Schaste*, reprinted in *Iskusstvo Kino* 5 (1992) 35–36.

47. RGALI, f. 2307, op. 2, d. 26 ll. 1–2.

48. Ibid., l. 1.

49. RTsKhIDNI, f. 445, op. 1, d. 60, l. 157.

50. Ibid., l. 68.

51. RGALI, f. 2307, op. 2, d. 15, l. 116.

52. RGALI, f. 2307, op. 2, d. 26, ll. 1–2.

53. RTsKhIDNI, f. 445, op. 1, d. 60, l. 180. Shteiger was arrested in 1937 and presumed shot.

54. RGALI, f. 2307, op. 2, d. 15, l. 62.; RTsKhIDNI, f. 455, op. 1, d. 60, l. 137.

55. RTsKhIDNI, f. 445, op. 1, d. 60, l. 70.

56. GARF, f. 406, op. 12, d. 1460, l. 9.

57. RTsKhIDNI, f. 445, op. 1, d. 60, l. 91.

58. Ibid., ll. 77–78.

59. Thorpe, "The Academic Theater," 396–97.

60. RTsKhIDNI, f. 445, op. 1, d. 60, l. 173; See also Ibid., ll. 139, 147.

61. Ibid., l. 172.

62. RTsKhIDNI, f. 445, op. 1, d. 183, l. 136.

63. RTsKhIDNI, f. 445, op. 1, d. 60, l. 178.

64. RGALI, f. 2307, op. 2, d. 15, ll. 134–35.

65. RTsKhIDNI, f. 445, op. 1, d. 183, l. 93.

66. Ibid., ll. 94–95.

67. Ibid., l. 102.

68. Ibid., ll. 97–98.

69. Ibid., l. 10.

70. Ibid., ll. 2–4.

71. Ibid., l. 5.

72. Ibid., l. 9.

73. Ibid., ll. 12–13.

74. Ibid., l. 14; GARF, f. 406, op. 12, d. 1460, l. 98.

75. RTsKhIDNI, f. 445, op. 1, d. 183, l. 18.

76. Ibid., l. 24.

77. Ibid., l. 55.

78. Ibid., ll. 60–61.

79. Ibid., l. 62.

80. Ibid., l. 64.

81. Gitelman, *Jewish Nationality and Soviet Politics*, 382.

82. A. Vaynshtayn, "Fraynt funm melukhishn yidishn teater," *Der emes*, December 16, 1926.

83. RTsKhIDNI, f. 445, op. 1, d. 183, ll. 72–74.

84. Ibid., l. 75.

85. RGALI, f. 2307, op. 2, d. 26, l. 4.

86. Ibid., l. 5.

87. Ibid., l. 8.

88. RTsKhIDNI, f. 445, op. 1, d. 183, ll. 108, 115.

89. Ibid., l. 47.

90. RGALI, f. 2307, op. 2, d. 26, ll. 6–7.

91. Ibid., ll. 14–18.

92. RTsKhIDNI, f. 445, op. 1, d. 183, l. 43.

93. Ibid., l. 46.

94. RGALI, f. 2307, op. 2, d. 26, l. 13.

95. Michael David-Fox, *Revolution of the Mind: Higher Learning among the Bolsheviks, 1918–1929* (Ithaca: Cornell University Press, 1997); Mally, *Culture of the Future*, 243–45.

96. RGALI, f. 2307, op. 2, d. 177 (*Tenth Commandment*), l. 28. The Second International was regarded by Lenin as a hotbed of nationalism and syndicalism. It equated the German Social Democratic supporters of the Second International with both the religious and the nouveaux riche Jews of contemporary Europe.

97. Ibid., l. 7.

98. Ibid.

99. RTsKhIDNI, f. 445, op. 1, d. 183, l. 142.

100. G. Ryklin, "Desiataia zapoved," *Izvestiia*, January 26, 1926.

101. A. Tsenovskii, "Desiataia zapoved," *Trud*, January 21, 1926.

102. S. Margolin, "Desiataia zapoved," *Vecherniaia Moskva*, January 29, 1926; M. Bleiman, "Desiataia zapoved, " *Leningradskaia pravda*, August 24, 1926.

103. Boris Gusman, "Desiataia zapoved," *Pravda* (February 16, 1926).

104. A. Gvozdev, "3 Iziuminki–10ia zapoved," *Krasnaia gazeta*, August 23, 1926.

105. Moshe Litvakov, "Truadek," *Der emes* (February 5, 1927).

106. Moshe Litvakov, "In moskver melukhishn yidishn teater dos tsente gebot," *Der emes* (February 3, 1926).

107. RGALI, f. 2307, op. 2, d. 126 (*137 Children's Homes*), l. 71.

108. RTsKhIDNI, f. 445, op. 1, d. 183, l. 142; Kh. Tokar, "Tovarishch iz tsentra," *Pravda*, July 2, 1926.

109. RTsKhIDNI, f. 445, op. 1, d. 183, l. 142.

110. M. Zagorskii, "137 detskikh domov v Gosete," *Novyi zritel* 40 (October 5, 1926): 4.

111. P. M. "137 detskikh domov," *Pravda*, October 9, 1926.

112. G. Ryklin, "Sto tridtsat sem detskikh domov," *Izvestiia,* October 2, 1926.

113. See also A. Gvozdev, "137 detskikh domov," *Krasnaia gazeta* (Leningrad), August 26, 1926; Mikaelo, "137 detskikh domov," *Vecherniaia Moskva,* October 1, 1926; M. Bleiman, "137 detskikh domov," *Leningradskaia pravda,* August 27, 1926.

114. Moshe Litvakov, "Vegn tsvey oyfirungen," *Der emes,* December 4, 1927.

115. "Khronika," *Novyi zritel* 48 (November 30, 1926): 17.

116. IGTAM, G1 (Goset collection).

117. GTsTM, f. 584 (*Trouhadec* libretto), d. 55.

118. "Truadek," *Kharkov vesti,* August 17, 1927; M. Sheliubskii, "Truadek," *Kievskii proletarii,* August 27, 1927; "Truadek v gosudarstvennom evreiskom teatre," *Prozhektor,* February 15, 1927; V. A. Pavlov, "Sobesedovanie o Truadeke," *Vecherniaia Moskva,* January 27, 1927; G. Ryklin, "Truadek," *Izvestiia,* January 16, 1927; N. Volkov, "Truadek," *Trud,* January 14, 1927; A. Tsenovskii, "O muzyke Truadek," *Trud,* January 14, 1927; Mikh. Levidov, "Spektakli teatralnoi kultury," *Vecherniaia Moskva,* January 13, 1927.

119. Mikhail Koltsov, "Truadek v Goset," *Pravda,* February 17, 1927.

120. M. Zagorskii, "Truadek v gosete," *Novyi zritel* 1 (1927).

121. K. N., "Sobesedovanie o Truadeke," *Vecherniaia Moskva,* January 27, 1927.

122. Moshe Litvakov, "Truadek," *Der emes,* February 5, 1927.

123. Béatrice Picon-Vallin, *Le théâtre juif soviétique pendant les années vingt* (Lausanne: Editions la cité, 1973), 147.

124. RGALI, f. 2307, op. 2, d. 450. An English translation of Mendele's short story is available in S. Y. Abramovitsh, *Tales of Mendele the Book Peddler: Fishke the Lame and Benjamin the Third,* ed. Dan Miron and Ken Frieden, trans. Ted Gorelick and Hillel Halkin (New York: Schocken Books, 1996), 297–391.

125. Konstantin Rudnitsky, *Russian and Soviet Theater 1905–1932* (New York: Thames and Hudson, 1988), 195.

126. Grinvald, *Mikhoels,* 42.

127. A. Tsenovskii, "Veniamin Tretii," *Trud,* May 7, 1927; See also G. Ryklin, "Puteshestvie Veniamina Tretego," *Izvestiia,* May 4, 1927; Iak. Eidelman, "Puteshetvie Veniamina Tretego," *Komsomolskaia pravda,* May 7, 1927; Em. Beskin, "Don-Kikhot iz Tuneiadovki," *Vecherniaia Moskva,* April 27, 1927. For slightly less enthusiastic reviews see Ia. M., "Puteshestvie Veniamina Tretego," *Literaturnaia gazeta,* May 1, 1927.

128. A. S. Lirik, "Izrael shpielt mit zayn shaten," *Haynt,* May 24, 1928.

129. These figures are given in a report the theater submitted to the Jewish Section. RTsKhIDNI, f. 445, d. 183, l. 141. Considerably higher attendance figures (57,000 for the season) were reported in *Der emes,* May 26, 1927.

130. *Novyi zritel* 45 (October 1927): 21.

131. Moshe Goldblatt, "Der ufkum un umkum fun der yidisher teater-kultur in Sovetnfarband," DRI, P-51-21 (Goldblatt papers), 103.

132. A. Gidion, "Kolonialnye postanovki," *Sovremennyi teatr* 15 (December 13, 1927): 228–30.

133. Moshe Litvakov, "Tzvey oyfirungen," *Der emes,* December 7, 1927.

134. A. Ts., "Vosstanie," *Trud,* November 18, 1927; A. Z., "Vosstanie," *Pravda,* December 14, 1927; Ian. Roshchin, "Vosstanie," *Komsomolskaia pravda,* November 18, 1927; Iv. Astrov, "Vosstanie," *Novyi zritel* 3 (1928).

135. Em. Beskin, "Vosstanie v Gosete," *Vecherniaia Moskva,* December 4, 1927.

136. RGALI, f. 2307, op. 2, d. 26, ll. 28–29.

137. Ibid., ll. 30–32.

138. RGALI, f. 2307, op. 2, d. 12, l. 17.

139. RGALI, f. 2307, op. 2, d. 26, ll. 30–32.

140. Ibid., ll. 24–27.

141. RGALI, f. 2307, op. 2, d. 12, l. 25.

142. RGALI, f. 2307, op. 2, d. 26, l. 34.

143. Ibid., ll. 37, 48.

144. RGALI, f. 2307, op. 2. d. 45 (Imenitova's legal suit).

145. RGALI, f. 2307, op. 2, d. 26, l. 49.

146. Ibid., l. 57.

147. Goldblatt, "Der ufkum," 105.

148. Volosova, "Mnogo uslovnogo," unidentified newspaper clipping in IGTAM G1.

149. Cited in Max Erlik, "Menakhem-Mendl," *Der shtern* 5–6 (1935): 180–202; 8 (1935): 82–90.

150. Liubomirskii, *Mikhoels*, 44.

151. I. Kruti, "Chelovek vozdukha," *Sovremennyi teatr* (15) 1928.

152. O. Litovskii, "Chelovek vozdukha," *Pravda*, April 3, 1928. For similar reviews see A. Tsenovskii, "Chelovek vozdukha," *Trud*, March 31, 1928; D. Bukhartsev, "Na novuiu stupen," *Komsomolskaia pravda*, March 23, 1928.

153. G. Ryklin, "Chelovek vozdukha," *Izvestiia*, March 10, 1928. See also Uriel, "Chelovek vozdukha v Gosete," *Vecherniaia Moskva*, March 26, 1928.

154. Sh. Shamis, "Mikhoels—Menakhem Mendel," *Der emes*, July 12, 1929.

155. E. H. Carr, *Socialism in One Country, 1924–1926* (London: Macmillan, 1965), 2: 76–87; E. H. Carr, *Foundations of a Planned Economy, 1926–1929* (London: Macmillan, 1971), 2: 399–418.

156. Sheila Fitzpatrick, Alexander Rabinowitch, and Richard Stites, eds., *Russia in the Era of NEP: Explorations in Soviet Society and Culture* (Bloomington: Indiana University Press, 1991).

157. Michael S. Fox, "Glavlit, Censorship and the Problem of Party Policy in Cultural Affairs, 1922–28," *Soviet Studies* 44, no. 6 (1992): 1049–1050. See also Roger Pethybridge, "Concern for Bolshevik Ideological Predominance at the Start of NEP," *Russian Review* 44, no. 4 (1982): 445–53.

158. TsGAOR Ukr, F. 166, op. 6, d. 8233 (repertoire of Jewish theater).

159. Gitelman, *Jewish Nationality and Soviet Politics*, 141–48.

3. Wandering Stars

1. P. A. Markov, *The Soviet Theatre* (London: V Gollancz, 1934), 19.

2. *Teatr i muzyka* 35 (October 9, 1923), 1160.

3. Natalia Vovsi-Mikhoels, *Mon père Salomon Mikhoels: souvenirs sur sa vie et sur sa mort*, trans. Erwin Spatz (Montricher, Switzerland: Les Editions Noir sur Blanc, 1990), 39.

4. RGALI, f. 2307, op. 2, d. 15 (correspondence between Narkompros and Granovsky, 1921–1928), ll. 37–38.

5. Ibid., ll. 6, 9, 10.

6. Ibid., ll. 28–30.

7. Ibid., l. 34.

8. Ibid., l. 78.

9. RGALI, f. 2307, op. 2, d. 18 (correspondence regarding foreign tour, December 13, 1923–March 15, 1926), l. 115.

10. RGALI, f. 2307, op. 2, d. 15, l. 9; RGALI, f. 2307, op. 2, d. 18, l. 12.

11. RGALI, f. 2307, op. 2, d. 18, ll. 29–32.

12. Zalman Zilbercwaig, ed., *Leksikon fun yidishn teater* (Warsaw: Alisheve, 1934), 2: 572–76.

13. RGALI, f. 2307, op. 2, d. 18, ll. 12, 21–22, 25–28.

14. Nahma Sandrow, *Vagabond Stars: A World History of Yiddish Theater* (New York: Harper and Row, 1977), 302.

15. RTsKhIDNI, f. 445, op. 1, d. 60 (correspondence between Jewish Section and Moscow State Yiddish Theater, September 1920–December 1925), l. 64.

16. RGALI, f. 2307, op. 2, d. 15, ll. 65, 74.

17. RGALI, f. 2307, op. 2, d. 18, l. 39.

18. Ibid., l. 47.

19. Ibid., ll. 63–65.

20. Ibid., ll. 29–32.

21. Ibid., ll. 102–103.

22. Ibid., l. 98.

23. Ibid., ll. 66–71.

24. Ibid., l. 119. After returning to the Soviet Union as a journalist, Talmy became active in the Jewish Anti-Fascist Committee and was executed with many of his colleagues in August 1952.

25. Ibid., l. 135.

26. RTsKhIDNI, f. 445, op. 1, d. 183 (correspondence from Jewish Section regarding Jewish theater, 1926–1927), l. 67.

27. RGALI, f. 2306, op. 2, d. 27 (Granovsky's correspondence regarding foreign tour, 1926–1928), ll. 8–42.

28. RGALI, f. 2307, op. 2, d. 15, l. 122.

29. RTsKhIDNI, f. 445, op. 1, d. 183, ll. 69–71.

30. RTsKhIDNI, f. 445, op. 1, d. 185 (correspondence between Jewish Section and the Moscow State Yiddish Theater regarding foreign tour, February 1928–October 1929), l. 11.

31. RGALI, f. 2307, op. 2, d. 27, ll. 117–22.

32. RGALI, f. 2307, op. 2, d. 27, l. 163.

33. RGALI, f. 2307, op. 2, d. 33 (certificate from Narkompros RSFSR to Moscow State Yiddish Theater artists).

34. RGALI, f. 2307, op. 2, d. 26 (material regarding conflict between trade union and Moscow State Yiddish Theater, 1926–1929), l. 52.

35. RTsKhIDNI, f. 445, op. 1, d. 185, l. 97.

36. Ibid.

37. Moshe Goldblatt, "Der ufkum un umkum fun der yidisher teater-kultur in sovetn-farband," DRI, P-51-21 (Goldblatt papers), 109.

38. *Literarishe bleter* 17 (April 27, 1928).

39. Goldblatt, "Der ufkum," 112.

40. Ibid., 120.

41. Ibid., 123.

42. Ibid., 121.

43. Alfred Kerr, "Moskauer jüdisch-akademisches Theater," *Berliner Tageblatt*, April 12, 1928.

44. Herman Swet, "Der ershter aroystreyt fun moskver yidishen kamer teater in Berlin," *Der moment* (Warsaw), April 22, 1928.

45. A. S. Lirik, "Shmuel Soroker als revoliutsioner," *Haynt* (Warsaw), April 20, 1928.

46. Bernhard Diebold, "Folkstück mit gesang," *Frankfurter Zeitung,* May 19, 1928.
47. Goldblatt, "Der ufkum," 129.
48. RTsKhIDNI, f. 445, op. 1, d. 185, l. 10.
49. Ibid., l. 100.
50. Ibid., l. 101.
51. Ibid., l. 12
52. Ibid., l. 13.
53. Ibid., l. 99.
54. Ibid., l. 53.
55. Ibid., l. 101.
56. Ibid.
57. Ibid., l. 102.
58. "Moskovskie teatry gastrolnykh poezdkakh," *Pravda,* June 26, 1928.
59. Nakhman Mayzel, "Mir un di velt," *Haynt,* July 6, 1928.
60. Chaim Weizmann, *The Letters and Papers of Chaim Weizmann,* 25 vols. (Jerusalem: Israel Universities Press, 1968–), 13: 136. *Der emes* had also begun a campaign to discredit Weizmann's scientific research. See p. 27.
61. Ibid., 160.
62. *Literarishe bleter* 30 (July 27, 1928): 595.
63. RTsKhIDNI, f. 445, op. 1, d. 185, l. 20.
64. Ibid., l. 21.
65. RTsKhIDNI, f. 445, op. 1, d. 185, l. 102.
66. "Dos moskver yidishn akademishn teater in Vien," *Der moment,* October 15, 1928.
67. RTsKhIDNI, f. 445, op. 1, d. 185, ll. 57–61.
68. Ibid., ll. 68–70.
69. Ibid.
70. Ibid., l. 71.
71. Ibid., ll. 46–49 in Russian; 42–45 in Yiddish.
72. Anatolii Lunacharskii, "Goset za granitsei," *Vecherniaia Moskva,* October 6, 1928.
73. *Literarishe bleter* 42 (October 19, 1928): 833.
74. RTsKhIDNI, f. 445, op. 1, d. 185, l. 76.
75. Ibid., l. 75.
76. Ibid., l. 76.
77. Ibid., l. 77.
78. Ibid., l. 84.
79. Ibid., ll. 85–86. See also Aleksandr Granovsky, "Pismo v redaktsiiu," *Izvestiia,* October 21, 1929.
80. Herman Swet, "Fun Tuneiadovke keyn Monte-Karlo," *Der moment,* October 12, 1928.
81. *Literarishe bleter* 44 (November 2, 1928): 874.
82. RTsKhIDNI, f. 445, op. 1, d. 185, l. 93.
83. Ibid., l. 108.
84. Ibid., ll. 95–96.
85. "The Great World Theatre," *Theatre Arts Monthly* XIII (January 1929): 5.
86. C. Hooper Trask, "Le Bourgeois Gentilhomme," *New York Times,* March 24, 1929.
87. Nakhman Mayzel, "A. Granovski," *Haynt,* March 19, 1937.
88. Yosef Sheyn, *Arum moskver yidishn teater* (Paris: Commission du plan d'action culturelle, 1964), 102.

89. Sheila Fitzpatrick, *The Cultural Front: Power and Culture in Revolutionary Russia* (Ithaca: Cornell University Press, 1992), 1–15; Lewis Siegelbaum, *Stakhanovism and the Politics of Productivity in the USSR, 1935–1941* (Cambridge: Cambridge University Press, 1988); J. Arch Getty and Roberta Manning, eds., *Stalinist Terror* (New York: Cambridge University Press, 1993); Hiroaki Kuromiya, *Stalin's Industrial Revolution: Politics and Workers, 1928–1932* (New York: Cambridge University Press, 1988); Stephen Kotkin, *Magnetic Mountain: Stalinism as a Civilization* (Berkeley: University of California Press, 1995); David Hoffman, *Peasant Metropolis: Social Identities in Moscow, 1929–1941* (Ithaca: Cornell University Press, 1994).

90. RTsKhIDNI, f. 445, op. 1, d. 185, l. 132.

91. Ibid., l. 133.

92. "Di efnung funm vinter sezon in moskver melukhisn idishn teater," *Der emes,* September11, 1929.

93. I. Lashevich, "Evreiskii teatr i ego zritel," unidentified newspaper clipping in IGTAM G2 (Goset collection).

94. "Rabkory v evreiskom teatre," (1935), unidentified journal clipping iin IGTAM G1 (Goset collection).

95. RGALI, f. 2307, op. 2, d. 12 (list of theater employees, 1920–1937), ll. 17–18.

96. RGALI, f. 2307, op. 2, d. 4, l. 1.

97. RGALI, f. 2307, op. 2, d. 12 (correspondence between RABIS and Goset, 1929–1935), ll. 17–18.

98. RGALI, f. 2308, op. 1, d. 44 (curriculum of Moscow Jewish Theater School), ll. 1, 43–44.

99. Cited in Sheyn, *Arum moskver yidishn teater,* 120–21.

100. "Inem moskver melukhishn idishn teater," *Der emes,* August 22, 1929.

101. Peretz Markish, *Mikhoels* (Moscow: Der Emes, 1939), 24.

102. See Aharon Steinberg, "Mayn Dvinsker khaver Shlomo Mikhoels," *Di goldene kayt,* 43 (1962), 142–52.

103. Erwin Piscator, "Dos teater fun haynt un fun morgn," *Literarishe bleter* 8 (February 24, 1928): 153–54.

104. John Willett, *The Theatre of Erwin Piscator* (New York: Holmes & Meier, 1979), 79.

105. "Gezegenung mitn moskver idishn melukhishn teater in Kiev," *Der emes,* May 30, 1928.

106. RTsKhIDNI, f. 445, op. 1, d. 185, l. 144.

107. "Pismo v redaktsiiu," *Izvestiia,* October 26, 1929.

108. "Pismo v redaktsiiu," *Rabochii i iskusstvo,* September 30, 1929.

109. "V mosgubrabis," unidentified press clipping in IGTAM G1.

110. "Tvorcheskii metod Goseta," *RABIS* 3 (1931).

111. Solomon Mikhoels, "Navstrechu novomu zriteliu," *Sovetskoe iskusstvo,* November 7, 1933. See also Benjamin Zuskin, "Put evreiskogo teatra," *Komsomolskaia pravda,* March 30, 1939.

112. "Vystuplenie v komitete po delam iskusstv 1936–37 g," IGTAM, uncatalogued.

4. The Court Is in Session

1. For more on Soviet censorship see Herman Ermolaev, *Censorship in Soviet Literature, 1917–1991* (Lanham, Md.: Rowman & Littlefield, 1997); and Arlen V. Blium, *Za*

kulisami "Ministerstva pravdy": tainaia istoriia sovetskoi tsenzury, 1917–1929 (St. Petersburg: Akademicheskii proekt, 1994).

2. Norris Houghton, *Moscow Rehearsals: The Golden Age of Soviet Theatre* (1936; reprint, New York: Grove Press, 1962), 81.

3. See, for instance, Richard Stites, *Russian Popular Culture: Entertainment and Society since 1900* (Cambridge: Cambridge University Press, 1992), 64–97; Régine Robin, *Socialist Realism: An Impossible Aesthetic,* trans. Catherine Porter (1986; reprint, Stanford, Calif.: Stanford University Press, 1992), 183–90; George Lukács, *The Meaning of Contemporary Realism,* trans. John and Necke Mander (1963; reprint, London: Merlin Press, 1979); Katerina Clark, *The Soviet Novel* (Chicago: University of Chicago Press, 1981).

4. Houghton, *Moscow Rehearsals,* 195–96.

5. Liubomirskii, "Der idisher teater in rekonstruktion period," *Prolit* (Kharkov) 10–11 (1930): 127–37. Similar articles appeared in *Sovietskii teatr* 9–10 (1930); and *Nayerd* 7–8 (1930).

6. See Arlen V. Blium, *Evreiskii vopros pod sovetskoi tsenzuroi* (St. Petersburg: St. Petersburg Jewish University, 1996), 64–77.

7. See, for instance, "Alfarbandishe baratung fun di yidishe teaters," *Der emes,* January 9, 1935; "Di alfarbandishe baratung di yidishe teaters," *Der emes,* January 12, 1935.

8. Cited in Robin, *Socialist Realism,* 34.

9. Iakov Grinvald, *Mikhoels: kratkii kritiko-biograficheskii ocherk* (Moscow: Der Emes, 1948), 47.

10. Dobrushin and Zuskin, "L. Pulver: fardinstpuler kunst tuer," *Der emes,* April 18, 1934, 4.

11. Yekhezkel Dobrushin, *Der gerikht geyt* (Moscow: Tsentraler felker farlag fun FSSR, 1930),19.

12. Ibid., 32.

13. Nojach Prylucki, *Yidishe Folkslider* (Warsaw: Bikher far ale, 1911); Ruth Rubin, *Voices of a People: Yiddish Folk Song* (New York: Thomas Yoseloff, 1963).

14. For the normalization of language see Robin, *Socialist Realism,* 165–83.

15. RGALI, f. 2307, op. 1, d. 178a (*The Court Is in Session*). For a published version see Dobrushin, *Der gerikht geyt.*

16. "Sud idet," *Rabochii i iskusstvo,* January 15, 1930. This sentiment was echoed in a wide variety of reviews: "Sud idet," *RABIS* 49 (1929); "Sud idet," *Komsomolskaia pravda,* December 1, 1929; V. Mlechin, "Sud idet v Gosete," *Literaturnaia gazeta* (Leningrad), October 16, 1929; "Sud idet," *Sovremennyi teatr* 43 (1929).

17. G. Ryklin, "Sud idet—sut prishel," unidentified newspaper clipping in IGTAM, P26 (Sud idet).

18. "Der ershter ovnt fun der gezelshaft fraynt funm moskver melukhishn yidishn teater," *Der emes,* October 24, 1929.

19. M. Zagorskii, *Literaturnaia gazeta,* October 28, 1929. For similar comments see O. Liubomriskii, "Der gerikht geyt," *Der emes,* October 16, 1929.

20. George Lukács, *The Meaning of Contemporary Realism,* trans. John and Necke Mander (1963; reprint, London: Merlin Press, 1979), 94.

21. This argument was also put forward by Osip Liubomirskii, "Der idisher teater in rekonstruktion period." *Prolit* (Kharkov) 10–11 (1930). See also *Sovietskii teatr* 9–10 (1930) and *Nayerd* 7–8 (1930).

22. Liubomirskii, "Sud idet," *Novyi zritel* 4 (1929); see also his "Der gerikht geyt," *Der emes,* October 16, 1929.

23. "Sud idet," *Rabochii i iskusstvo*, January 15, 1930.

24. For anti-Semitism in the workplace see Nora Levin, *The Jews in the Soviet Union since 1917: Paradox of Survival* (New York: I. B. Tauris, 1990), 259–65.

25. See, for instance, Lukács, *The Meaning of Contemporary Realism*, 129.

26. "Di gastroln fun moskver melukhisn idishn teater," *Der emes*, May 17, 1930.

27. "Vi azoy zeynen durkh di gastroln fun vaysruslandishn melukhishn idishn teater," *Der emes*, May 13, 1930.

28. RGALI, f. 2307, op. 2, d. 454 (libretto for *The Dams*).

29. "A groyser idielogisher un kunstlerisher zig," *Der emes*, July 18, 1930.

30. M. Zagorskii, "Grebles," *Vecherniaia Moskva*, October 29, 1930.

31. For more on Markish see Esther Markish, *The Long Return* (New York: Ballantine Books, 1978). Markish was arrested as part of the Jewish Anti-Fascist Committee in 1948 and executed on August 12, 1952.

32. Uriel, "Vchera i segodnia," *Sovetskoe iskusstvo*, March 29, 1931.

33. Em. Beskin, "Novyi shag Goseta k sovremennoi tematike," *Vecherniaia Moskva*, February 26, 1931.

34. Levin, *The Jews in the Soviet Union*, 227.

35. Ibid., 238.

36. Konstantin Rudnitsky, *Russian and Soviet Theater 1905–1932* (New York: Thames and Hudson, 1988), 185.

37. See "Little Heroes and Big Deeds: Literature Responds to the First Five-Year Plan," in Sheila Fitzpatrick, *Cultural Revolution in Russia, 1928–1931* (Bloomington: Indiana University Press, 1978), 189–206.

38. This scene was published in *Deklamater fun der sovetisher yidisher literatur* (Moscow: Der Emes, 1934), 375–79. For a synopsis of the play see RGALI, f. 2307, op. 2, d. 453 (libretto for *The Deaf*). Bergelson's short story can be found in David Bergelson, *Oysgevaylte verk* (Moscow: Melukhe farlag fun kinstlerisher literatur, 1961), 21–54.

39. Osip Liubomirskii, *Mikhoels* (Moscow: Iskusstvo, 1938), 66.

40. V. Mlechin, "Glukhoi," *Vecherniaia Moskva*, January 20, 1930.

41. I. Krugi, "Novye postanovki Glukhoi," *Rabochii i iskusstvo*, September 5, 1930.

42. Cited in Liubomirskii, *Mikhoels*, 96.

43. See, for example Solomon Mikhoels, *Stati, besedy, rechi* (Moscow: Iskusstvo, 1965), 157–58.

44. "Moskovskii gosudarstvennyi evreiskii teatr," *Izvestiia*, October 17, 1931.

45. R. Imenitova, "Zaem i . . . kolduniia," *Sovetskoe iskusstvo*, October 3, 1931.

46. I am grateful to Joshua Rubenstein for directing me to this information.

47. M. Daniel, *4 teg* (Minsk: Melukhe farlag fun vaysrusland, 1932).

48. RGALI, f. 2307, op. 2, d. 439 (foreign-language librettos, 1922–1944).

49. Peretz Markish, *Mikhoels* (Moscow: Der Emes, 1939), 25–26.

50. M. Shteingauzr, "V evreiskom teatre," *Elektrozavod*, March 3, 1935.

51. "4 teg in moskver melukhishn idishn teater," *Der emes* (November 15, 1931).

52. Iakov Grinvald, "Chetyrie dnia," *Vecherniaia Moskva*, November 17, 1931.

53. V. Z., "Zlobodnevoe i aktualnoe," *Literaturnaia gazeta*, December 3, 1931. See also G. Ryklin, "Chetyrie dnia," *Pravda*, November 28, 1931; V. Mlechin, "Put tvorcheskoi perestroiki. Iulis v Gosete," *Sovetskoe iskusstvo*, November 25, 1931.

54. Mlechin "Put tvorcheskoi perestroiki."

55. "4 Teg (Iulis) in moskver melukhishn yidishn teater," *Der emes*, November 5, 1931.

56. Flavius Josephus, *Toldot milkhamot ha-Yehudim im ha-Romaim*, trans. Naftali Simchoni (1923; reprint, Tel-Aviv: Shtibel, 1938).

57. Flavius Josephus, *Di idishe milkhomes* (Vilna: B. A. Kletskin, 1923).

58. Yael Zerubavel, *Recovered Roots: Collective Memory and the Making of Israeli National Tradition* (Chicago: University of Chicago Press, 1995), 60–64.

59. "Teater un kino," *Der emes,* February 17, 1932.

60. "Moskovskii gosudarstvennyi evreiskii teatr," *Izvestiia,* October 17, 1931.

61. "Teater un kino," *Der emes,* February 11, 1932.

62. "10-letnie gos. evreiskogo teatra," *Izvestiia,* January 5, 1931.

63. "Sheferishe baratung bam moskver melukhishn yidishn teater," *Der emes,* January 15, 1932.

64. "Ongehoyben arbetn der kunst-politrat bam moskver yidishn melukhishn teater," *Der emes,* February 24, 1932.

65. B. Rozentsveig, "Pered otkrytym semaforom," *Komsomolskaia pravda,* April 17, 1932.

66. Iakov Grinvald, "Protivorechiia rosta," *Vecherniaia Moskva,* April 3, 1932.

67. Markish, *Mikhoels,* 26.

68. "Chto pokazhet goset," *Vecherniaia Moskva,* September 10, 1932; "Erev dem nayem teater-sezon," *Der emes,* September 20, 1932.

69. "Moskver melukhisher yidisher teater," *Der emes,* February 3, 1933; "Der moskver melukhisher yidisher teater shpilt vider in zayn gebayde," *Der emes,* April 20, 1933.

70. See, for example, "Der groyser oktober ovnt in klub komunist," *Der emes,* November 11, 1932.

71. *Nosn Beker fort aheym,* directed by Shpis and Milman, USSR. 1932 (film).

72. Felix Cole to Secretary of State, September 15, 1932, NARA, RG 59, 861.4061/ 88.

73. "A fardislekher durkhfal," *Der emes,* November 20, 1932.

74. "Khronik," *Der emes,* January 22, 1933.

75. "Haynt hoyb zikh on di spekteklen fun moskver melukhishn yidishn teater midat hadin," *Der emes,* October 8, 1933.

76. Liubomirskii, *Mikhoels,* 106.

77. "Geefnt zikh der sezon fun moskver melukhishn yidishn teater," *Der emes,* October 10, 1933; see also "Novyi spektakl Goset," *Sovetskoe iskusstvo,* November 2, 1933; Iakov Grinvald, "Mera strogosti," *Vecherniaia Moskva,* October 13, 1933.

78. Moshe Litvakov, "Midat hadin," *Der emes,* October 24, 1933.

79. Raphael Mahler, *Hasidism and the Jewish Enlightenment: Their Confrontation in Galicia and Poland in the First Half of the Nineteenth Century* (Philadephia: The Jewish Publication Society of America, 1985), 11–13. See also Gershom Scholem, *On the Mystical Shape of the Godhead: Basic Concepts in the Kabbalah* (New York: Schocken Books, 1991), 61–64.

80. O. Liubomirskii, "Sovetskaia evreiskaia dramaturgiia," unidentified newspaper clipping, IGTAM, G1 (Goset collection), 36.

81. Cited in Vitaly Shentalinsky, *The KGB's Literary Archive,* trans. John Crowfoot (London: Harvill Press, 1995), 47. Mikhoels expressed a similar sentiment to Abraham Sutzkever. Abraham Sutzkever, "Mit Shlomo Mikhoels," *Di goldene keyt* 43 (1962): 156.

82. "Novyi zritel—novyi teatr," *Sovetskoe iskuustvo,* December 26, 1933.

83. Ibid.

84. Ibid.

85. O. Liubomirskii, "Der krimer kolvirtisher yidisher teater," *Der emes,* June 2, 1935.

86. Mikhoels, "Put vysokogo realizma" *Sovetskoe iskusstvo,* May 5, 1935.

87. Leon Mussinak, "Frantsuzskii vodevil v Gosete," *Izvestiia,* October 24, 1934.

88. Albert Gran, "Parizh v Gosete," *Literaturnaia gazeta*, November 16, 1934.

89. Iakov Grinvald, "Labish v Gosete," *Vecherniaia Moskva*, November 11, 1934. See also A. Petrovich, "Millioner bedniak i dantist," *Trud*, November 27, 1934; A. Gambrunis, "Millioner dantist i bedniak v Gosete," *Krasnaia gazeta* (Leningrad), June 11, 1935; and V. Potapov, "Vodevil v Gosete," *Izvestiia*, November 14, 1935.

90. Juri Jelagin, *Taming of the Arts*, trans. Nicholas Wreden (New York: E. P. Dutton & Co., 1951), 81.

91. RGALI, f. 2307, op. 1, dd. 86–104 (personal files of employees).

92. Jelagin, *Taming of the Arts*, 18.

93. Houghton, *Moscow Rehearsals*, 236.

94. Ibid., 238.

95. RGALI, f. 2307, op. 2, d. 12 (list of theater employees, 1920–1937), ll. 55–56.

96. Ida Kaminska, *My Life, My Theater* (New York: Macmillan, 1973), 134.

97. "Inim moskver yidishn melukhe-teater Konig Lir," *Der emes*, March 18, 1934.

98. For more on Shakespearean productions in the 1930s see Joseph Macleod, *The New Soviet Theatre* (London: George Allen & Unwin, 1943), 208–218.

99. Grinvald, *Mikhoels*, 56.

100. Komitet po delam iskusstv pri SNK soiuza SSR, *Rezhisser v sovetskom teatre* (Moscow: Iskusstvo, 1940), 75.

101. N. A. Ravich, *Repertuarnyi ukazatel GRK* (Moscow: Teatr-Kino, 1929), 124–25.

102. See Vladimir Markov, "An Unnoticed Aspect of Pasternak's Translations," *Slavic Review* 20, no. 3 (October 1961): 503–508; Anna Kay France, *Boris Pasternak's Translations of Shakespeare* (Berkeley: University of California Press, 1978).

103. Cited in Lev Loseff, *On the Beneficence of Censorship: Aesopian Language in Modern Russian Literature* (Munich: Verlag Otto Sagner, 1984), 49.

104. Ibid., 46.

105. Mikhoels, *Stati, besedi, rechi*, 104–105.

106. Grigori Kozintsev, *Shakespeare: Time and Conscience*, trans. Joyce Vining (New York: Hill and Wang, 1966), 60–61.

107. Ibid., 65.

108. Liubomirskii, *Mikhoels*, 80.

109. *King Lear*, 1.5.36.

110. Cited in Liubomirskii, *Mikhoels*, 97.

111. Ibid., 83.

112. Cited in Marvin Rosenberg, *The Masks of King Lear* (Berkeley: University of California Press, 1972), 21.

113. Grinvald, *Mikhoels*, 57.

114. Rosenberg, *The Masks of King Lear*, 130.

115. E. Dobin, "Korol Lir," *Leningradskaia pravda*, April 9, 1935; see also B. S., "Korol Lir v Gosete," *Za industrializatsiiu*, February 14, 1935.

116. O. Litovskii, "Korol Lir," *Pravda*, February 27, 1935. For other reviews see M. Zagorskii, "Dva aktera," *Vecherniaia Moskva*, March 4, 1935; Adr. Piotrovskii, *Krasnaia gazeta* (Leningrad), May 28, 1935; V. Morskoi, "Korol Lir," *Krasnoe znamia* (Kharkov), July 11, 1939.

117. Karl Radek, "Bolshaia pobeda sovetskogo teatra," *Izvestiia*, February 27, 1935.

118. Grinvald, "Korol Lir."

119. B. Rozentsveig, "Korol Lir," *Komsomolskaia pravda*, February 14, 1935.

120. Radek, "Bolshaia pobeda."

121. "200 i spektakl Korolia Lira v Gosete" *Sovetskoe iskusstvo,* December 10, 1938.

122. "15 yor moskver melukhisher yidisher teater," *Der emes,* March 5, 1935.

123. Robin, *Socialist Realism,* 292.

124. Zvi Gitelman, *A Century of Ambivalence: The Jews of Russia and the Soviet Union, 1881 to the Present* (New York: YIVO Institute, 1988), 42.

125. According to Judel Mark, there were approximately 160,000 Jewish students attending Yiddish schools in the Soviet Union in 1931. Jacob Frumkin, Gregor Aronson, Alexis Goldenweiser, and Joseph Lewitan, *Russian Jewry (1917–1967)* (New York: Thomas Yoseloff, 1969), 253. For more on clandestine religious education see David E. Fishman, "Preserving Tradition in the Land of the Revolution: The Religious Leadership of Soviet Jewry, 1917–1930," in Jack Wertheimer, ed., *The Uses of Tradition: Jewish Continuity in the Modern Era* (New York: Jewish Theological Seminary of America, 1992), 23–84.

126. Sutzkever, "Mit Shlomo Mikhoels," 158.

127. Markish, *Mikhoels,* 15.

5. Where Are the Maccabees?

1. Richard Stites, *Russian Popular Culture: Entertainment and Society since 1900* (Cambridge: Cambridge University Press, 1992), 78; Boris Groys, *The Total Art of Stalinism: Avant-Garde, Aesthetic Dictatorship, and Beyond,* trans. Charles Rougle (Princeton: Princeton University Press, 1992), 37.

2. Régine Robin, *Socialist Realism: An Impossible Aesthetic,* trans. Catherine Porter (Stanford: Stanford University Press, 1992), 74.

3. For an analysis of kitsch in the Soviet context see Svetlana Boym, *Common Places: Mythologies of Everyday Life in Russia* (Cambridge, Mass.: Harvard University Press, 1994), 15–19.

4. Edward W. Said, *Culture and Imperialism* (New York: Knopf, 1993).

5. Although the party never officially accepted the existence of a Jewish nation, it did, in many ways, treat the Jews as a national minority in practice. The establishment of the Jewish Autonomous Region in 1934 and the Jewish designation on passports are just two examples of the means by which Jews were treated as a nation.

6. Katerina Clark, *The Soviet Novel* (Chicago: University of Chicago Press, 1981), 162.

7. Cited in Natalia Vovsi-Mikhoels, *Mon père Salomon Mikhoels: souvenirs sur sa vie et sur sa mort,* trans. Erwin Spatz (Montricher, Switzerland: Les Editions Noir sur Blanc, 1990), 125.

8. "Tsum 15 iorikn iubili funem moskver yidishn melukhishn teater," *Der emes,* March 4, 1935.

9. "Der iubili ovnt funem moskver idishn teater," *Der emes,* March 6, 1935.

10. M. Zinenberg, "Piatnadtsatiletie Goseta," *Govorit SSSR,* May 1935.

11. Unidentified press clipping, IGTAM, G2.

12. "15 yoriker iubili funem moskver melukhishn yidishn teater," *Der emes,* March 6, 1935.

13. Solomon Mikhoels, "Put vysokogo realizma," *Sovetskoe iskusstvo,* May 5, 1935; "Piatnadtsat let moskovskogo gosudarstvennogo evreiskogo teatra," *Krasnaia gazeta* (Leningrad), March 5, 1935; "XV let gosudarstvennogo evreiskogo teatra," *Rabochaia Moskva,* March 5, 1935; "Piatnadtsat let evreiskogo teatra," *Leningradskaia pravda,* November 11, 1935.

14. RGALI, f. 2307, op. 2, d. 439 (foreign-language librettos, 1922–1944).

15. "Novyi zritel—novyi teatr," *Sovetskoe iskusstvo*, December 26, 1933.

16. Zinenberg, "Piatnadtsatiletie."

17. Osip Liubomirskii, *Mikhoels* (Moscow: Iskusstvo, 1938), 103.

18. Ts. Fridliand, "Teatr tragicheskikh komediantov," *Literaturnaia gazeta* (Leningrad), March 6, 1935.

19. "O iubileinom slavoslovnii," *Sovetskoe iskusstvo*, March 17, 1935.

20. "100 spektaklei Goseta," *Vecherniaia Moskva*, July 23, 1935.

21. "Plany evreiskogo teatra," *Teatralnaia dekada*, May 1935; "Repertuarnye plany goset," *Sovetskoe iskusstvo*, May 23, 1935; "Postanovski Goseta," *Izvestiia*, October 10, 1935; "Premery evreiskogo teatra," *Vecherniaia Moskva*, November 15, 1935; "Novye postanovki evreiskogo teatra," *Vecherniaia Moskva*, January 11, 1936; "V Gosete," *Literaturnaia gazeta*, February 14, 1936; "Shefstvo teatra," *Krasnaia zvezda*, February 5, 1936.

22. Barukh A. Hazan, *Soviet Propaganda: A Case Study of the Middle East Conflict* (Jerusalem: Keter, 1976).

23. RGALI, f. 2307, op. 2, d. 460 (libretto for *Wailing Wall*).

24. G. Ryklin, "Stena placha," *Pravda*, November 25, 1935.

25. Em. Beskin, "Stena placha," *Rabochaia Moskva*, November 29, 1935; S. Levman, "Stena placha," *Sovetskaia torgovlia*, December 13, 1935; V. Potapov, "Stena placha," *Sovetskoe iskusstvo*, December 5, 1935; A. Moiseev, "Stena placha," *Leningradskaia pravda*, May 16, 1935; Is. Kats and Ia. Sinelnikov, "Stena placha," *Rabochii put* (Smolensk), June 6, 1936.

26. I. Berezark, "Stena placha," *Krasnaia gazeta*, May 14, 1935.

27. E. J. Hobsbawm, *Bandits* (London: Weidenfeld and Nicolson, 1969), 13.

28. Jeffrey Brooks, *When Russia Learned to Read* (Princeton: Princeton University Press, 1985), 166–213.

29. See Barbara Kirshenblatt-Gimblett, "Contraband: Performance, Text and Analysis of a Purim-Shpil," *The Drama Review*, 24, no. 3 (September 1980): 8–9.

30. Hobsbawm, *Bandits*, 34–36.

31. Matvei Geizer, *Solomon Mikhoels* (Moscow: Prometei, 1990), 138–39.

32. Moyshe Kulbak, *Oysgeklibene shriftn* (Buenos Aires: Ateneo Literario, 1976), 157–226: 205.

33. Ibid., 157–226; RGALI, f. 2307, op. 2, d. 439, ll. 76–79.

34. For some works dealing with the social strife within the *kahal* see Jacob Katz, *Tradition and Crisis: Jewish Society at the End of the Middle Ages* (New York: New York University Press, 1993) and Raphael Mahler, *Hasidism and the Jewish Enlightenment*.

35. Solomon Mikhoels, "Razboinik Boitre," *Izvestiia*, October 9, 1936.

36. Iakov Grinvald, "Razboinik Boitre," *Vecherniaia Moskva*, October 13, 1936. See also O. Litovskii, "Razboinik Boitre v Goset," *Sovetskoe iskusstvo*, October 17, 1936.

37. A. Gofman, "Razboinik Boitre," *Zvezda*, July 7, 1936.

38. Isidor Kleiner, "Razboinik Boitre v evreiskom teatre," *Za kommunisticheskoe prosveshchenie*, October 20, 1936. See also S. Levman, "Razboinik Boitre," *Sovetskaia torgovlia*, October 21, 1936; A. Moiseev, "Razboinik Boitre" *Leningradskaia pravda*, May 22, 1936; V. Golubov, "Razboinik Boitre," *Izvestiia*, October 14, 1936; and E. Dobin, "Radostnoe dostizhenie goseta," *Literaturnaia Leningrad*, May 24, 1936.

39. Grinvald, "Razboinik Boitre."

40. Levman, "Razboinik Boitre."

41. Golubov, "Razboinik Boitre."

42. I. Berezark, "Razboinik Boitre," *Krasnaia gazeta,* May 9, 1936; O. Litovskii, "Razboinik Boitre."

43. *Vecherniaia gazeta* (Petrograd), March 16, 1918.

44. Iakov Grinvald, "Gershele Ostropoler," *Vecherniaia Moskva,* May 10, 1937. See also "Gershele Ostropoler," *Kurskaia pravda,* June 22, 1937.

45. A. Khasin, "Hershele Ostropoler," *Der emes,* June 6, 1937.

46. For Kaganovich's biography see Stuart Kahan, *The Wolf of the Kremlin* (New York: William Morrow and Company, 1987).

47. Cited in Yosef Sheyn, *Arum moskver yidishn teater* (Paris: Commission du plan d'action culturelle, 1964), 148.

48. Ibid., 148–49.

49. Irving Howe, Ruth R. Wisse, and Khone Shmeruk, *The Penguin Book of Modern Yiddish Verse* (New York: Viking Penguin, 1987), 379.

50. Gennadi Kostyrchenko, *V plenu u krasnogo faraona* (Moscow: Mezhdunarodnye otnosheniia, 1994), 14.

51. Solomon Mikhoels, "Undzer grunt problemen," *Der emes,* March 22, 1938.

52. Iakov Grinvald, *Mikhoels: kratkii kritiko-biograficheskii ocherk* (Moscow: Der Emes, 1948), 72.

53. See, for instance, George L. Mosse, *The Image of Man: The Creation of Modern Masculinity* (New York: Oxford University Press, 1996), 107–132.

54. For the Zionist creation of the New Jewish Man see Michael Berkowitz, *Zionist Culture and West European Jewry before the First World War* (Cambridge: Cambridge University Press, 1993).

55. Nakhman Mayzel, *Dos Yiddishe shafn un der yidisher shrayber in Sovetnfarband* (New York: Yidisher Kultur Farband, 1959), 253.

56. A. Gurshtein, *Izbrannye stati* (Moscow: Sovetskii pisatel, 1959), 181.

57. Ch. Shmeruk, "Yiddish Literature in the U. S. S. R.," in Lionel Kochan, ed., *The Jews in Soviet Russia since 1917* (London: Oxford University Press, 1970), 250–51.

58. Tamar Alexander, "'The Weasel and the Well': Intertextual Relationships Between Hebrew Sources and Judeo-Spanish Stories," *Jewish Studies Quarterly* 5, no. 3 (1998): 257. See also Zipora Kagan, *Me-agadah le-siporet modernit bi-yetsirat Berdits'evski* (Kibbutz hameuchad: Kibbutz hameuchad publishing, 1983), 95–114.

59. While the legend itself never appears in the Talmud, a reference is made to it in Ta'anit 8a of the Babylonian Talmud. The Hebrew version of the legend tells of a rat and a well. However, in English it has conventionally been changed to a wildcat or weasel. The earliest written version of the fable was composed by Nathan ben Jehiel of Rome in the eleventh century. A new version was later written by Goldfadn's grandfather, Eli Mordecai Werbel, in 1852.

60. Taanit 8a.

61. Shmuel Halkin, *Shulamis* (Moscow: Der Emes, 1940), 4.

62. Ibid., 9–10.

63. See the commentary on Lekh Lekha in *Midrash Tanhuma* and *Sefer ha-yashar.* Also Louis Ginzburg, *Legends of the Jews,* Book 1, 221–22.

64. Halkin, *Shulamis,* 18.

65. "Stenogramma," "Sulamif." IGTAM, uncatalogued.

66. Ia. Eidelman, "Sulamif v gosudarstvennom evreiskom teatre," *Literaturnaia gazeta,* May 10, 1937.

67. M. Zh[ivov], "Sulamif," *Izvestiia,* April 16, 1937. See also I. Bachelis, "Sulamif,"

unidentified press clipping from IGTAM, P. 27; and A. Anastasev, et al., eds., *Istoriia sovetskogo dramaticheskogo teatra,* 6 vols. (Moscow: Institut istoriia iskusstv, 1966), 4: 636.

68. Moshe Litvakov, "Shulamis," *Der emes,* May 20, 1937.

69. Moshe Litvakov, "Shulamis," *Der emes,* May 15, 1937.

70. Em. Beskin, "Sulamif," *Vecherniaia Moskva,* April 13, 1937.

71. Efim Dobin, "Goset na novykh putiakh," unidentified press clipping from IGTAM, G. 1.

72. V. Vitebskii, "Sulamif v Goset," *Sovetskoe iskusstvo,* February 11, 1937.

73. V. Potapov, "Proshloe i nastoiashchee Goset," *Sovetskoe iskusstvo,* June 11, 1937. Incidentally, prior to the murder of Mikhoels a decade later, when the Ministry of State Security was working out a scenario for a show trial instead of a murder, the director's preference for Tyshler over Ryndin was to be one of the central pieces of evidence proving his Jewish nationalism. Lidiia Shatunovskaia, who was arrested in 1947, recounts how during her interrogation, she was asked to confirm this. Shatunovskaia replied to her interrogator with the question, "Are you sure Ryndin is Russian?" to which the surprised interrogator replied, "You think he is Jewish?" Having no idea whether this was indeed the case, Shatunovskaia silenced her adversary by remarking, "I am not sure, but it sounds very close to the Jewish names, Gyndin and Myndin." Lidiia Shatunovskaia, *Zhizn v kremle* (New York: Chalidze, 1982), 342. The author incorrectly identifies Ryndin as an artist for the Bolshoi theater and incorrectly identifies *Shulamis* as the first production directed by Mikhoels.

74. Yael Zerubavel, *Recovered Roots: Collective Memory and the Making of Israeli National Tradition* (Chicago: University of Chicago Press, 1995), 96.

75. Shmuel Halkin, *Bar-Kokhba* (Moscow: Der Emes, 1939), 8. For Josephus's interpretation see *War of the Jews,* Book IV, Chapter IX.

76. RGALI, f. 2307, op. 2, d. 462.

77. M. Shekhter, "Obraz Bar-Kokhby," *Dekada Mosk. zrelishch* (1938), no. 19.

78. M. Zhivov, "Pesa o Bar Kokhbe," *Sovetskoe iskusstvo,* March 24, 1938. See also B. Borisov, "Bar-Kokhba," *Voroshilovgradskaia pravda,* August 3, 1939; Gr. Slutskii, "Bar Kokhba," *Krasnoe znamia* (Kharkov), July 16, 1939; A. Gurshteyn, "Bar Kokhba," *Der emes,* March 24, 1938 and March 27, 1938.

79. Iakov Grinvald, "Bar Kokhba," *Vecherniaia Moskva,* n.d. 1938.

80. V. Potapov, "Bar Kokhba," *Izvestiia,* May 28, 1938.

81. G. Ryklin, "Bar-Kokhba," *Pravda,* March 26, 1938.

82. Halkin, *Bar Kokhba,* 5.

83. Ibid., 6.

84. Ibid., 49.

85. Ibid., 54.

86. Ibid., 107.

87. Ibid., 50.

88. Ibid., 52.

89. Ibid., 58.

90. Ibid.

91. Zhivov, "Pesa"; Potapov, "Bar-Kokhba."

92. Potapov, "Bar Kokhba."

93. Zhivov, "Pesa."

94. Gurshteyn, "Bar Kokhba."

95. Halkin, *Bar-Kokhba,* 127. Halkin had used this same parable before to express his ambivalence toward his Soviet homeland. The pledge of allegiance in his 1923 poem *Russia*

is tempered by the final line which declares: "But now we have fallen in step with you / Though of your kisses we die."

96. Wendy Goldman, *Women, the State and Revolution: Soviet Family Policy and Social Life, 1917–1936* (Cambridge: Cambridge University Press, 1993), 296–343.

97. Clark, *The Soviet Novel*, 86.

98. David Bergelson, "Freylekhs," *Der emes*, August 30, 1945.

99. "Puti goseta," *Sovetskoe iskusstvo*, October 23, 1936.

100. For more on Birobidzhan see Robert Weinberg, *Stalin's Forgotten Zion: Birobidzhan and the Making of a Soviet Jewish Homeland—An Illustrated History, 1928–1996* (Berkeley: University of California Press, 1998).

101. V. P. Naumov, *Nepravednyi sud. Poslednii stalinskii rasstrel* (Moscow: Nauk, 1994), 64–65.

102. See for example Solomon Mikhoels, "Novaia zemlia," *Sovetskoe iskusstvo*, October 17, 1937.

103. Peretz Markish, *Semia Ovadis*, translated from Yiddish by M. A. Shambadal (Moscow-Leningrad: Iskusstvo, 1938), 42.

104. Ibid., 70.

105. Ibid., 79–80.

106. Clark, *The Soviet Novel*, 87, 116.

107. S. Nels, "Tema Mikhoelsa," *Teatr* 2–3 (February–March) 1939: 163.

108. Peretz Markish, *Mikhoels* (Moscow: Der Emes, 1939), 27.

109. Dobin, "Goset na novykh putiakh."

110. M. Zhivov, "Semia Ovadis," *Sovetskoe iskusstvo*, December 17, 1937. See also M. Anatolev, "Semia Ovadis," *Voroshilovgradskaia pravda*, September 5, 1939; I. Levi, "Semia Ovadis," *Krasnoe znamia*, July 6, 1939; A. Zorin, "Semia Ovadis," *Komsomolets donbassa*, April 12, 1939; S. Dorminov, "Semia Ovadis," *Rabochaia Moskva*, December 16, 1937; I. K., "Semia Ovadis," *Vecherniaia Moskva*, November 16, 1937; S. Z., "Semia Ovadis," *Izvestiia*, November 15, 1937.

111. Iakov Goroskoi, "Semia Ovadis," *Sovetskaia Ukraina* (Kiev), July 5, 1938. Despite this praise, after Markish was arrested in 1949 he was forced to renounce the play for "nationalist deviations," a crime for which the author was executed. Naumov, *Nepravednyi sud*, 70.

112. Cited in M. Zhivov, "Mechty i stradaniia Teve-Molochnika," *Teatr* 1 (January) 1939: 117.

113. Ibid., 118.

114. "Blizhaishie zadachi goseta," *Bolshevistskoe znamia* (Odessa), July 23, 1938.

115. See Zachary M. Baker, "Yiddish in Form and Socialist in Content: The Observance of Sholem Aleichem's Eightieth Birthday in the Soviet Union," *YIVO Annual* 23 (1996): 209–231.

116. Zhivov, "Mechty i stradaniia," 122.

117. Ibid.

118. Jacob Weitzner, *Sholem Aleichem in the Theater* (Madison, Wis.: Fairleigh Dickinson University Press, 1994), 89.

119. Nels, "Tema Mikhoelsa," 169.

120. Mikhoels, "Tevye Molochnik," *Vecherniaia Moskva*, October 21, 1938; See also *Ogonek* no. 35/36 (1938).

121. "Doklada narodnogo artista SSSR tov. Mikhoels na zasedanii delegatov evreiskoi konferentsii organizovannoi vsesoiuznym domom narodnogo tvorchestvo. 13 XII 1939," IGTAM, uncatalogued.

122. Weitzner, *Sholem Aleichem*, 89.

123. Moshe Beregovskii, "Kegnzaytike virkungen tsvishn dem ukrainishn un idishn muzik-folklor," *Visenshaft un revoliutsie 2*, no. 6 (April–June 1935): 79–101.

124. Katerina Clark, *Petersburg: Crucible of Cultural Revolution* (Cambridge, Mass.: Harvard University Press, 1995), 212–23.

125. See Boris Groys, "From Internationalism to Cosmopolitanism: Artists of Jewish Descent in the Stalin Era," in Susan Tumarkin Goodman, ed., *Russian Jewish Artists in a Century of Change, 1890–1990* (Munich: Prestel, 1995), 81–84.

126. For glowing reviews see B. Liberman, "Zamechatelnii spektakl," *Komsomolskaia pravda*, December 30, 1938; A. Gurvich, "Tevye Molochnik," *Trud*, December 26, 1938; Iakov Grinvald, "Tevye Molochnik," *Vecherniaia Moskva*, December 2, 1938; B. Rozanov, "Tevye Molochnik," *Izvestiia*, December 1, 1938; Bor. Valee, "Tevye Molochnik," *Leningradskaia pravda*, March 29, 1938.

127. Kh. Tokar, "Tvorcheskaia udacha," *Sovetskaia Ukraina* (Kiev), July 15, 1938.

128. M. Khashchevatskii, "Tevye Molochnik," *Krasnoe znamia*, June 5, 1941. See also B. Borisov, "Tevye der milkhiker," *Voroshilovgradskaia pravda*, July 27, 1939; V. Morskoi, "Tevye molochnik," *Krasnoe znamia*, July 4, 1939.

129. Ia. Eidelman, "Tevye Molochnik v gosudarstvennom evreiskom teatre," *Robochaia Moskva*, January 6, 1939.

130. Markish, *Mikhoels*, 27.

131. Itzik Fefer, "Premiere Tevye der Milkhiker inem moskver melukhisn yidishn teater," *Der emes*, July 16, 1938.

132. "Tevye Molochnik," *Radio-programmy*, November 23, 1939.

133. A. S. Baslavskii, "Evreiskii teatr v dvortse kultury," *Dognat i peregnat*, February 24, 1940.

6. One Generation Passes Away

1. "Stenogramma torzhestvennogo zasedaniia posviashchennogo dvatsatiletniiu gosudarstvennogo evreiskogo teatra," IGTAM, uncatalogued, 10.

2. "Ibid.," 18.

3. Kessel, "Radost evreiskogo naroda," *Za tiazheloe mashinostroenie* (Sverlovsk), April 14, 1939.

4. "Sumbur vmesto muzyka," *Pravda*, January 28, 1936; "Baletnaia falsh," *Pravda*, February 6, 1936; "O khudozhnikakh," *Pravda*, March 2, 1936.

5. Iakov Etinger, "The Doctors' Plot: Stalin's Solution to the Jewish Question," in Yaacov Ro'i, ed., *Jews and Jewish Life in Russia and the Soviet Union* (Essex: Frank Cass & Co., 1995), 103.

6. Terry Martin, "The Origins of Soviet Ethnic Cleansing," *Journal of Modern History* 70 (December 1998): 853.

7. V. P. Naumov, *Nepravednyi sud. Poslednii stalinskii rasstrel* (Moscow: Nauk, 1994), 83.

8. For recent studies of the purge process see J. Arch Getty and Roberta Manning, eds., *Stalinist Terror* (New York: Cambridge University Press, 1993); J. Arch Getty, *Origins of the Great Purges: The Soviet Communist Party Reconsidered, 1933–1938* (Cambridge: Cambridge University Press, 1985); Sheila Fitzpatrick, *Stalin's Peasants: Resistance and Survival in the Russian Village after Collectivization* (New York: Oxford University Press, 1994); Robert W. Thurston, *Life and Terror in Stalin's Russia, 1934–1941* (New Haven: Yale University Press, 1996).

9. "Dos ovnt funem Iudvokans in emes," *Der emes*, February 9, 1936.

10. "Fragn fun yidisher muzik un gezang," *Der emes,* May 9, 1937.

11. A. D. Mirol, "Ver ufmerkzamkayt der yidisher muzik," *Der emes,* July 18, 1937.

12. "Kegn formalizm un naturalizm in teater," *Der emes,* March 24, 1936.

13. "Vystuplenie v komitete po delam iskusstv 1936–37 g," IGTAM, uncatalogued, 7.

14. "Puti goseta," *Sovetskoe iskusstvo,* October 23, 1936.

15. "Vystuplenie." See also Solomon Mikhoels, *Stati, besedy, rechi* (Moscow: Iskusstvo, 1965), 90–93.

16. "Vystuplenie," 6.

17. "Stenogramma torzhestvennogo zasedaniia posviashchennogo dvatsatiletniiu gosudarstvennogo evreiskogo teatra," IGTAM, uncatalogued, 2–3.

18. Samuel Halkin, "Iubilei Goseta," March 20, 1939, unidentified newspaper clipping, IGTAM, G2 (Goset colletion).

19. I. Nusinov, "Dvadtsat let Goset," *Sovetskoe iskusstvo,* March 7, 1939. See also Kh. Tokar, "Moskovskii gosudarstvennyi evreiskii teatr," *Sovetskaia Ukraina,* March 29, 1939; Peretz Markish, "Dvadtsatiletie Goseta," *Pravda,* March 29, 1939; Iakov Grinvald, "Put teatra," *Vecherniaia Moskva,* March 29, 1939; Aleksandr Deich, "Put Goseta," *Izvestiia sovetov deputatov trudiashchikhsia SSSR,* March 20, 1939.

20. Solomon Mikhoels, "20 let moskovskogo gosudarstvennogo evreiskogo teatra," *Kurotnye izvestiia* (Crimea), February 3, 1939. See also Solomon Mikhoels, "20 let moskovskogo gosudarsvennogo evreiskogo teatra," *Rabochaia Moskva,* January 25, 1939.

21. "Stenogramma torzhestvennogo," 4.

22. Ibid., 5.

23. Kh. Tokar, "Demonstratsiia druzhby narodov," *Sovetskaia Ukraina,* April 2, 1939.

24. Komitet po delam iskusstv pri SNK soiuza SSR, *Rezhisser v sovetskom teatre* (Moscow: Iskusstvo, 1940), 14.

25. Solomon Mikhoels, *Stati, besedy, rechi* (Moscow: Iskusstvo, 1965), 201–218.

26. Joseph Macleod, *The New Soviet Theatre* (London: George Allen & Unwin, 1943), 18.

27. "Postanovlenie o likvidatsii teatra im. Vs. Meierkholda," *Teatr* 1 (January 1938): 5.

28. "Okonchanie gastrolei moskovskogo Goseta," *Dnepropetrovskaia pravda,* June 30, 1939; Io. Zhernovoi, "Vstrecha artistov Goset so stakhanovtsami," August 4, 1939, unidentified press clipping, IGTAM, G1.

29. A. Baslavskii, "Goset," *Voroshilovgradskaia pravda,* July 22, 1939.

30. Solomon Mikhoels, "K nashim zriteliam," *Voroshilovgradskaia pravda,* July 22, 1939.

31. Katerina Clark, *Petersburg: Crucible of Cultural Revolution* (Cambridge, Mass.: Harvard University Press, 1995), 212–23.

32. Natalia Vovsi-Mikhoels, *Mon père Salomon Mikhoels: souvenirs sur sa vie et sur sa mort,* trans. Erwin Spatz (Montricher, Switzerland: Les Editions Noir sur Blanc, 1990), 131.

33. Ibid., 135.

34. Yosef Sheyn, *Arum moskver yidishn teater* (Paris: Commission du plan d'action culturelle, 1964), 127–38.

35. Cited in Mordecai Altshuler, "The Jewish Anti-Fascist Committee in the USSR in Light of New Documentation," in Jonathan Frankel, ed., *Studies in Contemporary Jewry* (Bloomington: Indiana University Press, 1984), 1: 265.

36. Vitaly Shentalinsky, *The KGB's Literary Archive,* trans. John Crowfoot (London: Harvill Press, 1995), 34, 47.

37. "Sterets litsa zemli predatelei rodiny," *Sovetskoe iskusstvo,* March 1938.

38. Vovsi-Mikhoels, *Mon père,* 132.

39. Mikhoels, *Stati,* 178.

40. Ben Zion Goldberg, *The Jewish Problem in the Soviet Union: An Analysis and a Solution* (New York: Crown Publishers, 1961), 60.

41. Komitet po delam iskusstv pri SNK soiuza SSR, *Rezhisser v sovetskom teatre,* 73–74.

42. RGALI, f. 2307, op. 1, d. 5 (orders from Committee of Artistic Affairs to Moscow State Yiddish Theater, January 4, 1939–August 29, 1939), ll. 16, 32.

43. "Novye spektakli v Goset," *Sovetskoe iskusstvo,* April 16, 1938.

44. "V partiorganizatsii Goset," *Sovetskoe iskusstvo,* November 2, 1938.

45. Baslavskii, "Goset."

46. "Repertuarnyi plan evreiskogo teatra," *Sovetskoe iskusstvo,* May 5, 1938. See also "Repertuarnyi plan Goset," *Sovetskoe iskusstvo,* January 16, 1939.

47. RGALI, f. 2307, op. 2., d. 439 (foreign-language librettos, 1922–1944), ll. 106–107.

48. G. Ryklin, "Bespokoinaia starost," *Pravda,* November 12, 1938. See also M. Zhivov, "Bespokoinaia starost v Gosete," *Sovetskoe iskusstvo,* November 20, 1938.

49. "Po novomu ustavu," *Sovetskoe iskusstvo,* April 27, 1939.

50. For biographical information, including Party affiliation of all members of the troupe, see RGALI, f. 2307, op. 1, dd. 87–104 (personal files of employees of the Moscow State Yiddish Theater).

51. Solomon Mikhoels, "Undzer grunt problemen," *Der emes,* March 22, 1938.

52. Benjamin Zuskin, "Dvadtsat let Goseta," *Teatr* 5 (May 1939): 67.

53. "Dvadtsatyi sezon Goset," *Sovetskoe iskusstvo,* September 26, 1938; "Repertuarnyi plan Goset," *Sovetskoe iskusstvo,* 6 Jan 1939.

54. Nakhman Mayzel, *Dos Yiddishe shafn un der yidisher shrayber in sovetnfarband* (New York: Yidisher Kultur Farband, 1959), 203.

55. Peretz Markish, *Dor oys dor ayn,* 2 vols. (1929; reprint, Warsaw: Yidish Bukh, 1964).

56. Ibid., Vol. 2, 15.

57. RGALI, f. 2307, op. 2, d. 439, ll. 118–23.

58. S. Levman, "Pir," *Moskovskii bolshevik,* December 2, 1939.

59. Iogann Altman, "Rozhdenie muzhestva," *Izvestiia,* December 4, 1939.

60. Solomon An-sky, "Khurbn," in *Gezamelte shriftn,* 4: 85–87. See also Aviel Roshwald, "Jewish Cultural Identity in Eastern and Central Europe during the Great War," in Aviel Roshwald and Richard Stites, eds., *European Culture in the Great War: The Arts, Entertainment, and Propaganda, 1914–1918* (Cambridge: Cambridge University Press, 1999), 94.

61. Altman, "Rozhdenie muzhestva."

62. G. Ryklin, "Novyi spektakl v Gosete," *Pravda,* December 16, 1939; V. Potapov, "Obilnyi Pir," *Literaturnaia gazeta,* January 10, 1940. For less enthusiastic reviews see Iakov Grinvald, "Pir," *Vecherniaia Moskva,* December 3, 1939; Kh. Tokar, "Pir," *Sovetskaia Ukraina,* August 9, 1940.

63. "Bluzhdaiushchie zvezdy na stsene," *Vecherniaia Moskva,* November 19, 1939.

64. RGALI, f. 2307, op. 2, d. 439, ll. 108–117.

65. Iakov Grinvald, "Arn Fridman," *Vecherniaia Moskva,* January 10, 1940.

66. I. Berezark, "Realizm i uslovnost," unidentified newpaper clipping, IGTAM, G1.

For a more positive review see I. Avin, "Arn Fridman," *Birobidzhanskaia zvezda,* January 27, 1940.

67. "Gastroli Goseta na Ukraine," *Sovetskoe iskusstvo,* July 4, 1940.

68. For a picaresque account of Maimon's life, see his popular autobiography, published in 1792–1793; for an English translation see *Solomon Maimon: An Autobiography,* ed. and trans. Moses Hadas (1947; reprint, New York: Schocken Books, 1967).

69. RGALI, f. 2307, op. 2, d. 439, ll. 124–33.

70. Solomon Mikhoels, "Nashi premery," *Izvestiia,* September 28, 1940; see also Solomon Mikhoels, "Geroi, volnuiushchie moe voobrazhdenie," *Vecherniaia Moskva,* October 5, 1940.

71. I. Bachelis, "Solomon Maimon," *Izvestiia,* November 17, 1940.

72. M. Khashchevatskii, "Solomon Maimon," *Krasnoe znamia* (Kharkov), June 6, 1941. See also V. Potapov, "Dela i mysli," *Literaturnaia gazeta,* October 27, 1940; G. Ryklin, "Solomon Maimon," *Pravda,* November 4, 1940; Bachelis, "Solomon Maimon"; S. Zamanskii, "Solomon Maimon v Gosete," *Sovetskoe iskusstvo,* October 27, 1940. For more favorable reviews see L. Nakhlev, "Solomon Maimon," *Bezbozhnik,* November 20, 1940; Lev Kvitko, "Solomon Maimon," *Komsomolskaia pravda,* December 26, 1940.

73. Ia. Eidelman, "Dva spektaklia," *Moskovskii bolshevik,* December 17, 1940.

74. S. Zamanskii, "Solomon Maimon."

75. Lulla Adler Rosenfeld, *The Yiddish Theatre and Jacob P. Adler* (1977; reprint, New York: Shapolsky Publishers, 1988), 48.

76. Avraam Goldfadn, *Di beyde kuni-lemels. operete in 4 akten un 8 bilder* (New York: Hebrew Publishing Company, 1901).

77. S. Valerin, "Tsvei Kunileml," *Vecherniaia Moskva,* December 17, 1940; Ia. Eidelman, "Dva spektaklia."

78. A. Gurstein, "Grustnye pazmyshleniia," *Literaturnaia gazeta,* January 12, 1941.

79. G. Roshal, "Tsvei Kunileml," *Sovetskoe iskusstvo,* December 29, 1940.

80. M. Khashchevatskii, "Tsvei Kunileml," *Krasnoe znamia,* June 13, 1941; see also S. Valerin, "Tsvei Kunileml."

81. Sholem Aleichem, *Wandering Stars,* in David S. Lifson, ed. and trans., *Epic and Folk Plays of the Yiddish Theatre* (Rutherford, N.J.: Fairleigh Dickinson, 1975), 16–58.

82. I. Bachelis, "Bluzhdaiushchie zvezdy," *Sovetskoe iskusstvo,* September 18, 1941.

83. "Bluzhdaiushchie zvezdy," *Krasnoe znamia,* June 11, 1941. See also V. Potapov, "Bluzhdaiushchie zvezdy," *Literaturnaia gazeta,* September 17, 1941.

84. S. Zamanskii, "Bluzhdaiushchie zvezdy," *Vecherniaia Moskva,* September 16, 1941.

85. RGALI, f. 2307, op. 1, d. 40 (orders from Committee of Artistic Affairs to Moscow State Yiddish Theater, 1947), ll. 310, 340.

86. "Goset v 1940 godu," *Sovetskoe iskusstvo,* December 9, 1939.

87. S. M. Mikhoels, "*Ispantsy* Lermontova," *Teatralnaia nedelia* 16 (1941).

88. L. Grossman, "Lermontov v evreiskom teatre," *Sovetskoe iskusstvo* (May 11, 1941); and A. Novikov, "*Ispantsy* Lermontova," *Teatralnaia nedelia* 18 (1941).

89. Cited in Altshuler, "The Jewish Anti-Fascist Committee," 257.

90. Matvei Geizer, *Solomon Mikhoels* (Moscow: Prometei, 1990), 146.

91. RGALI, f. 2307, op. 1, d. 7 (contracts with writers, musicians, etc., 1940–1944), l. 1.

92. Solomon Mikhoels, "Geroi, volnuiushchie moe voobrazhenie," *Vecherniaia Moskva,* October 5, 1940.

93. Cited in Geizer, *Solomon Mikhoels,* 146.

94. Jan Kott, *Shakespeare, Our Contemporary*, trans. Boleslaw Taborski (1964; reprint, New York: W.W. Norton, 1974), 5.

95. Ibid., 10.

96. Ibid., 17.

97. Ibid., 23.

98. James Norris Loehlin, "Playing Politics: Richard III in Recent Performance," *Performing Arts Journal* 15, no. 3 (September 1993): 80–94.

99. *Izvestiia*, April 1, 1939.

100. RGALI, f. 2307, op. 1, d. 4 (orders from Committee of Artistic Affairs to Moscow Jewish Theater, 1939–1949), l. 1.

101. M. Belenkii, "A shul fun aktiorishe kadren," *Der emes*, July 5, 1938.

102. Vovsi-Mikhoels, *Mon père*, 136.

103. Cited in Altshuler, "The Jewish Anti-Fascist Committee," 256.

104. Levin, *The Jews in the Soviet Union*, 219–20; Vaksberg, *Stalin against the Jews*.

105. Aleksandr Nekrich, *"June 22, 1941": Soviet Historians and the German Invasion*, trans. Vladimir Petrov (Columbia: University of South Carolina Press, 1968); Alexander Werth, *Russia at War, 1941–1945* (London: Pan Books, 1965).

106. Getty and Manning, *Stalinist Terror*; Gabor Tamas Rittersporn, *Stalinist Simplifications and Soviet Complications: Social Tension and Political Conflicts in the USSR, 1933–1953* (Chur, Switzerland: Harwood Academic Publishers, 1991); Getty, *Origins of the Great Purges*.

7. Brother Jews

1. Iakov Grinvald, *Mikhoels: kratkii kritiko-biograficheskii ocherk* (Moscow: Der Emes, 1948), 76.

2. See Jan Gross, "The Jewish Community in Soviet-Annexed Territories on the Eve of the Holocaust," in Lucjan Dobroszycki and Jeffrey S. Gurock, eds., *The Holocaust in the Soviet Union* (Armonk, N.Y.: M. E. Sharpe, 1993): 156.

3. Cited in Alexander Werth, *Russia at War, 1941–45* (London: Pan Books, 1965), 173.

4. The Jewish Anti-Fascist Committee, however, was evacuated to Kuibyshev together with most governmental institutions. Mikhoels initially went with the Anti-Fascist Committee but soon joined the theater in Tashkent.

5. Shimon Redlich, *War, Holocaust and Stalinism: A Documented Study of the Jewish Anti-Fascist Committee in the USSR* (Luxembourg: Harwood Academic Publishers, 1995); Shimon Redlich, *Propaganda and Nationalism in Wartime Russia: The Jewish Antifascist Committee in the USSR, 1941–1948* (Boulder: East European Quarterly, 1982); Mordecai Altshuler, "The Jewish Anti-Fascist Committee in the USSR in Light of New Documentation," in Jonathan Frankel, ed., *Studies in Contemporary Jewry* (Bloomington: Indiana University Press, 1984), 1: 253–91; Leonard Schapiro, "The Jewish Anti-Fascist Committee and Phases of Soviet Anti-Semitic Policy during and after World War II," in Bela Vago and George L. Mosse, ed. *Jews and Non-Jews in Eastern Europe, 1918–1945* (New York: Wiley, 1974); Yehoshua Gilboa, *The Black Years of Soviet Jewry*, trans. Dov Ben-Abba and Yosef Shachter (Boston: Little, Brown and Company, 1971), 42–86.

6. Benjamin Pinkus, *The Jews in the Soviet Union: The History of a National Minority* (Cambridge: Cambridge University Press, 1988), 195.

7. Redlich, *War, Holocaust, and Stalinism*, 3.

8. Cited in Leni Yahil, *The Holocaust: The Fate of European Jewry* (1985; reprint, Oxford: Oxford University Press, 1990), 606.

9. RTsKhIDNI, f. 17, op. 125, d. 35, ll. 64–65. English translation in Redlich, *War, Holocaust and Stalinism,* 173.

10. Mordechai Altshuler has argued that significant information about Nazi treatment of the Jews in the occupied territories reached the Russian interior rapidly through informal channels, particularly through the testimonies of refugees fleeing the occupied territories into Russia. See Mordechai Altshuler, "Escape and Evacuation of Soviet Jews at the Time of the Nazi Invasion: Policies and Realities," in Dobroszycki and Gurock, *The Holocaust,* 77–104.

11. *Brider yidn fun der gantser velt* (Moscow: Der Emes, 1941), 12.

12. Ibid., 9.

13. "Bratia evrei vsego mira," *Pravda,* August 25, 1941.

14. See Samuel A. Portnoy, trans., *Henryk Erlich and Victor Alter: Two Heroes and Martyrs for Jewish Socialism* (New York: Ktav Publishing House, 1990).

15. RGALI, f. 2693, op. 1, d. 195 (Mikhoels's correspondence on JAFC, 1941–1947).

16. *Pravda,* May 25, 1942. English translation in Redlich, *War, Holocaust and Stalinism,* 203.

17. H. D. Meritt to George Allen, January 11, 1945, NARA, RG 226, INT 18JE 140. The American cultural attaché in Moscow also noted an easing of Soviet anti-American propaganda in general. A report to the Secretary of State on the anniversary of the Revolution noted that "special effort was made to show courtesies and display friendliness to the Americans, the British and the Japanese." Henderson to Secretary of State, November 9, 1942, NARA, RG 59, 861.00/11964.

18. Meritt to Allen.

19. Chaim Weizmann, *The Letters and Papers of Chaim Weizmann* (Jerusalem: Israel Universities Press), 20: 196. While the Jewish Anti-Fascist Committee was aware of Weizmann's support, it is not clear whether Weizmann's letter actually reached the Committee.

20. Summaries of Jewish press, October 8, 1942, NARA, RG 226, INT 18JE 177.

21. Ibid.

22. Dickerson to Jewish Daily Forward, December 19, 1941, NARA, RG 59, 861.00/11921.5; J. Baskin to Secretary of State, December 19, 1941, NARA, RG 59, 861.00/11925; William Green to Secretary of State, NARA, RG 59, 861.00/11926.

23. Breckenridge Long to Mrs. Roosevelt, January 29, 1942, NARA, RG 59, 861.00/11927; Breckenridge Long to William Green, January 28, 1942, NARA, RG 59, 861.00/11931.5.

24. Maksim Litvinov to William Green, February 23, 1943, NARA, RG 59, 861.00/11986.

25. Redlich, *War, Holocaust and Stalin,* 165–71; Lukasz Hirszowicz, "NKVD Documents Shed New Light on Fate of Erlich and Alter," *East European Jewish Affairs* 22, no. 2 (1992): 65–85.

26. Report from Office of Strategic Services Foreign Nationalities Branch to A. A. Berle, NARA, RG 59, 861.00/11997. See also Portnoy, *Henryk Erlich,* 194–232.

27. Cited in Lukasz Hirszowicz, "The Soviet Union and the Jews during World War II: British Foreign Office Documents," *Soviet Jewish Affairs* 3, no. 1 (1973): 107.

28. GARf, f. 8114, op. 1, d. 792 (Shakhno Ephshteyn to A. S. Shcherbakov, August 18, 1942). For an English translation see Redlich, *War, Holocaust and Stalinism,* 315.

29. V. P. Naumov, *Nepravednyi sud. Poslednii stalinskii rasstrel* (Moscow: Nauk, 1994), 170.

30. CAHJP, P. 166, B. 139 (Mikhoels to Anastasia Pototskaia, March 1943). English translation in Redlich, *War, Holocaust and Stalinism,* 306.

31. Interview with Natalia Vovsi-Mikhoels, Tel Aviv, August 13, 1995.

32. Gennadi Kostyrchenko, *V plenu u krasnogo faraona: politicheskie presledovaniia evreev v SSSR v poslednee stalinskoe desiatiletie* (Moscow: Mezhdunarodnye otnosheniia, 1994), 38.

33. CAHJP, P. 166, B. 155 (Mikhoels to Pototskaia).

34. Naumov, *Nepravednyi sud,* 171.

35. Ben Zion Goldberg, *The Jewish Problem in the Soviet Union: An Analysis and a Solution* (New York: Crown Publishers, 1961), 47.

36. CAHJP, P. 166, B. 139.

37. Cited in Hirszowicz, "The Soviet Union and the Jews," 110. For American intelligence see Report from Foreign Nationalities Branch of Office of Strategic Services, August 14, 1943, NARA, RG 226, INT 18JE 252.

38. Interview with Natalia Vovsi-Mikhoels, Tel Aviv, August 13, 1995.

39. Abraham Sutzkever, "Mit Shlomo Mikhoels," *Di goldene keyt* 43 (1962): 164–165.

40. GARF, f. 8114, op. 1, d. 830, l. 40 (Fefer to his family, November 3, 1943). English translation in Redlich, *War, Holocaust and Stalinism,* 310.

41. "Soviet Delegates Urge Unity Here," *New York Times,* July 9, 1943. The U. S. Office of Strategic Services estimated attendance at "over 45,000 people." See Report from Office of Strategic Services, July 15, 1943, NARA, RG 226, INT 33RS 5.

42. CAHJP, P 166, Z 1 (British Jewish Fund for Soviet Russia letter).

43. *Pravda,* July 16, 1943. English translation in Redlich, *War, Holocaust and Stalinism,* 308.

44. Report from Office of Strategic Services.

45. Solomon Mikhoels, "Azoy hot tsu mir geredt der lebediker sholem aleykhem," *Eynikayt,* December 30, 1943.

46. "Visitors from Soviet Union Honored by Consul," *New York Times,* June 30, 1943.

47. Joseph Brainin to Franklin Roosevelt, July 5, 1943, NARA, RG 59, 711.61/908.

48. Sumner Welles, the undersecretary of state, had sent a statement to the April 4th mass meeting of the Committee of Jewish Writers and Artists. Chaim Zhitlovski to Sumner Welles, March 30, 1943, NARA, RG 59, 711.61/886. Later the White House discouraged a letter-writing campaign initiated by the Russian War Relief. See Edward Carter to Harry Hopkins, April 8, 1943, NARA, RG 59, 711.61/890.

49. "The Michoels-Feffer Mission," August 14, 1943, NARA, RG 226, INT 18JE 252.

50. Ibid.

51. Letter to Zacharia Shuster, July 15, 1943, NARA, RG 226, INT 18JE 247.

52. H. Rabinavicius to Office of Strategic Services, c. August 21, 1943, NARA, RG 226, INT 18JE 254.

53. Horace Marston to Mr. Poole, June 28, 1943, NARA, RG 226, INT 18JE 237.

54. OSS report, June 30, 1943, NARA, RG 226, INT 18JE 239.

55. H. Rabinavicius to Office of Strategic Services.

56. Cited in Hirszowicz, "The Soviet Union and the Jews," 109.

57. See for instance, "Closer Ties Urged with Soviet Union," *New York Times,* September 20, 1943.

58. Naumov, *Nepravednyi sud,* 300–301.

59. See Kostyrchenko, *V plenu,* 32–57; Shimon Redlich, *Propaganda and Nationalism in Wartime Russia: The Jewish Antifascist Committee in the USSR, 1941–1948* (Boulder: East European Quarterly, 1982), 130–33; Arkady Vaksberg, *Stalin against the Jews,* trans. An-

tonina W. Bouis (New York: Alfred A. Knopf, 1994), 121–32; Louis Rapoport, *Stalin's War against the Jews* (New York: Free Press, 1990), 98–127.

60. Chaim Weizmann, *The Letters and Papers of Chaim Weizmann*, 25 vols. (Jerusalem: Israel Universities Press, 1968–), Series B, Vol. 2, 509–510.

61. Meyer W. Weisgal, *Meyer Weisgal . . . So Far: An Autobiography* (London: Weidenfeld and Nicolson, 1971), 144–45.

62. Natalia Vovsi-Mikhoels, *Mon père Salomon Mikhoels: souvenirs sur sa vie et sur sa mort,* trans. Erwin Spatz (Montricher, Switzerland: Les Editions Noir sur Blanc, 1990), 196.

63. Kostyrchenko, *V plenu,* 354.

64. Redlich, *Propaganda,* 128.

65. Ibid., 146.

66. H. Rabinavicius to Office of Strategic Services.

67. Aharon Steinberg, "Mayn Dvinsker khaver Shlomo Mikhoels," *Di goldene keyt* 43 (1962): 142–52. Steinberg, a childhood friend of Mikhoels, acted as his interpreter at the London conference. See also Vovsi-Mikhoels, *Mon père,* 191.

68. Ibid., 192.

69. "Stennogramma doklada tov. Mikhoelsa," 49; and Solomon Mikhoels, *Stati, besedy, rechi* (Moscow: Iskusstvo, 1965), 283.

70 "Narodnyi artist S. M. Mikhoels," IGTAM, uncatalogued; "Stennogramma doklada tov. Mikhoelsa," 11–12; Mikhoels, *Stati,* 270–71.

71. O. Litovskii, *Tak i bylo* (Moscow: Sovetskii pisatel, 1958), 161.

72. Mikhoels, *Stati,* 271–72.

73. "Stenogramma doklada tov. Mikhoelsa," 28.

74. "Ibid.," 46.

75. Mikhoels, *Stati,* 275.

76. Ibid., 276.

77. Ibid., 280; CAHJP, P. 166, Z. 1.

78. "Stenogramma doklada tov. Mikhoelsa," 45; Mikhoels, *Stati,* 281.

79. "Stenogramma doklada tov. Mikhoelsa," 50–51.

80. Ibid., 52.

8. Our People Live

1. Cited in Alexander Werth, *Russia at War, 1941–1945* (London: Pan Books, 1965), 242.

2. Gennadi Kostyrchenko, *V plenu u krasnogo faraona: politicheskie presledovaniia evreev v SSSR v poslednee stalinskoe desiatiletie* (Moscow: Mezhdunarodnye otnosheniia, 1994), 23. The phrase was first used in the 1936 Soviet constitution.

3. See Richard Stites, ed., *Culture and Entertainment in Wartime Russia* (Bloomington: Indiana University Press, 1995).

4. See Harold B. Segel, "Drama of Struggle," in Stites, *Culture and Entertainment,* 108–125; See also his *Twentieth-Century Russian Drama,* 2nd ed. (Baltimore: Johns Hopkins University Press, 1993), 295–318.

5. Yehoshua Gilboa, *The Black Years of Soviet Jewry,* trans. Dov Ben-Abba and Yosef Shachter (Boston: Little, Brown and Company, 1971), 32–35; Ben Zion Goldberg, *The Jewish Problem in the Soviet Union: An Analysis and a Solution* (New York: Crown Publishers, 1961), 54–59.

6. RGALI, f. 2307, op. 1, d. 9 (orders from Committee of Artistic Affairs to Moscow State Yiddish Theater, December 18, 1941–December 28, 1942), l. 2.

7. RGALI, f. 2307, op. 1, d. 8 (orders from Committee of Artistic Affairs to Moscow State Yiddish Theater, November 19, 1941–September 20, 1943), ll. 6–7.

8. RGALI, f. 2307, op. 1, d. 13 (contracts with writers, musicians, etc., February 25, 1941–February 2, 1942), ll. 18–20.

9. Yon Barna, *Eisenstein: The Growth of a Cinematic Genius* (Bloomington: Indiana University Press, 1973), 229.

10. "Semia Oppengeim v moskovskom evreiskom teatre," *Vecherniaia Moskva,* August 30, 1941.

11. CAHJP, P. 166, F. 6 (Mikhoels to Lion Feuchtwanger).

12. Zvi Gitelman, "Soviet Reactions to the Holocaust," in Lucjan Dobroszycki and Jeffrey S. Gurock, eds., *The Holocaust in the Soviet Union* (Armonk, N.Y.: M. E. Sharpe, 1993): 3–27, 13–14.

13. Cited in Shimon Redlich, *War, Holocaust and Stalinism: A Documented Study of the Jewish Anti-Fascist Committee in the USSR* (Luxembourg: Harwood Academic Publishers, 1995), 350.

14. RGALI, f. 2307, op. 1, d. 19 (orders from Committee of Artistic Affairs to Moscow State Yiddish Theater, January 9, 1943–December 13, 1943), l. 33. The figure includes 122 theater workers, 115 dependents of theater workers, 11 instructors from the Yiddish theater school, and 38 students.

15. Kostyrchenko, *V plenu,* 15–16.

16. While the Jews constituted only 1.78 percent of the total population of the Soviet Union, they were awarded 2.5 percent of all medals for bravery in the Red Army. See I. Nusinov, "Di sovetishe yidishe kultur," *Eynikayt,* November 8, 1944.

17. At least sixty Jewish writers also volunteered to serve in the front, one-third of whom were killed, including Khashchevatskii, Godiner, Gurshteyn, and others. See Nusinov, "Di sovetishe yidishe kultur."

18. Iakov Grinvald, *Mikhoels: kratkii kritiko-biograficheskii ocherk* (Moscow: Der Emes, 1948), 82.

19. "Goset v Moskve," *Literatura i iskusstvo,* October 9, 1943.

20. "Postanovki Goseta," *Vecherniaia Moskva,* June 2, 1942.

21. Cited in A. Anastasev, et al., eds., *Istoriia sovetskogo dramaticheskogo teatra,* 6 vols. (Moscow: Institut istoriia iskusstv, 1966), 5: 668.

22. Khamid Alimdzhan, "Vozvrashchenie," *Pravda vostoka,* September 19, 1943.

23. RGALI, f. 2307, op. 1, d. 4 (orders from Committee of Artistic Affairs to Moscow State Yiddish Theater, 1939–1949), ll. 4–5.

24. Solomon Mikhoels, "Nashi tvorcheskie zamysly," *Pravda vostoka,* May 14, 1942.

25. Anastasev, *Istoriia sovetskogo,* 1: 288–306.

26. RGALI, f. 2307, op. 2, d. 439 (foreign-language librettos, 1922–1944), ll. 154–59.

27. "Pobeda teatra," *Pravda vostoka,* May 25, 1943.

28. "Goset v Moskve: beseda s V. Zuskina," *Literatura i iskusstva,* October 9, 1943.

29. I. Liubomirskii, "Khamza," *Eynikayt,* January 6, 1944.

30. Peretz Markish, *Oko za oko,* DRI, P-20/90, 1.

31. Ibid., 5.

32. Ibid., 7.

33. Ibid., 13.

34. RGALI, f. 2307, op. 1, d. 7 (contracts with writers, musicians, etc., 1940–1944), l. 3.

Notes to pages 240–249

35. RGALI, f. 2307, op. 1, d. 4, l. 10.

36. O. Liubomirskii, "A vunderlekhe geshikhte," *Eynikayt*, July 20, 1944.

37. Cited in Redlich, *War, Holocaust and Stalinism*, 228.

38. Solomon Mikhoels, "Nashi tvorcheskie zamysly," *Pravda vostoka*, May 14, 1942.

39. RGALI, f. 2307, op. 1, d. 19, l. 25.

40. The story is available in English in Sholom Aleikhem, *The Bewitched Tailor* (Moscow: Foreign Languages Publishing House, n.d.), 65–113.

41. See, for example, A. Deich, "Novye postanovsi Goseta," *Literatura i iskusstvo*, February 5, 1944.

42. "Premiera zakoldovannyi portnoi," *Vecherniaia Moskva*, January 10, 1944.

43. Vera Dunham, *In Stalin's Time: Middleclass Values in Soviet Fiction* (Cambridge: Cambridge University Press, 1976).

44. Natalia Vovsi-Mikhoels, *Mon père Salomon Mikhoels: souvenirs sur sa vie et sur sa mort*, trans. Erwin Spatz (Montricher, Switzerland: Les Editions Noir sur Blanc, 1990), 212.

45. RGALI, f. 2307, op. 1, d. 4, l. 10.

46. RGALI, f. 2307, op. 1, d. 7, l. 22.

47. "Kultur-khronik," *Eynikayt*, November 8, 1944.

48. RGALI, f. 2307, op. 1, d. 4, l. 16. 2307, op. 1, d. 4, l. 16. RGALI, f. 2307, op. 1, d. 4, l. 16.

49. Ibid., l. 18.

50. I. Goldberg, *Undzer dramaturgie* (New York: Yidisher Kultur Farband, 1961), 356.

51. Shmuel Rozshansky, *Yidishe literatur—yidish lebn* (Buenos Aires: Ateneo literario en el iwo, 1973), 2: 466.

52. David Bergelson, *Prints Reuvayni* (New York: Yidisher Kultur Farband, 1946), 125–26.

53. S. Niger, *Yidishe shrayber in Sovet-Rusland* (New York: S. Niger Book Committee, 1958), 332.

54. Vovsi-Mikhoels, *Mon père*, 225.

55. "Vystuplenie v komitete po delam iskusstv 1946 g," IGTAM, uncatalogued, 2.

56. RGALI, f. 2307, op. 1, d. 4, l. 10.

57. Ibid., l. 14.

58. Ibid., ll. 15–27. Ibid., ll. 15–27.

59. RGALI, f. 2307, op. 1, d. 38 (contracts with writers, etc., 1946), l. 30.

60. Goldberg, *The Jewish Problem*, 91.

61. Yitzhak Rosenberg, "Meetings with Soviet Jewish Leaders," *Soviet Jewish Affairs* 3, no. 1 (1973): 67.

62. RGALI, f. 2307, op. 1, d. 29 (orders from Committee of Artistic Affairs to Moscow State Yiddish Theater, 1945), ll. 134–77. In the fall of 1945, the staff numbered 111.

63. RGALI, f. 2307, op. 1, dd. 7, 13, 32, 38 (contracts with writers, musicians, etc., 1940–1946).

64. RGALI, f. 2307, op. 1, d. 32 (contracts with writers, musicians, etc., 1945), l. 30.

65. Anastasev, *Istoriia sovetskogo*, 5: 671.

66. Vovsi-Mikhoels, *Mon père*, 211.

67. O. Litovskii, *Tak i bylo* (Moscow: Sovetskii pisatel, 1958), 164.

68. CAHJP, P. 166, Kh. 9 (Boris Shimelovich to Mikhoels).

69. RGALI, f. 2307, op. 1, d. 52 (orders from Committee of Artistic Affairs and Chief Management of Dramatic Theaters to Moscow State Yiddish Theater, 1948), l. 26.

70. RGALI, f. 2307, op. 1, d. 38 (contracts with writers, musicians, etc., 1946), l. 35.

71. RGALI, f. 2307, op. 1, d. 4, l. 23.

72. Moshe Broderzon, *Oysgeklibene shriftn* (Buenos Aires: Ateneo Literario, 1972). "Moishe Broderzon, Yiddish Dramatist," *New York Times*, August 21, 1956; "Jewish Poet Ends Ordeal in Soviet," *New York Times*, August 6, 1956. See also entry in A. A. Roback, *The Story of Yiddish Literature* (New York: Yiddish Scientific Institute, 1940), 272, 305.

73. A. Moiseev, "Prodolzhat rabotu nad sovremennoi temoi," *Leningradskaia pravda*, July 28, 1948.

74. For the effects of the war on the Soviet infrastructure see J. D. Barber and M. Harrison, *The Soviet Home Front 1941–1945: A Social and Economic History of the USSR in World War II* (London: Longman, 1991), 42.

75. "Neie spektaklen inem moskver melukhishn yidishn teater," *Eynikayt*, June 18, 1946.

76. "Premiere fun Itsik Fefers piese di zun fargeyt nit," *Eynikayt*, February 15, 1947.

77. Itzik Fefer, "Budushchie knigi," *Literaturnaia gazeta* (Leningrad), April 1, 1945.

78. "Groys derfolg fun der piese di zun fargeyt nit," *Eynikayt*, March 25, 1947.

79. Ewa M. Thompson, "The Katyn Massacre and the Warsaw Ghetto Uprising in the Soviet-Nazi Propaganda War," in John Garrard, ed., *World War 2 and the Soviet People* (New York: St. Martin's Press, 1993), 212–33. For reviews of several contemporary books on the Warsaw ghetto uprising see L. Goldberg, "Tsvey naye bikher vegn dem oyfshtand fun varshaver geto," *Eynikayt*, May 24, 1947.

80. RGALI, f. 2307, op. 1, d. 7, l. 21. The text of Halkin's never-performed play can be found in Samuel Galkin, *Dalnozorkost. Stikhi, ballady, tragediia* (Moscow: Khudozhestvennaia literatura, 1968).

81. Ia. Eidelman, "Na puti k geroicheskomu spetakliu," *Sovetskoe iskusstvo*, September 12, 1947. Markish's play can be found in DRI, P-20/94.

82. RTsKhIDNI, f. 17, op. 128, d. 459, ll. 24–31 (Shcherbakov to Kuznetsov, October 7, 1946). English translation in Redlich, *War, Holocaust and Stalinism*, 418.

83. Redlich, *War, Holocaust and Stalinism*, 419. The letter is dated October 7, 1946.

84. Kostyrchenko, *V plenu*, 40.

85. Broderzon was released from prison in 1955 but died the following year of a heart attack.

9. This Is a Bad Omen

1. See Vera Dunham, *In Stalin's Time: Middleclass Values in Soviet Fiction* (Cambridge: Cambridge University Press, 1976).

2. Cited in Gennadi Kostyrchenko, *V plenu u krasnogo faraona: politicheskie presledovaniia evreev v SSSR v poslednee stalinskoe desiatiletie* (Moscow: Mezhdunarodnye otnosheniia, 1994), 9.

3. See Jack Miller, ed., *Jews in Soviet Culture* (New Brunswick: Transaction Books, 1984).

4. Juri Jelagin, *Taming of the Arts*, trans. Nicholas Wreden (New York: E. P. Dutton & Co., 1951), 20.

5. Kostyrchenko, *V plenu*, 12.

6. Benjamin Pinkus, *The Jews in the Soviet Union: The History of a National Minority* (Cambridge: Cambridge University Press, 1988), 146.

7. Mikhail Heller and Aleksandr Nekrich, *Utopia in Power: The History of the Soviet Union from 1917 to the Present* (New York: Summit Books, 1986), 484.

8. Pinkus, *The Jews in the Soviet Union*, 147.

9. "Vystuplenie v komitete po delam iskusstv 1946 g," IGTAM, uncatalogued, 3.

10. Solomon Mikhoels, "V chem byli nashi oshibki," IGTAM, uncatalogued.

11. The project actually involved two separate commissions, one headed by Ehrenburg, which was responsible for the Russian edition and the other headed by Mikhoels, which was responsible for the foreign-language edition. For more on the Black Book see Shimon Redlich, *War, Holocaust and Stalinism: A Documented Study of the Jewish Anti-Fascist Committee in the USSR* (Luxembourg: Harwood Academic Publishers, 1995), 95–108; Shimon Redlich, *Propaganda and Nationalism in Wartime Russia: The Jewish Anti-fascist Committee in the USSR, 1941–1948* (Boulder: East European Quarterly, 1982), 65–71.

12. GARF, f. 8114, op. 1, d. 912, ll. 1–28 (protocols of Black Book Commission, October 13, 1944). For an English translation see Redlich, *War, Holocaust and Stalinism,* 352–53.

13. *The Black Book: The Nazi Crime against the Jewish People* (New York: Duell, Sloan and Pearce, 1946), 11. The book was published in New York in the spring of 1946 as a joint project of the World Jewish Congress, the Jewish Anti-Fascist Committee of Moscow, the Jewish National Council of Palestine in Jerusalem, and the American Committee of Jewish Writers, Artists and Scientists. For more on Grossman see John Garrard and Carol Garrard, *The Bones of Berdichev: The Life and Fate of Vasily Grossman* (New York: Free Press, 1996).

14. *Black Book,* xxix.

15. Ibid., 414.

16. RTsKhIDNI, f. 17, op. 125, d. 436, ll. 216–18 (Aleksandrov to Zhdanov, February 3, 1947). For English translation see Redlich, *War, Holocaust and Stalinism,* 366.

17. RTsKhIDNI, f. 17, op. 125, d. 438, ll. 219–20 (Mikhoels to Zhdanov, September 18, 1947). For English translation see Redlich, *War, Holocaust and Stalinism,* 367.

18. Redlich, *War, Holocaust and Stalinism,* 37–54.

19. GARF f. 8114, op. 1, d. 972 (Mikhoels and Epshteyn to Molotov, October 28, 1944). For English translation see Redlich, *War, Holocaust and Stalinism,* 248. The *Jewish Daily Forward* had earned the ire of the Soviet press by criticizing Soviet communism from a socialist perspective.

20. GARF, f. 8114, op. 1, d. 792, l. 63 (Molotov to Popov, October 29, 1944). For English translation see Redlich, *War, Holocaust and Stalinism,* 249.

21. RTsKhIDNI, f. 17, op. 125, d. 317, l. 285 (Aleksandrov to Malenkov, October 17, 1945). For English translation see Redlich, *War, Holocaust and Stalinism,* 258.

22. CAHJP, P. 166, kh. 3 (correspondence to Mikhoels regarding JAFC).

23. RTsKhIDNI, f. 17, op. 125, d. 246, l. 204 (Bregman to Lozovskii, November 27, 1944). For English translation see Redlich, *War, Holocaust and Stalinism,* 302.

24. GARF, f. 8114, op. 1, d. 792, ll. 32–36 (Mikhoels, Epshteyn, Fefer to Stalin, February 15, 1944). For an English translation see Redlich, *War, Holocaust and Stalinism,* 264–67. For a comparison of the two letters see Kostyrchenko, *V plenu,* 44–48.

25. Ibid.

26. Redlich, *War, Holocaust and Stalinism,* 314–44.

27. Abraham Sutzkever, "Mit Shlomo Mikhoels," *Di goldene keyt* 43 (1962): 164–65.

28. Ibid., 425–33.

29. Ibid., 417–25.

30. Kostyrchenko, *V plenu,* 84–87.

31. Pinkus, *The Jews in the Soviet Union,* 180; Lidiia Shatunovskaia, *Zhizn v kremle* (New York: Chalidze, 1982), 335–36.

32. Kostyrchenko, *V plenu,* 96–97.

33. Vaksberg, *Stalin against the Jews,* 155–62.

34. Natalia Vovsi-Mikhoéls, *Mon père Salomon Mikhoels: souvenirs sur sa vie et sur sa mort,* trans. Erwin Spatz (Montricher, Switzerland: Les Editions Noir sur Blanc, 1990), 219.

35. *Vecherniaia Moskva,* December 22, 1947.

36. Vaksberg, *Stalin against the Jews,* 160–61.

37. Shatunovskaia, *Zhizn v kremle,* 272.

38. Ibid., 246.

39. V. P. Naumov, *Nepravednyi sud. Poslednii stalinskii rasstrel* (Moscow: Nauka, 1994), 308.

40. Petr Leonidovich Kapitsa, *Vospominaniia, pisma, dokumenty* (Moscow: Nauka, 1994), 86.

41. After its discovery by Borshchagovskii in 1992, this letter was widely published in Russian journals. See, for example, *Novyi mir* 10, no. 822 (1993): 105–51; *Argumenty i fakty* 19, no. 604 (May 1992); *Kaleidoskop,* January 15, 1993; *24 chasa* 22, no. 260 (June 2, 1992); Aleksandr Borshchagovskii, *Obviniaetsia krov* (Moscow: Kultura, 1994), 5–8. An English translation is available in Redlich, *War, Holocaust and Stalinism,* 448–50.

42. Vaksberg, *Stalin against the Jews,* 182.

43. Iakov Grinvald, *Mikhoels: kratkii kritiko-biograficheskii ocherk* (Moscow: Der Emes, 1948), 84.

44. Itzik Fefer, "Mikhoels," *Eynikayt,* February 5, 1948.

45. *Eynikayt,* January 15, 1948 and January 17, 1948.

46. "Di ershte Mikhoels farlezungen," *Eynikayt,* May 8, 1948.

47. RGALI, f. 2307, op. 1, d. 4, l. 37.

48. Ibid., l. 29.

49. Cited in Redlich, *War, Holocaust and Stalinism,* 451–64.

50. Smith to Secretary of State, January 27, 1948, NARA, RG 59, 861, 00/1-2748.

51. The theater was scheduled to perform Grossman's *The Old Teacher* and Fefer's *To Life.*

52. RGALI, f. 2307, op. 1, d. 4, l. 36.

53. "Velder royshn," *Eynikayt,* December 18, 1947.

54. A. Moiseev, "Prodolzhat rabotu nad sovremennoi temoi," *Leningradskaia pravda,* July 28, 1948.

55. "Premiere in yidishn melukhishn teatr ofn nomem fun Sh. Mikhoels," *Eynikayt,* May 4, 1948.

56. Advertisement in *Eynikayt,* March 23, 1948.

57. RGALI, f. 2307, op. 1, d. 39 (orders from Committee of Artistic Affairs to Moscow State Yiddish Theater, February 8, 1947–December 29, 1948), l. 15.

58. Ben Zion Goldberg, *The Jewish Problem in the Soviet Union: An Analysis and a Solution* (New York: Crown Publishers, 1961), 152–53.

59. RGALI, f. 2307, op. 1, d. 50 (orders from Committee of Artistic Affairs and Chief Management of Dramatic Theaters to Moscow State Yiddish Theater, 1948), ll. 12–13.

60. RGALI, f. 2307, op. 1, d. 4, l. 43; RGALI, f. 2307, op. 1, d. 50, ll. 78, 92.

61. RGALI, f. 2307, op. 1, d. 4, l. 39.

62. "Gastroli evreiskogo teatra imeni S. M. Mikhoelsa," *Leningradskaia pravda,* June 16, 1948.

63. "Dem tsaytvaylikn prezident fun der melukhe Yisroel," *Eynikayt,* May 20, 1948.

64. Redlich, *War, Holocaust and Stalinism,* 373–89.

65. Ibid., 390–92.

66. RTsKhIDNI, f. 17, op. 128, d. 608, ll. 5–10 (Baranov to Suslov, June 5, 1948). English translation in Redlich, *War, Holocaust and Stalinism,* 395.

67. Golda Meir, *My Life* (Camberwell, Eng.: Futura Publications, 1976), 205.

68. Ibid., 207.

69. "Priezd evreiskogo teatra," *Vechernii Leningrad,* December 16, 1948.

70. Goldberg, *The Jewish Problem,* 153.

71. Ibid., l. 143. According to Ala Perelman-Zuskin, her father was hospitalized on December 19th.

72. Ibid., l. 151.

73. RGALI, f. 2307, op. 1, d. 39, ll. 1–4.

74. RGALI, f. 2307, op. 1, d. 4, l. 49.

75. RGALI, f. 2307, op. 1, d. 53 (regulations, 1948).

76. RGALI, f. 2307, op. 1, d. 4, l. 47.

77. Ibid., l. 48.

78. Ibid.

79. RTsKhIDNI, f. 17, op. 132, d. 239 (closing of Jewish theaters), ll. 8, 18. See also Kostyrchenko, *V plenu,* 162–67.

80. RTsKhIDNI, f. 17, op. 132, d. 239, l. 10.

81. Ibid., ll. 11–15; RGALI, f. 2307, op. 1, dd. 86–104 (biographical information).

82. Ibid., ll. 16–17.

83. Ibid., ll. 20–23. For English translation see Gennadi Kostyrchenko, *Out of the Red Shadows: Anti-Semitism in Stalin's Russia—From the Secret Archives of the Former Soviet Union* (Amherst: Prometheus Books, 1995), 143.

84. RGALI, f. 2307, op. 1, d. 4, l. 52.

85. Ibid., l. 55.

86. RGALI, f. 2307, op. 1, d. 50, l. 12.

87. RGALI, f. 2307, op. 1, d. 4, l. 58.

88. Ibid., l. 59.

89. Ibid., l. 60.

90. RGALI, f. 2307, op. 1, d. 79 (order from Committee of Artistic Affairs to end liquidation of Moscow State Yiddish Theater, 1950), l. 1.

91. RGALI, f. 2307, op. 1, d. 67 (protocols of liquidation committee, July 1949–July 1950), l. 5.

92. E-mail to the author from Ala Perelman-Zuskin, August 22, 1999.

93. RGALI, f. 2307, op. 1, d. 67, l. 1.

94. RGALI, f. 2307, op. 1, d. 76 (inventory of property, October 10, 1949), ll. 36, 77.

95. RGALI, f. 2307, op. 1, d. 79, l. 47.

96. Ibid., l. 46.

97. Ibid., l. 2.

98. Avraham Greenbaum, ed., "Rehabilitation of the Jewish Anti-Fascist Committee," *Soviet Jewish Affairs* 19, no. 2 (1989): 60–71.

99. Cited in Shimon Redlich, ed. and trans., "Rehabilitation of the Jewish Anti-Fascist Committee," *Soviet Jewish Affairs* 20, nos. 2–3 (1990): 94.

100. Naumov, *Nepravednyi sud,* 61–62.

101. Ibid., 306.

102. Ibid., 70.

103. Ibid., 305.
104. O. Litovskii, *Tak i bylo* (Moscow: Sovetskii pisatel, 1958), 166–68.

Conclusion

1. For a description of this play see Joseph Macleod, *The New Soviet Theatre* (London: George Allen & Unwin, 1943), 25–26.

2. Richard Stites, *Culture and Entertainment in Wartime Russia* (Bloomington: Indiana University Press, 1995).

3. George O. Liber, *Soviet Nationality Policy, Urban Growth, and Identity Change in the Ukrainian SSR 1923–1934* (Cambridge: Cambridge University Press, 1992).

4. Yuri Slezkine, "The USSR as a Communal Apartment, or How a Socialist State Promoted Ethnic Particularism," *Slavic Review* 53, no. 2 (Summer 1994): 414. See also "Nationalities in the Soviet Empire," *Russian Review* 59, no. 2 (April 2000).

Bibliography

Archival Sources

Tsentralnyi gosudarstvennyi arkhiv Oktiabrskoi revoliutsii Ukraina (TsGAOR Ukr), Kiev
    Fond 166 Narkompros
Rossiiskii gosudarstvennyi arkhiv literatury i iskusstva (RGALI), Moscow
    Fond 2307 Goset
    Fond 2308 Goset Theater School
    Fond 2693 Solomon Mikhoels
Gosudarstvennyi arkhiv rossiskoi federatsii (GARF), Moscow
    Fond 2551 Narkompros
    Fond 8114 Jewish Anti-Fascist Committee
    Fond 2306 Commissariat of Enlightenment
Rossiiskii tsentr khraneniia i izucheniia dokumentov noveishei istorii (RTsKhIDNI) Moscow
    Fond 445 op. 1 Jewish Section of the Communist Party of the Soviet Union
    Fond 17 Central Committee of the Communist Party of the Soviet Union
        op. 125 Management of Propaganda and Agitation, 1939–1948
        op. 128 International Information, 1944–1950
        op. 132 Department of Propaganda and Agitation, 1948–1956
Gosudarstvennaia publichnaia istoricheskaia biblioteka (GPB) Manuscript division, St. Petersburg
    Fond 30 N.N. Arbatov
    Fond 1220 I.P. Makhlis
    Fond 1035 L.R Koganov
    Fond 1126 Natan Altman
    Fond 1067 M. A. Milner
Bakhrushin Theater Library (GTsTM), Moscow
    Fond 584 Goset
    Fond 626 A. Ia Burshtein
Central Archives for the History of the Jewish People, Jerusalem
    INV 2709 Itzik Fefer
    P 166 Solomon Mikhoels
Diaspora Research Institute, Tel-Aviv
    P-51 Moshe Goldblatt
    P-20 Peretz Markish
    T-31/50 Natalia Vovsi-Mikhoels

Library of Jewish Music, Jerusalem
  63 Moses Milner
  47, 50, 59 Aleksandr Krein
National Sound Archives, Jerusalem
  uncatalogued material on Soviet Jewish music
Theater Archive of Hebrew University, Jerusalem
  398 Natalia Vovsi-Mikhoels collection
  G1–G3, P1–P34, B1–B4, GRT1–GRT18 Goset Collection
  M1–M3 Mikhoels Collection
National Archives and Records Administration, College Park, Maryland
  RG 59 State Department Records
  RG 226 Records of the Office of Strategic Services (OSS)
  RG 208 Records of the Office of War Information (OWI)

Newspapers and Journals

IN RUSSIAN

Bezbozhnik (November 20, 1940)
Birobidzhanskaia zvezda (January 27, 1940)
Bolshevistskoe znamia (Odessa, July 23, 1938)
Budushchnost (1900–1902)
Dekada Mosk. zrelishch (1938)
Dnepropetrovskaia pravda (June 30, 1939)
Dognat i peregnat (February 24, 1940)
Elektrozavod (March 3, 1935)
Ermitazh (1922)
Govorit SSSR (May 1935)
Iskusstvo kino (1992)
Izvestiia (1923–1940)
Izvestiia sovetov deputatov trudiashchikhsia SSSR (March 20, 1939)
Kharkov vesti (August 17, 1927)
Kievskii proletarii (August 27, 1927)
Komsomolets donbassa (April 12, 1939)
Komsomolskaia pravda (1927–1940)
Krasnaia gazeta (Leningrad, 1925–1936)
Krasnaia zvezda (February 5, 1936)
Krasnoe znamie (Kharkov, 1939–1941)
Kurotsnye izvestiia (Crimea, February 3, 1939)
Kurskaia pravda (June 22, 1937)
Leningradskaia pravda (1926–1948)
Literatura i iskusstvo (1943–1944)
Literaturnaia gazeta (Leningrad, 1927–1945)
Moskovskii bolshevik (1939–40)
Novy put (1916)
Novyi zritel (1924–1929)
Ogonek (1938)
Pravda (1919–1949)
Pravda vostoka (1942–1943)

Prozhektor (Feburary 15, 1927)
RABIS (1929–1931)
Rabochaia Moskva (1935–1937)
Rabochii i iskusstvo (1929–1930)
Rabochii put (Smolensk, June 6, 1936)
Radio-programmy (November 23, 1939)
Rampa i zhizn (1910–1917)
Sovetskaia torgovlia (1935–1936)
Sovetskaia Ukraina (Kiev, 1938–1940)
Sovetskii teatr (1930)
Sovetskoe iskusstvo (1931–1947)
Sovremennyi teatr (1927–1929)
Svoboda i ravenstvo (1907)
Teatr (1938–1940)
Teatr i iskusstvo (1905)
Teatr i muzyka (1922–1923)
Teatralnaia dekada (1935–1936)
Teatralnaia Rossiia (1905)
Teatralnaia zhizn (10 May 1990)
Trud (1926–1938)
Vecherniaia gazeta (Petrograd, March 16, 1918)
Vecherniaia Moskva (1925–1944)
Vechernii Leningrad (December 16, 1948)
Voroshilovgradskaia pravda (1939)
Voskhod (1900–1905)
Za kommunisticheskoe prosveshchenie (October 20, 1936)
Za tiazheloe mashinostroenie (Sverdlovsk, April 14, 1939)
Zhizn i iskusstvo (1905–1916; 1929)
Zhizn iskusstva (1921–1924)
Zrelishcha (1922–1924)
Zvezda (July 7, 1936)

IN YIDDISH

Baginen (1919)
Der emes (1920–1938)
Eynikayt (1942–1948)
Forpost (Birobidzhan, 1936–1940)
Haymland (1948)
Haynt (Warsaw, 1928, 1935, 1937)
Literarishe bleter (1928–1934)
Literatur un kunst (1931)
Moment (Warsaw, 1928)
Nayerd (1925, 1930)
Oktyabr (Minsk, 1925–1931)
Prolit (Kharkov, 1928–1930)
Di royte velt (Kharkov, 1925–1931)
Shul un bukh (1926)
Der shtern (Minsk, 1927–1941)

Sovetishe literatur (Kiev, 1938–1941)
Sovietish (1935–1938)
Vissnshaft un Revoliutsie (1934–1935)

IN OTHER LANGUAGES

Berliner Tageblatt (1928)
Le figaro (Paris, 1928)
Frankfurter Zeitung (1928)
New York Times (1928–1929, 1943, 1956)
Theatre Arts Monthly, 1927–1929

Interviews

Markish, Esther. Interview by author, July 31, 1995, Tel-Aviv.
Mikhoels, Natalia. Inteview by author, August 13, 1995, Or Yehuda.

Motion Pictures

Nosn Beker fort aheym. Directed by Shpis and Milman. Moscow, 1932.
Skvoz slezy. Directed by Grigori Gricher-Cherikover. Moscow, 1927.
Tsirk. Directed by Grigori Alexandrov. Moscow, 1936.
Yidishn glikn. Directed by Aleksandr Granovsky. Moscow, 1925.
Zayn Eksilants. Directed by Grigori Roshal. Moscow, 1928.

Published Versions of Plays Discussed

In most cases the published version is substantially different from the version performed at
the Moscow State Yiddish Theater. I have provided the closest version to that which
was performed. Where possible, I have also given information about English translations.

Abramovitsh, S. Y. *Benjamin the Third.* In *Tales of Mendele the Book Peddler: Fishke the Lame
and Benjamin the Third,* edited by Dan Miron and Ken Frieden, translated by Ted
Gorelick and Hillel Halkin. New York: Schocken Books, 1996, 229–391.

Aleichem, Sholem. *Agentn.* In *Ale verk fun Sholem Aleychem,* Vol. 3, bk. 2., 197–218. New
York: Farvert, 1942.

———. *Agents: A Joke in One Act.* In *Marc Chagall and the Jewish Theater,* 164–171. New
York: Solomon R. Guggenheim Foundation, 1992.

———. *The Bewitched Tailor.* Moscow: Foreign Languages Publishing House, n.d.

———. *Blonzende shteren: a roman fun Sholem Aleykhem.* New York: Hebrew Publishing
Company, 1920.

———. *Der get.* In *Ale verk fun Sholem Aleychem,* Vol. 3, bk. 1., 11–39. New York: Farvert,
1942.

———. *A doktor.* In *Ale verk fun Sholem Aleychem,* Vol. 3, bk. 1., 101–115. New York:
Farvert, 1942.

———. *Dos groyse gevins.* In *Ale verk fun Sholem Aleychem,* Vol. 3, bk. 1., 151–256. New
York: Farvert, 1942.

———. *Mazl tov.* In *Ale verk fun Sholem Aleychem,* Vol. 3, bk. 2., 135–68. New York:
Farvert, 1942.

———. *S'align.* In *Ale verk fun Sholem Aleychem,* Vol. 3, bk. 4., 153–162. New York: Farvert, 1942.

———. *Teve der milkkiger.* In *Ale verk fun Sholem Aleychem,* Vol. 3, bk. 3., 165–235. New York: Farvert, 1942.

———. *Wandering Stars.* In *Epic and Folk Plays of the Yiddish Theatre,* edited and translated by David S. Lifson. Rutherford, N.J.: Fairleigh Dickinson, 1975.

Asch, Sholem. *Amnon un Tamar.* Warsaw: Progres, 1909.

———. *God of Vengeance.* In Joseph Landis, *Three Great Jewish Plays,* 69–113. New York: Applause Theatre, 1986.

———. *Got fun nekome.* In *Dos vert* (Wilna) no. 12 (August 12, 1907): 32–40.

———. *Winter.* In *Six Plays of the Yiddish Theater,* edited by Isaac Goldberg. Boston: J. W. Luce, 1916.

Bergelson, David. *Kh'vel lebn.* In *IKUF almanakh* (1967): 131–80.

———. *Midas ha-din.* Kiev: Kultur-Lige, 1929.

———. *Prints Reuvayni.* New York: Yidisher Kultur Farband, 1946.

———. *Der toyber.* In *Oysgeveylte verk,* 21–54. Moscow: Melukhe farlag fun kinstlerisher literatur, 1961. Segments of the dramatic version were published in *Deklamater fun der sovetisher yidisher literatur,* 375–379. Moscow: Der Emes, 1934.

Daniel. *4 Teg (Iulis).* Minsk: Melukhe farlag fun vaysrusland yidsekter, 1932.

Dobrushin, Yekhezkel Moissevich. *Der gerikht geyt.* Moscow: Tsentraler felker farlag fun FSSR, 1930. Soviet Jewish Library, Givat Ram.

Dobrushin, Yekhezkel Moissevich, and Nakhum Oyslender. *Teve-Molochnik.* Moscow, 1938.

Goldfadn, Avraam. *Di kishufmakherin: opereta in 5 akten un in 8 bilder.* Warsaw: Sh. B. Lande, 1905.

———. *Di tsvey kuni-lemels: operete in 4 akten un 8 bilder.* New York: Hebrew Publishing Company, 1901.

———. *Dos tsehnte gebot.* Cracow: Joseph Fisher Press, 1897.

———. *Shulamis.* In *Oysgeklibene shriftn.* Buenos Aires: IWO, 1972.

Gutzkow, Karl. *Uriel Acosta: tragedye in finf akten.* Translated by Y. L. Lerner. St. Petersburg, 1888.

Halkin, Shmuel. *Arn Fridman.* In *Fir piesn,* 100–173. Moscow: Sovetski pisatel, 1977.

———. *Bar-Kokhba.* Moscow: Der Emes, 1939.

———. *Shulamis.* Moscow: Der Emes, 1940.

Kulbak, Moyshe. *Boytre: dramatishe poeme in 6 bilder.* In *Oysgeklibene shriftn,* 157–226. Beunos Aires: IWO, 1976.

Markish, Peretz. *Dor oys dor eyn.* Kharkov: Melukhe farlag fun Ukraine, 1929.

———. *Pir.* Translated by M. A. Shambadal. Moscow-Leningrad: Iskusstva, 1941.

———. *Semia Ovadis.* Translated by M. A. Shambadal. Moscow-Leningrad: Iskusstvo, 1938.

———. *Vozvrashchenie Neitana Bekera.* Moscow: Sovetskaia Literatura, 1934.

Peretz, Isaac Leyb. *Baynakht oyf'n alten mark.* In *Ale verk fun I. L. Peretz,* Vol. 10, bk. 17, 3–67. New York: Idish, 1920.

———. *Night in the Old Market.* In Mel Gordon, "Granovsky's Tragic Comedy: *Night in the Old Market.*" *Drama Review* 29 (Winter 1985): 91–122.

Reznik, Lipe. *Oyfshtand.* Kiev: Kulture-Lige, 1928.

Romains, Jules. *Le marriage de Le Trouhadec.* 3rd ed. Paris: Gallimard, 1959.

Vayter, A. *Far tog.* Wilna: Vilner farlag fun B. A. Kletskin, 1922.

Memoirs and Contemporary Accounts

Allilueva, Svetlana. *Only One Year.* Translated by Paul Chavchavdze. New York: Harper and Row, 1969.

Ben-Ari, Raikin. *Habima.* New York: Thomas Yoseloff, 1957.

Broda, Meir. *Kilisn un hinterkulsn, zikhronot, bagegnishn, geshtoltn in idishe teater in soviet Rusland.* Tel Aviv: Hamenorah, 1974.

Bukhwald, Nathaniel. *Teater.* New York: Farlag-komitet teater, 1943.

Buloff, Joseph. *From the Old Marketplace: A Memoir of Laughter, Survival, and Coming of Age in Eastern Europe.* Translated by Joseph Singer. Cambridge, Mass.: Harvard University Press, 1991.

————. *On Stage, Off Stage: Memories of a Lifetime in the Yiddish Theater.* Cambridge, Mass.: Harvard University Press, 1992.

Carter, Huntley. *The New Spirit in the Russian Theater.* New York: Benjamin Bloom, 1970.

Chagall, Marc. "Mayn arbayt in Moskver idishn kamer-teater." *Di idishe velt* 2 (May 1928).

————. *My Life.* New York: Orion Press, 1960.

Dobrushin, Yekhezkel Moissevich. *Mikhoels der aktior.* Moscow: Der Emes, 1940.

Fail, I. *Zhizn evreiskogo aktera.* Moscow: Der Emes, 1938.

Folkovitsch, Aliah. *Mikhoels, 1890–1948.* Moscow: Der Emes, 1948.

Fueloep-Miller, Rene. *The Mind and Face of Bolshevism: An Examination of Cultural Life in the Soviet Union.* Translated by F. S. Flint and D. F. Tait. London: G. P. Putnam's Sons, 1927.

Goldberg, Ben Zion. *The Jewish Problem in the Soviet Union: An Analysis and a Solution.* New York: Crown Publishers, 1961.

Grinvald, Iakov. *Mikhoels: kratkii kritiko-biograficheskii ocherk.* Moscow: Der Emes, 1948.

Houghton, Norris. *Moscow Rehearsals: The Golden Age of Soviet Theatre.* 1936. Reprint, New York: Grove Press, 1962.

Jelagin, Juri. *Taming of the Arts.* Translated by Nicholas Wreden. New York: E. P. Dutton & Co., 1951.

Kaminska, Ida. *My Life, My Theater.* New York: Macmillan, 1973.

Kapitsa, Petr Leonidovich. *Vospominaniia, pisma, dokumenty.* Moscow: Nauka, 1994.

Kersten, K. "Das Maskauer jüdische Akademische Theater." *Das Neue Russland* 5 (1928): 8–10.

Khrushchev, N. S. *Khrushchev Remembers.* Edited and translated by Strobe Talbott. Boston, Little, Brown and Company, 1970.

Libermann, M. *Aus dem Ghetto in die Welt: Autobiographie.* Berlin: Verlag der Nation, 1977.

Litovskii, O. *Tak i bylo.* Moscow: Sovetskii pisatel, 1958.

Liubomirskii, Osip. *Mikhoels.* Moscow: Iskusstvo, 1938.

Lyons, Eugene. *Assignment in Utopia.* London: Harcourt, Brace and Company, 1937.

Macleod, Joseph. *The New Soviet Theatre.* London: George Allen & Unwin, 1943.

Markish, Esther. *The Long Return.* New York: Ballantine, 1978.

Markish, Peretz. *Der fertsikieriker man.* Jeruslame: Farlag Y. L. Peretz Israel, 1978.

————. *Mikhoels.* Moscow: Der Emes, 1939.

Markov, P. A. *The Soviet Theatre.* London: V Gollancz, 1934.

Meir, Golda. *My Life.* Camberwell, England: Futura Publications, 1976.

Moskver yidisher kamer teater. Kiev: Kultur Lige, 1924.

Rapoport, Yakov. *The Doctor's Plot of 1953.* Cambridge, Mass.: Harvard University Press, 1991.

Rosenfeld, Lulla Adler. *The Yiddish Theatre and Jacob P. Adler.* 1977. New York: Shapolsky Publishers, 1988.

Shatunovskaia, Lidiia. *Zhizn v kremle.* New York: Chalidze, 1982.

Sheyn, Yosef. *Arum moskver yidishn teater.* Paris: Commission du plan d'action culturelle, 1964.

Steinberg, Aharon. "Mayn Dvinsker khaver Shlomo Mikhoels." *Di goldene keyt* 43 (1962): 142–52.

Sutzkever, Abraham. "Mit Shlomo Mikhoels." *Di goldene keyt* 43 (1962): 153–69.

Teatry moskvy: albom postanovok vedyshchikh teatrov. Moscow: Krestianskaia gazeta, 1936.

Vovsi-Mikhoels, Natalia. *Mon pere Salomon Mikhoels: souvenirs sur sa vie et sur sa mort.* Translated by Erwin Spatz. Montricher, Switzerland: Les Editions Noir sur Blanc, 1990.

Weisgal, Meyer W. *Meyer Weisgal . . . So Far: An Autobiography.* London: Weidenfeld and Nicolson, 1971.

Zagorskii, M. *Mikhoels.* Moscow: Kinopechat, 1927.

Writings by Key Figures

Arbatov, Boris Ignatevich. *Natan Altman.* Berlin: Petropolis, 1924.

Beregovski[i], Moshe. *Old Jewish Folk Music.* Edited and translated by Mark Slobin. Philadephia: University of Pennsylvania Press, 1982.

Beregovskii, Moshe, and Itzik Fefer. *Yidishe folks-lider.* Kiev: Melukha farlag far di natsionale minderhaytn in USSR, 1938.

Bergelson, David. *The Stories of David Bergelson: Yiddish Short Fiction from Russia.* Edited and translated by Golda Werman, with a foreword by Aharon Appelfeld. Syracuse: Syracuse University Press, 1996.

———. *The Jewish Autonomous Region.* Moscow: Foreign Language Publishing House, 1939.

The Black Book: The Nazi Crime against the Jewish People. New York: Duell, Sloan and Pearce, 1946.

Brider yidn fun der gantser velt. Moscow: Der emes, 1941.

Broderzon, Moishe. *Oysgeklibene shriftn.* Edited by Shmuel Rozshanskii. Buenos Aires: Ateneo Literario en el Iwo, 1972.

Deich, A. I. *Maski evreiskogo teatra: ot Goldfadena do Granovskogo.* Moscow, 1927.

Der Nister. *Di mishpokhe Mashber.* 2 vols. New York: Yidisher kultur farband, 1943.

Dobrushin, Yekhezkel Moissevich. *Binyomin Zuskin.* Moscow: Der Emes, 1939.

———. *Di dramaturgie fun di klasiker.* Moscow: Der Emes, 1948.

———. *Evreiskie narodnye pesni.* Moscow: Pomgrafkniga, 1947. Lenin Library.

———. *Gedankengangn.* Kiev: Kultur-Lige, 1922.

———. *Kinder teater.* Minsk: Tsentraler felker-farlag fun F.S.S.R. Vaysrusishe optaylung, 1931.

———. *Literaturno-kriticheskie stati.* Translated by A. Belova. Moscow: Sovetskii pisatel, 1964.

Dobrushin, Yehezkel, and A. Yuditsky. *Yidishe folks-lider.* Moscow: Der Emes, 1940.

Efros, Abram. *Iskusstvo Marka Shagala.* Moscow: Gelikon, 1918.

———. *Kamernyi teatr i ego khudozhniki, 1914–1934.* Moscow: Navka, 1996.

———. *Portret Natana Altmana.* Moscow: Shipovnik, 1922.

Ehrenburg, Ilya, and Vasily Grossman, eds. *The Black Book: The Ruthless Murder of Jews* by German-Fascist Invaders throughout the Temporarily-Occupied Regions of the Soviet Union and in the Death Camps of Poland during the War of 1941–1945. Translated by John Glad and James S. Levine. New York: Holocaust Library, 1981.

———. *Chernaia kniga. O zlodeiskom povsemestnomubiistve evreev nemetsko-fashistskimi zakhvatchikami vo vremenno-okkupirovannykh raionakh Sovetskogo soiza i v lageriakh unichtozheniia polshi vo vremia voiny 1941–1945 gg.* Yad Vashem Martyrs' and Heroes' Remembrance Authority. Israel Research Institute of Contemporary Society. Jerusalem: Tarbut Publishers, 1980.

Fefer, Itsik. *Lider, balades, poemes.* Moscow: Sovetski pisatel, 1967.

Gorkii, Maksim. "M Gorkii—Sholom Aleikhemu." In *Sholom Aleikhem. Pisatel i chelovek,* edited by U. A. Guralnik. Moscow: Sovetskii pisatel, 1984.

Halkin, Samuel. *Dalnozorkost. Stikhi, ballady, tragediia.* Moscow: Khudozhestvennaia literatura, 1968.

———. *Stikhi, ballady, dramy.* Moscow: Goslitizdat, 1958.

Howe, Irving, and Eliezer Greenberg, eds. *Ashes Out of Hope: Fiction by Soviet-Yiddish Writers.* New York: Schocken Books, 1977.

Howe, Irving, and Ruth R. Wisse, eds. *The Penguin Book of Modern Yiddish Verse.* New York: Viking Penguin, 1987.

Ivanov, Viacheslav. *Rodnoe i vselenskoe.* Moscow: Respublika, 1994.

Khashchevatskii, Moisei, and Der Nister. *Yidishe folkslider.* Odessa: Kinderfarlag, 1940.

Komitet po delam iskusstv pri SNK soiuza SSR. *Rezhisser v sovetskom teatre.* Moscow: Iskusstvo, 1940.

Litvakov, Moshe. *Funf yor melukhisher yidisher kunst teater, 1921–1925.* Moscow: Shul un bukh, 1924.

Lunacharskii, A. V. *O teatre i dramaturgii,* 2 vols. Moscow: Iskusstvo, 1958.

Markish, Peretz. *Milkhome.* 2 vols. New York: Yidisher kultur farband, 1956.

Mayakovsky, Vladimir. *Polnoe sobranie sochinenii.* Moscow: Gosudarstvennoe izdatelstvo khudozhestvennoi literatury, 1955.

Mikhoels, Solomon. *Sholem Aleikhem: aiinokters.* Moscow: Der Emes, 1940.

———. *Stati, besedy, rechi.* Moscow: Iskusstvo, 1965.

Orshanskii, Ber. *Teater shlakhtn.* Moscow: Tsentraler felker-farlag, 1931.

Prylucki, Nojach. *Yidishe folkslider.* Warsaw: Bikher far ale, 1911.

Ravich, N. A. *Repertuarnyi ukazatel GRK.* Moscow: Teatr-Kino, 1929.

Stalin, Joseph. *Marxism and the National and Colonial Question: A Collection of Articles and Speeches.* London: Lawrence and Wishart, 1936.

Trotsky, Leon. *Literature and Revolution.* Ann Arbor: University of Michigan Press, 1960.

———. *The Revolution Betrayed: What Is the Soviet Union and Where Is It Going?* Translated by Max Eastman. New York: Harcourt & Brace, 1937.

Weizmann, Chaim. *The Letters and Papers of Chaim Weizmann.* 25 vols. Jerusalem: Israel Universities Press, 1968–.

Yidishe Teatrale Gesellschaft. *Dos yidishe kamer teater.* Petrograd, 1918.

Document Collections

Kommunisticheskaia partiia sovetskogo soiuza v rezoliutsiiakh i resheniiakh sezdov, konferentsii i plenumov TsK. Moscow: Izdatelstvo politicheskoi literatury, 1970.

Naumov, V. P. *Nepravednyi sud. Poslednii stalinskii rasstrel.* Moscow: Nauka, 1994.

Redlich, Shimon. *War, Holocaust and Stalinism: A Documented Study of the Jewish Anti-Fascist Committee in the USSR.* Luxembourg: Harwood Academic Publishers, 1995.

Books, Articles and Manuscripts

Adler, Lois. "Alexis Granovsky and the Jewish State Theatre of Moscow." *The Drama Review* 24, no. 3 (September 1980): 27–42.

Alexander, Tamar. "'The Weasel and the Well': Intertextual Relationships between Hebrew Sources and Judeo-Spanish Stories." *Jewish Studies Quarterly* 5, no. 3 (1998): 254–76.

Alter, Robert. *After the Tradition: Essays on Modern Jewish Writing.* New York: Dutton, 1969.

Altshuler, Mordechai. "The Agony and Liquidation of the Jewish State Theater of Belorussia (1948–1949)." *Jews in Eastern Europe* 3, no. 25 (Winter 1994): 64–72.

———. "The Jewish Anti-Fascist Committee in the USSR in Light of New Documentation." In *Studies in Contemporary Jewry*, edited by Jonathan Frankel. Vol. 1. Bloomington: Indiana University Press, 1984.

Altshuler, Mordechai, ed. *Ha-teatron ha-yehudi bi-verit ha-moatsot.* Jerusalem: Hebrew University Press, 1996.

Anastasev, A. *Istoriia sovetskogo dramaticheskogo teatra.* 6 vols. Moscow: Institut istorii iskusstv, 1966–1971.

Apter-Gabriel, Ruth, ed. *Tradition and Revolution: The Jewish Renaissance in Russian Avant-Garde Art, 1912–1928.* Jerusalem: The Israel Museum, 1988.

Arendt, Hannah. *The Origins of Totalitarianism.* 1951. Reprint, New York: Meridian Books, 1958.

Armstrong, John. *The Politics of Totalitarianism: The Communist Party of the Soviet Union from 1934 to the Present.* New York: Random House, 1961.

Ascher, Abraham. *The Mensheviks in the Russian Revolution.* Ithaca: Cornell University Press, 1976.

Aucouturier, Michel. "Le Futurisme Russe ou l'art comme utopie," *Revue des études slaves* 56 no. 1 (1984): 51–60.

Baker, Zachary M. "Yiddish in Form and Socialist in Content: The Observance of Sholem Aleichem's Eightieth Birthday in the Soviet Union." *YIVO Annual* 23 (1996): 209–231.

Barber, J. D., and M. Harrison. *The Soviet Home Front 1941–1945: A Social and Economic History of the USSR in World War II.* London: Longman, 1991.

Barghoorn, Frederick. *Soviet Russian Nationalism.* New York: Oxford University Press, 1956.

Barna, Yon. *Eisenstein: The Growth of a Cinematic Genius.* Bloomington: Indiana University Press, 1973.

Baron, Salo Wittmayer. *The Russian Jew under Tsars and Soviets.* New York: Macmillan, 1964.

Beloff, Max. *The Foreign Policy of Soviet Russia, 1929–1941.* New York: Oxford University Press, 1947–1949.

Ben Meir, Orna. "Biblical Thematics in Stage Design for the Hebrew Theatre." *Asaph* 11 (1989): 141–67.

Berkowitz, Michael. *Zionist Culture and West European Jewry before the First World War.* Cambridge: Cambridge University Press, 1993.

Besançon, Alain. "R. R. Falk (1886–1958)." *Cahiers du monde Russe et Soviétique* 3, no. 4 (October–December 1962): 564–81.

Beth ha-têfutsot. *The Closed Curtain: The Moscow Yiddish State Theater.* Tel Aviv: Diaspora Museum, 1980.

Birnboym, Y. *Yidisher teater in Eyrope tsvishn beyde velt-milkhomot.* New York: Congress for Jewish Culture, 1971.

Blium, Arlen V. *Evreiskii vopros pod sovetskoi tsenzuroi.* St. Petersburg: St. Petersburg Jewish University, 1996.

———. *Za kulisami "Ministerstva pravdy": tainaia istoriia sovetskoi tsenzury, 1917–1929.* St. Petersburg: Akademicheskii proekt, 1994.

Borshchagovskii, Aleksandr. *Obviniaetsia krov.* Moscow: Kultura, 1994.

Bowlt, John E., and Olga Matich. *Laboratory of Dreams: The Russian Avant-Garde and Cultural Experiment.* Stanford: Stanford University Press, 1996.

Boym, Svetlana. *Common Places: Mythologies of Everyday Life in Russia.* Cambridge, Mass.: Harvard University Press, 1994.

Braun, Edward. *The Theatre of Meyerhold: Revolution on the Modern Stage.* London: Methuen, 1986.

Braun, Joachim. *Jews in Soviet Music.* Jerusalem: Hebrew University Press, 1977.

Brenner, Michael. *The Renaissance of Jewish Culture in Weimar Germany.* New Haven: Yale University Press, 1996.

Brooks, Jeffrey. *When Russia Learned to Read.* Princeton: Princeton University Press, 1985.

Broszat, Martin. *The Hitler State: The Foundation and Development of the Internal Structure of the Third Reich.* London: Longman, 1981.

Brown, Deming. *Soviet Literature since Stalin.* Cambridge: Cambridge University Press, 1978.

Brzezinski, Zbigniev. *Ideology and Power in Soviet Politics.* New York: Praeger, 1962.

Carr, E. H. *Foundations of a Planned Economy, 1926–1929.* 2 vols. London: Macmillan, 1971.

———. *Socialism in One Country, 1924–1926.* 2 vols. London: Macmillan, 1965.

Clark, Katerina. *Petersburg: Crucible of Cultural Revolution.* Cambridge, Mass.: Harvard University Press, 1995.

———. *The Soviet Novel: History as Ritual.* Chicago: University of Chicago Press, 1981.

Clayton, J. Douglas. *Pierrot in Petrograd: The Commedia Dell'Arte/Balagan in Twentieth-Century Russian Theatre and Drama.* Montreal and Kingston: McGill-Queen's University Press, 1993.

Cohen, Stephen. *Bukharin and the Bolshevik Revolution.* London: Wildwood House, 1974.

Conquest, Robert. *The Great Terror: Stalin's Purge of the Thirties.* London: Macmillan, 1968.

———, ed. *Soviet Nationalities Policy in Practice.* London: Bodley Head, 1967.

Cukierman, Walenty. "Isaak Babel's Jewish Heroes and their Yiddish Background." *Yiddish* 2, no. 4 (1977): 15–27.

Daniels, Robert Vincent. *The Conscience of the Revolution: Communist Opposition in Soviet Russia.* 1960. New York: Clarion Books, 1969.

David-Fox, Michael. *Revolution of the Mind: Higher Learning among the Bolsheviks, 1918–1929.* Ithaca: Cornell University Press, 1997.

Dektor, Felix, and Roman Spektor, eds. *Kovcheg: almanakh evreiskoi kultury.* Moscow: Khudozhstvennaia literatura; Jerusalem: Tarbut, 1991.

Deutscher, Isaac. *The Prophet Outcast: Trotsky, 1929–1940.* Oxford: Oxford University Press, 1963.

———. *Stalin: A Political Biography.* 1949. Reprint, New York, 1966.

Dobroszycki, Lucjan, and Jeffrey S. Gurock, eds. *The Holocaust in the Soviet Union.* Armonk, N.Y.: M.E. Sharpe, 1993.

Dubnow, Simeon. *History of the Jews in Russia and Poland from the Earliest Times until the*

Present Day. 3 vols. Translated by I. Friedlander. Philadelphia: Jewish Publication Society of America, 1916–1920.

Dunham, Vera. *In Stalin's Time: Middleclass Values in Soviet Fiction.* Cambridge: Cambridge University Press, 1976.

Eckman, Lester Samuel. *Soviet Policy towards Jews and Israel.* New York: Shengold Publishers, 1974.

Ermolaev, Herman. *Censorship in Soviet Literature, 1917–1991.* Lanham: Rowman & Littlefield, 1997.

Estraikh, Gennady. *Soviet Yiddish: Language Planning and Linguistic Development.* Oxford: Clarendon Press, 1999.

Fischer, George. *Soviet Opposition to Stalin.* Cambridge, Mass.: Harvard University Press, 1952.

Fishman, David E. "Preserving Tradition in the Land of the Revolution: The Religious Leadership of Soviet Jewry, 1917–1930." In *The Uses of Tradition: Jewish Continuity in the Modern Era,* edited by Jack Wertheimer. New York: Jewish Theological Seminary of America, 1992.

Fitzpatrick, Sheila. *The Commissariat of Enlightenment.* Cambridge: Cambridge University Press, 1970.

———. *The Cultural Front: Power and Culture in Revolutionary Russia.* Ithaca: Cornell University Press, 1992.

———. *Cultural Revolution in Russia, 1928–1931.* Bloomington: Indiana University Press, 1978.

———. *Education and Social Mobility in the Soviet Union. 1921–1934.* Cambridge: Cambridge University Press, 1979.

———. "The Emergence of Glaviskusstvo: Class Wars on the Cultural Front, Moscow, 1928–1929." *Soviet Studies* 23, no. 2 (October 1971): 236–53.

———. *Stalin's Peasants: Resistance and Survival in the Russian Village after Collectivization.* New York: Oxford University Press, 1994.

Fitzpatrick, Sheila, Alexander Rabinowitch, and Richard Stites, eds. *Russia in the Era of NEP: Explorations in Soviet Society and Culture.* Bloomington: Indiana University Press, 1991.

Fox, Michael S. "Glavlit, Censorship and the Problem of Party Policy in Cultural Affairs, 1922–28." *Soviet Studies* 44, no. 6 (1992): 1045–68.

France, Anna Kay. *Boris Pasternak's Translations of Shakespeare.* Berkeley: University of California Press, 1978.

Frost, Matthew. "Marc Chagall and the Jewish State Chamber Theatre." *Russian History/ Histoire Russe* 8, nos. 1–2 (1981): 90–99.

Frumkin, Jacob, Gregor Aronson, Alexis Goldenweiser, and Joseph Lewitan. *Russian Jewry (1917–1967).* New York: Thomas Yoseloff, 1969.

Gabler, Neal. *An Empire of Their Own: How the Jews Invented Hollywood.* New York: Crown Publishers, 1988.

Garrard, John, ed. *World War 2 and the Soviet People.* New York: St. Martin's Press, 1993.

Garrard, John, and Carol Garrard. *The Bones of Berdichev: The Life and Fate of Vasily Grossman.* New York: Free Press, 1996.

Gassenschmidt, Christoph. *Jewish Liberal Politics in Tsarist Russia, 1900–1914: The Modernization of Russian Jewry.* New York: New York University Press, 1995.

Gay, Peter. *Freud, Jews and Other Germans: Masters and Victims in Modernist Culture.* New York: Oxford University Press, 1979.

————. *Weimar Culture: The Outsider as an Insider.* New York: Harper & Row, 1968.

Geizer, Matvei. *Solomon Mikhoels.* Moscow: Prometer, 1990.

German, Mikhail, ed. *Art of the October Revolution.* Translated by W. Freeman, D. Saunders, and C. Binns. New York: Abrams, 1979.

Gessen, Iulii. *Evrei v Rossii.* St. Petersburg: A. G. Rozen, 1906.

Getty, J. Arch. *Origins of the Great Purges: The Soviet Communist Party Reconsidered, 1933–1938.* Cambridge: Cambridge University Press, 1985.

Getty, J. Arch, and Roberta Manning, eds. *Stalinist Terror.* New York: Cambridge University Press, 1993.

Giatsintova.S. V. *S pamiatiu naedine.* Moscow: Iskusstvo, 1985.

Gilboa, Yehoshua. *The Black Years of Soviet Jewry.* Translated by Dov Ben-Abba and Yosef Shachter. Boston: Little, Brown and Company, 1971.

Gitelman, Zvi. *A Century of Ambivalence: The Jews of Russia and the Soviet Union, 1881 to the Present.* New York: YIVO Institute, 1988.

————. *Jewish Nationality and Soviet Politics: The Jewish Sections of the CPSU, 1917–1930.* Princeton: Princeton University Press, 1972.

Gleason, Abbott, Peter Kenez, and Richard Stites, eds. *Bolshevik Culture: Experiment and Order in the Russian Revolution.* Bloomington: Indiana University Press, 1985.

Goldberg, I. *Undzer dramaturgie.* New York: Yidisher Kultur Farband, 1961.

Goldman, Eric A. *Visions, Images and Dreams: Yiddish Film Past and Present.* Ann Arbor: University of Michigan Press, 1983.

Goldman, Robert N. *Einstein's God: Albert Einstein's Quest as a Scientist and as a Jew to Replace a Forsaken God.* Northvale, N.J.: Jason Aronson, 1997.

Goldman, Wendy. *Women, the State and Revolution: Soviet Family Policy and Social Life, 1917–1936.* Cambridge: Cambridge University Press, 1993.

Goodman, Susan Tumarkin, ed. *Russian Jewish Artists in a Century of Change, 1890–1990.* Munich: Prestel, 1995.

————. "Meyerhold's Biomechanics." *The Drama Review* 18, no. 3 (September 1974): 73–88.

Goren, B. *Di geshikhte fun yidishn teater.* New York: Max N. Mayzel, 1923.

Gray, Camilla. *The Russian Experiment in Art.* New York: Thames and Hudson, 1962.

Greenberg, Louis. *The Jews in Russia: The Struggle for Emancipation.* 1944. Reprint, New York: Schocken Books, 1973.

Grinbaum, A. "Ha-teatron ha-Idi be-Rusia ha-soveitit be-shanot ha-esrim." *Ha-avar le-divrei yemei ha-yehudim ve ha-yehudit be-resiah* 16 (April-May 1969): 109–117.

Groys, Boris. *The Total Art of Stalinism: Avant-Garde, Aesthetic Dictatorship, and Beyond.* Translated by Charles Rougle. Princeton: Princeton University Press, 1992.

Günther, Hans, ed. *The Culture of the Stalin Period.* London: Macmillan, 1990.

Gurevitz, Baruch. *National Communism in the Soviet Union, 1918–1928.* Series in Russian and East European Studies. Pittsburgh: University of Pittsburgh, 1980.

Hazan, Barukh A. *Soviet Propaganda. A Case Study of the Middle East Conflict.* Jerusalem: Keter, 1976.

Heller, Mikhail, and Aleksandr Nekrich. *Utopia in Power: The History of the Soviet Union from 1917 to the Present.* New York: Summit Books, 1986.

Hirsch, Francine. "Toward an Empire of Nations: Border-Making and the Formation of Soviet National Identities." *Russian Review* 59, no. 2 (April 2000): 201–26.

Hirszowicz, Lukasz. "NKVD Documents Shed New Light on Fate of Erlich and Alter." *East European Jewish Affairs* 22, no. 2 (1992): 65–85.

Hoberman, J. *Bridge of Light: Yiddish Film between Two Worlds.* New York: Museum of Modern Art, 1991.

———. "The Crooked Road of Jewish Luck." *Artforum* 28 (September 1989): 122–25.

Hobsbawm, E. J. *Bandits.* London: Weidenfeld and Nicolson, 1969.

Hoffman, David. *Peasant Metropolis: Social Identities in Moscow, 1929–1941.* Ithaca: Cornell University Press, 1994.

Howe, Irving. *World of Our Fathers.* New York: Harcourt, Brace, Jovanovich, 1976.

Idelsohn, Abraham Zebi. *Jewish Music in Its Historical Development.* 1929. Reprint, New York: Tudor Publishing Company, 1944.

Ivanov, Vladislav. "Poetika metamorfoz: Vakhtangov i Gabima." *Voprosy teatra* 13 (1993): 188–222.

———. "Teatr Gabima v Moskve: na vesakh Iova." *Znamia* 12 (1995): 168–92.

Jäckel, Eberhard. *Hitler's Weltanschauung: A Blueprint for Power.* Middleton, Conn.: Wesleyan University Press, 1972.

James, C. Vaughan. *Soviet Socialist Realism: Origins and Theory.* New York: St. Martin's Press, 1973.

Jelavich, Peter. *Berlin Cabaret.* Cambridge, Mass.: Harvard University Press, 1993.

———. *Munich and Theatrical Modernism: Politics, Playwriting and Performance, 1890–1914.* Cambridge, Mass.: Harvard University Press, 1985.

Jüdisches Museum der Stadt Wien. *Chagall: Bilder-Träume Theater 1908–1920, Jüdisches Museum der Stadt Wien.* Vienna: Brandstätter, 1994.

Josephus, Flavius. *Di letste teg fun Yerushaloim.* Vilna: B. A. Kletskin, 1923.

———. *Toldot milkhamot ha-Yehudim im ha-Romaim.* Translated by Naftali Simchoni. 1923. Reprint, Tel-Aviv: A. Y. Shtibel, 1938.

Kagan, Zipora. *Me-agadah le-siporet modernit bi-yetsirat Berdits'evski.* Kibbutz hameuchad: Kibbutz hameuchad publishing, 1983.

Kahan, Stuart. *The Wolf of the Kremlin.* New York: William Morrow and Company, 1987.

Katz, Jacob. *Tradition and Crisis: Jewish Society at the End of the Middle Ages.* New York: New York University Press, 1993.

Keegan, John. *The Second World War.* New York: Viking, 1989.

Kelik, M. "On Jewish Culture in Theatrical Arts." In *Tarbut Yehudit bi-Verit Hamoatsot.* Jerusalem: ha-Mahlakah le-tarbut shel ha-Kongres ha-Yehudi ha-olam, 1972.

Kenez, Peter. *The Birth of the Propaganda State: Soviet Methods of Mass Mobilization, 1917–1929.* Cambridge: Cambridge University Press, 1985.

———. *Cinema and the Cultural Revolution.* Cambridge: Cambridge University Press, 1992.

Kersten, K. "Das Maskauer Jüdische Akademische Theater." *Das Neue Russland* 5 (1928): 8–10.

Kirshenblatt-Gimblett, Barbara. "Contraband: Performance, Text and Analysis of a Purim-Shpil." *The Drama Review* 24, no. 3 (September 1980): 5–16.

Kholodov, E. G., et al., eds. *Istoriia russkogo dramaticheskogo teatra.* 7 vols. Moscow: Iskusstvo, 1977–1989.

Kleberg, Lars. *Theatre as Action: Soviet Russian Avant-Garde Aesthetics.* Translated by Charles Rougle. London: Macmillan, 1993.

Knopp, Josephine Zadovsky. *The Trial of Judaism in Contemporary Jewish Writing.* Urbana: University of Illinois Press, 1975.

Kochan, Lionel, ed. *The Jews in Soviet Russia since 1917.* London: Oxford University Press, 1970.

Koenker, Diane P., William G. Rosenberg, and Ronald Grigor Suny, eds. *Party, State, and Society in the Russian Civil War: Explorations in Social History.* Bloomington: Indiana University Press, 1989.

Komitet po delam iskusstv pri SNK soiuza SSR. *Rezhisser v sovetskom teatre.* Moscow: Iskusstvo, 1940.

Korey, William. "Ehrenburg: His Inner Jewish Conflict." *Jewish Frontier* (March 1968): 25–31.

Kornblatt, Judith Deutsch, and Richard F. Gustafson, eds. *Russian Religious Thought.* Madison: University of Wisconsin Press, 1996.

Kostyrchenko, Gennadi. *Out of the Red Shadows: Anti-Semitism in Stalin's Russia—From the Secret Archives of the Former Soviet Union.* Amherst: Prometheus Books, 1995.

———. *V plenu u krasnogo faraona: politicheskie presledovaniia evreev v SSSR v poslednee stalinskoe desiatiletie.* Moscow: Mezhdunarodnye otnosheniia, 1994.

Kotkin, Stephen. *Magnetic Mountain: Stalinism as a Civilization.* Berkeley: University of California Press, 1995.

Kott, Jan. *Shakespeare, Our Contemporary.* Translated by Boleslaw Taborski. 1964. Reprint, New York: W.W. Norton, 1974.

Kozintsev, Grigori. *Shakespeare: Time and Conscience.* Translated by Joyce Vining. New York: Hill and Wang, 1966.

Küenzlen, Gottfried. "Secular Religion and Its Futuristic-Eschatological Conceptions." *Studies in Soviet Thought* 33, no. 3 (April 1987): 209–28.

Kuromiya, Hiroaki. *Stalin's Industrial Revolution: Politics and Workers, 1928–1932.* New York: Cambridge University Press, 1988.

Lahusen, Thomas. *How Life Writes the Book: Real Socialism and Socialist Realism in Stalin's Russia.* Ithaca: Cornell University Press, 1997.

Laqueur, Walter. *The Soviet Union and the Middle East.* New York, Praeger, 1959.

Lenemen, Leon. *La tragedie des juifs en USSR.* Paris: Desclee de Brouner, 1959.

Lestshinsky, Jacob. *Dos yidishe folk in tsifern.* Berlin: Klal farlag, 1922.

Levin, Nora. *The Jews in the Soviet Union since 1917: Paradox of Survival.* New York: I. B. Tauris, 1990.

Levitan, Viktoriia. *I evrei-moia krov: evreiskaia drama na russkoi stene.* Moscow: Vozdushnyi Transport, 1991.

Levitats, Isaac. *The Jewish Community in Russian, 1772–1844.* 1943. Reprint, New York: Octagon Books, 1970.

Lewin, Moshe. *Lenin's Last Struggle.* London: Farber & Farber, 1969.

———. *The Making of the Soviet System.* London: Methuen, 1985.

———. *Russian Peasants and Soviet Power.* London: Allen & Unwin, 1968.

———. *Russia-USSR-Russia. The Drive and Drift of a Superstate.* New York: New Press, 1995.

Leyda, Jay. *Kino: A History of Russian and Soviet Film.* New York: Macmillan, 1960.

Liass, Fedor. *Poslednii politicheskii protsess stalina ili nesostoiavshiisia genotsid.* Jerusalem: F. Liass, 1995.

Liber, George O. *Soviet Nationality Policy, Urban Growth, and Identity Change in the Ukrainian SSR 1923–1934.* Cambridge: Cambridge University Press, 1992.

Lifson, David S. *The Yiddish Theatre in America.* New York: Thomas Yoseloff, 1965.

Liptzin, Sol. *A History of Yiddish Literature.* New York: Jonathan David Publishers, 1972.

Litovskii, O. *Tak i bylo.* Moscow: Sovetskii pisatel, 1958.

Lodder, Christine. *Russian Constructivism.* New Haven: Yale University Press, 1983.

Loseff, Lev. *On the Beneficence of Censorship: Aesopian Language in Modern Russian Literature.* Munich: Verlag Otto Sagner, 1984.

Lukács, George. *The Meaning of Contemporary Realism.* Translated by John and Necke Mander. 1963. Reprint, London: Merlin Press, 1979.

Madison, Charles A. *Yiddish Literature: Its Scope and Major Writers.* New York: Frederick Ungar, 1968.

Mahler, Raphael. *Hasidism and the Jewish Enlightenment: Their Confrontation in Galicia and Poland in the First Half of the Nineteenth Century.* Philadelphia: The Jewish Publication Society of America, 1985.

Maimon, Solomon. *Solomon Maimon: An Autobiography.* Edited and translated by Moses Hadas. 1947. Reprint, New York: Schocken Books, 1967.

Malia, Martin. *The Soviet Tragedy.* New York: Free Press, 1994.

Malin, Irving, and Irwin Stark, eds. *Breakthrough: A Treasury of Contemporary American Jewish Literature.* New York: McGraw Hill, 1964.

Mally, Lynn. *Culture of the Future: The Proletkult Movement in Revolutionary Russia.* Berkeley: University of California Press, 1990.

———. "The Rise and Fall of the Soviet Youth Theater TRAM." *Slavic Review* 51, no. 3 (Fall 1990): 411–30.

Marc Chagall and the Jewish Theater. New York: Solomon R. Guggenheim Foundation, 1992.

Markov, Vladimir. *Russian Futurism.* Berkeley: University of California Press, 1968.

———. "An Unnoticed Aspect of Pasternak's Translations." *Slavic Review* 20, no. 3 (October 1961): 503–508.

Martin, Terry. "The Origins of Soviet Ethnic Cleansing." *Journal of Modern History* 70 (December 1998): 813–61.

Mayzel, Nakhman. *Kegnzaytike hashpeot in velt-shafn.* Warsaw: Yidisher kultur farband, 1965.

———. *Dos Yiddishe shafn un der Yidisher shrayber in Sovetnfarband.* New York: Yidisher Kultur Farband, 1959.

———. *Yidishe tematik un Yidishe melodies bay bavuste muziker.* New York: Yidishe Kultur Farband, 1952.

Medvedev, Roy. *Let History Judge: The Origins and Consequences of Stalinism.* Edited by D. Joravsky and G. Haupt, translated by C. Taylor. New York: Alfred A. Knopf, 1971.

Miller, Jack, ed. *Jews in Soviet Culture.* New Brunswick: Transaction Books, 1984.

Mosse, George L. *The Image of Man: The Creation of Modern Masculinity.* New York: Oxford University Press, 1996.

Murza, S. A. *Akterskaia sistema Solomona Mikhoelsa.* Ph.D. diss., St. Petersburg Institute of Theater, Music, and Film, 1992.

Nakhimovsky, Alice Stone. *Russian-Jewish Literature and Identity: Jabotinsky, Babel, Frossman, Galich, Roziner, Markish.* Baltimore: Johns Hopkins University Press, 1992.

Nekrich, Aleksandr. *"June 22, 1941": Soviet Historians and the German Invasion.* Translated by Vladimir Petrov. Columbia: University of South Carolina Press, 1968.

Neuberger, Joan. *Hooliganism: Crime Culture and Power in St. Petersburg, 1900–1914.* Berkeley: University of California Press, 1983.

Nicoll, Allardyce. *The World of Harlequin: A Critical Study of the Commedia Dell'Arte.* Cambridge: Cambridge University Press, 1963.

Niger, Shmuel. *Di tsveyshprakhikayt fun undzer literatur.* Detroit: Louis La Med Foundation for the Advancement of Hebrew and Yiddish Literature, 1941.

————. *Yidishe shrayber in Sovet-Rusland.* New York: S. Niger Book Committee, 1958.
Novietskii, Pavel Ivanovich. *Obrazy akterov.* Moscow: Iskusstvo, 1941.
Oyslender, Nakhum. *Idishe teater, 1887–1917.* Moscow: Der Emes, 1940.
Parrott, Ray J. Jr. "Aesopian Language." In *The Modern Encyclopedia of Russian and Soviet Literature,* vol. 1. Gulf Breeze, Fla.: Academic International Press, 1977.
Pethybridge, Roger. "Concern for Bolshevik Ideological Predominance at the Start of NEP." *Russian Review* 44, no. 4 (1982): 445–53.
Picon-Vallin, Béatrice. *Le Théâtre juif soviétique pendant les années vingt.* Lausanne: Editions la cité, 1973.
Pinkus, Benjamin. *The Jews in the Soviet Union: The History of a National Minority.* Cambridge: Cambridge University Press, 1988.
Pipes, Richard. *The Russian Revolution.* New York: Vintage, 1990.
Portnoy, Samuel A., trans. *Henryk Erlich and Victor Alter: Two Heroes and Martyrs for Jewish Socialism.* New York: Ktav Publishing House, 1990.
Posner, Solomon. *Evrei v obshchei shkole.* St. Petersburg: Razum, 1914.
Powell, David E. *Antireligious Propaganda in the Soviet Union: A Study of Mass Persuasion.* Cambridge, Mass.: MIT Press, 1975.
Prylucki, Nojach. *Yidishe folkslider.* Warsaw: Bikher far ale, 1911.
Rapoport, Louis. *Stalin's War against the Jews.* New York: Free Press, 1990.
Rassweiler, Anne. *Generation of Power.* New York: Oxford University Press, 1988.
Redlich, Shimon. *Propaganda and Nationalism in Wartime Russia: The Jewish Antifascist Committee in the USSR, 1941–1948.* Boulder: East European Quarterly, 1982.
Ringer, Alexander L. *Arnold Schoenberg: The Composer as Jew.* New York: Oxford University Press, 1990.
Rittersporn, Gabor Tamas. *Stalinist Simplifications and Soviet Complications: Social Tension and Political Conflicts in the USSR, 1933–1953.* Chur, Switzerland: Harwood Academic Publishers, 1991.
Roback, A. A. *The Story of Yiddish Literature.* New York: Yiddish Scientific Institute, 1940.
Robin, Régine. *L'Amour du yiddish: écriture juive et sentiment de la langue (1830–1930).* Paris: Éditions du Sorbier, 1984.
————. *Socialist Realism: An Impossible Aesthetic.* Translated by Catherine Porter. 1986. Reprint, Stanford: Stanford University Press, 1992.
Ro'i, Yaacov, ed. *Jews and Jewish Life in Russia and the Soviet Union.* The Cumming Center Series. Essex: Frank Cass & Co., 1995.
————. *The Struggle for Soviet Jewish Emigration, 1948–1967.* Cambridge and New York: Cambridge University Press, 1991.
Rosenberg, Marvin. *The Masks of King Lear.* Berkeley: University of California Press, 1972.
Rosenberg, William G. *Bolshevik Visions: First Phase of the Cultural Revolution in Bolshevik Russia.* Ann Arbor: University of Michigan Press, 1984.
Rosenberg, William G., and Lewis H. Siegelbaum, eds. *Social Dimensions of Soviet Industrialization.* Bloomington: Indiana University Press, 1993.
Rosenfeld, Lulla Adler. *The Yiddish Theatre and Jacob P. Adler.* 1977. Reprint, New York: Shapolsky Publishers, 1988.
Rosenthal, Bernice Glatzer, ed. *The Occult in Russian and Soviet Culture.* Ithaca: Cornell University Press, 1997.
Roskies, David G. *A Bridge of Longing: The Lost Art of Yiddish Storytelling.* Cambridge, Mass.: Harvard University Press, 1995.
Rowland, Richard. "Geographical Patterns of the Jewish Population in the Pale of Settle-

ment in Late Nineteenth-Century Russia." *Jewish Social Studies* 48, no. 3–4 (1986): 207–34.

Rozshansky, Shmuel. *Yidishe literatur—yidish lebn.* 5 vols. Buenos Aires: Ateneo literario en el iwo, 1973.

Rubenstein, Joshua. *Tangled Loyalties: The Life and Times of Ilya Ehrenburg.* New York: Basic Books, 1996.

Rubin, Ruth. *Voices of a People: Yiddish Folk Song.* New York: Thomas Yoseloff, 1963.

Rudnitsky, Konstantin. *Russian and Soviet Theater 1905–1932.* New York: Thames and Hudson, 1988.

Said, Edward W. *Culture and Imperialism.* New York: Knopf, 1993.

Sand, Maurice. *The History of the Harlequinade.* New York: B. Blom, 1968.

Sandrow, Nahma. *Vagabond Stars: A World History of Yiddish Theater.* New York: Harper and Row, 1977.

Sawyer, Thomas E. *The Jewish Minority in the Soviet Union.* Boulder: Westview, 1979.

Schapiro, Leonard. *The Communist Party of the Soviet Union.* 2nd ed. New York: Vintage Books, 1971.

———. "The Jewish Anti-Fascist Committee and Phases of Soviet Anti-Semitic Policy during and after World War II." In *Jews and Non-Jews in Eastern Europe, 1918–1945,* edited by Bela Vago and George L. Mosse. New York: Wiley, 1974.

———. *1917: The Russian Revolutions and the Origins of Present-Day Communism.* London: Temple Smith, 1984.

———. *The Origin of the Communist Autocracy.* Cambridge, Mass.: Harvard University Press, 1977.

Scholem, Gershom. *The Messianic Idea in Judaism.* New York: Schocken Books, 1971.

———. *On the Mystical Shape of the Godhead: Basic Concepts in the Kabbalah.* New York: Schocken Books, 1991.

Schulman, Elias. *Di sovetish-yidishe literatur.* New York: Tsiko, 1971.

Schwartz, Solomon. *Di yidn in Sovetn-Farband milkhome un nokhmilkhome yorn, 1939–1965.* New York: Yidishn arbeter komitet, 1967.

Schwarz, Boris. *Music and Muscial Life in the USSR.* 1972. Reprint, Bloomington: Indiana University Press, 1983.

Schwarz, Solomon M. *The Jews in the Soviet Union.* Syracuse: Syracuse University Press, 1951.

Segel, Harold. *Twentieth Century Russian Drama.* 2nd ed. Baltimore: Johns Hopkins University Press, 1993.

Shaffer, Harry G. *The Soviet Treatment of Jews.* New York: Praeger Publishers, 1974.

Shchedrin, Vasilii. "Istoriia gosudarstvennogo evreiskogo teatra na idish (GOSET) v Moskve, 1919–1948." MA thesis, Russian State University of Humanities, 1994.

Shehori-Rubin, Zippora. "Habimah in Russia—Theater with a National-Zionist Mission, 1918–1926." *Shevut: Studies in Russian and East European Jewish History and Culture* 6, no. 22 (1997): 79–103.

Shentalinsky, Vitaly. *The KGB's Literary Archive.* Translated by John Crowfoot. Introduction by Robert Conquest. London: Harvill Press, 1995.

Sicher, Efraim. *Jews in Russian Literature after the October Revolution: Writers and Artists between Hope and Apostasy.* Cambridge: Cambridge University Press, 1995.

Siegel, Lee. "Persecution and the Art of Painting." *New Republic,* August 31, 1998, 33–41.

Siegelbaum, Lewis. *Soviet State and Society Between Revolutions, 1918–1929.* New York: Cambridge University Press, 1992.

————. *Stakhanovism and the Politics of Productivity in the USSR, 1935–1941.* Cambridge: Cambridge University Press, 1988.

Siegelbaum, Lewis, and Ronald G. Suny, eds. *Making Workers Soviet.* Ithaca: Cornell University Press, 1994.

Silber, Jacques. "Some Demographic Characteristics of the Jewish Population in Russia at the End of the Nineteenth Century." *Jewish Social Studies* 42, nos. 3–4 (1980): 269–80.

Slezkine, Yuri. "The USSR as a Communal Apartment, or How a Socialist State Promoted Ethnic Particularism." *Slavic Review* 53, no. 2 (Summer 1994): 414–52.

Slonim, Marc *Russian Theater: From the Empire to the Soviets.* New York: Collier, 1961.

Starr, S. Frederick. *Red and Hot: The Fate of Jazz in the Soviet Union, 1917–1980.* New York: Oxford University Press, 1983.

Stites, Richard. *Culture and Entertainment in Wartime Russia.* Bloomington: Indiana University Press, 1995.

————. *Revolutionary Dreams: Utopian Vision and Experimental Life in the Russian Revolution.* New York: Oxford University Press, 1989.

————. *Russian Popular Culture: Entertainment and Society since 1900.* Cambridge: Cambridge University Press, 1992.

Strassler, David. "The Dictator Feared the Actor." *Jerusalem Post,* August 14, 1992.

Suny, Ronald Grigor. *Looking toward Ararat: Armenia in Modern History.* Bloomington: Indiana University Press, 1993.

Tartakower, Aryeh, and Zelda Kolitz, eds. *Jewish Culture in the Soviet Union: Proceedings of the Symposium Held by the Cultural Department of the World Jewish Congress.* Jerusalem: World Jewish Congress, 1973.

Taylor, Brandon. *Art and Literature under the Bolsheviks.* London: Pluto Press, 1991–1992.

Taylor, Richard, and Ian Christie, eds. *Inside the Film Factory: New Approaches to Russian and Soviet Cinema.* London: Routledge, 1991.

Thorpe, Richard G. "The Academic Theater and the Fate of Soviet Artistic Pluralism, 1919–1928." *Slavic Review* 51, no. 3 (Fall 1992): 389–410.

Thurston, Robert W. *Life and Terror in Stalin's Russia, 1934–1941.* New Haven: Yale University Press, 1996.

Timasheff, Nikolai. *The Great Retreat: The Growth and Decline of Communism in Russia.* New York: Dutton, 1946.

Tolstoy, Nikoali. *The Secret Betrayal.* New York: Charles Scribner, 1977.

Tucker, Robert. *Stalin in Power: The Revolution from Above.* New York: W.W. Norton, 1990.

Tumarkin, Nina. *Lenin Lives! The Lenin Cult in Soviet Russia.* Cambridge, Mass.: Harvard University Press, 1983.

————. *The Living and the Dead: The Rise and Fall of the Cult of World War II in Russia.* New York: Basic Books, 1994.

Ulam, Adam. *Expansion and Coexistence: A History of Soviet Foreign Policy, 1917–1967.* New York: Praeger, 1968.

————. *Stalin: The Man and His Era.* New York: Viking Press, 1973.

Vaksberg, Arkady. *Stalin against the Jews.* Translated by Antonina W. Bouis. New York: Alfred A. Knopf, 1994.

Virpi, Tuulia Donner. *O sydbakh Goset, 1918–1948.* Ph.D. diss., Helsinki University, 1988.

von Geldern, James. *Bolshevik Festivals, 1917–1920.* Berkeley: University of California Press, 1993.

von Geldern, James, and Richard Stites, eds. *Mass Culture in Soviet Russia: Tales, Poems, Songs, Movies, Plays and Folklore, 1917–1953*. Bloomington: Indiana University Press, 1995.

Weinberg, Robert. *Stalin's Forgotten Zion: Birobidzhan and the Making of a Soviet Jewish Homeland—An Illustrated History, 1928–1996*. Introduction by Zvi Gitelman. Berkeley: University of California Press, 1998.

Weitzner, Jacob. *Sholem Aleichem in the Theater*. Northwood, Middlesex: Symposium Press; Madison, Wis.: Fairleigh Dickinson University Press, 1994.

Werth, Alexander. *Russia at War, 1941–45*. London: Pan Books, 1965.

Wertheimer, Jack, ed. *The Uses of Tradition: Jewish Continuity in the Modern Era*. New York: Jewish Theological Seminary, 1992.

Willett, John. *The Theatre of Erwin Piscator*. New York: Holmes & Meier, 1979.

Wirth-Nesher, Hana. *What Is Jewish Literature?* Philadelphia: The Jewish Publication Society, 1994.

Wisse, Ruth R. "By Their Own Hands." *New Republic*, February 3, 1997, 34–43.

Wright, A. Colin. "'Superfluous People' in the Soviet Drama of the 1920s." *Canadian Slavonic Papers* 30, no. 1 (March 1988): 1–16.

Yahil, Leni. *The Holocaust: The Fate of European Jewry*. 1985. Reprint, Oxford: Oxford University Press, 1990.

Yerushalmi, Josef Hayim. *Zakhor: Jewish History and Jewish Memory*. Foreword by Harold Bloom. 1982. Reprint, Seattle: University of Washington Press, 1996.

Youngblood, Denise. *Movies for the Masses: Popular Cinema and Soviet Society in the 1920s*. Cambridge: Cambridge University Press, 1992.

———. *Soviet Cinema in the Silent Era, 1918–1935*. 1980. Reprint, Austin: University of Texas Press, 1991.

Zerubavel, Yael. *Recovered Roots: Collective Memory and the Making of Israeli National Tradition*. Chicago: University of Chicago Press, 1995.

Zilbercwaig, Zalman, ed. *Leksikon fun yidishn teater*. Warsaw: Alisheve, 1934.

Zivanovic, J. "Little-Known Theatre of Widely Known Influence." *Educational Theatre Journal* 27, no. 2 (May 1975): 236.

Zohn, Hershel. *The Story of Yiddish Theater*. Las Cruces, N.M.: Yucca Tree Press, 1979.

INDEX

Page numbers in *italics* refer to illustrations.

Fininberg, Ezra, 61, 135
Finkelkraut, Daniil, 198, 204, *218*
Fishman, G. B., 234
Fishzon, Abraham, 24, 25
Five-Year Plans, 106, 112, 118, 216
Flame from the Boiler (Toller), 130
folk art/literature, 37, 39, 44
folk music, 11, 13, 45, 59, 116, 171, 181
folklore, 108, 150, 151, 237
For Life and Unto Death (Halkin), 246
formalism, 110–11, 186, 190–93, 213
Four Days (Daniel), 119, 125–29, *127*, 135, 243
Fox, Michael, 86. *See* David-Fox, Michael
French Revolution, 21, 206
Freud, Sigmund, 14, 15, 111
Freylekhs (Shneer-Okun), 246–49, *247*
Friedland, Zvi, 153–54
futurism, 21, 37

Geizer, Matvei, 156
generational conflict, 15, 42, 118, 147; national themes and, 174, 177, 182; World War II and, 240
genocide, 23, 123
German language, 26, 29, 90, 109
Germany, 4, 44, 93, 275; Granovsky's defection to, 103; Jews of, 95; rise of fascism in, 199; tour of, 90
Gershenzon, M., 158, 159
Gershwin, George, 230
Gielgud, John, 225, 231
Gitelman, Zvi, 9, 147–48, 235, 240
Gladkov, Fedor, 113
Glinka, Mikhail, 46
God of Vengeance (Asch), 42, 59
Gogol, Nikolai, 209
Goldberg, Ben Zion, 222, 246
Goldblatt, Moshe, 82, 84, 99, 191; on European tour, 93–94, 94–95; Mikhoels's death and, 263; state-awarded title of, 139; Yiddish theater studio and, 49; Zionist scandal and, 98
Goldenweizer, Aleksandr, 253
Goldfadn, Abraham, 28, 45, 68, 73, 94; anniversary of birth of, 207; birth of Yiddish theater and, 24; as folk artist, 46; modernist interpretation of, 4; socialist realism and, 115; stylized social types and, 144; theater's return to, 151; tsarist ban on Yiddish theater and, 1; Zionism and, 163
Goldmann, Nahum, 224, 228
Goldshteyn, Isaak, 258

Golem, The (Leyvick), 27
Goodman, Benny, 12
Gorbachev, Mikhail, 5, 16
Gordin, Jacob, 24
Gordon, R. Isaiah Hertz, 108
Gorky, Maksim, 22, 38, 233; on Aleichem, 177; Cultural Revolution and, 113; folklore and, 150, 183; plays of, 115, 209; seen as deviationist, 89
Granovsky, Aleksandr, 4, 22, 54, 144; appeals to Party, 60; authority of, 55; backstage intrigues and, 67–73; carnivalesque staging of, 51; cinema and, 65; Communist Party control and, 46; control of troupe's daily activities, 86–87; defection from Soviet Union, 76, 92, 102–103, 105, 109–10, 275; depiction of revolution on stage, 81–82; directorial methods, 167; European tour and, 89–97; falling fortunes of, 89; films of, 103; folk art and, 150; formalism and, 190; honored by Soviet state, 64; Jewish Theatrical Society and, 29, 31; legacy of, 191; Litvakov and, 86; Mikhoels's defense of, 110–11, 153, 191–92; move to Moscow, 35–38; press releases and, 212; salary of, 49, 83; as symbolist, 76; ties to Party officials, 58; Yiddish Chamber Theater and, 31–34
Great Dictator, The (film), 3, 230
Great Terror (1937–1939), 1–2, 4, 185–88, 209–14; Aleichem and, 206–209; anti-Semitism and, 10–11; arrests of theater artists, 194–97; art of theater and, 190–93; Goldfadn and, 206–209; historians on, 281n17; music and, 188–89; plays performed during, 197–206
Gricher-Cherikover, Grigorii, 65, 241
Grinvald, Iakov, 126, 130, 138; on heroism in theater, 161; on Jewish bandit plays, 157, 158; on *King Lear*, 145, 146
Gromyko, Andrei, 259, 260
Gropius, Walter, 109
Grossman, Vasilii, 245, 264
Guide to the Perplexed (Maimonides), 14
Gurshteyn, Aron, 162, 171, 207
Gusiatinskii, A. M., 154
Gutzkow, Karl, 33

Habima troupe, 27, 36, 45; campaign against, 60; *Dybbuk* production, 48; Falk's work with, 62; harassment of, 56; Moscow State Yiddish Theater and, 90, 96; in Palestine, 98

JEFFREY VEIDLINGER is Assistant Professor of History and Jewish Studies at Indiana University, Bloomington.

The Circle of Fire

by
Jenny Robertson

Illustrated by
Jan Skelsey

ARK PUBLISHING
47 Marylebone Lane, London W1M 6AX

Also by Jenny Robertson:
Fior – Son of the King
The Circle of Shadows
King in a Stable
The Book of Bible Stories in Colour
The Ladybird Bible Book Series
This story is a sequel to 'The
Circle of Shadows'

© Jenny Robertson 1979 Illustrated by Jan Skelsey

ISBN 0 85421 787 8

Printed in Great Britain by offset lithography by Billing & Sons Ltd.,
Guildford, London and Worcester.

Contents

Historical Note

At the end of the first century AD a freed slave, Dercc, makes his way home to his own people who live as I have described them in the first book about Dercc's adventures, *Circle of Shadows*, in the part of the country now known as Mid-Argyll. You can still visit several of the places spoken of: the stone circles; the High Fort – Dunadd; the burial mounds; the Ridge of the Reindeer, though there are no reindeer there now; and the Hill of the Maidens. Dercc's people, the Epidii, worshipped a goddess, Epona. Like the other Celtic tribes they lived a precarious life raiding and hunting, loving war and personal glory and adornment. There were three important festivals during the year and since these are mentioned in the story and one at least is very important I think that I should give you their names and dates.

The year began with Imbolc, the feast of lambs, which was at the beginning of the month we call February. March and April known as the 'misty, wet weeks of the year' brought kinder weather, and the first of May, the feast of Beltane, was the next important feast. Then, as the long dark winter began, November brought the dark feast of Samain – the feast of the dead. We call it Hallowe'en and, because folk memory is long, some of our celebrations today hark back to those of Dercc's people in the High Fort two thousand years ago.

I
Homecoming

'So you're on your way home at last?' The old woman looked up at the red-headed youth, stocky and strong for his eighteen years, who brought her four shining trout on the end of his borrowed spear.

'Ah, you've caught me some beauties,' she added. 'Well, it's no wonder they're so silver and sleek, for tonight the moon will be full.'

Dercc nodded, squatting down to set about the messy task of gutting the fish. Seagulls appeared out of nowhere.

'I had forgotten that old people believe the full moon is lucky,' he admitted.

'Forgotten? Ah, well, you've been away, over the sea. But I'm telling you that when the old people forget all our traditions and beliefs, you young ones will lose the sap of your being, just as the sap goes out of the willow and hazel and pine, or any wood that's cut when the moon is on the wane.'

Dercc nodded. It was so strange to be nearly home! At first, months ago, as the three-decked troop ship pulled away from Southern Gaul, he had kept looking back, remembering the friends he had just left behind in the busy port of Massilia. He could not believe then that he would actually arrive home in the North. Now the past was already becoming unreal. Increasingly the thought of home brought a tight knot to his stomach . . . especially the thought of seeing Liath again.

The old woman was still talking.

'Meat has no taste and wood has no goodness at the wane of the moon. So when we weave willow for our baskets we make sure it was cut when the moon was full. And we cut our peats and reap our corn only when the moon is new.'

He nodded again. He remembered the long wands of willow Liath and he used to cut, Dercc guiding his blind brother's hand, in the good days before the magic and the vision they'd seen in the stones. Soon they would be together again.

'I will set off today,' he told the old woman. 'As you say, the moon is full. I will be able to walk some of the night as well.'

'Yes, it's not so far, compared with all the distance you've been, to our High Fort, the Horse People's stronghold,' the old woman said. 'You deserve a good journey and a happy meeting with your kinsfolk, especially your brother. . . .' She checked and in a changed tone went on, 'You've done so much to help us here, though. Why, you delayed your long journey to harvest our barley. It's thanks to you that my small crop was gathered before the rain could damage it.'

'A traveller's return for his stay!' smiled Dercc, wiping his hunting knife in the heather. Shrieking gulls still squabbled for their feast as he carried the cleaned fish into the old woman's small round hut, bending beneath overhanging heather thatch. The small dwelling clustered with other identical round houses in an old dun, behind stone walls strengthened with criss-crossing spars of wood.

'So you're leaving us!' the old woman said again. 'May you walk well, laddie – for that's all you are, in spite of the broad shoulders on you. May you travel with the good influence of the moon, because I sense both sorrow and darkness ahead of you. Give me your hand.'

'In farewell only,' he said. 'Don't tell me my future, wise woman. I'm not afraid of the dark, and I've learnt

that sorrow can bring its own good.'

'Then it is you who are wise, laddie! Yes, yes, I can see in your face that you've learnt that sore lesson. So you're minded to go,' she said again. 'May blessings go with you.'

'May blessing stay with you, and with your kin here in the dun,' he returned. He picked up his heavy cloak, neatly rolled, checking first that a small bundle was tucked safely inside. Then he swung away into the hills on the last lap of his long journey home.

He left a long, still loch behind him and, walking now by moonlight, found his way through a pass that took him westward across rough, barren hills. Then, at last, he stopped to sleep as he had so often done, rolled up in his cloak. Disturbed perhaps by the bright harvest moon, excited, or overtired, he dreamed, slept fitfully, and dreamed again, haunted by the thin empty face and dark sightless eyes of his twin brother, Liath. Again and again that night, Liath's face swam before him, and there was no sign of welcome in it. He woke before dawn, shivering, with a cold, sick feeling and a bad taste in his mouth. He did not feel like eating, and strode on, until the rhythm of walking began to blot out the dream.

He walked on and on, sometimes following the grassy roadways of his people, sometimes taking remembered short cuts through now familiar countryside. Once or twice he passed ruined settlements with charred roof beams and crumbling walls; the work of raiders.

The sun was lingering low in the western sky when he halted. Below him was the grey smudge of the western firth, where, nearly four years before, he had been taken prisoner in an enemy ship. Dercc looked away, uphill to the farmstead, where he had been brought up, feeling the familiar chill of the mountain wind on his hot face. He heard the shouts of children herding goats home to the old dun close by, so similar to the little cluster of huts he had left the day before. Black-fleeced sheep bleated in the

distance. From the long glen of burial mounds and ancient stones, scores of rooks rose, flying home, ragged wings flapping. Strangely, at that moment, his thoughts returned to his friends in Massilia, and especially to Rudi, who had been so sure that the violent, red-headed, young prisoner would one day return to his home. Now the time had come! Soon he would be with Liath.

He was spotted as he climbed the hill. His foster-father, Uncle Mael, had always kept a good look-out, Dercc remembered. He waved, hearing the shouts as his three young cousins yelled the news of a stranger's arrival.

'It's a traveller. Do you think he speaks our language? Look at his odd clothes.' That was one of the girls.

'Foreigners always dress differently from us.' Gilla's voice was breaking. He would be about fifteen by now. His curly brown hair hung loosely round his shoulders. His bare arms and legs were sturdy and sun-tanned.

'Down, Penn, down! Hey, don't let her loose!' They tried to hold the dog back. 'Why, look. She seems to know him! Look! She's licking him like an old friend!'

Dercc, thrilled that the old sheep dog recognized him, flung his arms round her as she leapt up at him. He ran his hands through her heavy coat, tickling her white throat as he had always done. She had been his puppy when they were both small.

Hearing the commotion his foster parents came hurrying down the hill.

'What stranger is this our dog welcomes?' Black-haired and bearded, Uncle Mael boomed his question to the world at large. But Dercc suddenly found his voice stick in his throat. Fondling Penn, he bent and buried his face against the dog's neck.

'Can it be Dercc, come back at last?' Aunt Ala cried out. 'But he's got the shoulders and hands of a man!'

'Penn knows him though!' Uncle Mael hurried towards them. His tunic blew against his bare knees, and his wooden shoes hammered the grassy slope.

Dercc stood up.

'Yes, I am Dercc. It is good to see you again, Uncle Mael!'

His aunt stifled a cry.

'Is it your brother's strange powers that have brought you back here?' She pushed her unbraided greying hair back from her face and drew her fair-haired daughters Vin and Alarch close beside her.

There was an uneasy silence which his uncle broke.

'Powers or not, we're still your kin. Come on in to our home, Dercc, son of my brother Coll.'

It was only after he had washed his hands and face in the discoloured iron pan Gilla held for him, and eaten and drunk, and answered questions, that he dared to ask,

'Where is Liath?'

He noticed Gilla silence eleven year old Alarch with a dig of his elbow.

'Liath is a priest now. He is one of the Great Ones. Young as he is, he is one of the most powerful people in our tribe,' Uncle Mael said. There was a silence.

'A priest? Liath?' Dercc's voice sounded unnaturally loud. 'But you have to train for years to be a priest. . . . Liath has never been trained like that. . . .' His voice trailed away.

'Liath was different,' said Aunt Ala. She got up and began to pour more ale into their cups. 'There,' she said, 'drink that, Dercc. I should think you'll have missed good ale on your travels.'

'I've missed more than ale, Aunt. I've missed my home, all of you . . . and Liath.' He checked himself. Yes, he had missed the farm and the old haunts, but not everything he remembered had been good. There were old, bitter memories of a childhood without too much love, when Aunt Ala had been too busy with her own children to care for her husband's nephews. And Uncle Mael too was not a man to show affection, or know how to treat a sensitive blind boy and his fiercely loyal twin

brother. Liath and Dercc had been left to themselves. Even the other children ignored them in their games because Liath's blindness was a handicap. 'Was Liath still unwanted?' Dercc wondered, watching their faces. He had to find out more.

'Liath's very gifted, of course,' he suggested.

'Gifted, yes, if gifts that come from darkness and all the powers of the dark are what you're after,' Uncle Mael said. He spat into the palm of his hand, warding off evil. Dercc recognized the gesture.

'The gods of our tribe have been good to me,' Uncle Mael went on. 'My ponies down on the flat land are the finest amongst the Horse People. You should know, Dercc. You've sold them yourself at the High Fort.'

Dercc nodded.

'I expect you sell them now,' he said to Gilla, who smiled shyly.

'Long before our tribe settled here other people made their living in this wide glen,' Uncle Mael continued. 'And I respect the memory of those ancient people who carved the old stones with their strange markings. Of course I pay my dues to the gods of our tribe and I honour our king and our customs, but the fighting for power, and the dark magic that takes the priests down into the burial chambers to disturb the dead, now that I've not time for. You went with the priests once, didn't you?'

Dercc knew his cousins were staring at him curiously. He met his uncle's gaze and felt a sudden new liking for Uncle Mael as he looked into the steady grey eyes in the lined weatherbeaten face.

'We went to the stone circle in the woods,' he began slowly. 'There was a strange message in the stones. I guided Liath's hand and he found it too.' Vividly Dercc recalled the scene. Nineteen stones, each towering above the two half-frightened boys, encircled an empty grave. Shadows stretched away on every side. The place was still and full of mystery. Liath, the dark lonely boy, was

shivering as Dercc laid his hands over his and guided them towards the stones.

'There is power here,' Liath had whispered. 'I feel it running through my hands. We will have power – the twins nobody wants – '

Later the priests had taken them down into one of the burial chambers. They too had talked about power. . . . Dercc shivered, driving away bad memories.

'It's over now,' he said, 'for me anyway. I chose a way of light instead of darkness. It has led me home.'

The rush lights flickered. The fire reddened his cousins' wide-eyed faces, and stained the wooden chest which was the only furniture in the round house apart from Aunt Ala's loom. Dercc smiled at his family.

'It's so good to be with you here at last!' he told them, and this time he meant it. 'I should like to stay here with you and learn more from you, Uncle Mael, and help you. Liath and I ran free all the time. I hardly ever bothered to give you a hand, except at the horse fairs and at harvest. Forgive me.'

'You've changed, Dercc,' Aunt Ala said, quietly.

'Well, now, I often thought that you could have done more to help us,' Uncle Mael agreed. 'Foster parents generally mean as much to their foster children as to their own flesh and blood, more even, but you two were always wrapped up in yourselves. No one else seemed to matter.'

'I know. I'm sorry,' Dercc said and added, 'I'm glad I've come home to say it!' He got up and unrolled his cloak.

'I bought these for you on my way home.' He held out several small bundles.

His cousins jumped up and crowded round, holding the rush lamps close to see.

'Thank you for your mothering, Aunt Ala.' The words brought tears to his aunt's eyes. She pinned his silver brooch to her plain woollen tunic.

'It's much too fine a thing for me, Dercc. Oh, I wish

your mother could see you now: you've come home with such confidence in your bearing and so little pride in your ways! Yet, Dercc, I fear your brother will hate you for it,' she added.

Not questioning her words, he unpacked the other presents: a hunting knife with a decorated handle for his uncle; knuckle stones and dice for Gilla; and necklaces of small clear amber beads for Vin and Alarch. One bundle remained still rolled in his cloak and he stowed it carefully away.

'Does Liath still play his harp?' he asked.

'Oh, yes,' his cousins were eager to tell him. 'They say he can make the tribe see things with his music that they've never seen before, even though he's blind himself.'

'I must find Liath,' he said.

'Even though he may not want you now? Do you not understand how powerful Liath is?'

'Yes,' Dercc answered at once. 'Remember, I once gave myself to the dark force too. It brought me dark and more dark. I have heard Liath play his harp and seen him lay a kind of spell on everyone.'

'It's not just that, Dercc,' his uncle said. 'The priests have had him in their clutches ever since that time you're speaking about. He's been made a teacher, as we told you. Many of the chiefs and great lords hate him, but they are no match for him. He is very wealthy now and it is even said,' Uncle Mael dropped his voice, 'that he will be the next king.'

'But Liath can never be a warrior,' exclaimed Dercc.

'No, but he will be a priest king,' said Aunt Ala. 'As your Uncle says, we don't interfere in the high affairs of our tribe, but we hear things, many things.'

'There are ambassadors from the eastern tribes at the Fort now. Liath is often in their company,' said Uncle Mael.

'The priests talked to us about uniting the tribes,' Dercc recalled. 'I did not understand then. But I know

how strong the message of the stones was – how it filled us with the power of the dark. But it leads only to disaster. Tomorrow I will go to the Fort and tell Liath of all I have learnt.'

The next day Dercc remembered his words to his Uncle. Anxious as he was to be off he spent the morning helping Gilla and Uncle Mael with the animals: goats; long-haired, sturdy ponies, eleven hands high; a cow and her calf; and a flock of black-fleeced sheep. He cut wood for the fire that blackened the rafters of the roof. There was no ceiling in the round house. The smoke found its way out through the rafters which were overlaid with split birch branches and heather thatch.

Then he offered to help his aunt who was pounding barley to make ale.

'Let me do this for you, Aunt Ala.'

'You've been helping your uncle, Dercc. You don't want to do women's work – slave's work even.'

'I've been a slave, though, as I told you.' Dercc set to work with the heavy grinding stones. His aunt sat back on her heels and rubbed her wrists and swollen finger joints.

'I wish your mother could see you now,' she said softly. 'Ah, what puny babies you and your brother were! We never thought you'd live. We fed you with goat's milk dripped into your wee mouths from a rag, for I had no bairns of my own then. To think I held you both, all wet on my knee, through that winter, coaxing you every hour to take some milk!'

'Some foster parents might have put us both out,' he said, 'especially when you found that Liath was blind. Here you are, Aunt Ala. What happens now?'

'This.' She tipped the powdered barley into a big jar and stirred the mixture to which she carefully added water.

'Of course! I'd forgotten. Or perhaps I hadn't really noticed before! Then you let the mixture stand?' Dercc watched with interest.

'Yes, till it ferments. Then it will be boiled and strained.'

'What a lot of work!' he observed, feelingly.

'Yes, indeed, but the men will have their ale,' Aunt Ala returned. 'And you need your breakfast,' she added, feeding him generously with porridge and honey and pieces of smoked fish washed down with home-made ale.

Then he knotted his heavy cloak on his back, took the gift for Liath and put a small bundle of food in the wallet at his belt. He went towards the Fort following the course of the winding river, then over the moorland, already at that season touched with melting frost.

II
The High Fort

Out of a huge rock the Fort rose above him, like a lion frozen in its leap.

He made his way up to the grassy roadway from the field where the warriors trained, and paused for a moment, bewildered by the crowd of people surging around the gateway. From their dress Dercc recognized the Seal People, one of the clans of his tribe, who lived by the western shore and came to the Fort to trade sealskins, creels of fish and stores of seal fat, which fed the lamps in the great hall of the Fort.

Close beside the gateway a small group of half-naked boys were struggling with a rearing half-wild pony, jerking hard with heather ropes that bit across the frightened animal's flared nostrils. Watching, Dercc suddenly remembered a far-away port and himself, wild and sick and bound. He ran up to them.

'Let me help you with your pony.'

'Hey!' they protested. 'Hands off! He's our pony! We're going to sell him.'

'But you're terrifying him,' Dercc replied, putting his hand on the ropes.

The boys laughed and jerked the pony's head harder, trying to shake Dercc off.

'Who do you think you are?' demanded one of the boys.

'He's foreign, of course. You can tell by his clothes,' another said.

'No, I'm not foreign,' Dercc said. 'I've led ponies up here to sell in the fort since I was smaller than you.'

'Out of the way! The chiefs are returning!' A naked runner, one of the young warriors, elbowed his way through the crowd. His straight blond hair, darkened with sweat, lay limply across his shoulder blades.

A hunting horn rang out. Startled by the sound, which distracted his captors' attention for the moment, the pony broke free, running amok in the crowd. He knocked over a group of elderly men in long hooded cloaks, and charged across the path of the mud-flecked ponies who were cantering up with the leading chariot. With a deft pull the charioteer checked his team. The crowd pressed back, clearing the way to the gate. As the charioteers, dressed in short coats of deerskin, drove the chiefs back to the Fort, the small boys chased the pony slapping at him with their wooden sandals, making futile grabs at the rope, frightening the poor beast into a blind panic.

The king and lords of the Horse People rode by, followed by the easterners, a gay cavalcade, with decorated shields and rich trappings. Dercc watched eagerly for the first sight of his brother, and suddenly – with a shock – he saw him. That was Liath – that haggard, white face, crowned with owls' feathers.

But at the moment of recognition there came a distraction. The wild pony, rearing frantically among the gang of small boys, charged Liath's chariot. The charioteer swore; the other charioteers, craning their necks to see, yelled enthusiastically; but some spat in their hands and turned away. Dercc hurled himself forward and caught the trailing rope, but the pony with a scream had checked itself, rearing up, foaming. He looked up. He saw the sightless eyes, the contorted face, the outstretched hand, almost above him. A black whirlpool began to swim inside his brain. He smelt the burial mound, the blood, and heard again the high inhuman scream. He remembered the madness, and then, the Name.

'Jesus! Light – oh Light.'

The pony turned aside, dragging Dercc after him, while Liath's charioteer, mastering his two black mares, drove on to the fort, followed by ranks of young warriors and finally by the slaves.

It took a long time to calm the pony. Dercc, badly shaken, coaxed the young thing gently, his hand on the rough mane. The boys hung back in awed silence and let him lead the pony to the high gateway in the rock.

'Well, you got him under control then! That's a wonder! The way he bolted I didn't think we'd ever see him inside our gates. You boys needed the help of the stranger then? . . . If you are a stranger,' the gatekeeper added, staring at Dercc. 'There's something very familiar about you.'

'You have seen me before,' he answered. 'I've been in and out of these gates since I was small, usually with ponies to trade. I came here to tryst with the warriors when the enemy ship sailed down the Sound. I'm one of the Horse People.'

'But you're not one of the warriors now?' enquired the gatekeeper. 'I know them all, and, although, as I say, you look familiar. . . .'

'I was made one, a warrior of our tribe,' Dercc explained. 'Not much of one though,' he smiled. 'I'm only now returning from my first fight more than three years ago.'

The boys gasped and the gatekeeper roared with laughter.

'Oh, that's rare! It was a long fight then?'

'Yes,' Dercc returned amicably.

'What's your name? I'm racking my brains but I still can't place you. And it's not often that happens, I can tell you.'

'My name is Dercc, the son of Coll,' he said.

The gatekeeper looked startled.

'The Lord Liath is also a son of Coll.' He spat to his left, muttering.

'He is my brother. I don't know *your* name,' he added pointedly.

'Garan,' said one of the boys, and the gatekeeper turned on him at once.

'Don't you be so free with my name, nor with the one whose company you're keeping. For though he wears trousers like the commonest servant, he's kin to one of the great ones. I see now why your face and your voice are so familiar – though your colour is different.'

Dercc nodded.

'I red and he black, as our names say. We are twins.'

The gatekeeper spat to the left again as Dercc went past him, into the outer enclosure. Slaves were grooming the weary horses, and one or two people were still unrolling their bedding for the night while their women cooked the evening meal.

Dercc went up the narrow steps into the inner enclosure, and on into the main hall. Here a great fire burned. All round the sides of the hall were alcoves where each chief sat with his most trusted friend, his charioteer, and other loyal men around him. Dogs fought over bones flung by the chiefs, who were already eating with loosened

belts. Dodging snapping curs and powerful hounds, which were trained to hunt and kill as skilfully as their masters, he made his way steadily forward to the fire in the centre of the hall. Sides of meat sizzled on spits turned by sweating slaves. Beside the fire sat the King and his guests, with the greatest lords. About them circled the Queen and her women and girls, their mouths and brows carefully painted. Bands of gold shone on their bare white arms. They carried heavy wine cups carefully, and Dercc checked and stood back for one of them to pass. At the same time she stood back for him. They looked at each other. She was dark-haired and wore a plain green dress.

'Go on with your cup,' he told her, still waiting, his eyes on the far side of the fire where his brother sat. Liath's high crown had been removed. A silver band circled his forehead holding back his black hair. A slave passed a silver wine cup around the priests. Each man tilted it back, took a great gulp and gave it back to the slave. When it came to Liath, the slave carefully placed the cup between the young man's long, slim fingers.

No one paid any attention to Dercc. They probably took him for one of the servants. He waited. When the slave bent down and took the cup from Liath, Dercc, swallowing hard, said hoarsely: 'May I speak, lords?'

They looked round then. One of the chiefs, Lord Leuchos, tore at the bone he held in his jewelled fingers and, even with his mouth full, managed to boom with annoyance:

'What do you want? Go and sit among the slaves. I'm surprised the gatekeeper let you in to disturb our meal!'

'The gatekeeper let me in when he heard my name,' Dercc replied. He was watching Liath all the time. Slaves stood round the chiefs holding torches of blazing pine branches. As each branch burned down to a charred stump, the slave tossed it into the fire and lit another. Behind drifting curls of blue smoke Liath's pale face was still for a moment.

'He heard your name?' Leuchos yawned and loosened his belt another hole.

'My name is Dercc, son of Coll. My brother, too, will know me by my voice.'

Dercc spoke clearly, confidently, looking always at his twin.

'My brother is dead,' Liath's voice was strangely loud, though flat and dull. As he spoke he touched a crest of white owl feathers he wore on the shoulder of his plain linen tunic. The chiefs, too, touched lucky things or made signs to ward off evil, and one of the priests threw a piece of meat out into the shadows beyond the fire.

'No – but I *am* Dercc,' he protested, shocked. 'The gatekeeper recognized me!'

'He deserves to be whipped,' Leuchos rumbled.

'Stay, Leuchos!' The King spoke. 'The young man is not unlike the Lord Liath, though his hair is red, and his shoulders broad.'

Dercc turned gratefully to the King and met his eyes for the first time.

The chief of all chiefs of the Horse People was slight and dark. People whispered that the blood of the old, long-ago people flowed in his veins. Dercc remembered that many of the priests hated him for that.

'Lord King, let the eastern lords see that the chief of the Horse People listens to a stranger's request,' he pleaded. 'Please let me speak to my brother. I have brought him a gift.'

He saw the King look quickly at the eastern ambassadors. Those who understood were explaining in their own language to the others.

'Brother?' Liath cut in before the King could reply. 'My brother is dead. Which one of you doubts my words?' he challenged the chiefs, who denied it loudly. Dercc's heart sank.

'*I* doubt your word, Liath, because I am Dercc. Why do you say that I am dead?'

Liath's blank eyes stared at him. He spoke but the words came as singing. Although his voice was low, everyone, even the slaves in the remotest corners of the hall furthest from the fire, paid attention.

'There was an augury, a seeing. In the middle of the stone circle where the power first made itself known to us, over the grave, the priests killed a black cock. In its wet guts appeared a ship, a foreign ship, not unlike the one that was sighted in the Sound when the sorrow came and my brother was parted from me, but this ship was far away. My brother was dead in the depths of that ship. He is dead. The seeing showed us. They saw it. I placed my hands over the black cock's guts and I too knew it. I knew. All the Horse People know that at that time the brown horse, the one that carries the black sorrow, came to me from our Goddess's stables on the far holy hill. No one sees the brown horse with his eyes, but we feel the sorrow that he brings, and we know, then, that the Mother has sent him to us. He brought such sorrow, lords, that even though the Mother has sent me great power, my song is death. My brother is dead. . . .' His voice died away and there was quiet in the hall, except for the whispering of the eastern ambassadors.

Dercc, fighting against the spell of his brother's singing, cried out: 'No, my brother, you have not seen the truth!'

There were startled angry cries from the priests. He turned from one side of the hall to the other, and back to the ring of lords and priests.

'I – Dercc – did not die in the hold of the enemy ship. I was taken to a foreign country and sold as a slave. Those who bought me treated me with kindness, but I escaped from them into the hands of a cruel, one-eyed man, who tricked me and sold me as a slave again, this time to pull with an oar in the depths of another ship to the end of my days. But even in that dark place, light reached me. A friend came beside me, who brought me news that set me

free. Not free from the hold of the ship, but from the terror that gripped me. It was the news of the Son of God who loved me and died for me. Died but rose again so that I might live. I turned from the old magic then, Liath, so that I could follow him and accept his life. Then it was you saw me dead, in your "seeing". For I *am* dead to the old powers, Liath, but I am alive because I belong to the Lord Jesus Christ.'

But the last words were drowned in a shriek from Liath and a furious outburst from the priests. Dercc saw the King glance anxiously at the eastern lords, then look keenly at him. He wondered if the King believed him. Then the King spoke and the uproar died down.

'Lord Liath, this matter concerns you alone. Take this stranger into one of the alcoves and question him.'

After that one shriek Liath's face had become composed and cold. He bowed stiffly, and guided by an old slave, he made his slow, groping way towards an alcove at the end of the hall. The long-robed priests followed closely, and then came Dercc, miserably remembering the days when he had guided his twin in all weathers over the hills, the blind boy lifting his face to feel the rain, or leaping with Dercc into places that he could never have reached by himself.

He stood in front of Liath in the alcove, aware of the hostility of the listening priests.

'What do you want? Why have you come here?' Liath's voice was cold and hard.

'Because we have always been together, Liath,' he said simply.

'I mourned with the others when the augury showed my brother was dead. We light a fire for him each Samain, as we remember the dead. Are you a ghost come to worry me now?'

'Touch me. I am quite real.'

He drew back.

'My brother is dead. I don't know you. What do you

hope to gain?'

'Let us talk alone, Liath. I beg you.'

'We can have nothing to talk about.'

'Nothing about the years since we parted? Nothing about our childhood? Nothing about our future?'

'My brother and I had a great future together. We would have ruled the tribes together. Now I will rule alone, and by my power there will be unity – by the power of the Standing Stones.'

As Liath spoke Dercc began again to feel the creeping blackness, the smell of the dead, and to hear the wail of the wind through the stones. . . . He cried out in horror,

'There is a greater power – the power of Jesus!'

'There is no greater power,' screamed Liath. 'Impostor! Almost I believed you were he, returned from the dark places of death to share with me in the triumph of kingship, and the power of priesthood. But you deny my power, and the beliefs of our people. Cast him out!' He shook with frenzy, and the priests thronged forward.

Dercc had been holding his gift all this time. Now he held it against his brother's trembling pointing hand.

'At least take my gift and play your sweet music again for me.'

It was a little harp with a frame of carved wood and ivory, strings of white bronze. He had bartered his doctor's instruments for it, thinking of the joy it would give his brother.

Liath's hand felt and grasped the harp. Then he flung it away behind Dercc.

'Not for me,' he cried, as the priests seized Dercc and began to hustle him triumphantly towards the middle of the hall, with cries of 'Impostor', and 'Cast him out.' Dercc saw the harp, which had struck the rocky wall and he darted forward to retrieve it. He heard Liath's scream, like and yet unlike the voice he remembered,

'He means to harm our people!'

Slaves rushed towards Dercc from all parts of the hall,

cheered on by the young men. He did not defend himself. Clutching the harp, kicked, bruised and beaten he was dragged through the main hall. He heard the royal women jeering and a wine-cup was emptied at him. As he turned his head away he glimpsed the dark-haired girl in green, and he thought there was pity in her face. The tribesmen swept him down the steps and across the outer enclosure. The wooden gate opened and he reeled through and heard it shut behind him. He got to his feet and found to his surprise that his fur-lined cloak lay on the grass. Someone had cast it out with him.

Confused and utterly weary he wrapped it around him and stumbled away, still clutching the harp. It was too late to make the journey home now. Further on, he re-membered, was a kind of shelter that had once been a den for a pair of motherless boys: a grassy hollow at the foot of a semi-circular cliff. Stunted trees grew precariously out of the limestock rock. He had gathered primroses there for the soup small children loved. He and Liath used to try to scramble up the sheer rocks.

'Oh, Liath, will you ever listen to me?' he thought, sadly. Rudi, who had helped him to know Jesus, had warned him it would be hard to make Liath understand.

'Please help Liath, Lord Jesus,' Dercc prayed. 'It's for this I've come here, after all,' he thought. He rolled over in his cloak and fell asleep, an outcast from the Fort, but not without hope.

III
Of Treachery and Trial

Dercc woke up aching all over, and with a weight of sadness that would have made him drift back to the nothingness of sleep, but he was too sore and uncomfortable, and now too much awake in the first light of an autumn morning. A morning such as he had often longed for far away from home and from Liath.

He sat up and examined the little harp. It was none the worse for the battering it had received. He stowed it away, thankful for that, and for his warm cloak someone had flung out to him.

He decided to go back to where it had all started; back to the stone circle in the woods, where he and Liath had first linked themselves to the dark power.

Resolutely he swung away over the moorland, startling a heron beside the swift burn that ran through the glen of high burial mounds. Soon he was crunching through frosty drifts of fallen leaves in the woods about the circle.

With a lifting of his heart he saw the ring of stones: saw them, and felt no fear. They had no power over him now. He was at peace.

If only Liath were too!

Far from home, Dercc had often thought about the old stones, but even so he had not remembered that they were so beautiful! Very slowly he walked around the inside of the circle. The sun, still strong, beating back the frost, shone straight between two stones. Dercc walked towards them, and saw that the path of the sun was a

straight line that led from the east directly through one of the high burial mounds. He walked on, sun-wise around the circle, occasionally stopping to finger the weathered carvings: the rings and hollows, marks of magic and endlessly intertwining lines.

The Horse People avoided the stones and their mystery out of fear. They could not understand their purpose, and were afraid of their great age.

Their centuries-old silent stance, their careful positioning, the skill with which master craftsmen had carved their weathered designs, were all a message. But it was a new message that Dercc read now. It was a message of joy and he could read it as clearly as he had once read the evil knowledge there. The stones stood still, but pulsed with rhythm; they stood stock-still in a frozen dance, a timeless motionless movement, carved by a long-vanished people as a statement of truth.

The new message of the stones was one that brought joy. Glimpsing something true and timeless, the ancient people had carved the stones and set them in their circle.

They were part of a people's worship of light and eternity and the things they sensed were good. Their shadows danced the dance of the sun. The stones echoed the sun's laughter, the falling and rising again of light.

Confidently he walked round the circle again, until he reached the point he had started from, opposite the risen sun. Standing directly in the golden path of light, he lifted his hands into the morning sky.

'The darkness is light to you, Father in Heaven. Long ago Rudi prayed that you would take the darkness from Liath as you did from me. Show him light, Lord – the light of the sun, the dance. Teach him the music of light. And let me share your message with him. You are the Risen Christ and the Lord of Light.'

He stayed there for a long time, praying and looking about him at the woods awash with sunlight, at the stones, at the pale sky and the world around, wonderfully warm

before the hard dull days of winter, so soon to set in. And as he prayed for Liath he began to understand that lust for power had entered into his brother, and that he wished to rule and would use any means to do so. Encouraged by scheming priests and filled with despair at the loss of Dercc, he no longer cared for anything else. He had been unable to believe that his brother whom he had lost had come back, for the dark power to whom he had given himself had blinded his mind. So that he was blind twice over. And Dercc prayed again for the light to enter him.

At last he moved away, and realised at once how hungry he was. In a clearing in the woods a fire crackled. He smelt it, and something else that was good; the scent of roasting venison. He looked at the food Aunt Ala had given him the day before – meat and flat barley loaves. He would not willingly go empty-handed to someone else's fire, but now he could ask to eat his food beside it.

Whistling, he approached the blaze.

'A traveller gives you welcome, friends,' he called.

The two men, squatting by the fire, looked up at him and grunted something that might be taken for a welcome in return.

'I have food with me,' Dercc went on.

'We have plenty of food here. Come and sit down.'

He saw that they were slaves. Like the boys who had led the pony to barter for corn, they belonged to the Seal Clan who eked out a living along the western shore. He guessed from the charms and amulets they wore round their foreheads and necks that they had taken up service with the priests in the shrine close by. They would eat better now, being slaves, than they had ever done before when they lived with their own clan. It was quite common for the poor among the Seal People to sell their freedom for bread.

'We are Winwaloe and Cradawg from the Seal People. We belong to the priests,' said one, confirming Dercc's guess. They shifted along on their haunches, making a

place for Dercc.

'I am one of the Horse People, like yourselves, though not from your clan. I am Dercc.' He squatted beside them and held out a cold hand to the blaze. 'I'm glad of the place at the fire.' He took out his food and shared it with them and they passed him venison. They washed down their food with water and Dercc made himself useful by finding a well-remembered path to a racing burn and refilling the leather bottles.

He sat by the fire, his hands clasped round his updrawn knees, listening to the fitful conversation – a few remarks interspersed with long silences – the relaxed communication of two men who knew each other so well that each was to the other a well-worn, comfortable garment.

With the food inside him and warmed by the fire, Dercc felt sleepy. His head nodded forward. He must have dozed, glad of the warmth, the food and the quiet. When he was next aware of the talk, it was to hear Liath's name mentioned.

He kept his eyes closed and let his head drop lower, but he was fully awake now, straining his ears, and hanging on to every word.

'It will be the fire,' said one voice.

'Surely,' the other agreed. Then after a pause, 'The test of fire.'

'He will be held prisoner until the Feast of Samain, surely. Unless none dare touch him for fear of the dark power on him.'

Dercc raised his head.

'I was sleeping, but I heard some of your words. Who is to be held prisoner until the Feast of Samain? And for what offence?'

'It is the Lord Liath, a priest possessed by such power that he wishes also to make himself king,' said the slave Winwaloe.

Dercc felt a thrill of fear. Had he not realised this

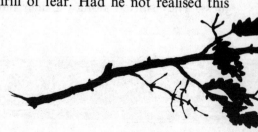

already at the Standing Stones?

'He has been plotting with the eastern lords to poison our King – the King of the Horse People,' said Cradawg. 'Some words spoken were reported to the King. The eastern lords fled from the Fort at first light this morning, but the King has challenged the Lord Liath with his treachery, and he does not deny it, but trusts in the dark power to save him.'

The slaves were eager to tell the story.

'The ghost of his dead brother appeared to him in the hall and warned him to turn away from the power he worships,' said Winwaloe, 'but he would not. And now this trouble has come to him.'

'But what will the punishment be?' asked Dercc, trying to speak calmly and with only a stranger's interest.

'He would be buried alive, but they fear the dark magic,' said Cradawg, 'so they will see if the fire will burn him.'

Dercc could not speak again, and as the slaves' talk turned to other things he rose and, thanking them for their food and fire, went towards his foster-parents' home.

On the way, not wishing to return empty-handed, he stopped and lay down beside the fast-flowing burn. It had always been a good place to fish and he had been used to watch there for hours together, with Liath beside him listening as the fish leapt the small foaming waterfalls. He spent the last couple of hours of daylight with his hands in the cold water and caught half a dozen trout. And all the time he was thinking of Liath.

Then he went on to the farm. His wet tunic clung uncomfortably to him in the windless frost that had already begun to whiten the earth. The last few leaves on birch and oak looked like a cold beggar's sparse rags. The earlier warmth of the day had been short-lived, and with the frost winter seemed very close. Samain Feast was only two weeks away – the darkest Feast of the year. Every-

where fires would burn to drive away the restless spirits of the Underworld. On the night of Samain gods and men might walk together, and a simple ring flung by a slave girl could forecast the future of an entire people. It was a time of sooth-saying and augury, a time when offerings were made to the embalmed heads of defeated enemies which were stuck high on poles. At Samain such a head might well speak, foretelling disaster for the tribe. It was a time when the powers of darkness seemed to gather themselves in force, and therefore Dercc knew he would have to fight for Liath. But what could he do, rejected and cast out from the Fort as he now was?

At the farm, sitting around the fire in the middle of the house, he talked long with his uncle and the family. He told of his trouble at the Fort, and then of the news he had heard from the slaves. They ate their supper of mutton stew and herbs, dipping their hands into the big cauldron which hung from a cross-beam above the fire. The goats, tethered to hooks beside the door, champed and twitched, butting each other. Hens roosted on the beams that supported the roof. Outside on the hill the stags clashed their antlers in locked battle, churning up the rough grass and bracken with their feet.

'Listen,' said Uncle Mael. 'The stags are fighting, as they do each night at this time of year. The saying is that desire is hot in them for the pure white hind of the Otherworld. She is white indeed, but her ears are red, a sign of her immortality, and they long to win her.'

'Does one win her?' Vin asked.

'Ah now, is she not one of the Lordly Ones with the protection of *yon* place and the power of timelessness? She'll evade them, but they fight each year to win her.'

'Now I begin to feel at home,' said Dercc, 'hearing that tale again.'

'Stay with us,' Aunt Ala said. 'We'd given up all hope of seeing you again. Liath has made his choice and we cannot save him.'

'But I will go to the Fort again,' said Dercc. 'There may be something I can do.'

'You will be recognised,' said Aunt Ala. 'We do not want to lose you, too.'

'But I came westwards over the sea to find Liath. Not only for home, but to be with *him* – to share my new life with him,' he said wretchedly. 'And he is so full of the priests' magic he would not even believe I was alive, though I stood beside him.'

'Magic! It's best not meddled with,' said Uncle Mael, shaking his head and nursing the ale-cup in his large, countryman's hands. 'There are plenty of people in the tribe who think like me and don't want to meddle with magic. Why, Dercc, it's magic enough for me to see the barley shoot up green, and turn yellow and ripe for the harvest. It's magic enough to see the birth of one trembling young foal, or to smell a fat ox roasting over a charcoal fire.'

'You are right.' Dercc remembered the way the sunlight had fallen on the stones. 'But I have a weapon I can use against the dark that has hold of Liath. I can pray.

'A sacrifice you mean?' said his uncle. 'I'll burn a fire with you beside some sacred place – we'll offer a gift to

whichever god you choose.'

'There is another way of prayer,' said Dercc, 'in the name of Christ, the Anointed One. He himself was the sacrifice; he let himself be put to death so that those who believed in him could pray to the one true God who loves us all.'

They looked at him wonderingly, and he longed to make them understand the faith which he had found. As they settled for the night, curling under the sheepskins around the fire, he prayed again for Liath, asking for help, asking for love.

Next morning Gilla came to Dercc with a plan. He suggested that he and his cousin should take ponies to sell at the Fort. If Dercc's red hair was kept hidden, he would not be noticed, and perhaps they would gain some information about the plot and Liath's trial.

Dercc rejoiced to have something to do. He borrowed a cloak of his uncle's, and braided his hair under the hood. Then he set off with Gilla leading five ponies and followed by the pleased and faithful Penn.

Instead of going across the moorland and along by the winding river as Dercc had done before, they took the easier route along the grassy trackway the tribe kept carefully in repair. Dercc remembered having worked hard on this stretch, pulling up weeds and cutting back brambles the summer before he had begun his training as a warrior.

Outside the settlement, in the old dun, children were playing with carved animals. They obviously knew Gilla and ran up to him, showing him the little carved objects, and talking about the glittering band of foreign lords who had dropped them in the roadway very early yesterday.

Dercc looked on, feeling uneasy. They must mean the easterners. A closer look at the little carved animals confirmed this: they were so like the designs worked on the easterners' armour and jewellery. But why were they riding this way, due north from the Fort? They had said

they were anxious to be home before winter. He thought of the high hills to the north: the Hill of the Maidens was there – a holy place, before the Horse People came with their weapons of iron from the south and drove away the little dark race. There were hills beyond too, where he had never been; another tribe lived there, the Cre People. They were bitter enemies of the Horse People and lost no opportunity to raid and harry the duns and farmsteads along the border.

Liath had talked of unity, of ruling all the tribes, and he had been involved with the easterners. Were the Cre People somehow involved in the treachery? Dercc felt more and more uneasy as they approached the massive hump that was the High Fort, the stronghold of the King and the nobles of the tribe, the centre of the scattered clans. The walls and defences were the rocks themselves. Perhaps soon this stronghold would be threatened, betrayed by his own brother.

Once again there was a crowd at the gates, this time admiring a group of new warriors, who were boasting of their first raid. The cousins managed to elbow their way through unnoticed and settle the ponies in a corner of the outer enclosure. Here they gave them hay, and talked, sitting in the frosty sun, waiting for customers. Gilla said,

'Dercc, you could have had a hero's welcome at the Fort if Liath hadn't insisted you were dead. Your name is honoured, as one of the first to board the ship, and one of the first to kill an enemy. Every year they light a fire for you at Samain, and the bards sing the tale of the battle and the ship.'

'I could sing a different song,' said Dercc with feeling, 'of being a prisoner, mad in the dark. The desire for fighting has gone out of me. I would rather heal. And I do not care about the hero's welcome if only Liath would know me.'

It took them two days to barter the long-maned ponies, but they gained spears and throwing sticks, a

silver brooch and a gold ring (which they could exchange
for corn later), a pair of embroidered, leather-soled shoes
and a large quantity of wool. From snatches of conversation they discovered that Liath was still walking free,
and they wondered if the King was afraid to touch him.
But Dercc's heart leapt when he thought that he could
find Liath and persuade him to leave the Fort before it
was too late. And he prayed for power to accomplish this.

On the second afternoon he left Gilla with the last two
ponies and went quietly into the main hall, Penn following behind. There he found Liath teaching a group of
boys, but when he heard Dercc speak his name he
screeched out,

'Ghost! Ghost! Let me alone!'
and all the little boys shrank away from him. Even Penn
cringed into a corner, all her hackles up, and Dercc wished
he, too, could hide from his brother's voice. It was like
and yet unlike the voice he remembered and brought a
cold sweat to his forehead and made his clenched palms
clammy.

'Come with me, Liath,' he said, making his voice steady. 'Come home.'

'To the halls of death?' came the strange voice.

'No, to our foster parents' house,' he said, thinking of the quiet ordinariness of the home, that now meant more to him than dreams of power.

'You haunt me,' said Liath, 'and yet you cannot now be with me when I triumph. The King is afraid to lay hands on me. The fire cannot burn me. When I make my music in the great hall each evening the power fills me and overflows and they are all afraid. Soon I will rule three powerful tribes – not one but three!'

'Think for a moment,' Dercc said. 'How can you achieve this without ruining your own people? The poor folk will suffer when the chariots drive across their barley. Where will they shelter when their homes are burnt? You will not rule the tribes without fighting.'

'No, but Corn King will enrich them,' cried Liath, flinging his arms up in ecstasy, 'Corn King never dies!'

He began to sing and in his music were barley fields, richer and more golden than any of the tribe. Grains of wheat spilled into magnificent garners built of gleaming stones. Ships settled lower into a distant blue sea as the golden harvest from the fields of a wealthy ruler poured into their dark holds.

Looking beyond Liath, Dercc saw that the King was in the hall, listening, with the lords and young men. Some had their eyes shut, others smiled, and Dercc knew that in their ears field after field of barley rustled. The countryside was clothed with gold – ruled by Liath. But Dercc thought of Jesus. And then he saw again the chariots driving over the barley and he said with strength,

'Liath, Liath, there is gold in your song, but no food for the hungry. You sing of power and wealth for yourself, not bread for the poor. You're deceiving yourself, Liath. You need peace to bring in the harvest, and in your song there is war.'

He forced his words through his brother's music and he saw with distress the young priest's face grow dull and heavy. Liath shuddered. His song died. He was like a guttering wick. Dercc saw that without the dark power to hold him Liath was empty.

'Lord Jesus,' he whispered, 'he is my brother. Give him light.'

Liath screamed,

'Ghost! Get away from me, ghost! You've spoilt my music with your haunting!'

Then he began to sob. At this the King made a signal and ten of the strongest warriors rushed forward and seized him, trampling down the slave who trembled beside him. Dercc understood that the King had chosen this moment of weakness to arrest his brother and he stood appalled.

'Let me go with him,' he cried to the King.

'Traitor,' screamed Liath. 'It is you who have done this! I curse you with your talk of light. You have spoilt my singing. Keep away from me with your haunting.'

His screams died away as they led him from the hall.

Slowly, blindly Dercc stumbled out to the enclosure and Penn followed him. Gilla, seeing his face, asked no questions, but hastily packed up the goods they had gained, and untied the remaining pony. They left the Fort in silence and they were close to the farm before Dercc spoke. He said,

'I shall go back to the stone circle tonight. Tell my foster parents I have failed to bring back Liath and now he has been imprisoned by the King. And it is my doing – for it was my voice which spoke and made him weak.'

'What will you do at the stone circle?' asked Gilla fearfully.

'I will fight in prayer, Gilla. The circle is no longer dark for me,' and seeing that the boy did not understand, he said,

'Listen, warrior-to-be, what do the young men most

long for when they go to battle?'

'Oh to be first at the kill! First at the wounding and at the capture,' Gilla said at once. 'If they die bravely they have an honoured place in a glorious kingdom beyond the western islands.'

'I have a place in a kingdom too,' Dercc said, 'only I didn't win it. It was bought by the bravery of my King. He went to his death, just as our warriors do, stripped naked, and the fight was long and very great, for it was with death itself. The King who is God went without weapons, and died, bleeding and wounded. But death could not hold him. He rose again. I believe He who lives can save Liath from the dark.'

'You are brave, too, Dercc,' said Gilla. 'None of our warriors would go to the circle now that the dark is coming.'

Then Dercc embraced Gilla, and handing him the goods he had been carrying went down the hill. The last splendid light of the autumn day brought him to the circle of standing stones.

IV

'I'm afraid for Liath...'

'The light must be stronger than the darkness,' Dercc thought desperately. He had been here for hours now, crouched by the empty grave in the centre of the circle. Perhaps he had slept. It was raining. As darkness had filled the woods and silenced the birds a toad had hopped beside him, and he had watched it, just making it out in the dark.

There had been times in the past when he felt as though he were in some dreadful, living nightmare, and longed to waken, but this was worse, far worse. All he wanted was to go back to the Fort and be with Liath, but Liath did not want him. There was nothing more he could do; he had prayed until he had no words left, no thoughts and no silence even. Nothing.

He supposed he could offer that nothing. Into the emptiness and silence and darkness he offered all the emptiness, and hopelessness and darkness he felt inside himself. He offered the tears he could not shed. He offered the despair that knotted his heart. He offered all darkness and all hopelessness. He offered the darkness and dark things of Samain. He offered Liath. He offered fire.

Drained, he got up. He had a picture in his mind: a white rod. Kingship. The rod of kingship that only the king might wield, the sign of his power over the life and death of his people. If the King wished he could set Liath free. But he would never, never let him go, not now. Dercc sighed and shook his head. Still the vision of the white rod filled his mind. As he stood there one of the laws of his tribe suddenly came to him. It was the right of any tribesman to come before the king with a request. He had to stand in the great hall, waiting among the slaves until the king noticed him, and he had to wait fasting, but this gave him the right to speak. There was no guarantee, of course, that a request would be granted, but at least it would be heard, and the plaintiff had the right to stay in the hall until it was. Often the sight of a persistent, pleading figure, day after day, would make the king relent; if only to get the man out of the hall where his presence spoiled the feasting. Or if the man came from a powerful family the king would be forced to pay attention for fear the relatives would take up his cause more violently if he were allowed to starve to death.

Dercc rebelled. It was nonsense. The King would never listen to him. Besides, he had been cast out of the Fort once; they might not even let him into the hall again. He was not going back.

Yet he was going. He had prayed. He had given everything, and into his emptied, exhausted mind had come this one idea. He must follow it.

And now he must sleep! He did not want to sleep in the wet woods. The farm would be barred and bolted but he could sleep in one of Uncle Mael's barns. Stumbling sometimes in the dark, he made his way home.

But they had left the door unbolted. Penn lay across the threshold. The kindness of his foster family comforted him. Carefully he pulled the door shut behind him and bolted it. A very dim glow from the banked fire which never went out was enough for him to grope his way to it. He lay down beside Gilla. Penn followed him across the room. They had left a sheepskin out for him. Shivering he pulled it over him and fell asleep, glad of Penn's warmth across his feet.

When the family awoke next morning he told them what had happened at the Fort and the idea that had

come to him at the standing stones.

'I will do what our laws allow,' he explained. 'Liath's a prisoner. I will stand and plead for him in front of the King.'

'Stand before the King? But that is for Liath to do,' Uncle Mael said. 'He should make his own plea for mercy. Then they will let him stand fasting before the door of the hall and put his case to the King in that way.'

'Liath will never plead for himself, Uncle Mael. I must be his plaintiff,' Dercc replied. 'Perhaps they won't put him to the trial.'

'Will he go to the fire?' Gilla asked. 'Did you see something in the stones?'

Dercc shook his head. 'I prayed for light for Liath. But perhaps he will have to go through the fire first. That's why I must go. I am afraid for Liath when the fire burns, and I am afraid, too, that his power may be great enough to stop the fire from harming him. Then what will become of our tribe?'

'That is my fear too,' said Uncle Mael. 'Then Dercc, I advise you to wait here a while yet. There are still nine days till Samain Feast. Stay here and let everyone's anger cool, then go and plead on the day before the feast.'

It seemed good advice and Dercc agreed to follow it, hard though he found it to wait.

There was plenty to do before winter set in, and he was glad to be able to help his foster family during the next few days. He cut a stack of wood for the fire. With Penn at his heels he went over the moorland after wild duck and brought three down with javelins and throwing sticks. One day he and Gilla hunted and caught a fine young stag and hung the antlers in the Round House.

Whatever he did, his thoughts were never far from Liath and as often as he could he paused in what he was doing to pray.

The girls had been working busily at the loom for days. Dercc had often gone over and watched as they

stood for hours together, tucking the shuttle in and out of the dyed woollen threads, but they had never told him what they were making. Two days before Samain Feast Vin called him, and held up a long hooded cloak. Alarch showed him a tunic. The wool had been dyed yellow and green with lichen and moss, and woven into a soft, flecked pattern.

'Did you do this for me?' he said wonderingly. 'They are beautifully made. You've put in so many hours of work for me.'

'You must wear them when you go and plead for Liath,' Vin told him.

'I shall go tomorrow,' he said.

The next morning he ate no breakfast. He went outside to wash at the spring that poured out of the hillside above the farm. Gilla went with him. He took leather jugs and oil, and, as a shield-bearer helps a warrior prepare for battle, Gilla helped Dercc, pouring water into his cousin's cupped hands, and over his head and feet, rubbing oils into his body when the wind had dried him, and plaiting his long red hair, binding it with leather thongs.

Then for the third time Dercc made his way to the Fort. This time he went alone to plead before the King.

The gatekeeper remembered him in spite of the new clothes, yet looked at him with some respect.

'You have been cast out once, red-headed son of Coll. And now they are all against your brother, too. But you had the power to stop the evil charm in his music, they say. Has the King summoned you to him?'

'No, but I have come as plaintiff before the King, to plead for my brother,' he said.

'Then in you go, in you go, son of Coll. I'll not keep you back. Though there's a power of pleading yon lad will need to do,' Garan told the world at large. Dercc, overhearing, squared his shoulders and walked firmly into the fort, across the first enclosure up to the main hall.

He stood inside the doorway, waiting. He ached for himself, knowing that he must be patient. He ached for action, and longed to be able to talk to Liath, and then rush off and find the King, who was in the hills leading the last hunt before Samain. He began to daydream. He imagined how wonderful it would be to bring the quarry to bay himself, to brave the boar, or the wolf, or the mountain bear, and be first at the kill. In fact, anything would be better than this waiting in the near empty hall, with the women in their bower and the idling slaves. Yet as plaintiff for his brother, he knew he had to wait . . . and wait . . . for days maybe.

It was all the harder because he knew that Liath was a prisoner somewhere, perhaps close by, under the hall itself.

He waited, trying to pray, and became more and more despairing, more and more bored.

Scenes from his past life, memories of the people he had known in the other country where he had been a slave flashed through his mind. He tried to turn these memories into prayer for the people he would never see again.

It helped.

Hunger rumbled inside him. His mouth was dry. He would not think of food or drink!

Slaves started to bustle about, tending the fires and lights, pouring fresh tallow into sheeps' gullets in which long wicks floated. They stacked pine branches ready for burning as torches and began to prepare food. A meal was taken to the women in their part of the hall.

Later he heard horns in the distance, the rumble of chariot wheels, oncoming horses, men shouting and calling. The noises grew louder as the hunt returned home.

He prayed for the hunters.

The first runner, who was always ahead, clearing the way for the King, stumbled into the hall and slumped swinging his arms slackly, drawing breath.

Dercc ached to be as exhausted as the runner. Then his heart beat faster, for into the hall came the lords, with the slight dark figure of the King in their midst.

His head swam. He ran and bowed down before the King.

'Great King of the Horse People!' He swallowed hard. The words stuck in his dry throat. The lords, hungry and anxious to be washed and at their supper, urged the King on. The rest of the hunt was clattering up the stone steps outside and came crowding into the hall.

The King stopped. His hard, shrewd eyes stared at Dercc trying to guess his purpose.

'We'll hear you when we have eaten, young warrior,' he said after a moment, and moved on. Dercc watched him go with his train of lords. Their bare legs were spattered with mud, their bright tunics and kilted cloaks were torn and their amazingly styled hair was sadly dishevelled, but they glittered with a splendour of gold and gems.

Now the white-armed women circled the hall with jugs of ale for the chiefs. A girl holding a jug on her shoulder paused before Dercc.

'Drink,' she murmured. 'I've seen you stand there all day.'

Dercc shook his head. 'Not ale or wine. I may not eat or drink until the King grants my plea.'

'When will he hear you?'

'When he has eaten,' Dercc replied.

'I'll bring you water.' She turned on her heel and disappeared in the crowds in the hall. She seemed familiar but he could not place her.

At his post at the doorway, thinking now of water, Dercc remembered a man, who, years ago, had brought water to a despairing line of slaves in a distant harbour.

The girl came back with the leather bottle freshly filled. Dercc ran his tongue over his dry lips.

'You were smiling as I came up to you,' she said.

'I was remembering a friend. I thank you, lady.' He lifted the bottle to his lips.

'You are Liath's brother,' she said as he drank. 'I saw you when you came to the Fort before and he would not believe you were alive. To think he should refuse such good news!' Her face was sad as she said this, and she looked wistful, as if she too had known the death of a brother.

'I saw you too,' he said. 'When they cast me out you did not laugh as the others did.'

She shook her head.

'I threw your cloak out to you,' she said. 'I'll bring you water again as often as I can,' and she left him.

It was hard but while the others ate he continued to stand by the door and wait and try to pray. At length the King sent for him. There was a stir and a sudden silence as he walked for the second time since his homecoming to the fire in the centre of the hall where the King sat with his nobles.

'So, young warrior whom the tribe cast out, what urgent matter brings you to your King?'

Kneeling, Dercc looked at the King's lined face, framed by carefully-arranged curls and oiled beard.

'Lord, I come as a plaintiff.'

'What cause have you come to plead? By all the rare and shining ones, you should be out on the fields with the warriors, not standing all day fasting within the hall.'

He met the King's brown eyes.

'I follow the customs of the Horse People, Lord. Though it's not easy to stand waiting hour long to plead.'

'What is your plea then? For your place as a warrior in the tribe that cast you out?' the King asked sympathetically.

'No, Lord. I plead for my brother, my twin, that he may go with me from the Fort.' He was aware of the hostility in the half-circle of chieftains. 'Liath is sick. Let me take him away and I will let him do no more harm to the tribe.'

'You plead for my enemy!' the King roared. 'I shall not grant your plea – not if you stand and wait in the great hall for forty feasts of Samain.'

Dercc remained kneeling.

'Lord King, nevertheless it is my right as plaintiff to stand in your hall, and so I shall until you grant my plea.'

He got up and turned back to his place by the door. As he went he heard a muted sound of approval from the watching tribesmen in the alcove furthest from the fire.

He remembered the King's white rod. He must wait until the King allowed him to touch it, granting his request. Wearily he leant against the wall. He had had no idea his homecoming would lead to this! The air in the hall became thick with smoke as the wicks in the hot tallow guttered and burned low. Slave children cried and were hushed. People put down animal skins and prepared to sleep. Dercc wrapped his new cloak round him and lay where he was. His last thought was of Liath. Now again, they would sleep under one roof together. Curled in his cloak, his arms pressed against a very hollow stomach, he slept soundly, waking to hunger and to another seemingly endless day beside the door of the great hall. He watched the chiefs waken, eat and leave on their different concerns. The hall emptied steadily, but the slaves were busy, preparing food for the feast.

The girl came by in the middle of the morning.

'Not water this time.' She held an earthenware jar out to Dercc. 'I've just milked the goats.'

He drank the frothy milk gratefully.

'Lady, what is your name? And why are you kind to me?'

'Thanew – I will come with some more milk this evening' – and she hurried away without answering his second question.

The waiting went on. He sat with his head against the wall. It was no easier to pray, but the thought came,

comforting him, that this whole long, hungry, hopeless waiting was like a prayer.

'It is harder than fighting,' he thought, 'harder than fighting with weapons. I offer this to you, Lord Jesus, as I offered the darkness before I offer it for Liath.'

As the day went on and he sat, waiting like a slave for the return of an absent master, something – a gladness – came alive inside him. And this gladness, too, he offered for Liath. He knew now that the Lord he served was near him.

But the day dragged on. Tonight they would light the Samain fires. Tonight they would feast. Tonight Thanew would bring him milk. Tonight he would see Liath. Tonight Liath would be tried. . . . His thoughts became desperate.

'I told them I would plead. It was so easy to say it! How hard it is, Lord.' Again a sudden understanding came to him. 'Hard for me, because I am Dercc. But you are the Lord who fought with death and returned alive. You are stronger than the powers of death and of evil.'

He leant back, resting his head against the wall and felt a deep peace flow through him, dulling his hunger, lifting his tired spirit.

Someone called his name.

'The King wants to speak with the son of Coll.' A slave came up to him.

Dercc stood up. 'Go with me to the King, Lord Jesus,' he prayed silently.

The King sat with a circle of priests and soothsayers. They were aloof men with secretive faces. Slaves stood behind them and Dercc saw Winwaloe and Cradawg staring at him.

'So you're waiting, fasting yet another day. Why do you do it?' The King's voice was quiet.

'Because our laws say I may do this,' Dercc answered, 'and because there is nothing else I can do for my brother.'

'So you really are his brother? You wait and fast not

for yourself but for him! Would you like to try another
way?'

Dercc tried to concentrate, wondering what new test
there could be.

'What other way is there?'

'I have watched you,' said the King. 'Your will and
your heart are strong. The cause you plead is hopeless, yet
you refuse to give up. I heard your strange story in the
hall. Then I heard you again, and you spoke the truth to
your brother with great power – greater than his – so that
he became weak. Dercc, the son of Coll' (this was the first
time his name had been acknowledged in the hall, and
Dercc's heart lifted), 'you are honoured as a warrior of the
tribe. Now let me see what strength you have in wrestling.
You will wrestle before me and if you win you shall have
your place among the warriors.' Dercc raised his hand to
speak again for Liath, 'Enough,' said the King. 'I have
commanded you.'

Dercc bowed his head. He felt weak and utterly
desolate. In the still line of slaves a figure stirred.
Winwaloe of the Seal People came forward and stood at
Dercc's side.

'I shall hold your shoes and your tunic,' he said. He
lifted a jug of warmed wine and honey and gave it to
Dercc. 'Let it strengthen you after your fasting,' he said.

Dercc took a little wine. It set his body on fire.

The King gave orders. Horns and drums announced
the contest. The entire tribe, with the King at the head
went out and gathered on the frosty field where Dercc's
opponent already waited. The November day was nearly
at its end. Before long the festival fires would flame out.
Soon the soothsaying and magic would begin.

Noisy spectators crowded round the edge of the field.
Stripped, the wrestlers faced each other. Horns brayed.
There was a moment's hush, for on to the field the priests
led a bound, white-robed figure. Liath's black hair was
crowned with owl feathers. Dercc saw, with a tug at his

heart, that his brother was very sick. From his own experience of the dark powers Dercc recognized the madness that lay like a shadow over his blind twin's sunken face.

V

The Dark Feast

It was to be the best of three falls.

For one still moment Dercc and his opponent waited. Both shivered as the cold bit their naked bodies. Dercc's palms were clammy. He rubbed them together but it didn't help. A horn rang out. The crowd roared. It was the signal for the fight to begin. Warily, the wrestlers circled, each getting the measure of the other, neither anxious to make the first move. Then the young warrior of the Horse People, whose summer had been spent in the hills after deer, and with the fighting bands on raids into other territories, sprang in under Dercc's guard.

Dercc staggered back, regained his balance, and grabbed his opponent's arms, drawing him closer in a bear hug. For a long time they wrestled, locked together, neither giving ground. It seemed as if the two grappling bodies were completely still, but they were both struggling desperately. Sweat shone on their shoulders. The crowd cheered encouragement. Above the straining and heaving, the crack of every joint, the wrenching that seemed to be tearing him apart, Dercc heard voices shout for him, and, close by, was a girl's voice.

He held on with all his strength. His shoulders and his broad wrists ached, but he would not give ground. All the agony of his vigil of the last two days spurred him on. The motionless struggle had his breath coming in searing gasps, and every muscle screaming with pain.

He felt his opponent weaken, and felt in his own body

the sag of shoulder and spine. Delicate as dancers the wrestlers' bare feet began to move across the hard ground. Dercc slithered, and felt his opponent's hold tighten. He bent his head lower, strained for all his worth, and the young warrior loosened his grip and sank to his knees.

The crowd roared its approval as Dercc too gave way, and stood back panting, giving the other a chance to get to his feet.

'Fair play! The red warrior fights fair!' chanted the onlookers. But the other warrior goaded him breathlessly:

'Fool! Or coward? Or is it a woman's way of fighting?' He leapt on Dercc who braced himself for the shock. He stood firm and with one toss of his shoulders had his opponent on the hard earth.

Dercc stood back again, wiping sweat out of his eyes. Winwaloe came up with excited encouragement and a basin of water, and he splashed his face and hands. The spectators relaxed, chewing herbs and hazelnuts and laying bets. Thanew broke free from the women round about her and ran to him with a dish of goat's milk.

'I promised,' she said. 'Drink it, Dercc.' He drank it thankfully.

Friends had gathered round his opponent. From time to time they glanced at Dercc who stood with the slave and the girl in the beginnings of the frosty sunset. High on the ramparts sentries watched for the first glimpse of the moon, the signal for the feast of Samain to begin.

A horn announced the start of the second round, and the supporters dropped back. Everyone became attentive. The two wrestlers took up their positions. A second signal. This time Dercc rushed in first. The young warrior staggered backwards, but before Dercc could send him sprawling he recovered and now Dercc was reeling as the young man gripped his waist. He felt the ground slipping under his feet as he was forced down. His opponent's head was against his chest. For a moment he saw the sweat gleaming on the warrior's shoulders and then he was

down, rolling on the trampled earth.

Winwaloe helped him to his feet. He held water for him, but Dercc hardly noticed. All his concentration was centred on the need to win the final fall. Impatiently he splashed his face. 'Help me, Lord Jesus,' he muttered, 'help me to set Liath free.' The horns sounded again, and the third round began.

For a long time neither seemed anxious to begin. While the crowd cheered them on, the wrestlers circled round each other. This time Dercc dived for the warrior's legs. The young man sprang back and Dercc found himself on the ground. In a flash his opponent was on top of him. Now Dercc was pinned down. He arched his back, forcing the warrior upwards until he had him at arm's length.

The tribe loved Dercc for that show of strength. The warrior could not break free. Now Dercc had him on his back on the ground. His shoulders strained. Once again the wrestlers seemed completely motionless. The young warrior fought hard, trying to get up. Dercc forced him down. The crowd yelled madly. The fight was over.

He got to his feet. His breath came in tearing gasps. He helped the other man to stand.

'I didn't choose this fight,' he gasped.

'I am the champion of all the young warriors, but I give this fight to you, son of Coll,' his opponent said generously.

At that moment the sentries on the ramparts shouted, 'Oh, see! See! The moon! The moon!'

Now everyone's attention was turned away from the frosty field and the two warriors. People spat in the palms of their hands and held their arms high to the moon.

Dercc looked up. Purple clouds hung low in the sky. In the pale north-east the moon yellowed as daylight faded. It was so quiet that the tribespeople on the field could hear the bleating goats plainly, as slave girls drove them in through the gateway of the fort.

Winwaloe flung Dercc's cloak around his shoulders.
Glad of its warmth he pulled it round him, thanking the
slave with a smile, which the other returned as he cried
with the rest:

'The moon! The moon!'

Dercc alone was silent. His eyes were on the fading
colours in the west. Into himself he gathered the joy of
being home. Moments like these were almost too great to
be borne. He turned his head, searching for Liath. Very
pale in the growing dusk, Liath stood quite still, his blind
face turned up towards the sky. Dercc watched him and
his soul ached to go to him.

The King lifted his arms high. Torches blazed on all
sides of the field, and all around the ramparts. Arms
outstretched, the King and the priests took up the chant.
People passed lighted torches from hand to hand. Led by
their King they turned towards the Fort and the brightly-
lit hall. No one looked behind. Evil lurked in the
gloaming. Ghosts were astir. Along the ramparts and all
round the gateway they were lighting the Samain fires.

Inside the hall, the King, still chanting, stood beside
the roaring fire, and when all the tribe were in their places
he beckoned the two wrestlers.

'Dercc, here is the hero's portion for you. The meat of
an ox fed on milk and corn only. There are loaves baked in
honey.'

Cradawg waited with a dish heaped with the best cuts of
meat and fragrant brown loaves. Dercc hardly dared look
at it. He was starving and could scarcely keep himself
from taking the food. The smell of it made him ravenous.
But Liath's fate was still to be decided. He knelt before the
King.

'Lord King, I care not for the hero's portion. I
wrestled for my brother.'

The King grew impatient.

'There is your brother. Ask him if he will go with you.
Ask him if he wants the trial of the fire.'

The priests led Liath forward. All round the hall men made signs to ward off evil. The young wrestler, already eating a thick red piece of roast ox, spat to his left.

'Eat your portion, red-head,' he advised, tearing at the hot flesh. 'Your brother's mad enough to want the fire. There's no need to go hungry for him.'

Dercc did not listen.

'Will you come away from the Fort with me, Liath? The power of the past is defeated. . . .'

'A lie!' Liath shouted. 'The power is far from being defeated. It is still with me!' His face ran with sweat. He was shaking with fever. 'If you *are* my twin brother you could share it – yes, even you!' His voice rose, unintelligible sounds broke from his lips, a meaningless, evil-sounding jangle which rose and fell, like a wheel running out of control down a rutted trackway. Dercc's dry lips moved, forming one name. He whispered,

'Jesus!'

Liath shuddered. He stopped babbling. He thrust his ashen, contorted face close to his brother's.

'Power of the dark, power for the people, power, come!' he cried. 'The power *has* come! It is here! The power is Liath! Liath is the power!' Turning to the tribe he screamed,

'Follow me! I shall rule you! They've tied my hands. I'm so strong, they fear me. The King fears me. He knows my plans and I care not – he does not know all things! I'm not afraid of the fire, but the King's afraid!'

'Cut out his tongue!' roared the King. 'We bury men alive for this kind of treason!'

'Bury me alive! I'll leap out from the darkness! Cut out my tongue! I'll go on speaking! The severed heads of slain warriors cry, and so will I! Take me to the fire – I'm not afraid – I am protected by my power.'

He started to stumble towards the blaze.

'Lord King, do not hear him,' begged Dercc. 'His evil charms have made him mad.' Turning he cried, 'Oh will

you not save him, Lord Jesus? You came to me and saved me! Jesus! Jesus! Jesus! Save Liath from this evil thing!'

A yelping moan broke from Liath's lips.

'I see! I see! I who was blind. I see the flames like warriors leaping. I see war hosts clashing together. I see Liath leaping and harping and singing between the flames.'

With his bound hands held in front of him, he started to spring like a dancer. Then he staggered. Froth bubbled out between his bloodless lips. His eyes rolled.

'It fades . . . it darkens . . . don't leave me . . . not the dark again. . . .'

He began to moan, staggering sideways as if something blocked his way, and he stumbled over a protruding log. He fell at the very edge of the fire. Sparks singed his tumbled hair and set his long robe alight.

The spell was broken. Dercc leaped forward and dragged him away. All around them was commotion as the warriors rushed forward shouting. Dercc flung his heavy cloak over his brother, and leapt on him, rolling him over and over until the flames were out. His hands began to throb painfully. He could hear the tribesmen shouting

'Burn the priest! He is guilty! The fire has shown it!'

Then he heard the cry,

'Our King is our leader! Health to our King!'

It was taken up by everybody in the hall. Dercc moved away from his brother now that the fire was out. He looked towards the King, and met his eyes.

'Health to our King.' He knelt before him. 'Lord King, let me take my brother away from the Fort. He cannot harm anyone now.'

The King looked hard at Dercc for a long moment. Then his face relaxed. He signalled to a slave. Dercc saw with relief that the slave fetched the white rod, the sign of the King's authority. Holding it high, the King stood and the tribesmen fell silent.

'The fire has shown the guilty one, and Liath, the son of Coll, has lost his powerful magic. The young red-headed warrior came as plaintiff for him. He has fasted, waiting my word of mercy. He has wrestled with our champion. Did he not wrestle well?'

'He wrestled well,' the tribesmen agreed.

'He is Dercc, the son of Coll,' said the King. 'He was not killed as we supposed, but has returned home after many adventures. He has wrestled, not for his own honour, or for his place in the tribe, but for the body of his brother who now lies there harmless. Do you hear my word, my people?'

'Give Dercc, the son of Coll the prize he wants,' said one of the lords, and the others took up the shout.

'They're both mad,' growled Leuchos, from the place beside the fire where he sat, stroking a striped cat curled peacefully on his plump knee. 'Send them away.'

'It is time to kill the black cock and cast rings in the water,' said the King. 'Let the whole matter of Liath be forgotten. Take your brother away, Dercc. Never let him return to the High Fort.'

Dercc touched the King's white rod. He gathered up Liath's unconscious body and turned to leave the hall.

'Dercc, you deserve better than this!' the King said suddenly. 'You shall not go out into Samain night. I am a son of our Horse Goddess and you are my guest. Sleep here tonight and break your long fast. Leave at first light tomorrow.'

Winwaloe stepped up to Dercc's side.

'My master has found another slave to hold blazing branches. Lord King, tonight let me help this young warrior look after his brother's hurts.'

'You have won friends as well as wrestling matches,' the King observed gently. 'You have a power with you, and a story I would know more of. Lay your brother on a bed of fresh grass, and then come and eat. You have deserved your prize.'

He waved away Dercc's thanks. Winwaloe spread grass in one of the alcoves and Dercc carefully carried Liath there and laid him down.

'Honey.'

He looked round at the sound of Thanew's voice, not understanding what she meant. Queen-like, with her long hair coiled in thick plaits around her head, Thanew held burning branches in either hand.

'Honey,' she said again. 'Don't you know anything? Honey is what you put on burns.'

'That is so,' Dercc said, 'but where can I get any tonight?'

'I'll get some for you.' She gave Winwaloe the torches and hurried away, her dress rustling over the dried grass.

While all the Horse People in the High Fort, in farmsteads and scattered villages, in wretched hovels, caves and fortified round houses kept the Feast of Samain, Dercc looked after his brother, helped by Winwaloe and Thanew. Liath's right arm was burnt, but his clenched hand, the hand Dercc hoped would still play on the carved harp with strings of white bronze, had been tucked under him and was unmarked. They smeared honey over the burns, and wrapped strips of linen round them, binding them tightly. They moistened his lips with water and sprinkled it over his face.

Then at last Dercc ate, sharing the food with Winwaloe, while Thanew brought him a beaker of ale.

That night of Samain, with the yellow moon outside in its last quarter, and all the fires burning low, Dercc slept fitfully beside his brother who moaned and babbled. Many times Dercc got up and bathed his brother's face, trying to cool the fever. Winwaloe slept on his other side, breathing steadily and giving an occasional snore, undisturbed by the movements. Liath cried out in his sleep, turning towards Dercc but unable to recognise his brother, who had won him at last.

VI
The Darkest Weeks

Thanew came early in the morning, her arms full of bundles. Winwaloe had already gone to see if one of the ox-carts which carried the priests to the High Fort was returning to the Temple that day. He hoped to drive it and carry Liath to the farm. Dercc was smoothing his brother's brow with a piece of linen.

'His fever is still high,' he said.

Thanew hesitated, putting her bundles down but unwilling to go away.

'What is it, lady?' asked Dercc, looking up.

'I am not a lady,' she said, and began to talk of her life on her father's farm at the Ridge of the Reindeer before the Cre raiders from the north had burnt it. Only she had escaped and taken refuge with her aunt at the Fort.

'I used to carry water, make ale and bread, crush herbs and nuts. I used to milk the goats,' she said. 'I was bringing them home that evening when I saw the smoke going up – the farm in ruins – ' she stopped, choking on tears.

After a silence, Dercc said, 'There was no one left?'

'No one. That day when you came back – from the dead – back to Liath, and he wouldn't believe – ' she wept again, and Dercc understood why she, of them all, had been the one to pity him. Then he said,

'And your life at the Fort, Thanew, what will it be now?'

'I have a good shelter, food and clothes. I do not mind it, but soon – ' her face clouded and she stopped again.

He waited, then he said, 'They will choose a man for you.'

She nodded.

'I do not know whom they will choose. . . . The gods grant it is not Leuchos.'

Winwaloe was coming across the hall and she turned away.

'My foster parents live beyond the old dun,' said Dercc quickly. 'Come and see us. Please come. You will be welcome.'

'I'll try,' she said over her shoulder, and he thought, 'She is crying again.'

He watched her make her way back to the women's quarters.

'I have not thanked her,' he said to Winwaloe.

She had brought more honey and more linen, plenty of it, wrapped together, a small leather bottle of ale and some dried meat, hazelnuts, bread and herbs. There were also skins and a thick woollen cloak. She had thought of everything. Winwaloe said, 'I have a cart. There is much stuff belonging to my master, but room for Liath to lie. We must go slowly. There is a thick mist.'

In the dim alcove they shared their breakfast, then lifted Liath and carried him through the quiet hall. He slept heavily now. They put him in the cart and wrapped him round with skins. Then they went into the swirling mist, Dercc walking beside the cart and holding Liath steady.

As they went they began to talk. Dercc said, 'Winwaloe, you have been a friend to me. Yesterday when I stood alone before the tribe to wrestle for my brother, you came and stood beside me and gave me comfort. I have nothing to offer you but my friendship in return.'

And Winwaloe said, 'Your friendship is much for me, a slave. You are a champion wrestler and you are

a free man. I was about your age when they put the iron collar round my neck. I scarcely felt it then for the hunger in my cold guts. Only later, the pain of slavery begins – knowing that you belong, full or hungry, to a man who scarcely knows your name.'

'I know; I too have been a slave.'

'Aye, your strange adventures are being told around the Fort, and the power of the new God you serve.'

'Then my slavery and all my sufferings have not been in vain,' said Dercc. 'My God gave me light in the darkness of my mind when I was still a slave, Winwaloe, and in serving Him I have found freedom for my innermost self.'

'You make me feel like a free man again,' said Winwaloe, and they continued to talk and sometimes sing along the way, and Dercc told Winwaloe more of the God who makes men free.

But all this time Liath slept, pale-faced, in the cart.

When they reached the farm, Dercc carried him inside but Winwaloe had to hurry the oxen on to the Temple.

'So you have won your plea,' said Uncle Mael, looking at Dercc and his burden in a mixture of amazement and fear. Liath began to wake and moan as Dercc put him down in a warm place by the wall. Aunt Ala fussed around them both, bringing sheepskins and warmed wine. Dercc explained about Liath's burnt arm and side, and she said, 'It's a bad time for healing to begin with the moon on the wane, but it may be that as the new moon grows full the burns will heal.'

They spoke kindly to Liath, telling him where he was, and they made him comfortable. They thought perhaps he understood them, but he turned and lay with his face to the wall, his blind eyes closed and his body shivering.

Later when Liath had fallen again into a deep sleep, Dercc told of the two days of fasting, and of the fire, and a little about his wrestling, while Penn lay against his feet.

All through the darkest weeks of the year they did

their best to help Liath's healing. He did not rave any more and Dercc believed the dark power had left him at last. But Liath was silent and without spirit, like an empty shell. He never spoke directly to anyone unless it was to tell them what he needed. He never called them by their names. But sometimes Dercc heard him sigh to himself and heard the words 'cold' and 'dark'. Dercc tended his burns, watching him closely, and he prayed that a deep healing might take place, but he saw no sign.

As the weeks wore on, food became less and less plentiful. As often as possible Dercc went into the hills or across the frozen moorlands, but what he brought back was scanty. Often it was too wild for him to go at all. They ate salted meat from the autumn's stores. The loaves Aunt Ala and the girls baked became smaller and less filling. Dercc felt that he and Liath were a burden on their foster parents. Now when they gathered round the cooking pot he sat back in the shadows, or played with Penn, or slipped across the room to be with Liath, making it look as though he had already eaten.

Then there were days of snow. The water in the well outside froze. They had to bring water from the spring further up the hill.

Everyone except Liath had coughs and colds. They stayed huddled beside the fire which never went out.

At night wolves howled in the hills. One night they sounded very close at hand. The next day Gilla found their footprints right outside the gate.

That evening Dercc felt uneasy. He moved from his seat beside Liath and went to the pile of spears and javelins. He began to sort through them but without any concentration or interest. Soon he propped them again beside the wall and drifted over to the other side of the round house, stopping to play with Penn.

'What is it, Dercc? You are restless,' said Uncle Mael.

'It is hunger,' said Aunt Ala. 'You've not eaten enough for days – I have been watching you.'

'It is the wolves,' Dercc said quickly. 'They've come very close again tonight. Look how Penn's hackles are up! And how she growls. . . .'

But it was Liath, not the wolves, nor even hunger. He was stifled by longing for his brother to be as he had been before. If he would only show that he knew them!

Suddenly he remembered that harp he had brought home for his brother. It might be that if Liath felt a harp in his hands again the music that flowed through his fingers would heal him.

He fetched the harp.

'Dercc, is this wise?' asked Uncle Mael. 'His music has been full of darkness. We dreaded to listen and yet we could not turn away.'

'I know. I remember, Uncle. But before that, when we were young boys and Liath had sorrow for his blindness, it used to help him to play the harp. It may be it will help him now.'

Uncle Mael said,

'After you were taken away from him, Dercc, and he was much with the priests, his music became darker and more powerful still. The evil magic took all his playing.'

'I believe that the evil power was cast out of him at the fire,' said Dercc. 'I called out to my Lord Jesus, and for one moment Liath saw a vision, then the power left him, and he has been like this ever since. But I wish that he were filled with light, and my hope is that the harp may help him.'

They looked at one another as a wolf howled outside.

'Like hunger, like all the bad things of the dark, the wolves press closer,' Uncle Mael said. 'It's not so long now till the Festival of Lambs, but longer till the lighter days of spring. Try Liath with his harp then, Dercc, for I too feel ill at ease.'

Dercc sat beside his brother.

'Liath, will you not take my gift now?'

'What is it?' he said dully. 'Have you brought me the

gift of light at last?'

'I cannot give light to your eyes,' said Dercc, 'no matter how I long to. But my Lord can fill your mind and your thoughts with light – yes and your music too.'

'I have used my music to serve the dark gods, and now they have left me, and I am awake from the evil dreams. But the darkness is still all around me – oh why cannot *I* have light too? For one moment . . . in the Fort . . . and then, all dark again . . . oh, Dercc. . . .' He wept, but Dercc was overjoyed – his brother had called him by his name! He held the harp, forgotten, in his lap, and Liath began to speak again, slowly, stumbling for words.

'I saw the flames, the glorious colours of them, I saw the warriors, and me leaping in the midst, leaping like the flames. I thought they would make me their king, Dercc – there I've said your name again. I have known it was you but something stopped me saying your name. Now, Dercc, my brother, forgive me, for I have done you a great wrong. I have wronged my king and my tribe, but you more than all.'

Then they embraced with great joy and Dercc said,

'I too need your forgiveness. It was I who first guided you into this evil, showing you the darkness in the stones. But now I serve the Lord who has defeated all dark powers. I returned to the stone circle to pray for you, and I knew the power was defeated for the stones were changed. They were full of light, and I saw the sun's laughter in them. I longed for you to see it too!'

'The light! The laughter!' said Liath. 'I do know it – you bring it.'

'*I* bring it? But you have been so unhappy. . . .'

'The light you've brought near as you've cared for me . . . this light has been hurting me. I am afraid of it and want to hide away, but I can pretend no longer. It is there and I know it. I am afraid of what it will call upon me to do. I didn't want to call any of you names, though I knew you all, and all that you have done for me. Yet I have been

afraid of truth.'

'But if you are willing, this Truth will fill your mind with light,' said Dercc.

Liath thought long, then he said, 'What is the name of the God you pray to?'

'Jesus.'

'It is a very powerful name. It tormented me when the power was in me. What does it mean?'

'It means, "The One Who Saves". Without him helping me I should never have come home; or spoken with power at the Fort. But he is far stronger than all dark powers. He is stronger than death itself.'

'I knew this when I first heard his name,' said Liath. 'He is a God to fear.'

'He is a God to love, Liath, because he loves us.'

'No one has ever loved me except you. I have been shut out, always, different. Dercc, you said you had brought me a gift, it is a great gift, this gift of the One Who Saves – this Lord of power and love.'

'But I have brought this also,' Dercc said smiling, and put the harp into his brother's hands. Liath fingered from it single notes like a bird's swift flight. Dercc looked at his brother's face with joy for it was lit with happiness.

The wind drove rain against the door. The rush lights guttered. Gilla was sharpening a knife. The girls were sleeping, curled together. Wolves howled and a pony screamed. Penn snarled.

'I am afraid no more,' said Liath softly, 'We two are together. And I have two great gifts.'

He began to play the harp quietly. Feeling very tired and weak, Dercc leant back, listening. Liath's long unhurt fingers wove music as a skilful weaver works cloth: colourful music, warm as heavy wool, and music that shimmered like webs of silk. On an ordered weft and warp Liath wove patterns of sound that drove away hurt and hunger, the winter and the wolves.

'Thank you, Liath.' It was Uncle Mael's voice in the

silence when at last the music stopped. 'That was the best playing we've ever heard, from you or anyone else. Gilla, we've still a little wine and some honey bread. Bring them to your cousin for his harping.'

Gilla brought the wine and brown bread to Liath.

'No, Gilla, I've been eating your best food. Give the bread to my brother,' he said. 'He gave me this harp and he gave me the music too.'

'Oh, light of the long ago people!' Uncle Mael exclaimed. 'Dercc's new way comes like the gentle misty spring and conquers all the dark. Eat bread, Dercc. Tomorrow we'll kill the ponies. It's not a thing we Horse People like to do, but horse flesh is better than hunger.'

But they did not need to kill the ponies that winter, for to everyone's surprise Winwaloe appeared next day, his ox cart laden with provisions and treasures. He had brought them from Liath's own supplies in the priests' store rooms.

'I've missed you, Dercc,' he cried. 'But you're as lean as a birch stripped by the autumn gales! I can see the food's come at the right time. How is your brother? He looks well.'

'I am well,' Liath called out, 'and you're welcome.'

'Aye, welcome,' said Uncle Mael. 'Stay and eat with us, for you have shown great kindness to my foster sons. And you have risked being robbed to bring these treasures.'

'The gods and powers were kind,' said Winwaloe. 'It may be because I came for the sake of friends as a free man might do. I saw no one on the way.'

They unpacked the cart with delight. There were stores of grain and salted meat, which Liath's slaves had laid aside for him in the autumn. It was good to sit round the fire and eat till all had had enough, and to know there was still plenty. It was good to tell stories and hear laughter – most of all the laughter of Liath. Winwaloe told of the wrestling match again – but in full this time –

and all but Dercc pressed for the tale to be told yet again.

Then Liath took his precious harp and began to play. He made music of the wrestlers and the cheering crowds, the hard falls and the struggling for a grip. And Dercc remembered how they too had wrestled when they were boys, the blind twin feeling for each hold. Then they sang songs to the harp and Winwaloe taught them songs of his own clan.

But at last he had to leave and Dercc went out with him to the cart.

'What news of Thanew?' Winwaloe queried, looking keenly at him and stirring the unwilling ox into motion.

'I know nothing – she has not been here,' said Dercc.

'All winter they have been celebrating weddings,' said Winwaloe.

'Has she been given to one of the lords?' said Dercc and the loss showed on his face.

'Some royal maidens did not. . . .' Winwaloe's ox at last made up its mind to move and jolted away, leaving the bitter east wind to toss away its master's words unheard.

VII
Raiders

There came a day when Liath's bandages could finally be unwound.

'There's more than burns have been healed,' Uncle Mael said. 'When I first saw you the day after Samain, I did not think we'd soon be thrilling to your harp again, Liath.'

'But now that I am well,' said Liath, 'what am I to do? Dercc has an honoured place in the tribe if he wants it. But I am an outcast. And I can do nothing.'

'I have no place with the warriors,' said Dercc. 'I have been a slave and seen the unglorious side of fighting. I well remember the thrill of the drawn spears before the battle, and the strong taste of the heather ale when all the warriors drink at the trysting. It puts the fire inside you – ' he looked at Gilla's eager face and nodded, 'but I also remember the stink of the slave ship, the men's screams as the pirate ship rammed us – oh, I have had enough of killing.'

'Let me tell you,' Uncle Mael broke in, 'what you two should know already. You both have a place with us.

'Yet it is not right to go on eating your food and taking a place at the fire,' said Liath. 'My treasure will not last for ever and then what? Dercc can go hunting, but I . . .?'

'Why! Did you not go hunting with Dercc in the old days?' cried Gilla. 'You helped him with your sharp hearing and your careful fingers, skinning the game. . . .'

'We could go hunting – today – the three of us,' said

Dercc, eagerly.

'Often a hard winter like this brings the mountain bears down from the high hills,' said Uncle Mael. 'If Liath gets used to hunting again, he'll be a great help to us.'

So they set off, Liath's hand on Dercc's shoulder as in the old days. He was soon breathless, but excited as a child.

'I am set free,' he gasped. 'I was caged up at the Fort – pacing up and down all day in the alcoves.' He gave a leap for joy, like a spring lamb, then froze.

'Listen!'

'Your ears are so sharp; *I* hear nothing,' said Dercc after a time.

'It may be a peewit,' said Gilla

'No – crying – a woman,' said Liath. 'Somewhere there.' He pointed.

Gilla, his hand on his hunting knife, wanted to go on but Dercc said,

'No, we must go down and see.'

They went downwards where Liath had pointed. The hill was steep, but around its shoulder and further down they saw someone crouched in the grass. A face turned upwards at their coming.

'Thanew!' cried Dercc, and turning only to put Liath's hand on Gilla's shoulder, he went leaping down to her. She was crying bitterly and trembling, and he put his cloak around her. She pointed to her foot, trying to control her sobbing, biting her lips.

'I've hurt my foot . . . I fell, running away from them . . . I thought you were them.'

'Who?' he asked.

'Raiders – the Cre people. I knew their battle gear.'

'The battle gear – of the Cre people?' repeated Dercc, with foreboding. 'What are they doing so far south?'

'They are on their way to the Fort,' said Liath. He had become very pale.

'Yes,' said Thanew with bitterness, 'but it was lucky for me. They had no time to come after me.'

'What were you doing alone out here?' said Dercc, and, 'Is the Fort unprepared for them?' cried Gilla at the same time.

'Oh yes. They know nothing of an attack,' she said to Gilla.

'Then we must warn them,' he cried. 'I'll run to the Fort, shall I?'

'No wait,' said Dercc. 'You must go to the shoulder of the hill and make a fire: the people in the dun will see it. Then you must return to the farm. You must let *me* go to the Fort.'

Gilla raced off and Dercc turned to Thanew.

'You have not answered me, Thanew . . . quickly, I must know. I have thought of you so much through the dark months I must know about your trouble.'

She buried her face in her hands.

'They chose Leuchos. They would have given me to him before, but I became ill.'

'So you were running away from the Fort? Where were you going to go?'

She gestured helplessly.

'Anywhere. Nowhere. I don't care. . . .'

'But you are not yet given to Leuchos?'

'Not yet.'

'Oh, Thanew, my love,' he said with relief. 'Are you well now? You must go to my foster-parents. Go with Liath. You can lean on him – and be his eyes.'

He turned to his brother who was standing, pale as death.

'Take Thanew back and tell Uncle Mael to get word to Winwaloe. He will gather the Seal People, and they can make a show of strength in the back of the enemy. And now if I go across the moorland I – '

'Dercc,' Liath interrupted. 'This is all my doing. And this is the result of my plotting. It is I who must make

recompense. I will offer all my treasure in return for a
treaty of peace. Tell the King this, and that I will come
soon. It may be that our God will help us to prevent the
battle.'

Then they parted and Dercc ran along the muddy
track towards the Fort. In a little while he caught sight of
a glimmer of gold in the woodland. His ear picked up the
vibration of marching feet. The raiders were keeping
amongst the trees and were making slow progress. He at
once left the trackway and crossed the moorland. He
knew every step of the way and dodged bogs and low-
lying marshes easily. At last, bent against the wind, he
came clambering to the gateway of the Fort and alerted
Garan, who began to sound the alarm.

Dercc rushed up through the gates shouting his
warning. Already the quickest of the athletes from the
training field was at his heels. In the hall the minstrels left
off playing to the King, who leapt up and began to arm
himself as Dercc gasped out his warning of the Cre attack
and Liath's offer for peace. More warriors came running
from the field and river and seized weapons. Dercc
wondered what he should do; he had no wish to fight, yet
knew he must help in the defence of the Fort. He began to
take down spears from the wall.

'This is your brother's doing,' Leuchos said, not
quietly, but in the uproar of the hall only the slaves close
to him heard.

'Son of Coll!' It was the King's voice. Dercc went to
him and knelt. 'I will give your brother the chance to set
right this treachery, for your sake only,' the King said
quietly. 'Go and bring him here, with the treasure he
offers. We can lose no more, and we may gain peace
by it.'

Thankfulness filled Dercc's heart. He raced away to
the enclosure where the horses were being led out from
their stables to be harnessed to the light wicker chariots. A
slave brought him a horse by the King's orders and he

mounted gladly, recognising it as one of the ponies that had belonged to his uncle, and turned its head towards the gate.

A rain of flaming throwing sticks flew in an orange arc above his head, but he turned from the direction of the attackers, heading the pony towards the moorland.

'The son of Coll is fleeing for his life!' He heard Leuchos' taunt and ignored it, thought it stung like any arrow. On and on. . . . As he galloped over the moorland he saw the people of the dun marching with their weapons to join the warriors behind the gates. Gilla's signal had done its work. More and more tribesmen were streaming across the moor to the defence of their High Fort.

As he came to the farmstead he saw the family waiting half-way down the hill, and Thanew with them. Gilla came running to meet him.

'Let me carry your shield at the battle,' he begged.

'No, I shall go unarmed to the fighting with Liath,' said Dercc dismounting. 'We must try to make peace before too much evil has been done. The King has sent me to bring Liath and the treasure he offers.'

'*I* shall fight,' said Thanew fiercely. 'I will be revenged upon those who murdered my family. *I* can throw a spear – '

'You might be killed!' cried Alarch.

'It would be better than being given to Leuchos – ' she broke off, biting her lips. Dercc tried to put his arms round her, but she stood rigid.

'I thought *you* were a warrior, Dercc!' she said bitterly. 'I brought you the wine cup because I admired your courage, when you stood alone against the whole tribe – '

'And he *is* brave,' Liath broke in. 'He has never been cowardly, Thanew. It may be he has a different kind of bravery now – '

'One *I* don't understand,' she said quickly and turned away from them.

Penn started to bark. Liath had also heard something.

'They are coming – the Seal People. Dercc, lead me to the things Winwaloe brought. They are still in sacks in the stable. We must go now.'

Dercc went sorrowfully with Liath. It was hard to be thought a coward by Thanew. He loaded his brother's stuff onto two ponies, Liath holding their heads, and then led them out of the stable in time to see Winwaloe march up with his army. Poorly-equipped, led by a slave, the Seal People had left their hovels by the shore to defend the Fort.

'We're yours to lead,' Dercc,' Winwaloe spoke with pride.

'Mine?'

'Our weapons are poor, but our war-horns make a wonderful din. If they do not see us at first, we can make the raiders think an enormous war-host has come upon them!'

To prove this the musicians flourished their long, black, curled horns and blew a blood-curdling blast, making the ponies rear.

'Your plan's a good one! Hidden in the woods you can surprise them from the rear. But Winwaloe, these are your people and you must lead them,' said Dercc. He turned to the Seal People.

'Will you not follow Winwaloe to this fight?'

'We will! He is one of us!' cried the tribesmen.

'Let me march with them too!' pleaded Gilla, and when Uncle Mael consented, he armed himself with spears and throwing sticks and took his place among Winwaloe's men.

'My foster sons have returned but now my own son is leaving,' Aunt Ala said quietly.

'I will go with you to the Fort also,' said Thanew, who had armed herself with a spear.

'Thanew must have a pony!' Vin said to her father. 'She cannot walk.'

'Very well,' said Uncle Mael. 'Take a pony, Thanew.

Throw your spear at the Cre people to avenge the deaths of your family and the destruction of your home. Then ride back to us, quickly.'

'You will be welcome here,' said Aunt Ala.

They helped her onto a pony and there were tears on her cheeks as she kissed them. Then without more words she rode after the Seal People.

Dercc and Liath followed as quickly as they could with the laden ponies. Seeing Thanew ahead Dercc longed that she would let him speak to her.

'She looks so alone,' he said to Liath.

'You love her,' said Liath. 'I know this though I am blind. What is she like?'

'She is Thanew,' he said, smiling in spite of his distress. 'She is different. Beautiful and queenly.'

'Is it wrong to feel happy?' Liath asked after a while. 'I do, riding into the wind like this. If they would only accept my treasures instead of destroying our tribe. . . .'

They urged the willing ponies forward towards the High Fort and the clash and clamour of fighting. Dercc saw the charioteers charging into the midst of the attackers. Where they charged they mowed men down crushing the raiders closer and closer together. Ponies, screamed, rearing and dragging their wounded drivers from broken chariots. There was great confusion and the noise of war-horns.

'Winwaloe's sending his army into the battle,' said Dercc. 'They're running out of the trees now, Liath. With the noise they're making they seem like a huge war-band. The raiders are breaking ranks. I think they may be glad to accept your treaty now without losing any more lives.'

He saw the King's chariot and urged their ponies towards it, slithering on the churned-up mud. Wounded men lay in their path, and Dercc saw the boy he had wrestled with, bent over and groaning.

The Seal People's surprise attack had been successful and it was followed by a lull in the fighting, while the

warriors reformed for a new attack. As soon as he saw Dercc and Liath with the treasures they brought the King made a signal, and from the ramparts of the Fort, waiting priests blew high, silvery notes from the trumpets they carried.

There came a stillness on both sides.

In this stillness the brothers walked towards the raiders, leading the ponies. Behind them, carrying shields but no weapons came a score of chiefs with the priests in their midst, and made a half-circle in the centre of the battle field. It was then that Dercc saw Thanew again. She was over towards the trees, mounted on her horse with her battle spear in her hand. Winwaloe stood beside her.

Then Liath cried in his melodious voice,

'Who will speak peace with us?'

The other side debated. Six of the leaders, three of them easterners who had helped to plan the attack, stood forward.

'What terms do you offer?' their spokesman called.

'Here is my treasure,' Liath said. 'Divide it amongst your two tribes and let there be an end to the fighting.'

'What is your wealth?' called the spokesman after more deliberation.

'See here,' said Dercc, pointing to the ponies.

The sacks were unloaded and the treasure spilled out onto the mud. On both sides the warriors rested on their spears, lowering their shields, watching the low rays of winter sunlight catch on Liath's gold and silver.

'Divide it among you,' Liath said again, 'and let there be peace between the tribes.'

His pony whinnied. Brighter than the gleam of sunlight on silver a weapon flashed. Dercc heard a cry of pain, and saw the blood gushing through a northerner's woollen tunic. The man toppled forward and Dercc turned at once towards Thanew as the yells of outrage rose up all about them. She had no spear now, staring, white-faced and set, as the warriors all around her seized

their weapons and the fury of killing broke loose again. A throwing stick knocked him to his knees, and when he got up he could not see her.

'What is it? What's happening?' came Liath's bewildered voice, and Dercc turned back to help his twin, but in desperate fear for Thanew. Spears hurtled around them – and then, there was Winwaloe coming to them among the milling tribesmen.

'Come!' he shouted, and took Liath's arm. But as he turned to lead him from the battle, a spear struck with full force and he was thrown forward against Dercc.

Dercc lifted him. He put Liath's hand on his shoulder. 'To the trees,' he yelled above the din. 'Winwaloe is hurt.' He swung Winwaloe into his arms and tried to run forward.

Not far now. He could see trees ahead of him. He felt his burden ease and saw that Liath supported Winwaloe's other side. They laid the slave beside a beech tree away from the fighting. He was barely conscious. Dercc ripped open his tunic and tried to staunch the blood. Winwaloe opened his eyes.

'No use,' he said feebly. 'Their spears are barbed.'

Then Dercc knew that the wound was fatal. It was impossible to pull a barbed spear from a wound.

'You saved me, Winwaloe,' Liath said. 'That spear was surely intended for me. I heard it coming and felt you fall. Why did you come to help me?'

'The giving.' His voice was very faint. 'the love of you two brothers. It's dark now – Dercc – Dercc where are you?'

'I am here,' said Dercc, gripping his hands.

Liath groaned, 'All this is my doing.'

But Dercc said, softly, 'There is no greater love than this – that a man lays down his life for his friends.'

Winwaloe's eyes were dull. His face was white but a smile came to his dry lips.

'Again – Dercc – '

So Dercc said the words again. Then he said,

'Our Lord gave his life for us – you too, Winwaloe.'

'Me? A slave?' He could only just catch the words.

'I too was a slave when I believed, my friend.'

Winwaloe smiled. There was peace in his grey face.

It was not long before Dercc leant forward and touched the slave's still face.

'His iron collar doesn't hurt him any more, Liath.'

'We've no coins for his eyes,' Liath said, weeping.

'There's no need. The price of his journey has been paid.' Dercc pulled his cloak over the body of the dead man. They sat side by side in silence for a time.

'We have failed to bring peace,' Liath said brokenly.

'Yes.'

Then after another silence Dercc roused himself and said,

'I will go and look for Thanew. Perhaps she did not ride from the battle when she threw her spear.'

And he left Liath beside Winwaloe and went to the edge of the wood. He saw that the battle was almost ended, and if there was victory, it was to the Horse People. He saw the Lord Leuchos leading the chariots against the last of the raiders, and heard the horns of the Seal People as, armed with the weapons of their fallen enemies, they came sweeping back into the battle. He saw Gilla in the midst of them brandishing a spear and shield.

But the dead and wounded lay strewn over the trampled blood-stained grass. He knew that it would take him many hours to search for Thanew, and that he would not be able to refuse help to the wounded or pass them by.

He returned to Liath, who said.

'Lead me back to the battle, Dercc. I will be able to help you.'

He was glad that Liath could not see the misery and horror of the carnage. But Liath knew it.

They stepped over costly battle equipment ground

into the mud by the chariots. Some of Liath's treasure was still scattered about in the place where they had stood to parley.

'Liath,' said Dercc, 'I think you have done some good. It seems to me that many of the raiders took your treasures and scattered, and there were few left to fight. The battle is over, and I see Gilla returning to the Fort with trophies.'

'I hear men on the ramparts shouting "Victory",' said Liath, 'but I hear women lamenting as they look for their dead.'

The Seal People, with Gilla among them marched triumphantly back to the Fort. The least-honoured clan of all had slain the king of the northerners and carried his head and gold-embossed shield among their plunder. Cradawg was leading them and he came to Dercc.

'Where is Winwaloe?'

They told him.

'We will honour his burial,' said his clansmen. 'We will take him back to his own village where he belongs.'

The brothers went on over the battle-field but they did not find the body of Thanew. Gilla came to them and asked them to come to the Fort to share the triumph. He said,

'I was in a rowan tree when I saw her fling the spear that began the fighting the second time. But then the warriors came round and I could not see her. It may be she has gone safely home to the farm.'

Then Dercc begged drugged wine from the mourning women and went about the battle-field easing the last moments of many a dying warrior. The short winter day darkened. They carried many wounded back up the rocky slope to the Fort, the way lit by flares and flaming pine branches. They passed the gate many times and saw that a new gatekeeper sat there. Garan, the old man had been killed by a spear.

At last it was time for the gate to be shut, and it was then that Gilla came running to say,
'The King calls for the two sons of Coll!'

VIII
The House by the Rowans

They went into the King's hall where he sat, distributing gifts to those who had earned them by valour in the fight. Behind the flickering fire, in places of honour, sat Cradawg and several of the Seal People, with awkward pride. But Leuchos was not among the lords.

'Welcome, twin sons of Coll,' said the King. 'The tribe has sent for you.'

They knelt before him.

'Lord King,' said Liath clearly, so that all the tribe could hear, 'I have done you and the whole tribe a great wrong. I have been the cause of much evil in the hall, and without my brother's pleading you would all have killed me at Samain Feast. In your mercy you set me free. Now I am in my right mind and I no longer serve dark powers, but the Risen Lord my brother has shown me. I brought my treasures to the fighting to make reparation, but I fear they have done little good, for today many have died, and many are in great pain and sorrow. I still have some gold and silver left. Let me give them to you now for the tribe's benefit and your wealth.'

Then the lords whispered to one another, and the King looked at Liath wonderingly. Then he said, 'You are forgiven your treachery, for we all see now that you are changed and no longer possessed by evil powers. Besides your treaty was not in vain, for many of the raiders seized your treasure and fled, and after that the victory was easy.' He turned to the tribe.

'Is it not agreed by us that these young men used their power first for the harm of the tribe, but now they return as from death, with a new power to heal the hurt of the first. Dercc and Liath, sons of Coll, from this time you have a place with the tribe in the High Fort.'

Then the King held out his hands to the brothers, but they drew back because they were dirty and Dercc's hands were stained with blood. Slaves put basins of water, oils and fresh clothes in an alcove and when they were ready they were led back to the King who sat them beside him. And he gave a gift to their cousin Gilla, praising him for his bravery in the battle and for giving warning to the people of the moorland. He gave him the shield of the northern king, and all the tribe cheered him. They shared the remains of the victory meal: flat bread baked on the hot stones of the fire; fish flavoured with cummin, and ale from huge vats.

'Dercc, I do not know how to reward you,' said the King.

'I did not fight, Lord King,' he said.

'Nevertheless you brought the warning to the Fort, then helped in Liath's attempt to bring peace, and I wish to reward you, for you have played a great part in saving our Fort. Will you take your place among the warriors? Shall I give you spear and shield?'

'Lord King, I have a dream,' Dercc said slowly. 'I would build a round house. I would cut willow and weave the walls, then thatch the roof with heather. It would be a place of healing.' Remembering Winwaloe he said, 'For the unfree people too. Before I returned to the tribe I had instruments of healing and was taught to use them. But these I no longer have. This is all that I desire, for I wish to bring healing and not death any more.'

'Then,' said the King, 'I will do all in my power to help you in your dream. And you shall obtain your instruments of healing again, and have land for the building of your house.'

'There is one more thing,' said Dercc, and he did not know how to go on. 'There is a girl, one of the Queen's maids,' he said at last, and the King laughed and said at once,

'You shall have her, son of Coll!'

'She is promised to another whom she hates.'

'And what would you do? Wrestle for her?' The King's eyes brightened still more at the idea.

'It is the Lord Leuchos,' said Dercc, looking about the hall but still seeing no sign of him.

'Leuchos? He was killed in the last charge. He was a brave man in battle, but hasty and ill-tempered. So – the way's clear for you, Dercc. But who is the maiden?'

Dercc told him about Thanew and her burnt home by the Ridge of the Reindeer, and the King said,

'Find her, and if she lives she shall be yours.'

'If she will have me,' said Dercc under his breath.

The King turned to Liath.

'And you, Liath. Have you a dream too?'

Liath said sadly, 'Once it was to see the light, colours, and the faces of my friends, to see the way before my feet –'

Dercc said to him immediately, 'Liath, Liath, I would give *my* dream if yours could come true –'

But Liath answered, 'Now it is different; if I could find some way to serve my Lord in spite of my blindness; if I could give light through my music, I would be content.'

'Come to the burial ground tomorrow night and dance among the warriors when we honour the dead,' said the King to them both, and they promised.

That night they slept beside the fire in the great hall, but early in the morning Dercc left to look for Thanew. Instead of going back to the farm, he turned at once towards the Ridge of the Reindeer. Something told him she would go back to her old home, as a hurt wild creature seeks its lair. He climbed into the hills using the long,

loping pace of the hunter.

'She must never be caged again,' he thought, 'yet she must never be lonely.'

But would she share his dream? Would she come with him? Did she not think he was a coward?

Just before the Ridge of the Reindeer he came upon the ruins of Thanew's home. He recognised the spot straight away from what she had told him. He could see the southern slope where thyme and bell heather must have scented the air each summer, giving honey to Thanew's bees. At the doorway, beside the burnt-out walls, grew two rowans. Buds on their bare branches promised leaves. The intertwining boughs must have borne their scented, creamy blossom when Thanew had last seen her home. They would bloom again year after year and bear red berries. Birds would scatter the seeds of the rowans and little by little small saplings would crow in the roofless ruined dwelling.

Unless . . . unless someone came and rebuilt Thanew's home!

He stood in the doorway. Brown branches fretted their pattern against the changing shapes of the clouds.

She was huddled inside, sheltering from the wind in the southern corner of the ruin. He walked up to her but she turned her face to the wall.

He sat beside her. She edged away, still not looking at him. He did not move. He stayed sitting beside her, waiting, and praying too, as he had learnt in the fort when he pleaded for Liath.

After a very long time he said: 'Leuchos is dead.'

There was more silence, and at last he said, 'I have often dreamed I should like to build a house of willow – a place for the healing of wounds. Could we not rebuild the house here?'

She was still silent but he became more sure.

The rowans must be beautiful when they're in flower. . . .'

'Oh, they are,' she exclaimed eagerly. 'The smell of the blossom is so fragrant. But I prefer them when the berries come. Sometimes they're simply laden with berries. Their branches quiver and shake all day because little birds hide away and eat their fill.'

'I expect they were in blossom when the house was burnt,' he said, quietly.

'Yes, yes, they were! It was a wonderful year for blossom and it seemed to float all over them; like foam on a waterfall I used to think as I brought the goats down from the hill. . . .' Thanew's voice broke. She started to cry. Dercc bit his lips, seeing he had hurt her. Something had made him go on talking about the rowans. Yet he sensed that it was good that Thanew was crying now, pouring out her desolation, perhaps for the first time since the farm and her family had been destroyed. He put his arm round her and stroked her hair, speaking gently to her.

'No one else knew. No one cared. You came alone to the High Fort and your aunt told you not to cry. Princesses don't bother with their maids. They certainly wouldn't have liked it if you had cried. Cry now, Thanew. It's good to cry.' He felt tears prick his own eyelids. 'Your family is dead. It must have been so hard to believe it. Perhaps you didn't believe it properly until you came back here.'

'How did you know, Dercc?' she said through her tears.

'I knew. I've been sick with longing for my home too. How I wish I'd taken you with me, too, when I took Liath home after Samain Feast. I wanted to, but I didn't dare to think you'd come.'

He saw her smiling through her tears then, and suddenly they were both laughing together, talking and planning the future.

At last he rose, and began to gather scattered twigs from the foot of the rowans. He laid them in the centre of

the floor where the hearth had been, set amidst stones on which Thanew's mother had baked her flat barley scones, oatmeal bannocks and brown bread.

'What are you doing?'

'Kindling a fire.' He struck sparks from a blue flint. A small flame flickered. With a crackle the short-lived fire burned in the hearth. 'A fire will burn there again soon,' he promised, 'but now come with me to the farm.'

It was evening when they climbed the hill to his foster home.

'There's Penn coming to welcome us,' he said. But Thanew stood still. He turned back to her. Behind her the wide sky in the west purpled. Sombre clouds smudged the quiet horizon. A glow of torchlight showed along the grassy road from the Fort as the Horse People walked in procession to bury the dead warriors.

'What is it?'

She did not reply immediately and he came closer with Penn jumping up to his hands.

'Dercc,' she said, 'it was I who threw the spear that broke Liath's peace treaty.'

'I know.'

'But you still came to look for me? Why?'

'I understood that you were hurt – I understood because I love you, Thanew. I have been hurt too. I had to accept healing.'

'That is what makes you different,' she said slowly. 'Forgive me that I called you a coward. It is better to heal than to hurt.'

'Let us learn the way together.'

They went hand in hand into the house.

Later Dercc and Gilla ran through the dusk to the long silent glen where high mounds of stones hid the long-ago dead.

Liath was there among the King's minstrels, carrying the harp Dercc had given him. Dercc touched his hand.

'Gilla and I have come, Liath. Thanew is with our

foster parents now.'

Quickly he told him what had happened and while Liath listened, his hands were busy on his harp: music shimmered and hummed about them. 'Like bees over a patch of bell heather and thyme all through a long, lazy summer day,' thought Dercc.

'Yes, yes, it was just like that, Thanew's ruined home. And soon it will be rebuilt. Listen, they're lighting the fires,' he said aloud.

The wail of women mingled with the crackle and roar of many fires. Leuchos lay in a huge grave with his chariot beside him. Two slaves crouched there. They would die with their master to serve him beyond death. On separate sides of the fires men and women danced to the accompaniment of ancient dirges. Dercc did not join in. Unnoticed in the dark he withdrew to one side and watched, aware of the flight of an owl, the quacking of startled ducks and the never-ceasing rush and boom of burn water. He saw the warriors dance – Gilla was with them. Among the shifting shapes Dercc recognized the champion wrestler, bandaged, and moving stiffly through the shuffle and stamp of the dance.

None of the Seal People had come. They had gone back to their own place, taking Winwaloe's body. Dercc was glad. He had said his good-bye to Winwaloe already.

Liath danced beside the King. Much later, as the long winter night drew on, and the fires faded, Liath danced alone. Dercc's eyes were heavy with sleep. He was stiff and chilled but he watched his brother weave a pattern. Liath danced a slow dance of wounding and death shot through with hope and mounting, wild joy. His black hair spilled over the ground. His body bent low. His hands covered his blind eyes. The whole tribe watched, wondering how long he could maintain his perfect mimicry of grief and guilt, wrong and sorrow when suddenly he leapt high, his hands raised, his head flung back, and now he was singing. Listening in the shadows Dercc caught the tune

and the words:

Not with weapons of war, with spear and long
Javelin I come amongst you, but with a song
And a harp filled with music I try to right a great wrong.

Stones mark where our dead lie; stones grind our grain;
Stones in stark circles dance on every green plain:
Stones dance through long centuries, feeling no hurt, neither pain.

For pain there's a Healer. A bright lord stooped low,
Bore wounds and sorrow; tasted death's heavy woe.
What god over death's black boundaries ever dared go?

From death leaps my Hero: this bright Lord brings healing.
Warriors, listen: Liath brings a new harping.
Like red flames that burnt me I dance the Name of my saving.

As Liath danced on, singing became a wordless mouth music that set the warriors first swaying and then wildly dancing in spite of their weariness. And now Dercc understood that Liath's very blindness helped him to see bright visions, which spilled out in music to enrich the tribe.

When day came, Dercc roused himself. He must have dozed, for since Liath's dance he hadn't been aware of much. Beside him, on an overhanging branch, a robin sang, announcing the grey winter dawn. The glen was emptying. The tribespeople returned to their own duns and settlements or to the Fort. Grey ash drifted beside a score of newly dug graves. Liath, clutching his harp, stumbled in his direction. Dercc ran to his brother.

'I'm here, Liath.'

'Dercc, the King has asked me to become one of his musicians. I have a place in the Fort with the tribe. Let us go home past the stone circle.'

'What about Gilla?'

'He went home hours ago.'

'Aren't you tired, Liath?'

'I was. It comes then leaves me. I danced, Dercc.'

'I saw you. It was beautiful and so was your song. I can

see that you must stay with the tribe.'

'You gave me the dance and the song, Dercc. It was a song of our King, a song of our Jesus.'

They walked to the stone circle in the woods. As they had done once before, Dercc guided Liath's fingers over the rings and swirling patterns carved centuries before on the standing stones.

'Rings, Dercc. There are the rings of the long-ago people inside the rings of our people, inside the rings of the people who'll come after, and those after that. Perhaps one day people will come, not to plunder and raid, but to tell our tribe about the love of our Lord. People who will build small places of healing.'

'Do you think so?'

'I feel it. The stones know it.' Liath spoke oddly. Then he laughed. 'That's enough of visions! *Our* story is here, too; the story of twins who found a strange power here; the story of twins who found each other after a long parting, because one of them came back to the High Fort with a new Master and a different kind of power. We are the first to tell the story of Jesus here, the first of many. All through the years people will keep coming here with the love of Jesus, and go from here to bring the love to others. Perhaps someone will come one day and see these stones and find our story.'

'You will sing it, Liath, in the evenings in the fort.'

'I will sing it. Let's run now. It's so good to run!'

With hands on each other's shoulders the twins ran across the long glen, leaving the still circle of carved stones to the empty sky and the awakening day.

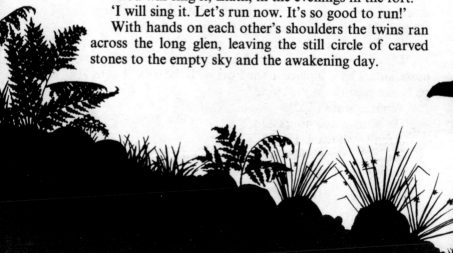